Washed Away?

The Invisible Peoples of Louisiana's Wetlands

Washed Away?

The Invisible Peoples of Louisiana's Wetlands

Donald W. Davis

University of Louisiana at Lafayette Press
2010

Jacket Image Credits: All color images are courtesy of the author; image of three men holding fish is from the *Jefferson Parish Yearly Review,* 1938; all other black and white images are courtesy of the Library of Congress, Print and Photographs Division, FSA-OWI Collection (LC-USF34- 057080-D, LC-USF33- 011647-M2, LC-USF34- 056818-D).

University of Louisiana at Lafayette Press
P.O. Box 40831
Lafayette, LA 70504-0831
http://ulpress.org

ISBN 13 (paper): 978-1-887366-96-0
ISBN 10 (paper): 1-887366-96-2

Library of Congress Cataloging-in-Publication Data

Davis, Donald W. (Donald Wayne), 1943-
 Washed away? : the invisible peoples of Louisiana's wetlands / Donald W. Davis.
      p. cm.
 Includes bibliographical references and index.
 ISBN-13: 978-1-887366-96-0 (paper : alk. paper)
 ISBN-10: 1-887366-96-2 (paper : alk. paper)
1. Gulf Coast (La.)--Social life and customs. 2. Gulf Coast (La.)--Social
conditions. 3. Gulf Coast (La.)--Geography. 4. Wetlands--Louisiana--Gulf
Coast. 5. Landscapes--Louisiana--Gulf Coast. 6. Landscapes--Social
aspects--Louisiana--Gulf Coast. 7. Human ecology--Louisiana--Gulf Coast. 8.
Coastal settlements--Louisiana--Gulf Coast. 9. Community
life--Louisiana--Gulf Coast. 10. Cultural pluralism--Louisiana--Gulf Coast.
I. Title.
 F377.G9D38 2010
 976.3--dc22
                              2010014944

CONTENTS

PREFACE

. . . man may alter nature directly by clearing forests, substituting introduced for native vegetation, changing drainage, depleting or increasing soil productivity, causing erosion, or polluting land, atmosphere, and water. Man also alters the land by creating fields, levees, highways, orchards, and by constructing houses, towns, and cities. The manner in which man alters the earth varies with time and with the traditions of different groups of people. Indians and Europeans differed greatly in their technological capacity, for example, to hunt, to till the ground, and to ascend waterways. Among the Europeans themselves, there were traditional differences in the manner in which they carried out the activities of living. For instance, French and British stock in the Mississippi Valley built different kinds of houses out of the same materials. The French lived in compact settlements and practiced a distinctive manner of dividing land, in direct contrast to British stock living under the identical natural conditions (Kniffen 1990:3).

In less than a century, Louisiana's fragile and ephemeral wetlands have dwindled from nearly ten million to about three million acres. (For reference, the state of Connecticut encompasses roughly 3.5 million acres). These wetlands are more than a simple habitat; they constitute a natural system that has been superseded by human-induced modifications. Some of these transformations are dramatic, others are subtle, but in all cases, humankind has been the active agent of change (Ko and Day 2004). In fact, the term "wetlands" is so new it cannot be found in Mencken's 1948 edition of *American Language*. However, more than thirty meanings of the word "swamp" are recognized.

In Louisiana, swamps, or watery forests, are formed at those sites where the land dips below the mean water table (Viosca 1933). Within the swamp "land and water are not readily separable" (Conner and Day 1976:1359); it is a place where terrestrial plant material is replaced by flood-tolerant vegetation varieties. Therefore, because of these myriad environmental changes, wetlands (including marshes that are part of the transition zone between land and water) have collectively become the focal point of a wide variety of scientific disciplines that routinely ignore the landscape's human population. Yet, if Louisiana's living, evolving, and intensively exploited coast is to be fully understood and appreciated, its human population must be studied and valued.

From the earliest historical times, Louisiana's marshes have appealed to a broad cross-section of ethnic groups. Still the coastal lowlands are a landscape in which humans seem tiny and inconsequential. Further, their cultivated plots and settlements, within this near sea-level locale, were temporary, since they could be washed away in the blink of an eye. In many instances, they were indeed lost just that quickly to unannounced hurricanes that destroyed them completely. In the process, these hamlets vanished from the historical record, for the marshlands gave no quarter. It was a place that humankind avoided. It seemed to be a landscape type that could not be mastered and was at the "edge" of human existence.

Unlike their Eastern Seaboard counterparts, who avoided wetlands as settlement sites, some early Louisianians "considered it undesirable and unsafe to start a community where there was not adequate marshland" (Vileisis 1997:31). Hence, shortly after the Louisiana Purchase (1803), pioneers were settling and exploiting the marshlands and adjudicating private land claims (Gates 1956). Marshland pioneers often lived in villages or dwellings perched upon stilts over "semi-liquid soil" on unsurveyed land that was open to settlement because of lingering confusion over titles and boundaries that had "been defined by wars, treaties, diplomatic letters, territory purchases, legislative acts, and court decisions" (Miller 1997:204).

Although settled well before the arrival of Europeans, the state's working coast was an afterthought for many Louisianans living inland—little more than a surveyor's nightmare, as the lasting achievements of humankind could only be established inland, beyond the danger zone. Consequently, for nearly all of Louisiana's history, the marshes can be best described as "the forgotten landscape," more a public nuisance that required corrective measures than a valuable environment (Vileisis 1997). Therefore, for more than 250 years Louisiana's wetlands were considered a geographic province that should be converted to a more functional and purposeful landscape. Government land grants, laws, and subsidies collectively encouraged this transformation and promoted this idea.

Well before governments decided that these lowlands should be made into something better, these green-fringe lands were settled in North American, Europe, and other regions of the world. Following in the wake of Indian occupancy, European, and Pacific-rim immigrants left their own distinct imprint on the marshes. These were "boat-minded" people (Hubbard 1990:9), who were a census taker's nightmare. Their communities—St. Malo, Ostrica, Chênière au Tigre, Grand Prairie, Camp Dewey, Fort Boulaye, Filipino, Oyster Bayou, Mauvais Bois, Chênière Caminada, Balize, Monsecoeur, and many others—are part of the marshlands' human story. In such inaccessible, remote, and self-sufficient villages, everyone knew everybody else; there were no secrets in these close-knit communities. When a house needed to be erected, the owner fabricated the structure out of the materials at hand. Quite often, the community rallied to help complete the assemble process. Although not pretentious, their homes were designed to withstand a tropical storm using techniques derived from European, West Indian, and aboriginal forms.

The diversity of this wetland-dependent folk landscape has been neglected by most scholars, and the dim remaining memories survive only in a faded photograph, or a word, sentence, or paragraph in a newspaper, book, map, or other print-based media. Yet, this surviving material helps define the marshland's topography as first and foremost a people place. This is a landscape of people and that point should never be forgotten, for the people give this dynamic and constantly changing environment its character and its "face" through the numerous forms of human-induced alterations to the surface and their unyielding pride in their culture.

This work seeks to discover and interpret the intertwined ingredients producing the great diversity of natural and cultural environments that for more than two centuries have helped define Louisiana's marsh and swamplands. Furthermore, a better understanding of cultural attitudes toward this ecosystem can help us recognize the importance of traditional beliefs, which, because they seldom change, may be an important benchmark guiding decisions about this landscape's future (Vileisis 1997).

The factors that produce this

cultural landscape are varied and complex, and they may be summarized under three broad headings: man, the constant as a group, demanding a pattern of activities to satisfy his wants; nature, a combination of climate, relief and situation resources, and situation, relatively constant in time but highly variable in space; and culture, which is man's inheritance of knowledge and skill, variable both in time and space. Clearly the important variable here is culture, and the knowledge of a culture is our chief key to the knowledge of any particular complex of land and people, any particular cultural landscape (Kniffen 1978C:166).

The Marshdweller Was Tough

"Il [elle] est raide comme une babiche
He [she] is as tough as a rawhide" (Read 1931:80).

The marshlands support a traditional way of life that has been maintained by local inhabitants for centuries. Consequently, the "marshdweller" or "fishermen" is an integral part of Louisiana's folklore and heritage. As one resident remarked, the marshlands are "a great place to live; just ask anybody lucky enough to be living here" (Ditto 1980:47). Living and working in the state's alluvial lowlands gives that landscape meaning. Through time, the marshlands have developed into a kind of living archaeological-anthropological-geographical museum that was inhabited by proud, self-reliant, tough-minded, independent individuals who never worked for wages and maintained the individualistic spirit of a frontiersman. In the province's settlement clusters public schools were scarce. Consequently, many of the residents were illiterate, and contact with persons outside of their community was rare. Much of the produce they grew, the fish they caught, and the fowl, fur- and hide-bearing animals they killed were sold or bartered to others from their secluded frontier outposts. These folks were like the residents of the Appalachian Mountains and other pockets of strong-willed, single-minded, rural Americans. They were self-sufficient, suspicious of outsiders, poor, had their own language, and were reluctant to learn or speak English. They just wanted to be left alone and make a living from the wetland's assorted habitats.

In their communities they valued the "heart over the intellect, spontaneity over calculation, instinct over reason, music over the [printed] word, forgiveness over judgment, impermanence over permanence, and community over the isolated and alienated individual" (Starr 2001:63). With this background, marshdwellers developed an exceptional capacity to manage and benefit from the natural environment. They had a life "hidden" from the outside world and recognized quickly that a difference of "six inches in elevation could mean success or failure to a crop or a home" (Kane 1944:14). These folks lived, worked, and loved their remote marsh and swamp environments and understood their seasonal rhythms. They hunted, fished, and trapped this little known geographic province. (To some degree, many marshdwellers still have a hunter-gatherer lifestyle). Their living conditions were primitive by today's standards. They obtained their drinking water from cisterns (*cuves*). They had no electricity or formal education, but they could build a home or boat without plans. They were self-reliant, humble, proud (but not arrogant), and often intolerant of outsiders and their laws. They spoke French, Spanish, Chinese, and other foreign languages; yet, they were bound together by a common cultural element. They preserved their close-knit community and adhered to their regional "tribal codes" (Gowland 2003:414).

The ethnic diversity existing within the wetlands spawned cultural concepts that are rooted in each pioneer group's settlement philosophy and incorporated into their land-use ethics and patterns of economic production. Distinct attitudes toward the regional resource base developed, along with material elements that assisted the population in harmonizing with their surroundings and maximizing its yields. The relationships between different cultural elements evolved into a distinct human landscape imprint. These elements are now a part of the area's cultural ecology and ethnohistory. It is important to comprehend the region's ethno-history, since the layers of culture are very deep and very important to understanding the genesis of the human landscape, particularly as we see the "homogenization of American culture and the washing away of the peculiar characteristics that make Louisiana distinctive, quirky, and irreplaceably enriching to the rest of the country" (Richard 2003:177).

This is the story of Louisiana's "No Man's Land" that in actuality is a human landscape. From Indian communities, marked by a range of pottery and stone tools, to relocations prompted by Hurricanes Katrina (2005), Rita (2005), Gustav (2008), and Ike (2008), South Louisiana's near sea-level marshes and swamps served a range of culture groups—Acadians, Dalmatians/Yugoslavians, English, Filipinos, African Americans, American Indians, Italians, Germans, Creoles, Vietnamese, Danes, Isleños, Irish, Portuguese, Greeks, Norwegians, Swedes, Poles, and Americans.

To these permanent and transient settlers, the marsh and swamp was home. An analysis of these communities reveals eight all-encompassing categories: 1) agricultural; 2) industrial; 3) fishing; 4) trapping; 5) commercial hunting; 6) government service; 7) recreational, and 8) a combination of one or more of these groups. Overlap between types was not uncommon. Even so, each component constitutes a thread in the warp and weft of the fabric of human usage that characterizes the geography of Louisiana's wetlands.

Like the lands of the Navajo and Hopi, the marsh Arabs of the Tigris-Euphrates Delta, the reclamation marshdwellers of the Sacramento Delta, the Indians and *pantaneiros* in Brazil's Pantanal, and Canada's First People, Louisiana's coastal lowlands is a land apart, characterized by the "wild intricacies of nature" (Vileisis 1997:2). The marsh was the backdrop that defined these cultural groups' shared lifestyle. In turn these people shaped the topography to meet their needs. They gave the marsh meaning. In the process they became marsh denizens, whose cultural diversity had a profound impact on the region's somewhat eccentric character and their individual outlook on life.

These wetlands pioneers discovered an environment that effectively resisted their attempts to change its character to meet their needs, so they adapted—and adapted well. The resulting cultural landscape unfortunately is usually entirely overlooked in campaigns to save Louisiana's endangered wildlife habitats. Habitat preservation is certainly important, but so is conservation of the human factors associated with the natural environment. It is the sum of the environment's natural and human elements that is important in defining the significance of Louisiana's wetlands. "Save the land, save the people" could be the rallying phrase for the state's near-sea-level citizens. From the Sabine River to the Pearl River the wetlands have vital significance. The residents living on the "built" environment adjoining the marshlands need greater awareness of the wetlands' direct and indirect influences on their daily lives.

The coastal lowlands are to Louisiana what the Everglades are to Florida, the Rocky Mountains are to Colorado, or the Grand Canyon is to Arizona; they are an easily identifiable landscape symbol as well as Louisiana's landscape icon. In the judgment of most of Louisiana's citizens and others, the state cannot afford to lose this unique, irreplaceable, and defining landscape. Even so, as the coastal landscape changed, so did the residents who gave the environment its distinctive character. New cultural forms emerged with distinctive variations among the culture groups that produced them (Kniffen and Russell 1951).

For tens of thousands of people, the wetlands were their workplace. In most cases these culture groups never thought about owning the land. This real estate was considered free for all to use. For most of its settlement history, the marsh was by most accounts worthless, largely because of the "fictional, exaggerated, and misleading depictions of mythic marshes and swamps" by the popular literature (Vileisis 1997:60). "Because few people had firsthand knowledge of the landscape, the wetland lore and legends became accepted and integrated into the dominant Euroamerican culture" (Vileisis 1997:60). This false image became pervasive and nearly omnipresent.

Popular perceptions began to change in the twentieth century, when the coastal lowlands became an important source of a wide-range of renewable and non-renewable resources. As the region's population exploited these resources, some land was cleared, some land was created through reclamation, and some existing land was protected from flooding. As the migrating population moved onto this marginal land, they required federally subsidized levees and pumps to keep their properties dry. In essence, these engineered barriers served as dams to hold back floods and cordon off the overflow from the Mississippi and the area's other rivers. The net result was the loss of sediments that kept the coastal wetlands in balance, which, in turn, produced dramatic wetland loss and a corresponding disappearance of many early coastal settlements. Although an important chapter in the region's human occupancy and settlement succession, the historic retreat from Louisiana's marshlands has not been examined systematically.

Prior to the twentieth-century changes in the state's levees, people moved onto near sea-level sites and made a living off the land. They were at risk. Hurricanes destroyed and killed large numbers of coastal inhabitants who were never memorialized in the historical literature. Risk was a way of life, and marshdwellers were willing to take a chance. If their homes were destroyed, they moved. The occupation site was abandoned, and a new one was occupied. In some cases, marshdwellers were constantly on the move. In others, they settled the high ground, and their communities were more permanent, but always vulnerable. They were aware of, and playing by, Nature's rules.

Even so, marshdwellers' individual cultural heritage dictated how they solved their problems. They had the technological capacity and a value system that allowed them to live and work in the coastal plain. They also used their technological expertise and accumulated knowledge to guide their economic and settlement decisions. Furthermore, their value system and culture determined what kind of house to build, how to dress, the types of food to eat and when, and the form and kind of transport to use. Free will, at least in this context, was a myth, as there was clearly a right and a wrong way to do things, which was determined by each ethnic group's culture (Kniffen 1978C:164).

Further, cultural forces are linked to sustained environmental changes that inevitably make for a better understanding of a geographic province's land-use evolution and the human imprint on the topography. Cultural awareness, therefore, tempers the tendency to oversimplify causal relationships between culture groups and nature, and instills a respect for historical processes. This notion is particularly true in trying to understand an area's cultural evolution, which at the most basic level consists simply of people interacting with one another.

Cultural practices and customs helped formulate Louisiana's alluvial wetlands' land-use ethic and patterns of economic development. Moreover, in a region's geographic evolution, many cultural forces served as a marker defining the significance of each morphological unit—barrier islands, natural levee ridges, *chênières*, Indian middens, marshes, and swamps. However, the cultural heritage and morphology of the marshdweller's natural canvas has continuously changed and evolved, offering fresh challenges; nevertheless, the marsh became home to a highly diverse group of individuals making a living from the area's renewable natural resources.

With the oil boom in the second half of the twentieth century, families were no longer just farming, minding their cattle, fishing, and trapping. Many coastal dwellers could live off of their oil royalties and could afford amenities that were unthinkable prior to the petroleum boom. The "countryside" and the people changed significantly with this development. Even so, the marsh was still home to many near subsistence groups, and the memory of numerous lost villages remains part of their folk heritage. They recall places that are now underwater, but which at one time were sites for fishing and oyster camps, that perhaps were identified by rows of orange trees. Today, these sites are gone, but they should not be forgotten.

This story is thus bound together by two topical threads—one physical and one cultural. No attempt is made to provide a detailed analysis of the area's geology, biology, botany, climatology, and hydrology. These disciplines are discussed only in the context of how they influence and affect settlement. Drainage, reclamation, natural levees, and the Mississippi are also part of the settlement story. Although each of these subjects could generate an impressive bibliography, no attempt has been made to encapsulate the definitive works, or the sizeable body of relevant documentation compiled by scientists who have looked carefully at each of these elements. The author's object is instead to provide the reader with the geographical/geological background of South Louisiana in the context of the swamps and marshes and the culture groups that lived and worked within these environments.

The marshdwellers themselves are the key to the story, because in the final analysis, the coast is a people place made up, and influenced by, a wide variety of cultural assemblages. Each community left its own imprint, in the process becoming important parts of the story that makes the wetlands a human landscape. Therefore, this story is about those people and their life within or near Louisiana's "little known landscape." In some cases all the landmarks are gone, but the locals can tell you, even without any geographic markers, what was where, and who lived there, and why. They intimately know the territory we call "the marsh," or "the swamp," for it has been home for generations. Their "stories" and heritage are not well-known. These elements, however, give this land an identity and a place in the broader society (Vileisis 1997).

* * *

Over the wine I heard at least six languages in light-hearted conglomeration. The father, born French, had learned Spanish from his wife; he had picked up the Slavic tongue from others, and knew a little Italian, a Filipino dialect, and considerable English. An ancient neighbor used only French and his shoulders to express himself. Several visitors spoke fluently in Slavic, moderately well in French, and hesitantly in English. One robust oysterman seemed to comprehend every one of the tongues, but his remarks were always Tocko. A good-humored couple managed easily: he spoke to her only in French; she answered only in Italian. Their daughter listened to both of them and interjected comment—only in English; both knew what she said but neither essayed the speech that she chose. And when an acquaintance passed, everyone yelled at him, each in a different language (Kane 1944:269).

ACKNOWLEDGMENTS

The idea for this book began in April 2002 when Dr. Jess Walker, Dr. George Stain, and Mark Davis, suggested, within four weeks of each other, that I transform a lecture entitled: "Living on the Edge: Culture, Humankind, and Economics Within Louisiana's Coastal Lowlands" into a book-length manuscript. After considerable thought, I decided to focus on producing a document that addressed the many faces of Louisiana's wetlands, which Harnett Kane (1944:2) described as a place "that seems unable to make up its mind whether it will be earth or water, and so it compromises."

Although I am responsible for the final product, this book has been shaped by the writings and input of many individuals. In addition to those persons whose names appear in the bibliography, in the text accompanying photography, and historic maps, many individuals agreed to let me incorporate them into the final manuscript. Thanks are also in order to a broad cross-section of individuals who made this project viable. Early on in my career, I was encouraged to gather, catalogue, and organize photography, and other paper goods. The focus was simple: "Don't quote it, unless you own it." This philosophy has allowed my wife and me to accumulate a large collection of wetland-related material that served as the foundation for this effort. Even so, JSTOR and other Internet services added to the material reviewed for this book.

Without the assistance of Dr. Carl Brasseaux and his staff at the University of Louisiana at Lafayette Press, this volume could not have been finished in a timely manner. Dr. Brasseaux's faith in the project, quiet encouragement, knowledge of the publication process, and willingness to provide editorial comments, were most helpful. Many hours of copying photos, maps, and other paper media into a digital format were required. The Press's staff was supportive and efficient in this time-consuming endeavor. In addition, editing and reediting, formatting the document, and helping to reduce thousands of images into a few key visuals were daunting and time-consuming tasks performed admirably by the Press's staff.

Individuals and institutions that provided resource material and advice for this book include Special Collections at Louisiana State University's Hill Memorial Library, Tulane University, McNeese State University, University of Louisiana at Lafayette, University of Southeastern Louisiana, and Nicholls State University; the State Library; public libraries in New Orleans, Morgan City, Franklin, Jennings, and New Iberia; The Historic New Orleans Collection; individuals within Coastal Environments, Incorporated, United States Geologic Survey's National Wetlands Research Center, United States Fish and Wildlife Service, Minerals Management Service, Louisiana Wildlife and Fisheries, State Lands, Louisiana Department of Conservation, Louisiana Department of Environmental Quality, Louisiana's Oil Spill Coordinator's Office, Louisiana Geological Survey, and Department of Public Works; Mid-Continent Oil and Gas Association; the National Archives and Records Administration; and the Smithsonian Institution also provided important documents as well. Special thanks are extended to the faculty in LSU's Department of Geography and Anthropology, Louisiana Sea Grant, Coastal Studies Institute, Energy Studies, and the School of Agriculture.

Librarians throughout south Louisiana were particularly helpful. Obscure, misplaced, or miss-shelved references were uncovered and copied where appropriate. Interlibrary loan personnel worked tirelessly in finding material I needed. These chronically underfunded information professionals provided highly useful and timely reference material. I extend kudos to their dedicated professionalism.

For more than forty years, I have wandered Louisiana's back roads seeking information on the people and resources of Louisiana's wetlands. I extend a special thanks to all of my university colleagues, friends, and former students, along with a large number of trappers, fishermen, hunters, boatmen, engineers, and small business owners who provided advice and encouragement, along with important stories, photography, family ledgers, and manuscripts. On more than one occasion, lodging was provided and key insights were obtained over a strong cup of coffee, a beer, or just evening banter. Each of these contacts added to the story, whether dealing with coastal erosion, settlement history, oil, oysters, canals, or the finer points of the shrimp-drying business.

I also extend special thanks to Fred Kniffen, Bob West, Jess Walker, Bill McIntire, and Bill Haag for honing my interest in physical and cultural geography. Each of these individuals, and others, provided key insights into the value of folk customs and traditions in understanding the many faces of Louisiana's wetlands. These scholars set the benchmarks. I only followed the paths they laid down before me. Using a vast assortment of reference material, I have tried to synthesis into one volume the highly diverse and somewhat complicated interplay between cultures and the region's renewable and nonrenewable resources.

This book is dedicated to the following individuals: Dr. H. J. Walker, friend, mentor, and dedicated scholar; along with my parents, Don and Vana Davis; my wife, Karen Davis, who always encouraged my research and never questioned my eclectic collection of Louisiana-based paper goods; our daughters, Shaunna Landry and Jacelyn Gray, and their respective families; and three coastal scholars, Rod Emmer, Jim McCloy, and Shea Penland, who contributed to the broad spectrum of coastal research and died well before their time. A special thanks to "The Pirates" who for nearly four decades have provided valuable insights and a wide array of visual and mapping materials. Thanks is also due to my "Tall Friends," who for nearly two decades have worried about my long hours, constant road trips, weekend work habits, and penchant to work on holidays and other "days of rest."

Chapter 1
INTRODUCTION

Humans have occupied lower Louisiana for millenia. The earliest evidence of human activity in South Louisiana is associated with a site on Avery Island. Stone tools, radiocarbon (C^{14}) dated, suggest this site is more than 11,000 years old (Weinstein and Gagliano 1985). Because written records are nonexistent, each prehistoric group is "finger printed" by its material culture, including pottery and stone tools. Artifacts found in or on the ground provide data necessary to unravel the regional Indian settlement succession (Yates 1967; Weinstein and Gagliano 1985; Kniffen, et al. 1987). Further, cultural remains provide many clues in determining the natural setting during aboriginal times.

The methods of classifying archeological material into chronological units have passed through a number of transitions from the original mound builders cataloging system to archeological stages defined as Paleo-Indian (10,000 B.C. to 6000 B.C.), Meso-Indian/Archaic (6000 B.C. to 2500 B.C.), and Neo-Indians (2500 B.C. to A.D. 1600). This later stage is further subdivided into Poverty Point (2000 B.C. to 600 B.C.), Tchefuncte (600 B.C. to A.D. 200), Marksville (A.D. 200 to A.D. 400), Troyville-Coles Creek (A.D. 400 to A.D. 1100), and Mississippian/Plaquemine (A.D. 1100 to the Historic period) (Neuman 1970; Neuman and Byrd 1977; Newton 1972; Neuman and Hawkins 1993).

Although the Meso-Indians are included in this chronology, W. McIntire (1978) reports that no evidence has been uncovered to suggest they lived in the coastal plain. Encampments may have been part of this geographic province, but their cultural remains have been apparently lost to subsidence and sea-level rise, placing these historical artifacts below present marsh levels.

These early cultures' economy was not the most primitive, since the tribes frequently hunted large, now extinct animals, such as mastodons (*Mammut americanum*), saber-tooth tigers (genus *smilodon*), and wooly mammoths (*Mammuthus primigenius*). They lived in small nomadic bands that moved when the food supply was exhausted. As hunters and gatherers, these wandering Indian encampments left few artifacts (Neuman and Hawkins 1993). Even so, early Indians were aware of the wetlands' productivity. With time, these early hunters were replaced by more sedentary peoples. These groups exploited the marsh's fish and shellfish and practiced horticulture. Their artifacts, particularly their pottery, have helped archeologists better understand their individual cultures and lifestyles (see http://www.crt.state.la.us/archaeology/homepage/index.shtml for more archeology information).

Aboriginal Settlers and the Deltaic Environment

Aboriginal populations were highly attuned to the Deltaic environment and its natural features, as evidenced in their selection of the elevated natural levees along river channels for their settlements. Refuse material, largely pottery and animal bones, provided archaeologists with the material required to confirm the purpose, as well as the date, of each site.

W. McIntire (1958 and 1978) was one of the first individuals to combine archaeological and geological data to date river channels and the associated Deltaic morphology. As the Mississippi changed course and wandered across South Louisiana's landscape, old channels no longer provided the necessary rudimentary subsistence elements necessary to maintain and support the aboriginal settlers. These Indian bands were forced to move and find new home sites. In the process, they established a direct relationship between the places they lived and the historic stages of Deltaic development.

Indian midden site used as a contemporary Euro-American cemetery, south of Chauvin, 2009. (Photo courtesy of Carl A. Brasseaux.)

S. Gagliano and others have synthesized, through a number of contract surveys, considerable data related to South Louisiana's Indian archeology (Gagliano 1963, and 1979; Neuman and Simmons 1969; Gibson, et al. 1978; Hahn and Pearson 1988; Kelly 1988; Pearson, et al. 1989; Pearson, et al. 1989B; Weinstein and Kelly 1992; Perrault and Pearson 1994). The result is a rather detailed paleo-geographical reconstruction of the terrain. For example, Pearson, et al. (1989), who investigated nearly 200 Indian sites on the Golden Ranch Plantation's Bayous Matherne, Château de Cyprès, Petit Bois, and Portuguese sites, developed a model of prehistoric and historic settlement patterns over time, and how this blueprint reflected larger patterns of cultural adaptation and contact with Europeans.

Evidence of these prehistoric settlers ranges from temporary hunting and fishing camps to more permanent villages. In the wetlands, some of the earliest sites date from the Tchefuncte period, when Indians camped on natural levees, salt domes, and *chênières*—a term derived from the French word *chêne*, meaning oak, and best described as a sand ridge surrounded by marshland (Russell and Howe 1935; Schou 1967; Weinstein and Gagliano 1985).

In the sequence of Louisiana's aboriginal American cultures, agriculture became increasingly more important. Even so, for considerable numbers of people brackish water clams (*Rangia cuneata*) were an important food stable well into the historic period. Discarded shell heaps and other waste that accumulated around the community, are identified by archeologists as "middens." These middens identify settlement areas and consist of refuse material intermixed with ash, bones, shell, dirt, pottery fragments, kitchen rubbish, and other discarded debris.

Pottery fragments or potsherds are of special interest. These artifacts help investigators correlate cultural remains with stages in the evolutionary sequence of the coast's geomorphology (McIntire 1978). Moreover, middens provided later European settlers elevated home sites, which were relatively safe havens from floods, and an elevated site for their cemeteries (Comeaux 1972). One writer (Wilkinson 1892:402) reports the mounds: "rise like oases in a desert waste of reeds and grasses." They are, in fact, vernacular historical markers. Archeologists inspect and often excavate each midden site to unearth a human story.

Indian Middens, Mounds, and Beach Deposits

Rangia cuneata shells dominate midden sites in South Louisiana. Depending on the location, and the site's local environment, oysters (*Crassostrea virginica* Gmelin) that required more salinity or *Unio* (a freshwater clam) can be part of the site matrix as well (Padgett 1960). Deep cross-section profiles at some localities reveal stratification of shell types. These spots are good indicators of local environmental changes (Neuman 1970; Comeaux 1972; McIntire 1978; Pearson and Davis 1995). As a result of this type of investigative research, archeologists have divided Indian occupation sites into five categories: shell middens, shell mounds, earth mounds, earth middens, and beach deposits (Kniffen 1935; Howe, et al. 1935; Kniffen 1936B; Kniffen 1945; McIntire 1958; Neuman 1970; Weinstein and Gagliano 1985; Kniffen, et al. 1987).

Furthermore, these topographic features have long been used to measure subsidence along watercourses that are now barely visible on aerial imagery. Built on natural levees, or *chênières*, many middens are now partially to completely submerged. Some are below marsh level and are only exposed by erosion or through canal excavations. Otherwise, they are lost (McIntire 1978).

Shell middens are by far the most numerous archaeological artifacts along the Gulf Coast. Many are quite large—representing continued occupation for hundreds or even thousands of years. In some cases, they cover several acres and can extend to depths of ten feet or more. Others may be quite small, frequently only a few inches thick covering only a few square feet (Weinstein and Gagliano 1985).

Earth middens are less numerous, but they become more significant with increasing distance from the source of mollusks. They are characteristically found in the uplands and lack shell as their primary constituent. Most are associated with the crests of natural levees, particularly in those locales where the levee is relatively wide and high (Weinstein and Gagliano 1985).

Shell and earth mounds are hillocks intentionally formed by their builders. Constructed as burial or ceremonial (temple) monuments, they vary in size and can measure more than fifteen feet in height and 135 feet in diameter. Mound shapes are usually conical or truncated pyramids—a characteristic of the Marksville culture. Earthen burial mounds are more numerous, but shell mounds can be found in the coastal plain (Neuman 1970; Pearson and Davis 1995).

Beach deposits are wave-formed accumulations of shell intermixed with waveworn artifacts. They are exposed when a beach that formerly extended beyond the regressive present shoreline of inland lakes, bays, or other waterbodies are cut by former river distributaries or beach-face erosion. The reworked midden or mound materials are then exposed (Howe, et al. 1935; Weinstein and Gagliano 1985). F. B. Kniffen (1968) notes that potsherds discovered on the beaches of the Chandeleur Islands are now in the Gulf of Mexico. These artifacts were eroded and covered as the Gulf's waters pushed the barrier island chain westward. In addition, as the beach deposits are reworked they are often tossed back on the treeless marsh surface where they may form a thin veneer (Weinstein and Gagliano 1985; Kniffen, et al. 1987).

Cattle grazing on a *chênière* ridge, 1982. (Photo by the author.)

South Louisiana's Historic Indians and Other Settlers

Indian tribes inhabiting central and eastern coastal Louisiana were culturally related to the native peoples of the Eastern maize area of North America, whereas groups living in southwestern Louisiana had cultural affinities with Indians that lived along the Texas coast (Kniffen 1935; Kniffen 1945; Neuman and Simmons 1969; Kniffen, et al. 1987). These tribal units included the Attakapa, Chitimacha, Houma, Washa, and Chawasha.

Overall, a rich and highly productive natural environment made it possible for a relatively large population to exist in the region on a full-time basis and to develop moderate-size villages. Even so, at the time of European contact there were perhaps only 15,000 Indians in all of Louisiana (Kniffen 1968). For example, during this period it is estimated that between 200 and 300 Washa and Chawasha occupied the general area parallel to Bayou Lafourche. Nevertheless, several tribal groups continue to work their ancestral land, such as the Chitimacha near Charenton, Louisiana (also known as *Lieu des Chetimachas* and Indian Creek). In fact, ancestors of the modern Chitimacha raised swamp living to a high art, built the best *pirogues*, and made fine cane baskets (Medford 1999). Along with the Chitimacha, a cluster of dispersed "Houma" in lower Terrebonne and lower Lafourche parishes still inhabit what they consider is their ancestral land.

Around 1900, Houmas families based in Golden Meadow pushed eastward through the Little Lake and Lake Salvador areas seeking new trapping, hunting, and shrimping areas. They settled eventually in the Barataria-Lafitte region in Jefferson Parish and further east in Plaquemines Parish. In the early 1930s, several Houma families moved west into St. Mary Parish and established communities that continue to the present. A few years later, Houma trappers from the Pointe aux Chênes community were recruited by St. Bernard Parish landowners to assist in the control of fur-bearing animals (Fisher 1965). During and after World War II, many families moved out of the Terrebonne-Lafourche region. They relocated across the Mississippi River from New Orleans in towns that are part of the "west bank" metropolitan area.

Although many individual Indians moved out of the coastal lowlands, a number remain a part of the folk landscape (Stanton 1971). These assemblages are most notable at Isle de Jean Charles and the lower extremities of the area's bayous, where hunting, fishing, and trapping are integral parts of the local way of life (Swanton 1911; Swanton 1952). The Houma Indians have been disappointed and frustrated that the Federal government's sponsored anthropologists and historians have determined there is no documented evidence of any cultural or archeological links between the modern Houma and the Houma of the colonial period. They are recognized as Indians, but not recognized as a valid tribe (Duthu 1997; Davis 2001).

Even so, Native American residents of the state's southeastern coastal plain maintain the region's oldest oral traditions which provide vital insights into the region's environmental history. Descendants of the Billiots and Naquins (common Native American names in southern Terrebonne Parish), who live on the Isle de Jean Charles ridge, recount that at the turn of the twentieth century lower Pointe aux Chênes (now underwater) boasted sugarcane fields. Isle Felicity, once the site of a few homes and small cattle herds, is also now under water (Rogers 1985). These recollections help frame changes in the modern landscape, and they are an important element in understanding the coastal lowland's environmental history.

For the post-Indian era there are no shell middens, but additional "diagnostic markers" do exist. Some are ephemeral and have disappeared. Others are more permanent and reflect the manner in which the marshlands were used (e.g. buildings, docks, roads, canals, place names, etc.). These relic "made" artifacts are preserved on maps, but the precise motivation behind their construction is frequently blurred or lost. As a consequence, the written record must be used to unravel the territory's "geographic personality." For example, in Fisk (1891) there is a reference to the community of Malagay. A query of the United States Geological Survey's (USGS) Geographic Names Information System (GNIS) reveals that this village was located in Lafourche Parish. No other information is provided. What happened to Malagay? How many people know that Malagay ever existed? One wonders if it was ever more than just a dot on a map.

In point of fact, local informants report Malagay was located several miles north of the Lafourche Parish community of Kraemer/Bayou Boeuf. It was a swamper's village that had a post office and school, and was named apparently for Bayou Malagay. This navigable bayou ran in front of the town to Bayou Boeuf. The school was moved to Bayou Boeuf and is the oldest one-room "little red schoolhouse" in continuous use in Louisiana. Students living on the same side of the bayou as the school originally walked or rode mules to class each day. Those living across the bayou traveled by boat (Landry 2006, pers. comm.; History of Bayou Boeuf 2006; Irvin 2007).

Another one of these "lost" communities is the Mermentau River village of Riverside, which had "three stores and several residences, post-office and shipping post" (Perrin 1891:1704). This site is not in the GNIS, so what happened to Riverside? Like so many wetland-de-

Abandoned Kraemer movie theater, 1983. (Photo by the author.)

pendent settlement clusters, it eventually disappeared. The population relocated to other places, and their former home became only a memory or a place name on a map of the period.

Wildlife and Fisheries Sister Lake Camp Facility, 1954. (Photo courtesy of Louisiana Wildlife and Fisheries.)

H. Moore (1899) commented that on "Grand Bayou de Large" approximately twenty camps between Sister Lake and the Gulf once harvested oysters. The problem is that in the late nineteenth century maps are so poor that many settlements and physical features were not reported. Lake Barré, for example, was not shown on any of these charts, yet the lake was at the time eight-miles long and three- to four-miles wide.

The only visible artifact of the swampers' village of Cousins, near Boutte in St. Charles Parish, is Cousins Canal. The village is gone. Gray (1985) reports that seventy or more homes—which lacked electricity, telephones, or indoor plumbing—formed the village's nucleus. They were built high on cypress blocks to protect against flooding. Moreover, a small Catholic church was serviced by a "circuit priest" from Luling. The canal was built in 1910 to harvest cypress. At the cypress industry's zenith, more than 100,000 board feet were cut daily from logs removed from the swamp around Cousins. Moss pickers, trappers, hunters, and cattlemen subsequently used the property. Each group left an imprint on the area and, as is frequently the case; "history is sometimes swallowed by relentless time and faltering memories" (Gray 1985:3).

In some cases, communities change names. For example, the Plaquemines Parish village of Filipino appears on the 1939 and 1944 edition of the USGS Pointe à la Hache quadrangle. By 1949, however, the name had been changed to Grand Bayou Village (Anderson 2006, pers. comm.). In addition, several place names reference China: China Bayou, Chinaman Bayou, China Pass, Bayou Chine, and China Island. Nothing has been discovered that would suggest that these places were named by Chinese for Chinese settlers. It is also quite likely that Filipino and Chinese cemeteries were part of the marsh landscape as well, like Alombro cemetery on the USGS 1935 Bay Dosgris 7.5 minute quadrangle (Anderson 2006B, pers. comm.). These references, and others, suggest the marsh and swamp were being permanently inhabited by a diverse assemblage of cultures.

The Marsh and Fringe Settlements

In Europe, a linear long-lot agricultural settlement plan emerged when wetlands' environments were reclaimed by dikes. In South Louisiana this form follows the crest of natural levees and *chênière* ridges, with agriculture dominating the available arable land. Consequently, natural levee settlements typify the complexity of linear settlement types. There is, therefore, a continuous row of houses along the highways parallel to the "back" country's north-south trending waterways. In a sense, these elongated communities are considered a homogenous unit. People regard a bayou settlement, regardless of its length, as a single entity with varying degrees of continuity, with the bayou serving as the community's main street. Locals deem populations residing outside definite community settlement nodes as being rural, even though the house-to-house line settlement may be several miles long and would be defined as clearly rural to outsiders. From the local perspective, this is not the case.

A second natural levee settlement grouping occurs on many autonomous, large, brick-and-mortar plantations. These nodes typically encompass from ten to more than thirty dwellings. The cluster contains a general store and may be either a linear or a block community. This category represents Louisiana's early agro-industrial capitalism. Today, they are relics of the pre-mechanization period (Rehder 1999; Follett 2007).

The third class is the compact urban district, with associated settlement outliers or subdivisions. The fourth is the remote individual residence, village, or hamlet established to harvest renewable resources and accessible only by boat. These remote hamlets can be subdivided into subsets based on purpose and resources. In general, they were primarily founded for fishing, trapping, and commercial hunting purposes.

In the early twentieth century, houseboat clusters were common sights along Louisiana's waterways, ca. 1910. (Photo courtesy of William Littlejohn Martin Collection, Archives & Special Collections, Nicholls State University.)

In the post-World War II era, recreational nodes are part of this subset as well (Padgett 1963; Padgett 1969). The renewable resource-base hamlets were often transient, self-contained, houseboat-based clusters, centered on a boat type that was more house than boat, for they were not seaworthy vessels. Other settlements were more substantial. The fifth is the industrial community built exclusively to exploit a renewable or non-renewable resource by profit-minded, risk-taking, entrepreneurs.

The People and the Landscape

Below us [Golden Meadow] there is . . . only wasteland, and the ruins of Chênière Caminada, until you reach Grand Isle (Ramsey 1957:110).

Why I can remember no more'n fifty years ago when dis whole marsh was nuttin' but wasteland . . . My *p'père*'s camp was down at da mouth of Palmetto Bayou and we made good livin' wit our lil lugger goin' shrimpin' in summer, catchin' us a few minks and 'rats in winter. We made good livin' . . . and we felt da land was ours awright . . . *mon dieu*, we couldn't felt no better if da whole earth was ours, mais sho! There ain' no system in them days, ma *chère* . . . an' that make plenty difference (Ramsey 1957:164).

The bayou is the focus of economic activity in Louisiana's coastal wetlands, 1950. (Photo courtesy of the Standard Oil Collection, University of Louisville, negative no. 67492.)

The world's coasts are changing continually. They represent perhaps our last frontier; yet, the wild seacoast is vanishing. As the coast evolves, humankind is either the region's worst enemy or its best friend. The difference between the two depends on how the coast is perceived and used with respect, carelessness, undisciplined development, or appreciation of its resources. There is, regardless of a culture group's objectives, a never-ending interplay between the forces and processes that reshape and realign coastal contours. Land-building and land-losing elements are at work constantly. People have had relatively little influence on these agents; thus, the inherent instability of beaches, dunes, sea cliffs, marshes, and barrier islands presents a challenge. All of these landscape elements have served as focal points for settlements during the Pioneer Period of American history and reflect the population's social heritage.

The settlement and economic development within the coastal lowlands was related to the larger processes of community development, trade, and resource exploitation. In the process, settlers deliberately modified and also unintentionally disrupted the natural balance. They reshaped the landscape to meet their needs and became the most active agent in changing the wetlands' geographic personality (Dunbar 1974). Through the processes of diffusion and migration, the human imprint within Louisiana's coastal plain has habitually been transient. In time and space, culture is the wetlands' dominate settlement force.

Culture is thus the variable that also reflects the landscape's human qualities through occupancy patterns (Kniffen 1954). There are no universal laws that allow us to study culture's interaction with the land and the associated relationships. "Therefore," Kniffen posits, "the study of man in a particular site must be historical" (Kniffen 1960:22). "Perhaps nowhere else in the United States does the landscape so clearly reflect the imprint of varied cultural strains as it does in Louisiana" (Kniffen 1936:179). With less than two persons per square mile, Louisiana's rural wetlands represent in the nineteenth and early twentieth centuries a frontier of occupancy (Hart 1974)—characterized by an exceedingly diverse assemblage of material and non-material culture elements or identifiers from a complex and decidedly diverse assemblage of cultures (Owens 1999B; Spitzer 1999). This is especially the case within Louisiana's coastal marsh and swamplands.

With time, these earlier pioneer and transient settlers realized the biological productivity of these "wet" habitats would sustain them physically and economically. They learned from the region's aboriginal population—including the Chitimacha and Houma tribes—how to survive in this geographic province (Roy and Leary 1977; Kniffen, et al. 1987). For example, the extensive use of palmet-

Where available, palmetto was an important building material for wetland inhabitants, 1907. (Photo courtesy of Swanton Collection, Smithsonian Institution, negative book IV, negative no. 155.)

to (*Sabal minor*), or *latanier*, as a building material was learned from contact with local Indian groups (Kniffen, et al. 1987). Palmetto was also woven into hats to use while working in the sun and Choctaw-inspired cane baskets were the pioneers' clothes hampers and storage containers.

Making these articles from the native plant material was not part of the immigrant's cultural baggage. Plants were utilized because they were available. Building and weaving techniques were borrowed from local Indian tribes, as was the case with other material and non-material folk culture elements that are now part of the vernacular landscape. Further, the marsh and swampland inhabitants developed a commitment to the land and a unique sense of togetherness. Their adaptability and resourcefulness permitted them to survive. They acquired the tools and techniques that allowed them to exploit the local resources and became an integral part of their folk economy (Comeaux 1972).

In the process, these "brethren of the coast" acquired a idiosyncratic cultural and regional identity that is a subset of the larger, more defined, and more thoroughly studied, ethnic island identified with Louisiana's French-speaking inhabitants. Although French was the dominate language, over time it was joined by English, *Créole*

(*Criollo*—literally those born in the colonies), Chinese, Spanish, German, Filipino, Italian, Vietnamese, and Serbian/Croatian. Clearly, Louisiana's wetland population was not predominantly Anglo-Saxon. Consequently, immigrant groups added cultural diversity to the bayou country's folk landscape and contributed

With arrival of the Vietnamese, Louisiana's business community had to adjust their signage accordingly, 1985. (Photo by the author.)

to the convergence of cultures within the alluvial plain (Dillard 1985; Gregory 1999).

A constant flow of immigrants brought these language groups into New Orleans and the surrounding marshes and swamps. By 1840, the Crescent City was one of the most ethnically diverse municipalities in America and the nation's fourth largest city (Jordan 1985; Magill 2000; Campanella 2006). The metropolis became so distinct ethnically, Henry Hopkins (1809:855) reported, that "let a company of Militia be assembled and there is no one language in which the word of command can be given that will be intelligible to all." Each cultural assemblage left its mark on the city's physiognomy while also clinging tenaciously to its individual uniqueness and love of life. The influx of these various ethnic groups proved an important labor pool in meeting the assorted needs of the expanding city.

After the Civil War, however, there was a labor shortage in the state. The need for an expanded workforce prompted Louisiana's legislatures to pass an act in 1866 to organize a Bureau of Immigration. The Bureau advertised "the state's many physical merits and natural resources and to assist those who wished to migrate to Louisiana" (Williams 1974:155). The immigration service functioned well until 1869, when its structure was modified. After this largely administrative adjustment, the Bureau became less effective and did not aggressively entice new immigrants. In 1873, the legislature made the Bureau a self-sustaining entity, thereby divesting itself, for a time, of the responsibility for underwriting the costs associated with the state's immigration policy. Private interests began to assist in recruiting immigrants.

In 1880, Louisiana was again in the immigration business with a revamped State Immigration Bureau (Williams 1974). Although rural parishes, such as St. Tammany, Caddo, Franklin, Calcasieu, Union, and St. Mary were interested in new residents, many of these post-Civil War immigrants flocked to New Orleans and rapidly adapted economically. In spite of hurricanes, floods, yellow fever (also known as the Saffron Scourge and the Strangers' Disease), and Asiatic cholera, life in New Orleans could be very pleasant for the business elite. New Orleans, "offered a cultural life of great diversity as well as grand recreational facilities" (Clark 1967:122). As a result, the city attracted thousands of immigrants, who took advantage of the municipality's economic climate and became successful entrepreneurs, artisans, tradesmen, and craftsmen—fruit dealers (who would establish the United Fruit Company [now Chiquita Brands International] and Standard Fruit Company [now Dole Food Company]), barbers, blacksmiths, carpenters, masons, hatters, tailors, watchmakers, bricklayers, butchers, clerks, accountants, physicians, teachers, and artists (Magnaghi 1986; Reeves 2007).

Ancillary to this growth was the fact the "Mississippi River and delta only began to be utilized intensively after becoming a center for colonization in the eighteenth and nineteenth centuries" (Walker and Davis 2002:61). In the early nineteenth century, New Orleans was expanding, but its death rates exceeded its births. Largely because of "violent" yellow fever epidemics, the city was the necropolis of the South. Even so, new immigrants assisted the city expand by leaps and bounds. "The menace of yellow fever did not seem to discourage the great hordes who flocked to the Crescent City annually" (Carrigan 1963:14). Moreover, in an age when no one understood how to combat yellow fever effectively, epidemics could not be prevented and/or controlled, as was the case with the great 1853 outbreak. In reference to the 1853 epidemic, J. A. Carrigan (1963:31) reported a number of tall tales that revealed "the fever was so bad at the St. Charles Hotel, that as soon as a man arrived and registered his name they immediately took his measure for a coffin, and asked him to note down in which cemetery he desired to be interred." Further, "as soon as a man arrived on one of the steamboats, the officers of the Board of Health immediately took his name and entered it in their books as deceased, to save all trouble in calling upon him again."

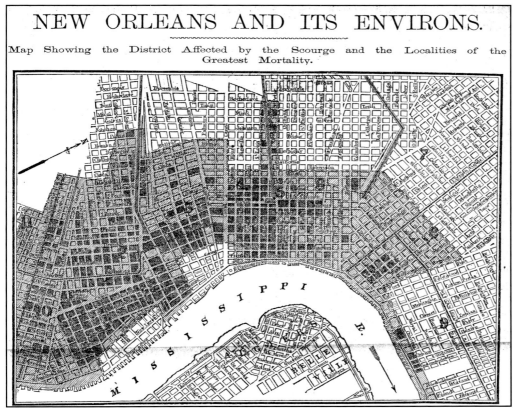

The boundaries of the 1878 yellow fever outbreak in New Orleans. (Image from the *New York Herald*, September 1878.)

These "plagues" and the associated "urban legends" had to run their course "until cold weather curtailed mosquito activity, or until the supply of susceptible victims gave out" (Carrigan 1963:27).

New Orleans was a hotbed for "yellow jack," and the mosquito-borne disease struck regularly, killing more adults than children, leaving a sizeable orphan population. In addition, "tens of thousands of Louisianans fled north to escape the 'fever of death'" (Shanabruch 1977:212). Even with all of the social issues associated with this disease, New Orleans had a population of more than 200,000 by 1890 and was an important market for the distribution of wetland-dependent resources (Campanella 2006).

Major yellow fever epidemics in South Louisiana, 1847-1905
(From Carrigan 1994; Bergerie 2000; and Campanella 2006)

Date	Issues
1847	In New Orleans between 2,300 and 3,000 died
1852-1853	About 8,400 died in New Orleans
1854	About 2,500 died in New Orleans
1855	About 2,600 died in New Orleans
1858	4,855 died in New Orleans

Date	Issues
1867	3,320 died in New Orleans
1878	2,700 ill, 4,046 died and 40,000 left New Orleans
1897	298 died in New Orleans
1898	South-central Louisiana
1905	452 died in New Orleans

Every year trappers had to transport all their belongings to their marsh camps. (Photo from the *Louisiana Conservationist,* vol. 10, 1958.)

Ultimately, the population expanded. Although the French are the most recognizable ethnic immigrants, villages within the swamp, marsh, or on the *chênières*, and barrier islands were colonized by a distinct assemblage of nationalities. This cultural and ethnic montage founded communities throughout the wetlands. To these secluded encampments, settlers brought pigs, poultry, and cattle that roamed freely over the near sea-level landscape. Cattle and feral hogs continue to roam and graze the marsh landscape.

Settling and Using the Coast: The Home of the Marshdweller

James Daisy doesn't even need to work a full eight months to live well, much less work twelve hours a day, so why does he do it? And with his considerable oyster income, why does he spend the rest of the year trapping on the side? 'Well,' he pauses in a curl of smoke, looking out the window again, 'out there's where I live' (Rushton 1979:96).

Louisiana's inland fishing vessels provide quick and easy access to harvesting sites, 1970. (Photo by the author.)

The marshdwellers' understanding and knowledge of the coastal lowlands is legendary. Their prodigious energy allowed them to survive and prosper without electricity, plumbing, or an evening newspaper. Whether such a life is desirable or not depends on the temperament and background of an individual. Even so, without any *Periplus*—navigational guides—or instruments, their *pirogues*, luggers, sloops, and Lafitte skiffs wend their way in the worst weather through the maze of ponds, lakes, bayous, and *traînasses* into their trapping, hunting, or fishing grounds with ease. Collectively, they are among the last of this country's hunters and gatherers.

Even though they struggled for habitable space, the marshdwellers understood the landscape and knew how to use it; and they used it well. They developed the stamina and tenacity to make a living in the near sea-level marshes. The same can be said about residents of the Atlantic seaboard's *pocosin* and California's "tule" settlements (Thompson 1982). These "folks" lived as close to the sea as the land would allow. They knew the interdependence of both well enough to know where to find their own place (Rushton 1979). This is a landscape of water and it is from the water and adjoining marshes that these folks made their living. It was a hard and primitive life, but one they enjoyed.

To the marshdwellers, their wetland retreats were a form of escape from their detractors. In the process of "hiding" in the "uninhabitable" marshes, the marshdwell-

Moving through the marsh. (Image from *Harper's Weekly*, March 1887.)

Coffee and camaraderie after a hard day in the marsh, 1941. (Photo from the *Louisiana Oyster Bulletin*, no. 1, 1941.)

Often not mapped, the trappers' "pirogue trails" provided access to isolated marsh sites. (Photo from the *Jefferson Parish Yearly Review,* 1939.)

ers preserved their ethnic folk culture in the camaraderie of their out-of-the-way wetland-oriented hamlets. City dwellers always had to go someplace to unwind. To marshdwellers, there was nothing more peaceful than getting out on the water unaccompanied and alone; they enjoyed the solitude and were grateful for the independence. To these people the human body was like a machine that was going to get stiff and useless through disuse. As a consequence, old men never retired. They simply worked as hard as they could teaching their children and grandchildren and in some cases their great-grandchildren the ways of the marsh or swamp. One generation passed on the traditions to the next generation and each survived on the abundant readily available local resources.

Folk speech and the art of storytelling became the vehicle for conveying their folklore and traditions (Perrin 1985). "No John Henry appears in Louisiana/folk songs; any Mike Fink or Paul Bunyan, no deeds of mighty workers or work efforts. Instead, the songs they sang and passed on to their children tended to be songs of love and courtship, narrative adventure, satirical comment, or pure fun, to be enjoyed with eating, drinking and dancing" (Dormon 1983:38).

Over time, this attitude about life allowed these marshdwellers to develop a unique capacity to manage and benefit from the natural wetland environment. The land was their sanctuary. By developing unique boat types, occupancy patterns suited to wetland environments, and a lifestyle based on renewable resources, they were content, happy, and independent. They only answered to themselves and their families. Life was harsh and often short, but enjoyable. Eventually, permanent settlers migrated to these remote landscapes and acquired cultural practices identified with an annual-use-cycle tied to the marketable natural resources.

Wetland-oriented communities were founded by numerous ethnic minorities representing a kaleidoscope of cultures that mingled and fused together. Based on different situations, viewpoints, and values, each group interpreted the environment differently. By the late nineteenth and early twentieth centuries, small settlements, hotels, dancehalls, and other recreation endeavors—lavish hunting clubs and camps—followed these wetland pioneers. The end result is a geographic region whose "personality" is identified by the early settlers' material and non-material culture elements.

For example, dances were an essential part of South Louisiana's culture. The dancehalls were frequently adjuncts to other businesses, like the lower Bayou Lafourche Lee Brothers Dancehall and Machine Shop (Cheniere Hurricane Centennial 1995). Trucks were sent out along the road by dancehall owners to transport people to the weekly dances (*fais do-do*)—separate trucks for men and women so that the occupants could be packed more closely.

At the dancehall, this popular social activity required a gentleman to pay five cents to dance with a lady, while her mother sat on the sidelines keeping a watchful eye on the couple (A picture history ca. 1986). Before automobiles, groups traveled to weekend dances on barges and in boats, or families held "house dances," known as *bals de maison*, where the local fiddlers played *mazurkas*—Polish folk dances, jigs, reels, cotillions, *lanciers, dance rondes*, and handkerchief dances. The Cajun two-step and waltz survives (Rickels 1978). In later years, dancehalls supplanted the *bals de maison*, but the *fais do-dos* met their demise with passage of a law banning children from establishments serving alcoholic beverages. Prior to that time, children would "make do-do"—sleep—under a table and around the room until it was time to go home. The dancehall was, in fact, the primary place to hear Cajun music that is based on the French accordion, guitar, violin, *'ti fers* (triangles), and a high-pitched singing style—the Cajun equivalent to "soul-vocals" (Savoy 1999).

Therefore, well before Wilson Pickett and James Brown were adding screams to their lyrics, Cajun roots bands were interrupting their music with a shrill cry of their own—Hay-hee!! The purpose was a cathartic release by musicians giving their all to make people dance. Indeed, the best complement one can pay a Cajun band is to dance to their music. The Hackberry Ramblers, with their authentic folk art-based music, have been meeting this mantra for more than seventy years and were the first musicians to bring electronic amplification to area dancehalls (Sandmel 2004).

As a result, "dancers across South Louisiana were shocked in the mid-1930s to hear music which came not only from the bandstand, but also from the opposite end of the dancehall through speakers. In places not yet reached by the rural electrification project (REA) these early sound systems were powered by a Model T idling behind the building" (Ancelet 1989:29). Throughout the coastal lowlands the most general form of recreation

Throughout South Louisiana, music is an important manifestation of the local *joie de vivre*, ca. 1941. (Photo courtesy of Luderin Darbone Scrapbook, Center for Louisiana Studies, University of Louisiana at Lafayette.)

Little Temple, an important landmark in the Barataria Basin, was used by pirates and locals. (Image from *Frank Leslie's Illustrated Newspaper,* 1868.)

Early twentieth century fishing camp. (Photo from Gates 1910.)

was dancing. In the marshes of southeastern Louisiana, prior to mass communications, a messenger was sent out to fire a gun before the door of each dwelling to announce a *"bal ce soir chez"* (Crété 1981). In some cases, young people were singing folk songs and dancing folk dances that are "almost forgotten in France" (Evans 1963:49). These non-material folk elements survived in the marshes virtually intact.

When not enjoying their *"laissez les bon temps rouler"* attitude, the wetlands landscape provided the local inhabitants with their recreation and income. Many "have never been in an airplane, never owned a credit card, never read a book, never seen a hill much taller than the thirty-foot Indian mounds. . . ." (Tidwell 2003:13). Even so, these marshdwellers were happy. Their lives have changed, accelerated partly by coastal land loss, but the wetlands are in their blood.

The Folks, the People, the Marshdweller: The Coastal Prospectors

It takes a formidable breed of men, you see, to match such a fabulous land. You wouldn't believe what a melting pot the Delta is . . . and how its peoples live in peace together. The English and French and the Tockos, Spanish and Irish, Italian and Chinese, Negro and Philippine . . . all living and sharing their work and their pleasures . . . the few big planters that are left and the *petits fermiers* in their narrow rows of truck garden, the orange growers and lily growers and the wine makers, the oystermen and shrimpers, frog hunters and trappers, alligator hunters and *remedie* men, the oil geologists and river pilots . . . and us few religious working among the whole great pack of them (Ramsey 1957:269-270).

The marsh and swamp are landscapes where faiths, culture, races, and ethnic groups coexist and contribute to the wetlands' persona, as well as to its dynamism and creativity. In many ways, these ethnic minorities reinvented the physical environment to meet their needs. In the process, they created an ethnically heterogeneous setting that is like a parenthetical thought, a land and a people uncertain—frankly, not caring—how or even whether they fit in. They were marshdwellers and proud of it. They did not need to explain their modest lifestyle, reason for being, and *c'est la vie* attitude. To them the marsh and swamp was of inestimable value; it sustained them and was their home. Consequently, the earliest immigrants utilized the wetlands to support their subsistence economies. By necessity these water-based communi-

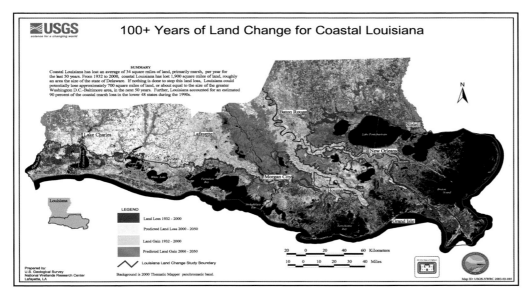

(Image from U. S. Geological Survey, 2003.)

ties were tied directly to the region's waterbodies. Without these watercourses many settlement clusters would never have come into existence, as the watercourse was the community's link to the outside.

With water as each settlement's constant, early marshdwellers established their homes, villages, and hamlets on protected and well-drained land. Stranded beach ridges, natural levees, barrier islands, "hammocks," stilt complexes, or barges in the marsh or swamps were the anchor points for their communities. Regardless of location, their home was a world of water (Job 1910). In fact, one of the most outstanding characteristic of these communities is their location. They were always near a waterbody which provided location stability.

The by-product of these quaint and picturesque settings is they became the subject matter for the photography of Fonville Winans, Elemore Morgan, C. C. Lockwood, George François Mugnier, Neil Campbell, and Julie Sims, or the paintings of John James Audubon, Thomas Bangs Thorpe, Everett B. D. Julio, Charles Giroux, Louise Amelia Green Woodward, and Charles Wellington Boyle (Bonner 2007-08). These photogra-

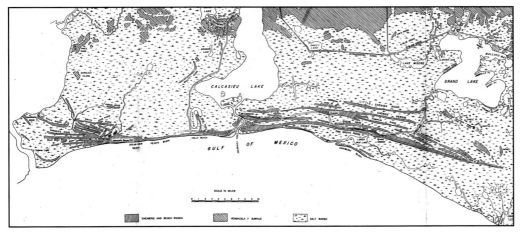

Former beach ridges mark the habitable land on the *chênière* plain. (Image from Howe, et al., "Physiography," *Geological Bulletin* 6, 1935.)

phers and artists, following the convictions of Ansel Adams, utilized photographs, as well as paintings, to "help us see more clearly and more deeply, and to reveal to others the grandeurs and potentials of the one and only world which we inhabit" (Kemp 1997:18). These images are important historic markers that preserved and captured the spirit, and perhaps heart, of the marshdweller's waterborne domain.

Houseboats provided a floating settlement for swampers, ca. 1895. (Photo courtesy of George François Mugnier Photograph Collection, Louisiana Division, New Orleans Public Library.)

Other than *chênières*, exposed salt domes, and isolated levee remnants, the marshes and swamps were devoid of high land, so land above the normal high-water mark, called by many the "front lands," or natural levees, regularly became the focal points of colonization (Kniffen 1990). As a result, a settlement succession pattern was initiated that evolved from the area's distinctive deltaic morphology that formed a complex, interconnected network of estuarine channels, and wetland habitats.

From a temporal-spatial perspective, these sites left a small geographic footprint. If the site was completely cut off from the outside, the form was simply a cluster of homes, or perhaps a single campboat or oystermen's, trapper's, or market hunter's camp. In the early twentieth century, this assemblage of subsistence settlements was joined by the orderly camp settlements associated with the exploitation of oil, natural gas, and sulphur—the exploitation of which added a large number of industrial communities to the wetland's settlement history.

Whether an industrial site, or a village occupied by trappers or oystermen, each community was economically homogeneous, in that all inhabitants were supported by variations of the same means of livelihood. Each settlement category had its own specific-trait-signature. This cultural or economic identifier gives the site functional meaning to the marshdweller's sense of place. Consequently, the people of the wetlands lived in obscurity in the most humble of circumstances. They were "aquatic men" who "flourished in the coastal lowlands and clung to their own customs and way of life" (Crété 1981:282).

The wetlands' farmer-trapper-fisher folk, outfitted in faded cotton-velveteen clothes developed skills that allowed them to harvest local estuarine-dependent wildlife in their "half-agricultural, half aquatic life" (Kane 1944:215). "Where the wheel stops, the keel begins" describes how these folks gained access to their harvesting and settlement sites. In actuality, where roads and power lines end, there is inevitably a settlement. These communities were frequently an unconscious gathering of

The seasons determined a waterman's livelihood, 1997. (Photo by the author.)

an individual clan. Since everyone was related, they lived together for a lifetime in a rural setting shaped by their cultural heritage (Kniffen 1978B). This was the way of the people of the marshes, swamps, natural levees, and *chênières*. On Bayou Lafourche this attitude is described simply as *la vie lafourchaise*.

Because in the wetlands chance rules, the inhabitants had no guarantees; therefore, by necessity, all occupations were seasonal. This meant all possible time was devoted to maximizing the harvest of aquatic, avian, and hide- and fur-bearing animals. When the shrimp (*crevette*) supply in inland waters became scarce, shrimp boats turned to oyster or crab fishing; and numerous watermen became trappers. When not at work in the marshes, marshdwellers tarred their hoop nets (also known as fyke nets in other parts of the United States) so they could withstand the rigors of underwater service. In addition, they knitted new nets, repaired their boats and engines, or built a *pirogue* or skiff (*esquif* in Louisiana French).

Whether Acadian, Isleño (Canary Islanders), Yugoslavian (Dalmatian), African American, American Indian, Chinese, Anglo-Saxon, Philippine, or Portuguese, these peasant fisherfolk were, in most cases, carrying on the occupation of their ancestors, some of whom were fishing for cod off Nova Scotia long before Columbus discovered America. Even though wetland residents considered the marsh to be of little monetary value, they always profited from harvesting the geographic province's aquatic and avian resources. Their income depended upon their harvest that in turn depended on the weather.

Louisiana's sea-level citizens learned to live and adapt to subsidence, sea-level rise, hurricane-induced storm surges, volatile winds, and coastal land loss/erosion. These natural phenomena, compounded by engineering "solutions," have created, in many cases, below sea-level citizens. As a result, South Louisiana's geographic complex is a product of two distinct ingredients: one natural and the other cultural, or human (Kniffen 1978).

Natural ingredients, such as relief, soils, landforms, rocks, vegetation, climate, and other features and agents have been studied extensive, and their importance is often self-evident. Cultural elements—demography, ethnicity, economy, learned skills, acculturation and assimilation, cultural adaptation and heritage, and historical and evolutionary change—are not observed so easily. In reality, these cultural and/or social identifiers are frequently the foundation for the coastal zone's importance as a productive environment.

Moreover, exploitation patterns cannot be explained by land characteristics alone. Many social/cultural factors complicate the interpretation of land use, including peo-

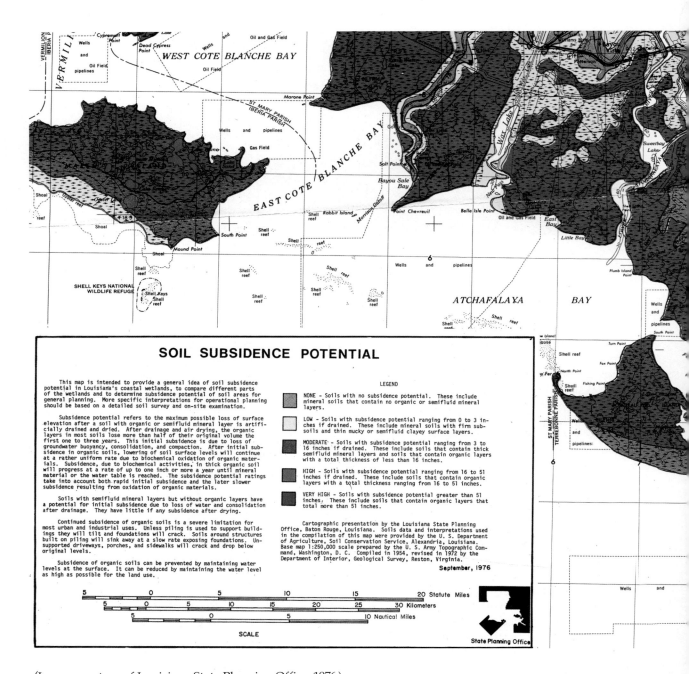

(Image courtesy of Louisiana State Planning Office, 1976.)

ple's tastes, desires, and traditions. Because they are vague, less fixed, intangible, and difficult to study, culture and its associated social phenomena are disregarded frequently by the science-based, policy-making community. The natural sciences are easier to incorporate into models that help drive policy decisions, whereas interpreting cultural/social elements in the decision-making process can be difficult. Hurricanes, like Katrina and Rita in 2005, along with Gustav and Ike in 2008 showed clearly the shortcomings of many standardized policies, because they lacked a human component (Piazza 2005). As a result, coastal residents suffered, as numerous television specials, documentaries, special scientific reports, books, public hearings, and editori-

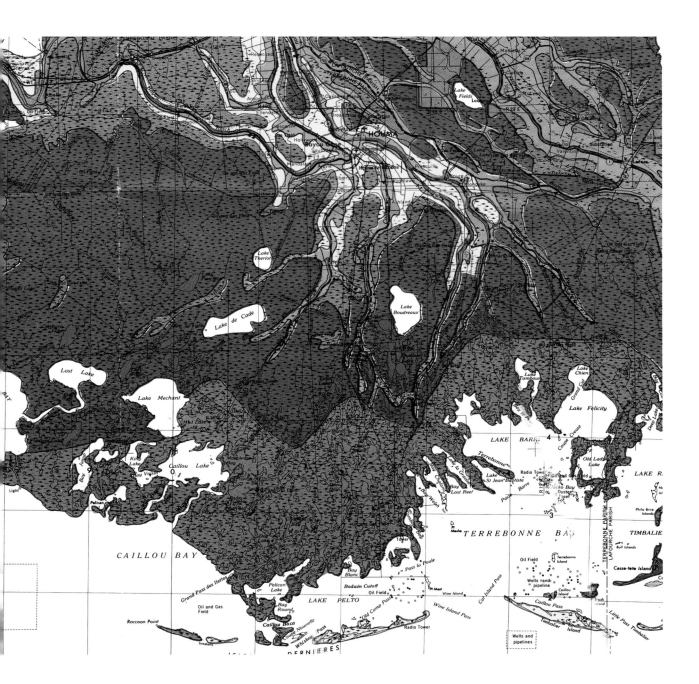

als made abundantly clear during the 2005 and 2008 summer tragedies.

These cultural/social elements are habitually considered too abstract to be a part of the decision-making process, as there is often a perception they cannot be explained easily because they regularly involve more qualitative than quantitative analysis. Research techniques are available to incorporate these human-based components into management plans, but, unfortunately, they have been ignored, underfunded, or misunderstood.

Estuarine Habitats

"Ask a Cajun where he is from, he will likely tell you, 'Man, if I'd be born any further south I'd be a sof' shell crab by now'" (Ditto 1980:10).

Estuaries are, by definition, a semi-enclosed embayment located in transition zones between continental and oceanic environments. The freshwater and nutrients they provide are critically important to a broad range of living resources; they are incubators, delivery rooms, and nurseries for an extensive array of plant and animal species. Although there are many variations of the definition, all reflect the "concept of the mixing of sea water and fresh water within a semi-enclosed body of water that has a free connection with the sea" (Walker and Prior 1986:180). In addition, barrier islands outline the seaward limit of these estuarine ecosystems.

The diversity of game, linked directly and indirectly to barrier island/marsh/swamp complexes, engendered the settlement and utilization these wildlife environments by early colonists. Consequently, barrier islands are well-defined coastal features that have served humankind since the seventeenth century, when "Pilgrims" settled the lee side of Cape Cod (Echeverria 1991). The estuarine ecosystems behind the barrier islands—despite high value, intense use, and frequent overuse—are considered superb places to live, work, and recreate (Basta, et al. 1990; Culliton, et al. 1990; Psuty 1992).

The highly diverse human activity, associated with the Industrial Revolution, transformed many estuaries into extremely stressed natural systems (Siry 1984; Dugan 1993). Although the industrial focus may have been on the uplands, the coast's green fringe of marshes was also impacted. In fact, few people anticipated the industrialization of Louisiana and the communities within the Mississippi River drainage basin would affect the wetlands, but they have had a profound impact. The end result is that the coastal plain has lost a great deal of its value as natural wildlife sanctuaries. The problem is acute, particularly as estuarine fisheries and waterfowl production are intertwined with human affairs (Haedrich 1983).

The health of an estuary system is defined by a number of indicators, such as

The *habitants* feared debt and often became swampers living off the land debt-free. (Photo from Coulon 1888.)

white and brown shrimp abundance, oyster density, the number of Atlantic croaker, red drum, spotted sea trout, largemouth bass, and freshwater catfish, along with alligator nest density, and the population of mottled duck. Furthermore, the number of acres of marsh damaged by nutria is also an important gauge as to the health of Louisiana's estuary system. These and other biological markers help define the estuary's productivity and usefulness (Barataria-Terrebonne n.d.).

Since the late 1970s, the nation's multi-faceted estuaries have begun to surface as important research themes. A number of government agencies recognized the value of estuarine environments and began to fund estuary-related research initiatives. From this body of research, estuarine systems became the focus of special management inquiry and concern, largely through the National Estuary Program (established in 1987 to support long-term state and local commitments to maintain the viability of selected estuaries).

Swamp, Marsh, and Natural Levee Communities

In the marshes and swamps, settlement is not always restricted to land unsuited for any other uses, although this was often the case. Until comparatively recent times, swamp and marsh tracts were not surveyed, for they were considered useless, impractical, unworkable, and of no monetary value. They were "unwanted portions of the public domain, of interest only to hunters, fishermen, and trappers" (Kniffen 1990:5). For example, "swampers" moved into secluded swamp tracts because they could not afford natural levee lands. They feared debt and lawsuits, and Anglo American sugar planters were willing to purchase bayou frontage at almost any price. Few individuals among the country-dwellers possessed the necessary $40,000 to become sugar farmers, so many became swampers (Comeaux 1972; Rehder 1971; Rehder 1973; Ditto 1980; Din 1988; Kniffen 1990). As a result, swamp dwellers made their living as subsis-

Moss picker's camp. (Photo from *Louisiana Conservationist Review*, Autumn 1937.)

tence farmers, supplementing their diet and income by utilizing the swamp's aquatic-dependent resources—fish, crabs, crawfish (*écrevisses*), frogs, timber, Spanish moss (*Tillandsia usenoides*)—*barbe espagnole* to the Cajuns, *Itla-okla* "tree hair" to the Indians, *mousse* to the Creoles, and Spaniard's Beard or *cabello francés* to others—turtles, and swamp game (Ramsey 1957; Martinez 1959; Adkins 1972; Comeaux 1972). Eventually, these avocations became regional economic specialties.

The Folk Landscape

Even during the depths of the depression frogs, crawfish, deer, alligator, catfish, and a host of waterfowl kept the marsh dweller's table filled with a menu that many would envy today. Small crops of vegetables were grown in back of each shack. . . . [K]erosene lamps burned dimly for a few hours as the sun set over a golden marsh that had sheltered generations of Cajun hunters . . . (Frank 1985:130).

In Eric Sloane's *America* (1956) and *Sketches of American Past* (1965), line drawings are used to capture the design and simplicity of many culture elements—covered bridges, fences, barns, boats, tools, and containers—that were used by early pioneers

Harvesting Spanish moss was a time-consuming and labor-intensive occupation, 1946. (Photo courtesy of Standard Oil Collection, University of Louisville, negative no. 44453.)

to reshape their surroundings; nothing like Sloane's books are available for Louisiana. Even so, many cultural components survive as part of the conventional folk landscape and give the region great diversity—dispersed and agglomerated settlements; linear hamlets, T-towns, and grid cities; plantations; folk houses, boats, fences, and barns; above ground graveyards; cattle brands; colloquialisms; foodways; net weaving (*tissage de filets*); land-division systems; furniture; spinning and weaving techniques; embroidered scarves; buggies; *la cuite*; farm equipment, like a grist mill (*moulin à gru*); music; *boucheries*; cockfighting; decoy carving; quilt-making; and *café noir* are all part of the cultural landscape and regional heritage (Kniffen 1978B). These are all unifying features of the South Louisiana cultural landscape and give the province its visual character. For example,

Prior to rural electrification, kerosene lamps provided all necessary light, 1946. (Photo courtesy of Standard Oil Collection, University of Louisville, negative no. 44513.)

> The Acadians built their own houses, made their own furniture, manufactured mattresses, dishware, shoes, cotton goods, clothing, sheets, and bread—in short, virtually all their household needs (Crété 1981:278).

These are the material and non-material vernacular elements that serve as part of the area's cultural fabric. To some, these cultural artifacts are not important; to others they are links to their heritage. In all cases, the environment is the common denominator, as it provided people with the raw resources necessary to survive, prosper, and embrace Louisiana's alluvial wetlands as their home. Until the 1930s, marshdwellers continued to cling to their centuries-old way of life. Only in the 1930s did new influences creep into their small communities. Electricity and plumbing arrived on the scene. A single light bulb attached to a power cord hanging from the ceiling appeared in every room. Kerosene lamps were no longer needed. The ice box was replaced by a small refrigerator, and a radio provided entertainment. "Modernization" had begun along the bayous, on the prairie, in the swamps, and throughout the wetlands. Life was changing, as was the cultural landscape. Many natural levee communities evolved into the principal settlement node, as people abandoned their remote sites for higher ground and greater security on the natural levees.

Natural Levee Communities

... the Lands on the Mississippi below Orleans are very rich and fertile and high enough for any kind of cultivation ... [B]ut are obliged to be defended from the overflowing of the river during the great freshes [*sic*] by a bank or levy [*sic*]. the Lands on the River below Orleans is in a kind of margin of fine rich Land extending back from the River from a mile to a mile and a half in width thence falling into a dead low Swamp Scarchly [*sic*] fit for anything being generally innundated [*sic*] with water. and as you decend [*sic*] the River this margin of rich high Land grows narrower and narrower and at about the distance of forty miles below Orleans the whole sinks into a very low swamp or marsh producing only a little branch willow Cottonwood and some Sycamore these Lands would be valuable for the cultivation of Rice for Hay and pasture and would the owners of these Lands turn their attention to Grazing what numbers of fine cattle might be raised and fattened here (Landreth 1819:153).

The first Europeans to traverse South Louisiana's wetlands were explorers, trappers (*coureurs de bois*), and traders. Farmers soon followed. The earliest arrivals established their homes and villages on the area's high ground. A settlement pattern was initiated that evolved from the distinctive natural levee morphology (Kollmorgen and Harrison 1946). Consequently, knowledge of the physiography of South Louisiana is essential to understanding settlement patterns and associated land use.

During the first half of the nineteenth century, cotton, rice, and sugar were the principal crops produced on the better-drained natural levees. Sugarcane—a sucrose-laden, freeze-sensitive, perennial tropical grass requiring a growing season of at least 250 days—was concentrated along the Mississippi River, Bayou Lafourche, along the bayou channels south of Houma, and west to Bayou Teche, Bayou Salé, and Bayou Cypremort— the two distributary chan-

Until the early twentieth century, cotton was an important crop at Leeville. (Photo from Cheniere Hurricane Centennal 1993.)

nels of the Teche (Post 1962). Plantation-type operations emerged within these regions between 1803 and 1820.

By 1860, sugarcane was the major commercial crop (Green Fields 1980; Rehder 1971; Rehder 1999). At its zenith, Louisiana's sugar-plantations were concentrated on nearly 12,000 square miles in twenty parishes (Rehder 1971; Rehder 1973). West of Bayou Teche, territorial boundary disputes hindered land settlement and plantation expansion. This land became home to Louisiana's rice industry and a settlement site for Midwestern farmers (Kollmorgen and Harrison 1946; Rehder 1971; Rehder 1973).

In many places, cotton and rice were phased out of production between 1890 and 1910. Although at remote marsh sites, like Leeville south of Golden Meadow, cotton and rice were grown as late as the 1920s (Cheniere Hurricane Centennal 1994). On the *chênière* ridges, such as Chênière au Tigre (south of Abbeville) and the *chênières* further west, cotton was an important agricultural crop until the 1940s. In the early part of the twentieth century, rice became the agricultural product of choice in the prairies of southwest Louisiana. As a result, this cereal grain is served in almost every dish at

almost every meal (Broussard 1977; Rushton 1979).

Further, in all of these areas, bees were an important adjunct to farming. Often overlooked, bees played an important role in South Louisiana farming, with several general stores providing cypress bee-keeping supplies. In 1924, Houma entrepreneur Walter T. Kelley began building cypress bee hives for nationwide distribution. When cypress became difficult to obtain, the Walter T. Kelley Bee Company moved to Kentucky. From their Houma origins the company continues to furnish bee keepers with supplies and accessories (Pitre 1993). Although reduced in number, clusters of bee hives are still a part of the agricultural landscape.

The Plantation and the Petit Habitant

With the influx of Anglo-American investors, available front lands on the natural levees were developed as plantations, but the area was settled first by small farmers know as *petit habitants*, who used a hoe, spade, broad axe, and pickaxe to build their farms. In the process they "preserved probably the purest example of a seventeenth century peasant culture to be found in the United States" (Kammer 1941:63).

Sugarcane plantation on the marsh fringe near New Orleans, from a postcard, ca. 1910.

Where front lands were not available, agricultural estates were developed behind the *petit habitants'* farms (Kollmorgen and Harrison 1946). Gradually, plantation owners consolidated the front holdings and imprinted the landscape with a plantation or truck-farming economy. The process continues today, but frequently the landowner is no longer farming sugarcane—the traditional crop. The land is being used for alternate row crops, pasture, or commercial and residential developments. These country-folk also farmed small natural levee plots alongside the eye-catching, modern plantation tourist attractions.

For more than 200 years, the plantation was the focal point of the economy. This system was based in part on the fertility of the alluvial soil, and in part on access to markets by means of a network of navigable waterways. The layout of these plantations was a result of conscious planning. Some plantations are built perpendicular to the bayou. Others, called the nodal-block form, are constructed in a grid pattern towards the back of a levee ridge (Labouisse 1985; Rehder 1971; Rehder 1999). Regardless of the design, each plantation is distinguished by the conspicuous "Georgian" mansion (colloquially called the "big house"), overseer's home, organized cluster of quarter houses, sugar "factory" (in some cases a sugar "refinery"), groups of barns, sheds, and other outbuildings, and perhaps a company store. Such a large assortment of outbuildings was typical in these water accessible plantations (Kniffen 1978B).

The importance of water to the plantation landscape is shown on the 1846 La Tourette map of Louisiana. This important historical document clearly indicates that small land holdings and larger tracts are settlement points that parallel the region's bayous. These ribbon-like farms are distinguished by their dwellings and outbuild-

ings. From the air, the length of these narrow cultivated strips is many times their width. Each plot stretches back from a waterway at a right angle to the stream's center. This pattern is shaped by a riverine-land-ownership arrangement that is based on the *arpent* which is a French land measurement unit. In 1903, the Louisiana Supreme Court established an *arpent* as 192 linear feet.

This land division configuration is identified in Canada and elsewhere as long-lots. These ownership patterns are derived from the European feudal—*seigneuries*—land division schemes. The system diffused into Louisiana and Texas by way of northern France, Québec, and the French colonies (Parenton 1938; Jordan 1974; Ditto 1980). The long-lot remains vividly imprinted on the landscape settled by French-speaking peoples (Long Lots: How 2006). Along the St. Lawrence River, territorial divisions follow the long-lot pattern with a width along the river of from ten to thirty miles, but extending at right angles to the watercourse for 100 miles or more (Semple 1904).

This is not the case in Louisiana, as the "back" property boundary was simply defined as "the trees." Therefore, an *arpent* extends from the waterway to the swamps, rarely more than three miles. The stream served as the survey base with bound-

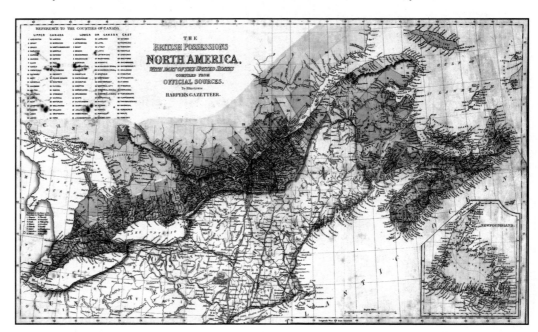

Long lots, which are commonplace in South Louisiana, are also prevalent in eastern Canada, 1855.

ary lines radiating out from the stream on either side to some predetermined depth. Because of the meandering nature of the waterbodies, the width of these strips varied widely. On the meanders the resulting land holdings were pie shaped, "broadening away from the river on the convex side of the meander and narrowing on the concave side" (Kniffen 1990:15). The end result is a survey system adapted from one used in northwestern France and in the reclaimed lands of Flanders.

Like the metes and bounds and township and range surveys, long-lot boundaries left an imprint on the landscape geometry through the road patterns. These routes follow the cadastral surveys and are visible reminders of the importance long-lots are to the coastal plain's pattern of ownership. By comparison, in Hawaii the basic land division is the *ahupua'a*. Like the Louisiana *arpent* and the Canadian long lots, these linear swathes run from the ocean (rather than a river) to the mountains. As a result, the countryside, from the air, has the same banded appearance one encounters in South Louisiana.

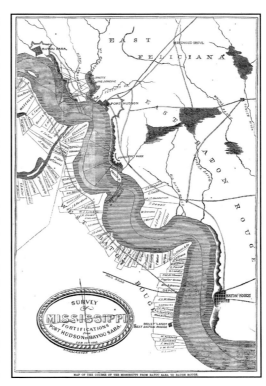

(Image from *Harper's Weekly*, April 1863.)

Land grants insured all settlers received bayou frontage, with a normal depth of forty *arpents*. Inheritance subdivisions were—and are—divided lengthwise, so the bayou evolved into a linear or line settlement type (Kollmorgen and Harrison 1946). These strip holdings were individually owned and occupied primarily by countryfolk who were more numerous than planters and owned from six to eight *arpents* of bayou access. The *petit habitants*, therefore, constituted a substantial portion of the bayou country's riparian occupants. Each linear community had access to local markets, either by using the bayou or the highway running parallel to the watercourse, but the farm's size reflected Louisiana's legal heritage.

Since these landholdings were quite narrow as a result of Louisiana's forced-heirship laws, children and grandchildren regularly built homes one behind the other perpendicular to the bayou, with the property line becoming the street. As generation followed generation, the *arpents* were continually subdivided. Consequently, there is a tendency for neighbors to be closely related to one another, with kinship being a key element in each community.

As each new generation inherited land, farms along the winding bayous grew smaller and smaller, and houses grew closer and closer together. Since all settlers built on the waterways, homes were side-by-side, and everyone had neighbors (Knipmeyer 1956). Like an urban neighborhood, these line communities are characterized by numerous local businesses. Yard signs advertise pet grooming services, tanning salons, beauty parlors, swings for sale, auto repairs, net mending, duck cleaning, nurseries, cake shops, catering services, and *la boucherie de campagne*. Each of these businesses is attached to a home. This is a living landscape and well before the concept of tele-commuting, the bayou country's inhabitants had established small businesses that allowed them to live and work on the same site.

The end result is a chain of small farms facing the bayous extending to the less fertile swamps or marshes (Ramsey 1957). The end of cultivation, therefore, is not a property line, but a contour that outlines the uncultivatable wetlands. The regional land-use pattern is, therefore, identified by a long line of habitations, with occasional breaks. Small urban centers developed every eight to twelve miles. As the width of the natural levee narrows towards the Gulf of Mexico, the economic focus changes from agriculture to water-oriented activities. "In the back" is the marsh and the homes and camps of the marshdweller, where one can absorb the sights and sounds of the *prairie tremblant,* gaining access to the "floating prairie" through natural waterways or a maze of canals.

Chapter 2
LOUISIANA'S ORGANIC LOWLANDS: A LANDSCAPE IN MOTION

Across the southern end of the State, from Sabine Lake to Chandeleur Bay, with a north-and-south width of from ten to thirty miles and an average of about fifteen, stretch the Gulf marshes, the wild haunt of myriads of birds and water-fowl, serpents and saurians, hares, raccoons, wild-cats, deep-bellowing frogs, and clouds of insects, and a few hunters and oystermen, whose solitary and rarely frequented huts speck the wide, green horizon at remote intervals (Cable 1886:2).

Louisiana's near featureless marshes and adjacent waterbodies span the entire coast and actually vary in width from fifteen to fifty miles. Without distinct relief, they can be compared to a green and gold carpet that is frayed at the edges, jagged, and full of holes. In these marshes organic material continually accumulates and decays, forming peats that serve as one of the bonds between the land and sea. Decomposition maintains an organic layer that thickens as the mass subsides to a depth of ten to twenty feet. Unless there is continuous sediment renourishment by flooding, marshland compacts, de-waters, subsides, and eventually sinks below the water surface (Boumans and Day 1993; Boumans and Day 1994).

This is some of the youngest land in America, and it is in a constant state of change. Peninsulas, islands, points of land, bayous, lagoons, lakes, sounds, and bays are part of the regional syntax—landscape elements that are being modified continually to change the character of these grassy water-lands. From a geological perspective, marshes are short-lived features—a product of currents, waves or rivers carrying sediments into shallow coastal waters. Over time these deposits vertically accrete to a point where the surface is then vegetated by a few hardy pioneer species—mostly grasses that can tolerate the stress of tidal flooding and salt water inundation. Species of the genus *Spartina* are the dominate marsh plants. *Spartina* is also notable in terms of tonnage produced, space occupied, and ability to withstand nearly constant contact with salt water. As it colonizes the fringing mudflats, *Spartina* stabilizes the surface and spreads slowly outward changing the water into an extensive grassy flat.

In the marsh, tree growth is limited to the *coteaux* and cheniers (English) or *chênières* (French)—toponymic generic names that are part of the cultural landscape (Detro 1970). These names are not simply parochial entities, but they are also a link to acculturation. They provide a unique perspective on the region, which is constantly reinventing and renewing itself, but the names often stay the same. Therefore, "marsh," refers to the marshland, rather than the vegetation cover of grasses, sedges, and rushes. Older residents still refer to the area as "prairie" and *"marais"*—a grassland, either wet or dry that was described as early as 1523 by the French sailor Giovanni as a treeless *"campaign"* or meadow (Vileisis 1997:14).

The *marais* is distinguished according to its stability. Conditions vary from surfaces that are firm and can be walked upon, to those that require the use of a boat. Areas of fresh marsh are also characterized by a type of "trembling marsh," locally called *flotant* or *prairie tremblant* (similar to the translation of the Seminole term "Okefenokee" as "land of the trembling earth") and can adjust vertically to rising water levels through "buoyant uplift" (McBride, et al.

Map showing the location of the principal culture groups in Louisiana. (Image from Cable 1883.)

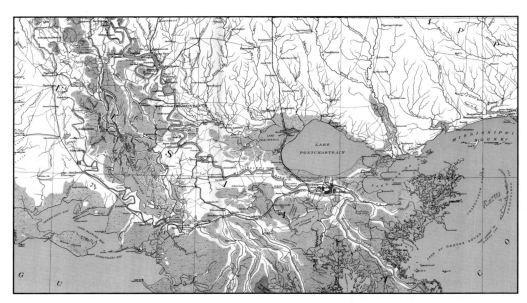

Outline of the marshes of southeastern Louisiana, with the natural levees, shown in white, 1891.

1991:1010). *Flotant* exists throughout the marshes of southeast Louisiana. It is a trembling vegetative layer or mat floating on subaqueous organic ooze. This vegetative carpet is difficult to navigate and requires special transportation equipment, because as one foot is pulled out of the quagmire, the other one continually sinks. This repetitive process, which can exhaust the uninitiated, has prompted some to report that "the country is so wet that we scarcely saw an acre of land upon which a settlement could

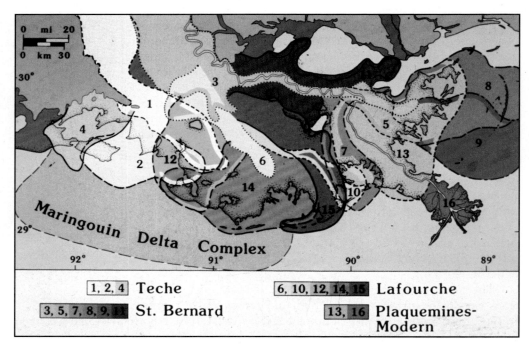

Louisiana's deltaic plain is a product of the historic shift of the Mississippi delta. (Image modified from Frazier 1967.)

Flotant or *prairie tremblant*, 1973. (Photo by the author.)

be made" (Vileisis 1997:61).

For convenience, the *marais* has been subdivided into four vegetative types: saline, brackish, intermediate, and fresh marsh (Russell 1942; Chabreck 1972; Sasser 1994). O'Neil (1949) published the first detailed vegetation map of these marsh zones. The relative distribution, or pattern, of these marsh bands changes during a delta's growth and deterioration cycles. Freshwater marsh dominates a new Deltaic lobe, like the emerging Atchafalaya delta, while a salt marsh will blanket the largest area in a delta, like the Lafourche or Terrebonne regions that are undergoing decay (Neill and Deegan 1986). Freshwater marshes will also have a larger number of plant species than salt water habitats, since fewer plants can survive the stress of salt water flooding. However, freshwater marshes are grazed by animals that can do serious damage to this plant zone by feeding on underground roots and rhizomes. This is not the case in salt water habitats, for foraging herbivores do not crop vegetation down to the root zone.

Salt marshes generally conform to the twenty parts/thousand (ppt) salinity contour (Gulf Coast wetlands n.d.). This *marais* is dominated by oyster grass (*Spartina alterniflora*), whose abundance is in direct proportion to the water table and salinity conditions. Brackish plants tolerate salinities between ten and twenty ppt and are categorized as either salt meadow or rush. Salt meadows are dominated by wiregrass (*Spartina patens*)—a plant that makes up 25 percent of the coastal vegetation and is generally underlain by peat. Its major competitor is oyster grass. The intermediate band is characterized by a heterogenic vegetative assemblage capable of surviving in salinities that vary from two to ten ppt (Penfound and Hathaway 1958; Wright, et al. 1960; Gulf Coast wetlands n.d.). Included are salt grass (*Distichlis spicate*), roseau cane (*Phragmites australis*), and bulltongue (*Sagittaria falcata*). Freshwater marsh occupies an area where salinities are less than two ppt. It is a region dominated by *canouche* (*Panicum hemitomon*)—a place where a type of *prairie* may develop. Along with the *canouche*, saw grass (*Cladium jamaicense*)—whose serrated leaf blades are nearly as sharp as a sword—is found on surfaces where the drainage has been altered due to industrial, highway, or canal construction.

Unlike the marsh, swamps or "wet forests" exist where the soil is saturated for one or more months of the growing season with water not too deep to prevent germination or to drown year-old swamp plants. Gulf Coast swamp forests are best developed within floodplains. These riverine bottom lands afford an ideal habitat for bald cypress (*Taxodium distichum*) or tupelo gum (*Nyssa aquatica*). These two primary plant species provided the raw materials for "swampers" who logged these water-forests so successfully that restoration efforts are an ongoing issue (Shanklin and Kozlowski 1985; Conner and Flynn 1989; Myers, et al. 1995; Turner and Streever 2002; Coastal restoration builds 2007). Also, the swamp's numerous lakes and bayous provide habitat for a large and diverse array of commercial and recreational freshwater fish and

For the first time in 1947, O'Neil showed the four marsh vegetation types (fresh [gray], intermediate [purple,

served as important pathways for the region's inhabitants.

As one surveys this broad expanse of land, the difference in height between marsh habitats and adjacent natural levees, *chênières*, and beaches is generally less than five feet. Tree growth requires an elevation of only eighteen inches above sea level. In the entire region, relief is often less than seven to ten feet/mile over hundreds of square miles. Elevations of three feet can provide firm, habitable land.

All of the wetlands' elevated landforms were sought out by prehistoric populations for settlement; they continue to sustain human population today. There is, accordingly, a wide and highly diverse assortment of natural forces and processes that contribute to the creation, degradation, and destruction of the habitats which support these communities. The Mississippi River is one of these forces, along with hurricanes that has reshaped Louisiana's coastal lowlands and contributed to medications of this landscape element.

Modification of the Coast's Geomorphology

The land was vast. There was no need to think about what we did to the land, at least not initially. . . . Americans continue to coexist, only warily, with na-

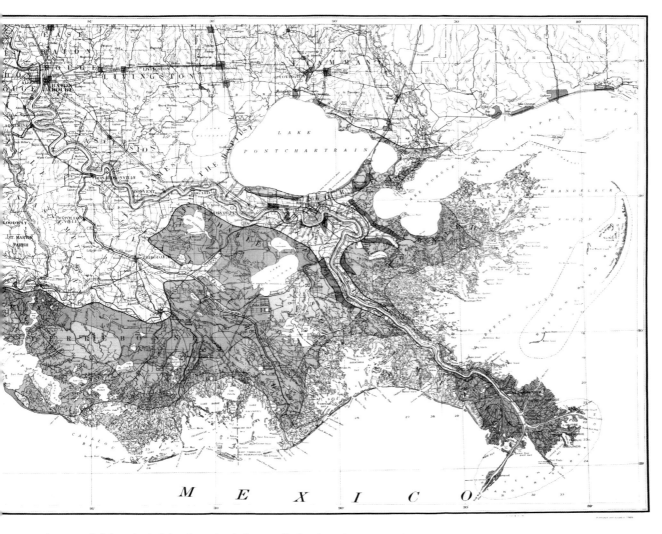

burgundy], brackish [olive], and salt [orange]) that band Louisiana's coastal lowlands. (Image from O'Neil 1949.)

ture, despite our now flaunted environmental stewardship. Nowhere is this compromised relationship more concentrated and evident than in the Mississippi River delta, an area that an astounding number of people, from New York to San Francisco, have told me they don't even know exists (Hallowell 2001:xvii-xviii).

The sea has "reclaimed" and modified the coastal zone's geometry over time. Many of the features along the land/water interface have been altered, damaged, or destroyed repeatedly by the forces of the ocean. At the same time, many of these elements, beaches in particular, have been rebuilt. Like lemmings, humankind continues to move towards the land/water interface in a quest to see and hear the ocean, regardless of the consequences. Our coastal citizens, specifically those on barrier islands, or in communities facing the sea, are at risk—at the mercy of hurricanes, nor'easters, and tropical depressions. Their homes and businesses are particularly vulnerable, as they live on the mainland's seaward limit. In many cases, they are dangerously close to the water's edge, and crisis response costs are great (The H. John Heinz 2000). Hazard consideration, in fact, provides a compelling argument for the preservation and protection of Louisiana's undeveloped wetlands.

This danger is most evident when the barrier islands and associated coastal lowlands are overrun by a hurricane-generated primary storm surge fifteen to nearly thirty-feet high, followed, in some cases, as during Ike (2008), by a secondary surge, making landfall several hours after the primary event (Wold 2009A). A hurricane like Katrina (2005) hits the barrier shoreline with such intensity that it sweeps far inland, like a liquid bulldozer, flattening everything in its path. In the case of Hurricanes Katrina and Rita in 2005, an area nearly as large as the United Kingdom was flooded. Three years later, Hurricanes Gustav and Ike (2008) added to the area's enduring flooding misery and have prompted many parishes to reconsider their general antagonism towards zoning and land-use planning. The devastation caused by these storms has led some in Texas to consider building the "Ike Dike" a fifty-five mile long, seventeen-foot high barrier (Lozano 2009). The purpose would be to reduce the type of flooding prompted by the storm's passage. Louisiana's Morganza to the Gulf of Mexico Hurricane Protection Project is a similar plan.

Unlike Texas, Louisiana's coastal lowlands are the first line of defense against the destructive forces of hurricanes and tropical storms. The Morganza to the Gulf spillway may be needed, but the marshes proved their value in 2005, as their sponge-like capacities absorbed the full force of Katrina and Rita (McCulloh, et al. 2006). Frequently, destruction is total. Audrey (1957), Betsy (1965), Camille (1969), Juan (1985), Andrew (1992), Lili (2002), Ivan (2004), Katrina (2005), Rita (2005), Gustav (2008), and Ike (2008) have left their mark on Louisiana's landscape. Although the damage each of these storms inflicted was extensive, the destruction would have been much worse if the wetlands had not absorbed some of the physical forces unleashed by these storm events.

A storm's wind and waves are altered by the wetlands and although the winds are important and are the defining element of a hurricane, it is the water that poses the greatest threat to marshdwellers. Before storms were named, high water from hurricanes in the late nineteenth and early twentieth centuries destroyed entire communities, including Village Bayou, Chênière Caminada, and Oyster Bayou. Survivors suffered, rebuilt, or relocated to higher ground (Davis 1992B).

Population and industrial growth increased the stress on this band of coastal real estate. In the United States, more than half of the population lives within sixty miles of the coast. In the latter part of the twentieth century, human occupancy within two miles of the shore has increased at more than three times the national growth rate, providing challenges to local governments (Crossett, et al. 2004). Consequently, urban agglomerations, agriculture, and natural erosion are collectively responsible for the nation losing a considerable portion of its wetlands.

Louisiana best exemplifies this problem, as the state is facing a serious coastal dilemma. The problem is related directly to humankind's interference with the Mississippi River's flow regime and the effects of erosion induced by natural processes, like subsidence and sea-level rise—together the two processes are referred to as relative sea-level rise. Erosion accounts for a fluctuating land loss rate that, on average, claims twenty to twenty-five square miles each year. At that rate, an area greater than New Orleans (180.6 square miles) is lost every 7.2 years. Some believe that unless corrective measures are initiated soon, the damage to the fragile ecosystems may reach the point of irreversibility (Subsidence and sea-level . . . 2007). Further, wind and waves are causing the state's barrier islands to move landward at rates up to sixty-five feet per year. Between 1900 and 2000, some islands lost nearly half of their surface area; others have completely disappeared. The marsh is also at risk because of subsidence, muskrat (*Ondatra zibethicus rivalicius*) and nutria (*Myocastor coypus*) eat-outs, salt water intrusion, and change in the regional hydrology. Collectively and individually, each of these elements has had serious effects on this productive habitat (Gosselink and

Baumann 1980; Houck 1983; Dunbar, et al. 1992; Williams, et al. 1992; Barras, et al. 1994; Boesch, et al. 1994; Day, et al. 2000; Barras, et al. 2003). One of the most important agents of change is hurricanes and their cumulative impacts.

Hurricanes: A Constant Reminder of the Risk Factors of Living at the Edge

> September 11, 1722. A hurricane began in the morning which lasted until the 16th. The winds came from the southeast passing to the south and then to the southwest. This hurricane caused the destruction of beans, corn, and more than 8,000 *quarts* of rice ready to be harvested. It destroyed most of the houses in New Orleans with the exception of a warehouse . . . the *Espiduel*, three feighters [sic], and almost all the boats, launches, and pirogues were destroyed (de la Harpe 1971:156).

Coastal Louisiana's climate is generally described as humid and subtropical. As the state borders the Gulf of Mexico, this waterbody plays a significant role in moderating local climatic patterns. Hot summers and mild winters are the norm. Winter extremes, when they occur, are a product of cold fronts that quickly change the daily weather pattern. Temperatures can plummet thirty to forty degrees in just a few hours. In addition, about two-thirds of the coastal rainfall is associated with frontal activity.

In summer and fall, warm-humid-wet conditions are the norm. This pattern can be altered dramatically by the periodic arrival of hurricanes that have a striking effect on estuarine systems. High storm surges and increased freshwater inflow are the primary issues. Although summers are hot with July and August being the warmest months, the temperature rarely exceeds 100°F. Even so, "summer heat is completely democratic; sending planters, field workers, and merchants is [sic] search of shade and a cool breeze. In the days before air conditioning, they would all seek refuge in their gardens and on their porches" (Boykin 1999:1).

For six months, hurricanes are a threat and a reminder of how fragile life and work in the *marais* can be. June first begins the hurricane season, and there is the perennial possibility that coastal Louisiana will be hit by "the big one"—a Category 5, large diameter storm, whose northeast quadrant passes to the west of Lake Pontchartrain (the Indians called the lake *Okwa-ta*—wide water) and New Orleans. Hurricane Katrina (2005) came close to making landfall as a Category 5 storm, and, the year before, Ivan (2004) just missed as well. These storms travel, in general, from east to west and are reminders of the destructive forces of these dynamic energy turbines.

Hurricane Dynamics

Tropical cyclones originate off the West African coast and have their own distinct personalities and unpredictable routes. Between May and October they move in a north-northwest direction across the Atlantic Ocean and are always of some concern, because they can carry high winds, extreme low pressure, and vast quantities of precipitation. In 1856 and 1893, unannounced hurricanes wreaked havoc across Louisiana's coastal lowlands, particularly at Last Island (Isles Dernières), the communities in the Barataria Basin, and in Calcasieu Parish (Tannehill 1943).

In profile, counterclockwise winds move out from the hurricane's center or eye, where there is a relatively calm space. As the storm crosses land, the greatest storm surge heights occur in the northeast quadrant, where the onshore winds are strongest. In the final analysis, a hurricane is essentially a massive turbine that generates enough energy to blow an armada into kindling, completely erase one of Louisiana's barrier island communities, or destroy the architectural integrity of two or three cities

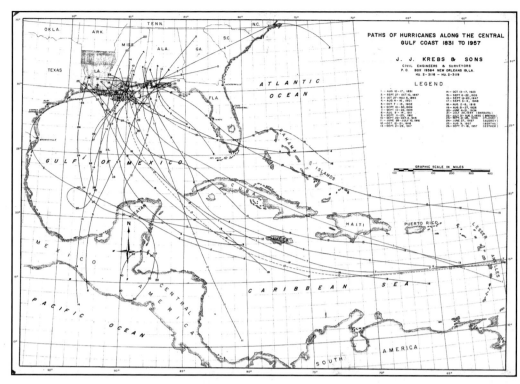

Prior to 1957, Louisiana's hurricanes were largely unannounced; consequently, the coastal population was perennially at risk.

(Schwartz 2007).

To categorize a storm's intensity, the Saffir-Simpson damage-potential scale is used. The rating system is designed to indicate the damage potential from wind and storm surge on a scale of one to five—most Louisiana hurricanes fall into Category Two or Three. The twelve deadliest hurricanes of this century were all Category Four or above. Louisiana has been part of this history; Katrina, Rita, Gustav, and Ike serve as recent reminders of the damage one of these monstrous storms can cause.

Although the Saffir-Simpson wind-scale is used by climate professions to categorize hurricanes, water height would be a much better measure in the coastal lowlands. Wind should not be underestimated, but water is the element that kills, destroys property, and scares coastal inhabitants. Consequently, hurricanes were a problem to all of the wetlands' remote commercial hunters, trappers, fishermen, oystermen, and military personnel assigned to wetland-oriented fortifications. Yet, although hurricanes continue to be a concern, they are regularly underestimated, perhaps precisely because they have been such a long-standing problem.

Louisiana's Hurricanes

Hurricanes are not new to Louisiana; in fact, prior to joining the Union, the state was pounded, bruised, or affected by ten storms (Hurricanes in Louisiana 1865; Ludlum 1963; Hurricane study 1972). From 1831 to 2005, sixty-two storms have crossed, or brushed, the coast. In more recent history, Hurricanes Andrew, Georges, Isidore, Lili, Katrina, Rita, Gustav, and Ike were vivid reminders of the massive force contained in one of these storms.

In the mechanics of these low-pressure events, the greatest potential for loss of life is from the system's storm surge. Water pushed toward the shore by the force of the winds, combines with the normal tides to cre-ate the hurricane storm surge. These processes can increase the mean water level fifteen feet or more. In Katrina, the storm surge at Constance Beach in southwest Louisiana was 14.9 feet; while south of Abbeville the USGS measured a surge height of 9.5 feet. (For comparison purposes, a standard door is six feet, eight inches.) At some sites, water rose at a rate of five feet an hour (Dunne 2006B:2B). It has been shown by Swenson (1994) that a reduction in storm surge of approximately 2.7 feet per linear mile is achieved when the surge passes over fairly solid marsh. If this is the case, and this "exact" number is debatable, a rehabilitated marsh has the potential of reducing hurricane-induced property damage significantly. In the right scenario, this reduction in damage could easily pay for a significant role of the coastal restoration/rehabilitation effort.

Whether a rain event or a hurricane, evacuation was often prudent. (Image from *Harper's Weekly*, October 1866.)

Hurricanes that affected coastal Louisiana, 1722-2008
(From: Ludlum 1963; Hurricane study 1972; Roth 2003)

1722	1723	1756	1779	1780	1787	1793	1794
1800	1811	1812	1831 Great Barbados storm	1837 Racer's Storm	1846	1856 Isles Dernières storm	1860
1865	1877	1879	1882	1887	1888	1892	1893 Chênière Caminada storm
1901	1902	1905	1909	1915	1918	1926	1931
1932	1934	1936	1940	1943	1947	1955 (Brenda)	1955
1956 (Flossy)	1957 (Audrey)	1957 (Bertha)	1960 (Ethel)	1961 (Carla)	1964 (Hilda)	1965 (Betsy)	1969 (Camille)
1970 (Felice)	1971 (Edith)	1974 (Carmen)	1977 (Babe)	1979 (Bob)	1979 (Claudette)	1985 (Danny)	1985 (Elena)
1985 (Juan)	1986 (Bonnie)	1988 (Florence)	1992 (Andrew)	1995 (Opal)	1996 (Josephine)	1997 (another Danny)	1998 (Francis)
1998 (Georges)	2001 (Allison)	2002 (Isidore)	2002 (Lili)	2004 (Ivan)	2005 (Katrina)	2005 (Rita)	2008 (Gustav)
2008 (Ike)							

Hurricanes have become part of Louisiana folklore and are reference benchmarks in time. For example, Audrey (1957), Betsy (1965), Camille (1969), Ivan (2004), Katrina (2005), Rita (2005), Gustav (2008), Ike (2008), and the storms of 1893, 1909, or 1915 are etched into the regional psyche. They are the mental storms of record.

Consequently, the threat of any storm provokes highly punctuated dialogues that reference these hurricanes and others. In some cases, the stories have been told so fre-

quently that those recounting tales of a storm's fury are two generations removed; nevertheless, they recount the event vividly (Perrin 1985). The concern is justified. For example, the 1893 weather event, a hurricane that was unforgiving, killed hundreds of marshdwellers. At Bayou André, just north of Grand Isle, sixty-three Chinese immigrants were lost and not a trace of the $16,000 shrimp factory could be found (Forrest n.d.; Sampsell 1893). One hundred died at Bayou Lafond

Unannounced hurricanes sounded the death knell for many Louisiana shrimp platforms. (Photo by Thomas B. Cobb, ca. 1930. From *A Pictorial History of Terrebonne Parish* 1967.)

(Bayou Dufond or Defond)—a shrimp-drying platform built perhaps as early as 1840 (Campanella 2007). At Bird Island, where there had been about 150 people, fifty died (Forrest n.d.; Van Pelt 1943). At Razor Island, no one survived to tell the story of this Sunday morning storm. Of Bayou Cook's 300 to 500 inhabitants, only twenty-three survived. The settlement was destroyed completely, and Louisiana lost the source of its best oysters (Sterns 1887; Forrest n.d.).

The same can be said of the people living at Chênière Ronquill, Grand Lake, Chênière Caminada (also called Caminadaville), and Sandrez Canal. Of the forty camps on Bayou Challon, none remained (Forrest n.d.). The destruction was complete at Oyster Bayou, at Grand Bayou, as well as at Simon Bayou—making the body count during the 1893 storm nearly 2,000 (Forrest n.d.; Sampsell 1893). The storm was unprecedented in Louisiana's history. The region's inundated communities quickly became ghostly reminders of the "fisherfolk" who lived and worked in the bays, lakes, and bayous. This weather phenomenon is nevertheless the forgotten hurricane. It is recorded primarily in folklore, not in publications, such as *Isaac's Storm*.

Prior to Katrina, the 1893 storm was, in terms of mortality, one of the most devastating in Louisiana's history, a natural disaster comparable to the 1900 storm that destroyed Galveston (Larson 1999). Hurricanes, therefore, have always played a role in determining who survives in the states near sea level marshes, and they will continue to do so.

The Benchmark Storms and Numerous Forgotten Communities

Perhaps the earliest recorded example of how hurricanes influence settlement is associated with the Spanish Isleño colony between Lake Salvador and Bayou Barataria. This small village, one of the earliest marsh-oriented settlements, began with about 150 Canary Islanders. Living on a site barely above sea level, the village was repeatedly flooded, damaged, and eventually abandoned. Hurricanes in 1779 and 1780, along with poor soils, deplorable living conditions, and their inability to prosper, prompted the Spanish government to transfer these settlers to the St. Bernard Parish community of Terre aux Boeufs. As a result, little remains of the Spanish Barataria community; it is a forgotten part of Louisiana's marsh-oriented settlement landscape (Din 1986; Din 1988). This was often the case with Louisiana's "cut off" coastal communities; they are simply an ignored part of the wetlands landscape.

The 1893 hurricane exemplifies how these settlement sites have vanished from the historic record. Even with the risk involved, and the number of people who died, most of Louisiana's Slavic oystermen went back into the oyster business nearly immediately after the clean up; however, other groups left the area. The Croatian oystermen constructed new camps that were larger and safer. They built better boats and restocked their reefs. The oyster industry would take several years to recover. The hurricane did not deter these hardy fishermen. They regrouped, rebuilt, and continued to pursue their lifestyle as oystermen.

The Storms of the Twentieth and Twenty-First Centuries

There were other storms in the nineteenth century that were just as severe as the 1893 hurricane, but never again was the loss of life so great to the state's marsh-dwellers. As communications and warning systems improved, human safety increased to the extent the population heeded weather bulletins. Even so, there were other storm events that affected the people of the marsh. For example, the headlines in the New Orleans papers reported on the September 20, 1919 hurricane: "Louisiana Gulf Coast Swept by Tidal Wave—Two Hundred or More Lives Lost on Bayou Terrebonne and Vicinity."

The water-accessible community at Seabreeze was severely damaged by the 1909 hurricane, ca. 1897. (Photo courtesy of the Randolph A. Bazet Collection, Archives & Special Collections, Nicholls State University.)

The whole Louisiana coast, from Grand Isle to some point westward, probably as far as Cote Blanche Bay in Vermilion, was swept by a great tidal wave that poured in on the unsuspecting fishermen living along the coast, destroyed their homes and took the lives of untold hundreds (Louisiana Gulf coast 1919:1).

According to newspaper reports, thousands of fishermen were affected by this tempest. In addition, camps, like those clustered at Seabreeze, and along the bayous south of Houma were being swamped. One account remarked the "waves were dashing completely over the house, which was ten feet above the ground, and the roof nearly ten feet higher." Further, "a big wave, it must have been twenty feet high, engulfed us, and the roof floated off with its human freight. We clung desperately to our frail craft, holding to each other and tossing about like a cork" (Louisiana Gulf coast 1919:1).

And so it was throughout the coastal plain. Refugees found their way to Houma—exhausted, famished, bruised, and battered—their only possessions were the clothes, or what was left of them, on their backs. In 2005, Hurricanes Katrina and Rita caused comparable suffering. Nearly ninety years after the 1919 storm event, people are still becoming nomadic evacuees, looking for a place to stay, planning how to return, or making preparations to start a new home. For many, relocation has become an important option (Piazza 2005). In 2008, Gustav and Ike added to the suffering, misery, trauma, and uncertainties about the future. Even so, countless lowland residents have decided to

After the hurricanes of 2005 and 2008, rather than move, many people adapted their homes to possible floods, 2009. (Photo courtesy of Carl A. Brasseaux.)

remain in the wetlands, as "the thought of living anywhere else is more daunting than losing it all" (Bahr 2006B).

In the post-1950s, radios, aircraft, and a generally better working knowledge about weather improved the warning system and reduced the death tolls. The exception is Katrina. The final tally may never be accurately determined, but at least 1,300 Louisianians lost their lives directly or indirectly from this weather event. Moreover, the storm's aftermath revealed the complex set of social problems associated with dealing with a storm of this magnitude, following a track that pummels one of North America's cities at risk.

On June 21, 1987, the front page of the *Baton Rouge Sunday Advocate* proclaimed: "Potential for storm disaster rising" (Anderson and Dunne 1987) and "Cameron residents remember horror of Hurricane Audrey" (Shelton 1987B). Elsewhere in this issue were articles titled "Louisiana evacuation plans untested" (Dunne 1987) and "Future holds bigger hurricanes, longer seasons, experts say" (Anderson and Dunne 1987B). The editor's note that preceded this series stated:

> Five years ago the *Morning Advocate* examined the lack of planning and potential disaster the state faces from a major hurricane. Since that time improvements have been made and more is known about the potential effects of storms. But the *Advocate* discovered that in other ways Louisiana's vulnerability is increasing and the potential for disaster still exists (Anderson and Dunne 1987:1A).

Hurricanes Katrina, Rita, Gustav, and Ike proved unequivocally the true vulnerability of the state's exposed southernmost hamlets, villages, towns, municipalities, parishes, and fragile aquatic habitats (Burke 2005). It will take several years to assess completely the damage to the state's communities and aquatic resources (Macaluso 2008). Preliminary information suggests the losses will be staggering. With nearly 30 percent of the state's wholesale/retail seafood dealers and 42 percent of the commercial fishing fleet in the impacted parishes the economic effects are significant. Further, wind and salt water burns require new habitat studies and management programs to appreciate and understand fully the recovery process (Burke 2005). Although the seafood harvest frequently spikes after a large disturbance, like a hurricane, and preliminary information suggests this is true in South Louisiana, the long-term viability and sustainability of the system is the principal concern. Only time will tell if the system will heal properly to allow Louisiana to continue to be a primary source of national fishery resources.

Clearly, Katrina, Rita, Gustav, and Ike altered a number of habitats, sediment regimes, and salinities in those regions closest to these storm's paths. Hurricanes Isidore and Lili in 2003 and Ivan in 2004 reminded the Louisiana's coastal dwellers of their vulnerability. Katrina, Rita, Gustav, and Ike proved it.

Hurricanes are inevitable; and levees are but a tool to mitigate their effects. But levees can give residents a false sense of security. Katrina overwhelmed the system at its weakest point, and the people of New Orleans suffered (Campanella 2006; McCulloh, et al. 2006). The end result will be a rebuilding effort unlike anything witnessed in this country; it will require a "collaborative effort to maximize the role of science in decisions made about the rebuilding" project (Groat 2005:341).

Lessons will be learned and improvements will be mandated. It is clear that levees and internal drains help, but they are not designed to retard all hurricane-induced storm surges. Moreover, A. Hinton and D. D. Thurston (2004:2) report "that a Category 3 hurricane would send a 10- to 12-foot storm surge—a miles-long wall of water pushed ashore by swirling winds—crashing through downtown Houma. The effects would be more devastating in low-lying bayou communities, such as Chauvin,

Dulac, du Large and Montegut."

The levees have their limits. With many parts of the coastal lowlands less than three feet above sea level, mean water flooding is a constant problem. Even though the landscape is drained, the natural system is superseded by an artificial one outlined by levees, flood gates, and residential, commercial, and industrial activity.

* * *

Aye, the two things happen at the one time. Things get better. And they get worse (Glassie 1994:968).

Barrier Islands

Without these barriers, the full force of storm surges and hurricane waves will directly strike the fragile interior wetlands, resulting in even more rapid deterioration than what is currently occurring. In addition, loss of barrier islands will increase salt water intrusion and accelerate the destruction of freshwater swamps and marshes at the upper ends of the state's estuarine basins (Penland, et al. 1986:23).

Louisiana does not have a single barrier island ten miles long. Last Island, Timbalier, Grand Isle, Grand Terre, and the Chandeleur chain fringe the coast and protect the delicate, salt water-sensitive wetlands. This barrier chain ranges from small, remote, sand shoals—such as Ship Shoal—scarcely above sea level and often exposed only at low tide, to islands covered with vegetation and small dunes. They are in essence a ribbon of sand fronting the Gulf of Mexico. Salt-tolerant xerophytic grasses and herbs dominate the dune face and crest, grading into brackish and salt marshes on the bay side (Coastal Louisiana 2007).

Unlike other barrier island assemblages, like those along the East Coast, these geomorphic features were never overwhelmed by commercial development, but were colonized by a modest population. Currently, Grand Isle is incorporated as a municipality. Even so, it does not possess an extensive array of hotels, motels, high-rise buildings, condominiums, apartments, townhouses, single-family residences, mini-golf complexes, water parks, and tourist-oriented strip malls. The other islands that fringe the coast metamorphosed from settlement nodes back to their natural states, with little trace of human occupancy. Small villages, recreational hotels, plantations, pirates, smugglers, and bootleggers, along with scattered trapper-fisher-hunter camps

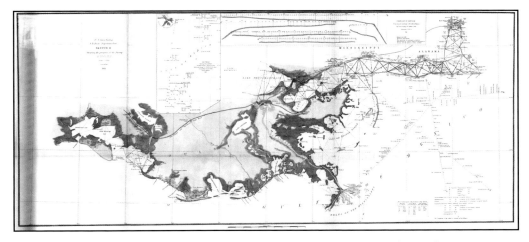

As early as 1855, federal surveyors were mapping Louisiana's coastline.

were a vivid part of their history and folklore. In the end, the folks living on these narrow strands were at risk, as the islands are in a constant state of change.

When in the path of a tropical depression, the barrier islands receive the full force of the storm's impact. The small land mass's permanent and seasonal recreational population is in constant danger. Because for more than two centuries hurricane winds and the associated storm surge have damaged the state's barrier complex, wash-over fans, new tidal passes, reduced dunes, altered beaches, and general profile changes initiated through accretion, deposition, and erosion are by-products of the passage of a hurricane, or, in some cases, a cold-front (Williams, et al. 1992). The barrier islands are the state's first-line-of-defense against the devastating impacts of hurricanes and their continual change is confirmation of their significance as a protective obstruction

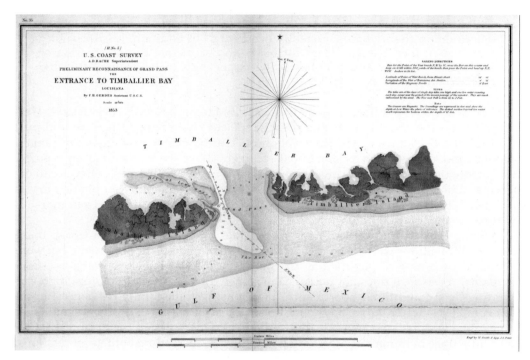

As surveys progressed across Louisiana, detailed maps were produced.

against the violent wind and waves generated by a severe storm.

When the islands and marshes are gone, they will no longer absorb ocean energies. Currently they cushion the mainland and landward aquatic habitats from normal wave action, current scour, and a hurricane's destructive forces. It is clear that these frail coastal features, and the related marshes, no longer provide the same defensive buffer they offered in the nineteenth and early twentieth centuries. Although the profile of these barrier islands suggests they offer some vertical relief, exposed salt domes constitute the marsh's dominant features. These geologic features have served humankind for thousands of years and continue to do so.

Salt Domes: The Wetlands' High Land

A dwelling is on a handsome bluff of regular shape, about one hundred and fifty feet above the level of the gulf. Beautiful shade trees and the sea breeze keep the yard and the house cool, even in the hottest summer days. The yard all around is well set in Bermuda grass. In front, the sea marsh extends over a

Louisiana's salt domes continue to provide products to a national market, 1987. (Photo by the author.)

hundred yards, and beyond this water of the gulf spreads out under a blazing sun . . . Redfish and many other fine fish are found in abundance in the bayou. There are oyster reefs not far off. . . . Fruit, also, appears to do well on all these islands (Perrin 1891:7).

In coastal Louisiana, the "Five Islands"—Jefferson (Orange Island, *Butte à Peigneur*; *Côte Carlin*; Pine and Miller's Island), Avery (*La Petite Anse*, McCall or Marsh Island), Weeks (*Grand Côte*), Côte Blanche and Belle Isle—are salt domes with topographic expression (Gifford 1892). Like all of these visible intrusive features, these domes vary in height and area. With elevations up to 230 feet they form distinct natural landmarks in the relatively flat, featureless marsh and prairie (*savane*) that typify the region. Salt, petroleum, and natural gas, along with Tabasco peppers, govern the economic interests linked with these features (Bernard 2005).

Most of these colossal vertical shafts of salt are buried. Some have pushed up conspicuous mounds. These round hills outline the subsurface plugs that remain one of the Gulf coastal plain's outstanding geologic features (Kupfer 1962; Kupfer 1990; Autin 2002). They are also of major economic importance. The structures consist essentially of a salt core covered by a mantle of cap rock. Hot, semi-plastic intrusions flowed upward through the sediments of the Gulf Coast geosyncline to form "bubbles." Their exact thicknesses are more or less undetermined with the total quantity of salt estimated in some domes, like Avery Island—the oldest continuously operating salt mine in the Western Hemisphere—to be in excess of two billion tons. Salt mined from these facilities is barged to Northern states to be used on highways and driveways for ice removal. The mined sodium chloride is also packaged for home use and is incorporated into the aging process of a number of Louisiana-branded hot sauces. Louisiana produces about one-fourth of the nation's salt—the most in the country.

Although five of these domes are exposed, most are buried, and in Texas and Louisiana, they are important both in the production of oil and natural gas and as storage receptacles for the nation's strategic petroleum reserves (SPR) (Steinmayer 1932; Bradley 1939; Oil, salt and 1968; Davis 1981; Neal and Magorian 1997). In 2008, there were five SPRs in the South. West Hackberry and Bayou Choctaw are in Louisiana. Like much of South Louisiana, the domes experience subsidence that plays an important role in understanding the dynamics and importance of coastal vegetation and sedimentation.

* * *

La Petite Anse salt dome has been active since at least the 1860s. (Image from *Harper's Weekly,* April 1883.)

Subsidence

It is stated that fifteen years ago [1884] there were no oysters above Bayou Lagraisse, nor in some of the small bayous of Lake Barré, and their presence there now is supposed to be owing to changes in the drainage due to the cutting of timber along the bayous and the washing of the islands. The topographical changes in the region between Timbalier and Terrebonne bays are quite extensive and rapid, and islands were observed there in all stages of destruction, some of them cut into pieces, others barely showing above the water, and still others whose former positions were marked merely by shoals or by dead brush projecting above the surface. It appears probably that these changes might have produced considerable alteration in the hydrographic characters, and thus have changed the adaptability of the waters for oysters (Moore 1899:73).

Subsidence can be classified as either endogenic or exogenic. Endogenic is associated with natural processes, while exogenic is related to humankind. Dolan and Goodell (1986:39) remark that the "rate of natural . . . subsidence rarely exceeds 10 mm/year [.39 inches/year], whereas man-induced . . . subsidence may be over 50 cm/year [1.9 inches/year]." This negative change is the result of compaction, dewatering, fluid withdrawal, and sediment consolidation (Walker, et al. 1987). S. Penland (et al. 1989) and others (Ramsey and Moslow 1987; Penland, et al. 1988; Penland and Ramsey 1990) have concluded the state's southeastern wetlands are subsiding at a rate of from 3.0 to 4.3 feet/century, while the marshes in the southwestern part of the state are subsiding between 1.3 and 2.0 feet/century.

There are at least 300 pumps in Terrebonne and Lafourche parishes, 2008. (Photo by the author.)

Worldwide, negative land surfaces are to a great degree a human-induced hazard. Largely unknown prior to the Industrial Revolution, subsidence can be slow and subtle or fast and dramatic. Coasts are particularly susceptible, since subsidence is an integral part of their destructive phase. While expected to occur, regional subsidence is accelerated by a number of variables. In the end, accretion cannot keep pace, so extensive defensive fortifications, including levees, dikes, sea walls, locks, and pumping stations, are constructed (Bryant and Chabreck 1998; Cahoon, et al. 2000). One of the best examples of subsidence is the number of prehistoric archaeological middens that have subsided. Some of these sites are at least eighteen feet below the present-day surface (Pearson, et al. 1989).

As one investigates negative land surfaces, subsidence is highest in peat and muck lands. In general, these histosols are subaqueous in origin. Frequently fifteen feet or more thick, they will undergo, when dried, an initial volume loss of as much as 75 percent. At this point, they will compact, shrink, and subside (Snowden, et al. 1977; Snowden, et al. 1979; Snowden, et al. 1980). Louisiana's wetlands are dominated by these soils. For example, in the southeast and east-central parts of Terrebonne Parish, some narrow natural-levee ridges, once used for cultivation, are subject to flooding or have subsided below the marsh. In analyzing the marsh, the flooding or subsidence problems are heightened by a landscape that is now more water than land. Further, Okey (1914:6) reported:

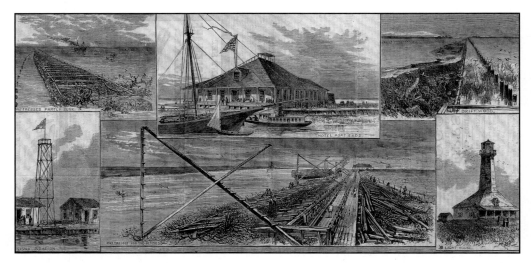

As people began to move into the wetlands, as at Port Eads, subsidence emerged as an important issue. (Image from *Harper's Weekly*, March 1878.)

In the very newest portions of the Delta at Port Eads, at the mouth of the river, a considerable subsidence of the land is yet going on, the measured rate being about 0.11 foot per year. That this subsidence is due to a compacting of the newer deposits is shown by the fact that permanent bench marks along the Mississippi River record a decreasing settlement as the distance from the mouth of the river increases. Except in this relatively small area near the mouth of the river, the remainder of this section of the State shows no change in elevation.

Subsidence, which is exceeding deposition in most of these regions, is increasing the open-water surface area. The problem is further compounded by a nearly imperceptible, but measurable sea-level rise. From a national perspective the changes may be small, but many of South Louisiana's sea-level citizens are living less than one foot above the high tide line, any change is critical.

Even with new data and increased awareness of subsidence problems, subsidence is not a new issue. One of the best early description of the problem is in Le Baron (1905:85), who observed:

At the head of the South Pass, the rails of a railroad track, which had been laid many years before for carrying coal from the barges to the coal pile for the United States Government, were found to be projecting from the bank and 2 or 3 ft. below the surface of the ground, and it may be said that they were relatively below the surface of the water. These rails had not sunk into the material, for the ground was hard and solid, but they had evidently gone down with it; and, as this ground went down, the annual deposits from the overflow of the river have kept the surface at about the same level in respect to the level of the water surface.

Further,

Two or three miles above Head of the Passes, was built, many years ago, a pilot's house, on brick piers 5 ft. high. The ground is now up to the sills of the house, but the surface of the ground bears about the same relation to the water surface in the river as when the house was first build.

And

> Without going further into these details of subsidence, it may be stated gener-
> ally that the question is one of great importance to the whole Delta country.

In 2005, a review of sixty years of National Oceanography and Atmospheric Administration (NOAA) data for southeastern Louisiana revealed 3.2 feet of relative sea
level rise per century. This is about one inch of relative mean sea level rise every thirty months for this period of record. The high rate is due apparently to land elevations
moving downward. Base levels had to be changed. New elevations were published
for coastal Louisiana in which elevations were lowered from six inches to a foot from
the last adjustment in 1995 (Osborne 2006, pers. comm.).

This ten-year-record suggests a negative elevation change from one-half-to-one-
inch per year depending on where the measurements were taken, which may explain
the rapid rise in coastal flooding. Estimates from a Terrebonne Parish engineering
company suggests about 8 percent or more of the parish is below two feet of elevation.
With a one foot or greater tide range, the parish floods more often. To monitor this
issue, local government created a vertical subsidence network to measure elevation
loss and to adjust known elevations every few years. These corrections are necessary
to offset the effects of subsidence on roads, levees, and other engineering structures
designed to help protect and evacuate the coastal dweller (Updated elevations 2006;
Sea levels online 2006).

Throughout the coastal lowlands the marsh surface is disappearing, putting the
inland citizens at greater risk from smaller storms or high-tide events. With about 50
percent of the state's population living in this area, the expansion of repetitive flooding is significant. Consequently, coastal
parish governments have real concerns
related to the potential loss of some unknown percentages of their population,
as families and businesses move (or fail
to return) to those areas that have seen so
much flooding. In this regard, Orleans,
St. Bernard, Plaquemines, Jefferson, Lafourche, Terrebonne, St. Mary, Iberia,
Vermilion, and Cameron parishes have
to make some difficult decisions. Vigi-
lance is now critical, especially after Hurricanes Katrina, Rita, Gustav, and Ike.

Also, the parts of the equation contributing to marshland habitat change
are: 1) shoreline erosion; 2) breakup of
flotant and fresh marshes by floods and
storms; 3) replacement of land areas by
canals and borrow pits; and 4) impoundment and flooding resulting from cross-
drainage spoil deposition (Holm 2003).

May and Britsch's work on land loss shows
an anomaly that appears to be a fault. (Image
from May and Britsch 1987.)

In addition, there is some evidence that imply oil, gas, and sulphur extraction may
have also played a role in site-specific subsidence.

Joel Bourne (2000), and Robert Morton, et al. (2002) report and document subsidence rates in producing oil and gas fields to be as much as 0.9 inches a year. It is speculated this increased subsidence is the product of the reactivation of stress faults, leading to rapid subsidence on the fault's down-thrust side. Prior to this research effort,
studies by Fisk (1944) Wallace (1957), Murray (1960), Gagliano and Van Beek (1993),

and Gagliano (2003) reported on the faults, fault pattern complexes, fault trends, and zones that may be rising, subsiding, and/or tilting.

As a result of regional subsidence, maps used to set insurance rates and flood control systems along with building codes may be inaccurate; hence they are being reassessed or surveyed. Further, Dokka (2007) reports the land is shifting southward "as a kind of avalanche of material, except that it is happening very slowly. It moved about the width of two credit cards this year [2006]" (Burdeau 2007:2B). Subsidence is, therefore, an issue of concern throughout coastal Louisiana that must be considered in the design of any engineered structure, such as new levees.

Sea-level Rise

It doesn't matter if the land is sinking or the water is rising, we still have to get taller boots. Com'on let's do something (Comments by Stevie Smith, during the October 2, 1998, the National Coastal Wetlands Summit, Today's Successes, Tomorrow's Challenges, Nicholls State University, Thibodaux, Louisiana).

Sea level is rising. In the twentieth century, a change of six inches was detected and "there is strong theoretical reason to expect that warming of the oceans already has led to more intense hurricanes and will continue to affect tropical storm characteristics" (American Geophysical Union 2006:3).

Tidal records along Louisiana's coast indicate relative sea-level rise is from .35 inches/year to .51 inches/year or about 35.8 inches/century to 3.9 feet/century (Ramsey and Penland 1989). Concern over sea-level rise has prompted publication of numerous projections. Most of these assessments are tied to carbon dioxide and other gases that effect air temperature, expected melting of polar ice, and thermal expansion of the world's oceans. The United States' Environmental Protection Agency (EPA) reports by the year 2100 it is likely a rise of sea level will be between 4.5 feet and 6.8 feet. Moreover, projects from as low as 1.8 feet to perhaps a high of 18.6 feet cannot be discounted. Further, most of the United States' Atlantic and Gulf Coasts will experience, according to some predictions, from a low of about seven inches to a high approaching twelve inches more rise than the global average (Titus, et al. 1987; Church, et al 2001).

These events are critical to Louisiana, since a rise in sea level of three feet during the next century would result in thousands of wetland acres being lost. Sea-level rise will exacerbate coastal flooding and expedite the already serious coastal erosion. Land that is just above sea level may be flooded by 2050. To counteract this problem, elaborate pumping schemes and other measures will be required to remove excess water, as gravity drainage will be ineffective.

Even a small rise in sea level increases the probability a hurricane-induced storm surge will extend further inland, enhancing coastal erosion and put more people at risk. As seas expand, wetlands are also threatened. Nowhere is that threat as great as in Louisiana. With current sea-level rise projections and the potential for hurricanes to be more frequent or more powerful, along with high barrier island shoreline erosion rates, coupled with regional subsidence issues and the break-up of the marsh, the state's estuaries are in danger of being lost, redefined, or altered permanently (National Research Council 2006; Dean 2007). To the state this is a serious issue. This real estate is an important economic driver. The income and taxes generated from the seafood products and/or hydrocarbons that are going to be gone or difficult to access are a vital part of the state's revenue stream.

While the state is focusing on wetland loss and rebuilding, or at least rehabilitating, the wetlands, a number of scientists and respected science-based organizations are reporting on global warming trends that are well above earlier predictions (Global

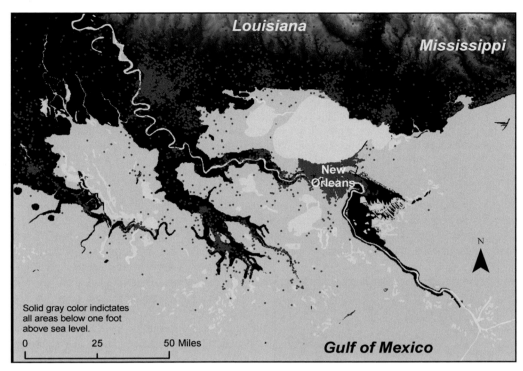

Possible future topography of coastal Louisiana, with each red dot representing 500 residences, distributed randomly within 2000 census block groups. (Image from Campanella 2006.)

Warming 2006; National Oceanographic 2006; Union of Concerned Scientists 2006). In the worst-case scenario, the Gulf Coast could run along the southern borders of Baton Rouge, Lafayette, Lake Charles, and Hammond by 2500. Further, sea-level rise impacts on Louisiana's coast must be factored into the entire Katrina, Rita, Gustav, and Ike reconstruction discussion. The current projections, right or wrong, need to be addressed, as sea-level rise will add considerable stress to the natural system and thus cannot be ignored (Dunne 2006B). In short, the system is hemorrhaging, and society needs to address the problem aggressively.

Little, if anything, can be done quickly to prevent sea-level rise. In the short term, sediment reintroduction can mitigate some subsidence issues, which requires considerable re-engineering of the natural system's plumbing (Day and Template 1989). However, sound, rational, long-term planning can mitigate the effects of both issues on existing and proposed intensive land uses. Options available to planners include 1) concentrating development on higher ground; 2) preventing encroachment into unsuitable zones; 3) flood-proofing buildings to reduce damage; 4) designing projects that can withstand the predictable problems; and 5) relocating communities at high risk.

Coastal Land Loss—Disappearing Coast, Disappearing Culture

At the edge of a large lagoon a man points out the boundaries of what was once a well-cultivated stretch. For some years, through the dark, soil-steeped liquids, the outlines of abandoned furrows could be made out; now they, too, are gone. Near a sagging back levee stands a small wreck, the frame that housed a powerful drainage machine; the waters that it once held back slip about and through it. A seventy-year-old Deltan nudges my arm: 'See that place way out there in the water? When I was eighteen I walked with my uncle there, and the crops rose higher than his head. Now they hunts ducks in the same place!' He is silent a moment, then he asks, almost to himself, 'Did any of us ever think this could happen?' (Kane 1944:150).

We're sinking, . . . Sinking. And not just a little. Dey say every twenty minutes or so, a football field of land turns to water in Louisiana. Every twenty minutes! Most of dat land is marsh . . . Don't you see dose telephone poles in de water along de bayou? Ten years ago dose poles were in grass. Didn't you see de 'tree cemeteries,' dose clusters of dead oaks in de water? All does trees were on land twenty years ago. And de big stretch of open water south of Golden Meadow all along de bayou? Cattle pastures fifty years ago (Tidwell 2003:18).

Although well documented in Louisiana, the land loss problem is not new—merely rediscovered. Of the estimated 214 million acres of wetlands that were in the United States when the first Europeans arrived, more than 50 percent have been lost and the rate is accelerating. Coastal wetlands are being destroyed—changing from near-sea-level marshes to open water. Subsidence, sea-level rise, and human interference with natural flow regimes are the principal factors responsible for this change. In Louisiana, an area the size of Connecticut is washing away. Vegetated marsh is reverting to open water and as a result no other coastal region in the United States is experiencing such large-scale wetland change.

Statistically, every ten months, an area the size of Manhattan disappears. Place names found on old maps are gone. The landscape has changed dramatically and only the old marshdwellers remember the lost bayous, bays, and lakes. In their mind, there will be no retreat without a struggle. They may move, but the decision will be difficult and the fight will be contentious. To the state's near sea-level citizens, humans are responsible for the present high rates of wetland loss; therefore, humans should fix the problem. To them, it is a black and white issue; there are no shades of gray.

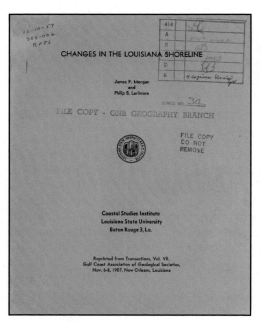

After World War II, Louisiana scientists initiated the first study of coastal change, 1957.

Wetland Loss

Since the preparation of the Coast Survey charts of this region [Plaquemines Parish] the topography has greatly changed, the marshes formerly existing in the northern and western part of the bay [Whale Bay and Grand Pass] being cut up into numerous small islands and channels (Moore 1899:80).

And

Throughout the region [Terrebonne Parish] . . . , there are rapid and extensive changes taking place in the topography. In the section between Cat Island

Lake and Timbalier Bay there are islands in all stages of disintegration: some of them are barely above the surface of the water, while the former location of others is marked by the tops of dead grass and bushes which alone extend above the water. Farther inland there has been a very noticeable increase in the area of many of the lakes, and some of them are several times as large as they were fifteen or twenty years ago (Louisiana State Board 1907:7-8).

In fact, "if wetland loss in Louisiana continues to go unchecked the total amount of wetlands lost by 2050, set end to end in a one-foot wide strip, would reach from the Earth to the Moon and back 11 times" (The cost of 1999:3). We have a wetland loss rate that is globally unparalleled. Maps have been used extensively to illustrate this change and the change is striking. The lost area is about the size of Delaware, thirty-one times the size of the District of Columbia, the size of New York, Chicago, Los Angeles, San Diego, and Houston combined, and it continues daily (Plot line 2004; Knapp and Dunne 2006). The state is falling apart "like old rotten cloth" because even, with fewer people living in its remote bayous, lakes and bays, the Mississippi River is no longer re-nourishing its surfaces (McPhee 1989:62).

Prior to 1950, the Mississippi carried a stable load of about 485 million tons of suspended material each year. Dam construction on the system after 1950 reduced the quantity of sediments reaching the delta by nearly 50 percent. In fact, since the 1850s the sediment supplied by the Mississippi River and its tributaries has decreased by almost 80 percent (Coastal Louisiana 2007). These sediments are funneled through the Atchafalaya Basin and channeled into the water on the edge of the Gulf of Mexico's continental shelf. They are lost to the near-shore sediment budget.

> "I put a 'No Hunting' sign on my property in September, don't you know. Dat sign, it was four feet from de water's edge when I put it up. But when I come back in April, it was four feet in de water. De shore moved eight feet in seven months" (Tidwell 2003:103).

Because the sediment is being dumped into deeper water, the coast is deprived of the material required to build new land at a rate slightly greater than subsidence (Coleman 1966; Baumann, et al. 1984). Land building by river-flood-flow deposition has been replaced by extensive and rapid wetland loss. Few regions can compete with Louisiana in production of renewable and non-renewable resources; yet because of land loss, those resources are threatened and may even vanish.

Between 1955 and 1975, it is estimated that in the contiguous United States more than 540,000 acres of wetlands were lost annually and most of this is attributed to human activities (Wetlands: Their use 1984; Deegan, et al. 1984). In Louisiana's coastal lowlands, wetland losses in the 1980s exceeded thirty-eight square miles per year—a fluctuating rate that appears to be decreasing (Gosselink, et al. 1979; Craig, et al. 1979; Gosselink and Baumann. 1980; Gagliano, et al. 1981; U. S. Department of Agriculture 1986; Turner and Cahoon 1987; Britsch and Kemp 1990; Penland, et al. 1990; Dunbar, et al. 1992; Williams and Cichon 1994: Turner 1997; Day, et al. 2000). At the beginning of the twenty-first century, the land loss rate was estimated at about twenty-five square miles per year. When equated with the remainder of the United States, these land-loss assessments are exceptionally high.

The national rate of loss has decreased slightly, largely due to reduction of agricultural reclamation that was aggressively promoted by the agriculture press, such as the *Country Gentleman* and the *Farmers' Register* (Vileisis 1997). This has benefitted upland wetlands, but is insignificant in the coastal zone, where the land loss problem is critical. Quite simply, Louisiana's coastal area is presently out-of-balance, and since marsh losses are so well documented, they serve as a contemporary illustration of coastal modifications (subsidence, erosion, salt water intrusion, and sea-level rise) that are, to some degree, a part of all coastal states.

Louisiana is not alone in the battle to save its coast. Since the 1780s, twenty-two states lost 50 percent or more of their original wetlands. Ten—five with coasts—lost 70 percent or more of their original wetlands (Dahl 1990)—documenting continued loss of wetland real estate. Moreover, since 1954 approximately 990,000 acres of United

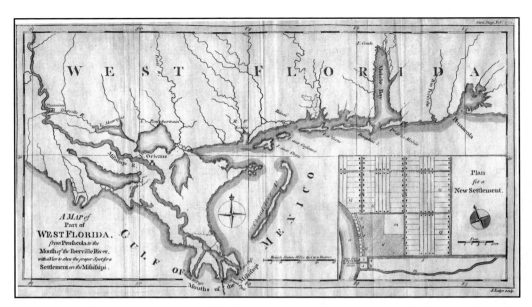

Until survey techniques improved, humankind had a poor understanding of Louisiana's coast. Ironically, in the twenty-first century, this depiction may be correct. A Map of Part of West Florida, 1772.

States' coastal marshes (3.2 times the size of the city of Los Angeles) were lost at a rate of 37,000 acres (57.8 square miles) per year. In Louisiana more than 15,000 square miles (for comparison purposes that is about half of the state of North Carolina) were eradicated in the twentieth century, affecting many of the wetlands' interlocking subsystems. All elements within this system—human and otherwise—must be analyzed to insure proper management decisions. This holistic strategy will maximize the marsh's productivity and minimize changes in the barrier island/marsh/*chênière* morphological character (Basta, et al. 1990; Psuty 1992).

Destruction of these wetlands is explained partially by natural processes—subsidence, sea-level rise, and long-term climatic change. Humans have relatively little control over these natural events. Human elements—specifically those levee-building activities that locked the Mississippi River into a controlled conduit—altered flow regimes, sediment patterns, and vegetative assemblages that created the original problem and continue to contribute to the land-loss predicament. Other factors include 1) change in the deposition site and stage in the delta cycle; 2) canal dredging; 3) biological degradation; 4) short-term natural and human-made catastrophic events; 5) fluid withdrawal; and 6) regional geosynclinal down warping (Walker, et al. 1987; Turner 1997; Turner and Streever 2002; Holm 2003) are important as well.

In 2000, just over 5,000 square miles of salt water, brackish, and freshwater wetlands remained in Louisiana. These wetlands supported a delicate ecosystem that is a spawning ground and nursery for a multitude of young fish, crabs, oysters, and shrimp. In addition, wetlands also filter pollutants out of runoff, reduce flooding, provide habitat for many waterfowl and other wildlife, and as previously noted protect the coast from storm surges, and rising sea level.

Annual floods re-nourished the land, but they were an aggravating aspect of living within the Mississippi's floodplain. To neutralize these seasonal disasters, natural levees were augmented by continental-scale manipulation of the Mississippi River through engineered structures high enough to counteract spring overflow events, or at least minimize their effects. The proliferation of levees became so efficient they deprived the marshlands of valuable sediment, influenced salt water intrusion, and disrupted flow regimes that contributed directly to Louisiana's high rate of land loss. The Mississippi's natural processes were altered. Erosion began to overshadow deposition. Indeed, even though the area is drained, the natural system is superseded by an artificial one outlined by levees. These engineering features are new additions to the landscape, since there is no record of leveeing the marsh in the 1700s (Nesbit 1885; Owens 1999). However, as early as 1814, Louisiana's natural hydrology was altered when Gen. Andrew Jackson issued an order to close and dam Bayou Lafourche and Bayou Manchac/Amite River to prevent the ascent of British forces by these routes, as these waterways constituted backdoors to the Gulf (Randall, et al. 1846; Dranguet and Heleniak 1985). The process of altering the natural system continues, and the end result is a collapsing coastline and a heightened hurricane threat to coastal communities like New Orleans.

Coming to terms with this wetland crisis was not a national priority, although the National Research Council in 2006 published *Drawing Louisiana's New Map: Addressing Land Loss in Coastal Louisiana* as a blueprint for action that incorporated and considered all of the state's previous plans, including the Louisiana Coastal Wetlands Conservation and Restoration Task Force 1998 study entitled *Coast 2050: Toward a Sustainable Coastal Louisiana* and the report *Louisiana Coastal Area (LCA), Louisiana—Ecosystem Restoration Study* (Reed and Wilson 2004). In January 2006, *A New Framework for Planning the Future of Coastal Louisiana after the Hurricanes of 2005* (A Working Group 2006) was issued, followed in November by the *Comprehensive Coastal Protection Master Plan for Louisiana: Preliminary Draft* (The coastal protection 2006). These studies are making headlines. Congress has approved coastal restoration funds derived from offshore oil and gas revenue produced in the outer continental shelf to help restore and protect the coastal wetlands. A number of bills and measures have been passed and the state in 2009 was entitled to nearly $500 million, a five-fold increase from the $50 million allocated in the early part of the twenty-first century (Shields 2009). This is good news, because the coast continues to disappear.

In 1990, the National Academy published *Managing Coastal Erosion*. In 2000, the Coalition to Restore Coastal Louisiana released *No Time to Lose: Facing the Future of Louisiana and the Crisis to Coastal Land Loss* an update of the 1989 report *Coastal Louisiana: Here Today, Gone Tomorrow?* In the intervening years, Louisiana continued to lose valuable coastal real estate (Turner 1997; Streever 2001). Nothing was apparently learned, or perhaps the political will was not strong enough to force the government to take on this important problem. And then in August and September 2005, Louisiana was pummeled by Hurricanes Katrina and Rita. Three years later, Gustav and Ike battered the coast. In the resulting crises, the political will, at the national and state level, finally crystallized; the intersection of science and politics became real, and a "well constructed collaborative effort to maximize the role of science in decisions made about the rebuilding" gained critical importance (Groat 2005:341). Further, "long-term flood protection will likely require reestablishing some natural systems, such as wetlands that serve as a natural barrier, adding some protection from storm surge and flooding" (American Geophysical Union 2006:4).

> Recent events have transformed all aspects of life in coastal Louisiana and nowhere is that more true than in southeastern Louisiana. The vulnerability of our communities and way of life are clearer now than ever before. So is the connection between a healthy coast and effective storm protection. The pace and scale of coastal conservation, restoration and storm protection efforts have been proven to be out of sync with the threats facing our coast and its communities, a fact most recently demonstrated by the deficiencies in the Corps of Engineers 2006 LACPR [Louisiana Coastal Protection and Restora-

tion] Interim Report. That must change and change now. Fortunately the State and the Army Corps of Engineers have each embarked upon ambitious efforts to meld coastal conservation and restoration with storm protection. This is our best and perhaps last chance to save—ecologically, culturally, and economically—what we know as South Louisiana (Davis 2006B:1).

In the past, solving the wetland problem was too expensive, too environmental, too parochial, and too unfocused. Now it has to be done or the next storm may be worse. The solution requires a commitment to restore the wetlands, estuaries, and barrier island shorelines, and a commitment to provide real storm protection to the regional population centers. Protection that can only come from the integration of levees, coastal conservation, restoration and rehabilitation, effective land use planning, and building codes, and perhaps rethinking current settlement patterns (Turner and Streever 2002; Constanza, et al. 2006).

As solutions crystallize, "big picture" issues must be integrated into the plan. Some of these decisions will be difficult and painful, but necessary. They include staged retreat, which is not new, and acceptance of the reality that not all segments of the coast can be saved. In order to work, sea-level rise and climate change issues need to be considered. None of these issues can be ignored, as the future of the state's coast is at stake. Further, it is imperative that considerable local participation be encouraged, as this element is necessary so everyone involved is aware of the science driving the decisions. This approach is necessary to convince Congress to act in an appropriate manner (Wold 2009B).

We cannot gamble with the future of our coastal communities or on the future of the greatest wetland and estuarine treasure in our country. It is imperative we get it right (Davis 2006, pers. comm.). Ironically, the marsh nurtured the resources that allowed the marshdweller to survive is now vanishing; yet, as individuals begin to recognize the societal value of wetlands (Constanza, et al. 1998), the restoration and rehabilitation of these degraded wetlands is of critical national and state concern (National Research Council 2006).

> Business and political leaders began to understand in the 1990s that the loss of Louisiana's coast lands was leading to catastrophic costs—and not just for the state. Coastal Louisiana has been designated 'America's Wetland,' and it is no exaggeration to say that the entire nation has a stake in its survival. As erosion worsens, everyone stands to lose. . . . (Richard 2003:177).

". . . in this particular case nature is cannibalizing itself, eating up what was once the most productive wildlife habitats in North America, if not on earth" (Reisner 1991:274).

In 1881, an issue of the *New Orleans Democrat* praised Randall Lee Gibson from Terrebonne Parish for championing the cause of flood control and creation of the Mississippi River Commission in 1878. In their article, the *Democrat* notes Gibson was

> the first to advocate the improvement of the river on the ground that it was a grand national and commercial highway, a vast inland sea, whose commerce and trade exceeds even now in value our whole foreign commerce, and which therefore should be improved by the general government in the interest of the whole country (McBride and McLaurin 1995:409).

The same can be said of Louisiana's disappearing coastal wetlands. They are a national treasure, and it is in "the interest of the whole country" to take notice of the region's looming environmental catastrophe and begin the process of rehabilitating this ecological system.

The Mississippi River: A Powerful Agent of Change

Transgression, sea-level rise, subsidence, vibracores, seismic profiles, and sediment loading are part of the lexicon of coastal geology and geomorphology. These terms, and others, are used to describe the fluvial and regional history of Louisiana's wetlands. The descriptive techniques employed are used to unravel the sequential record of the Mississippi's sedimentary patterns. More than 12,000 years of geomorphic history are recorded on the contemporary map of delta switching. The landscape is a product of repetitive floods laying down layer upon layer of new material, delta by delta. As the Mississippi changed its course, by following the shortest route to the Gulf, it created a new delta, and the old delta began to degenerate for lack of building materials and nutrients. This process was repeated through time, and what remains is the foundation of South Louisiana's marshland landscape. The Mississippi River is, therefore, the great architect of the state's coastal topography. The bird-foot delta still functions, but the Mississippi has been so manipulated, re-engineered, and controlled, its waters can no longer freely roam over the marsh and build up the fragile land. The Mississippi has been subdued and one might ask "why on Earth did those foolish settlers manage their land in ways that caused such obvious damage? Didn't they realize what would happen? Yes, they eventually did, but they couldn't at first, because they were faced with an unfamiliar and difficult problem of land management . . ." (Diamond 2005:201).

Superimposed, therefore, on this natural sequence of deltaic events are the engineered structures that have harnessed and trained the Mississippi River's tributaries to follow a designated route. The river can no longer overflow at random; it must follow a course outlined by earthen mounds constructed to control spring inundations and "rife with imperfections" (McPhee 1989:33). The national government ignored flood control issues after the 1882 flood, but after the record deluge of 1927, Congress appropriated the necessary funds to use engineered levees to prevent the Mississippi River from inundated the Valley. The $300 million earmarked for this work "was more money in one bill than had been spent on Mississippi levees in all of colonial and American history" (McPhee 1989:42). As a result, the United States Army Corps of Engineers went into the levee business and locked the Mississippi River into a straightjacket of engineered guide levees that resembled the Maginot Line and the Great Wall of China—"with the difference that while the levees were each about as long as the Great Wall they were in many places higher and in cross-section ten times as large" (McPhee 1989:45). In the process, this public works initiative attracted workers from throughout the country, who moved into South Louisiana for the jobs, married, and settled in the communities along the river and became absorbed by the French culture.

Prior to this period of massive levee construction, flooding was a reoccurring concern. Once the Mississippi broke through its embankments or natural levees, it rushed over the country "with the force of a torrent, carrying ruin and destruction in its course" (Wilson 1850:4). During periods of high water, vast submerged tracts were common throughout the river's floodplain. Although a complete inventory of all overflow events has never been completed, a list of the great floods has been documented (Elliott 1932; Elliott 1932B).

From the first explorers to the present, there has been sustained interest in the Mississippi River, which was explored, claimed, and exploited by the English, French, and Spanish. In 1543, Hernando De Soto's expedition observed the Mississippi overflowing its banks for about eighty days (Elliott 1932). Garcilaso de la Vega wrote of the 1543 flood: "inundated areas extended for twenty leagues [fifty-two to ninety-two statute miles] on either side of the river" (Elliott 1932:105). Robert Cavelier de La Salle

---

Early Nineteenth Century Mississippi River Commerce

Prior to the Civil War, the Mississippi River was a busy waterway. James Hall in 1826 reported: "As the waters rise, trade and navigation are quickened into activity. . . . At this season the spectator who is stationed upon the shore . . . sees these vessels passing in rapid succession—not infrequently several at a time being visible—laden so heavily that the whole hull is immersed" (Lippincott 1914:636).

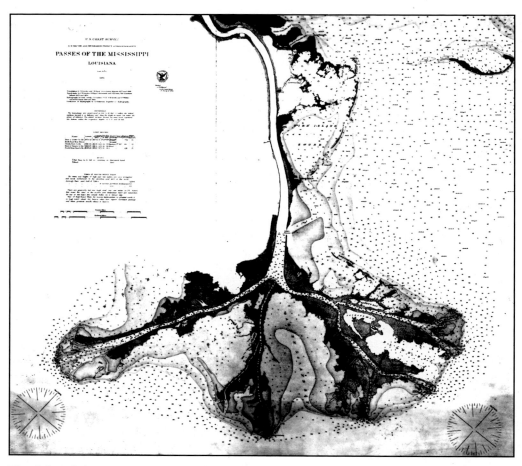

The delta of the Mississippi River has always been an important part of the commerce and development of the entire valley. Passes of the Mississippi, 1873.

in 1684 also reported the lower Mississippi out of its defined channel.

To these explorers, control of the Mississippi was paramount, but not in the sense of building a massive levee network to channel its flow. Political jurisdiction was deemed imperative; for over 150 years free navigation was critical. The sentiment was so strong that Thomas Jefferson became determined to gain authority over at least the river's east bank. Through the Louisiana Purchase the United States acquired over one million square miles, including most of the Mississippi's drainage basin (Richard 1995). For the first time, the river was under the jurisdiction of one government that began to exhibit an interest in the connectivity between flood management and navigation. Navigation was the key issue, and Congress used industrial development as a pretext to justify navigation improvement expenditures. As a result, Congress passed legislation in 1820 and 1822 ". . . for the purpose of facilitating and ascertaining the most practicable mode of improving the navigation . . ." (Lippincott 1914:634). In addition, the Louisiana Purchase insured that all immigrant groups residing in Louisiana would become American citizens regardless of where they were born (Richard 2003).

Flood control was not a new issue; ample evidence suggests flooding problems extended back to the founding of New Orleans. From the beginning, the Crescent City learned to endure the hardships that accompanied the river's annual submergence events. The site which the French explorer Jean Baptiste Le Moyne de Bienville selected for New Orleans was over the objection of Le Blond de la Tour, his chief engineer.

Without proper levees, the citizens of the Mississippi Valley were constantly at risk of repetitive flooding. (Image from *Harper's Weekly*, April 1882.)

(Middle) Image from *Harper's Weekly*, October 1869.
(Bottom) Image from *Harper's Weekly*, April 1882.

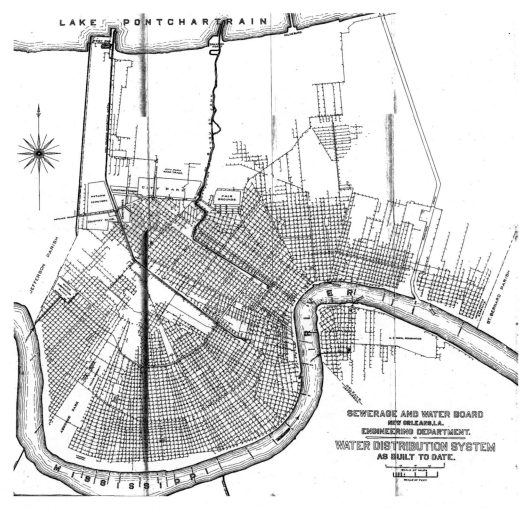

From its inception, New Orleans has always depended on a system of internal drains. (Image from Sewerage and Water Board of New Orleans, 1925.)

De la Tour felt the area would be flooded periodically. Because of these reservations, the new settlement was to be built above the surrounding terrain. Ironically, it could not be raised until the water receded from the 1717 flood (Martin 1827; Elliott 1932; Elliott 1932B; Campanella 2006). This was an omen of things to come.

De La Tour was correct, for New Orleans is in a constant battle with flooding. *Nouvelle-Orléans* flooded often (1735, 1775, 1782, 1785, 1791, 1799, 1816, 1823, 1844, 1849, 1882, and 1927), so much so it became a walled city. Levees formed protective barriers; without them the Mississippi River would easily engulf the city. Water nevertheless occasionally overwhelmed the "frail breastwork" (Twain 1901:296), entering into the city's reclaimed land. When this happened, a second reclamation effort was initiated to remove the flood water from the holding basin. Even though the area was drained, the natural system was superseded by an artificial one that, at times, could not accommodate the torrential rain storms or hurricanes in the summer and fall months.

While the situation in New Orleans was bad, other population centers fared even worse. Even so, the earliest emigrants recognized the narrow, elevated, fertile natural levees were capable of being quite productive. Colonists and traders settled the Mississippi's natural levees; others moved into the hinterlands, but "history is silent about the first settlers in the marsh areas" (Kammer 1941:6). To all of these newcomers, guarding against over bank flow was a massive undertaking. When the river was in flood stage, a thin sheet of water poured over the natural levees into the backswamps, destroying the crops in its path. At times, floodwater passed over both banks of the Mississippi for miles along the river's course (Ellet 1852; Richardson 1901). During flood stage, sediments built up the levees. The "frontlands" near the river banks are relatively high, while the "backlands" are low and outlined by swamps that absorb the overflow and seepage that always moved towards the "back."

Levees beyond New Orleans

Along the Mississippi and many other waterways, early settlers had to clear their land of a virtual thicket of trees and construct a levee, or levees, to protect their agricultural investment (Owens 1999). Mark Twain's mid-nineteenth century observations clearly illustrate the influence agriculturalists had on clearing timber to facilitate the sugar industry:

> Both banks, for a good deal over a hundred miles are shorn of their timber and bordered by continuous sugar-plantations, with only here and there a scattering of sapling or row of ornamental China trees. The timber is shorn off clear to the rear of the plantations, from two to four miles (Twain 1950:92-93).

To protect their investment, planters began to build crude, flimsy, mud embankments without any regard for the natural landscape. These earthen levees were the cheapest and most practical structure to keep floodwaters from their lands. These embankments did not work, and plantations were flooded regularly. Planters were not hydrologic engineers, so they paid little attention to the bayous or natural outlets that helped divert flood waters. These channels were stopped up by the extension of their levee network. Flood waters could no longer flow into the backswamp reservoirs. This water was forced down the main course. Flooding became a yearly issue, influencing everyone who lived on or near the Mississippi and its tributaries and/or distributaries.

> The advocates of river improvement have come to recognize in recent years that the deepening of the streams involves other betterments. Their plan is not at all simple. It includes a six- or- nine or a fourteen-foot channel, according to the river in question, a deep waterway from the Lakes to the Gulf, strengthening the levees against floods, reclamation of the overflow lands of the southern Mississippi, conservation of the forests along the watersheds of the streams, conservation of the rich soil which is now washed out to the ocean, and the utilization of water-power whenever that becomes profitable. President Roosevelt, speaking at the Memphis Deep Waterways Convention in 1907, stated the matter briefly as follows: 'The Mississippi River and its tributaries ought by all means to be utilized to their utmost possibility.' The latest platforms of the leading political parties pledge a vast system of improvement. This, then is the present program—the fullest use of the rivers of the interior with all that implies (Lippincott 1914:630).

Mississippi River Flooding Events from 1801 to 1927

From the beginnings of settlement, failure was the par expectation with respect to the river—a fact generally masked by the powerful fabric of ambition that impelled people to build towns and cities where almost any camper would be loath to pitch a tent . . .

Good Intentions Gone Wrong

"Man-made modifications in Louisiana's wetlands, which are changing the conditions of existence from its very foundations, are the result of flood protection, deforestation, deepening channels, and the cutting of navigation and drainage canals. . . . Reclamation and flood control as practiced in Louisiana have been more or less a failure, destroying valuable resources without producing the permanent compensating benefits originally desired. Reclamation experts and real estate promoters have been killing the goose that laid the golden egg. . . . [O]ur future conservation policy should be restoration of those natural conditions best suited to an abundant marsh, swamp, and aquatic fauna, but under some degree of control at all times, to the end that the state and nation may enjoy a more balanced diet, healthful recreation, and enduring prosperity" (Viosca 1928:216).

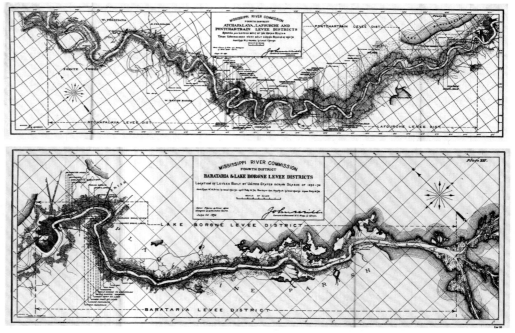

The Mississippi River levees south of Baton Rouge before 1900.

The message in the landscape could not have been clearer: like the aboriginal people, you could fish and forage and move on, but you could not build there without declaring war on nature. You did not have to be Dutch to understand this, or French to ignore it. The people of southern Louisiana have often been compared unfavorably with farmers of the pre-Aswan Nile, who lived on high ground, farmed low ground, and permitted floods to come and go according to the rhythms of nature. There were differences in Louisiana though. There was no high ground worth mentioning, and planters had to live on their plantations. The waters of the Nile were warm, but the Mississippi brought cold northern floods that sometimes stood for months, defeating agriculture for the year. If people were to farm successfully in the rich loams of the natural levees—or anywhere nearby—they could not allow the Mississippi to retain its natural state (McPhee 1989:31-32).

From 1801 to 1927, there were forty-seven major flooding events in Louisiana—nearly one every three years. The most notable was the flood of 1927, which contemporaries considered the "greatest peace-time disaster in our history" (Simpich 1927:245). It was the product of abnormally high rainfall in the thirty-one states and two Canadian provinces that comprise the Mississippi's drainage basin—a hydrologic unit that encompasses 1,240,000 square miles. Deluge after deluge increased the Mississippi's discharge rates. Parts of seven states were submerged. Simpich (1927:256) described the 1927 flood and observed: "at noon the streets . . . were dry and dusty. By two o'clock mules were drowning in the main streets . . . faster than they could be unhitched from wagons. Before dark the homes and stores stood six feet deep in water." The 1927 flood was a tragic event and changed national flood management policy.

On the lower Mississippi, thirteen crevasses—a natural break in the levee that served to alleviate flooding along the river—breached the levees, siphoning off enough flow to reduce flood stage downstream. These crevasses were a "source of terror no less effective than a bursting dam—and the big ones were memorialized, like other great disasters" (McPhee 1989:35). In total, the 1927 flood caused along the lower Mis-

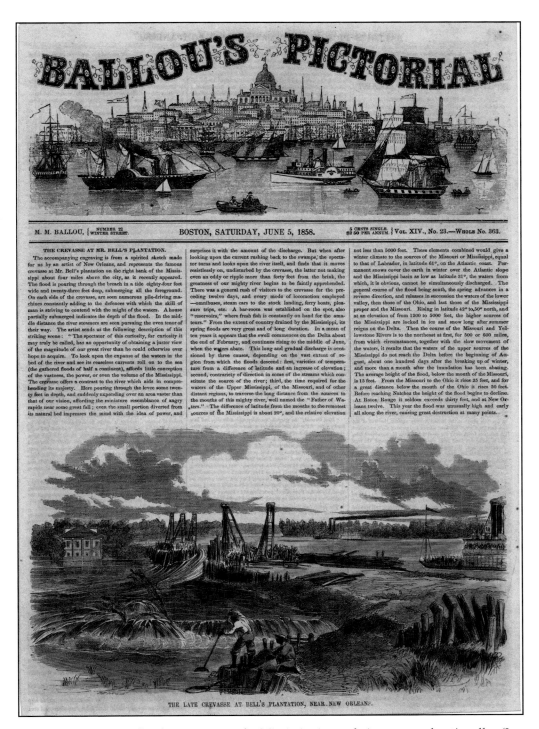

As early as the 1850s, flooding events on the Mississippi were being reported nationally. (Image from *Ballou's Pictorial*, June 1858.)

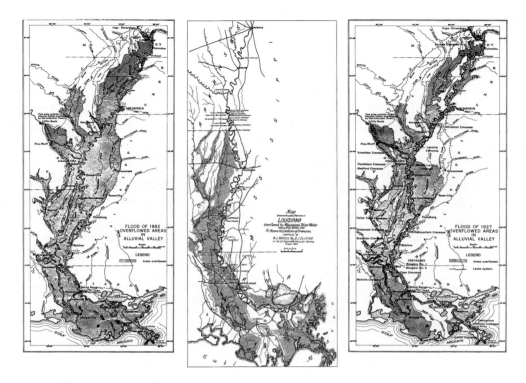

Before 1927, flooding issues were not a concern of the federal government. The flooding events in 1882, 1890, and 1927 convinced national leaders of the importance of becoming proactive in flood management issues.

sissippi more than five miles of levee to collapse. The current through these channels was so strong small homes were frequently tied to trees to hold them fast. Many floated off of their foundations, often lodging miles away from their original foundations.

More than 700,000 individuals—a number nearly equal to the 1927 population of Washington, D. C.—were driven from their homes and housed in tents, warehouses, schools, churches, and other shelters. Since the flood was considered "the most extensive health hazard ever experienced in America" (Simpich 1927:265), over half a

The 1927 flood was a catastrophic event south of New Orleans. At Caenarvon, the levee was blown up at the direction of the governor to protect the Crescent City. (Photo [left] courtesy of of the State Library of Louisiana, photo [right] courtesy of the National Archives and Records Administration, Still Picture Records Section, Special Media Archives Service Division, negative no. 27.G.1A.4.24967C.)

CANAL STREET, — LOOKING TOWARDS THE CAR-DEPOT.

COMING FROM MARKET.

COLLECTING THE MAIL.

Flooding was a perennial social and economic issue in the nineteenth century. (Image from *Every Saturday,* July 1871.)

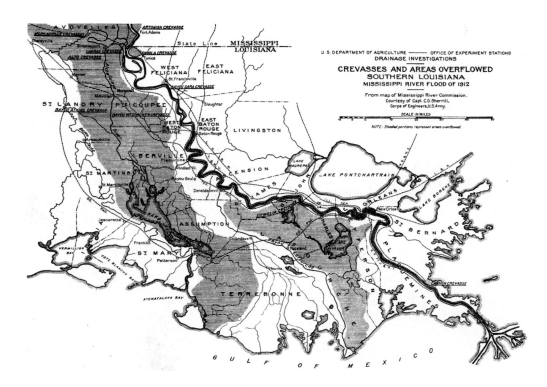

By the beginning of the twentieth century, survey and cartography skills had improved to better understand crevasse-induced flooding, 1912.

million people were "vaccinated, inoculated, or given malarial prophylaxis" (Simpich 1927:264). "Like a cataract, floods race[d] through crumbling levees" (Simpich 1927:257), and in the aftermath about 27,000 square miles were flooded to a depth of up to thirty feet. Barry (1997) estimated up to 1,000 people, most of whom were black, died in the Yazoo basin alone, but the precise number is difficult to tally.

Within the walled confines of New Orleans, the population began to demand action to reduce flooding. Crescent City residents wanted the levee cut. Vigilantes atop the levees used firearms to warn ships away from the earthen embankments. The locals were afraid the ships would be forced into the earthen knoll, thereby creating a crevasse. The crevasse they feared became a reality by official order. On April 26, Louisiana Gov. O. H. Simpson signed a proclamation giving permission to dynamite

Closing a crevasse was a labor-intensive effort. The Hagan Ave. crevasse, New Orleans, is pictured here. (Image from *Every Saturday,* July 1871.)

Street flooding was a common sight during and after the flood of 1927. (Photo courtesy of the Center for Louisiana Studies, University of Louisiana at Lafayette.)

Although farms flooded, if they were on the crest of the natural levee and elevated on piers, flood waters only inundated the home to a depth of a foot or so, 1927. (Photo courtesy of the Center for Louisiana Studies, University of Louisiana at Lafayette.)

Flooding events know no boundaries. When tombs are uprooted, finding and moving them back on site is a time consuming and emotional undertaking, 1927. (Photo courtesy of the Center for Louisiana Studies, University of Louisiana at Lafayette.)

the levee (Dabney 1944).

To reduce the floodwaters' height, the state utilized up to 1,500 pounds of explosives to blow up the bank at Caernarvon (also called Poydras), which had long been a vulnerable point for overflows and crevasses. This levee's Achilles' heel was formed five years earlier when a 1,400 foot section of the bank collapsed. The crevasse forced approximately 2,000 people from their homes. Nine days after the break all of Terre aux Boeufs, except for a few high points, was inundated. The event caused an estimated $300,000 in damages and nearly two months elapsed before the victims could return home (Din 1988). Blowing up the levee in 1927 simply replicated an earlier natural event.

The "engineered" crevasse created a 3,210-foot-wide artificial waterway that removed more than 324,000 cubic feet per second from the main channel into the fur-rich, tall-grass marshland of the Isleños. The break relieved the hydrostatic pressure on New Orleans' levees (Simpich 1927; Elliott 1932B; Cowdrey 1977; Meyer 1981), and the silt-laden, nutrient-rich water traveling through the break at Caernarvon "fertilized" the marsh, increasing the region's biological productivity (Pearson, et al. 1989). Regional fishing grounds were shifted, but the total oyster crop was not damaged significantly (Pearson, et al. 1989B).

Currently, Caernarvon is one of the largest freshwater diversions channels in the Mississippi Delta. This diversion, along with West Pointe à la Hache and Violet have been studied carefully. The results suggest these controlled crevasses are an effective coastal restoration tool and should be included in the state's wetland management plan (Crandall and Lindsey 1981; Chatry and Chew 1985; Haywood and Boshart 1998; Turner and Streever 2002; DeLaune, et al. 2003; Lane, et al. 2006). However, there are a number of uncertainties that need to be addressed before these projects are integrated into the state's restoration plan.

The Human Cost Associated with the Man-Made 1927 Caernarvon Diversion

Long lines of St. Bernard residents moved slowly up the highway toward New Orleans. They were described by one reporter as 'a highway of humanity on trucks, in pleasure cars, on wagons, horseback, muleback, afoot, on oxen, goading cattle, leading cattle.' Children brought a favorite toy or clutched a puppy, cat, or chicken. A young boy led a scrawny calf on a frayed rope. Another had a small pet alligator. What to take and what to leave behind was an agonizing decision. One woman pulled up a favorite rosebush and wrapped it in newspaper. Some families took furniture or farm implements. The farther a community was from the river, the harder it was for the inhabitants to accept the decision they had to evacuate. Some threatened to stay and fight the government. Mosquito-bitten and sunburned, angry trappers clenched their fists at the orders to leave. But as the hour of demolition on the levee grew near they all gave in (Jackson 1993:134-135).

A few refused to go despite everything. Let the water drown them if it wanted. Toward the lakes a number of bootlegging operators were reluctant. With everyone watching, it was impossible to move their commodities; none had any thought of deserting such valuables. In at least one instance, a rescue barge brought a large quantity, covered with fish. Most of the men stayed, with guns close at hand (Kane 1944: 196-197).

Locally the flood caused an estimated $5 million in damages (Russell, et al. 1936; Cowdrey 1977; Barry 1997). At a time when the federal budget barely exceeded $3 billion, the 1927 flood, directly or indirectly, caused nationally an estimated $1 billion in property damages ($12.3 billion in 2009). The 1882 and 1927 floods together submerged 57,600 square miles (Elliott 1932; Elliott 1932B)—an area larger than the land mass of Delaware, Connecticut, Hawaii, Massachusetts, Maryland, New Hampshire, New Jersey, Rhode Island, and Vermont combined.

The country's levees-only policy, which contributed directly to the flood, was an enormous political error. Proper flood control would require the mixture of levees, floodways, and spillways (Reuss 1982). The severity of the 1927 inundation event resulted in passage of the 1928 Mississippi River and Tributaries Act. This comprehensive legislation began the process of locking the Mississippi into a fixed channel, with spillways constructed along its course to protect against severe flooding. These spillways proved their worth during the post-1927 flood era.

The 1927 flood's effect on Louisiana's economy is frequently forgotten. The floodwaters inundated plantations reeling from the effects of the 1926 sugarcane mosaic virus (Leslie 1985). The successive disasters, coupled with America's Great Depression of the 1930s, resulted in the closure of many sugar mills and refineries. Banks foreclosed on plantation property they did not want and could not sell.

The 1927 "high water" also impacted the state's oyster industry. Freshwater introduced into Breton Sound from the Caernarvon "Crevasse," and Bohemia Spillway destroyed about one-third of Louisiana's oyster crop. In 1928, there was no production from this lease zone (McConnell 1930). High discharge through the Bohemia Spillway in 1932 and 1944—and the opening of the Bonnet Carré Spillway in 1945—also had an adverse and immediate effect on the oyster industry. The loss in 1933 was estimated at one million barrels east of the Mississippi River. The loss was so great in 1945 that the Federal government was asked to pay Mississippi and Louisiana up to $3 million in reparations (McConnell 1932; McConnell 1946).

In the wake of these natural disasters, the United States Army Corps of Engineers began to construct the Mississippi's "guide levees." Today, this network protects cities, towns, villages, farmland, and industrial complexes. In retrospect, the levees had a dramatic impact on the general ecology of the marshlands and modified the orderly distribution of fresh water from the river into the marsh-estuary complexes. Since the regional ecology is closely governed by, and geared to, the highly fluctuating deltaic environment, natural wetlands processes, inter-levee-basin drainage regimes, and vegetation patterns were altered permanently by this levee complex. Engineers brought about these changes through their use of large earthen embankments, internal drains, and pumps. Over time, the Mississippi's eye-catching levees were strengthened, eliminating over-bank flooding and the systematic sediment discharge to Louisiana's subsiding coastal lowlands.

Engineered to protect the population living within the river's alluvial valley, this array of engineered embankments also altered the region's natural topography—a landscape settled and used by a highly diverse mix of ethnic groups. Because of the Mississippi's movements through time, two geographic provinces have come to make up the wetlands—the *Chênière* and Deltaic Plains. These are natural laboratories for the study of a wide-range of biophysical processes. They are also the home to Louisiana's trapper-hunter-fisher folk, and part- to full-time "tough-as-leather" cowboys, many of whom where African Americans recruited from the Washington-Opelousas area (Jones 2007).

Frank Leslie's Illustrated Newspaper depicted the perils of living on the *chênière* plain, particularly Johnson Bayou in this October 1886 illustration.

Chapter 3
THE PHYSICAL AND CULTURAL LANDSCAPE OF THE *CHÊNIÈRE* PLAIN

> The terrain here was different . . . and the religion was predominantly Catholic. Many people spoke French; some couldn't speak English. They ate things, like crawfish, that our people wouldn't touch (Gomez 1998:65).

The coastal lowlands of Southeast Texas and southwestern Louisiana are about 100 miles in length and twenty to thirty miles wide. Bounded on the east by Bayou Teche, these lowlands encompass approximately 2,200 square miles (Gomez 1998).

Bayou Teche's wide natural levees suggest this route was at one time occupied by the Red River. The natural levee formed by this system, like that along the Mississippi, is used for large-scale plantation operations (Rehder 1971; Rehder 1999). The province's southern boundary is characterized by a smooth and regular shoreline. The regularity of this feature is occasionally fronted by beach or mud flats, backed by a marsh that in many places can support the weight of a horse and rider, to places that will support very little weight. The firmer surfaces are experiencing relatively low rates of subsidence and land loss.

However, lake edges and transportation channels or canals are subject to erosion. For example, the 64,000-acre East Cove marsh, adjacent to Calcasieu Lake's southeast corner, is characterized by a line of submerged fences that marked the boundaries of cattle pastures that are now under water.

An 1875 illustration showing the importance of the sugar industry in Louisiana. (Image from *Harper's Weekly,* October 1875.)

The district has been negatively impacted by the removal of the Calcasieu Pass oyster reef in 1876 and dredging of the Calcasieu Ship Channel in 1941. These two events, coupled with multiple hurricanes that blanketed the marsh with salt water, have contributed to the creation of large tracts of open water (Gomez 1998).

The marsh through the eyes of a *fin de siècle* artist. (Image from *The Century Magazine,* November 1900.)

Along this coastal lowland, there is an intervening series of beach ridges locally called *chênières* that parallel the shorefront for seventy miles, with widths varying from a few feet to a maximum of 1,300 feet and an average elevation of six to seven feet. Although the ridges make up only 3 percent of the region's geography, they are the most distinctive features on the landscapes of Cameron and Vermilion parishes. This land is best described as a sea of grass (whose surface is as flat as an inland lake on a calm day) that has supported farmers, fishermen, trappers, hunters, and cattlemen, who describe their country setting as "paradise" (Hanks 1988; Gomez 1998).

These elevated landforms tiptoe across the marsh and provide the marshdweller with a bit of "high" ground protection against hurricanes. As a result, they are rather densely populated. Even so, this is a remote and out-of-the-way landscape that until the 1970s had no incorporated towns, no city halls, no chambers of commerce, no fast food establishments, and no traffic lights.

In the geologic literature this chain of inland "islands" is referred to as the *Chênière* (or Chenier) Plain that is a product of wave action pushing sand up onto the shore. Each *chênière*, therefore, marks the position of a once-active shoreline. This ancient beach line varies from 1,200 to 2,500 years old and is related directly to the wandering habits of the Mississippi River and its associated delta (Cameron parish 1960). When the Mississippi occupied one of its western courses, clay, mud, and sand were carried

On the *Chênière* Plain, mail was delivered by a variety of water craft. (Image from author's collection.)

westward by littoral currents, advancing the *Chênière* Plain as a mud coast. Interruptions in the progradation process allowed coarser particles to accumulate as a ridge. An increase in sedimentation caused the shoreline to advance, leaving the conspicuous, oak-covered *chênières* as the region's most impressive and continuous topographic feature. Radio-carbon dates indicate a greater age for the northern or inland *chênières* than those closer to the Gulf.

Trees, particularly oaks, constitute an important part of the ridge's natural storm-protection system. In addition to the storm-dwarfed oak trees (*Quercus virginiana*), Chinese tallow (*Sapium sebiferum* L.), and Osage orange (*Maclura pomifera*) are also present (Okey 1914; Russell and Howe 1935; Wells and Kemp 1982; Schou 1967). On "islands" like Grand Chênière, early residents never cut the trees. Homes were built on the lee of these protective groves to insure the inhabitants had an added measure of security from the winds and storm surge associated with Gulf hurricanes. This was not the case at Last Island and Chênière Caminada in southeastern Louisiana, where the protective barrier of trees were harvested completely. At Grand Isle, like on the *Chênière* Plain, the residents built behind the trees and reduced drastically the number of hurricane-related casualties (Waldo 1962).

The trees, however, did not help break Hurricane Rita's storm surge, as nearly every structure on the *chênières* was destroyed; the devastation was nearly total due to the massive storm surge height. Using pressure sensors encased in pipes strapped or bolted to objects, which the USGS believed would survive Rita's storm surge, the water levels reached 14.9 feet at Constance Beach, 13.34 feet near Cameron, and 14.68 feet near Grand Chénière (Dunne 2006B). Three years later Ike's storm surge was also an issue.

In a description of the marshes of southwestern Louisiana, the *chênières* are "high" to the locals, but they were simply not high enough; and Rita and Ike proved their vulnerability. Although these *chênières* are inhabited by less than 10,000 people, and are the most sparsely populated territory in which Cajun culture predominates, they have always been at risk (Gomez 1998). Nevertheless, for a variety of reasons these weather-worn settlers have made a conscious decision to live in rural places, like Little Chenier (settled in 1849 by Ursin Primeaux) and Eugene Island, where the quantity of arable land is so small that individual homes are typically scattered at wide intervals.

Just like all the early chenier settlers, Ursin first cleared the land by hand and staked out a site for his house. This done, he returned to Lake Arthur, loaded up all the necessary lumber and building supplies on a raft, and floated southward down the waterways to Little Chenier where, on his newly-claimed property, he proceeded to build his house with the help of two or three of the Chenier Perdue settlers who would row their skiffs across the bayou.

Over the years, Ursin built up quite a little 'industrial complex' at his home place, consisting of a cotton gin, a sugar cane mill, and a grist mill which were the first of their kind in the Chenier Perdue-Little Chenier-Creole areas. This group of buildings became known as the Premo settlement . . . the original spelling of the name when the family first came to Breaux Bridge from France (Carter 1968:7-8).

The families also build the one-room Premo School for the community's children. From 1900 to 1913, Premo had its own post office and appeared on state maps from the time.

Clearly in the past, the fertile relic beach ridges in the *Chênière* Plain were cultivated, producing sugarcane, sea-island cotton, oranges, and bananas that were harvested and shipped in the holds of schooners (also called in French-speaking Louisiana a *goélette*) to various Gulf of Mexico markets (Carter 1968). Journalist William Henry Perrin (1891:177) reported:

> The cultivation of fruits in Cameron is one of its great industries, and perhaps always will be. [And,] when the marsh lands are reclaimed, then it will become also a great rice-growing region. But it will always be a fruit country. Further, when its marsh lands are reclaimed . . . the country [will] become thickly settled.

Fruits, some vegetables, and oranges were important early agricultural commodities, but the belt of *chênières* was also distinguished by cattle. Cattle herds ranged throughout the marsh, and ranching continues to be a vital part of the local culture. The blending of Anglo-American and Spanish-American ranching traditions began in this geographic province. This part of "Cajun Country" is also "Cowboy Country." At Johnson Bayou, the first *chênière* community east of the Texas line, "western attire is popular, and the local grocery posts flyers advertising events in Port Arthur, the nearest city. As a result, Johnson Bayou has a decidedly Texas feel . . ." (Gomez 1998:23).

Harvesting rice along the margins of the marsh, ca. 1940. (Photo courtesy of Louisiana State Library, Louisiana Department of Conservation.)

Further east, cowboys speaking a French *patois* fasten *hidalgo* spurs to rubber boots that withstand the wet conditions better than the traditional leather cowboy boots, swing 8-to-10-foot-long, plaited-leather whips behind their herds, and ride horses, frequently descendants of Louisiana's wild ponies, giving a western look to the landscape. Texas lies just across the Sabine River, but the cattle drives on the *chênières*

east of Johnson Bayou at Holly Beach are characterized by folks who have a cowboy/cowpuncher attitude and who regularly speak with a French accent that often can be used to identify a particular community. These wranglers moved herds that were described as "all-horn-and-hide-with-no-meat to market each spring along bayous used by shrimp and oyster boats" (Millet 1974:339).

These cattle drives were so big that children were excused from school for a week in the spring to help gather, brand—often up to 1,000 calves a day—and trail cattle from the marsh to sites around the marsh fringe communities of Ged, Edgerly, Starks-Big Woods, Kinney, Lawton, Vincent, Vinton, and Toomey. Cowpunchers used boats occasionally to move their herds, so a "trail drive" regularly involved floating the cattle to market. With from 15,000 to 20,000 head grazing north of Johnson Bayou, along with up to 100 horses, these drives to summer pastures were impressive events. With 60,000 hooves, 30,000 horns, and about fifteen million pounds of force, it took a great deal of skill to keep this mass walking in the same direction (Jones 2007).

Trail bosses in the late 1800s and early 1900s moved marsh cattle to the Russell Greene weighing station at Cow Island and on to the rail yard at Kaplan or Welsh. From this point, 800 to 900 head were shipped to Oklahoma City, New Orleans, or Morgan City. The trip took up to seven days and the cattlemen frequently received as little as four cents a pound for their herd (Hanks 1988). The practice continues today, with truck transportation replacing the long cattle drive.

A whip-toting *chênière* wrangler, with a Cajun accent, ca. 1985. (Photo courtesy of Sherrill Sagrera.)

When cattle are moved, traffic must wait its turn, 1987. (Photo by the author.)

The *chênières* also served as important entry points into the valuable fur habitat that surrounded these islands (Carter 1968). Freshwater *marais* dominates the regional geography and trapping was vital to these marshdwellers, as they worked to maximize their income from this sustainable resource, supplemented by hunting, farming, and perhaps a bit of bootlegging during Prohibition. All of these elements allowed the *chênière* dweller to make a living, as the marsh is an unforgiving environment.

The people of the *chênières* accepted the challenges and have survived. They live on a landscape whose connection to humankind dates to 1766 when the Spanish, by accident, first encountered the *chênières*. A hurricane in that year sunk the *El Nuevo Constante,* forcing the crew to take refuge on nearby *chênières*. This historical episode imprinted the name "Constance" on the area at such locations as Big Constance Lake, Constance Bayou, Little Constance Bayou, Little Constance Lake, Constance Ditch, Constance Beach, Big Constance Bayou, East Constance Bayou, East Little Constance Bayou, and East Constance Lake.

Later, the Federal government also called attention to the *chênières*. Engineers surveyed the ridges and set aside selected oak groves as naval reserves. Oak was needed for construction of the wooden boats of the period. This policy was eventually rescinded and the property was offered to War of 1812 veterans. It appears that no one came to the *chênières* as a result of this program. Instead, these tracts were sold to individuals willing to come into Louisiana and establish their homes on the ridges (Cameron parish 1960).

The first settlers—not explorers or travelers, but people who planned to establish a permanent residence—arrived during the second quarter of the nineteenth century. Between the 1830s and '40s, a wave of mainly Irish Americans and Scottish Americans homesteaded east of Grand Chênière (Diamond 1973). By 1860, they could buy public land for one dollar and twenty-five cents an acre. Some of this property was subdivided into *arpents*. This pattern is particularly evident at Holly Beach—the only *Chênière* Plain example of long lots perpendicular to the Gulf of Mexico (Meyer-Arendt 1981; Meyer-Arendt 1982; Hanks 1988). Within a generation of this initial settlement, "practically all of the available farming land was under fence and broken to the plow" (Cameron parish 1960:12). The most important crop was oranges. Although money was scarce, the barter system worked well. The ridge communities flourished, but not without risk.

European Marsh Pasture

In Europe, cattle and horses use marsh pasture with each animal grazing a particular niche or habitat (Menard, et al. 2002). As early as the 1630s, Massachusetts' farmers were harvesting marsh hay to feed their livestock (Vileisis 1997).

Hurricanes Audrey (1957) and Rita (2008) were devastating storm events. Hurricane Rita was one of the six strongest storms on record. When it came ashore nearly everything in its path was damaged and/or destroyed. The exceptions included several structures on the Rockefeller Refuge and a number of truss-supported-homes that allowed the surge to move under the elevated floor, thereby allowing the home to "stand-up" to the high water.

Residents paid the price for living on the *Chênière* Plain. The storm was so intense that areas previously considered safe were flooded. Lessons have been learned. Like many of New Orleans residents, these marshdwellers' roots go deep. They want to rebuild. They do not want to leave their ancestral real estate. In contemporary terms, this land is the marshdwellers 401K and their cattle herds are their interest. Bank failures and foreclosures are not part of their investment heritage. Their bank accounts have hooves. With the loss of their land, they lose their family's legacy and their retirement income. They may have to move, or be forced to relocate because of new governmental rules and regulations. This may be a prudent decision and one that would reduce the permanent population at risk. Their address and post office box may change, but these folks will always be marshdwellers.

These ridge dwellers have seen the hurricane-induce changes to their countryside. They want to remold this landscape so they can continue to live and work "their" property. They have always taken risks and probably will continue to do so; it is part of their life, as nothing has come easy. Even after Hurricane Audrey (1957) many, not all, moved back "home," because this land is their historical birthright and the link to their cultural heritage.

Hurricane Audrey: Name retired by the National Weather Service

They took us in small boats for about a mile to where the bridge had washed out. We got out on the road and waited for Army trucks to come after us. We waited there for over two hours, as they were taking the hurt, the aged and mothers with young children first. We rode about 14 miles on the truck; then we were transferred to a school truck and brought in to Lake Charles. Daddy had just registered at the Red Cross when someone grabbed us and it was Francis and Alton (two of the Coast Survey men who had been there all day checking every possible source to see if they could find a trace of us). Their voices sounded wonderful to us. They took us to Al's and they gave us clothes so we could take a shower and get cleaned up. Bonny fixed dinner, but I wasn't too hungry. All that I wanted was something cool to drink. That was Friday evening about 7 o'clock and we hadn't any food or water since Wednesday night, except Friday when the trucks came in they brought water to us in milk cartons (Smith 1957).

I never went back to where I once lived. It took two years before I could go visit my family in Creole. For ten years I relived that hurricane in my dreams. Hurricane Audrey drastically changed my life. My Momma and Daddy were not there for my wedding, my children being born, nor the births of any of my grandchildren. My children never saw their grandparents. So many others have gone through the same nightmare. Some lost husbands, wives, and children. I thank God for helping me to overcome the terrible memories of that day (Menard 1997:79).

Hurricane Audrey (1957) remains the earliest storm of any Atlantic hurricane season to reach Category 4 intensity in the recorded hurricane history of the Gulf of Mexico. On June 27, 1957, a rare early-season tropical storm spun into being in the Gulf. Intensifying quickly, Hurricane Audrey moved toward the Texas/Louisiana coast as a Category 4 storm, but unconfirmed reports put the winds offshore at 185-miles per hour (Menard 1997). Until Hurricane Danny (1985), Audrey was the strongest storm to form prior to August, and it was one of the first hurricanes to be observed by weather radar. Due to the storm's rapid motion and forward speed, coupled with the Weather Bureau's reputedly "flawed" forecast, this additional meteorological information was not effective in preventing loss of life. The Bureau's predictions were accurate, but the storm's unforeseen speedup caught everyone unprepared (Wright 1997).

People were urged to evacuate, and most of the newer residents did leave. Many old-timers, who had seen only weak tropical storms thought their *chênière* communities would survive. For more than 200 years hurricanes were part of the region's oral traditions and folklore. None of these "tales" offered any evidence that Audrey would be dangerous. As a result, the June 1957 tropical depression represents one of the last storms where modern technology came up against the attitudes and beliefs of a slower, simpler time, with tragic results.

After the tempest's passage, destruction along the coast was nearly total. Water levels approached twelve feet along the shoreline and decreased towards the Pleistocene terrace. Audrey's wind-driven water inundated the *Chênière* Plain. Nearly every frame house was pushed off its foundation. To escape the rising water, people who did not leave climbed into their attics and onto their roofs. In some cases, the roof became a survivor's raft. Some homes floated more than thirty miles into the marsh. Houses and tombs had to be retrieved. Some caskets floated over twenty miles from their respective cemeteries.

Officially, Audrey was responsible for 390 deaths, although unofficial sources claim the number actually exceeded 500. Many corpses were buried in a mass grave and never identified (Menard 1997). No other twentieth-century storm caused as many fatalities in Louisiana. In addition, an estimated 65,000 head of dead cattle had to be burned. Cattle that survived the storm surge were saved by feed shipments airlifted by Air Force helicopters assigned to the "Cattle Rescue Project" (Menard 1997).

Audrey's devastation caused surprisingly little impact upon the architectural decisions of the storm's survivors. Those who chose to return to their inundated home sites recreated structures like those that were destroyed. That did not replicate the dwellings of their ancestors. Instead, they chose a house type that had just failed.

Originally, houses on the ridges were built close to the road, and the style reflected the building traditions of the migrants. Many Anglo-Saxon settlers were from the land of log and half-timber homes. These house types were not part of the local vernacular landscape. The *chênières* could not provide sufficient lumber for local home construction; hence, building materials were imported. The primary style of home built was one "currently popular in the larger world immediately outside the marshes" (Kniffen and Wright 1963:5). These were not the styles of the original settlers whose homes were rigid, elevated, and designed to work with the wind and water, not against these elements. They may not be "popular," but they were solid and built according to the tenets of local folk knowledge.

The post-hurricane tendency to abandon "traditional" architectural styles was not new. Beginning perhaps as early as 1886, new *chênière* settlers stopped duplicating the housing styles first used on the ridges, possibly because of the damage and loss of life associated with the unmanned hurricane of that year (Perrin 1891). Despite the fact these vernacular homes had survived more than 150 years of hurricanes, they were not the dwellings of choice. Clearly, the proven value of locally developed "folk" architecture did not neutralize the more compelling temptation to build a more popular, "modern" slab home, as opposed to one built on low piers, or elevated several feet above the *marais/chênière*'s surface. In fact, "early in the period of post-Audrey reconstruction, there was a strong campaign to induce the building of homes on pilings . . .

Snake Patties and Hurricane Audrey

". . . Out there in the mud, it looked like cow patties. Just one pile after another, I mean solid in my yard. Every 'patty' was a snake coiled up. Some of 'em was fighting others; they'd be hooked up, just a 'poling at one another. If you made a racket on the ground, all of 'em would start striking at you. That was some mad snakes" (Jones 2007:123).

These sketches of Sabine Pass in the late nineteenth century may be stylized, but they clearly show the importance of this waterway. (Image from *Frank Leslie's Illustrated Newspaper*, September 1890.)

as expert opinion advocates piling construction as both sturdy and the best protection against high water" (Kniffen and Wright 1963:7).

Since this suggestion was not legally mandated, it was largely ignored. In one survey, only four of the hundreds of new homes built were elevated on piers. However, this was not the case for many oil company support buildings, government services, and recreation camps that were placed on piers or pilings. But with the exception of the government service buildings, none of these structures are occupied by full-time marshdwellers.

In the twenty-first century, many *chênière* structures, particularly those at Holly Beach and elsewhere along the coast, were directly in the path of the wind field and storm surge from Hurricane Rita. There was no marsh or *chênière* buffer. Although many beach homes were elevated, they were not built as concrete bunkers, designed to withstand the full force of the winds and waves generated in Rita's northeast quadrant. Even raised structures that had survived numerous hurricanes did not "weather" Audrey. Even so, elevated pier or strut-supported homes built according to traditional guidelines and plans have always fared better than "modern" slab homes. Thus, new engineering standards, building materials, and design decision patterned after the vernacular forms can further aid the marshdweller in building a hurricane-resistant structure.

In reflecting on construction decisions after Audrey, it is clear that the notion that humans generally resist change is true. Their decisions and behavior are shaped by conformist ideals as they strive to live within the context of their near-sea-level-landscape. When they abandon their architecturally distinct folk houses that, however absurd they may seem to the outsider, have survived for generations, they forgo "common sense" for the prestige afforded by change and "modernism." The old is not bad. Unfortunately, this lesson in housing style was not learned from Audrey. Rita demonstrated the folly of this "new" construction "designed to be swept away by the next storm" (Kniffen 1978C). The people "must feel literally that it is better to be dead than to be out of style" (Kniffen and Wright 1963:8).

The notion that "it won't happen again" is a gamble that a half-century after Hurricane Audrey (1957) the residences of the *Chênière* Plain lost to Hurricanes Rita and Ike. One wonders how the damage report would have read if Kniffen and Wright's (1963) suggestion that traditional house types built according to long-standing folk guidelines and elevated on piers would have been mandated and followed.

* * *

The radar station near Cameron was down that night. As Audrey approached, [Rodney] Guilbeaux called his parents, who resided near the coast, and asked them to come inland to his home. His father refused because he had 10 house guests, including his own parents, and his son's house would be over crowded.

The weather was quiet all night long, no wind or rain. But at 4 a.m., the coastal waters began to rise, driving Guilbeaux Sr. and his family up two floors, then to the attic, where they were forced to cut through to the rooftop. On the roof of his home Guilbeaux stood in water up to his chest and was pummeled constantly by waves. When the last wave hit, the house exploded and the family said their good-byes (Remembering Audrey 2002/2003:72).

Erosion, Settlement, and the Coastal Chênières

The southwest Louisiana shoreline is eroding rapidly; as a result, beaches are frequently quite narrow and low-lying areas are often inundated by minor storms. Although Hurricane Audrey (1957) had considerable impact, so did storms in 1865, 1886, and 1915. Each tempest killed many people, and, in the case of the 1886 hurricane, it wiped out the communities of Sabine Pass and Johnson Bayou, settled in 1790 by Texan Daniel Johnson. To many coastal citizens, the 1915 hurricane was referred to as "the storm," and it develop into the region's benchmark hurricane event. Even so, the population's resolve is evident in the continued survival of the *chênière* settlements (Ferguson 1931; Waldo 1962; Hurricane study 1972).

In Texas, Highway 87 is over-washed and closed repeatedly, while Louisiana Highway 82—the Hug-the-Coast-Highway—has been relocated north because of shoreline erosion. These routes are part of the coastal plain's modern road complex, but the earliest transportation corridor was not a paved modern highway. It consisted mainly "unfenced strips of land cleared of stumps and trees that had been set aside for public use" (Hollister and Denny 1989:14). Even though the *chênières* are now connected by means of a highway, and modern conveniences are readily available, many old folkways endure.

Nearly all homes on the *chênières* face the road, which was laid out along the southern side of the ridges. This is the highest and best drained land (Cameron parish 1960:12). Up until the 1920s, *chênière* residents rode to church in wagons, buggies, and horseback. They traveled along the coast, as the beach was their highway. Their contemporaries in Georgia, Oklahoma, Iowa, or Kansas also used wagons and buggies to move about, but this mode of transportation just lasted longer on the *chênières*, as "real" roads came late to the coastal ridges.

For more than 130 years, *chênières* residents going north,

Highway 82 had to be relocated because of shoreline erosion, 1983. (Photo by the author.)

or in some cases east or west, required a small boat, schooner—the *Chafana*, *Ramsey*, and *Flower France* made regular trips—or paddlewheel steamer. Watercraft served as the most important means of communication with the "outside" (Hollister and Denny 1989; Gomez 1998; Block n.d.). The *Crescent*, *Tuber*, *The Delta*, and *Margie* operated along the Mermentau River. Skiffs from Chenier Perdue (probably settled by Jean Vileor about 1847) and Little Chenier met the larger boats in the Mermentau channel. These small boats carried additional passengers to the steam vessels and met the weekly mail boat (Carter 1968; Hanks 1988). The automobile changed this pattern and began the modernization and Americanization processes and helped introduce a multitude of new goods and services to the *Chênière* Plain.

Although isolated, the community of Chênière au Tigre depended on boats for their mail and the transportation of their produce, 1947. (Photos courtesy of the Standard Oil Collection, University of Louisville, negative no. 50336 and 50337.)

For the first settlers and others, the *chênières* served as land corridors and nodal points for rows of farms and hunting camps that followed their crests. Settlements like Chênière au Tigre, Pecan Island, Grand Chênière, and others supported by cotton, rice, watermelon, citrus, cattle, duck, alligator (*Alligator mississippiensis*, known colloquially as simply gator), and fur-bearing animals. Along with these activities, local residents regularly served as hunting guides, operated rum-running vessels, worked as roustabouts, cooks, or helpers, in the on- and offshore oil industry, or labored at shore sites, like Columbia Gas Transmission Company, ExxonMobil (Humble), Shell Oil, or Stone Oil. These jobs offered decent pay, and the opportunity for advancement, and the acquisition of new marketable skills.

Oil offered locals other new avenues to wealth—leases, royalties, and jobs in the "oil patch" were welcomed. The industry's myriad challenges were not insurmountable, and as a result, by the mid-1900s the petroleum industry was beginning to transform the landscape and seascape; this economic province was shifting from its subsistence roots to a market economy. The barter system was being replaced by one based on income. As oil money filtered through the economy, everyone benefitted.

With arrival of oil and gas, the coastal population had a new income stream and new employment options. Their seasonal occupancy pattern changed throughout the coastal lowlands, and the landscape began to show the signs of the oil and gas industry.

* * *

Before Roads, the Chênières *Were Isolated*

Being isolated meant that basic foods—coffee, sugar, lard, flour, potatoes, shoes, cloth (typically a blue cottonade), and farm implements—were carried by *goélettes* from Galveston or Lake Charles and sold at local *chênière* stores. Coffee, sugar, lard, and flour were often purchased by the sack or barrel (210 pounds). Sometimes so many trading schooners were waiting to sail over the Calcasieu River (also called Bayou Quelqueshue or Culcashue) bar "one could almost step from one boat to another" (Leesburg n.d.:n.p.). Schooners plied the river delivering lumber to Galveston—for a long time the trading hub for Calcasieu Parish—and returning with basic food stuffs. For example, "the sloop *Emma* took lumber and cowhides to Galveston and returned with a cargo of salt bacon, 50 sacks of meal, 12 sacks of flour, black pepper, salt, furniture, chinaware, pants, shirts, muzzle-loading shotguns, powder, shot, wads, and caps" (Millet 1974:348-349). Not all of these goods went to the residents of the *chênières*, but many of these items did find their way into the local economy.

Building materials were not easily obtained, so most homes were made of mud and palmetto supported by a wooden frame, similar to the primitive, but livable, Midwestern sod houses. Like sod homes, this structure was cheap, cool in summer, and relatively warm in winter. Framing lumber from sawmills near the swamps, such as those at Lake Arthur, was freighted to the *chênières*. Local builders used this milled timber to construct a four-room framed homes with a central hall, batten shutters instead of glass panes, outside chimneys of mud and moss wrapped around a wooden skeleton, and stairways rising diagonally across the porch to the

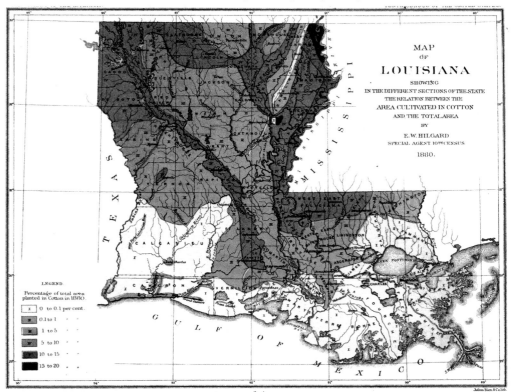

Historically recognized as an important north Louisiana crop, cotton was the economic mainstay of the *chênières* in the late nineteenth century, 1880.

grenier, or attic bedroom. These features are key identifying elements of the Cajun vernacular/architectural style.

Porches provided shade and to take advantage of Gulf winds, nearly all homes faced south. On the side of the house was a wing for the kitchen, dining room, and pantry. At night, huge draperies of cheese cloth, locally called mosquito bars or nets (*baires*), enclosed the beds. Timber was used to fence in the row-crops that characterized *chênière* communities.

Many housewives spun their own yarn and wove durable fabrics for home use. Furniture was plain and simple. In addition, mosquitoes (*maringouins*) and *frappe d'abords* (deer flies) were like a pestilential blanket. A man "could take both hands and run them up the length of [his] hip boot, from the foot to the hip, and scoop up whole handfuls, filled to the top with mosquitoes" (Gomez 1998:65). The mosquito issue was so bad it was reported that "the Indians were at times so badly bitten . . . they looked like lepers" (Rabalais 1985:59).

Most crops were for home use. Blue ribbon sugarcane was grown for use as syrup. Later these plots produced rice and cotton which was shipped to markets in New Orleans and Galveston. On the *chênières*, everyone would go up and down the rows with a cotton sack slung over their backs picking cotton. "Following the harvest, folks would get together nightly first at one house and then another for what the French called a *'grobote'* during which everyone gathered around the large pile of harvested cotton bolls and proceeded to separate the cotton from the bolls" (Carter 1968:11). While a *"grobote"* meant work, it was also a sign of prosperity, as cotton was a valuable product.

Although cotton was once the settlers' main source of income, emergence of the pink bollworm (*Pectinophora gossypiella*) prompted federal authorities to reduce cotton plantings to no more than ten acres per family. The limited acreage was designed to stop the spread of the pest. This ten-acre rule effectively suspended *chênière* cotton production, for such small plots made it difficult for a farmer to make a living. Sugarcane was also grown, but cotton and sugar fields have disappeared (Cameron parish 1960; Hollister and Denny 1989; Gomez 1998). These crops were replaced in some instances by watermelons, but cattle became the mainstay of the economy. In the third decade of the twentieth century, roads gradually replaced cattle "trails" and the steamboat and schooner waterways that linked the ridges to the "outside."

In the 1930s, that state under the direction of Huey Long, completed a highway from Hackberry to Cameron (the only community on the *chênières* that has the look and feel of a town, known originally as Leesburg) and from Sweet Lake to Creole (settled about 1855 by Sosthène Richard) (Carter 1968). This marked a new era in wetland transportation. Land was appropriated for roads that began to cross the *marais* north and south and east and west—where the roads connected *chênière* to *chênière*. The "outside world" was coming to Louisiana's marsh communities.

Even so, a road from Kaplan to Pecan Island was not finalized until 1954. By comparison, a shell road was completed between Houma and New Orleans in 1918—thir-

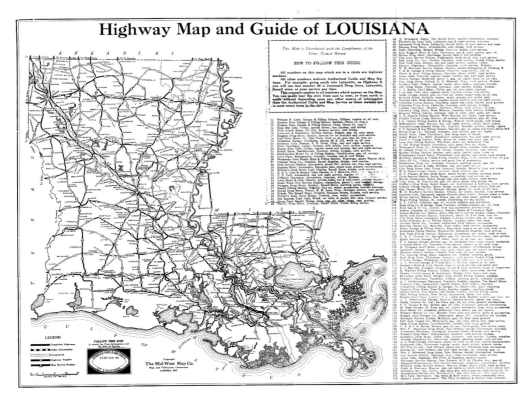

Highway Map and Guide of LOUISIANA

In the mid-1930s, the road system in the coastal zone was still limited. Cars remained uncommon, so maps used a number system to show the driving public where they could find fuel, ca. 1930s.

ty-six years before the Kaplan highway. These transportation arteries had a profound effect on the lives of *chênière* residents. Prior to construction of Highway 82 to Pecan Island, the only way to reach the *chênière* was by boat from Abbeville, south down the Vermilion River, through the Intracoastal Canal, west across White Lake then through a series of narrow canals to a landing north of the Island. The mail boat made three trips a week, and each journey took eight hours (Bradshaw 1997C). But the canal was considered too narrow, and in 1916 the *Abbeville Meridional* noted the channel needed to be deepened or the people on the island were not going to be able to get off unless they "hoof it" (Pecan Island 1916:n.p.).

With completion of the highway, the residents of Pecan Island no longer had to rely on watercraft. "Strangers" began to appear on the *chênières*. The region was being

(Below) The prairie and the marsh are both treeless, and their mutual boundary is blurred. (Photo from the author's collection.)

transformed from inaccessible hamlets to part of "mainstream" America. The same was true throughout Louisiana's coastal lowlands. Bridges and public works changed the folk landscape into a commercial one. From virtually governing themselves, these communities became part of the large political, economic, and cultural systems.

Initially, economies were of the subsistence type. In time, local economies became increasingly commercialized. The end result was the slow demise of the region's cultural isolation. This process began during the initial phase of highway construction, but accelerated after World War II. Nearly seventy years after a "talking telegraph" company was incorporated in New Orleans (Estaville 1987:134) and just about sixty years after New Orleans got its first electric lights, electric and telephone lines began to cross the marsh.

All across Louisiana's coastal lowlands, World War II was the most disruptive force on the marshdweller's way of life. The war brought together trends that gradually changed the wetland's human character (Bernard 2001; Sanson 2001). Not since development of pre-Civil War agricultural estates had the state seen such massive changes. The marshdwellers did not want to retreat into their postwar isolation. Many watermen, who entered the armed services and the war industries, did not return to the wetlands, but others did, for the *marais* was home. Many chose to live at the end of the roads: "where there is inevitably a settlement composed of those drawn to a focus of city conveniences" (Kniffen 1978B:203).

Radio, newspapers, and the departure of local men mobilized into the armed services increased the *chênière* population's awareness of the size of the United States and the world. Contact with these "unfamiliar" people had a profound effect on the typical marshdweller's life (Bernard 2001). They could not escape Americanization any longer, as acculturation had become the rule (Smith and Parenton 1938). "The walls of Cajun cultural isolation had been breached," and this culture island became "culturally curious about the outside world" (Conrad 1978:17).

Cajun grandparents—members of the largest French-speaking minority in the United States, witnessed the emergence of the first generation of local marshdwellers who failed to learn French, an indication of the "rapid decline of the French language as the basic method of communication" (Stielow 1986:189). Along with their language, the marshdwellers' customs, habits, and ways of thinking were also influenced by the radio, better roads, marine engines, newspapers, and automobile travel. There was, in effect, a sharp cultural awakening and an increased involvement in the commercialized world—professional bakeries, inside stoves equipped with ovens, and store-bought goods were being incorporated into the culture (Kniffen 1960B; Kniffen 1978B).

The Settlers of the Chênières

Even though the French are the predominate culture group in South Louisiana, in parts of the *Chênière* Plain settlement began during the Spanish and French colonial periods. Surnames, such as Rutherford, Johnson, Miller, Canik, Doland, Baccigalopi, Welch, LaBauves, Blanco, Dupré, Landry, Sagrera, Romero, Carinhas, Santos, Viator, and Nunez, along with place names, like New Iberia (Din 1986), are reminders of the diverse ancestral origins of the early settlers who came to this region from Africa, England, Scotland, Ireland, France, Germany, Holland, Denmark, the Philippines, Portugal, Cuba, Italy, Spain, Syria, Lebanon, and, most recently, Vietnam and Laos. In fact, the Spanish settlers moved west from New Iberia to Spanish Lake (also known as Lake Flamant and Lake Tasse), where many of their descendants continue to live (Millet 1964; Bergerie 2000).

In Iberia Parish, the Acadians in the early nineteenth century were joined by

Americans and later Germans—Lutzenbergers, Brunners, Emmers, Fishers, Indests, and others. Germans introduced the Acadians to the accordion—which was loud enough to cut through the noise of a crowded dancehall and greatly changed the area's music—and showed Southerners how to celebrate *Oktoberfest* (Kolb 2004; Comeaux 1999). Germans also introduced a barn type that evolved into the south-central Louisiana "Cajun barn" (Comeaux 1989). Along the bayous and in the prairie these three groups were considered poor whites. The Acadians were the most numerous; the Germans, the most prosperous; and the "Americans," the poorest (Crété 1981). Italian immigrants—Jennaro, Briganti, Culotta, DiCorti, Drago, Bassigalopi, Pecoraro, and others—along with a number of Syrians and Jews—Wise, Dreyfus, Levy, Kahn, Silverman, Wormser, Gugenheim, and Strauss—joined the ethnic mix (Bergerie 2000; Merrill 2003).

There has been considerable co-mingling of these culture groups throughout South Louisiana; they thus have become acculturated. L. C. Post (1962:88) notes these immigrants "contributed more in numbers to the settlement of the prairies than did the French Créoles, despite the fact they were not an integral part of the larger ethnic island of Acadians." Regardless of their origin, each of these groups represents a subculture that has contributed to the marshlands' character either directly or indirectly.

In the period between 1815 and 1842, settlers moved into the prairie and *chênières* because of an international land dispute involving the territory between the Sabine and Calcasieu rivers—individually called *rio, arroyo,* or *hondo* by the Spanish. The original land title was based on a Spanish grant to the settler in return for some stipulated military service (Ferguson 1931). Also known as the Neutral Strip, The Free State of Sabine, The Bastard State, Stinking Hell, and No Man's Land (Perrin 1891; Ulmer 1935; Nardini 1961; Schwartz 2005), this territorial buffer between the western edge of the Louisiana Purchase and the Spanish boundary of Texas was not well defined. It was one of the state's most remote and out-of-the-way territories that "festered like an infected wound" (Schwartz 2005:56). As early as the late 1700s, the poor soils were supporting a rudimentary cattle industry that became the birthplace of the state's prairie/marsh cowboy culture.

Under the Neutral Strip Pact, the Spanish and the United States governments were forbidden from entering this "No Man's Land." It was, as a result, a haven for lawless individuals—bandits, pirates, cattle rustlers, fugitive slaves, smugglers, and treasure hunters (Schwartz 2005). Jean Lafitte—pirate and patriot—used the bayous within the Neutral Strip to off-load and hide his contraband and as his back door into the United States (Ferguson 1931; Nardini 1961). Bayou Contraband evokes the enduring popular memory of this illicit activity. Further, ". . . the Mermentau and Calcasu [*sic*] are the harbours and Dens of the most abandoned wretches of the human race[—]smugglers and Pirates who go about the coast of the Gulph [*sic*] in vessels of a small draught [*sic*] of water and rob and plunder without distinction every vessel of every nation they meet with and are able to conquer . . . their unlawful plunder they carry all through the country and sell at a very low rate and find plenty of purchasers" (Landreth 1819:118). In 1821, the United States took control of this "No Man's Land, but the transition was difficult, as the newly acquired territory contained innumerable land claims."

Jean Lafitte. (Image from Schoonover 1911.)

In order to solidify its claim to this property, the United States made liberal land deals with the new settlers. This offer of land brought into the area farmers, traders, and merchants from Tennessee, the Carolinas, and Georgia "whose . . . long rifles did more to settle the boundary question than any display of force could have done" (Cagle 1967:1). The Perkins, Ryans, Smiths, and Clarks were a few of the settlers who came to the *Rio Hondo* from the United States (Millet 1964).

It is thus hardly surprising that, in many ways, the Spanish era is a forgotten part of the region's history. Yet place names, along with some surnames, are the primary reminders of southwestern Louisiana's Spanish colonial era, but one must not overlook the area's ranch culture. Although Spanish authorities allocated Acadians land, many of these early pioneers were squatters, whose poorly designed palmetto, and mud houses were located in the woods on parcels so small that had no yards or gardens (Millet 1964:35). Further, their horses and cattle roamed the open, unfenced range. They learned to ride and use a firearm at a young age. These were important skills, since cattle drives regularly went from the Calcasieu River to the Mississippi River.

On the *chênières,* one can find the seventh or eighth generation whose ethnic identity is a blend of Spanish, English, French, German, Polish, and Irish, but whose roots are firmly imbedded in southwest Louisiana's cowboy culture. The feeling towards their horses is as intense "as it is in Tidewater Virginia or the English Midlands" (Looney 1974:76). Riding a Creole or Cajun pony is a way of life (Hansen 1971). These small to medium sized, sure-footed "pessel tails," as the wild marsh ponies are called, were tougher than can be believed and well suited to run cattle through the marsh. They may have been wild, but, once ridden, these small horses were invariably reliable.

Southwest Louisiana's last wild horses were captured in the 1980s, when the herd was infected with *equine encephalitis* and had to be removed. In the previous decade, Bang's disease and tuberculosis resulted in "depopulating" several entire cattle herds in compliance with a government program to eradicate these diseases. The resilient southwest Louisiana cattlemen, within a short period of time, were back in the cattle business. They were determined to continue the 200-year tradition of using the marsh for winter grazing and trailing their cattle to "high" ground in the spring. Trucks are used, but this continues to be horseback country, with horses and drovers moving cattle, for example, from Chênière au Tigre to cattle pens with highway access (Jones 2007). From Johnson Bayou to Pecan Island, the landscape is reminiscent of any of the country's cattle producing regions. The one primary difference is much of this ranch land is only slightly above sea level. Consequently, the settlements reflect the culture and grazing traditions of the "American West."

Although cattle is the unifying element across all of the ridges, Johnson Bayou, Constance Beach, Holly Beach, Cameron, Creole, Oak Grove, Grand Chênière, Little Chenier, Murière, Pecan Island, and Chenier Perdue have evolved from small insular communities into regional business, recreation, fishing, or oil and gas centers. Prior to Hurricanes Rita and Ike, Holly Beach, frequently referred to as the "Cajun Riviera," was a cluster of stilt-supported camps that emerged as highway-access connected the *chênières* to the "outside." Permanently- and seasonally-occupied residents, and cabins for rent made up the Holly Beach community—largely a summertime resort that dated to the late nineteenth century, when recreationalists arrived by schooner from Lake Charles (Meyer-Arendt 1982). The site was damaged by Hurricane Audrey (1957) and obliterated by Rita (2005), as no buildings were left standing. Holly Beach was leveled, but within two years new camps were built on this site. The memory of Rita and three years later Ike will not die easily, but access to the beach is a powerful force in the rebuilding process.

Cameron developed into one of the country's top five fishing ports, largely because

---

Jake Cole Settled Pecan Island

"The first known settlers to come to Pecan Island were in 1840 when Jake Cole, an East Texas cattleman, explored the countryside following the Gulf coast to Grand Chênière in Cameron Parish. He and two local residents made the trip across the marsh. . . . The men started on their journey early in the morning on horseback, fighting the . . . wet grass, insects and the twelve to fourteen foot alligator[s]. . . . Cole reported that he had never seen so many different kinds of fruits and animals such as racoons, opossum, deer, bears and wildcats."

"Cole had blazed the trail for others [who] began to homestead claims on the Chênière of Pecan Island. Cole gathered pecans to prove his discovery and named the newly discovered haven 'Pecan Island'" (Vermilion Historical Society 1983:36).

Louisiana cattlemen migrated to Texas as well. In fact, the "largest Anglo-American ranching empire on the west side of [Galveston] bay was established by southwest Louisiana families" (Gallaway 2004:7). These saltgrass cattlemen migrated from Calcasieu Parish in 1840; the same year Jake Cole homesteaded Pecan Island.

as many as three menhaden (*Brevoortia species*) plants located there. At one time, the port was constantly in contention for the title of the country's busiest fishing port. A flotilla of menhaden vessels was responsible for this distinction, as they annually provided local processing plants from 300 to nearly 500 million pounds. These small fish were pressed into fish meal, fish oil, and fish solubles used in feed, fertilizer, and soap, which was marketed in the Midwest, Europe, and elsewhere. The shrimp fishery was also an important element in the local economy. After packaging the canned products were sold to Canada and elsewhere (Wakefield 1977).

Chênière farms also grew oranges, cantaloupes, watermelon, peaches, plums, persimmons, pears, and other seasonal crops. Wild grapes were so abundant, that they were purged periodically because the vines choked the valuable island oaks—some of these trees were more than twenty-five feet in circumference (Segura 1973).

The menhaden fishery allowed Cameron to become one of the nation's most important commercial fishing ports, 1982. (Photo by the author.)

Since farm produce ripened early, it commanded a high price in Northern markets. It is reported orange growers harvested enough citrus to ship barge-loads to the Galveston market (Perrin 1891; Ulmer 1935; Cameron parish 1960). Orange trees, some of which were described as "being a foot in diameter and over twenty-five feet in height produced yearly from three hundred to five hundred oranges . . ." (Millet 1971:354). Orange groves, as a result, stretched for miles and were common on all of the *chênières*. Harris (1881:124) reported there were "about 100,000 trees" within Cameron Parish. Severe freezes, the 1895 hurricane, and San Jose scale (a sucking insect that as it feeds injects a toxin into the plant) ended this industry—a now largely forgotten part of the area's agricultural history (Perrin 1891; Cameron parish 1960; Hollister and Denny 1989; Leesburg n.d.). With end of orange exports, cotton developed into the main crop, with cotton fields "cover[ed] large parts of the highest and most accessible" land (Howe, et al. 1935:3). Consequently, from 1895 to the 1930s, cotton was the *chênières'* single most lucrative agriculture commodity.

Non-renewable resources were insignificant to the local economy until the second decade of the twentieth century, when oil was discovered. With hydrocarbon discoveries at Sweet Lake in 1926 and around the Hackberry salt dome's perimeter in 1927, the economy and landscape changed, as the boom progressed from the Pleistocene uplands into the marsh fringe. Men and equipment had to be staged and shuttled into the impassable, subaqueous marshes. This was a new challenge for the wildcatting community. They were unfamiliar with the wetlands and needed to rethink their exploration model. As a direct result of oil activity in the 1920s, the boomtown of Ged,

At the marsh's edge, the community of Ged represented the oil industry's frustration. Oilmen suspected that oil was in the marsh, but they did not yet know how to tap this promising oil-producing province, ca. 1920. (Photo courtesy of the Gray Family Estate.)

south of Vinton on the marsh's northern rim, prospered and grew to a population of 3,000. At Ged, built on the Gray Ranch, the Gray family allowed all who worked in the oilfield to erect their homes on ranch property. The family built and donated a school for the oilmen's children. Ged was a hub of activity and became a jumping off point for new fields developing along the marsh's northern boundary. Oil was so important regionally that John Geddings Gray noted: "I bought land to run cows on, and found an oil well under every cow" (Jones 2007:30). In addition to oil, this "boundary" evolved into an important appendage to the prairie's rice industry.

Rice at the Boundary of the Chênière *Plain*

> A German who settled the region in the early 1870s . . . cultivate[d] the first large field of rice ever grown in Southwestern Louisiana (Millet 1964:187).

In South Louisiana's agricultural history, rice has evolved into a major farm product. In fact, within five years of New Orleans' establishment (and about thirty years after its introduction into South Carolina), rice was cultivated along the Mississippi River (Glenk 1934). Before sugarcane began to compete with cotton in the state's agricultural statistics, rice was generally the crop of choice. Rice farming, after the turn of the twentieth century, was vital to the growth and prosperity of southwest Louisiana's prairie. In this geographic province, Cajun farmers planted small rice plots in places that could not be plowed—along coulees and ditches, next to bayous or in ponds. When the cereal grain was ready to be harvested, farmers cut the small stalk with a sickle, threshed the product by hand, and hulled it with a wooden mortar and pestle (Post 1962).

Louisiana's French and Spanish settlers eventually used rice as a food staple. They incorporated the grain into many recipes—none of which were written down. Cooking was one of the most important aspects of the regional folk culture; and no meal was complete without rice on the table (Rickels 1978). Ironically, this culinary item was not part of the gastronomic tradition in France, where rice is almost nonexistence in the diet. Rice, therefore, as a dietary stable, was acquired by the Acadians after they settled in Louisiana and incorporated into their cooking traditions (Bultman 2003). For example, rice and gravy is a unique South Louisiana tradition, just like red beans and rice, which developed into a Monday dinner meal—"dinner" is served at noon, while "supper" is the evening meal. Rice was consumed every day and when added to the nearly ubiquitous potatoes and bread, the marshdweller's food regimen was laden with starches.

When Midwesterners settled at Welsh, Iowa, Lacassine, Roanoke, and other prairie sites, they introduced wheat machinery (specifically the McCormick Harvester) to the emerging rice industry. The rural geography was distinguished by twine-binders, gang plows, seeders, disc harrows, irrigation techniques, and the two-story I-house. All of these items were introduced into what evolved into the rice district.

Midwestern pioneers revolutionized the industry. Rice developed into a crop distinguished by large-scale, mechanized, farms that required investment in modern equipment and water management systems. To meet the equipment demands, the William Deering Company in 1890 shipped to Lake Charles twenty-two railroad cars loaded with 300 improved binders built for rice. Such shipments, coupled with the first steam irrigation pump (perfected in 1885 by W. W. Duson), and the successful construction and promotion of a system of levees, and canals, along with improved roads and railroad service, remade the prairie's agricultural landscape. Immigrants had successfully transformed the open range into farmland, and, by 1890, Louisiana had become the nation's leading rice producing state (Post 1962; Millet 1964; Comeaux

After the Civil War, the rice industry spread throughout South Louisiana. (Image from *Harper's Weekly,* April 1876.)

SCIENTIFIC AMERICAN

[Entered at the Post Office of New York, N. Y., as Second Class matter.   Copyright, 1896, by Munn & Co.]

A WEEKLY JOURNAL OF PRACTICAL INFORMATION, ART, SCIENCE, MECHANICS, CHEMISTRY, AND MANUFACTURES.

Vol. LXXIV.—No. 19.
ESTABLISHED 1845.   NEW YORK, MAY 9, 1896.   [$3.00 A YEAR.
                                                                              WEEKLY.

A RICE CUTTING MACHINE.

PUMPING ENGINE AND FLUME FOR A 1,000 ACRE
RICE PLANTATION.

RICE CULTURE IN SOUTHWESTERN LOUISIANA.

BY H. H. CHILDERS.

At present rice is a leading industry in only two States of the Union, though at one time it was grown in many States. Louisiana and South Carolina are now the rice-producing States, and in these States its production continues to be profitable. Within the last few years some impetus has been given this industry in Southeastern Texas, but so far it amounts to little more than an experiment. At one time rice was planted in the States of North and South Carolina, Alabama, Georgia, Florida, Mississippi, Louisiana, Texas, Virginia, Tennessee, Missouri, Kentucky, Arkansas, Michigan, Minnesota and California, and for some reason, perhaps by the law of the survival of the fittest, the acreage decreased until the quantity produced in all except the two States mentioned was no longer appreciable. This falling off may have been caused by destructive competition with foreign countries and by the discovery that the soil chosen for rice production in those States above mentioned was found to be inadequate and unsuited for lucrative results.

Rice is grown in Louisiana in the lower Mississippi, La Fourche and Terre Bonne River valleys

HARVESTING RICE ON A LOUISIANA PLANTATION.

A RICE PLANTATION WAREHOUSE, 480 FEET LONG.

western portion of the State, in the parishes of Calcasieu and Acadia. Rice growing for commerce began in Southwestern Louisiana in the year 1884. Before that time the largest field that could be found was five acres in size. But that year a colony of Iowa farmers settled in Calcasieu Parish, and each year since that time the acreage has continued to increase in that belt of prairie country, taking in Acadia and St. Landry Parishes.

The older authorities on rice growing have claimed that this cereal must be grown in alluvial soil, but this statement is successfully contradicted by the facts, and other wet soils have been found that have in them the elements that enter into the body of the rice grain. The soil in Southwestern Louisiana is clay loam, with clay subsoil. It is thoroughly saturated with moisture and the underlying subsoil acts as an impervious basin, preventing anything like a perfect absorption, or the disappearance of the water from the surface. Unlike the prairies of Western Texas, all during the winter, and not unfrequently during the summer seasons the water stands ankle deep even in places covered by the "feather top" or "broom sage" grass; and the pedestrian who would (Continued on p. 295.

Improved machinery and reclamation efforts allowed the rice industry to expand. (Image from *Scientific American*, May 1896.)

1978; Kondert 1988; Bultman 2003).

Promoters skilled in advertising, real estate sales, transportation, large-scale farming, and engineering took the lead and publicized South Louisiana's potential for rice production. Through ingenuity and skill, they succeeded. Added to the improvements introduced by Midwestern settlers, German immigrants—including members of the Vondenstein, Achten, Grein, Thevis, and Gielen families—found a way to water rice fields by building levees and installing irrigation systems. They were so successful their irrigation techniques were adopted quickly throughout the state.

The rapid development of the prairie was made possible by the Kansas City Southern and Southern Pacific railroads. These "roads" cut across the region and encouraged people to settle the land. These railroads also attracted new commercial and industrial businesses, along with increased capital investment, and real estate speculation and development (Shanabruch 1977; Bradshaw 1997; Bradshaw 1997E). Parenthetically, the railroad served as the impetus for the founding of Erath—named after Auguste Erath, a New Iberia businessman born in a German-speaking Switzerland canton, who was instrumental in having a railroad built from New Iberia to Abbeville.

By 1892, 100,000 tons of Acadiana rice was shipped by the Southern Pacific railroad—10,000 railroad carloads. Rice mills were being constructed, a system of primary and secondary irrigation canals were excavated, and rice fields were expanded, with Vermilion Parish having the state's largest network of irrigation canals (Did you know 1917). During the harvest, entire communities would work together to bring rice bundles from the field to the nearest threshing machines. The rice was then separated from the straw and sacked. Mule or horse-drawn wagons made continuous trips from the fields to the threshing machines (Bradshaw 1997).

This agricultural development led to the demise of the tall-grass prairies' large-scale ranching tradition, with the exception of thousands of acres in and along the northern fringes of the coastal *marais*. In the late 1800s, ranching operations in these areas shipped to Cuba and the Midwest cattle that grazed the marsh. As the farms encroached upon cattle country, newly established farmers employed range hands as "bird miners." Originally, they would ride a horse around the rice levees cracking their whips to scare off the blackbirds. Later, when they could afford firearms and ammunition, they would fire rifles and shotguns to kill or scare off the birds. Today, automated carbide guns and airplanes are used to keep ravenous birds out of the rice fields (Coreil 2007, pers. comm.; Jones 2007).

On the *Chênière* Plain, settlers devoted small plots to rice, but ranching was mainstay of local agriculture. For more than a century, the *chênières* supported a vibrant beef business. Yet, in less than a day, Hurricane Rita, followed by Ike devastated the local industry, decimating livestock holdings on the *chênières* and submerged traditional pastures with salt water. An important part of Louisiana's agriculture history was injured, and battered, but not destroyed, as ranchers regrouped, bought new head, monitored their calf crop, repaired their fences, cared for their pastures, drained off salt water, and went back into the business. The lingering effects of the 2005 storm, coupled with a prolonged drought, and saltwater flooding from Ike were extraordinary events, but they did not end the careers of many coastal cattlemen.

The Cattle Industry

Southwest Louisiana possessed almost ideal conditions for development of a livestock industry. The area early became the center of one of the largest, if not the largest, cattle-producing sections of the United States. Although little attention was given to the improvement of stock before the 1880s, the period following saw many efforts made at scientific breeding. . . . By the end of the century, though other agricultural enterprises were beginning to compete with cattle raising, the industry continued to flourish. In the last decade of the century, cattle were being shipped to many parts of the United States and to Cuba (Millet 1964:180-181).

Watching over the herd. (Photo from *Progressive Farmer*, October 1989.)

Freshwater marshes have served Louisiana's coastal cattlemen well, as has pasturage in confined levee districts. Cattle husbandry, a cash-and-carry business with strong cultural connections, serves in many ways as a link to the past as the area's agrarian residents maintain the pastoral traditions of their forefathers.

The southwestern Louisiana ranching tradition, once centered in the inland prairie, is now concentrated in the marshes. Throughout coastal Louisiana, early efforts to reclaim large tracts of Louisiana's wetlands were largely unsuccessful. Smaller reclamation efforts, however, were ideally suited for livestock, encouraging marshdwellers to drain and reclaim areas for use as pasture. They did so by extending the boundary of their agricultural land through projects involving pumps, canals, and levees. On Louisiana's southeastern Deltaic Plain, the reclamation projects were generally associated with natural levee land. On the *Chênière* Plain, cattlemen grazed the marsh and used pumps to provide freshwater and expand their *chênière*-oriented pastures, largely south of Highway 14 — The Hug the Marsh Highway or The Reclamation Road (Waldo 1965; Waldo 1965B). Along with these managed tracts, local boat builders constructed cattle boats that permitted stockmen to maximize accessible pasture by transporting their herds from one grazing site to another (Millet 1987). In fact,

cowhands sloshed by day through knee-deep mud and slept at night in the marsh with its myriad mosquitoes and other insects. At appointed places along the lake or river bank, a small vessel—the chuck wagon of the coastal country—met the herd. Manned by one or two men, each being both sailor and cook, these vessels sometimes served as sleeping quarters for the cowhands. After a herd had safely reached the marshlands, saddles and cowhands were loaded aboard the vessel for a two-to-three day trip back home (Millet 1987:317).

Cattle roamed the open range at will and were rounded up in the spring when stockmen drove a common herd—consisting of cattle drawn from many different ranches—along the beach about eighty miles from the Sabine River to Vermilion Bay. These drives could involve 6,000 head or more. They were organized each year to move livestock from Constance Bayou, Dan's Ridge, Eugene Island, Long Island, Oak Grove Ridge, Pecan Island, Chenier Perdue, Little Chenier, Creole, and Chênière au Tigre. Using sternwheelers or barges, the animals were shipped to unloading facilities in the Vermilion Parish communities of Boston, Abbeville, or Intracoastal City (once a small community for fishermen, trappers, and farmers that has evolved into an important logistic support base for the offshore oil business).

At times, the livestock were herded across the marsh directly to market, a trip that could take five to seven days. From Chenier Perdue, stockmen used the same route to move their herds out of the *marais* on a seasonal basis. As a result, the migrating animals fashioned a small canal that "winds its way from the eastern end of the ridge to the Mermentau. . . . For over a half century, the canal provided the residents of Chenier Perdue, East Creole, and Creole with a link to the Mermentau River and thence to the outside world" (Carter 1968:4).

> The extensive prairies and sea-marsh of this parish [Vermilion] furnish abundance of pasturage for thousands of cattle, horses, and sheep. Stock-raising has always been the principal business in Vermilion parish, and many handsome fortunes have been realized from the profitable pursuit. Cattle and horses require no shelter, and keep fat winter and summer upon no other food than the native grasses. New Orleans and the Mississippi River parishes always afford a ready market at good prices (Harris 1881:237).

With discovery of oil, many small subsistence communities became important logistic support centers, no date. (Photo courtesy of the Morgan City Archives.)

On the larger, annual, New Orleans cattle drives boats moved up to 15,000 head of cattle along the Atchafalaya-Red-Mississippi River route, or from Washington through Bayou Courtableau to New Orleans via Plaquemine, or from Berwick's Bay via "round boats" that went "around" the bays into the Crescent City. In some cases, cattlemen followed Bayou Teche, crossed the Atchafalaya to Bayou Black and then trailed their herd along the Old Spanish Trail. The "drive" eventually cut across the swamp to Bayou Lafourche, then north along Bayou Lafourche to the Mississippi River, and east to New Orleans—a journey that took two weeks and subjected the wranglers to numerous hardships. In some cases, *chênière* cattlemen took their cattle to Texas by swimming the herd across the Sabine River and then trailing their livestock along the beach to pasture in the Lone Star State, or along well-worn regional trails (Jones 2007).

Before the Civil War, cattle were moved to stockyards for shipment by either rail or steamboat, no date. (Photo courtesy of the Morgan City Archives.)

Once the railroad into the prairie was completed, long cattle drives ended. Since no roads existed in the marshes, steamboats and other watercraft moved the animals to the nearest rail shipping point. The *Hazel* and *White Lily* provided transportation service to Lake Charles. In the spring of 1899, one cattle shipment from the marsh ranches included 1,900 head. It took seventy-five rail cars to transfer the herd to pastures on government land in Indian Territory (present-day Oklahoma) (Millet 1964; Millet 1974; Millet 1987).

Southwest Louisiana's ranching heritage was presumed to be established with the signing of the Dauterive Compact (named for pioneer rancher Antoine Bernard Dauterive) in April 1765. Under the terms of this agreement, Acadian immigrants secured cattle for breeding purposes. After six years, one-half of the offspring, according to the Compact, along with the original number of cows were returned to Dauterive (Jones 2003). "It was a good deal for both sides, Dauterive got free care of his cattle, one-half the profits and a source of skilled labor [and] . . . Acadians . . . got a start in the cattle business without having to come up with the capital" (Jones 2003:61). New evidence, however, suggests the deal fell apart after about three weeks (Brasseaux 2006, pers. comm.).

Cowboys: *Vachers* Versus French

East of Cameron, the cowboys were called *vachers*, west of the Calcasieu River, "French." Most settlers west of the river had less than a hundred head of cattle, unlike the big herds that grazed the marsh north of Johnson Bayou.

Acadians then began to buy cattle. Since the prairie was unfenced, and the open range was populated by wild and free-roaming cattle and horses, local pioneers needed only catch these itinerant animals to become part of a setter's "herd." Indeed,

> it was in Louisiana that the methods developed by the French-Acadian grazier and the cattle handling customs of the Mexican *vaqueros* were combined with the existing knowledge of Anglo-American stockmen and that of their African-American slaves. The new ways to handle cattle were incorporated into a blend of methods that facilitated the raising of stock in the grass-rich, wet coastal prairie of South Louisiana (Gallaway 2004:3).

Over time, Acadians quickly adapted to the open range and became highly skilled in breaking and racing horses and managing their livestock. This is a custom that goes back to at least the Spanish colonial period. In fact,

> in 1769, when Spanish governor Alejandro O'Reilly sent envoys into the southwest interior to learn what was out there on the prairie, they noted that Acadians were beginning to prosper as ranchers. The envoys found over two thousand head of branded cattle at the Opelousas Post and a thousand head at the Attakapas Post [current parishes of St. Martin, St. Mary, Lafayette, Vermilion, and Iberia]. By 1803, when Louisiana became a territory of the United States, branded cattle in the Opelousas district numbered over 50,000 head (Jones 2003:62).

In 1790, twenty-one years after Governor O'Reilly's envoy surveyed the prairie, members of a *Chênière* Plain pioneer family registered a cattle brand at the *Poste des Attakapas* (later known as St. Martinville) and started grazing livestock in what is now Vermilion Parish. Many followed their example. The *Chênière* Plain cattle industry—whose herds consisted of cattle reflecting a blend of Spanish and British breeds—expanded into Texas along a cattle trail from New Orleans to the Trinity River community of Anahuac. The early local cattle business represents an Anglo-Texan tradition that extended from southwest Louisiana into Texas to compete with the industry that expanded north out of Mexico. These *vacheries* are to the Acadians what a *rancho* or a *hacienda* was to Spanish-speaking people of Texas and Mexico (Millet 1987). The Acadians may, in fact, be North America's first cowboys.

From Bayou Teche to the Sabine River, there were extensive *vacheries* (ranches) (Millet 1974; Post 1962). Since wild cattle roamed the prairie and marshlands, they were originally a blessing, but they became a curse as ownership became an issue. To solve this problem cattle bands have been registered in Louisiana since 1739—twenty-one years after the founding of New Orleans. The *Brands of the Attakapas and Opelousas Districts, 1760-1888* records more than 2,700 brands belonging to *vachers* with French, Spanish, Acadian, and Anglo-Saxon surnames.

From this early beginning, prairie cowboys learned to twist a lariat from Spanish moss and to rope, corral, and break wild horses that they trained to cut and work cattle like their Mexican *vaquero* counterparts. In the coastal plain, there was a clear blending of Anglo-American and Spanish-Mexican ranching traditions. Further, it is highly likely southwest Louisiana was the birthplace of the black cowboy (Gallaway 2004).

Before the arrival of rice and fences, cattle husbandry was the prairie's main industry and dates back to the Avoyelles Indians, who introduced domesticated livestock into the area (Bradshaw 1997; Bradshaw 1997C). With time, cattle became an important agricultural commodity to the settlers on the *chênières* as well. These stockmen raised this livestock on pastures that were natural "saltgrass prairies." Between 1820 and 1840 these pioneer cattlemen brought the concept of grazing the marsh grasslands to East Texas (Jordan 1969). The industry established itself quickly. Like their prairie and *chênière* counterparts, Texas drovers were soon moving herds to New Orleans.

One rancher near Galveston Bay drove 1,000 head of cattle to New Orleans in 1834, a drive which took three weeks and cost $4.12½ per head. His motivation for undertaking this long and difficult drive can be understood when one considers that his yearlings were worth $5.00 per head in Texas and $12.00 or more at New Orleans. Eventually, in the late 1840s, the overland trails were partially superseded by steamship transport of cattle from Galveston to New Orleans, and still later came the railroad. Even into the post-bellum period, New Orleans remained a major market for the cattle of Texas (Jordan 1969:76).

In the 1870s, stockmen discovered marsh grasses would support their grazing herds. Therefore, the history of the marsh cattle business mirrors those of western cattleman. Brahma or Zebu (*Bos indicus*) became the coastal rancher's animal of choice (Cavendish 1948; Ward 1914; Cobb 1946). The Brahma was introduced into the United States in 1849. The diffusion process began in the Eastern Seaboard states and moved westward across the Lower South, through Louisiana, and into the coastal prairie corridor of southeastern Texas and into the semi-arid portion of Texas. Richard Barrow, a plantation owner near St. Francisville imported the strain in 1854, making the Louisianian a pioneer in Brahma use. By 1866, the breed was established in Texas, where extensive tracts of salt grass provided pasturage (Parr 1923; Gayden 1952). Despite numerous environmental hardships, this Brahma stain continues to prosper on marsh vegetation.

Through natural selection and selective breeding emerged a variety of cross-bred cattle that can endure heat, withstand insects, and, when necessary, graze belly-deep in water (Massey 1969). Part-Brahma range herds are now found in the coastal marsh and fringe areas extending from near New Orleans to Brownsville, Texas (Black 1935; Rhoad and Black 1943). Not many beef breeds can survive in the *marais*; yet the Brahma-hybrid is making profitable use of these grasslands (Guillot 1977).

This trait has not been lost on *chênière*-based ranching families, who helped improve the breed and encouraged the use of marsh pasture. Consequently, from their *chênière*-based homesteads cattlemen gain access to the *paille fine* (*canouche* or *caniche*), oyster grass (*Spartina alterniflora*), marsh hay cordgrass (*Spartina patens*), and other vegetation assemblages that serve as seasonal pasture that are classified as excellent, good, fair, and poor. The grade is determined by the climax vegetation's potential use for grazing. All four categories are used. For example, three to four acres of excellent range or ten to twelve acres of poor range will provide enough fodder to support one cow (Williams 1955). The determining element is the status of the climax vegetation. A highly degraded marsh will be rated poor, while one that has not been broken up will be considered excellent pasture land. These range conditions provide cattle growers with a guide they can adjust to maximize beef production.

Since cattle are selective grazers, they eat constantly the most palatable, nutritious grasses, and leave the less edible varieties to increase. These foraging habits affect the nutritional quality of each pasture, so proper grazing is the key to successful management. To use the marsh profitably, a stockman must maintain vigorous and productive fodder. Otherwise, overgrazing destroys the better pastures and permits deterioration of the grass resource. A similar pattern was discovered by Reimold, et al. (1975) in an analysis of grazed and formerly grazed marshes on Georgia's Sapelo and Ossabaw islands.

When marsh pasture is covered with water, as was the case after Hurricanes Rita and Ike, cattle will not forage more than about a quarter of a mile into the *marais*. Near

Wild Cattle Roamed the Prairie

Wild cattle roamed the prairie and wetlands; *Ile des Vaches*, Cow Island, an isolated section of the marsh, documents this fact. These unbranded animals were originally a blessing. They became a curse as ownership became an issue. To solve this problem cattle brands have been registered in Louisiana since 1739. *The Brands of the Attakapas and Opelousas Districts, 1760-1888*, records more than 2,700 brands belonging to *vachers* with French, Spanish, Acadian, and Anglo-Saxon surnames.

the ridges, this practice results in destructive overgrazing. To improve interior graz-ing, cattlemen in the 1950s began to build cattle walkways at a cost of between $1,500 and $2,000 a mile. Draglines excavated spoil from ditches on each site of the right-of-way to construct a levee. The end result is a twelve-foot-wide walkway, elevated above the surface and flanked by a series of small staggered ditches or ponds that ex-tend into the pasture for up to a mile. Once completed, cattle could easily move from the walkway into the *marais* to graze, even if the grassland was partially submerged.

Cattle do particularly well in *paille fine* pastures, as this grass has a protein content of 12 to 15 percent. The additional *canouche* and other grazing lands, made accessible by the elongated walkways, helped boost *chênière*-based cattlemen's profits by nearly 100 percent (Shiflet 1960; Reimold, et al. 1975).

Marsh cowboys' yearly work-cycle has always involved driving cattle out of the marsh. Before property and ownerships issues were being addressed by the courts, the marshlands were largely free range. As property titles were secured, many old cattle trails had to be replaced with new routes capable of handling the large herds that were a product of better range management practices. Each October and April herds were trailed or trucked, sometimes as far as seventy to 100 miles. This practice permitted the cattle to escape the summer mosquitoes and to take advantage of the marsh's excellent winter range. The rotation system works well and is an important part of the *chênière's* cowboy's lifestyle (Williams 1955; Shiflet 1966).

To move their herds, the Gray family, for example, bought a right-of-way from the Texas Company (now Chevron) in 1924 and built an eight-mile-long levee known as the "Dump" or "Gray's Ditch." This first and still longest cattle walkway in the marsh allowed cattle to be moved from Johnson Bayou directly to the north. Prior to cre-ation of this route, cattle were trailed along the shore face to Holly Beach, north to the "Big Marsh"-Gum Cove Ridge trail, and then west and north. The new passageway speeded up the process, and it made the journey easier on the cattle and the drovers.

Herds could now be trailed from the marsh to upland pasture in about three days. Before completion of the "Dump," the drive took more than a week. Beyond the "Dump," the cattle path followed high ground along Pine Ridge/Perry Ridge, where the Grays maintained a camp, then across Black Bayou through a channel outlined by booms to prevent the swimming animals from drifting downstream, and eventually across the Intracoastal Canal. Along this new track, cattlemen took nearly a day to swim the herd across each waterway to pastures that were open range before World War II.

On this unfenced land, cattlemen did not pay lease fees, for open-range laws were in effect. Unless the property was fenced, it was considered free range, and many families grazed this property for generations. In fact, between 1880 and 1930, the *marais* was considered open country. Cattle freely roamed the unfenced range. Brah-ma stock from different owners mixed and ran together as a single herd. In the late fall, winter, and early spring livestock grazed marsh pastures improved by the local cattlemen.

Using controlled burns, cattlemen enhanced their marshland pasture's produc-tivity. This pastoral tradition was an annual event that was evident by the large, black, columns of smoke that drifted over the marsh. Each spring, throughout the *chênières*, a *coup de main* (cooperative community) rounded up these "wild" animals so they could be moved to upland pastures or sold (Vermilion Historical Society 1983; Jones 2003). Shortly after World War II, truck transportation replaced the multi-day trail drives. The roundup nevertheless continues on a smaller scale, as there are not as many days involved. Dogs and whips are used to corral the animals that are then moved to an appropriate loading facility. This communal activity provides participants with a connection to the past, and it is one of the country's last horseback trail drives.

Eventually, large landowners controlled the range, so traditions had to change, as there were no longer unfenced pastures. Out of necessity herds became smaller. Even so, ranching remains an integral part of the local culture. Horses, cowboy hats, boots, cattle, bridles, ropes, belt buckles as large as small plates, and jeans are as much a part of the cultural heritage of the *Chênière* Plain as they are a part of western grazing tradition. Like the American and Canadian West, "cowboying" on the *chênières* has not changed too much since its inception.

(Image from the author's collection.)

1. A Cotton Pickery. 2. Drying Sheds. 3. Mixing. 4. Picking or Cleaning a Bale. 5. Making up a Bale. 6. A Lint Room. 7. Sunning Racks. 8. A damaged Bale.
9. A Cotton Float. 10. European Steamer loading. 11. Cotton Presses on Levee. 12. Packing Cotton in a Steamer's Hold.

Throughout the coastal plain, cotton is often the forgotten crop. (Image from *Harper's Weekly*, July 1883).

Chapter 4
THE PHYSICAL AND CULTURAL LANDSCAPE OF THE DELTAIC PLAIN

East of Marsh Island (also known as *Grosse Ile du Vermilion*) is the Delta or Deltaic Plain—land built by alluvial material deposited by the Mississippi River as it enters the Gulf of Mexico. Within the region's boundaries are between 8,000 and 12,000 years of Deltaic morphology, exemplified by a highly irregular shoreline—characterized by natural levees, marshes, swamps, bays, lakes, and barrier islands (Russell, et al. 1936; Weinstein and Gagliano 1985). This geographic province consists of a series of shifting, prograding sedimentary lobes, deposited by the Mississippi River and linked to long-term climatic events and cycles. Since it formed over the last 600 years, the modern "bird foot," or Balize, delta "is more an artifact of engineering efforts to stabilize the river channel for navigation than a result of natural processes" (Padgett 1966:425).

Each of the delta's principal lobes and sub-lobes advanced into the shallow waters of the continental shelf and was distinguished by numerous distributaries. Through time these channels continued to branch and subdivide, thus aiding the distribution of river-borne sediments within the coastal lowlands and the coast's progradation—the outward building, over time, of the delta into the Gulf. Most authorities agree there are at least seven historic lobes: Sale-Cypremort, Maringouin/Cocodrie, Teche, St. Bernard, Lafourche, Plaquemines, and the Modern/Balize. A new lobe is developing in association with the Atchafalaya River in Atchafalaya Bay (Fisk 1952; Kolb and Van Lopik 1958; Frazier 1967).

These recurring channel changes created an intricate pattern of levee fingers extending into the wetlands and also assisted in providing the geologic framework for the backswamps, marshes, and waterbodies that characterize the physical landscape. Each change represents a major shift in the Mississippi River's course and consists of a network of distributary waterways that radiate out from a main or trunk channel or channels with each of these features separated by interdistributary troughs or basins. The end result is a landscape whose age is determined by each of the Mississippi's deltaic lobes. Every historic delta is being altered, with the older deltas deteriorating faster than the newer ones. The one visible constant is the natural levee ridges.

In as much as subsidence takes place simultaneously with sea level rise, only remnants of some of these natural levees are evident, such as Marmande Ridge and Isle de Jean Charles in Terrebonne Parish, and Lafourche Parish's Petit Bois Bayou and Bayou Château de Cyprès. These geomorphic-remnant features represent the destructive processes (root production of flood-stressed plants cannot keep pace with subsidence) that today easily overshadow constructional processes. Other areas, because of vertical growth through the input of sediments and the associated underground mat of plant growth, are countering the effect of submergence (DeLaune, et al. 1983; Salinas, et al. 1986).

Natural Levees

Repetitive flooding along all of South Louisiana's rivers, and bayous diverted sediments and water into the surrounding lowlands. These events elevated the surface at a rate that counteracted subsidence and sea-level rise. These recurring events resulted in a landscape distinguished by a broad plain that is gently sloping away from the watercourse. The nearly imperceptible backslope descends as little as six inches per mile for up to five or six miles and terminates at the backswamp or "the trees." The height and width of these topographic elements are directly proportional to the size of the waterbody that created them (Welder 1959; Hatton, et al. 1983; Kesel 1988; Kesel

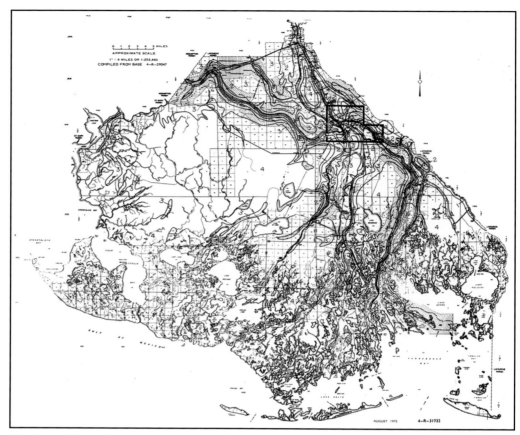

The United States Department of Agriculture General Soil Map of Terrebonne Parish, ca. 1970, illustrates the natural levee fingers south of Houma.

1989; Mossa 1996; Roberts 1997; Davis 2000; Day, et al. 2000). These surfaces are identified as natural levees. In all cases these topographic elements furnished the essential high ground for colonization and flank both sides of the Mississippi, and all of the associated distributary channels. Differences in elevation between the levees and the marsh are slight, but vital from the standpoint of human occupancy. In fact, south of New Orleans (29.95°N latitude), with the exception of exposed salt domes, there are no elevations more than twenty-five feet above sea level.

The Mississippi River's Flood Control Levees

The history of the levee system of the Mississippi River is replete with the records of failures, breaks in the embankments and crevasses (McDaniel 1930:4).

From 1840 to 1860, a series of highly destructive and injurious floods made it apparent the Mississippi River's flooding problem was too large to be handled at the local level. It was a national issue. Much of the unprotected/unoccupied land was in the public domain. According to some, if this property was reclaimed and protected against overflow it would become an economic asset and no longer be "worthless" (Waddill 1945). Two severe Mississippi River floods in 1849 and 1850 "left the alluvial land in waste" (Harrison 1951:8) and convinced the Federal government to provide financial assistance to construct a continuous, serpentine levee system. This public

The Civil War had a profound effect on South Louisiana's levee system and hydrology. (Image from *Frank Leslie's Illustrations: The American Soldier in the Civil War*, 1865.)

During the Civil War, a common strategy of the Confederate forces was to blow up the levee systems to cover their retreat. This practice resulted in repetitive flooding. (Image from *Frank Leslie's Illustrations: The American Soldier in the Civil War,* 1865.)

After the Civil War, the Mississippi's levees were in total disrepair. During flood events, crews were dispatched to make the necessary repairs under the watchful eye of a gun-toting guard. (Image from *Harper's Weekly,* March 1884.)

Whether repairing a levee break or working in the sugarcane fields, Chinese immigrants were contract laborers. Some migrated into the wetlands, but this part of Louisiana's ethnic history has not been well recorded. (Image from *Harper's Weekly*, June 1871.)

works plan would add worthless property to the tax rolls by building an uninterrupted levee that included unoccupied lowlands. Although this notion was identified as necessary, the plan never materialized. The Civil War intervened.

A decade before the Civil War, there were in Louisiana 1,400 miles of privately built levees, protecting more than five million acres (twice the size of Jamaica) of swamp and overflowed lands (Harrison 1951). An 1850 survey described these levees as about five-feet high, seven-feet wide at the top, with a base width of thirty feet. Even so, all levees built during the pre- and post-Civil War period were insufficient in height and cross-sectional profile to protect the population from overtopping and crevasse-induced floods (Thorpe 1853; Elliott 1932B, Waddill 1945).

When natural levees are overtopped, the water moves gently across the landscape. This sheet flow does not cut crevasses, which produce far more destructive torrents. The documented number of crevasses identified with each flood event, provides ample evidence of the early levee system's deficiencies. During every flood, frequent levee gaps were observed, simply because of the levee system's deficiencies. Although in 1851, the Baton Rouge-to-Pointe à la-Hache levee segment was continuous, with a mean height of 4.5 feet, many of these levees were too close to the river and failed because of overtopping, crevassing, seepage, and bank collapse, or burrowing animals and abandoned rice flumes (Elliott 1932B). It was a weak sys-

Louisiana's sea-level citizens were in a constant battle with water. (Image from *Every Saturday*, July 1871.)

Crevasses were a common issue. (Image from *Harper's Weekly*, May 1866.)

After a flood event, relief boats were a welcome sight. (Image from *Harper's Weekly*, March 1882.)

Crevasses were a hazard to navigation and residents alike. (Image from *Collier's Weekly*, April 1897.)

tem, easily breached, creating crevasse-induced flooding (Conrad and Brasseaux 1994). Nevertheless, in the Lower Mississippi Valley, earthen embankments afforded the only practicable means to prevent property damages triggered by floods.

If the Valley was going to reach its economic potential, crevasses needed to be terminated. They were complex natural phenomena that needed to be properly considered in the design and construction of levees. To inhibit normal overflow, plantation owners constructed artificial or engineered levees that, because of their design, also encouraged crevasse development. Clearly, engineering design was the key element in harnessing a river's flood potential, because, when a crevasse does occur, a channel is scoured allowing the outlet to function during high water. The break usually silts up in a few years and is normally associated with a river's cut bank side—a natural erosion point and an ideal location for a crevasse. Many crevasses can be dated from the historical record, and much of their development during the past few hundred years can be traced by reviewing historical maps (Coastal Louisiana 2007).

When a levee was breached, the related crevasse furnished a pathway, or vent, for water and sediments to be discharged into the backswamps and interdistributary basins (Kesel 1988; Kesel 1989). Overbank sedimentation, through a crevasse, was a vital process in building the sub-aerial land in the lower Mississippi River delta and much of the marsh was created through sequential and reparative flooding and sedimentation (Coleman 1988; Turner and Streever 2002).

Before construction of artificial levees, crevasse splays were a common occurrence that directed sediments out of the main channel and reduced flood stages downriver. Archaeological evidence suggests these geomorphic features are natural phenomena that remained open and functional for several hundred years (Gagliano and Van Beek 1970). Vogel (1931) shows a crevasse splay will encompass an average of about 650 square miles—the largest involved 2,160 square miles (an area slightly larger than the

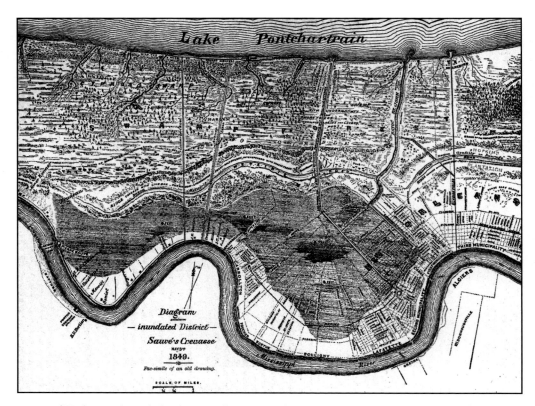

state of Delaware)—while the smallest was about 210 square miles. Regardless, large crevasses, which can discharge water and sediment over considerable area, were a constant reminder of the fragile nature of the Mississippi River's engineered levees. This was particularly true in New Orleans—America's crevasse-prone city.

The 1849 Sauvé's Crevasse, for example, flooded to a depth of six feet inundating more than 2,000 homes in a 220 block area of New Orleans. "Many occupants of houses with high-ceilinged rooms stuck it out by building floating floors inside their houses." Unfortunately, "people who were evacuated had nowhere to go. Many families that were moved to dry land found themselves without shelter and worse off than they had been in their flooded homes" (Carruth 1979:153). One hundred and fifty-six years later the same can be said of Hurricane Katrina and its affect on the displaced families of New Orleans.

It is important to note once a large crevasse, like Sauvé opens, closure was difficult. The breach could not be repaired until the flooded areas, influenced by the crevasse splay, were sufficiently inundated to reduce materially the current flow through the break. Once the flow was no longer a raging torrent, usually during the next low-water period, closure procedures could be initiated to seal the fissure, but not always.

In 1850, a 1.2 mile-wide crevasse broke through the levee at Bonnet Carré. For more than six months, the channel diverted water flowing at an estimated rate of more than 149,000 cubic feet per second into Lake Pontchartrain (Ellet 1852, Elliott 1932). As long as water passed through the gap with considerable velocity, the opening continued to widen. Along with Bonnet Carré, many other crevasses actively removed water from the Mississippi during the winter and spring of 1850—with an estimated cumulative discharge between 306,350 and 548,120 cubic feet per second (Ellet 1852).

From 1849 to 1874, this crevasse overflowed four times (1849, 1850, 1871, and 1874). The 1874 break remained open until 1883 and raised the level of Lake Pontchartrain by about two feet (Gunter 1955). Water poured through a gap 1,370 feet wide, with an average channel depth of twenty-two feet (Millis 1894; Warfield 1876). The rupture was triggered by a muskrat burrow that weakened the levee's integrity. The flood waters, estimated as high as 229,800 cubic feet per second, swept away "dwellings, sugar-houses, crops, and fences like chaff before the wind, tearing out railroad embankments for many miles, interrupting railroad communication from the north with New Orleans, and even threatening the safety of the city itself. . ." (Morey 1875:7). The steamer "*Katie*, one of the largest and finest steamers on the western waters, was drawn into the vortex of Bonnet Carré . . . and was only pulled from her peril by tugs . . ." (Warfield 1876:6).

As a result of this long-term flood event, it was reported in 1876 that

> the lake itself is rapidly filling up with the sediment with which the crevasse water is charged, and which is deposited, as soon as the crevasse current is checked, in the placid waters of the lake. Navigation of the lake is becoming dangerous and difficult. The trade of the lake, which engages and employs three hundred vessels and three thousand men, and supports, perhaps, forty thousand people, is threatened with utter ruin. The city of New Orleans, impoverished and almost bankrupt, has just ordered a hydrographic survey of the lake, for the purpose of determining accurately the effects of the crevasse in filling up the lake, thereby raising the water-line and threatening to overflow the city itself . . . (Warfield 1876:8).

Along with the Bonnet Carré crevasse, the 1884 Davis Crevasse, approximately twenty miles upriver from New Orleans (on the west bank at the railroad station of the same name, in St. Charles Parish), was directly attributed to an abandoned rice flume removed a few months prior to the high water (Ewens 1885), although a muskrat hole may also have been responsible for the break. The event was catastrophic and ruinous to land owners southwest of New Orleans.

According to one eyewitness, this incident was

> . . . by far the most destructive single crevasse known in the history of overflows in Louisiana. Its waters extend in a sea o' desolation for a distance of more than a hundred miles along the west bank of the Mississippi river. The right banks of St. Charles, St. John and St. James parishes above the break, for 40 or 50 miles, are wholly or partially submerged. Below the crevasse the richest agricultural portions of Jefferson, Orleans and Plaquemines parishes, to a distance of 60 miles, are under water, which sweeps over them in a wide waste, whose depth varies from two to eight feet. Thirty or 40 miles away to the westward the great flood spreads out like a modern deluge to the banks of the Lafourche, above Thibodaux (Daily States 1884:4).

This experience led to the conclusion "that rice flumes are the great crevasse makers, and that they should be abolished" (Ewens 1885:108). The warning of 1884 concerning flume-induced crevassing was ignored, and, consequently, rice flumes gave rise to a considerable number of crevasses in the late 1800s. In the floods of 1897, flumes were responsible for thirteen crevasses in the vicinity of New Orleans (Gillespie, et al. 1897). South of the city, where the levee was small and quite vulnerable to crevassing, raceways were responsible for more than a dozen breaks.

Although flume-induced levee fractures were easily identified, most crevasses reported between 1850 and 1920 were caused by the abandonment and neglect of the levees designed to protect the human population. Breaks were the result of 1) paths worn across the levee by livestock; 2) poor maintenance where, in some cases, a shovel-full or two of dirt could have prevented the fissure; 3) defective rice flumes; 4) crawfish and/or muskrat holes; 5) waves from passing steamboats; 6) loggers' activities; and 7) sand boils or "blow outs" (Warfield 1876:7). From these events, it was apparent artificial levees were not high enough to guard against overflows. Because they were poorly engineered, they could not keep flood water confined to the main channel; as a result, a breach was a disastrous event (Stielow 1977B).

The Beginning of the Flood Protection Levee Systems in Louisiana

> On occasion questionable engineering has resulted from good political decisions; at other times, excellent engineering decisions have caused political confusion. Sometimes neither politics nor engineering has determined the course of a project. Rather a crisis of calamitous proportions forces Congress and the Corps to act without a thorough investigation of either social or engineering requirements. The history of flood control on the lower Mississippi illustrated vividly all these problems (Reuss 1982:131).

Immediately after New Orleans was founded, an earthen mound was created to defend the city from floods. Completed in 1727, the mud embankment was 5,400 feet long, three-feet high, with a crown width of eighteen feet. Over time the levee expanded as plantations were established along the river's lower reach (Elliott 1932B). By 1735, an earthen bank extended from English Turn (twelve miles southeast of New Orleans) to approximately thirty miles northwest of the city. A flood in that year proved the levee's inefficiency, for it broke in many places (Le Page du Pratz 1774).

In 1743, Gov. Pierre François de Rigaud, marquis de Vaudreuil-Cavagnal decreed that Louisiana property owners must complete their levees by January 1, 1744 or forfeit their land as a penalty for their negligence (Frank 1930). The colony's administrators wanted Louisiana to become a self-sufficient, agriculturally-based, exporting colony, and they recognized the need for adequate drainage and flood control. Their efforts to promote self-sufficiency were futile, but the mandated levee construction bore fruit. When Louisiana became a state in 1812—nearly 100 years after construction of New Orleans' first levees—the embankment extended 155 miles on the Mississippi's east bank and 185 miles on the west bank (Frank 1930).

While flooding was of local and regional concern, the nation's attention was focused on enhancing river navigation in the first half of the nineteenth century. Protection against flooding attracted little legislative attention. However, in 1823 a survey by S. Bernard and J. G. Totten determined the only practical approach to decrease the number of "snags" in the Mississippi's main channel was to construct levees. It was believed these levees would prevent the lateral currents responsible for the snags, thereby enhancing navigation (Frank 1930).

A quarter-century after Bernard and Totten's survey, the Federal government recognized the Mississippi Valley's flooding problem by enacting the Swamp Land Acts of 1849 and 1850. This legislation provided Louisiana and other flood-prone states with the necessary financial assistance to combat the flooding issue (McCrory 1919; Tomlinson 1926; Schneider 1952; Vileisis 1997). Perhaps more importantly, these Acts marked the culmination of legislative that transferred the wetlands from the control of the Federal government to the states. As early as 1826, attempts were made in Congress to grant the wetlands to the states; the abortive agrarian-based transfer reflected the ideology that every man had the right to own land, even "wetland" (Harrison 1951; Vileisis 1997).

As a result of the Swamp Land Acts, Louisiana and Florida received the largest share of frequently flooded, federally-owned swamp and overflowed lands—approximately 64 million acres, an area slightly larger than Wyoming—that were transferred to the states (Wooten and Jones 1955). Louisiana's share was eight and a half million

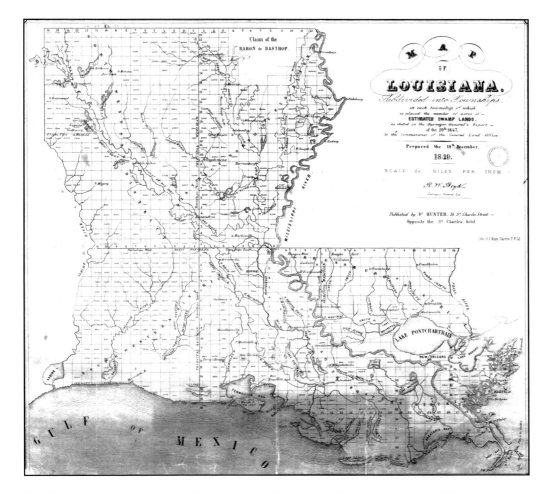

The Swamp Land Acts provided Louisiana with considerable acreage to be sold for the benefit of levee construction, 1849. (Image courtesy of the National Archives and Record Administration.)

acres (McPhee 1989). The Acts constituted the first important federal attempt to foster land reclamation by promoting the notion that "farm production formed the very basis of the nation's wealth" (Vileisis 1997:74). However, by not appropriating drainage funds, the Federal government effectively blocked development of the transferred wetlands by yeoman farmers. Local politicians consequently claimed the "national government was 'morally bound' to expedite drainage and agricultural settlement, emphasizing the ethical nature of the obligation" (Vileisis 1997:75).

The Federal government, however, intended that these donated swamp and overflowed lands were to be sold to underwrite the cost of both levee construction to control annual flooding and reclamation projects required to make the land fit for cultivation and settlement (Harrison 1951). South Louisiana's swamps and marshes were ideally suited for such reclamation endeavors, for they were considered "nearly valueless until reclaimed by drainage" (Morse 1854:1). As a result, the new owners, largely absentee Northern investors, demanded the protection of their "new" land from frequent flooding (McPhee 1989).

In states, like Louisiana, where the administration and use of the swamp land funds was a major political, economic, and social issue for more than 30 years, the reclamation carried out under the Swamp Land Acts left a permanent impression on the agricultural economy. The experiences in flood control and drainage engineering gained in trying to meet the provisions of the grants formed the basis for the elaborate projects later undertaken by the Federal government for the control of floods and the drainage of land in the Lower Mississippi Valley. Likewise, most of the legal and administrative concepts and machinery set up under the Swamp Land Acts became a permanent part of flood control and drainage practice. Even more important than these considerations is the influence of the methods used in disposing of the 'swamp and overflowed' areas on the ownership and tenure situation which developed and thereby upon the level of living which the social and ethnic groups of the Valley have been able to achieve. Certainly the Swamp Land Acts cannot be dismissed as unimportant in the agricultural history of Louisiana. Indeed, a thorough understanding of the history of land development and settlement throughout the Alluvial Valley of the Lower Mississippi requires and [an] examination of the scope and nature of the reclamations initiated under these acts and review of the ultimate disposition of the 'swamp and overflowed' lands (Harrison 1951:2).

To manage the "swamp and overflow" lands, the state created levee districts. Sales of the swamp and overflowed properties generated capital to operate these districts (Harrison 1951). Even though not much was known concerning the extent of these "wet lands," or even what was meant by the term swamp and overflowed land, the wetlands were for sale. Unfortunately, the levee boards, which were rife with corruption, sold "untold numbers of acres of public property to land speculators" (Wilt 2005:43). Many transactions were of dubious legality, and many deeds bear the warning "no guarantee of title."

Money raised through the Swamp Land Acts was utilized to build a contiguous levee along the Mississippi—at the cost of reclamation projects. Hence, in the post-Civil War era, it became clear that funds generated from the sale of swamp and overflowed lands would be insufficient for their reclamation. Meanwhile, every effort was made by Louisiana's governmental officers to secure federal funds to repair and strengthen the state's levees. This endeavor was only partially successful because of insufficient coordination and cooperation between flood-prone states and the Federal government's only occasional gestures of assistance (Harrison 1951). The Swamp Land Acts were thus ultimately failures.

Even so, the governmental effort to protect the banks of the Mississippi River through Louisiana's various reclamation programs, as outlined in the Swamp Land Acts, took on new purpose and direction. Clearly the state's floodplain swamps could not be effectively drained without controlling the Mississippi—a slow and arduous process. And although the acts did not accomplish the results envisioned by its legislative sponsors, "the engineering experience gained in trying to implement the acts laid the foundation for successful drainage projects undertaken later in the century. Furthermore, many legal and legislative concepts established with the Swamp Land Act became permanent fixtures in the spheres of drainage and flood-control" (Vileisis 1997:91). Further, the concept of levee boards and their ability to collect taxes on wetlands that could be defined by recognized boundaries, like other properties, was paramount to the privatization of the nation's swamps and overflow lands.

Flood Control and the Federal Government

'Without levees,' Senator Gibson wrote to a friend, 'our country is a waste and we are beggars' (McBride and McLaurin 1995:390).

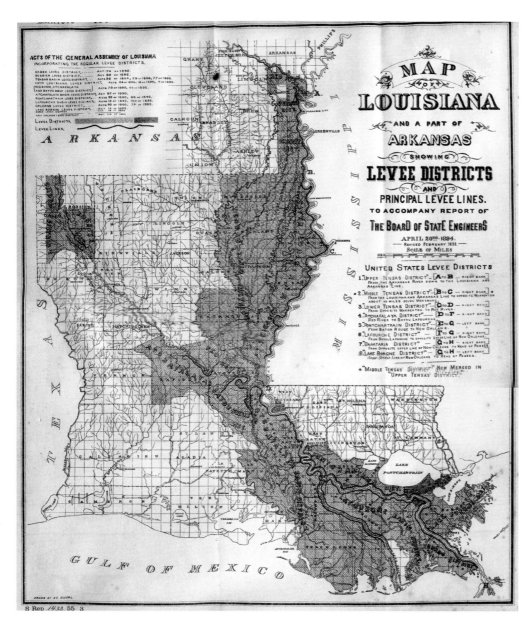

By the end of the nineteenth century, Louisiana was beginning to organize its principal levee districts, 1894.

In the strictest sense, the Swamp Land Acts were not a flood-control measure, but the legislation nevertheless marked the beginning of federal participation in flood-related issues and affected permanently the agricultural economy of the states involved (Cowdrey 1977).

Nationally, appropriation debates were centered on improvement of navigation. As late as 1855, there was no mention of levees to defend against floods—only to augment navigation. The business community lobbied successfully for navigational improvements, while agricultural and urban communities said practically nothing. In 1835, Henry Clay suggested to the Secretary of the Treasury the government should study carefully the cost of raising a levee on the Mississippi's west bank. The suggestion fell on deaf ears.

While the Federal government was arguing the merits of flood control, the states organized levee districts and levee boards (Morgan 1909). These quasi-public corporations were empowered to construct the drains necessary to reclaim the swamp and overflowed lands. Also, they were authorized to fight the battle against floods. With these boards and the Federal government working together, there were by 1858 more than 2,000 miles of eight-to-ten-foot-high levees (with a base of fifty to seventy feet) outlining the Mississippi; Louisiana invested $18 million to build 745 miles (Forshey 1873; Morey 1874). By 1927, between Cape Girardeau, Missouri, and New Orleans, twenty-eight levee boards worked on a two-to-one match, meaning that for every two federal dollars spent on a project, the local district spent one (Simpich 1927). Thirteen of these levee districts were incorporated in Louisiana. They were empowered to levy taxes, issue bonds, and generally do whatever was necessary to construct and maintain levees within their respective districts. Along with the money each district generated internally, the proceeds of a one mill ($0.001) tax throughout Louisiana were dedicated to levee work (Richardson 1901).

Floods in 1862, 1865, 1867, 1874, 1882, 1883, and 1884 breached the levees, vividly demonstrated the need to raise and strengthen their height and base. The frequency of post-bellum floods indicates clearly the rival Civil War armies had done their jobs well; the levee system was variously destroyed, neglected, or in disrepair, and the labor force required to repair it was no longer available (Waddill 1945; Ferleger 1982).

Because Louisiana experienced the nation's longest period of military Reconstruction, its post-bellum government and economy were in disarray. Citizens roamed the state or emigrated to the North or West. They became nomads; refugees looking for a home were not available to work anywhere in their forsaken home state. In the postwar chaos, many of these exiles returned to face numerous problems, not the least of which was rebuilding the crumbling Mississippi River levees (Sutherland 1980).

Crevasse after crevasse helped demolish the post-bellum earthen mounds. Indeed, "before any repairs had been made, the waters rushed through the crevasses and breaks, sweeping off the embankments for many miles in length" (Henderson 1868:3). The problem was so severe, some individuals considered abandoning levees and allowing the river to overflow its banks and periodically flood formerly protected adjacent fields. Faced with imminent disaster, Mississippi Valley farming interests became increasingly shrill, as the following plea indicates: "[T]he General Government must come to the rescue; otherwise the fairest and most fertile portion of the valley of the Mississippi must be abandoned and become depopulated. . . . There is no illusion in this. It is a simple fact" (Westphal, et al. 1980:30).

The heightened sense of urgency among the region's leading business interests compelled the Federal government to take an interest. The detailed and scholarly delta survey conducted by A. A. Humphreys and H. L. Abbot was submitted to the Bureau of Topographical Engineers in 1861. In 1865, Sec. of War Edwin M. Stanton commissioned Gen. Humphreys to investigate the status of the Mississippi River's levees. With delivery of Humphreys' report, Congress sought to determine the cost of repairing the deteriorating levee system. Meanwhile, Pres. Andrew Johnson (1865-69) urged Congress to pass legislation necessary to rebuild the Mississippi River's protective levees, as Humphreys had reported fifty-nine crevasses, one of which, measuring two miles in length, had flooded thousands of acres.

The uncertainty surrounding federal flood control legislation during Reconstruction killed the antebellum momentum for swamp/marsh reclamation. During Reconstruction many planters were financially unable—or unwilling—to expand their agricultural operations into the flooded backlands. Levees needed to be repaired, but funds were unavailable, and labor was in short supply. As a result, the river tempo-

---

The Swamp Land Act May Have Robbed Peter to Pay Paul?

"It is possible that no friend of Peter had ever been so generous in handing over his money to Paul. The federal government deeded millions of acres of swampland to pay for the levees. The Swamp Act gave eight and a half million acres of river swamps and marshes to Louisiana alone. . . . The new owners were for the most part absentee. An absentee was a Yankee. The new owners drained much of the swampland, turned it into farmland, and demanded the protection of new and larger levees" (McPhee 1989:36).

rarily regained control of the struggle between Man and Nature. The quest for suitable habitation sites and agricultural land consequently focused on the natural levee.

Interest in land reclamation and flood protection waned, but it had not disappeared. Floods in 1868 and 1874, rekindled the issue of flood control. In 1871, Louisiana made revolutionary changes in the methods used to manage its levee program by creating the Board of State Engineers and the Louisiana Levee Company to build and maintain levees. The Board of State Engineers was to act as an advisory body concerning all levee and drainage work. Managing, financing, and protecting Louisiana's communities from overflow was the responsibility of the Louisiana Levee Company—a private corporation (Harrison 1951).

After the flood of 1874, it became apparent the Louisiana Levee Company could not meet the state's levee needs. There was no residual confidence in the program. The company directors had become so intoxicated with power and privilege they had forgotten their mission, and the state consequently lost ground every year in the battle for flood control (Harrison 1951). The Louisiana Levee Company was abolished in 1877 and a new and better levee program was organized. Even with this change, a national levee policy was needed—one that included the entire Mississippi River Alluvial Valley. After the 1874 flood, Congress began to mobilize itself in support of flood-control legislation, particularly when it was reported that "gaps in the levees equaled from one-third to one-half of the entire length of the levees" (Frank 1930:39).

After 1874, the Federal government convened a board of engineers, called the "Levee Commission" (Waddill 1945:3). Five years later, the Mississippi River Commission was created by an act of Congress approved June 28, 1879. This legislation immediately launched the United States government into the flood-control business along the entire Mississippi River system (Camillo and Pearcy 2004). Section four of the Act provided that:

> It shall be the duty of said commission to take into consideration and nature such plans and estimates as will correct, permanently locate, and deepen the channel, and protect the banks of the Mississippi River; improve and give safety and ease to the navigation therefore; prevent destructive floods; promote and facilitate commerce; trade and postal service . . . (Lippincott 1914:656).

The commission recognized that Gen. Andrew Jackson's closure of Bayou Manchac during the War of 1812 constituted the first step in confining the Mississippi to a single channel. Building upon this precedent, the commission in 1882 adopted a levee policy based on "the theory that confinement of flood water would periodically flush out the channel, thus removing obstructing bars and preventing the formation of new obstructions" (Waddill 1945:5).

Creation of the commission marked the end of the country's non-systematic approach to levee construction. Levees erected through the cooperative efforts of interested landowners had been built without effective supervision from a central authority (Ellet 1852). The era of uncontrolled, unstructured, and unsupervised construction was over. It had become obvious that government aid was essential to building a levee system that would provide adequate protection (Ockerson 1901), and the Commission began to discharge its new responsibilities in earnest (Camillo and Pearcy 2004).

Initially, these hand-built levees used spoil derived from parallel drainage ditches excavated by "station men" contracted to work on 100 linear feet of levee. As the levee increased in height and volume, mules and scrapers were added to the construction effort, replacing the station men's wheelbarrows (Cowdrey 1977; Barry 1997). Over time, mules were replaced by dredging equipment powered by coal, gasoline, diesel, fuel oil, or electricity (Waddill 1945). Once completed, these machine-made levees

The Mississippi's Levees

". . . it must be remembered that the lands on the Mississippi River are protected from annual inundation by embankments known as 'levees.' In the spring of the year, the Mississippi, . . . rises not only until its banks are full—but would, if left to itself, overflow for a season the whole lower country through which it passes. To remedy this evil, from below New Orleans and up toward the north for hundreds of miles, the river is lined by an embankment, which, in time of flood, confines its waters within its usual channel. These embankments vary from six to twelve feet in height" (Thorpe 1853:755).

The Mississippi's Great Wall

"Nothing on earth rivals these levees, not even the Great Wall, and they have worked much better against the Corps's chosen enemy nature than the Great Wall worked against the Mongol hordes. The Mississippi escaped briefly from its confinement in 1973, during a very large flood, but has been confined from source to sea, for the most part, since the thirties" (Reisner 1991:282).

Before mechanization, repairing a levee was a labor-intensive effort, ca. 1890. (Photo courtesy of the State Library of Louisiana.)

were regularly set back and raised in order to maximize high-water protection. By 1901, most of the levees as far south as New Orleans averaged twelve feet in height. In some areas they were over twenty-feet high. South of New Orleans, however, the height varied from five to six feet (Richardson 1901).

The agricultural community generally benefitted from this aggressive approach to levee construction. Large-scale plantations devoted to the production of indigo, cotton, sugarcane, flanked the Mississippi and their owners were actively engaged in protecting their lands at all levels of government.

Sugarcane, Plantations, Drainage, and Reclamation of the Marshes

Throughout Louisiana's history, agricultural activities have occupied an important position in the wetlands' social and economic environments. Originally, the most successful commercial crops were indigo and cotton, neither of which is cultivated in South Louisiana today (Holmes 1967).

Sugarcane cultivation filled the resulting economic void, growing in fields restricted to the natural levees (Davis and Detro 1977; Jones 2003). The first mention of this food staple in Louisiana occurred in 1725 (Surrey 1922). By 1733, the colonists had taken up its cultivation for the production of syrup. When Etienne de Boré planted cane on his plantation—which is now part of New Orleans' Audubon Park—he began experimenting with a granulation process. He was successful in 1796, and the Louisiana sugar industry was established. De Boré's achievement prompted other planters to follow his example, and ever increasing numbers of sugar factories were established with each succeeding year (Glenk 1934; Glenk 1934B; Rehder 1971, Rehder

Louisiana's early sugar "mills" were mule-powered. (Image from *Frank Leslie's Illustrated Newspaper,* October 1871.)

1973, Rehder 1999; Conrad and Lucas 1995).

By 1861, the state boasted 1,291 steam-powered sugar mills (Rehder 1999). These "factories" handled the "Bourbon," "Ribbon," "Otaheite," and "Creole" cane varieties. Each was distinguished by a large diameter stalk, low-fiber content, and a sucrose level high enough to permit granulation (Thorpe 1853; Begnaud 1980). Twenty years later, more than eighty-five sugar houses were operating within Terrebonne Parish alone; today, there are none. Scores of these antebellum mills were small operations. They made use of humans or mules to crush and squeeze the sugarcane in a screw press; collecting the juice in a vat (Leslie 1985). This juice was then evaporated in a series of large kettles over an open fire. The surface skimmings were set aside for fermentation into *tafia* (a low-grade rum). The remaining thick crystalline mass was ladled into conical molds or hogsheads that held sixty-three gallons (Read 1931).

In the first six decades of the nineteenth century, the sugar industry enjoyed explosive growth. This expansion was largely through the efforts of Northern capitalists who introduced Anglo-American names to the regional landscape. These toponymic generic names, such as creek and river, mingled freely with those of the early French planters. But sugar-based prosperity evaporated quickly with the Civil War. Nearly two decades were required for the industry to recover from the conflict's lingering after-effects (Butler 1980).

To help the industry, Louisiana State University (LSU) incorporated the Audubon Sugar School (part of the Louisiana Sugar Planters' Association's sugar experiment station) into the university's academic programs. As a result, by 1900 LSU, in conjunction with the school's links to the Caribbean sugar industry, graduated sugar chemists who became the backbone of the Caribbean sugar industry. Known collectively as Louisiana's "sugar tramps," they also helped foster the centralization process that improved the industry's productivity and took part in the industrialization of the sugar business (Garcia-Muñiz 1999).

The rapid expansion of South Louisiana's sugar industry resulted in no small part from the introduction of steam equipment. Sugar industry pioneers transported their cane to mills by means of mule-drawn wagons. Following the advent of the steam locomotive, most of the area's major sugar operations used narrow-gauge steam railroads to haul their sugarcane from the field to the mill. At one time, the Lower Terrebonne Sugar Refining and Manufacturing Company in Montegut, one of the world's largest and best-equipped sugar refineries, operated its own railroad, consisting of four locomotives and 500 sugarcane cars and over thirty miles of company-owned track. This was the longest plantation railroad in the Sugar Belt. In the 1950s, the railroad component of plantation operations faded away as trucks replaced narrow gauge railroad tracks and locomotives. Sugar mills now use trucks to deliver their cane and many of the original locomotives have been recycled. One Godchaux Sugars locomotive has been restored for operation at Walt Disney's Disneyland, while two Enterprise Plantation locomotives were rebuilt for use by Six Flags over Texas (Butler 1980).

Steam technology was also essential on the sugar country's myriad streams. Along these routes, steamboats pushed shallow-draught wooden barges laden with sugarcane to mills with water access (Maier 1952; Becnel 1989). On Bayou Lafourche, these boats traveled from Donaldsonville as far as south as Harang's Canal (a distance

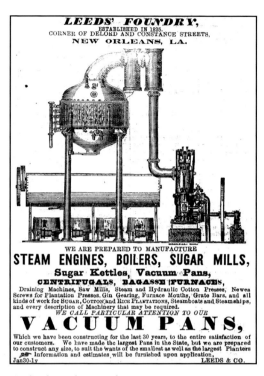

With the advent of steam power, Louisiana newspapers advertised the availability of steam engines. (Image from the New Iberia *Louisiana Sugar Bowl*, 1880.)

After the Civil War, sugar plantations required large numbers of wagons, mules, and barges to haul cut cane, ca. 1909. (Photo from the author's collection.)

Offloading a wagon of sugarcane into a waiting barge on Bayou Terrebonne, ca. 1930. (Photo from Butler 1980.)

of sixty-eight miles), but they generally terminated their trips at Lafourche Crossing—thirty-eight miles south of the Ascension Parish seat of justice (Heuer 1887).

Bayous were the sugar country's principal commercial arteries. These watercourses not only facilitated movement of raw and refined sugarcane to market, but they also served as conduits for the coal used in the sugar mills. Wood fueled the original sugar business. Coal was first used about 1850, and it eventually developed into the fuel of choice. Common sights along the region's bayous were "black mounds of coal" (Cole 1892:12) piled against the levees, waiting for the grinding season to begin. Bagasse burners were introduced about the same time (Glenk 1934B). Oil and natural gas eventually replaced coal, but bagasse remained an important sugar house fuel throughout the twentieth century.

Throughout the Sugar Belt, the effective use of technology and alternate fuels encouraged small reclamation efforts. Individual agricultural-based estates sought to protect their natural level land, while seeking to secure additional cultivable property by building back levees and pumping this "new" land dry. In the process, sugar farmers became increasingly aware of flooding issues. They quickly realized that levees, pumps, canals, and drainage programs would have to be employed to guarantee their natural levee lands would not flood and thereby protect their valuable crops (Lytle, et al. 1960; Campanella 2006). Sugar was king, but levees insured the "king's" survival and were paramount in maintaining an uninterrupted planting and harvesting schedule.

Forced Drainage: A Contemporary Engineering Solution

When or where the idea of diking marshes to prevent the overflow of tides had its inception, is not known. The nations of the Old World banked out the waters of their seas and rivers to make room for increasing population many centuries before Columbus crossed the Atlantic, and the early colonists from Holland, Sweden, England, and Scotland, with an unexplored continent before them, began the work of excluding the tides from the rich meadows bordering their rives. The subject is not new . . . (Nesbit 1885:5).

Forced drainage is perceived by South Louisiana's citizens as the most acceptable solution to flooding. As a result, about 17 percent of the "deltaic plain is in active forced drainage districts . . . , in abandoned districts . . . , or in areas where pumps assist drainage during emergencies . . ." (Kemp and Mashriqui 1996:i). In general, pumps were installed to increase the available "fastlands." Pumps and drain machines permitted agriculturalists to expand beyond the natural levees' "high" land into the marshes or swamps. Private funds from these expansionists sustained numerous early small-scale individual plantation reclamation endeavors. Forced drainage efforts, however, were larger, much larger. They required the support of regional governments and required a substantial geographic footprint. They were frequently constructed under the rubric of hurricane protection. This was particularly the case in Terrebonne, Lafourche, and Orleans parishes, as well as along the Mississippi River in Plaquemines and St. Bernard parishes. G. Paul Kemp and H. S. Mashriqui (1996) found within the Deltaic Plain 116 forced drainage areas encompassing 443,497 acres—nearly 693 square miles, or about two-thirds the size of Rhode Island.

Regional drainage plans were created in the 1970s in response to continued flooding because of 1) the absence of pumping facilities to remove excess runoff; 2) moderate tidal flooding; and 3) backwater flooding from high-water stages associated with the Atchafalaya and other rivers and bayous (U. S. Army Corps of Engineers 1983; Pumped land drainage n.d.). There was a need to improve the region's ability to remove excess water. For example, since the 1800s, people have occupied the ridge along

Throughout Louisiana's coastal lowlands, pumps have become an integral part of the land-scape. In fact, they are so common that they have become virtually invisible, 2007. (Photo by the author.)

Terrebonne Parish's Bayou du Large. As water encroached on this linear settlement, levees were constructed. In addition, new residents moved onto areas less than five feet above mean sea level. These tracts became flood prone, in part because natural gravity flow could no longer handle the increased runoff. On some previously dry lands, subsidence and a rising sea level also contributed to the parish's flood problem (U. S. Army Corps of Engineers 1983; Subsidence and sea-level 2007).

With the aid of pumps, agriculturalists began to systematically drain their backlands, ca. 1895. (Photo courtesy of George François Mugnier Photograph Collection, Louisiana Division, New Orleans Public Library.)

The boundaries of forced drainage projects generally follow old agricultural levees, existing canals, or newly constructed levees. In order to develop an envisioned drainage scheme, an individual assessment and permit application is required. Maximum levee heights are ten feet, but this depends on existing project-site elevations. Material required to build the levees was dredged from "borrow canals." The resulting "fastlands" are surrounded by "artificial" levees designed to provide protection from river and storm flooding. Each of these individual drainage districts requires at least one pump. The number and size of pumps required depends on the drainage area. Moreover, within the "fastlands" a system of drainage canals and ditches funnels water towards the pumps.

Rapid removal of floodwater produced unexpected side effects. Protective levees prevent aggradation, and soils consequently shrink and compact. The end result is that surface elevations within the "fastlands" are subsiding (Louisiana Coastal Wetlands 1998).

Forced drainage districts range from ten acres to slightly more than 10,000 acres. To minimize wetland impacts and maximize the availability of "uplands," the associated levees are located within the wetland-non-wetland interface. Any project's ultimate objective is protection of existing property and "all undeveloped agricultural and other non-wetlands that are probable for development in the future" (U. S. Army Corps of Engineers 1982:II-4). This is not a new concept, since plantations regularly relied on large drainage machines, similar to water wheels used in early flour mills, to move water from sugarcane fields to the backswamps (Begnaud 1980).

The levee network south of Houma, for example, only provides protection from minor tidal flooding; it is not designed as a hurricane-protection levee, while the levee system in south Lafourche meets all federal criteria and guidelines for a hurricane protection levee. North of Houma, the levees protect against minor backwater flooding associated with the Atchafalaya River's high-flood stages. These earthen mounds are not designed to impede a major flood. Nevertheless, marginal lands are protected and become more attractive as development sites, particularly as they are incorporated into forced-drainage districts (U. S. Army Corps of Engineers 1983).

Hurricane induced high water adds to the flooding risk. To those living near the marshlands, the drainage district concept offers an admitted short-term solution—one designed for only minor flooding events. The national flood insurance program requires structures be built above anticipated flood levels. As people and businesses move into some of these areas, they can expect to be flooded from one-to-five times over the next fifty years, particularly as the sea rises and subsidence becomes more significant. Parts of this system will be obsolete in fifty years. In the interim, the forced drainage network has contributed to changing the region's natural hydrology, and when at capacity led to localized flooding and litigation. Projects with a forty- to fifty-year life expectancy may seem ill advised. In fact, the long-term flooding problem may require more drastic means. Over the short-term, the current projects provide the region with some level of protection, while more detailed and massive bulwarks are planned—such as rebuilding the barrier islands and reconnecting the region's natural plumbing (Committee On Coastal Erosion, et al. 1990).

Drainage districts protect some lands known to be only marginally suited for development. In many cases, the drainage districts are designed so part of the protected real estate is left in its natural wetland state. Discharge from some of the drainage pumps have assisted parish engineers develop new marshlands because of the high nutrient loads associated with the pump outfall. As long as they remain in their natural state, these enclosed wetlands serve as natural absorption zones. Unfortunately, vacant lands within expensive drainage districts are frequently converted to homes and other forms of development.

Several of these drainage district levees will soon be exposed to the direct impact of Gulf processes. Marshlands are deteriorating, and the barrier islands are eroding—the protective forelands consequently are disappearing. In the last half of the twentieth century, "some barrier islands have submerged entirely . . . , and more are on the verge of total submergence" (Coastal Louisiana 2007:2). After Hurricane Ivan, the small islands of Curlew and Grand Gosier, within the Breton Island Refuge, vanished. In addition, Breton Island and parts of the Chandeleur chain were breached. "Waves breaking over submerged sandbars offer[ed] the only hint of where the islands were located" (McNamara 2004/2005:53). Further, during Hurricane Katrina, the Chandeleurs were nearly obliterated. "Outside of the fastlands, the coastal ecosystem is in a state of collapse. The combined effect of regional subsidence, alterations of hydrology at all scales, episodic storms, and local factors, such as herbivory and canal bank erosion, can lead to conditions across the coastal landscape which cause severe stress to wetland plants and ultimately their death" (Louisiana Coastal Wetlands 1998:42).

Once these marsh/barrier island complexes have disappeared, replaced by open water, the regional drainage district levees will have to withstand the full force of waves and storms. To counteract the problem, many drainage districts are rebuilding and stabilizing their levees and parish governments are entering agreements to re-nourish the barrier islands. Of course, maintenance costs will be necessary, as the levees are undermined or washed away and the probability of breaching is increased. History demonstrates this to be a predictable problem. As a result, Terrebonne and Lafourche parishes have built a system that will not be plagued by most storm events. A record hurricane or rain event however, can thwart the best plans, but, in the eyes of the local population, some protection is better than none at all.

Much of South Louisiana became polderized—although this term is used widely in the Netherlands, it can also be applied to South Louisiana. The polderization pro-

---

Marsh Fertility and Reclamation

"This class of marshes can be easily and cheaply drained, and, when so improved, they afford exceedingly rich soils. Along the outer margins of these vast morasses, some hundred thousand acres have been won to culture. These lands are remarkably fertile; and I am told that they often yield fifty bushes of shelled maize to the acre, and that they endure tillage for a period of many years without fertilizing" (Shaler 1886:233).

cess resulted from construction by private corporations and individuals in drained areas after petitioning parish levee boards—600 levee districts had the power to issue bonds—and the Army Corps of Engineers to construct the required protective levees. In the process, the Corps became the most conspicuous and influential hydrologic engineering entity in the country. By opening offices in nearly every state after the Civil War, the Corps supervised and maintained river navigation, opened blocked channels, built revetments, removed snags, and dredged shallow areas. All of this activity gave the Corps the expertise, the political leverage, and the capital necessary to embark on large-scale drainage reclamation/levee projects (Vileisis 1997).

By using the Corps' engineers, individual property owners avoided the cost of levee construction, and Louisiana's lower-tier of parishes became interlaced with an elaborate levee and pump system (Emmer 1971). In the process, the organized reclamation endeavors altered the natural sediment distribution system. When levees were built to channelize a watercourse, they also stopped natural sediment renourishment. Without continued sediment deposits, the marsh and associated alluvial wetlands became sediment-starved.

Farmers concerned about flooding, built levees to protect their properties, but they also deprived the wetlands of the sediments required to keep pace with subsidence (U. S. Department of Agriculture 1986). Too much reclamation, buttressed by too much levee construction, with too much emphasis on immediate results, and no apparent concern about the long-term effects, has caused too much subsidence, erosion, and salt water intrusion. These are problems that must be carefully addressed by modern society, as they affect humankind's long-term use of the coastal lowlands.

The Wetland's Ethnicity

". . . Over the wine I heard at least six languages in light-hearted conglomeration. The father, born French, had learned Spanish from his wife; he had picked up the Slavic tongue from others, and knew a little Italian, a Filipino dialect, and considerable English. An ancient neighbor used only French and his shoulders to express himself. Several visitors spoke fluently in Slavic, moderately well in French, and hesitantly in English. One robust oysterman seemed to comprehend every one of the tongues, but his remarks were always Tocko. A good-humored couple managed easily: he spoke to her only in French; she answered only in Italian. Their daughter listened to both of them and interjected comment—only in English; both knew what she said but neither essayed the speech that she chose. And when an acquaintance passed, everyone yelled at him, each in a different language" (Kane 1944:269).

The French Quarter became the meeting place for Louisiana's diverse culture groups. (Image from *Frank Leslie's Illustrated Newspaper* March 1883.)

Chapter 5
THE HUMAN MOSAIC: A KALEIDOSCOPE OF CULTURES

Thousands of people at the edge of the marshlands that skirts the Gulf of Mexico spend their lives trapping animals for fur, dredging oysters, trawling for shrimps, or pursuing other forms of marine and marsh life that thrive in this fertile and wet region. They do not lead a hand-to-mouth existence. They sell their daily harvests for cash. In this way they have moved closer to the mainstream of American economic life, but with one foot resting on deeply planted traditions quite foreign to the lives most of us lead (Hallowell 1979:16).

Louisiana's wetland habitats support at least 40 percent of the nation's marsh eco-systems (Gosselink 1980) and a large array of renewable and non-renewable resources (Davis 1976, Davis 1978). Within the narrow band bordering the land/water interface, small hamlets were founded by numerous ethnic minorities representing a kaleido-scope of cultures. Originally, the economy was subsistence driven, but with time it became more money and entrepreneurial oriented. Agricultural products, sulphur, oil and natural gas, fresh and salt water fisheries, and the region's trapping resources developed in response to national and international market demands. There evolved, therefore, a large concentration of people confined to wetland-dominated habitats who were exploiting these resources to meet the demand.

Since early cultures had to adapt to an ever-changing environment, settlement sites were rarely continuously occupied. In Louisiana, prehistoric cultures followed the changing patterns of the Mississippi River. These relic encampments are found throughout the coastal lowlands and represent a range of aboriginal cultures. These early pioneers established their villages on the area's natural levees, exposed salt domes, beach ridges, and other high-ground features. In the process, they developed a close relationship with the land they occupied. For thousands of years, these Lower Mississippi River Valley nomads witnessed most (if not all) of the Mississippi's delta-switching events. Their settlement sites corresponded to the regional topography, as determined by the Mississippi River. Therefore, the interrelationships between the wetlands' archaeology and geology are particularly evident. This interplay is well documented in the work of Kniffen (1936) and Russell, et al. (1936).

Kniffen (1936) commented on the consistent association of prehistoric sites with natural levee landforms. As a result of this work and others (Fisk 1944; Ford 1951; Phillips, et al. 1951; Fisk and McFarlan 1955; McIntire 1958; Gagliano 1963; Saucier 1963; Phillips 1970; Saucier 1974; Saucier 1981; Weinstein and Gagliano 1985; Stein 1986), the marshlands' archaeological chronology became the basis for assigning dates to Mississippi River delta landforms. This link between geology and archeology has become a key element in the interdisciplinary approach to studying Deltaic processes.

It is no accident that this methodological approach developed in the Mississippi River Delta, because many of the changes occur at a rate that can be measured on a "human" scale (Pearson and Davis 1995). As new natural levees were built, and old ones decayed because of the reduction of fresh water and sediments, the Indians moved. They had no choice; their sources of sustenance were no longer available.

For at least 12,000 years, the native population followed the coastal zone's changing topography (Weinstein and Gagliano 1985; Kniffen, et al. 1987; Walker and Davis 2002). As they moved, they left extensive artifacts. Relic Indian encampments are distinguished, therefore, by shell middens. These elevated sites served as marker points

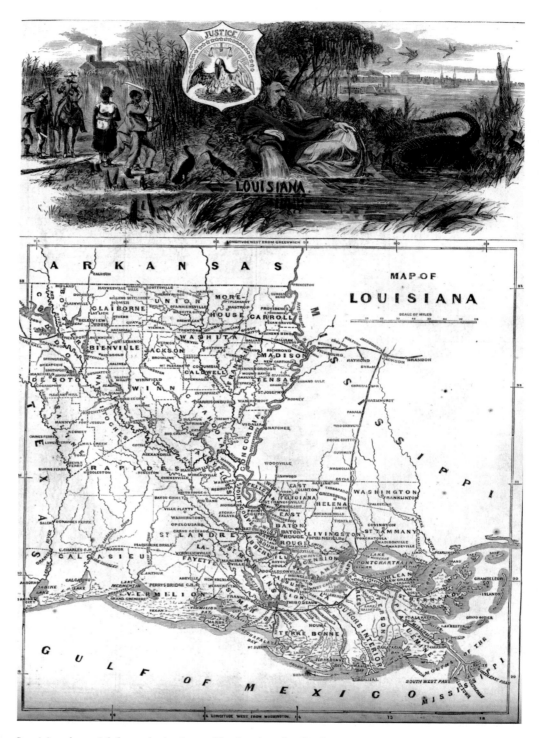

Louisiana's parish boundaries immediately after the Civil War. Note the cartographer's recognition of the marsh. (Image from *Harper's Weekly,* February 1866.)

for squatter "shanties," the inhabitants of which mined middens for their shells. When Europeans began to traverse the area, Indian settlements were quite numerous and their human occupants continued to build on the region's natural levees and other "high" ground features.

The Europeans followed their example and build according to the architectural tenets of the indigenous population. As the number of Europeans immigrated into the region increased, they mixed freely with the local aboriginal population and their lifestyles reflected the bounties afforded by the environment (Kniffen, et al. 1987). Moreover, their place names were frequently derived from local Indian languages.

Some South Louisiana place names of Indian origin
(From: Read 1927)

Name	Tribal Group	Name	Tribal Group
Acadia	Perhaps Micmac	Houma	Choctaw
Atchafalaya	Choctaw	Manchac	Mobilian or Choctaw
Bayou	Choctaw	Mermentau	Atakapa, also Attakapa
Calcasieu	Atakapa, also Attakapa	Mississippi	Algonquian
Cataouache, also Cataouatche	Choctaw	Pecan Island	Algonquian
Chacahoula	Choctaw	Plaquemines Parish	Mobilian
Choupique	Choctaw		

These indigenous peoples taught European settlers how to survive in the wetlands. In the process, the newcomers adapted local resources to meet their needs. Yet changes in the exiled Acadians' material culture altered only superficially their traditional way of life. As in their homeland, the vast majority of Acadian immigrants remained subsistence farmers, pastoralists, fishermen, trappers, or some combination of these occupations. They were also craftspeople who were self-sufficient, accustomed to hardships, fun-loving, gregarious, cooperative, and affable. They earned their living from a fundamental understanding of and relationship with the land and the sea, and developed "deep local attachments to their immediate realities" (Dormon 1983:11).

Their needs were modest and any surplus income was used to improve their surroundings—never for conspicuous consumption. They wanted only to complete a day's work and take care of their families. They took a communal approach to solving problems; everyone helped everyone else. If a roof was needed on a neighbor's home, the entire community pitched in to put on the roof quickly, not unlike a barn-raising among the Amish. This was simply part of their pragmatic cultural heritage (Brasseaux 1985). Most addressed each other by their given names, but more often by their nicknames: "T-Row" Cheramie, "Dido" Comeaux, "Coon" Guidry, "Blue" Landry, "Doc" Matherne, "Black" St. Pierre, and "Lay-Lay" Vizier. Nicknames are so widely used, that regional telephone directories once listed many customers by their sobriquets; in fact, an individual's given name may not be generally known to the community. Even today in the marsh, residents rarely addressed others by their "back" name (Wilkinson 1892; Parenton 1938).

Wetland inhabitants did not become large plantation owners. This was not part of their heritage. The region's plantations were established by British immigrants, not the local *habitant* or *petit paysan* (peasant) (Dormon 1983; Labouisse 1985). Indeed, Acadians were "independent, yet devoted to his family; equalitarian, yet tolerant of slavery; innovative, yet mired in tradition. He was . . . a man caught between two worlds" (Brasseaux 1985:40). Further, because of the culture's isolation, strong ethnic identity, geographic isolation, sense of community solidarity, the importance placed on the extended family, religion, and illiteracy, many marshland inhabitants retained their folklore, folkways, and oral traditions, frequently perpetuated by the family and evening visits (*veillées*) with neighbors (Rickels 1978; Perrin 1985).

With the exception of the east Texas "stock raisers," who migrated to the present Lone Star State directly from Louisiana, these settlers were not explorers. In fact, the large majority of cattle raisers on the Texas coastal plain were Anglo-Americans, who were "by birth and place of removal from states farther east in the coastal herder belt" (Jordan 1969:82). Louisiana Francophones did drift into southeastern Texas as cattle herders, but they constituted a very small part of the area's population. The one exception was Taylor White (born LeBlanc), who was the largest cattle owner between the Sabine and Trinity rivers. White is an anomaly, for Acadians lived on the land of their ancestors or as close to that land as possible. Until after World War II, there were no Daniel Boone-types among the Acadians; they were family-oriented and had no desire to live anywhere but South Louisiana. If they moved away from "home," they did not go to California or to the factory centers of the north. They went instead to Baton Rouge, New Orleans, Lafayette, Beaumont (Little Abbeville) or perhaps Houston, cities that were, in their mind, close to their ancestral property, so family members could easily keep in close touch with each other and continue to enjoy Sunday dinner (lunch) at *maman's* (Kollmorgen and Harrison 1946).

Marshdwellers were marginalized in this tightly-knit society. Even so, they thrived on what outsiders called a "simple," albeit frugal and unpretentious, lifestyle. Marshdwellers enjoyed a strong *esprit de corps* in part because they generally shared historical origins and traditions, as well as a common language and religion and a tendency to marry within the group (endogamy). They were inclined to maintain their common characteristics and values over a long period of time (Dormon 1983). They were in this respect profoundly conservative in "the manner of most traditional rural

Before Hurricane Katrina, the Isleño museum displayed the Canary Island migration to Louisiana, 2005. (Photo by the author.)

folk populations" (Dormon 1983:36).

The marshdwellers' Louisiana origins can be traced to about 1765, when French and German colonial farmers imprinted a subsistence pattern on South Louisiana that still endures (Richard 2003). Their long-lot property holdings—elongated, ribbon-like tracts—still appear on land-ownership maps. The colonial government typically proffered grants of forty *arpents* depth (*profondeur ordinaire*) by four-to-eight *arpents* frontage along bayous (*arpents de face*). Homesteads customarily bordered watercourses, and streams became South Louisiana's economic and communications lifelines. As a result, "in the early days of settlement, backlands [*brulés*] were of little use and presented no problem. It was the frontlands that counted for here were the houses, roads, fertile soil for cultivation, and perhaps a sugarhouse" (Millet 1971:63).

Bayou banks are crowded with habitations—though with occasional physical breaks and small urban centers. Waterfront settlements are frequently as dense as urban row housing, which reduces the problems associated with rural, agrarian isolation. Agriculture is important, but limited by the narrowness of the natural levees; as a result, cattle grazing has taken the place of traditional row-crop agriculture. Since Acadians lived under Spanish rule for nearly a third of a century, many elements of their pastoral economy were undoubtedly borrowed from their Spanish neighbors (Post 1962). *Pirogues* (the marshdwellers' Model T), instead of horses, and trained cow hounds were used to round up cattle. Over the past century, however, boat-oriented businesses and trapping became primary economic importance (Bowie 1935; Knipmeyer 1956; Padgett 1960; Bourg 1968; Padgett 1969; Hansen 1971; Butler 1985).

Isleños or Canarios

The Isleños were described as: "a diminutive specimen . . . clad in blue cotton made pants and hickory shirt, barefooted, with a palm-leaf hat upon his head, and an old rusty shotgun in his hands" (Din 1988:99). They "tended to be somber, taciturn, and suspicious of strangers, even of their French neighbors with whom they shared a common religion. They kept to themselves and married among their own" (Crété 1981:282).

In the 1770s, the Isleños—nearly 2,000 Canary Islanders who emigrated to Louisiana between 1778 and 1783 to serve as a buffer in the frontier area—settled four sites along a tongue of land locally known as Terre aux Boeufs or *Población de St. Bernardo* (Description of Louisiana 1803; Tinajero 1980; Din 1986). The 1778 Canarian immigrants, the only Isleños whose experienced is thoroughly documented, totaled 264 persons. Most of these colonists were citizen-soldiers recruited to complete the Louisiana Infantry Battalion (Tinajero 1980). They were drawn from Tenerife, Gran Canaria, Fuerteventura, Lanzarote, and Hierro islands. Ultimately, the crown's objectives were met by these soldier-settlers (Tinajero 1980).

Like their Southern Slavic neighbors, the Isleños—with surnames, such as Perez, Campo, Alfonso, and Nunez—continue to live in the Terre aux Boeufs area. Despite the fact they were convinced "that it [the area] was more suitable for cattle than for Christians" (Crété 1981:282), they continue to live at Delacroix, Reggio, Yscloskey, and Shell Beach. Lakes, swamps, marshes, and the Gulf of Mexico were part of the Isleños' physical landscape. As a result, they learned the marsh from childhood and knew it intimately.

The Canarios were considered ideal colonists because they were cheap, reliable, readily assimilated, geographically localized, and a readily distinguishable culture group (Parsons 1985). These Isleños maintained a closed society in which they could live free from interference, practice their customs uninterrupted, and make a living using traps, nets, and guns. It was a good life (Nunez 1979). Within these small com-

Hurricanes and Isleños

In St. Bernard Parish, a hurricane in 1915 resulted in the loss of fifty Isleños at Delacroix Island. Storms in 1919 and 1920 also displaced local inhabitants. In 1927 the levee at Caernarvon (also spelled Carnarvon) was blown up to save New Orleans. An unnamed 1947 storm, and Flossy in 1956, damaged severely Shell Beach. Betsy, in 1965 left only six homes standing of the nearly 600 within the community of Delacroix. In 2005, Katrina leveled or severely damaged the communities of Reggio, Yscloskey, Shell Beach, Hopedale, and Delacroix. But life goes on and has since the 1780s.

The Isleño museum in the aftermath of Hurricane Katrina, 2005. (Photo by the author.)

munities, the Canarios were able to retain their native language, Castilian Spanish. For more than two centuries their Spanish has survived in an oral form, despite the fact that it was never formally taught (Claudel 1945). A song structure of these oral traditions is the *metier* or *décima*. These are narrative ballads in the Spanish of Cervantes that run the gamut from tales of the Crusades to a parody of a man who hurt his back picking up a welfare check (Nunez 1979).

The Isleños adopted French material traits, particularly in house types, settlement patterns, recreation, and cuisine. They also learned French, or Cajun, and later English, thus becoming trilingual, as well as bi-cultural (Nunez 1979). Like the Acadians, twentieth-century Isleños were actually forbidden to use their native language in school, so they were forced to adapt. Also, like their French-speaking counterparts, these marshdwellers shared a sense of extended family. Families tended to form businesses jointly. And they normally lived together on the same land even after their children married and started their families. Also, they did not believe in welfare. If someone was in need, community members responded by passing the hat—the *limosna*. The practice of sharing was common to Isleño fishermen, trappers, and farmers. Indeed, the first of the catch went to the needy. As long as they could fish and farm, the Canarios were never destitute and no one in the community went hungry.

High land was scarce. High water, humid sub-tropical summers, and hurricanes brought numerous hardships; consequently, many Canarios left their remote communities. They dissolved into New Orleans' ethnic melting pot or relocated outside the Terre aux Boeufs region in St. Bernard Parish. Those who remained in the marshes became an almost forgotten people, but have preserved a way of life that has persisted for two centuries. When not hindered by the elements, their small farms, like those of the Acadians, provided vegetables for home consumption and for sale in New Orleans. The Isleño migrants also recognized the importance of the region's aquatic landscape provided them with fish, shrimp, crabs, and oysters. Muskrat, nutria, and alligator were also important. The wetlands and the sea profoundly shaped their Canary Island culture, and they managed to thrive as stewards of their immediate domain.

Like Acadians, and the Southern Slavs, the Isleños have maintained their identity, yet they are often regarded as a curiosity (Din 1988; Richard 2003). Even so, similar to their Cajun counterparts, these marshdwellers are talented, generous, and hospitable; they love life and people.

Movement of French, Germans, and Others into the Wetlands: An Introduction

Prestige is earned by purely physical accomplishment. The man who can shoot better than his neighbors, paddle a pirogue faster, run a bigger trap line, tong more oysters, or hold more liquor, is admired for these accomplishments . . . (Kammer 1941:33).

Over time, French/Cajun and German settlers displaced the indigenous Native American population, and these immigrants were later joined by Englishmen, Latin Americans, West Africans, Austrian/Yugoslavian (Southern Slavs), Canary Islanders

Bancker, one of South Louisiana's forgotten communities, was settled by Acadian, Spanish, German, and Danish immigrants, 2006. (Photo by the author.)

(Isleños), Mennonites, Spaniards, and Basques. Other immigrants entered the region from Ireland, Lebanon, Sweden, Switzerland, Philippines, Italy, Portugal, Cuba, Denmark, Norway, Poland, Russia, Greece, China, Vietnam, and Laos. As might be expected, bargaining was done in dozens of languages.

These immigrants initially established small ethnic enclaves throughout the coastal lowlands. Members of these communities became farmers, laborers, oystermen, shrimpers, crabbers, trappers, truck farmers, roustabouts, watermen, and entrepreneurs. The foreign fishing population, however, predominated (Collins and Smith 1893).

Each ethnic group's cultural baggage may have differed somewhat, but over time many of these assemblages became partially or totally assimilated by the Acadians. The Clements, Rommes, Chauffes, Haydels, Toups, and Zerinques are of German descent. The Blancos, Rodriques, and Dominiques are of Spanish ancestry, and so it goes throughout Louisiana's coastal lowlands (Smith and Parenton 1938; Dormon 1983). Today there are Acadians named Stanford, Hanks, Smith, Hoffpauir, Moore, Schexnayder, Webre, Miguez, Perez, Alleman, Young, Hernandez, and Miller (Post 1962; Smith and Parenton 1938).

> **Three Ways to Become a Cajun**
>
> In South Louisiana, a person could become a Cajun in three ways: "the blood, by the ring, and by the back door" (Rushton 1979:10).

Ancestors of the now culturally dominant Acadians consciously disassociated themselves from other groups while seeking out the security of the foreboding South Louisiana landscape. These settlers "were an equalitarian people whose long tradition of universal landholding and rugged frontier individualism had taught them to recognize no social superior" (Brasseaux 1985:36). Their pragmatism and innovativeness made possible life in the marsh and swamp lands, and, by the mid-1800s, Louisiana's coastal plain sustained hundreds of wetland-oriented communities. Accessible only by water, these somewhat secluded settlement sites were connected to their resource areas, markets, and sources of supplies by well-defined routes—the region's natural waterbodies and humanly altered waterways. An unorganized network of wetland-ridge villages comprised a large permanent populace. Boasting resident populations ranging from less than ten to more than 1,000, these rural hamlets of foreign-speaking *petit habitants* were engaged in a wide range of harvesting activities—all part of an annual-use cycle designed to maximize exploitation of the marshland's marketable products, but with an eye to sustainability.

This tough and independent group of coastal dwellers knew the landscape and how to maximize its productivity. They trapped, hunted, logged, fished, and farmed according to the seasons. When the cold months came, they would take their traps and heavy clothing and set out for their winter camps. In the warmer months, they harvested a wide array of aquatic species or did nothing. There was really no need to do anything for the marsh really satisfied their immediate needs, as a chicken neck tied to a string could fill a bucket with crabs in half an hour. Further, catfish bite on almost anything. "Oysters line the banks of many bayous" (Hallowell 1979:5) and are "very fine and in great plenty" (Landreth 1819:82). In addition, "rabbits thrive on the levees, and sometimes the marsh is overrun with ducks and geese" (Hallowell 1979:5).

By 1900, residents of this network of solitary and remote settlement clusters constituted an important part of southern Louisiana's population. The *émigrés* exploited the wetlands, but in most instances, never considered owning the property they utilized. Most of this real estate was regarded as a worthless, uninhabitable wasteland unfit for human habitation, so the question of ownership was moot (Phelps 1854:7). Unless reclaimed, the wetlands were of no monetary value. Early maps repeatedly show large blank stretches of unsurveyed land, as if the cartographers were either disinterested or unwilling to chart these vast near featureless, mosquito-invested, and inhospitable marshlands.

Within this "forgotten" landscape, marshdwellers embraced the Indians' concept of land ownership. An individual did not own land. The "village," like the tribe, controlled an area that was fixed in the locals' minds and used by them to support their hunting, fishing, and trapping activities. From their association with this land, these self-sufficient and independent settlers proved irrefutably that Louisiana's little-know coastal landscape was not useless.

Outsiders' negative perception of the *marais* changed dramatically in the early twentieth century, when muskrat coats—marketed as "marsh rabbit," "moleskin," or "Hudson Bay seal"—became the rage, and Louisiana's trappers began to make up to $4,000 in the seventy-five-day trapping season (Cottman 1939; Frost 1939). "Land grabbers" or "lease hounds" began to purchase or lease large tracts of trapping land. For example, in 1924, John R. Perez leased the trapping rights on nearly 100,000 acres (156 square miles) from the Phillips Land Company for $3,000 a year. This property was subleased to the Delaware-Louisiana Fur Trapping Company and eventually became a continuous issue between the land owners and the local trappers, who considered themselves the stewards of these traditional trapping areas (Jeansonne 1995; Din 1988).

Louisiana's wastelands suddenly had value, and large blocks were sold to land and/or timber barons for twelve-and-a-half cents to twenty-five cents an acre. When this property passed into private hands, the part-time trappers and hunters, who previously had roamed unimpeded over the marshes, were forced off "their" lands, often at gunpoint. The resident trappers reluctantly moved, but the indignation associated with this behavior intensified the trapper's disdain for these outsiders. Since they frequently had to pay a fee to hunt or trap on property they considered theirs, frustrated them further.

Ownership was a confusing issue, since their fathers, grandfathers, and great-grandfathers trapped and fished throughout the marsh, without giving a thought to the property's ownership. Because the marshdweller was "not a man for laws, nor for official dates, nor for artificial regulations not dictated by the more primeval legalities of the marsh itself. When his land is prepared for trapping, he traps . . . *comme ci, comme ça . . . mais sho*, it is simple, no?" (Ramsey 1957:167). This simple code changed when the marsh became important to entrepreneurs. The marshdwellers who appreciated the *marais* character and wanted to make a living from property they considered theirs by ancestral rights were now marginalized, exploited, and unappreciated; yet, they were the first Europeans to recognize the true value of the coastal lowlands. They were the pioneers.

Settlers Carve a Home from Louisiana's Wetlands

'Ah!' cried Mario, 'I do not like this place; it is inhabited.' He pointed to a wretched hut half hidden by the forest. Except two or three little cabins seen in the distance, this was the first habitation that had met our eyes since leaving the Mississippi.

A woman showed herself at the door. She was scarcely dressed at all. Her feet were naked, and her tousled hair escaped from a wretched handkerchief that she had thrown upon her head. Hidden in the bushes and behind the trees half a dozen half-nude children gazed at us, ready to fly at the slightest sound. Suddenly two men with guns came out of the woods, but at the sight of the flatboat stood petrified (Cable 1889:69).

The first French and German yeoman farmers who settled along the Mississippi River in the *Côte des Allemands* (German Coast)—the fourth oldest German settlement in the United States—were recruited by Louisiana's proprietary government, the Company of the Indies, through propagandistic literature extolling the soil's fertility and the abundance of game (Merrill 2003). Local place names like "Des Allemands" and "Kraemer" remind us of the Coast's German roots and heritage. German farmers planted food crops for the local market and for export to New Orleans. Many truck farms still exist there (Nau 1958; Merrill 1990; Stahls 2003). "It was often said that the German farmer with his luxurious vegetables made living more enjoyable for New Orleanians since he offered his wares by peddling from house to house or occupying a stall at the French market . . ." (Nau 1958:59). Although the German culture mixed with the French, the German part of the state can still be identified by surnames. Voltz became Folse. Himmel became Hymel. Huber became Oubre. Zweig was translated as La Branche. Vicknare and Schexnayder are also German in origin (Kolb 2004).

The Acadian Coast lay along the Mississippi immediately north of the German community. This strip of riparian land was opened to settlement shortly after Louisiana was partitioned by the Treaty of Paris (1763), by means of which Great Britain and Spain received respectively the eastern and western halves of the once vast former French colonial frontier. Destitute Acadian exiles were the initial settlers. Since the Mississippi River constituted the international border between the British and Spanish empires, Louisiana Gov. Antonio de Ulloa required these newly arrived Acadian exiles—expelled from their British-controlled Nova Scotia homeland during the *Grand Dérangement* (1755)—to settle at strategic points along the western riverbank to serve as the first line of defense against potential English encroachment (Brasseaux 1991). Although inter-colonial trade was prohibited, English settlers had iron tools and other goods, like powder and shot needed by the immigrants and the Acadians had pork, beef, horses, and mules needed by the English. As a result, both groups entered into—and benefitted from—an active, but illegal, trade across the Mississippi.

Bellin's map of Louisiana and adjacent territories showing French control of the Mississippi Valley, 1757.

By the 1880s, the moss industry was an important source of income throughout the South. (Image from *Harper's Weekly,* September 1882.)

The palmetto-roofed *habitant* home with external chimney and cistern, 1934. (Photo courtesy of Randolph A. Bazet Collection, Archives & Special Collections, Nicholls State University.)

The German and Acadian Coasts constituted an essential colonial-era agrarian beachhead. In fact, once the swamps were surveyed, French-speaking refugees began to establish permanent communities along the ribbons of dry land within these forested wetlands. The *habitants,* who frequently sold their "frontlands," moved beyond to ridges within the swamps. In this harsh and inhospitable environment, they burned off the vegetation and started new farms on marginal lands that could be purchased at a reasonable price, but, if the property was not for sale, the migrants became "squatters" (Comeaux 1972).

On these swamp ridges or *brulés*, pockets of Isleños and Acadians lived at near the subsistence level on small cultivated plots and supplemented their income by fishing, trapping, and collecting Spanish moss, which was regularly referred to as *Spanish beard*. In the Bayou Lafourche region, the most notable of these communities were at McCall, Capit, Maurin, Longvue, Sacramento, Pierre Part, Grand Bayou, St. Vincent, Big and Little Texas, and L'Abadie. The *brulés*, and others, would have been quite valuable and productive if they did not suffer from Mississippi River floods. Floods and their associated crevasses in 1874, 1878, 1882, 1890, 1892, 1893 and 1909 inundated the *brulés,* often for months at a time, forcing many people to live in palmetto-thatched huts in the Indian fashion (Din 1988; Edwards 1988).

Travel into many of these *brulé* encampments was usually accomplished by boat, frequently pulled by mules walking along bayou banks. Other than the trail along the waterways, roads did not exist, and, as a result, a great deal of their original material culture survived unblemished. Like the Isleños, the *brulé-,* swamp-, and marsh-dwellers managed to preserve their native languages in these remote, out-of-the-way places. Although they had to learn English, largely through contact with outsiders, "French-speaking parents often gave their children English first names and French middle names, thus retaining a certain ethnic connection but hiding it under a protective layer" (Ancelet 1999:1).

Throughout this diverse ethnic island, education was not important, since the Acadians lived in "an area blessed with great natural abundance, they found no need for educational tools to survive" (Brasseaux 1978:213). Therefore, before World War II, the swamp- and marshdwellers were overwhelmingly illiterate but hardly ignorant. French was the preferred language and resulted in a population that appeared uninformed to outsiders, but in reality they were like the American Indians and knew well the ways of the land. They just communicated this knowledge through a foreign language that in the twenty-first century is favored by older residents. This is, after all, their first language. The one they are most comfortable using.

Until the late 1970s, monolingual French-speakers utilized the Cajun *patois* exclusively for communication (Post 1962). Cajuns who came of age after the early 1920s were almost universally bilingual because in 1921 Louisiana school children were forbidden to speak anything but English, with predictable results. For example, "Randy Stelly still smarts from the times his knuckles were rapped by an angry teacher. . . . 'They hit ma hands good, them teachers, but I didn't know English good enough then. French was the only way I could of talked. But even now, I feel kind of, ya know, funny, speakin' French sometimes. It's like I was doin' something' wrong'" (Hallowell 1979:75).

While children were being punished for using their native language, businessmen learned to speak French, which was essential to conduct business successfully with the French-speaking swamp- and marshdwellers. English eventually became the dominant language, but many people remain bilingual. The first generation of bilingual Cajuns who used French at home and English in public venues learned English not only at school, but also through the popular media. On lower Bayou Lafourche, movies were shown on the lower deck of the *Mayflower*, which was eventually replaced by the Star and Buccaneer theaters (Cheniere Hurricane Centennal 1995). With a few exceptions, westerns staring Hoot Gibson, Gene Autry, Roy Rogers, and Tex Ritter were the features shown on Fridays, Saturdays, and Sundays. Double features were described as "cowboy and another cowboy" movies (Pitre 1993:56). These movies allowed people to gain a better working knowledge of English and its subtle nuances.

Unfortunately, Cajun French may not survive another generation. In the mid-twentieth century, bilingual parents frequently did not teach their children French, for they felt English was more important. Often the English currently used by many south Louisianians is merely a literal translation from the French, with English words substituted for the original French construction. Hence, "What time is it?" becomes "What time it is?"

Yet the Americanization process of the past century fortunately has not eroded the marshdweller's appreciation for the local environment. Since the *habitants* were small landowners, they enjoyed the isolation provided by South Louisiana's physical geography. The solitude of the wetlands was an ideal setting to start a new life. Unfortunately, many consider the wetlands only for their intrinsic and aesthetic qualities. The Acadians, and others, recognized the area for its resources and ecological value and were willing to make their living from these resources. Moreover, these newcomers believed Louisiana's semi-aquatic real estate was an attractive location for their settlements. They recognized the area's ecological value and were united by a "trilogy of values: God, family, and the land" (Brasseaux

A marshdweller's work kept him out of doors, and his skin reflected this aspect of his life. (Photo from *Louisiana Conservationist*, vol. 8, 1956-1957.)

Fornet Millet's Landing and Shrimp-Drying Platform, Bayou Rigaud. (Photo from *Jefferson Parish Yearly Review,* 1939.)

1978:213).

They embraced this environment, as it met all of their needs. Therefore, by the 1880s, several thousand people and a fleet of rough-hewn folk boats were engaged in a range of seasonal harvesting endeavors throughout the marshes and swamps (Knipmeyer 1956; Comeaux 1972). By the mid-1920s, many swamp- and marshdwellers had left their secluded encampments for natural levee communities. These folks would leave the dock each morning and return each evening to their linear villages, where hand-turned drawbridges were lifted time and time again for them to pass. Prior to World War II, from nodal points across the coastal zone a fleet of boats annually harvested millions of dollars worth of shrimp, oysters, speckled trout, redfish, sheepshead, and pompano. Shrimp,], and fish wholesalers were kept busy processing the catch. Consequently, these "fish houses" became important social centers that served as meeting places where local residents, fishermen, and factory employees came to talk, socialize, and play *bourré*. The "fish house" became the heart of the community, whether at Delcambre, Cameron, Morgan City, Houma, Golden Meadow, Grand Isle, or Empire.

Many of the wetlands serviced by these communities had polyglot populations. Besides the well-documented French Acadians and the Isleños, Austrian oystermen (made up of Yugoslavians, Dalmatians, Slovenians, and Croatians) colonized the bayous, bays, and lakes southeast of New Orleans (Moore 1899). Chinese and Filipino immigrants built shrimp-drying operations in the estuaries (Pillsbury 1964; Adkins 1973; Din 1988; Espina 1988; People long ago 2007). British, French, and American newcomers colonized the lowlands as well.

These newcomers learned to coexist, which allowed them to share their collective knowledge, experiences, culture, and folkways within the context of the marshlands. Thousands of watermen were scattered throughout the marsh-estuary complex. In the Barataria basin alone, there were at least 3,000 individuals whose livelihood evolved around the estuary's renewable resource base. Sprinkled throughout these aquatic lowlands were small enclaves—two homes on one ridge, three anchored to an Indian midden, four on an exposed shell reef, perhaps 100 or more on a shrimp-drying platform or *chênière*, along with a houseboat or two moored along a bayou. Individually, these dispersed sites were inconsequential, but collectively they represented a sizeable population that epitomized the coastal lowlands human mosaic.

For example, on Bayou St. Denis, there was an old settlement called St. Joseph that had three houses in 1917. Two miles further south was an unnamed community of four homes, identified as "resorts of fisherman and duck-hunters" (Harris 1881:165). At the mouth of Bayou Perot, near Little Lake, was a small village that included a store, while a few miles south was Clarksville, or Clark's Chenier, with a population estimated at from fifty to 100 people. There also were a number of small population centers along a number of bayous in the vicinity of Clark's Chenier.

Like small villages, shrimp platforms became transient settlement sites, ca. 1930. (Photo courtesy of the Louisiana Wildlife and Fisheries.)

In all of these communities, fishing, trapping, and hunting were the primary occupations (Barataria Bay 1917). Marketable aquatic and avian game was readily available. As a result, in the late 1800s, one hunter could market more than 1,000 alligator hides (Arthur 1931; O'Neil 1949). In addition, tons of catfish were shipped to the Midwest to be sold as tenderloin of trout. Large turtle pens enclosed herds of diamond-back terrapin being raised by the thousands for the restaurant trade (Sterns 1887; Cole 1892; Housley 1913). To add to their income base, the marshdweller hunted

A successful early twentieth-century hunting outing. (Photo from Hanks 1988.)

gulls, terns, and white egrets, frequently being paid as much as "$20 in gold per ounce for the wings of a white heron" (Louisiana has greatest 1905:15). In addition, millions of eggs, shells—as many as 100,000 in one season—and plumes were harvested for use by restaurants, glue manufacturers, photographic film makers, and in the millinery trade in New York and Paris. In winter, market hunters regularly shipped more than 1,000 brace of ducks a week to New Orleans's markets (Louisiana has greatest 1905; Barry 1979). Oysters and shrimp were harvested by the boatload. Furthermore, in the 1920s, after the misconception that quality furs came only from cold climates was disproven, Louisiana's marshes became North America's preeminent fur producing region (Davis 1978).

Louisiana's watermen navigated their shallow, sail-powered luggers through a labyrinth of waterways to exploit aquatic wildlife. In the late 1800s, a rather large fleet of luggers and other sailing craft employed in various trading activities. Locally, these sailing vessels were called *canots* (also known as a lugger) and

Without ice and power, shrimping was difficult, demanding great effort from hauling in the seines and sailing to a shrimp-drying platform. (Photo from *Report of the Conservation Commission of Louisiana from April 1, 1914 to April 1, 1916.*)

were often fitted with a cabin and deck. Steered with a rudder controlled by Malay, Chinese, Yugoslavian, Italian, Portuguese, or French fishermen, a *canot* moved easily through Louisiana's shallow lakes, bays, and bayous and could be operated easily by one or two watermen. These folk boats would be loaded to the gunwales with big, bell-shaped woven baskets, covered with Spanish moss, and filled with the day's harvest of shrimp, oysters, fish, or crabs, that were lashed to the deck with ribbons of "*latania*" (Cole 1892).

These fishermen frequently off-loaded their catch at one of the area's well organized shrimp-drying villages that dotted South Louisiana's landscape until the Hurricane of 1893 obliterated most of them (Sampsell 1893). Regardless of the destination, "the fishermen's relationship with his boat is not . . . unlike that of the cowboy with his horse. The shrimper has the privilege of naming his boat, the responsibility of feeding it and caring for it, and the joy of riding it across the plains of water on one adventure after another. His boat gives him temporary freedom from the rigors of life onshore and incredible independence" (Kelly and Kelly 1993:40).

Fresh shrimp waiting to be processed, 2007. (Photo by Carl A. Brasseaux.)

With their boats in constant use and their life dictated by the seasons, marshwellers kept the wetlands teaming with activity. Because the harvest was generally bountiful, moving the catch to New Orleans was arduous. When these men of the coast were in transit, they were not fishing, hunting, or trapping. Because they could not work when they had to transport their harvest, they did not make any money. To rectify this dilemma, canneries were built at isolated sites to package quickly various seafood products.

These sites usually consisted of a single cannery—which practically ceased to function during the off season—a store, and often a ramshackle cluster of workers' quarters or barracks that were crammed with cannery workers and their families. Crowding was the rule in rooms as small as ten feet by five-feet-eight inches that were outfitted with an iron bed or wooden bunks, wood-burning stove, oil lamps, rough table, and wooden benches. Newspapers were sometimes pasted on the walls to keep out the cold. Outside privies were scattered throughout the community; rarely was there a toilet for every family. Instead, facilities were shared (Paradise 1922).

One of these sites was constructed at Canovia along the Mississippi River. This largely forgotten community, was dominated by a "row of two-family shacks behind the cannery, a store, and a school . . . about 10 miles from New Orleans" (Paradise 1922:10). The community's Croatian inhabitants, and those in its sister oyster-harvesting community of Ostrica, "live[d] in constant fear of floods and storms" (Paradise 1922:10). At Ostrica and elsewhere, there was no church, no school, no physician, and no railroad. A mail packet delivered mail once a day and whatever provisions and foodstuffs the community needed from New Orleans.

The hamlet became inaccessible in the 1920s after the Orleans Levee Board cut off all land access to the village during creation of the Bohemia Spillway. Hurricanes Betsy (1965) and Camille (1969) forced the few families still occupying Ostrica to seek a less vulnerable location on the Mississippi's west bank. It was a hamlet, like so many in the coastal zone, which had "no conservation, no sheriff, no laws . . . [; yet, according to one inhabitant,] we never did have no trouble" (Casmier 1991:B-2). As late as 1991, the village boasted several herds of cattle, some horses, and a few goats. Thirty-two people were registered to vote in Ostrica, and twenty-six voted—all had to get to their designated polling site by a parish-run boat (Casmier 1991).

At these canneries workers were paid in metal or wooden coin-like objects called

Two examples of tokens used in South Louisiana, no date.

trade or barter tokens. Merchants started this practice about 1885 and it was adopted by a number of labor-intensive industries. These privately minted "coins" are now eagerly sought by collectors in a branch of numismatics called exonumia (Louisiana trade tokens 2007). The original value of these cannery tokens was based on a picker's abilities. The tokens varied from a "quarter cup" to a "half cup." Use of these "shrimp tokens" (also known as "shrimp nickels") became an accepted practice at the factory's commissary and in some cases within the local town (Fountain 1985; Louisiana seafood industry 2007). Denominations varied, but the most common was the "good for 5¢ in trade." Others were valued at: 2½¢, 6¼¢, 10¢, 12½¢, 25¢, 50¢, and $1.00. This payment method was common in the shrimp and oyster industry, but the tokens are difficult to come by and often command a premium price.

Tokens and script were also used on many of the state's lumber, cotton, and sugar businesses (Louisiana lumber mill 2007; Louisiana cotton 2007). The purpose of this quasi-currency was to allow employers to recover as much of an employee's wages as possible, a practice that was declared eventually illegal and terminated. In the lumber industry many mills also paid laborers daily in tokens and, in some cases, would only pay cash if the employee accepted a discount of between 5 and 20 percent (Louisiana lumber mill 2007). Where used as a form of local currency, this private tender/script was also declared illegal and stopped. By this time, "prohibition was in full bloom and more capital began to show up in South Louisiana" (Blum n.d.:7) and the need for privately minted tokens was no longer necessary. Rum-running paid well—and always in cash—so many marshdwellers developed another source of income and a new avocation.

Prior to prohibition and the associated wealth, shrimp nickels were the rule. Working in a cannery was hard work with a picker's income based on a ten-pound bucket of peeled shrimp, worth ten cents, a good picker could make twenty cents per hour. This labor-intensive piece work paid between $5 and $7.50 a week (Paradise 1922).

Since the shrimp fleet did not follow a definite schedule, cannery hours were irregular. When a boat arrived, a factory whistle summoned the pickers—mostly women and children—who rapidly beheaded and peeled the catch. Peeling and canning the load could take a few hours or all day. Frequently the employees worked from before daylight to after dark. Regardless of the hours, standing over a pile of shrimp and the repetitive motion involved in the processing of the raw product was hard work, as an acid in the shrimp heads made the "flesh raw and sore" (Paradise 1922:6). After two or three days' work, pickers had to take a day off to allow their hands a chance to heal. In some cases, a shrimp "thorn" could result in a serious infection. Most cannery workers were accustomed to "cuts, burns, infections, soreness, . . . rawness, . . . and occasionally serious

Well into the twentieth century packing shrimp was a labor intensive job, no date. (Photo courtesy of the Morgan City Archives.)

accidents" (Paradise 1922:6). Working in a shrimp cannery gave women and children a chance to add to the family income, and the nation enjoyed a product that became a key ingredient in such dishes as shrimp alfredo, coconut shrimp, shrimp salad, shrimp cocktail, and other delectable dishes for those not allergic to the product's iodine.

First You Make a Roux: At Breakfast You Are Planning Dinner

Even with the wide array of natural resources available to the wetland inhabitants, the driving force behind their harvesting activity was their willingness to utilize local estuarine-dependent wildlife. Nothing in their culture precluded collecting these edible foodstuffs. Because of their desire to use all available game, South Louisiana's marshdweller's devised a cooking style incorporating waterfowl, rabbit, deer, crawfish (also known locally as mudbugs), turtle, shrimp, oysters, crab, and a vast assortment of fish species, along with beans, rice, potatoes, spaghetti, grits, and salt pork. Using a well-cared-for cast iron pot or skillet, often handed down from one generation to the next, local cooks prepared gumbo, *gratons*, *pain perdu*, *courtbouillon*, *bisque d'écrevisses*, *jambalaya* (named for the French *provençal* version of *paella* called *jambalaia* from *jambon*, French for ham), *bouillabaisse*, *couche-couche*, *maque choux*, *sauce piquant*, *boudin*, *andouille*, *fricassée*, *étoufée*, white beans (*faillot*), and hog's head cheese, which all became part of the local diet. The best local cooks have in their repertoires dozens of these dishes that local family-own restaurants serve as plate lunches. In addition, seeds and nuts were used to add protein, enhance flavors, and thicken soups and stews.

In this culinary tradition, spices are critical. Onions, garlic, bay leaf, celery, red and green bell peppers, black and cayenne pepper, parsley, thyme, shallots, basil, cloves, and allspice were used in different combinations to enhance flavors. In many dishes pig fat was essential, simply because Acadian cooks preferred the taste of pork (Brasseaux 1987; Bultman 2004). The process began with a *boucherie*, the slaughter of a hog and the preparation of the meat for human consumption. For example, *boudin* or blood sausage—a favorite food throughout French-speaking Louisiana—is a spicy mixture of rice, pork, liver, and seasoning locked in a sausage casing. Basically everyone in South Louisiana "ate every bit of a hog but the oink" (Bultman 2004:88). In the late 1800s, marshdwellers kept a large number of "free ranging" hogs to guarantee they had the pork they enjoyed. There was no feed bill since grasses, roots, acorns, and nuts were readily available. Many of these animals escaped and are now part of the wetlands' feral or wild hog population.

It is the seasoning that makes South Louisiana's food distinctive—just the right combination of bacon fat, not burnt fish or dishes cooked in too much pepper. The various seasonings (especially celery, bell pepper, onion, garlic, and herbs) are mixed into a *roux*, the basis of many dishes, which is made by browning flour carefully in clarified butter (used primarily after World War II) or lard. With patience and simmering, the ingredients blend and thicken into the sauces required in many recipes. Habitually, three starches were part of the marshdwellers dinner meal: rice, bread, and potato salad. Rice, in fact, is used by south Louisianians as potatoes are used elsewhere. When it comes to eating, improvisation is the rule (Reeves 2007). In addition to idiosyncratic cooking styles, distinct folk ways also emerged, from palmetto houses to Creole cottages, to boat types, to a musical style, such as Zydeco, to a *joie de vivre* and other material and non-material culture elements that endows the region with an irrefutable flare and a passion for life. Even though the land provided most of the marshdwellers' needs, some items had to be purchased from local merchants.

Jambalaya, Pilar, Payloo, and Paella

"It was jambalaya—call it pilaf, payloo, *paella* or anything you want—but its main ingredients are rice and red peppers. Into this rice has been mixed shrimps, oysters, clams, crayfish, pork sausage, great white slabs of fish, chicken for the stock, and the whole business cooked together until it was one great big wonderful adventure. Pierre had cooked the rice with saffron, so that it came out yellow; and the juices from the seafood and the chicken had got married in the tremendous soupy ceremony so that the rice, while dry by grain, was damp by volume, and the hunks of fish and the shellfish hadn't lost any of their flavor but were nuggeted through the rice" (Casada 1996:18).

A Traiteur Replaced a Pharmacist

Since pharmacies were not readily available and doctors and dentists were frequently more than thirty miles away, the local dry goods store carried a large stock of patent medicines and simple remedies, like aspirin, Epsom salts, castor oil, liniment, iodine, mercurochrome, bandages, and adhesive tape. For more serious problems, the marshdweller consulted a *traiteur* or *remède*-maker—a practioner of Cajun folk medicine. The *traiteur* (or Spanish *curandero*) used only prayer, or sympathetic magic, to affect a cure, while the *remède*-maker used medicinal herbs, roots, and whatever to concoct solid and liquid remedies to cure the illness (Kammer 1941; Rickels 1978; Dormon 1983; Rabalais 1985). While in Hawaii the *lomilomi* used message therapy, the South Louisiana healers—predecessors of modern ethno-botanists—followed Indian healing practices and homeopathic medicine. These practitioners of folk medicine do not necessarily know how they obtained the "gift," but claim they have never failed to cure those whom they have treated. They make no attempt to treat a broken bone. They treat primarily: "sprained or sore backs, flowing of blood, snakebite, skin diseases, worms in children, liver trouble, toothache, and sunstroke" (Kammer 1941:141).

Common remedies included:

> the use of cocklebur leaves mixed with vinegar to help cure several ailments; swamp root was rubbed on the gums of babies while they were teething; dirt dobbers nests were crushed and dried into a powder and applied to a baby's navel when it refused to heal; cobwebs, placed on a fresh cut stopped the bleeding; alligator tongue oil was considered a good remedy for coughs and the croup; buttonwood flowers made into a tea was used in the treatment of chills and fever; asafetida bags hung about the neck were guaranteed to keep almost everything away; and elderberry was used in treating kidney ailments . . . (Case 1973:104-105).

In addition, turpentine was considered the universal antiseptic, and honey was used to treat hay fever (Pitre 1993).

World War II Disrupted the Region's Tranquility

> Over time, the coastal plain's population expanded, and the area began to acquire a wide range of ancillary services and structures that characterize modern society. Radio, telephone and power lines, associated communication facilities, sewage systems, good roads, potable water supplies, expanding urbanization, schools, churches, cemeteries, shopping centers, [bank loans, mortgages], and numerous other "modern" conveniences began to dominate this traditional rural landscape; country living could be compared favorably to life in the suburbs. On the natural levee ridges and *chênières*, baseball became an important sport, where balls and strikes were called in French and umpire abuse was enlivened by a French accent (Kammer 1941).

Consequently, "Louisiana has seen more change since the beginning of World War II than ever before in history" (Din 1988:194).

After World War II, the GI Bill allowed returning veterans, who were young and poorly educated, but aware there was an entirely different world beyond their sea level homes, to complete high school by taking their General Education Development (GED) exam. Also, they could go to trade schools to learn mechanics, air conditioning maintenance and repair, and other skills. With the experience of the War and completion of class/courses funded through the GI Bill came the realization that there was more to life than working in the marshes. While deployed in North Africa and Europe, these coastal Acadians returned home to families that "were now fervently American" (Falgoux 2007:18). They took from the war a new nationalism. Throughout the wetlands, the flag of choice was no longer French tri-color, but "Old Glory" (Falgoux 2007).

During the post-World War II period, the marsh was generally forgotten as a place where people lived and worked; yet its ethnic roots are deeper and more profound than in most regions of the country. Only trappers, watermen, and others, who chose to live in the region, appreciated its poignant qualities. The marsh was in their blood, and they liked just being there, and, in the mid-twentieth century, it was a good place to make a living. Prior to World War II, oystermen made about $90 a month. After the war, their incomes typically ranged from $225 to $300 a month (McConnell 1946). These earnings were not insignificant when compared to the country's median income. The $300 figure beat the average by $600 a year, as the census reported median family revenue in 1947 was $3,000.

With advent of good roads and automobiles, many former swamp and marsh residents continue to live near the swamps and marshes. Though they have become well-trained pipefitters, welders, and carpenters—earning their living outside the swamps and marshes—they continue to live as close to the swamp or marsh as possible. In many cases these environments exist just beyond their back doors. In this way, they are guaranteed the opportunity to hunt and fish effortlessly in these habitats. For many, their recreational venue is as close as next door—in their mind an ideal situation. The region's isolation provided comfort, quiet, solitude, and gave the early marshdwellers peace-of-mind. It was, and is, a perfect place from the marshdweller's perspective.

In a sense, the region's population is composed of "maritime man," "coastal man," and "inland man." The folks within the maritime category are dependent upon the open sea for their livelihood. They use natural levees for their ports and home sites, and their property is typically framed by docks and wharfs to which fishing and oil logistic support vessels are usually docked side-by-side. Coastal dwellers make their living from the near-shore zone. They harvest the resources of the wetlands—crabs, oysters, muskrats, nutrias, alligators, and shrimp. And finally, inland man does not depend upon the coastal zone for his livelihood; he is a "landlubber." Such landlubbers seek the Gulf for their leisure-time pursuits.

World War II and Patriotism

"Besides all the tension, the war [World War II] did generate a surge of nationalism on the bayou. The south Lafourche Cadiens, some of whom flew the French flag as late as the turn of the century, were now fervently American. Throughout the war, the Lafourche country was awash with American flags, red, white and blue signs and boat awnings. Up and down the bayou, 'victory gardens' grew in V-shaped rows" (Falgoux 2007:18).

House Types of the Coastal Dweller: An Element of Material Culture

The combination of all these [building] elements produced a building type of delicate beauty and an air or rightness from both a visual and an intellectual point of view (Labouisse 1985:190).

Wetlands settlers needed a dwelling that could be built without benefit of plans or architects. They initially utilized concepts and techniques embraced by their forefathers, while incorporating locally available building materials—hence the importance of termite-resistant cypress in all of the material goods produced by these ethnic groups. Kniffen (1936) and others (Newton 1971; Newton 1985) identify these structures as "folk housing." During the last half of the twentieth century, many occupants of local indigenous buildings abandoned their hand-made homes for more modern ones that incorporated manufactured components. Even so, the old and new can still be found standing side-by-side.

Within the coastal lowlands, and on the associated natural levees, virtually every structure falls into four generic categories: side-facing gables; gables facing the front; pyramidal roofs; and shed roofs. All are part of the folk landscape and keys to cultural diffusion (Kniffen 1965). These generic categories were further refined by Kniffen (1936) into nine groups of morphologically similar types: built-in porch; attached porch, porch-less, open passage, Midwestern, shotgun, bungalow, trapper, and oysterman. In South Louisiana, five house types are significant: Acadian or Cajun, Creole, Creole raised cottage, shotgun, and bungalow (Kniffen 1936, Newton 1985; Labouisse 1985). These buildings are conspicuous features on the landscape and "are an element of culture possessing great diagnostic value in regional differentiation" (Kniffen 1936:179). As cultural identifiers, houses survive as substantial landscape elements. Moreover, as cultural artifacts these structures are significant historic, social, and economic relics.

Houses are part of the "human universe" and cultural landscape that varies depending on personal tastes, economic status, and available materials. Regardless of the location, these structures share many common characteristics pioneered by the folk builder's basic form (Newton 1971). The folk house had no name, as it was built according to the traditions of the builder's family. In simple terms, the house was constructed in a particular manner because that was the way my "daddy built it."

A palmetto covered trapper's cabin about 100 years ago. (Photo courtesy of Swanton Collection, Smithsonian Institution, negative book IV, negative no. 244.)

Many of the earliest immigrant homes copied those of aboriginal Americans, who plastered their huts with clay (smectite, illitite, kaolinite, and chlorite) kneaded with Spanish moss and covered with cypress bark or a thick thatch of palmetto fronds which, according to one eyewitness, kept "out the rain very well" (Landreth 1819:108). Though effective, these temporary structures were replaced eventually with more permanent dwellings made of milled lumber.

Throughout the lowlands, sawed lumber was always used as a building material because the settlers never built log houses. Even when swamp timber was available, folk houses were invariably made of sawed or hand-hewn lumber, mortised and pegged, roofed with straw, grass, or wooden shingles, and floored with earth or roughhewn boards (Post 1962). The house consisted of an above-ground first floor, a cypress roof, and a "proper" layout (Pulliam and Newton 1973; Heck 1978; Ditto 1980). The walls were packed four-inches thick between a lattice of *barreaux* (bars) or bricks with *bousillage*—a mud, green moss, and water mixture—that dried to a concrete hardness and formed well-insulated walls. Once dried, the exterior was covered with thin plaster and frequently overlaid with horizontal cypress boards. Under the porch, these boards were always painted white (Hansen 1971).

The *bousillage* technique existed in Normandy, but was probably borrowed from the Indians. This construction method is also known as nogging. Some folk houses were constructed of half-timber (*colombage*) framing with either *briquette entre poteaux* (bricks between the beams) or *bousillage entre poteaux* (between wall posts) that were utilized as weatherboarding for the house and the chimney. These folk houses originally had earthen floors; as a result, the human occupants waged a continual war with dirt, bugs, snakes, and other critters. In the structure's evolution, the raised pillar construction came much later (Newton 1985; Edwards 1988).

Cypress was particularly important for it was difficult to burn and insect resistant, but it did not become a key building material until the great age of logging. Beginning about 1880 to1930, Northern interests began harvesting cypress, which was with for shingles, studs, siding, as well as in boats and barges. All of this lumber was cut using hand tools. In some cases, men went from place to place cutting timber and making the required planks needed by the local builder.

Principal Coastal Lowlands House Types

The first few settlers who built close to the ground and then watched the water rise over their floors learned the value of cypress stumps to elevate them . . . For the roof, the Deltan cut cypress shingles or used the not less serviceable palmetto leaves. When he wanted a chimney, he mixed river mud and Spanish moss and fashioned a tight and roaring fireplace (Kane 1944:81).

Creole

The colonial architecture style of the Creole house/cottage consisted of the side-by-side and back-to-back room arrangement with a central fireplace. High ceilings were the norm and windows and doors were arranged to maximize cross ventilation to help cool the home during the summer. This floor plan was asymmetrical, with no hallway, and was replicated as the family expanded. The structure was raised on cypress or handmade brick piers from twenty-four to thirty-six inches off the ground. Initially, these dwellings were constructed from hand-hewn heavy timber, using mortised and pegged joints. In the nineteenth century, rough-sawed timber was added to the list of building materials. Local craftsmen would number each pre-cut piece with roman numerals. This system guided the home's construction. The roof was covered with hand-split shingles. The front porch was included under the gable, and ran the full length of the front, with the walls under the porch being whitewashed, rather than weather-boarded. Protected by the overhang, the porch did not need to be covered by hand-hewn siding, and for ten months of the year it served as the main reception center for all social activities (Parenton 1938; Heck 1978; Kniffen 1978B; Edwards 1988).

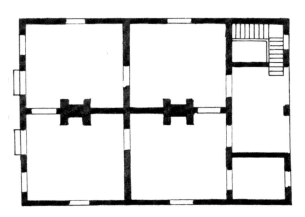

The simple Louisiana Creole home. (Image courtesy of the Fred Daspit Collection, Center for Louisiana Studies, University of Louisiana at Lafayette.)

Acadian

Some house-type scholars refer to the Acadian as the "smaller Creole house." The Acadian house was the typical dwelling of the small farmer. This structure's simple lines were characterized by one room under a continuous-pitched, sideward-facing gabled roof that resembled an inverted "V." The steep roof shed water well and made a spacious attic that could house a loom and spinning wheel—used to make cloth from flax or "brown" cotton. The upstairs space also provided a sleeping room for the boys, called in French the *garçonnière* (bachelors' quarters). A girl's bedroom, tucked behind the parents' bedroom, lacked access to the outside. This house type has a full gallery with a chimney built into the end wall. It is sometimes two rooms wide with a center chimney as well (Kniffen 1936; Newton 1985; Edwards 1988). This simple building is still part of South Louisiana's rural landscape. Many historic homes that do not have *bousillage* walls still have white fronts, as this is the regional custom (Post 1962; Sand and Koch 1975; Heck 1978). When a new owner moved into one of these homes, the front was nearly always repainted. The reason is unclear, but painting was simply the right thing to do. Glass windows were incorporated in a few of these Acadian-style homes, but most had wooden-batten-shutters called *contrevents*. Also, a small barn, *pieux*

Acadian house with cistern, 1968. (Photo by the author.)

fence, tin roof, and cypress cistern are additional diagnostic elements associated with this farm dwelling (Kniffen 1978B).

The larger Acadian or Cajun house was constructed by more prosperous people. It is characterized by a continuous pitched, sideward-facing gabled roof, with a full gallery. It may have two main rooms with one common chimney and a T-addition of three smaller rooms. Some versions have four basic rooms with a full center hall, gabled-end roof, built-in chimney, and the T-addition. On either side of the T-addition was a porch that guaranteed that one was always in the shade. The porch or *galerie* was open, deep, and wide. It ran the entire width of the house, and when screens and awnings were added, the occupant had a refuge from Louisiana's tropical heat. The porch was the home's social center, big enough to accommodate the large numbers of cousins, *tantes* (aunts), *noncs* (uncles), *parrains* (godfathers), and *nainaines* (godmothers) who gathered there constantly (Kniffen 1936; Ramsey 1957; Newton 1985). There were *passer la journée* visits in the morning, and *passer l'après-midi* visits in the afternoon, and *causeries*, or evening visits as well.

For the Acadians, family is the bulwark of their culture—"where no one is left out and where institutions like mental hospitals and old-folk homes were never developed to allow one class of people to throw another class out" (Rushton 1979:15). Among earlier generations, the entire family had to call on the "old folks"—*papa* and *maman*—at least once a week. Once a month everyone must get together (Ramsey 1957). It was not uncommon for three, or sometimes four, generations to live in close proximity or on the same piece of family land—a clear example of forced-heirship.

Raised Cottage

Similar to the Creole house, the raised cottage had a hipped roof and a brick ground floor that was elevated on cypress piers up to two to three feet off the ground. The framing was of heavy hand-hewn cypress timbers mortised and pegged together (Heck 1978). The West Indian Creoles, accustomed to heat and humidity, learned to build houses well suited to tropical environments. Their Louisiana homes were often raised a full story (Edwards 1988). In both examples there are usually a large number of front openings, full-length "French" doors and windows. The house evolved into a form with a sideward-facing gabled roof, a central hall, and light shutters which replaced the heavy board doors over the long windows (Kniffen 1936; Newton 1985).

Shotgun

The shotgun house is one room wide and at least three rooms in length, with a gabled roof facing the front of the house. Most include a small front porch and almost all are built of lumber. Chimneys may be external or internal—on the side of the house or on traverse walls. The shotgun is always raised on piers. This house is common in three contexts: as plantation quarters, as a working-class urban house, and as a fisher-trapper dwelling, often constructed on a barge. The origin is obscure. Some theorize that it has African origins. Others believe it evolved from the Indian palmetto hut or trappers' campboats; still others hypothesize that the structure was adapted to fit narrow rural and/or urban lots, and some theorize the shotgun's architectural beginnings are from Haiti. Regardless, the shotgun home is common throughout South Louisiana's wetland and urban landscape (Kniffen 1936; Newton 1985, Newton 1971; Kniffen, et al. 1987). It is claimed that the term "shotgun" is derived from the fact a person could stand in the front of the home and shoot a gun through the open interior doors and out the back without hitting any walls.

West Indian Creoles often built cottages raised a full story. (Photo by the author.)

The common narrow shotgun is found throughout South Louisiana. (Photo by the author.)

Bungalow

The bungalow is described as a double shotgun. The floor plan is two rooms wide and at least three rooms long, all under a gabled-front roof. Between 1930 and 1950, this was the most common house in Louisiana, after which emerged the "ranch-style" slab home. The bungalow is common in rural and urban landscapes. It was rarely used as plantation quarters, though it was frequently a small independent farmer's residence (Kniffen 1936; Newton 1985).

Regardless of the type of folk house under discussion, most of these old homes still exist and are still occupied. They have been upgraded with indoor plumbing and running water, replacing outhouses and cisterns—early breeding grounds for the yellow-fever-carrying mosquito (Viosca 1925). Metal roofs, nailed over the original

The distinctive South Louisiana bungalow is usually found in urban environments, ca. 2008. (Photo courtesy of James Terry.)

shingles, are common, as well as paint inside and out, along with electricity, air conditioning, and a yard decorated with ornamental plants and perhaps a small swing or some form of yard art, such as a cement and painted Virgin Mary. The homes became modernized, but not necessarily gentrified.

Folk Boats: Part of the Region's Material Culture

Platform they carry Horses or cattle as I am told they either Sail or row very well and Some of them will carry ten or twelve Horses at a time and they are considered safe Boats. These Boats run from Rentropes [*sic*] on the Teche across the Lakes to the Laforch [*sic*] canal about thirty miles the price of Ferriage [*sic*] for a single man four Dollars for a man and Horse twelve dollars (Landreth 1819:70).

Historically, movement through coastal wetlands presented humankind with a special challenge and resulted in development of unique boat types built, like homes, without the aid of a blueprint and mechanical devices, according "to forms handed down over time and learned by each generation of builders through imitation, oral instruction, and practices" (Comeaux 1985:161). These hand-made vessels were built by eye and feel, for no formal measuring was involved. Shared knowledge was the cornerstone of these building traditions, which helped delineate the Bayou Cajuns from their Prairie Cajun cousins (Jordan 1985).

Using an ax, the *pirogue* builder shapes a cypress *pirogue*, no date. (Photo courtesy of the Morgan City Archives.)

Pettyaugre or Pirogue

Arguably the most important boat found in French Louisiana is the *pirogue* (*pettyaugre*)—an aboriginal dugout copied by European settlers and powered by a push-pole to achieve a quick passage through shallow waters (Waldo 1965; Brassieur 1999; Butler 1985). These folk craft would probably be identified as canoes elsewhere in the United States, but the term "canoe" has never been used widely in South Louisiana. They were essential watercraft that brought settlers to part of Louisiana's coastal lowlands that were inaccessible otherwise. Nearly every man, women, and child in the wetlands learned to handle a *pirogue*, as they were utilized constantly.

For the first inhabitants, this shallow-draft vessel became an indispensable tool. *Pettyaugres* were the earliest craft to ply the waters of South Louisiana with any regularity. Made from a single tree, they were capable of carrying a large number of men and cargo. The modern counterpart is the hand-made, wooden *pirogue* made of marine plywood or cypress planks. It draws so little water, it is said to "float on a heavy dew." In reality, in the hands of skilled watermen, the watercraft could be pushed over solid mud, if the mud had "a bead of moisture on it" (Casada 1996:17).

The hand-crafted, locally-built, cypress *pirogue*—made with a hatchet, hand adz (or adze), drawknife, wooden jack plane, broken glass, wedges, and templates—was ideally suited for the state's meandering wetland waterways and wet grasslands (Waldo 1965). These simple tools are now historical artifacts, but they crafted a vessel that fit perfectly through the trappers' and hunters' hand-chopped narrow paths, or *traînasses*, utilized to harvest marsh resources. Hollowed-out cypress dugouts are no longer built, yet plank-type counterparts are abundant. The small one-to-two man *pettyaugre* continues to serve sportsmen and trappers who "paddle" the wetlands. Fishermen and trapper's bodies typically fill the *pirogue* to the point that they look like a proverbial "bump on a log." This narrow, sleek, shallow-draft, dinghy-like folk boat is the quintessential work vessel. Balance and experience, however, are the keys to the use, of what appears to the novice, as an unstable watercraft (Waldo 1965).

Flat-Bottom Small Boats

Chaland

Another major folk boat is the flat-bottom *chaland* that is perfectly rectangular, with no sheer, and a sharp angular upward slant to the bow and stern. The three-foot-wide and ten- to fourteen-foot-long *chaland* was used to cross a bayou. It was essentially a ferry. Always operated by hand and never used for going even a short distance, *chalands* transported goods and people from one side of a bayou to another. They are not the product of some form of chronological development, but evolved based on their functionality, like barges used for downstream transport, as a village utility vessel, as a houseboat foundation, and much more (Comeaux 1985; Brassieur 1999).

A variation is sometimes called a "plank boat." Occasionally used for logging and is distinguished by a narrow hull (Knipmeyer 1956). A special oar-driven *chaland*—called a punt or scow by English-speakers—was used for moss gathering (Knipmeyer 1956).

The French example of a *chaland* used to harvest bivalves, 1911. (Photo from the author's collection.)

Esquif

"Of all the folk boats in French Louisiana, none is more carefully distinguished than the *esquif* or 'skiff'" (Knipmeyer 1956:165)—a term used by boatmen throughout North America. European colonists introduced this craft into South Louisiana. The "Creole skiff" in particular is an "ancient form historically descended from boat-building traditions in southern France" (Brassieur 1999:2). Some *esquif* forms came

Using a skiff to tong oysters in Sister Lake, 1954. (Photo courtesy of Louisiana Wildlife and Fisheries Commission.)

from other regions as well; as a result, there are many regional skiff types found throughout Louisiana. However, in the wetlands, a skiff is flat bottomed with a squared transom, pointed bow, and blunt stern—an ancient design called by most people a rowboat (a term not used in French Louisiana).

Skiffs, propelled by sails and oars and identified as *chaloupe* and *galère* were utilized to carry goods (Knipmeyer 1956; Comeaux 1978B; Pearson, et al. 1989). They became more popular as *pirogue* use declined, and virtually every bayou dwelling had a skiff tied up in front of their home. With two oars placed amidships, the *esquif* became the typical wetland family's all-purpose mode of travel. One man or two children could handle it with ease.

A variation of this vessel is the English sloop, Dutch *sloep*, and German *sluppe* which are all phonetic adoptions of their French equivalent the *chaloupe* (Migchelsen n.d.). Between November and March, oystermen used their skiffs to "tong" or harvest Louisiana's oyster beds. In point of fact, during the oyster season, nearly any vessel big enough to hold a few barrels of oysters became a tonging boat. In some cases, a line of tonging skiffs was towed to the reefs, and the oystermen filled each individual skiff, "until the gunwales are awash" (Prindiville 1955:4). The *esquifs* were regularly overloaded, so any shift in the load would result in the boat capsizing.

The skiff continues to be an important folk boat, and it can be found throughout Louisiana. Poachers have used the skiff to maximize their net-based illegal fishery harvests. In one case, such "outlaws" were caught carrying more than 800 pounds of illicit fish in a car so loaded that the "rear bumper was hanging down about two inches from the pavement" and "they were laying a trail of fish slime all the way to Memphis cause in those days freezers was expensive and they shipped fresh" (Reisner 1991:175).

A contemporary example of a Louisiana *bateau*, no date. (Photo courtesy of the Morgan City Archives.)

The Swampdwellers Standing Skiffs

A variation of the *esquif* is the "standing skiff" which was operated in a standing position using a rowing device called a *joug*. A *joug* elevated the oars and "extended the fulcrum beyond the sides of the boat" (Knipmeyer 1956:169). In the late 1800s, this vessel was common throughout French Louisiana. It was a particularly common boat type in many Atchafalaya Basin swamp communities. At Pierre Part, for example, small houses lined the bayou and campboats, used to harvest moss, were tied to their docks, with standing skiffs scattered throughout the community.

Bateaux Plats (Flatboat) or *Bateaux*

Beginning about 1800, cargo *pirogues* were being replaced by keel-less, flat-bottomed boats with a blunt bow and stern called *bateaux plats* (Chambers 1922). These are not the same as the Midwestern flatboats or broadhorns (variations were known as Orleans boats, New Orleans boats, arks, family boats, and Kentucky boats) that traveled down the Mississippi River (Comeaux 1978B). Louisiana flatboats were from twelve to over twenty-feet long and up to five-feet wide. They were not decked, had flaring sides, no cabins, and were constructed with horizontal and elbow braces on the inside. Fish wells were common in these flatboats as well. *Bateaux plats* could be propelled by sails, but oars and poles were also utilized. They operated as trading vessels and when powered by a two, four, six or eight horsepower, two-cycle inboard "putt-putt" engine they served Atchafalaya swamp dwellers well (Knipmeyer 1956; Chapelle 1951; Comeaux 1978B; Butler 1985; Brassieur 1999).

This original folk boat type, now simply called *bateau,* remains common on many of the wetlands' small bayous. The term can refer to several types of vessels. These modern flatboats are made of plywood or aluminum, are shorter than traditional *bateau,* and are frequently powered by an outboard engine. With their wide bottom and raked bow, a flatboat can be made to plane; this adaptation has assured their survival (Comeaux 1985). The true "original" *bateau* has been almost completely replaced, as they are too heavy to plane, or "get up on the step," by an outboard engine (Comeaux 1978B; Comeaux 1985).

All of these vessels were shallow draft, relatively small, and tended to be flat-bottomed. These characteristics made these folk vessels well suited for the wetlands' shallow lakes, bays, and bayous (Chapelle 1951). Many of these channels were commercially important in the latter part of the eighteenth century and throughout nineteenth century, but were used rarely in the twentieth century, when many of these watercourses vanished from the historical record because of land loss.

Canot and *La Cordelle*

The *canot* is a generic term that referred to sailing and/or rowing craft smaller than a schooner. This boat type evolved into a large skiff powered by an inboard engine and was frequently fitted with a cabin and decking (Brassieur 2007, pers. comm.). If they were not motorized, they were rowed and served as a common fishing and utility vessel. When fitted with a four-cornered, fore-and-aft sail (called a lug-rig) and the right wind, a *canot* could move well in Louisiana's coastal lakes and bays. Because of their lugsails, English-speakers labeled them "luggers" (Brassieur 1999; 2007). Dalmatian immigrants altered these *canots* to meet their specific needs by outfitting them with a centerboard, or hinged keel that allowed the boat to operate in shallow waters (Chapelle 1951; Landry 1999). Therefore, "with the basic eighteenth century hull design and rig still intact, the *canot* sailed into the twentieth century

Pulling a boat along the *cordelle* was a difficult job. (Image from *Harper's Weekly*, October 1866.)

As in Louisiana, Chinese fishermen were harvesting shrimp in San Francisco Bay as early as 1888. (Photo courtesy of Bancroft Library, University of California-Berkeley.)

The *cordelle* at Spanish Fort in New Orleans, ca. 1895. (Photo courtesy of George François Mugnier Photograph Collection, Louisiana Division, New Orleans Public Library.)

as the famous New Orleans oyster lugger" (Brassieur 1999:2). The gasoline or diesel powered version retained the name "lugger"—a term still used in South Louisiana. Older fishermen continue to refer to their old luggers as *canots*.

To navigate along many bayous, *canots*, along with other shallow-draft folk boats, had to be dragged with a tow rope (*haler à la cordelle*). "*La cordelle*" referred to the cord or rope used to pull the vessel along the channel. This halter was attached from the boat's bow mast to a horse, mule, or Cajun "longshoremen" that pulled the vessel along a *cordelle* (path) worn in the bayou's bank. In some cases, a steam tow may have been available.

La cordelle paths—the forerunners of the region's highways—were used by local stores and others to haul groceries and merchandise to their customers. Flatboats were regularly pulled along *la cordelle*. They would leave the general store on Monday morning and returned on Friday "with money or barter" (Ditto 1980:60). Other boats, like the *Laura N* on Bayou Lafourche, made weekly trips to New Orleans to sell locally-produced farm products and to return to the coastal or bayou communities with groceries, furniture, clothes, and other necessities from the city. There was nearly a never-ending chain of folk boats carrying commerce and helping meet the local citizen's needs. Since these early vessels were wind-driven, when there was no sustained wind, *la cordelle* was crucial in the pick-up and delivery process.

"Frenchy" Hardee is one of Louisiana's typical fishermen, no date. (Photo courtesy of the Morgan City Archives.)

In the oyster industry, time was critical, for the oystermen had to transport their catch to market before it spoiled. If they had no wind and had insufficient time to *haler à la cordelle*, a power boat was hired in the late nineteenth and early twentieth centuries. A fee of twenty-five dollars to fifty dollars was levied for this service. That expense could easily equal the oysterman's entire profit, but when one was dealing with such a perishable commodity, the oysterman had to do what was necessary in order to save his perishable product.

***

> Vessels of large size while in the Gulf of Mexico turn aside from the mud-choked mouths of the Mississippi, and floating and cordelling through innumerable bays and bayous, finally work their way into the 'interior,' and mingle their rigging with the foliage of the forest. Here . . . fil' their holds with sugar and molasses, and, once freighted, wing their way to the north (Thorpe 1853:751).

Large Sailing and Engine-Powered Vessels

Luggers

The eighteen-to-forty-five-foot lugger was a boat type commonly identified with oyster fishermen. It was utilized in the same manner as a Chesapeake Bay skipjack or the San Francisco Bay Chinese junk to harvest fishery resources in inland waters (Warner 1988). More than 1,000 years ago, luggers evolved from Mediterranean sailing vessels that are identified as *felucca*. Lugsails or lateen sails, which originated in

Oyster luggers at work on Louisiana's "cabbage reef." (Photo from *Biennial Report of the Department of Conservation Commission, September 1, 1912 to April 1, 1914.*)

northern France, powered these nearly ubiquitous wooden boats. Because of their speed, maneuverability, and ability to handle severe weather events this narrow watercraft became the work-boat of choice on the Gulf Coast (Chapelle 1951; Butler 2000). The lugger's quadrilateral sails were bent upon a yard that crossed the mast obliquely, enabling the vessel to easily tack into the wind and "hold a light breeze" (Gates 1910; Muir 2001; Brassieur 1999). This type of sail was rare in North America, but it provided a powerful form of propulsion well adapted for Louisiana's coastal waters.

Handling the lugger was not for an amateur, because at every tack the sail had to be lowered and passed round to the other side of the mast. For this reason, this sail type was common on boats operating in open seas, where the sail could be dipped easily, and inland waterways. Frequently operated by a single mariner, this maneuver required plenty of sea room and considerable experience, particularly in Louisiana's narrow waterways (Knight n.d.; Chapelle 1951). South Louisiana's inland fishermen, who mastered this craft, were able to drop their sails with ease in the state's restricted bayous and canals.

A Louisiana oyster lugger at work. (Photo from *Sixth Biennial Report Department of Conservation from January 1, 1922–December 31, 1923.*)

The Louisiana lugger never diffused from its area of origin—Louisiana's inland waters. Italians, Acadians, Isleños, Dalmatians, and others who were active in the state's fisheries all mastered handling and maneuvering this folk boat. They were powerful and very sea worth vessels. Equipped with a center board, they sailed fast and well. Most shipwrights used cypress and longleaf pine in the lugger's design. The deck was nearly the same on all boats, "and consisted of a U-shaped cockpit, the forward portion of which was closed off, and had four to six hatch covers, the aft part had a U-shaped bench and steering well. The bow had a small cabin with at least two berths. The rudder was always hung overboard" (Butler 2000:18).

Since the lugger was the vessel of choice for Louisiana's watermen, their sails were visible from horizon to horizon. Working the state's oyster beds, lugger men did not get home for weeks at a time. They needed to be over the "salt" in order to make a living; as a result, they were subjected constantly to the weather. They were always over water traveling to their oyster beds and to market. These trips regularly involved more than 100 miles of sailing. Unfortunately, when there was no wind their perishable cargo was at risk. The only solution was to shovel everything overboard, wait for two tides, re-tong the oysters, and hope the wind was sufficient to reach the New Orleans' market.

The lugger eventually was replaced by inboard-powered boats, along with steel- or wooden-hulled fishing vessels introduced from Florida in the late 1930s. Yet, for more than fifty years, the lugger provided the local and New Orleans' markets with oysters and other fresh seafood.

Gas boats

In addition to the major folk boat types, other less common styles are also evident. Wooden barges, from which flatboats evolved, were used for carrying large, heavy loads, for seining, or as a base for a campboat or canning operation. Smaller versions evolved into Jo-boats, John boats, gas boats, and putt-putts. The putt-putt's name is derived from the distinctive sound a single cylinder engine made when used to propel these early modified flatboats. Automobile engines eventually replaced the single cylinder engine, leading to the demise of the traditional putt-putt (Comeaux 1978B).

With gas boats, the swamp denizen or marshdweller could go much further, much faster, in much less time. When powered by a practical and affordable twenty-horsepower Model T or a forty-horsepower Model A Ford engine, these vessels achieved from four to ten miles per hour. This was not fast by present standards, but was considerably better than paddling a skiff or waiting for the wind. Not as large as a lugger or *goélette*, these small, mid-engine, vessels were adapted to the lives of persons residing and working in Louisiana's wetlands. Their owners functioned as captain, navigator, and engineer. To these fishermen the four-cylinder Model A motor was the cheapest and easiest to install. It ran well and was inexpensive to maintain. Almost all fishermen could repair and keep them operating, as it was "not a pleasant experience to be on a broken-down gas boat with mosquitoes making life miserable for the passengers" (Case 1973:97).

Light-weight marine gasoline and diesel engines came later, but the early Ford engines provided the traditional sailing fleet with power. Even so, these early gasoline motors were large, heavy, slow, and had flywheels that had to be cranked by hand. "Many arms and feet were broken cranking these engines" (Blum n.d.:9).

As Henry Ford's assembly plants made affordable engines, the fishing boats began to modernize. The sailboat fleet was replaced by powerboats that greatly expanded the oyster and shrimp harvesting grounds. The industry was able to forage into new areas and with the ingenuity of new and refined gear, watermen began to move into areas beyond their traditional fishing areas.

The Lafitte Skiff

Designed by Schiro Perez or Emile Dufrene of Lafitte for shrimping in shallow, inside-estuarine waters, the indigenous Lafitte skiff evolved into a sleek, fast, and

A typical Lafitte skiff, 1982. (Photo by the author.)

shallow-draft folk boat (Brassieur 1999). From eighteen to thirty-five feet in length, this boat had a semi-V hull and great sheer and flare in the bow section. They were typically outfitted with a 200 to 275 horse power marine or automobile engine. A transom, culling board, ice hold, and outriggers identify the Lafitte skiff—a shrimp trawler that is still in use today (Brassieur 1999). Propelled by water-cooled automobile engines and employed widely in the inland shrimp industry, this watercraft was usually built in small backyard shipyards by master shipwright/craftsmen (Comeaux 1985; Reeves and Alario 1996). An experienced observer could merely look at a skiff's design and frequently tell where, and by whom, the boat was built. When internal combustion engines were installed, all-day trips were reduced to hours. Fishermen could efficiently harvest larger areas. Travel to, around, and between sites changed dramatically.

Few, if any, Lafitte skiffs have been built outside the area. They were made for Louisiana and their design is ideal in rough water; its broad-beam outfitted with a large working deck can withstand the punishment of daily use. The skiff's design was perfect for pulling an otter-trawl. Like packet boats, these vessels also carried freight.

The Atchafalaya skiff is a variation of this form; it is also motorized, but is powered by an outboard, not an automobile engine. On this boat the gunwales do not rake up at the stern and the rear bottom is very broad to increase the boats ability to plane when traveling at high speeds (Comeaux 1978B; Comeaux 1985). Regardless, these locally made shallow-draft vessels are consciously designed to outrun anything—including agents of the government.

The Lafitte skiff morphed into the popular large trawler. It is also called a skiff, but is much larger. From forty to fifty feet in length, these vessels also have a semi-V hull and great sheer in the bow section. When powered by a gas or diesel engine "these trawlers are built for serious commercial shrimpers" (Brassieur 1999:3).

The heavily laden oyster lugger *Capt. Wilbert*, no date. (Photo courtesy of Wilbert Collins.)

A modern steel hull shrimp vessel, 2007. (Photo by the author.)

The Modern Lugger and Shrimp Trawler

Modern luggers resemble the *canot* but are fitted with inboard engines and measure twenty- to thirty-feet from bow to stern. Some modern luggers, called "Biloxi oyster luggers," are from forty- to fifty-feet long, have V-bottom hulls supporting an overhanging deck upturned fore and aft (Padgett 1960; Hallowell 1979; Comeaux 1985). The vessel's foredeck is roofed with canvas stretched over a pipe framework. At the back is a small cabin with a tiny window and a short exhaust stack on the roof. Amidships, the gunwales are built up with a latticework extending vertically from the weather deck to increase the lugger's holding capacity. This addition is one of the key identifying marks of any Gulf oyster lugger (Hallowell 1979).

Since 1937, offshore shrimpers have used trawlers instead of luggers. Trawlers vary in size from the small "shrimp trawler" to the "South Atlantic trawler," which is fifty- to sixty-five feet long and designed around a steel or wood hull. Locally called a *Floridiane*, the boat was introduced into Louisiana by "Floridy-mens" and is distinguished by a wheelhouse that is in the front of the vessel, a deep draft, and refrigeration. These large boats frequently are rigged to tow two nets (Ramsey 1957; Comeaux 1985; Landry 1999; Brassieur 1999).

All of these vessel types were utilized on the state's natural waterways, but in order to facility travel east and west canals were necessary. Further, as the marsh became more industrialized other forms of canals became important, some for drainage and others for access, but all are a part of a coordinated effort to industrialize and commercialize the wetland's resources.

Natural Waterways, Canals, and Access

In order to remove . . . cypress and other timber from the swamps, it has been necessary to dig canals and cut pullboat runs throughout the length and breadth of our great swamp areas. Second, a large commerce has sprung up about the natural resources of our marsh lands and water areas, and in order to meet its requirements, there has been an enormous development of navigation canals which traverse our marshes and swamps in all directions. Third, in order to drain the ridge lands adjacent to the swamp and marsh

In the late nineteenth and early twentieth centuries, the dredge *Eclipse* was active in Lafourche and Terrebonne parishes, maintaining the navigability of canals and natural waterways, no date. (Photo courtesy of Randolph A. Bazet Collection, Archives & Special Collections, Nicholls State University.)

> country, many drainage canals and ditches have been dug from the relatively high lands, across the marsh or swamp to some natural lake or bayou. The result of this canalization of our wet lands has been to nullify the effects of the natural levees and to promote a rapid run off of water, not only from the high lands but from the adjacent wider areas of marsh and swamp (Pearson, et al. 1989:222).

Since New Orleans was established in 1718, Louisiana's waterways have played a pivotal role in development of the state's economic base. Movement of goods by water has long been an integral part of the coastal zone's transportation geography, despite the fact that it could take a day for a shipment to reach a point only a few miles away. Originally, large hand-hewn *pirogues*, flatboats, and keelboats (locally called *pointu les deux*) were used as commercial cargo carriers to thread their way through a maze of interconnecting natural waterways that wandered across the landscape (Pearson, et al. 1989). Although replicas of the thousands of keelboats employed on the Mississippi can be found, not one original remains (Sloane 1956).

On the Mississippi, these wooden boats routinely took a month or more to drift from Pittsburgh to New Orleans. During the early 1800s, more than 20,000 of these river craft floated downriver. The one-way trip to New Orleans ended with dismantlement of these flatboats and keelboats. The salvaged timber was used in home construction. Many of New Orleans' older homes, therefore, were built of material that originated 1,000 miles away. This timber was milled into wood panels and staircases for many of the mansions on St. Charles Avenue (Sloane 1956).

Pettyaugres, *bateaux plats*, and *pointu les deux* opened South Louisiana's commercial trade corridors. In the early 1800s, more efficient steam-powered vessels began to replace these traditional hand-powered boats. Safe waterways were then essential, as a steamboat was a fragile structure easily damaged and just small enough to navigate the narrow bayous. Sawyers and dredges were contracted to keep the principal channels clean. To increase the system's efficiency, and reduce travel time, arrow-straight canals were excavated, and they eventually crisscrossed the landscape (Becnel 1989).

Statewide, a 2009 search of the GNIS found 661 waterways with canal in the title. This is only a fraction of the total, as most canals were given a single name and rarely was the word "canal" officially incorporated into the place name. There are thousands of these engineered waterways. In some sections of the coast, the maze of channels looks like the countryside is trapped in a Salvador Dali painting.

Every planter with a reputed engineering background—and some with only the right political connections—began to contribute to the proliferation of canals. It was easier and cheaper to ship their commodities by ca-

Louisiana's prosperity was often tied directly to the canalization process, ca. 1910. (Photo courtesy of the Randolph A. Bazet Collection, Archives & Special Collections, Nicholls State University.)

nals, frequently nothing more than a ditch connecting a river or bayou to a wharf. Instead of hauling their commodities by horse- or mule-powered carts, they floated them down an engineered watercourse. The entire region became canal-minded. In the canalization process, many of these channels, over time, dramatically altered the hydrology of the coastal lowlands, bringing salt water into fresh marshes, influencing irrigation water used in the rice industry, impeding sheet flow, increasing tidal processes, and regularly endangering the potable water supply. But, at the time of their construction, no one knew or understood how these linear features would impact the region. The canal was simply an efficient way to move goods to market.

Named canals in the coastal plain in 2009
The canals listed are only an approximation, as several channels cross parish
boundaries and quadrangles and are consequently counted more than once.
(From: http://geonames.usgs.gov/domestic/)

Cameron	35	St. Bernard	41
Iberia	28	St. Mary	26
Jefferson	57	Terrebonne	40
Orleans	29	Vermilion	69
Plaquemines	67	Total	392

The original system was small, but adequate, furnishing local inhabitants with statewide connectivity that gradually expanded into something much larger. To make the canal patterns' geographic growth and development move understandable, the author has divided them into five categories: drainage and reclamation, transportation, trapping, logging, and petroleum (Davis 1973). These subdivisions, arranged historically, demonstrate the evolution of resource use and suggest changes that have

Over time, canals altered the coastal environment, 1998. (Photo courtesy of George J. Castille, III.)

occurred in the exploitation of South Louisiana's resource base.

In the United States, the nineteenth century was a period of increased economic specialization in which establishment of an efficient transportation network was tantamount to expanding local markets. Before the trucking industry's arrival, railroads were customarily hailed as the most notable force behind economic growth and the "single most important impetus to change in the nineteenth century" (Dormon 1983:63). Since railroad expansion was nationwide, its importance to the country's economic well-being was inescapable. Although, not as economically important as railroads, canals nevertheless played an essential role in the nation's industrial development. The collective impact of the Delaware, Erie, Ohio, Farmington, Cape Cod, and other Atlantic seaboard coal and general cargo canals was enormous (Miller 1914). Coastal Louisiana's canals engendered the same results on a smaller scale.

To capitalize on the alluvial wetlands' renewable and non-renewable resources, many engineering endeavors aided in the harvest or exploitation process. Canals were the most visible expression of humanity's interest in wetland resource utilization. These watery passages now dominate the marsh/swamp terrain and exemplify the engineer's ability to alter the natural environment; as a consequence, canals became an essential component of the marsh and swampdweller's daily water-based activities (Turner, et al. 1983).

South Louisiana's canalization began with the arrival of the earliest European settlers, and the process continues to the present. Since construction of Louisiana's first drainage project, dredged waterways have advanced unchecked in the state's quest to exploit the wetlands' natural riches—ducks and geese, oyster, shrimp, crabs, timber, fur and hides, hydrocarbons and sulphur, and even grazing and agriculture—until the last quarter of the twentieth century. As early as 1944, Harnett Kane remarked:

> Everywhere the surface is broken by curving rivulets, inlets, bayous, and green-fringed canals in which the skies are always to be seen in silver reflection. From almost any point to the other, the Deltan can find a route by boat among the weblike turnings (Kane 1944:ix-x).

The ease of communications afforded by wetland canals created environmental problems that had a profoundly detrimental effect on this fragile real estate (Davis 1973). As the canal networks expanded, land loss accelerated, and Louisiana found itself in a no-win situation. If canals were not constructed, valuable mineral fluids and other resources could not be exploited easily. If canals were excavated, valuable estuarine habitats were lost. Since many individuals considered the marsh itself worthless, land was readily sacrificed to provide access to subsurface mineral fluids and also to aid in the transport of renewable and non-renewable resources. In retrospect, the state paid dearly for the short-term gains associated with wetlands mineral

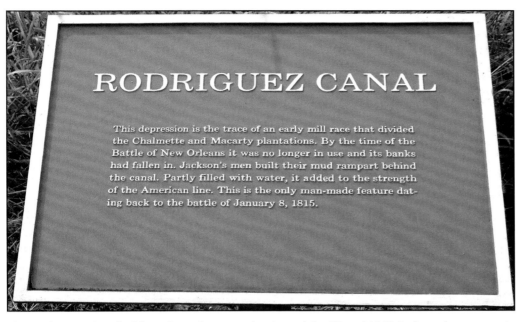

The Rodriguez Canal, although not in use at the time of the War of 1812, is the only man-made feature dating back to the battle and is a good example of the longevity of Louisiana's canals, 2005. (Photo by the author.)

To efficiently drain wetlands, a system of inter-connecting lateral canals were used in the reclamation and/or drainage process. (Image from Okey 1914.)

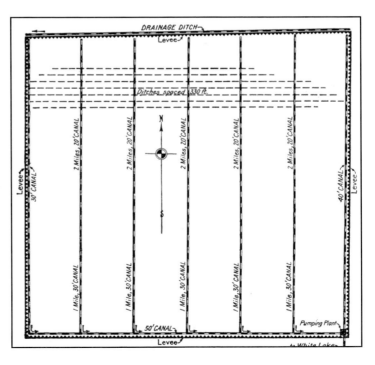

exploitation, but it should be noted that environmental concerns only entered the local consciousness during the early 1970s. Before this heightened environmental consciousness, wetland modification was not recognized as a major issue. Louisiana was simply following a national trend.

As a result of this canal construction activity, Louisiana's wetlands are criss-crossed, ringed, cut, and otherwise bisected by an intricate array of excavated access arteries. Until recently, new channels were being added constantly, and old ones were rarely filled in. As a consequence, the complex intertwines and expands into a well-defined, web-like design. Theoretically, a canal's life-expectancy is finite, but some of these artificial waterways have evolved into straight-channeled "bayous." They have lost their human-induced identity and are now a part of the natural topography, having become "lines" on the landscape (Davis 1992).

Drainage and Reclamation Canals

As early as 1720, two years after the founding of New Orleans, French colonists excavated drainage ditches to improve runoff from the natural levees. When New Orleans was surveyed, each block was ringed with canals (Nau 1958; Lewis 1976; Snowden, et al. 1977; Davis 1986). These ditches reflected the "Crescent City's" dependence on a drainage network. The Rodriguez canal, "a small abandoned waterway, reed-covered, extending all of the way from river levee back to dark cypress swamp," was probably one of the most famous drainage channels (Kane 1944:34). It became the fortified site for Andrew Jackson's stand against the British in the War of 1812.

In actuality, the Rodriguez Canal and all other small ditch-like channels were part of a great land reclamation enterprise. They were laid out to aid planters and urbanites drain potential agricultural, pastural, residential, and industrial land. Flood and water control procedures, in effect, extended cultivated land beyond the natural levee into the surrounding backswamp and the "earliest records . . . abound with references to land reclamation . . ." (Harrison 1951:3). Further, as land was cleared and it became apparent that better levees were needed, the state engineer and the Board of Swamp Land Commissioners, and later the Board of Public Works, were created to assist planters with flood control and drainage (Harrison 1951; Wagner and Durabb 1976). In some instances, drainage ditches were constructed for mosquito control.

Most of the channels built in salt marshes were a near carbon copy of drainage systems design widely used on the East Coast. For example, in Bergen County, New Jersey, the local health board spearheaded the construction and maintenance of nearly 285 miles of such mosquito-control ditches in an attempt to free the marshes of breeding mosquitoes (Vileisis 1997). A similar program was initiated in New Orleans, but on a much smaller scale, and more localized focus.

In many cases, South Louisiana's original drainage canals evolved into vital transportation links. Like canals elsewhere in the colonial period, they were multifunctional units serving as drainage and access waterways. Some of these original "ditches" remain indispensable transportation arteries today (Davis 1973). For example, when George Washington and others surveyed the Dismal Swamp of Virginia and North Carolina in 1763, they did so with a view to land reclamation. In 1787, the Dismal Swamp Canal Company was chartered. A canal was opened seven years later, and it served a dual role as a transportation artery and as a safeguard against regional flooding (Wooten and Jones 1955). The same evolutionary process produced many South Louisiana canals.

Representative sample of a few of the coastal plain's drainage canals
Since there is no directory of these channels, the list is based on location and apparent function. Some of the selected channels made be multifunctional channels. (From Davis 1973; http://geonames.usgs.gov/domestic/)

Abbeville	Algiers	Ardoyne	Ashland	Avery	Avondale Home Number One
Bancroft	Bardel	Bell City Drainage	Berg	Billiot	Bonvillain
Boston	Boudreaux	Braithwaite	Buras Drainage	Burke	Butte
Caro	Cameron	Canal Number Two	Carroll	Chalmette Vista	Charenton Drainage and Navigation
Citrus	Concession	Coulee Baton	Cow Island Number One	Creedmore	Crochet
Cross	Delahoussaye	De La Ronde	Dredge Boat	Dugues	Duplantis
Eickes	Elmwood	Eighty Arpent	Forty Arpent	Farrar	Franklin
Gannon	Gonsoulin	Gueydan	Hall-Schultz	Halpin	Hayes
Hopedale	Houma	Iberia	Jahncke	Jeanerette	Jefferson
Joe Brown	Jurjevich	Kelley	Kenliworth	Klondike	Lake Shore
Lapeans	London Avenue Outfall	Laurel Valley	Lening	Magnolia	Main Outfall
Marquez	Marshfield	Meraux	Meyers	Mingle	Minors
Morrison	New Iberia Southern Drainage	Number One	Number Two	Number Three	Number Eight
Number Four	Number Eleven	Number Twelve	Number Seventeen	Oaklawn	Orleans
Outfall	Patout	Patterson	Plaquemine	Pitre	Quintana
Rodere	St. Bernard	St. Mary	Sam Foret	Sandager	Scott
Sixth Ward	Suburban	Terrebonne	Terrebonne Lafourche Drainage	Theriot	Thorguson
Touchets	Vacherie	Verdunville	Vermilion	Westwego Drainage	Zigler

Drainage channels were confined customarily to tracts suitable for agriculture, primarily natural levees. When sugarcane became the dominant natural levee crop, planters spent considerable time and energy cleaning out their drainage ditches. Their slaves "ditched and cross-ditched fields to carry water off more quickly" (Vileisis 1997:46). These endeavors were one of the most important undertakings on a plantation, for standing water could damage crops. The custom was to cut parallel ditches about 200 feet apart from the front of the plantation to the rear, with cross ditches every 600 feet. As a result, ditches crossed and re-crossed the landscape creating a cubist design that resembled a checkerboard. Water gates controlled flow and there were plantations where one could find in one square mile "from twenty to thirty miles of ditching" (Thorpe 1853:755). This pattern is also visible on satellite images of the state's rice producing region, where private and semi-private companies manage

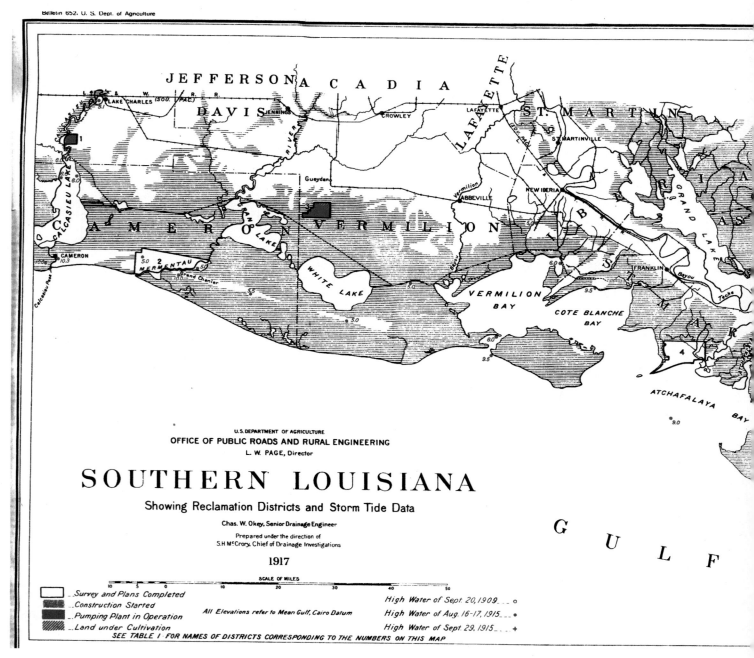

By 1917, reclamation projects were already reshaping Louisiana's topography.

an extensive grid-like canal network associated with rice cultivation.

Canal construction was an expensive process that often required installation of costly steam-driven drainage machinery. In fact, a plantation's productivity was related directly to its network of internal ditches that allowed the plantation to extend its fields "farther to the back than men had ever thought possible" (Kane 1944:46). With a spade and wheelbarrow, laborers kept these ditches clean and functioning properly. In the twentieth century, these hand tools were replaced with draglines and small "V"-shaped ditching buckets. The steam-driven traction ditcher, invented by James B. Hill in the late 1880s, cut the required channels to insure adequate runoff into a lat-

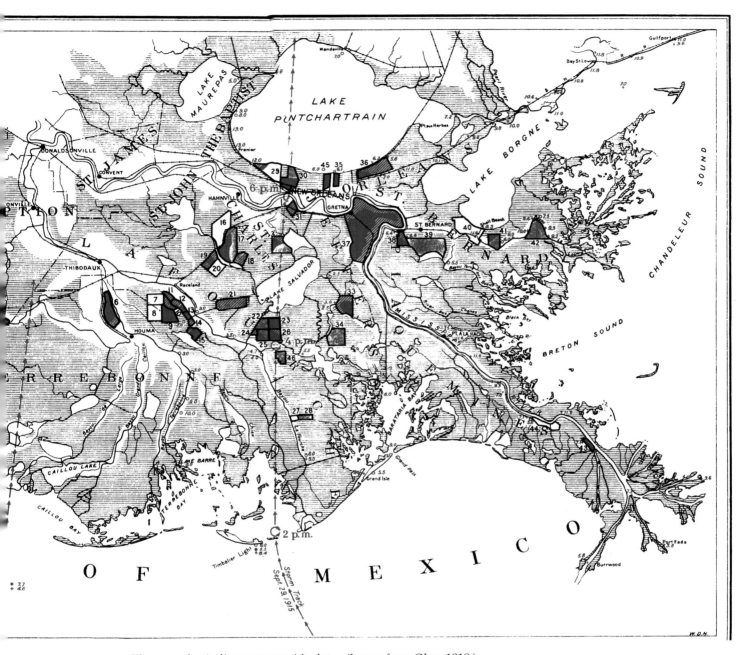

The map also indicates storm tide data. (Image from Okey 1918.)

tice work of interconnecting small ditches. These ditches frequently fed into special twenty- to forty-foot canals that moved the runoff into the larger natural drainage network (Maier 1952; Ditto 1980).

Planters became enthusiastic proponents of these reclamation methods. Along the lower Mississippi River, they cut drainage canals to force overflow waters "to the back," where smaller engineered channels were cut through the marsh or swamp to direct the overflow into the region's lakes and bays. These channels allowed river planters to maintain their estates during the flood season (Ramsey 1957).

From 1880 to 1930, the rush to drain land accelerated. One contractor working in

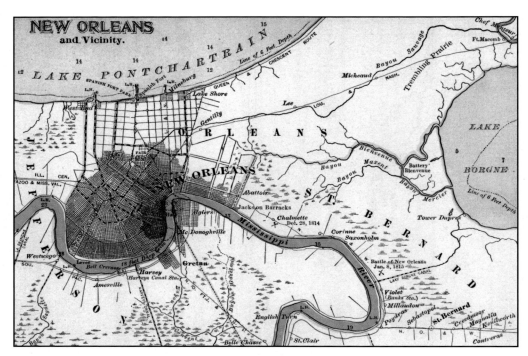

From its inception, New Orleans has pushed its reclamation boundaries toward Lake Pontchartrain. (Image from *Century Atlas*, 1897.)

the reclamation business was the Pennington Dredging Company. Owned by Willard Pennington, this company's advertising literature proudly trumpeted the slogan: "Reclamation of Swamp Land a Specialty" (A picture history ca. 1986).

Without drainage ditches and canals, much of South Louisiana's near sea-level agricultural land could not be farmed. In fact, American farmers have routinely drained land since the early days of settlement; it is part of the agricultural process. Unlike the large, well-ordered, polder projects completed by Northern businessmen, South Louisiana's planters drained their land by excavating a main "outfall" canal—at least twelve-feet wide and four-feet deep—through their plantations. In some instances, "drain machines" (or water wheels) were constructed to increase a canal's effectiveness (Davis 1973). As this equipment gained in popularity—and steam improved the machine's performance—the number of drainage channels multiplied. Back levees frequently were built to keep out river or tidal overflow, not unlike the levee systems currently utilized on many contemporary plantations.

During the decades before and after the Civil War, engineered waterways began to proliferate across South Louisiana. In some areas, the state invested in artificial waterways to decrease flood hazards and improve agricultural drainage. Other projects were initiated by plantation owners to increase runoff and drain "new" land. In Terrebonne and Lafourche parishes, the Ardoyne, Ashland, Dredge Boat, Sam Foret, Halpin, Lapeans, Laurel Valley, Pitre Lening, Minors, and Theriot canals were excavated as plantation "outfall" channels. But these channels constitute only a small portion of the labyrinth of drainage ditches that exists in the coastal zone. The fact that they remain on the landscape attests to their use, and with the continued clearing of "new" land, the system expanded into a landscape characterized by the linear configuration of these drainage and reclamation channels.

In the half-century between 1880 and 1930, Louisiana's coastal lowlands experienced intense reclamation activity, mirroring the seventeenth-century reclamation of the British Fenlands (Davis 1971) and the fourteenth-century reclamation of West Germany's North Sea coast (Kuratorium fuer 1978). South Louisiana's reclamation activity was frenzied during this period (Merry 1909; Morehouse 1910; Okey 1914). Okey's (1918B) cartographic documentation of forty-three of these well-organized marsh reclamation endeavors indicates that Louisiana farmers, like their counterparts throughout the United States, were reclaiming land on an unprecedented scale. Indeed, by 1926, American farmers were cultivating an additional sixty-five million acres cleared by steam-driven dredges and dragline excavators, using buckets with capacities as large as forty-cubic-yards (McCrory and Soo 1927; Vileisis 1997). In addition, a cadre of well-trained professional engineers and scientists provided considerable expertise to inform, improve, and accelerate the reclamation/levee process.

In South Louisiana, private drainage projects at Des Allemands, Delta Farms, Clovelly Farms, and near Westwego—the only town whose name forms a complete sentence—were initiated. Planters associated with these massive reclamation efforts, as well as more modest projects were "challenged from the very start to institute flood control and drainage measures" (Gagliano 1973:11). They became enthusiastic supporters of these programs as Alejandro O'Reilly, Louisiana's second Spanish governor had mandated that every immigrant family was to construct a levee and finish a highway with parallel ditches towards the levee within three years of settlement (Martin 1827).

To many individuals the marsh was reclaimable, fertile, and capable of producing record crops (Le Baron 1905). And a great many people were "willing to undertake the drainage of these marshes and tidal meadows if it [could] be shown to them that here will result a pecuniary profit" (Means 1901:2). With the help of the railroads and an aggressive advertising campaign by investors, this notion became a key ingredient in encouraging people to resettle in Louisiana's coastal lowlands.

Pumps like these at Clovelly Farms have allowed many reclamation sites to survive for more than 100 years, 1980. (Photo by the author.)

Reclamation Projects

> "Everyone we are certain will be gratified to know that these Michigan people who came here and invested over half a million dollars in this huge land reclamation project are once more in the saddle. Time has proven this land can be reclaimed and is as fertile as that of the Nile. . . ." (White Lake Land . . . 1916: no pagination).

Mr. Jewett Allin, in a letter to the 'Manufacturers' Record,' thus refers to the swamp land of Louisiana: 'My opinion is that the coast lands of southern Louisiana, for health, fertility, and marketing facilities combines, are unequaled by any other section of the United States. Their intrinsic value is evidenced by the fact that some of those who have these lands for sale are willing to sell them to satisfactory purchasers without any cash payment down, applying one-half of the crop to the purchasing of the land until the land is paid for, and releasing the purchaser from any personal responsibility for the purchase price of the land other than the one-half of the crop referred to, so that a man may use what capital he has entirely for the production of crops without personally going in debt; and if he subsequently becomes dissatisfied with his purchase, he is at liberty to leave the purchase without losing any original cash purchase payment or feeling obligated for any balance of purchase money. Only the best lands and conditions will stand such sales as these. As further evidence of their value, the State of Louisiana has authorized the organizing and bonding of drainage districts so that the drainage may be carried on at the least expense and greatest advantage to the party whose land is drained' (Merry 1909:9).

In the colonial period, the French and Spanish governments enacted laws requiring new settlers to clear their property to a depth of three *arpents* (approximately 600 feet), place two heavy mooring posts on their property for watercraft, construct and maintain a levee six-feet wide and two-feet tall, provide a foot and bridle path on the levee, construct a forty-eight-foot wagon road on the levee's landward side, run ditches into the swamp, and place culverts in ditches crossed by the road (Kniffen 1990). These early regulations guaranteed Louisiana's settled lowlands would be adequately leveed, drained, and connected to a transportation network within three years.

The rush to drain land was accelerated by implementation of land reclamation projects representing the climax of a century of reflection, writing, and experimentation. Since arable land was in increasingly short supply, the only practical way to resolve the land shortage problem was to reclaim swamps and marshes. The wetlands were recognized as a valuable though underdeveloped resource, one that could be reclaimed for cultivation. To meet the challenge, large-scale drainage districts were established. Land was reclaimed at a record rate. Reclamation efforts were widespread throughout Louisiana's lower tier of parishes, but the effort was destined to fail. Taxes, the cost of building and maintaining levees, pumping facilities, and an intricate network of drainage channels easily offset the monetary return on the generally low-value crops suitable for cultivation on reclaimed lands.

In 1878, during the land reclamation craze, the Louisiana legislature chartered the Louisiana Land Reclamation Company. The company was established to reclaim 13,000 acres in Terrebonne Parish (Bryson, et al. 1871; Bush and Wiltz 1878; Harrison and Kollmorgen 1947). After a complex of canals and levees was utilized to drain this immense wetlands tract, rice, jute, and vegetable crops were grown. The Terrebonne Parish venture, which served as a model for other Louisiana reclamation projects, was devastated by floods in 1883 and 1884 which destroyed the development's levees and inundated the reclaimed land.

Despite the catastrophic failure of Louisiana's first state-sponsored large-scale reclamation project, Louisiana entrepreneurs continued to levee tracts through reclamation enterprises that were considered the salvation of the wetlands for, in the claims of their promoters, they would open the marshes for agricultural-based communities (Merry 1909; Morehouse 1910). During this period, over fifty land reclamation efforts were started in coastal Louisiana. Reclamation entrepreneurs reclaimed tracts that

This breakwater, authorized in 1853, was the precursor to reclamation on the lakefront. Sketch of the Pontchartrain Harbour & Breakwater, 1853.

varied from 640 acres to more than 24,000 acres. Their efforts resulted in reclamation of more than 138,000 acres (about 3.5 times the size of the District of Columbia) in an ongoing effort to commercialize the wetlands (Davis and Detro 1980). Reclamation work reflected the widespread belief that this landscape was a physical impediment to commercial progress, as wetlands were a "resource to be converted into commodities" (Vileisis 1997:52). As a result, by the early 1900s, reclamation of tide lands was occurring on a national scale, and Louisiana was simply emulating the emphases on reclaiming marshlands (Wright 1907; Kemp and Mashriqui 1996).

The reclaimed property was touted as a first-rate truck-gardening venue, a new Citrus Belt, a second Corn Belt, a Rice Belt, and a new celery-producing region. Some believed the reclaimed marshlands would become "the site of the world's finest citrus groves" (Harrison 1961:268). In fact, the Lake Shore Land Company's Little Woods tract—centered on the community of Citrus—had seven miles of frontage on the south shore of Lake Pontchartrain with an average depth of two miles. To promote agriculture, the property was laced by a series of primary and secondary canals serviced by two main pumping units (Shaw 1917). As a result, the natural marsh buffer between Lake Pontchartrain and New Orleans was drained and developed, a land development best viewed in Theodore Lilienthal's 1867 image of the entrance to Bayou St. John (Van Zante 2006).

Attracted to wetlands reclamation sites by railroad companies' promotional literature and special low fares, settlers on most marshland reclamation projects were generally immigrants from Illinois, Indiana, Iowa, Michigan, and Wisconsin (Kollmorgen and Harrison 1946; Shanabruch 1977). The developers' high-pressure promotional tactics—and perhaps false advertising—led a large number of ultimately unhappy settlers to make many unwise investments. Their land acquisitions proved ill-advised because, in most cases, the large polders quickly proved untenable. Under cultivation, the organic soils within the ring levee shrank and settled. After ten years of cultivation, many of these peat- and muck-land sites subsided nearly seven feet. In the absence of proper levee maintenance, these negative surfaces were easily flooded. As the land sank, the costs of protecting the reclaimed property from overflow and tidal flooding and, conversely, pumping out surplus water generated by torrential rainfall were great; indeed, they were usually prohibitively expensive (Okey 1918B; Turner and Streever 2002).

In addition, unlike wetlands reclamation in the Netherlands, continuous grazing and farming were practiced in Louisiana; hence, the fertility of the reclaimed wetlands was soon exhausted. As a result, "ballyhooed" Louisiana reclamation projects were abandoned (Harrison and Kollmorgen 1947; Harrison 1961). It is thus hardly surprising that numerous rectangular lakes now dotting the marshes presently serve as monuments to poorly conceived reclamation schemes, and the surviving wetland reclamation operations endure more as a result of their oil and natural gas revenues than their successful levees, canals, and pump-drainage operations. The exceptions are those reclaimed tracts in urban areas where reclamation efforts and refinements

"Most development projects were legally organized as drainage districts, so they levied hefty taxes on the new owners to pay off bonds that had financed the drainage. Oftentimes lands beyond the sample lots were not fully drained and so yielded disappointing crops. Furthermore, once plots in a district were sold off, responsibility for their maintenance, including operation of the pumps and upkeep of the levees fell to a group of commissioners elected from the new farm owners. Most had no inkling of how to keep the complex system of pumps and levees in working order. As a result, most pump-drained development projects in southern Louisiana ultimately failed" (Vileisis 1997:133).

Canals were the backbone of Louisiana's reclamation endeavors, ca. 1912. (Photo from Okey 1914.)

continue, and at several sites straddling southwest Louisiana's marsh/prairie boundary, particularly those south of Highway 14—The Hug, the Marsh Highway, or Reclamation Road.

The Prime Movers in Marsh Reclamation and Settlement

After a full investigation, Edward Wisner became convinced that these lands could be reclaimed. He began to purchase at the Levee Board Sales, and eventually acquired vast holdings. The residents of New Orleans and that portion of Louisiana contiguous to these lands had always regarded them as valueless waste. When Mr. Wisner began his purchases they looked upon him with pity, some though him crazy and others declared him foolish. This, however, did not deter him (Merry 1909:21). In fact, "when Wisner died in 1915, he was a multimillionaire and owned 950,000 acres of marsh. . . . Wisner left 53,000 acres . . . to: The City of New Orleans, Charity Hospital at New Orleans, Tulane University, and the Salvation Army." The four beneficiaries were to share any income for the land known in New Orleans government circles as the Edward Wisner Donation. A later resurveying discovered the bequest actually amounted to 40,000 acres (Hallowell 1979:64).

The leading proponent of marshland drainage was Edward Wisner (The Father of Louisiana's Reclamation Movement), a Midwesterner of German and Dutch ancestry who considered the wetlands to be valuable agricultural real estate. He was so committed to reclamation that in the early 1900s, he purchased nearly 1.5 million acres (2,343 square miles—about twice the area of Los Angeles). The price he paid for this land ranged from twelve-and-a-half cents to seven-and-a-half cents an acre. At one point, Wisner owned eleven companies, and if all of his options would have been exercised, he would have owned most of eleven parishes (Hallowell 1979). Local swamp and marshland owners considered these schemes foolhardy and were glad to sell their "wasteland"—a move many would regret when hydrocarbons were discovered

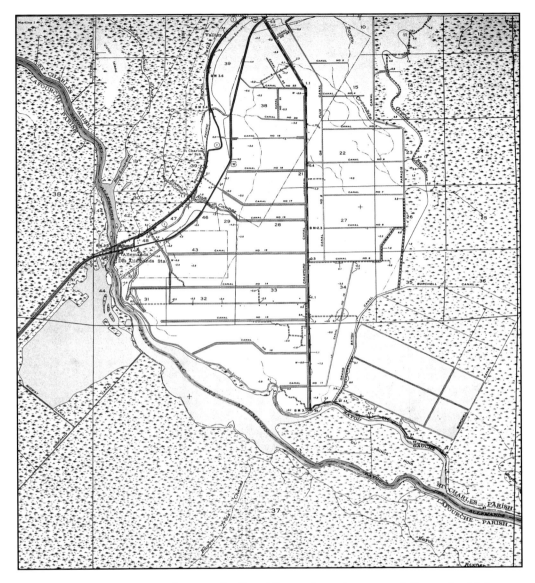

Like all land reclamation endeavors, the Des Allemands project was a laticework of interconnecting canals to facilitate drainage. (Image from USGS Lac Des Allemands fifteen minute quadrangle, 1938.)

in stratigraphic traps under these lands.

Wisner canvassed the Midwest encouraging prospective buyers to invest in small farms on his polderized property. The price of these reclaimed "estates" varied from $50 to $150 per acre for drained land and from $1 to $15 for virgin marshland (Hallowell 1979). These projects were moderately successful until 1915, when high prices associated with World War I and the passage of a highly destructive hurricane led to the decline of these speculative developments. Many of these endeavors subsequently encountered financial difficulties and were abandoned or survived as urban areas.

Wisner's reclamation efforts, as well as others, were based on a network of levees, internal drains, and pumping plants. Once the area was defined, outlet ditches were constructed by "hundreds of people" either by hand or with teams of scrapers (Hallowell 2001:44). With such methods, the ditch could not be more than five-feet deep, with a bottom width seldom exceeding four feet. In larger projects, such ditches provided inadequate drainage. Promoters consequently needed an economical means of constructing large open ditches. The first steam-driven dipper dredges were developed in 1883, followed in 1906 by the dragline excavator that became the standard excavating machines.

With this technical innovation, a large "dredge-boat canal" at least twenty-five-feet wide and five-feet deep could be excavated around the project's perimeter. In building these canals, spoil was used to erect a protective levee, with a height of five to six feet and a top width up to twelve. When the boundary channel and levees were completed, the reclaimed tract's internal drainage network was constructed. These "collecting" ditches were about four-feet wide and three-feet deep, somewhat smaller than the main reservoir channels that measured from ten to twenty-feet wide and up to eight-feet deep (Harrison and Kollmorgen 1947). This complex of internal drains served a dual role; they removed excess water and were deep enough for navigation, providing the farmer with a convenient transportation network. This pattern, with few exceptions, was replicated in all of the private and quasi-public reclamation schemes within the coastal lowlands.

Small lateral canals were the primary channels for managing runoff reclamation projects, ca. 1912. (Photo from Okey 1914.)

As reclamation endeavors proliferated, the landscape became laced with interconnecting channels. Such a watery labyrinth created a significant problem, for these engineered features were constructed in areas where the terrain was inundated frequently by storm surges. In addition, channel in-filling was so great that it quickly proved too expensive for most landholders to maintain existing canals and levees. Even so, reclamation companies and a number of railroads advertised the agricultural merit of these reclaimed parcels through public relations offices in Northern cities.

Pamphlets published by the Illinois Central Railroad, such as *Louisiana Reclaimed Lands Make Fertile Farms,* were distributed widely by the Louisville and Nashville Railroad (Merry 1909). The brochure proclaimed:

> Several Louisiana drained farms, that three years ago were wet prairie, are now owned and operated by farmers from Illinois, Michigan, Indiana and Ohio, and other northern and southern states. What has been done so successfully in the reclamation of low lands in foreign countries . . . is now being done in the United States (Merry 1909:4).

In order to promote these reclamation projects to the fullest, Merry (1910:6) further reported:

> For years the State of Louisiana has had many artificially drained plantations on which sugar cane has been grown with great profit. Truck gardening has also been an important industry on these artificially drained farms located within ten or a dozen miles of New Orleans. Such lands produce annually from $75 to $200 per acre, and cannot be bought at any price. The adjacent unreclaimed swamp lands, when properly drained, become equally fertile, and in time will be equally valuable.

The Louisiana Department of Agriculture and Immigration reinforced the ongoing promotional campaign by sponsoring trips for newspaper reporters and business leaders to successful drainage projects.

As a result of the advertising hyperbole and the state government's endorsement of these private reclamation efforts, engineers, draftsmen, and other professionals began to plan villages and house sites for the expected immigrants. It is thus hardly surprising that large numbers of settlers soon arrived from the Corn Belt and the Great Lakes region, with the intention of reaping the benefits of America's new "agricultural paradise." Initially, new agriculturalists achieved excellent yields. Optimism was high; there was no room for pessimism.

As homesteaders swarmed onto reclaimed properties, the state's leading proponent for land reclamation Edward Wisner's Louisiana Meadows Company (with offices in New Orleans, Chicago, and Kansas City) sought and found additional investors. The company owned and operated: the Truck Farm Land Company; the Terrebonne Land Company; along with the Pennington Dredging Company (A sketch of 1910). Operating out of offices in the Maison Blanche Building on New Orleans' Canal Street, along with publicity offices in Chicago and other Northern cities, Edward Wisner promoted aggressively his land reclamation endeavors.

Persuasive pamphlets boasted about the region's climate, soil, and low rates of infant mortality, while also highlighting glowing comments from settlers. The Company even shipped boxes of dirt to perspective settlers to show the quality of the peat soils (Vileisis 1997). Wisner's first project at La Branche, along the Illinois Central Railroad about fifteen miles northwest of New Orleans, was quickly cleared, leveed, and drained. The success of the initial corn and truck crops convinced investors and migrants of the property's value. This industrial enterprise became Wisner's showcase and the hub for his reclamation endeavors, with the Louisiana Meadows Company taking orders for small family farms at prices ranging from $150 to $600 per acre (Vileisis 1997).

Although Wisner had a head start, the marsh was too big for one man to own. Several entrepreneurs formed land companies, such as Delacroix, St. Martin, Miami,

Vermilion Bay, Orange-Cameron, Foster-Holcomb, Illinois-Indiana, White Lake, and Pan-American, which sent their representatives into Louisiana's marsh to claim what was left (Hallowell 1979). These land syndicates became the backbone of marshland ownership.

One of the most enthusiastic of these marsh landlords was Frederick Scully, who believed that if he could solve the problem of marshland reclamation, he would make a valuable contribution to Southern agriculture (Harrison and Kollmorgen 1947). In 1909, Scully purchased thousands of acres between Bayou Lafourche and Little Lake; and in 1916 he established Clovelly Farms—"The Little Holland of Lafourche"—at Cut Off. Like the Sunset Drainage District (formerly St. Charles Municipal Drainage District No. 1) at Des Allemands and the Raceland Prairie, Clovelly Farms is one of the few projects that continues to produce agricultural commodities. The homes on this site were either characterized as shotguns or were campboats moored in the canal surrounding the property's dikes.

Individuals and organizations actively involved
in reclaiming the marsh and swamp land, ca. 1910
(From: Merry 1909:7)

Individual or Company	Location	Individual or Company	Location
Louisiana Meadows Company	New Orleans, La.	Edward Wisner	New Orleans, La.
Winter Garden Drainage Company	New Orleans, La.	J. T. Badeaux	Lockport, La.
R. R. Barrow	Houma, La.	J. A. Brumbaugh	Elkhart, Ind.
E. W. Wickey & Company	East Chicago, Ind.	Oscar Bourg	Lockport, La.
Robert Downman	New Orleans, La.	J. C. Dupont	Houma, La.
Thomas Foret	Lockport, La.	John R. Gheens	Gheens, La
Godchaux Company, Ltd	New Orleans, La.	Senator Gueydan	Gueydan, La.
Wilson J. Guidry	Houma, La.	Dr. J. H. Jastremski	Houma, La.
George Koepp	Madisonville, La.	C. S. Matthews	Matthews, La.
McIlhenny Company	Avery Island, La.	G. A. McWilliams	Walnut, Ill.
R. S. Moore	Naomie, La.	Alfred Plaisance	New Orleans, La.
Dr. A. J. Price	Lockport, La.	Warren B. Reed	New Orleans, La.
A.V. Smith	Lockport, La.	Hon. H.C. Warmoth	Magnolia, La.
Hon. Theodore Wilkinson	New Orleans, La.	Frank B. Williams	Franklin, La.
Willswood Plantation	Waggaman, La.	Phillips Land Company	Chicago, Ill.
L. B. Langworthy	Chicago, Ill.		

Examples of Reclamation of the State's Marshes

"The marsh is reclaimable. The land is very rich when once placed under cultivation. The alluvial land is as rich as any in the world. It will produce in perfection all crops known to this latitude, as well as oranges, bananas and other tropical fruit" (Le Baron 1905:99). And, "a great many people seem willing to undertake the drainage of these marshes and tidal meadows if it can be shown to them that here will result a pecuniary profit" (Means 1901:2).

Simoneaux Ponds

In the early 1920s, a group of Mennonite farmers settled near Des Allemands and worked a piece of land that is now identified as Simoneaux Ponds. Their farming endeavor was not successful. Frustrated, the transplanted Northerners sold property to the McWilliams Dredging Company, which let the land go fallow. About 1929, the Simoneaux family purchased the tract and tried to turn the property into a muskrat and alligator farm. This also failed.

By the mid-1930s, a group of New Orleans business men, working with the Simoneaux family began a hunting club on the property. "The huge ten-foot pumps that had been used to irrigate the Mennonites' fields rusted into oblivion. The dams that had been constructed in a futile effort to grow rice fell into disrepair" (Frank 1985:126). Today, the Mennonite church in Des Allemands is the only visible, human reminder of this enterprise. There are Mennonite communities in East Carroll, Beauregard, and St. Tammany parishes, as well.

Many Mennonites were recruited to work on reclaimed land. This church is the only indication in Des Allemands that Mennonites were active during the reclamation era, 2004. (Photo by the author.)

Sunset Drainage District

Of the several pump-drainage projects started in St. Charles Parish, only the Sunset Drainage District survives. Begun in 1911, this endeavor has subsided by more than six feet and is served by an elaborate network of drainage canals that funnel into a main reservoir channel. Pumps successfully keep the property dry and a levee protects the property from external flooding. Originally settled by small owner-operated farms, this 10,000 acre tract is currently used for pasture and forage crops, with a small section being converted into residential property. South of this site is an example of the dichotomy in wetlands drainage. The success of the Sunset Drainage Districts borders the abandoned 2,000-acre St. Charles Drainage District No. 1, whose inundated fields serve local duck hunting interests (Harrison and Kollmorgen 1947).

Lafourche Drainage District No. 12 and Smithport Plantation: The Raceland Prairie

Probably the most successful of the Wisner projects were near Raceland on the west side of Bayou Lafourche. The 8,200-acre site in Lafourche Drainage District No. 12 has operated continuously since 1901. Unfortunately, the migrants who settled on Bayou Folse were grain farmers. As soil nutrients were depleted, these pioneers changed their principal occupation to become part of the labor force required to operate the Bowie Lumber Company's mill near Raceland (Cortez and Rybiski 1980). The tract became pasture land, and livestock continue to graze this former marsh.

South of this project is Smithport Plantation. This one-square-mile tract was reclaimed in 1911—ten years after the Raceland Prairie. Part of this farm was reclaimed from Lake Field. The venture was too expensive to operate. During the Depression, low yields and high prices forced the "Plantation" to close. Unattended, the two-foot high levees and poorly designed drains ringing the abandoned real estate failed and the site reverted to open water (Okey 1914; Harrison and Kollmorgen 1947). A square lake west of Lockport in the 1960s signaled the location of this failed business enterprise. However, current maps show that the tract is again being drained.

Delta Farms

Delta Farms was owned by New York businessmen Henry L. Doherty, founder of Cities Service Oil Company (that in 1965 became Citgo which was acquired by Occidental Petroleum, then the Southland Corporation and in 1990 by *Petróleos de Venezuela*, S.A.). In 1908, Doherty purchased 46,000 acres (71.8 square miles—about half the size of Detroit, Michigan) just south of Lake Salvador and east of the Bayou Lafourche community of Larose. This effort was one of more than 100 business interests he acquired in his career. Much of this land Doherty sold. He retained enough property to form Delta Farms that supported agriculture and pasture for race horses (American Poland-China 1914).

Like Clovelly Farms further south, this reclamation enterprise included a school, hotel, and store. The site was accessed through Yankee Canal (also known as Harvey Canal #2). In 1928, the levee broke, damaging the property. The levee was repaired, and the farm continued to produce agricultural commodities. Nearly 3,300 acres was used to raise livestock and as a truck farm for the New Orleans market. Delta Farm was abandoned after its northern levee was breached by a barge and water from the Intracoastal Canal flooded the entire farm in 1971 (Phillips 1970). This reclamation project is now readily identified by the angular

Most reclamation projects were characterized by thriving small communities. (Image from the author's collection.)

(Top) Raceland Prairie site, ca. 1900. (Image courtesy of Fred Dunham.)

(Middle) One of the earliest known color images of one of Louisiana's reclamation projects, ca. 1900. (Image courtesy of Fred Dunham.)

(Bottom) The Winter Gardens site after the 1915 flood. (Photo from Reeves and Alario 1996.)

geometry of the flooded fields that have produced a nearly square lake. For nearly twenty years after the site flooded, telephone poles marked the road that crossed the inundated property.

Clovelly Farms: The Little Holland in Lafourche and Golden Meadow

Clovelly Farms' principal drainage canal, 1980. (Photo by the author.)

From its very inception, Clovelly Farms, east of the Bayou Lafourche village of Cut Off, was heavily subsidized. The "Farm" continues to operate as a private reclamation venture. Like other reclamation projects, Clovelly was not started as a land-speculation or settlement enterprise. According to Harrison and Kollmorgen (1947), this is the only reclamation business enterprise that did not attempt to induce Northern farmers to settle its land; instead, local Cajun farmers were recruited as tenants. The "Farm" supported about fifty families—approximately 300 people. In the 1940s, the property produced Irish potatoes, selling about fifty to sixty train car loads annually, and also providing the industry with 4,000 to 5,000 bags of seed potatoes.

In the early 1930s, a small plot was used to experiment with CP2817—a variety of sugarcane that helped the sugar industry rebound from mosaic disease (Borne 1945). Unlike other reclamation tracts, the "Farm's" 2,500 acres have not been turned into pasture, but continue to grow sugarcane. The tract's principal drainage channel—Scully Canal—connects the property to Bayou Lafourche, and three pumps—with a capacity of 164,000 gallons a minute—could remove from the diked enclosure up to seven inches of rain and keep the property relatively dry (Borne 1945).

South of Clovelly Farms at Golden Meadow a group of "Michiganders" began in 1903 to drain land east of the community to grow rice at a site identified as Golden Meadow Farms. They dug a waterway the locals called Yankee Canal and planned a future Netherlands. They failed, but the geometry of the canals associated with this land survives as the project's environmental legacy (Falgoux 2007).

New Orleans Netherlands Company

In 1910, the New Orleans Netherlands Company was organized by Chicago attorney Cornelius Jon Ton. Dutch investors provided most of the financing, and by 1915, the company had constructed nine miles of levees and numerous structures, including a pump house on the western shore of Lake Cataouatche, south west of Westwego. The property was used to raise early vegetables and operated as a dairy farm. To promote urban expansion, the property was subdivided into "Winter Gardens" encompassing 398 lots; more that 110 were sold (Reeves and Alario 1996).

Early farms on the New Netherlands Company site, 1915. (Photo from Reeves and Alario 1996.)

For reasons that are not specified in the literature, the project failed. The location is visible on topographic maps as a small lake outlined by remnant canals. Primary access is through Bayou Bois Piquant or the Louisiana Cypress Lumber Canal. There are also no surviving place names that would help identify this property and the lots sold.

The New Netherlands Clubhouse, ca. 1915. (Photo from Reeves and Alario 1996.)

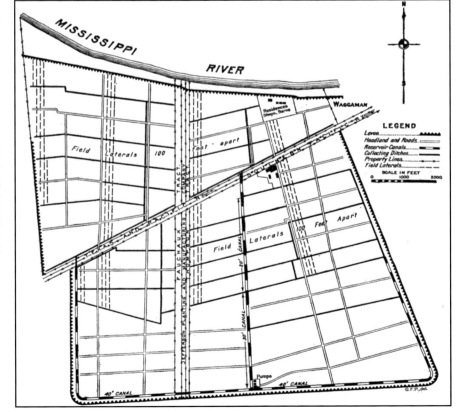

While the New Netherlands Company was reclaiming marsh, others were involved in draining land parallel to the Mississippi at Waggaman, Louisiana. These small natural levee-based-sites have evolved into part of metropolitan New Orleans. (Image from Okey 1914.)

Summary of South Louisiana reclamation projects
(From: Harrison and Kollmorgen 1947:676)

Drainage District	Parish	Town	Area in acres	Work Begun	First farmed
Gueydan, subdistricts nos. 1 and 2	Vermilion	Florence	7,400	1911	1912
Avoca	St. Mary	Morgan City	15,600	ca. 1913	ca. 1916
Upper Terrebonne	Terrebonne	Houma	4,240	1912	1915
Lafourche, no. 12 subdistrict no. 4	Lafourche	Raceland	4,240	1913	1915
Lafourche, no. 12 subdistrict no. 3	Lafourche	Raceland	2,250	1908	1910
Lafourche, no. 12 subdistrict no. 1	Lafourche	Raceland	835	1907	1909
Lafourche, no. 12 subdistrict no. 2	Lafourche	Raceland	940	1907	1909
Smithport Plantation	Lafourche	Lockport	647	1907	1908
Lafourche, no. 13 subdistrict no. 1	Lafourche	Lockport	2,000	1914	1909(?)
St. Charles	St. Charles	Paradis	9,860	1911	1916
St. Charles, no. 1	St. Charles	Paradis	2,840	1910	1915
Lafourche, subdistrict no. 6, subdistrict no 1	Lafourche	Des Allemands	1,880	1910	1912
Delta Farms, no. 4	Lafourche	Des Allemands	2,560	1913	1915
Delta Farms, no. 1	Lafourche	Larose	640	1910	1913
Delta Farms, no. 2	Lafourche	Larose	2,720	1910	1913
Delta Farms, no. 3	Lafourche	Larose	2,560	1911	1914
Lafourche, no. 9 subdistrict no. 1	Lafourche	Golden Meadow	1,780	1912	no date
Pontchartrain	St. Charles	La Branche	700	1913	1914
Kenner	Jefferson	Kenner	2,100	1912	no date
Willswood Plantation	Jefferson	Waggamon	2,600	1896	1897
New Orleans Netherlands Company	St. Charles	New Orleans	2,120	1912	1914
Jefferson, no. 3	Jefferson	Lafitte	5,000	1911	1914
N.O. Lake Shore Land Company	Orleans	New Orleans	6,950	1908	1909
Plaquemines Jefferson	Plaquemines - Jefferson	New Orleans	37,750	1912	no date
Reclamation, no. 1	Plaquemines	Poydras	2,500	1910	1912

Drainage District	Parish	Town	Area in acres	Work Begun	First farmed
Bayou Terre aux Boeufs	St. Bernard	Alluvial City	7,000	1913	no date
Venice	Plaquemines	Venice	1,100	1914	1915
Buras	Plaquemines	Buras	2,358	no date	no date
Jefferson, no 4	Jefferson	New Orleans	1,800	1915	no date
Lafourche, no. 20	Lafourche	Cut Off	2,500	1915	no date
	Total Acres	137,470			

Reclaiming the Marsh near Gueydan: A Non-Deltaic Plain Example

An inspection of topographic maps reveals that a great deal of the property south of Highway 14 was originally marshland. The highway served as the anchor point for access routes south into this easily reclaimed land. Many of these entry point roads were build on material dredged from the thirty-foot wide and eight-foot deep channels that delineate the reclaimed tracts (Merry 1909). These canals systems serve as reclamation identifiers.

Like the Wisner tracts, exaggerated advertising aggressively promoted the productivity of this reclaimed real estate. The principal difference was this land was being promoted twenty years before Wisner established his Louisiana Meadows Company and gained the advertising backing of the Illinois Central and Louisville and Nashville railroads.

Entrepreneurs in the early 1880s were reporting on the ease by which this land could be "turned under the plow." Harris (1881:122) wrote that: "with suitable drainage there is scarcely a foot of soil within the limits of Cameron [Parish] that could not be made to yield abundantly. At present not over one-fourth of the lands capable of cultivation without reclamation are being utilized." Further, J. M. Morgan reported in 1915: "Drainage and lots of it is what is needed to make this country blossom as the rose. The people are rapidly being educated along these lines and the White Lake project is a great object lesson in drainage and reclamation" (White Lake 1915:n.p.). The White Lake Land Company, the Illinois-Indiana Land Company, and others, were actively involved in reclaiming the *Chênière* Plain's green fringe along the southern boundary of the Pleistocene uplands (The Illinois-Indiana 1917:n.p.).

Southwest Louisiana's highly organized and focused approach to wetland reclamation can be traced back to May 1883 when Louisiana sold approximately 157,060 acres (245 square miles)—about the area encompassing Austin, Texas) of property "deeded under the Swamp Land Acts to developer Jabez B. Watkins for an unspecified consideration. Ten years later, he transferred title to the Orange

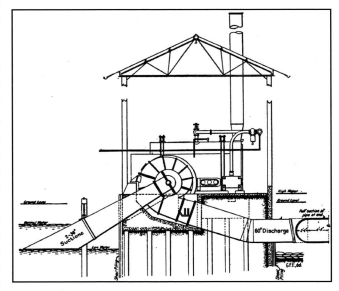

The elevated pump station at Gueydan. (Image from Okey 1914.)

Part of the complex used at Gueydan, ca. 1912. (Photo from Okey 1914.)

Land Company, Ltd., a land development company with headquarters in Lake Charles, for a consideration of $1,400,000 . . ." (Knapp 1991:6). Adjusted for inflation this sale, in 2009, is equal to $33 million. Along with this property it appears Watkins's North American Land and Timber Company purchased an additional 960,000 acres (1,500 square miles—about three times the area of Houston, Texas) in southwest Louisiana. To work this land the company began to systematically advertise for new immigrants. To aid in this venture, Watkins founded *The American* newspaper to advertise the amenities of this "new paradise" to potential migrants (Ferguson 1931:59). Once every month, 40,000 copies of *The American* were distributed, along with pamphlets, circulars, and other advertising material. These items were sent throughout the United States, Canada, and Europe. Thousands of farmers from the Midwest and elsewhere were encouraged to settle in the region. Shortly after Watkins began his advertising campaign, southwest Louisiana was transformed from a cattle province to one that was dotted with Anglo-Saxons familiar with farming the country's plain states.

As a result of Watkins's efforts and a number of other prairie/*chênière* land barons, large tracks of land have been reclaimed south of Highway 14. Under pump drainage, this "new" property was planted in rice, but salt water intrusion problems were a repetitive issue and were regularly described as the "grim menace" of the rice industry in these marginal lands.

A. L. Arpin, like Watkins, was intrigued by the possible rewards of reclaiming land south of Highway 14. Arpin moved in 1910 from Wisconsin to Crowley to be part of the Foster-Holcomb Investment Company's efforts to drain the marsh south of Gueydan. Arpin wanted to "prove that those so-called waste marshlands could be transformed into good farms" (Arpin, et al. 1999:18). After going bankrupt three times, he finally succeeded in 1912 when

Part of the Watkins' family legacy are the oil wells that bear their name. (Photo courtesy of Carl A. Brasseaux.)

> . . . the White Lake Land Company[,] headed by Arpin[,] and the Army Engineers, built a giant pumping plant. It, and a canal system, drained a large area of marsh land. It was bounded by a five mile Main Canal on the south side. The Spencer Canal along the north, which drained into Grand Lake, and a three-mile N/S canal every half mile. North/south roads were laid from the Main to the Spencer and midway between each canal. . . . Florence village . . . and the pumping plant were located at the SE corner where the two huge 36-inch steam drive turbines lifted the water from the Main into a drainage canal to the south (Arpin, et al. 1999:18-19).

On all of these reclaimed properties the drained organic soils subsided almost immediately either by oxidation or densification due to compaction, desiccation, and the loss of buoyant groundwater forces (Stephens and Stewart 1976). Therefore, each project required constant maintenance and monitoring. Further, developers launched each reclamation initiative without a clear understanding of the environment parameters that would affect the success or failure of each venture. As might be expected, these efforts were money driven, based on a quick return and not the logic of reclaiming land in an environment that was not easily drained. The investors did not realize that no suitable agricultural crop could produce the yields necessary to guarantee a profit and a return on their investment.

In addition, settlement plans were poorly developed and although federal and state agencies were involved, they did not investigate properly the social and economic effects of reclamation. Each project was capital intensive, and, to cover all of the associated reclamation costs, most of these projects ultimately became subdivisions whose tax base could maintain the system. Agricultural reclamation simply did not work (Emmer 1971). However, along the northern boundary of the *Chênière* Plain's marshes, there are still small sites that continue to support agriculture. Collectively these tracts encompass considerable land, but individually they are small-scale operations that are still identified by the canals and pumps that allow them to survive at the margin.

"Apron-traction ditcher" cutting the requisite lateral ditches at Gueydan, ca. 1912. (Photo from Okey 1914.)

Transportation Canals

In 1830, Congress appropriated funds to improve navigation through the Mississippi's delta. These funds were used to build the dredge *Balize*. "It proved an ignominous [sic] failure in two years of attempted dredging . . . The *Balize* was removed from service on the Mississippi and put to work digging holes in Mobile Bay" (Lowrey 1964:239).

Before construction of the Harvey lock, marshdwellers brought their boats to a site where, for a fee, they could be launched into the Mississippi, ca. 1880. (Photo courtesy of Rathborne Commercial & Industrial Properties, Harvey, La.)

Construction of the Harvey Canal and locks changed the transportation geography and the associated movement of cargo throughout the Barataria Basin, ca. 1928. (Photo courtesy of the United States Army Corps of Engineers, New Orleans District.)

Natural waterbodies were traditional shipping routes. Watercourses—such as bayous Lafourche, Terrebonne, Black, Grand Caillou, Petit Caillou, and Teche, as well as the Atchafalaya, Pearl, Vermilion, Mermentau, Calcasieu, and Sabine rivers—generally are aligned in a north-south direction, making east-west movement difficult. To rectify this navigational inconvenience, canals were excavated to increase the natural system's transportation efficiency, reduce travel time, and encourage regional economic growth. These artificial waterways regularly served as hubs for canal-based communities, designed so each home would have water frontage.

Maps produced in the mid-1700s clearly show transportation canals, or in some cases portages, linking the wetlands to the Mississippi River. These pathways served as funnels for goods moving into the New Orleans market and document the early influence of these transportation corridors. French colonists constructed canals to improve their contact with the Gulf of Mexico and to join the Mississippi with the bayous at the "rear" of their communities (Surrey 1916). In the 1850s, a small canal, probably the predecessor of the Harvey Canal, approached to within a "few hundred yards of the river bank" (Jackson and New Orleans 1854:1). In fact before construction of the lock into the Mississippi River, marshdwellers would sail their boats to the end of the canal, where they were hauled by mules over the levee on "cars" or by a "sub-marine railroad" and launched into the river.

Tolls were charged for this service: skiffs paid $0.25 each way, *pirogues* $0.35, and each hunter on horseback paid $0.15 (Swanson 1975). The service fees notwithstanding, this waterway allowed fishermen and hunters to transport their goods to the New Orleans market. By 1914, commerce through the lock included logs, lumber, railroad cross ties, general freight, oysters, shrimp, crabs, fish, diamond-back turtles, dried shrimp, shrimp bran, sugar, game, syrup, rice, potatoes, onions, cucumbers, squash, beans, corn, tomatoes, garlic, pumpkins, watermelons, cabbage, Spanish moss, furs, eggs, coal, fuel oil, gasoline, shells, machinery, cattle, ice, fertilizer, charcoal, gravel, empty barrels, beer, and cauliflower that were valued at $7,200,000 ($155 million in 2009)—all renewable resources destined for the New Orleans market (Barataria Bay 1917).

Frequently excavated by hand, these transportation routes served the local population well. With time they evolved into important commercial arteries. Although New Orleans merchants favored the Mississippi River over canal systems, transportation canals played an important role in South Louisiana's industrial history. One of these waterways, the Inner-Harbor Navigation Canal, embodies the twentieth century awareness of the importance of better connectivity. Further, by "making land available for lease to large industries, the canal encouraged the development of the city and at the same time brought more import-export business to the port of New Orleans" (Bolding 1969:54). This channel became the anchor point for the eventual construction of an alternate ship route to New Orleans along a seaway called the Mississippi River Gulf Outlet, whose construction proved to some that "modern New Orleans can no longer rely entirely on the ancient river" (Bolding 1969:60). This may have been true, but, in 2009, the route was effectively closed because of the damage it caused to the St. Bernard Parish marshes and its role in flooding New Orleans during Hurricane Katrina. Although designed as a transportation corridor, the route was branded a failure because the engineers did not understand or consider the dynamics of water movements through the channel. This fact was driven home during the storm surge from Hurricane Katrina and led to the route's closure.

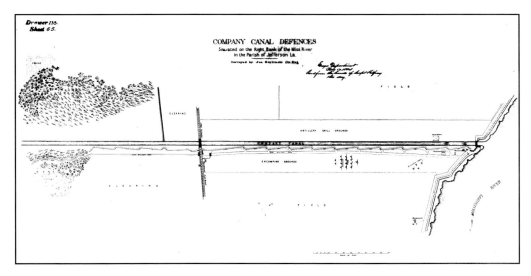

During the Civil War, transportation canals were critical, and Company Canal had its own resident defense force. (Image courtesy of National Archives and Records Administration, Division of Maps, Record Group 77, Drawer 133, Sheet 65, February 1894.)

Between 1829 and 1925 numerous ruler-straight transportation watercourses were built or improved (Becnel 1989). The Barataria Canal Company, for example, was charted by the state in 1829. The company, under the direction of Robert Ruffin Barrow, Jr. built a channel—the Barataria and Lafourche Canal or the Company Canal—from a lock in the Mississippi opposite New Orleans to Lake Salvador and Bayou des Allemands, via a canal to Bayou Lafourche at Lockport. From Bayou Lafourche, the canal extended through Lake Field (named after William Field who donated the prop-

This canal was cut to bring mail and supplies to Pecan Island, ca. 1910. (Photo from Hanks 1988.)

Oystermen used the Doullets and Ostrica canals to move their oysters from the west side of the Mississippi to the east side, ca. 1930. (Photo courtesy of Louisiana Department of Wildlife and Fisheries.)

erty on both sides of the bayou for the canal) and Lake Long to Bayou Terrebonne and into Houma. From Houma, the canal continued into Bayou Black and, finally, to Berwick's Bay (Ditto 1980; Becnel 1989). This became one of the state's most important early east-west corridors for waterborne traffic.

Further to the west, Delcambre, known originally as the *Marais Carlin* or *Grand Marais*, first became a shrimp processing center when Bayou Carlin was a narrow canal with a few small boats, one oyster canning factory, and a fuel dock. When Delcambre Canal was dredged in 1906, the community became synonymous with shrimping. Until the 2005 and 2008 hurricane seasons, the shrimp industry was a multi-million dollar business (Bradshaw 1997; Bergerie 2000). After four major storms in this three-year span, considerable thought is going into rebuilding the community's economic base in a more sustainable manner. Although the storm surge devastated the community, and the canal helped funnel the surge into the city, the citizens are working to revitalize the economy and prepare better for the next hurricane event and the associated flooding. Regardless, this canal is a good example of the importance of transportation canals in fostering economic development.

Commerce no longer had to take a circuitous route through the state's natural north-south trending waterways to the New Orleans' markets. Businessmen had a more direct shipping corridor. Eventually, parts of this route were incorporated into the Gulf Intracoastal Waterway—the twelve-foot deep, 125-foot wide, 1,066-mile waterway that developed into one of the world's great canals. The United States Army Corps of Engineers publication *Water Resources Development* (1957) delineates other transportation systems, including, but not limited, to Barataria Bay, Bayou Terrebonne, Johnson Bayou, and Bayou Petit Caillou. Other notable canals included the waterways from Empire to the Gulf of Mexico and from White Lake to Pecan Island, which was the primary trade route into the *chênière*.

By 1900, Louisiana's renewable resources were transported through a well-defined system of navigable channels (Davis 1985). In the 1930s, for example, a packet boat carried freight and passengers between New Orleans and the many river-accessible communities in Plaquemines Parish. During this period, as many as 500 sacks of oysters and 200 to 300 boxes of oranges were shipped weekly from the parish, with Buras serving as the region's orange-producing center (Hansen 1971). In addition, oysters were moved to market by a network of canals that ultimately connected to the Mississippi River. Local watermen moved their oysters through Doullut's Canal at Empire and the Quarantine Bay Canal at Ostrica (Vujnovich 1974). In fact, before construction

Dredging contractors introduced outside workers to excavate transportation canals used by the petroleum industry and others, no date. (Photo courtesy of the Morgan City Archives.)

in the early 1900s of these two locks, moving oysters from one side of the Mississippi to the other involved a long, dangerous, tedious, and indirect route. So, although the Mississippi River was the ultimate destination an interconnecting network of transportation canals were key links in the early supply chain to New Orleans. Many of these routes were not officially named and are now a footnote in history, since they are part of the state's expanding areas of open water.

By 1930, the coastal landscape was marked by engineered transportation-oriented waterways—such as the Boudreaux, Brady, Freshwater Bayou, Falgout, Sevin, and Lapeyrouse canals—and others that offered safe passage for campboats—introduced in the late 1890s—and used throughout the province during the annual trapping, fishing, hunting, and oyster seasons (Boutwell and Folse 1997). Also, as hydrocarbons became more important, these transportation corridors served the industry well by providing connectivity to individual fields and as feeder routes into a larger network of nationally significant waterways.

From 1945 until the end of the twentieth century, movement of crude petroleum and refined petroleum products dominated Louisiana's transportation statistics, with canals serving as the primary travel routes. This was not an accident, as these transportation corridors were built in direct response to Axis activity in the Gulf of Mexico. To counter the German U-boat menace during World War II, the Gulf Intracoastal Waterway (The Thousand-Mile Miracle) was completed in less than a year—providing a safe passage for shipment of goods from source regions along the Gulf of Mexico to Eastern markets (Wolfert 1961). When finished, this system—in tandem with the Mississippi River and other barge routes—made Louisiana the center for wartime Gulf Coast petroleum traffic. In addition, they served as a safe inland passage for powerboat and sailing enthusiasts. A by-product of this massive engineering effort was the Federal government's increased involvement in dredging in order to maintain adequate navigational depths.

Representative sample of a few of the coastal plain's transportation canals
(From Davis 1973)

Amoureux	Avery	Bayou LaCache	Belle Isle	Billot
Boudreaux	Breton	Bush	Caernarvon	Canal Blue
Canal St. Jean Charles	Cancienne	Company	Delcambre	Dupré
Falgout	Fasterling	Franklin	Freeport Sulphur Co.	Freshwater
Golden Star	Grand Pass	Gravolet	Gueydan	Hayes
Jimmie	Kings	Lapeyrouse	Last Point	Little Chenier
Madison	Marmande	McIlhenny	Meyers	Oaks
Peoples	Pecan Island	Rabbit	Sea Breeze	Sevin
Schooner Bayou	Sixmile	Socolo	Verdunville	Weeks
West Chenier Au Tigre	White Lake System	Wilkinson	Williams	

Evaluation of this expanding transportation network is difficult, for only a few twentieth-century canals were built exclusively for commercial traffic. Most were constructed for other purposes, their primary function being development of agricultural, mineral, forest, and fur resources, such as the Orange-Cameron Land Company's canal system designed to help improve muskrat habitat. The Company constructed canals eighteen-feet wide and six-feet deep to bring in fresh water from the Sabine River to improve accessibility across their 162,000 acre (30.6 square mile) "rat" ranch, stretching from the Sabine to Calcasieu Lake, and from the Intracoastal Canal to the Gulf (Arthur 1927).

Whether for agricultural, mineral exploration and development, forest access and removal, or to harvest or improve fur and alligator habitats, these routes operated only secondarily as transport couplings. Regardless, they furnished open-ended transportation links between points and extended for miles along well-defined right-of-ways. This paradigm, initiated in the early 1700s, persists today.

Although the Gulf Intracoastal Waterway is the best known, many routes predate it; at the same time, all serve the same basic role of providing connectivity. Each transportation artery influences the local economy, attracts industry, and alters property along the right-of-way. Because of constant use, the sides of many canals eroded to such an extent they became large waterways. In the process, they lost their fabricated character; they are now regarded as "natural." In addition, navigation channel deepening reflects, with time, the increased shipping demands made in the transportation industry.

Ancillary infrastructure responded accordingly. Ports in turn provided turning basins, tank batteries, off-loading services for liquid as well as bulk commodities, locks to provide safe connectivity and retard salt water intrusion, large onshore storage sites, and adequate quay space. Moreover, on the Mississippi River, large petrochemical complexes were constructed between the late 1960s and mid-1980s. These industries, and general technological advancements in bulk shipments, transformed the lower Mississippi into a major regional port, and New Orleans became the United States' largest port based on tonnage (Campanella 2006). Rivers, canals, and bayous became secondary links in cargo transport (Becnel 1989).

In the aftermath of Hurricanes Katrina, Rita, Gustav, and Ike, it is clear these transportation routes are at risk. The wetlands are a buffer, yet in view of continued land loss, this country's long-term refinery and associated energy needs and policies will have to be reassessed, as the transportation arteries become more exposed to open water, becoming the highways for salt water and hurricane waves (Turner 1987; Williams and Cichon 1994).

Trapping Canals: A Trapper's Access to the Marsh

While traveling along the Intracoastal Canal in the 1930s, the captain of the *Donie* reported:

> Once in a while a trapper's cabin would grace the banks of the canal, skins of muskrats or other swamp animals stretched out to dry on frames set against the walls. From a nearby clothesline, the wash of the trapper's family waved a lackadaisical welcome to the passing boat and its crew. Sometimes half-clad or naked small children playing along the bank of the canal looked up and shouted enthusiastically at the passing boat in French (Jackson 1993:169).

To exploit wetland resources, a *habitant* dug a *traînasse*—a term derived from a French word meaning "to drag," but in the local *patois* this word signifies: "a trail cut through the marsh grass for the passage of a canoe [*pirogue*]" (Read 1927:74). These liquid paths were hacked out by trappers using a *pirogue* paddle, "crooked shovel" (a shovel bent like a hoe), a hatchet (*casse-tête*), a rake, and a "sweeper" (a long-handled, steel-bladed knife). It took one man as much as three weeks to clean a mile of *traînasse*; but community participation in the construction process frequently cut this time considerably.

Marshdwellers dug their "push-pole" trails large enough to avoid depending on a current for channel completion and protected the route from erosional enlargement by damming their *traînasse*. This reduced the environmental damage connected with drainage, salt water intrusion, and erosion. As the number of individuals engaged in trapping increased, the trails gradually assumed their current chaotic pattern (Davis 1976). Later, ditch diggers, mudboats, and marsh buggies were employed to cut channels to gain access to trapping leases (Ensminger 1967). Additional ditches allowed individuals to trap larger areas, but, in creating the new passageways, many of the original safeguards were abandoned. Though small, the five-foot wide and six-to-twelve inch deep passages left about six inches of clearance on either side of a *pirogue*.

The channels are indicative of the marshdweller's painstaking exploitation of the coastal zone's avian, fur- and hide-bearing animals. The *traînasse* was crucial to the harvesting process (1941; Davis 1976). Since landowners never placed restrictions on the number of trails built, trappers had complete freedom to dig

The crooked shovel was one of the earliest tools to cut a *traînasse*, 1971. (Photo by the author.)

as many trapping canals as necessary. When large tracts were leased to fur-buyers and "outsiders," ditches were cut indiscriminately both between bayous and through ridges. The resulting system could easily encompass more than 300 miles of these meandering spider-web-like push-pole trails. Many leases were damaged by saltwater intrusion, because no dams or control structures blocked these channels in order to protect productive muskrat, alligator, and later nutria habitats, (Davis 1976). Through repeated use, storms, and current flow, a few of these trapping trails became larger waterways.

The elaborate *traînasse* network represents the wetlands' earliest large-scale canalization endeavors (Davis 1978; Davis 1976). Trappers became operating engineers. They opened the marsh to access through their use of canals that were so small they were not shown on many

The *traînasse* was the trapper's highway into the marsh. (Photo from O'Neil 1949.)

topographic sheets. The meandering ditches apparently appeared to photo interpreters as an insignificant feature—only nine appear on the GNIS database; Blackfish, Gang, LeBleu and Noah ditches are named. The other five are called "pirogue trails."

In reality, this chaotic assemblage of trails was the backbone of the trapping industry. Without these "water roads," a wetland trapper could not make a living.

In order to construct these routes quickly, two boat types were used—ditch diggers and mudboats manufactured by some unknown trapper or extending family member masquerading as a mechanical engineer. "Since the day of the bateau putt-putt, large inboard motors have been applied to a variety of flat boats. Many of these are used in the marsh as 'mudboats' capable of churning through very shallow marsh trails" (Brassieur 1999:3). Often powered by a 200-horse-powered,

Mechanization improved a trapper's ability to dig "pirogue trails." (Photo from Cheramie 1997.)

air-cooled inboard, these boats are quick, maneuverable, practical and ideally suited for moving through the state's marshes. With invention of the steel-hulled ditch-digging boats, trappers could cut four-feet wide, by two-and-a-half feet deep near surgically precise ditches. Two miles of these water roads could be cut in a day.

A ditch digger or *"traînasse* machine" was designed with two blades attached to the bow, one turning clockwise, and the other counterclockwise. These blades pulled the machine forward and chopped a *traînasse*. A deflector plate welded on the *bateaux*-type bow distributed the spoil evenly on both sides of the channel. It was a quick and efficient process that flailed a trail. The wooden mudboat was powered by an automobile engine. It used brute force to plow a trail through the marsh muck. As long as the *marais* was covered with a shallow layer of water, this boat could generate enough traction to tear through the substrate. Unlike the *traînasse* machine, the final incision was not nearly as exact, but the end result was the mudboat cut a *traînasse* at about the same speed

The rotating blades of the ditch-digger, 1997. (Photo courtesy of George J. Castille III.)

as a ditch digger. The ditch digger was used primarily on the delta plain, while the mudboat was preferred in southwest Louisiana and continues to serve recreational sportsmen interests, while most *traînasse* machines have been retired and when found are rusting away in someone's backyard.

Throughout coastal Louisiana *traînasses* have modified the landscape. Most ditches and associated land tracts have eroded extensively, making it difficult even to speculate on the number of *pirogue* trials excavated since the early 1900s. In some cases, a *traînasse* was cut from a remote secluded marsh camp or natural levee community, directly into a trapper's lease. These paths allowed marshdwellers to use their homes as base camps. Further, the number of "push-pole" trails was high, although documentation is unsatisfactory, and the written record shows, in many cases, evidence of few ditches. They were either overlooked in the maps of the period, or their scale was so small that they were never recorded. Even so, marshdwellers built many *traînasses* into, across, and around their trapping claims. Created for specialized use, *traînasses* have survived as silent reminders of humankind's abilities to change natural systems. They became marsh highways.

Logging Canals

By 1888, more than 1.7 million acres of Louisiana timberland belonged to forty-one companies, all owned outside the state. For a brief time, Louisiana was the world's leading lumber producer. But the business brought here by the timber industry came at a high price. With no thought to reforestation, the state's ancient and unique woodlands were wiped out (Richard 2003:111).

Lumber has been a major product of Louisiana almost from the beginning of European settlement. In the early 1700s, lumber was shipped along all major waterways, with consumers in the French West Indies being the leading customers. For example, in 1750, "forty vessels sailed from New Orleans loaded with lumber for French islands in the West Indies" (Moore 1983:204). In fact, the French term for swamp, *cyprière*, is adapted from the cypress tree. Milled timber was in demand and was the main cash crop of the colonists. Timber was so valuable, milled lumber could triple in value within one year.

Moving logs into New Orleans, ca. 1895. (Photo from Bridaham 1972.)

This kind of profit naturally increased the search for marketable cypress. Due to difficult working conditions, most timber was purchased from planters who were expanding their cultivatable land around New Orleans by clearing, channelizing, and draining the backswamp. A by-product was usable timber. Even with this source of lumber, early colonists dug canals between the Mississippi River and the Barataria Basin to retrieve additional marketable lumber.

Over time, New Orleans became a significant consumer of all kinds of building materials. Cypress was particularly important after fires in 1788 and 1794 destroyed most of the city (Campanella 2006). Reconstruction was extensive, and the construction trades required vast quantities of brick and lumber, especially cypress, which was less of a fire hazard than the available pine.

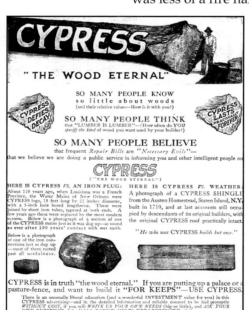

Louisiana settlers discovered homes constructed of cypress did not decay rapidly, and, in the era before Formosan termites, was not damaged by insects. In addition, when cypress was used for maritime planking, it was immune to saltwater borers. With all of these properties, cypress became the favored building material for a wide array of products and was eventually marketed as the "Wood Eternal."

The problem was getting the timber out of the *cyprière*. Oxen, horses, and wheeled carts were impossible to use in the swamp's water-logged soils. French axmen learned if they used a girdling technique in advance of cutting down a tree, the ring cut off the tree's moisture. When harvested, the sap-free log's buoyancy allowed the trees to float like a cork. These logs were removed from the swamp by lashing them into bundles, which were assembled into rafts to be floated out of the forest. To supplement hand-operated pit saws, the French logging community set up sawmills to meet their wood-product needs (Sand and Koch 1975). The problem was these mills could not be water-powered until a chain of levees were built along the lower Mississippi that could be cut to produce a raceway or chute. Water channeled through the race powered the mills.

When completed, the levees served as dams, so during periods of high water, water from the Mississippi flowing to the swampy backlands powered the mills, and then during the low-water season, some planters used the reverse flow to turn their waterwheels. To accomplish this feat, landowners excavated small canals linking the *cyprières* with the Mississippi. This technique worked until around 1820, when steam engines began to replace waterwheels. (Moore 1983B). Like the "tidal rice mills and sawmills on the coasts of South

Carolina and Georgia, the Mississippi River sawmills worked when the water level in the river was higher than in the swamp, or vice versa" (Moore 1983:204).

From a flooding perspective, these sluiceways were the Achilles heel of the levee system and eventually had to be outlawed, as they could easily trigger a crevasse. Immediately after the Civil War, swampers harvested cypress during low-water season and floated it out of the swamp during high water. Since levees interfered with their ferry system, breaks in the levee sometimes came from "the midnight work of the rafts men" (Westphal, et al. 1980:33).

As demand for lumber rose, planters began to excavate canals into the cypress swamps. These canals represented the first attempt in Louisiana to use artificial waterways to reach forest resources. They were multi-functional canals, providing drainage and transportation as well as timber access routes. Since most large planters owned sawmills, timber cut and milled "on the place" was used to build their own homes (the Gates house in Franklin is one example) or easily floated to the New Orleans market. As a result, by the end of the French era, loggers "had succeeded in cutting down the best of the cypress forests in the vicinity of New Orleans. The speed with which they did their work is most impressive. During 1824, a ship captain seeking logs for ballast could find no suitable timber left standing closer to the city than 'five or six leagues'" (Moore 1983B:36).

The planter's canals were useful to ship or raft timber and other commodities to market. Maps dated between 1817 and 1842 indicate that planters south of New Orleans had already constructed many of these multi-functional channels. The canals were frequently named after the planter who ordered construction. Hence, the Laronde, Larusles, Vileré, Jumonville, Philippon, Gentilly, Johnson, and other engineered waterways were dug to serve not only the planter's drainage and transportation needs, but also as important access routes to merchantable cypress.

Canals dug exclusively to assist commercial logging operation did not occur until after the Civil War, when the South's forests were considered the foundation for future economic and industrial growth. Because this resource was described as "inexhaustible," the U. S. Congress passed the 1876 Timber Act. This legislation encouraged the "sale of large parcels of federally owned forestland and provided tax breaks to lumber developers" (Vileisis 1997:117). By 1888, 5.7 million acres—about the size of the state of New Jersey—had been sold in five Southern states. Therefore, large-scale commercial logging began after the Timber Act, when vast cypress/tupelo tracts were sold for twenty-five cents to $1.25 an acre.

With passage of the Timber Act, entrepreneurs purchased large tracts of swampland. They logged it using an extensive array of canals, ca. 1900. (Photo courtesy of Milton Newton.)

Recognizing the timber's value, lumber companies purchased a considerable quantity of this land. Many of these businesses obtained clear title to more than forty or fifty square miles of wet forest (A sketch of 1910). About 1880, after the white pine forests around the Great Lakes were nearly depleted, many of these operators moved into the South (Stokes 1957). As a result, Timber Act incentives attracted Northern investors, who began the process of methodically logging Louisiana's swamps. Initially, these wet forests needed to be flooded to remove cut timber by floating them out of the cut forest. This was a labor-intensive, inefficient system that drastically limited logging. This changed with invention of the pullboat that made it possible to efficiently harvest untouched, large, stands of cypress with precision and became the symbol of the age of industrial logging in coastal Louisiana.

Pullboat Logging

A steel nose-cone on display at the Louisiana State Museum at Patterson, 2007. (Photo by the author.)

Prior to the pullboat's invention in 1889, lumbermen could not have operated year-round. With introduction of the steam-logging engine, steamboats, and pullboat, "cypress manufacturers were independent of [the annual spring] rise and unaffected by droughts" (Norgress 1935:34). Cypress now could be logged year-round. These inventions solved the problem of timber removal and were instrumental in increasing cypress output. The pullboat, developed by William Baptist of New Orleans and used until the 1940s, was originally equipped with a steam-logging engine (later, diesel was used). The barge-mounted engine operated two spools. The large reel carried a two-inch steel cable that could winch, along a run up to 8,000 feet, the cut cypress logs out of the backswamp. They were pulled into a logging canal. The second drum held a wire rope used to return the cable to the harvest site. The engines, using long cables attached to a steel-nose-cone placed over the end of a log to prevent the skidding tree from being buried in the mud, could handle up to 1,000 feet of logs per day. Heavy and cumbersome, the nose cones were difficult to use and inefficient. Eventually, loggers simply rounded off or "snipped" the front of the logs, and the cone was discarded in the swamp.

From the pullboat's anchor point, loggers pulled laser-straight paths through the swamp, spaced about 450 to 500 feet apart. From the air, this spoke-like pattern is easily distinguished and identifies the swamps that were harvested using pullboat logging. Moreover, these patterns indicate the areas harvested by industrial, mechanized logging that allowed a relatively small number of logging firms to quickly harvest the state's wetland forests.

Brownell and Drews, Louisiana Cypress Lumber Company, and Pharr and Williams were three of the earliest commercial cypress logging companies to harvest cypress using "liquid logging." These concerns had mills at Morgan City, Houma, and Patterson, respectively, and easily handled the flow of cypress from the surrounding swamps. Cypress rafts, also known as *chowtaws*, regularly a half-a-mile long, were towed to these mills, and eventually many others, for processing.

Other investors soon realized the value of the state's timber resources and began to make similar swampland acquisitions. By 1890, a sizeable percentage of Louisiana's swamps had been purchased by lumber interests. Access and timber removal were two problems that confronted these companies, problems that were easily solved by excavating canals into the prime harvesting sites. The distinctive canal patterns dredged by these firms, the names of the canals, and their locations serve today to define areas of intensive industrial cypress-logging activity.

A visual analysis of areas logged reveals some individual canals were seven miles long. G. E. Watson (1906) reported several of these routes were ten-feet deep and

The logging industry at work, ca. 1914.
(Above) Photo from the Report of the Conservation Commission of Louisiana, April 1, 1914 to April 1, 1916.

(Left) Photo courtesy of the George François Mugnier Collection, New Orleans Public Library, 1895.

(Left)   Photo courtesy of Rathborne Commercial & Industrial Properties, Harvey, La, no date.

(Above) Photo courtesy of the Standard Oil Collection, University of Louisville, negative no. 61754, 1948.

A pullboat working in the swamp, ca. 1900. (Photo from Bridaham 1972.)

fifty-feet wide and were connected with small feeder ditches that "radiate off in every direction like spokes in a wagon wheel. From the air, these watery radiants glisten like silver starbursts in the late afternoon" (Kemp 1997:10).

Representative sample of a few of the coastal plain's logging access canals
(From Davis 1973)

Ashland	Bayou Prevost	Bonvillain	Bowie	Cooke
Cotton	Cousins	Delery	Donner	Dry Cypress
F. B. Williams	F. B. Williams Storage	Franklin	Halpin	Hanson
Himalaya	Hollywood	Ivanhoe	Johnson	Kenta
Lewis	Louisiana Cypress Lumber	New Canal	Norman	Old Hanson
Pharr	Pitre Lening	Southwest Louisiana Lumber	St. Louis	Timber
Williams				

Abandoned logging channels are evident in most swamp areas, including the Atchafalaya Basin and around Boutte, Franklin, Gibson (also known as Tigerville), Houma, Kraemer, Lac Des Allemands, and Lake Verret. Sawmills in these communities and others like them produced 248 million board feet of cypress lumber in 1899 and one billion board feet in 1915. Ten years later, the state milled 296 million board feet—when placed end-to-end this was enough lumber to go around the world twice at the Equator.

Pullboat Watercourses: The Spokes of a Wheel

To utilize a pullboat effectively, lumber companies dredged primary and secondary watercourses leading to logging sites. These channels were indispensable to the timber operation. Further, they provided lumbermen with an essential link to their forest reserves. To remove the harvested cypress, the canal configuration incorporated a series of intersecting channels with fan-shaped cable runs radiating out in every direction from central points along the access routes. The end result is the pullboat runs or "drag paths" rotate out from a "set."

From the air, these runs resemble the spokes of a wheel. The pullboat remained in one location for up to two months, until all of the timber within a workable distance was dragged from the swamp into the canal. The boat and associated cable was then relocated to begin establishing another radial course to harvest the adjoining cypress timber. The process was repeated until the entire circle, with a radius of about 8,000 feet—1.5 miles—was cleared. These spoke-like designs were etched into the landscape by the cables required to "snake" the logs into the principal channel (Davis 1975; Cypress, wood eternal 1991).

Logging canals remain a part of the swamp's morphology. For more than fifty years, the channels were essential to the forest industry, but as swamp timber was depleted, wood-cutting operations were terminated. The cypress companies employed no methods of conservation to preserve their wood resources. They wanted the timber and short-term profits; they did not think of the future. Only canals and pullboat scars remain (Wurzlow 1976B). In a larger sense, these features are indicators of the once robust cypress trade and the nearly complete depletion of virgin cypress/tupelo

Pullboat logging scars are still visible in South Louisiana swamps, 2008. (Photo courtesy of Carl A. Brasseaux.)

swamps. These canals are conspicuous reminders of what will happen when South Louisiana's hydrocarbon resources are depleted. However, it must be emphasized the logging period occurred in a time when conservation and preservation were of no concern. The country was expanding and timber was vital to this expansion, so timber removal was simply an integral part of the industrial age.

The influence of humankind on this environment is clearly visible. It is estimated that during the systematic deforestation of Louisiana's timberland that 85 percent of , the state's cypress/tupelo forests had been logged (Pearson, et al. 1989). Since it takes about 100 years to grow a cypress tree sixteen inches in diameter, and natural reproduction is difficult, this industry will only return to Louisiana's swamps through aggressive management and stewardship programs.

One of the earliest pioneers in developing management techniques for their vast timber holdings was the Rathborne Lumber Company of Harvey, which, in 1947, contacted the United States Forest Service about improving and planting cypress on their land. (Kerr 1953). They planted 164,000 seedlings to try and regenerate a 45,000 acre cut-over tract near the community of Choctaw in Lafourche Parish. By the late 1960s the experiment was abandoned due to herbivory, escalating costs, and fluctuating water levels, but represents the only large-scale attempt to reestablish the state's cypress forests (Prophit 1982).

Canals and Oil Well Access

> . . . these canals are an asset in transporting the crude product to the refinery; and southern Louisiana is fortunate in having an intricate system of inland waterways, bayous and canals, which means cheaper transportation (Branan 1937:7).

> Just how important to petroleum companies are its dredging operations? Without them, scores of fields along the Gulf Coast would never have been discovered; thousands of miles of trunk and gathering pipelines could never have been laid; great volumes of crude oil could not be moved by barge. In short, without the dredges, a large share of the nation's oil and gas would be just where it was 25 years ago [1938]—beyond economic reach (McGhee and Hoot 1963:150).

During the last-half of the industrial logging era, oilmen began to appraise the coastal zone's hydrocarbon potential. Exploitation of the subsurface mineral wealth was a challenge since many considered the terrain "too thin to plow and too thick to drink" (Reilly 1956:138). Consequently, many favorable sites remained untested until drilling procedures, equipment, and geophysical expertise were developed to capitalize on the recoverable mineral fluids. Once engineering and logistic concerns were solved, along with regulations pertaining to the use of dynamite in public waters, the wetlands became a major hydrocarbon province provided all drilling and exploration functions were coordinated carefully (Moresi 1935).

In 1934, successful use of a submersible drilling barge marked the beginning of expanded drilling activity. To maximize the floating unit's potential, the industry needed to dredge canals to exploration and development sites (An unusual canal 1955). They were successful, as canals cost less to construct than a temporary board roadway into the various drilling locations. As a result of this practice, in the latter half of the twentieth century, almost one-third of the United States Army Corps of Engineers dredge and fill permits were issued in Louisiana (Mager and Hardy 1986). It is now difficult to locate a stretch of marsh where canals are absent, but excavating this canal network was a sizeable undertaking by all of the companies involved in

At times, access was so critical, two dredges operated on the same channel simultaneously, no date. (Photo courtesy of the Morgan City Archives.)

wetland hydrocarbon exploration and development (Drilling on land 1942). A search of the GNIS database reveals there are 801 named oilfields in the state. Those in the marsh and swamp are identified by their canal patterns.

In the marsh, soils presented no serious engineering impediments. Powerful suction dredges, bucket dredges, spud barges, and marsh buggies were quite adept at excavating the required petroleum access, pipeline, and transportation corridors (McGhee and Hoot 1963). Dredging contractors opened the coastal lowlands quickly to hydrocarbon development. In the process, operating engineers added an extensive agglomeration of interconnecting and dead-end canals. This was not always an easy task, as siltation issues required the redredging of some channels after drilling was complete. In some cases a dredge, after cutting a channel, had to dredge its own way out of the access route (Scott 1952).

Representative sample of a few of the coastal plain's oil company access canals
(Most of the canals associated with oil and gas fields were not officially named.)
(From Davis 1973)

Burton-Sutton	Bayou Couba Oil Field	California Company 12" pipeline	California Company	Cameron Canal Gas Field
Fohs	Gulf Refining Company 6" pipeline	Havoline	Humble	Magnolia
Magnolia Vacuum	Phillips	Shell	Stanolind	Superior
Sweet Lake	Voss			

Although there were no standards, the width of most canals was from seventy to ninety feet; this width would accommodate easily the largest drilling barge. Well location slips were dredged from 120-feet to 150-feet wide. Most of the channels were box cut giving the bottom approximately the same width as the top. A water depth of from eight to nine feet was considered adequate (Williams 1944) and as new reserves were discovered the interlocking system continued to expand. The canals and associated pipeline rights-of-way represented a maze of tributary lines that coalesced into an integrated, complex network of transportation arteries. The end result is Louisiana's wetlands are laced with canals and subaqueous pipelines, whose precise location is frequently unknown (Cappiello 2006).

For example, by the early 1950s the Venice dome, or "wagon wheel," was outlined by an eight-mile perimeter primary canal that involved nearly 150 wells. Using a submersible drilling barge, each well was completed in thirty to ninety days (Rose 1952). Slots extended outward and inward from the main circle and were utilized as drilling barge locations. The pattern outlines the subsurface salt dome and encompasses all holes drilled around the dome's flank (An unusual canal 1955). As was the case for most of Louisiana's access canals, through additions, the patterns enlarged into a complicated net of coalescing channels.

Without any regard for changes in natural drainage, the long-range hydrologic effects of all of the state's canals in many cases have been disastrous, but the severity of an individual waterway's impact varies with the environmental setting and the spoil placed along their banks (Swenson and Turner 1987; Turner and Streever 2002).

To develop an oil and gas field, a petroleum contractor cuts a series of initial service routes, and then adds supplementary passages as warranted. The canals extend from a maze of right-angle and dead-end channels that mark an oilfield and resemble an intricate city street map. Many of these channels end abruptly, "the banks tracing a shape that loosely resembles a keyhole, hence the name for them—'keyhole canal'" (Hallowell 2001:35). All of these waterways serve as tributaries that filter into the central traffic corridor, guaranteeing well access. The assemblage ultimately dominates the surface topography, with each appendage representing a new well. Constantly influencing larger quadrants, the geometric design grows rapidly. Once in use, the distinctive straight-sided canals can erode into a cuspate, serrated form. Some fields become so canalized that more than 20 percent of their surface morphology is devoted to these topographic elements. Within the complex are the pump jacks, gages, valves, and an intricate web of underwater pipes that are part of the essential technological elements that deliver the extracted hydrocarbon fluids to market.

The pipeline channels have become an integral part of the nation's energy policy. Tens of thousands of miles of pipelines cross the coastal lowlands, often with no official record of their exact location When pipelines cross the marsh or swamp their routes are marked by a canal, lines that cross waterbodies locations are not always well documented. The problem is that if the nation losses any part of this system for even a couple of days, the futures market and refinery industry react accordingly. In fact, the impressive number of these linear features has prompted some individuals to describe the unorganized network as a "spaghetti bowl." These interconnecting routes are now permanent features and represent at least 2.3 percent of the present wetland area (Turner and Cahoon 1987). In ad-

The keyway is an easy landscape identifier, 1975. (Photo by the author.)

After World War II, Louisiana's landscape was canalized, no date. (Photo courtesy of the Morgan City Archives.)

dition, Ko and Day (2004) report on a vast array of short and long-term impacts, other than canals and pipeline rights-of-ways, they attribute to the oil and gas industry.

In no other part of the United States is there such a chronology of resource utilization depicted in canal systems. A logical method of dealing with a distinct wetlands environment, canals nevertheless modified drainage patterns, altered flora and fauna, changed salinity regimes, and contributed to land loss. Whether the watercourse is the narrow trapper's *traînasse* or the complicated assortment of petroleum access routes, it has a decisive and cumulative impact on the alluvial wetlands. Regulatory agencies have slowed their growth, but it must be emphasized some canals are more than 200 years old. They are permanent landscape features. Canalization processes, therefore, illustrate how wetland habitats can be transformed through concentrated and uncontrolled dredging strategies.

While it is an arduous task to evaluate total wetland change, canal construction emerges as an important element in Louisiana's environmental modification. Although considerable controversy surrounds the effect of canals on marsh loss, exploitation patterns endure, even though resources are long-since depleted; their longevity is a visible reminder of humankind's capacity to unknowingly change the natural system. The function may change, but the "lines" persist. And, regardless of the original function, all of these engineered channels have altered water circulation patterns across the marshes and through the swamps.`

Reclamation was an attempt to entice settlers into the wetlands. In most cases these efforts failed, even so a wide array of settlements were scattered throughout the coastal plain. Some of these sites were used only during seasonal harvesting activity, others were permanent. (Image courtesy of The Historic New Orleans Collection, accession no. 1956.13.)

Chapter 6
REPRESENTATIVE EXAMPLES OF SETTLEMENTS
IN LOUISIANA'S COASTAL LOWLANDS

A small portion of its [Plaquemines Parish's] inhabitants live at the pilot villages and marine stations on Pass-à-l'Outre, Southwest and South Passes, while a few of its people dwell upon the 'chenieres' and ridges that rise above the sea marsh or upon the low sand islands of the coast (Harris 1881:182).

Living on the Edge

It has already been said that the whole Gulf coast of Louisiana is sea-marsh. It is an immense, wet, level expanse, covered everywhere, shoulder-high, with marsh-grasses, and indented by extensive bays that receive the rivers and larger bayous. For some sixty miles on either side of the Mississippi's mouth, it breaks into a grotesquely contorted shore-line and into bright archipelagoes of hundreds of small, reedy islands, with narrow and obscure channels writhing hither and thither between them. These mysterious passages, hidden from the eye that over glances the seemingly unbroken sunny leagues of surrounding distance, are threaded only by the far-seen white or red lateen-sail of the oyster-gatherer, or by the pirogue of the hunter stealing upon the myriads of wild fowl that in winter haunt these vast green wastes (Cable 1886:161).

Louisiana's coastal citizens face a triple threat—subsidence, sea-level rise, and hurricane-induced storm surges. Unfortunately, many coastal property owners deny that they are in danger. They have selected their residential/commercial/recreational sites without considering long-term geologic or meteorological processes. Their vision is obscured by either a faulty memory or the assumption that humankind can do almost anything. They typically downplay the threats of living in the coastal zone. They consider abandonment as unthinkable and not an acceptable alternative, even though settlement retreat has been a noteworthy part of the region's history.

Abandonment is not a new concept. Through time, Louisiana's coastal dwellers have adapted to the region's changing environments. The wetlands offer numerous restrictions and choices, settlement decisions are based on a wide array of socio-cultural and technological factors. The population has learned to adapt to these natural elements. For example, hurricanes became benchmark events and memory reference points. In the marsh, years do not mean much, so people frame their memories around storms. The sea level is rising, the land is sinking, and hurricanes are a constant threat, but these are not new problems. For nearly three centuries they have been an integral part of the wetland's settlement history, and abandonment has not been an acceptable option.

Marshdwellers lived, with rare exception, on the region's high ground—natural levees, *chênières*, or Indian middens. These sites were chosen because of their height above the surrounding marsh and because the waterways associated with the natural levees were a transportation artery. By late 1930, it was possible to visit nearly all of the Deltaic Plain's principal marsh communities by road. Even so, there were a few settlement clusters that were totally secluded at sites miles from a road "deep in the marsh" (Kammer 1941:22). They were accessible by boat, but were still culturally isolated and at the mercy of the environment. These "outlying" communities were at risk from an unexpected hurricane's wind and storm surge. In fact, landscape/landlord changes in coastal Louisiana occur at a rate that is observable on a "human" scale.

Damage to New Orleans, Last Island, Chênière au Tigre, Grand Bayou, Manila Village, Cabinash, St. Malo, Chênière Caminada, and numerous other communities

To the people of the marsh, hurricanes were a constant threat, ca. 1900. (Photo from Espina 1988.)

document the problems associated with living within Louisiana's coastal lowlands. Even with all of these environment issues, the wetlands' human-cultural-systems and their variability are inexorably tied to the natural environment.

In response to hurricane flooding and the associated devastation, wetland residents have made a conscious decision to move to communities less prone to hurricane-induced flooding. After Hurricanes Audrey (1957), Betsy (1968), Andrew (1992), Lili (2002), Ivan (2004), Katrina (2005), Rita (2005), Gustav (2008), and Ike (2008), a large number of people left their homes and moved to Lake Charles, Houma, Thibodaux, and other cities they perceived as safe; in South Louisiana, environmental adjustments are a way of life. Some residents have recently moved three or four times to escape the problems associated with hurricanes. Property owners overwhelmed by the accumulative devastation were slow to rebuild.

Historically, people have moved from the wetlands repeatedly to secure a safer, or at least less vulnerable, residence. Through time and across space, populations opted voluntarily, or were forced, to shift habitations to more desirable settlement locations. In some ways, abandonment has become part of their culture. Even so, prior to the 1930s, the world beyond the marshes and swamps was largely alien and remote. Yet, there was a remarkable give-and-take of people in the state's out-of-the-way and inaccessible, marsh communities. In the marshland, life was lived from season to season and the spirit of camaraderie helped many get through the good years and the bad (Hallowell 1979). The marsh provided a calm, unhurried environment that made people focus on each other during those turbulent hurricane-induced struggles. It was an area where people rowed to church, to the store, or to see a friend or family member. Gravel roads or automobiles were simply not a part of their communities; they were watermen.

Barrier Island Communities

As early as 1847 tourists from Attakapas . . . were able to make excursions to Last Island for a few days of bathing, fishing and related activities. Following is an excerpt from an advertisement that appeared in The Planters Banner of Franklin in 1847 titled 'A Pleasure Trip to Last Island'. It informed the reader that 'The steamboat Meteor No. 3 Captain Faussett, planned to leave Franklin Saturday, July 13 at 7:00 a.m. for Last Island offering a chance to the people to enjoy sea bathing and fishing, the boat was to remain six days at the island.' The advertisement further stated that 'The Meteor could provide berths for 60 persons but was able to accomodate [*sic*] 80 without crowding. The houses on the island were able to accomodate [*sic*] 40.' Also, according to the advertisement, a cotillion band was scheduled to be on hand for the trip (Southern 1990:19).

Last Island or the Isles Dernières: East Timbalier, Timbalier, Caillou, Wine, and Isles Dernières

. . . no ordinary island, but the proudest summering place of the Old South . . . [A] private little world dedicated to fine living. Here . . . wealthy planters and merchants, who bore the most illustrious names in all Louisiana, brought their families to escape the summer heat and to live according to the unchanging code of French and Spanish ancestors (Deutschman 1949:143).

In the early 1850s, Last Island, located off the coast of Terrebonne Parish, was described as "thirty miles long and half a mile in width" (*New Orleans Daily Picayune* 1850:2). At that time, a half-dozen summer cottages made up the "Village Bayou," also known as Fisherman's Bayou and Bayou Voisin. At this site Landreth (1819:86) wrote, ". . . the Pilot recommended us to go round to the Bayou to where the fishermens [*sic*] huts were . . . we could not find the mouth or entrance of the Bayou . . . the Pilot went in our Bateau and tried to find it . . . he brought back one of the Negro fishermen with him . . . and carried us into the Bayou up the Fishermen Hut where we arrived. . . ."

Landreth (1819:87) reported further that the two islands that made up the Isles Dernières were "about eight or nine miles easterly and westerly and from three to four in breadth northerly and southerly divided nearly equally by a Bayou which we call fishermens [*sic*] Bayou." In fact, "a Mr. Peter Dunett of New Orleans I am told has made a fortune by carrying on a fishery here. . . . [H]ere he always keeps three hands fishing and Turtling and three carry the fish and Turtle to New Orleans market which they can do in about Eighty or ninety miles by way of the Laforch [*sic*] through the Lakes and in this way the[y] can come by water within six miles of New Orleans" (Landreth 1819:85).

In 1850, thirty years after Landreth's trip, the island was being used for recreational purposes. Advertisements of the period note that "an extensive boarding establishment" was available for visitors (Southern 1990:25). "The houses are fine, particularly those of Lawyer Maskell and Captain Muggah. These houses serve for the reception of visitors during the summer season, at which time the enjoyers of elegant leisure flock to the isle in great number, and not as a dernier resort, but for the veritable purpose of enjoying themselves" (*New Orleans Daily Picayune* 1850:2).

By the middle of the nineteenth century, the Last Island community of Village Bayou was one of Louisiana's first coastal recreation sites. Families came to swim, fish, hunt, and enjoy the tranquility (Liddell 1849; Washburn 1956). It was a delightful place, where one could enjoy the sea breeze (Wailes 1854). The extensive beach served as a shell road where "one's buggy whirls over it with a softness, and airy, swinging motion, that is perfectly intoxicating" (*New Orleans Daily Picayune* 1852:1). Packet steamers and sail boats could moor in the safe harbor on the bay side of the Village Bayou.

On Caillou Island, near Last Island, a small "public house" was opened that also served as a summer resort in the early 1850s (*Thibodaux Minerva* 1854). This facility was also identified as "The Gulf House" and although no other references have been uncovered to suggest other islands were being used for recreational purposes, it is highly likely other sites were being used as well. Advertisements of the period note

Last Island was within a three-hour run from Morgan City and there was regular service to the island (*Thibodaux Minerva* 1855). Further, there were at least twenty-five "camps" located on or near the island's beach face (Southern 1990).

Two hotels, the Ocean House and Captain Muggah's Hotel (The Muggah Billiard-House), provided guest rooms on Last Island. The resort's light frame structures were not built to withstand the force of a hurricane, but no one asked if the Isles Dernières was a safe place (Silas 1890). Visitors were only concerned about enjoying the island's relaxed atmosphere. Consequently, in the legends of coastal Louisiana, Creole aristocracy danced until they died in the Last Island Hurricane of 1856 (Deutschman 1949): "Reality took them by surprise. Within a few hours, the worst antebellum hurricane would move from rumor to legend, changing the lives of generations to come" (Bultman 2002-2003:84).

The Storm of 1856

On that fateful Sunday, August 10, 1856, it is believed more than 400 people attended an evening ball in the Village Bayou—unaware of the hurricane about to make landfall. Late in the evening,

> the wind blew a perfect hurricane; every house . . . giving way, one after another, until nothing remained . . . [E]veryone sought the most elevated point on the island . . . at the same time [trying] to avoid the fragments of buildings, which were scattered in every direction . . . Many . . . were wounded; some mortally. The water . . . commenced rising so rapidly from the bay side . . . there could no longer be any doubt . . . the island would be submerged. The scene at this moment forbids description. Men, women, and children were . . . running in every direction, in search of some means of salvation. The violence of the wind, together with the rain . . . and the sand blinded their eyes, prevented many from reaching the objects they had aimed at (Ludlum 1963:166).

> The waters carried a depth of several feet of sand and debris on some parts of the island, and . . . so changed [the island's] surface . . . those formerly acquainted with it, could no longer recognize it (*New Orleans Daily Picayune* 1856B:1).

> It was a gloomy sight, not a house or shelter standing (Ellis n.d.:8).

The wind increased; the buildings shook; the water rose, and few escaped. During the night, every solid object became a mobile battering ram, destroying the island's man-made elements. Some died. Others rode out the storm on floating debris and were rescued fifteen miles from the resort or survived in the wreckage of the steamer *Star*, which made semi-weekly trips from the railroad stations at Bayou Boeuf and Morgan City, down the Atchafalaya River through Four League Bay to the resort (Schlatre 1937).

On the Sunday morning of the storm, the *Star* approached the island after a difficult voyage from Morgan City. Throughout the journey two men were required to steer the vessel. She was anchored behind Captain Muggah's Hotel. At some point, the pier used by the *Star* collapsed; the steamer parted its moorings and slowly drifted toward the island. Soon the steamboat's chimneys, pilot house, and hurricane deck were gone; only the hull remained (Ellis n.d.; Bultman 2002-2003). The wreck floated toward the island and lodged in a turtle enclosure for the remainder of the storm (*New Orleans Daily Picayune* 1856B).

Approximately 250 to 275 people survived the disaster in the wreck's hull (*New*

Marsh Outposts

"Clark Chênière, a shell bank on the eastern shore of Little Lake, supported a dozen houses and Juan Rojas's store. Sailing luggers and a few gasoline boats anchored offshore. Each yard had a charcoal furnace for cooking and a cistern for drinking water. Hundreds of families remained on these various cheniers, but the surplus population of Chênière Caminada, Grand Temple, Bayou Couba, Grand Coquille, and other marshy outposts flowed into Westwego" (Reeves and Alario 1996:18).

Since the Temple was about half way between New Orleans and Grand Terre, Jean Lafitte held contraband and slave auctions at the site, so New Orleans merchants and the region's planters did not have to make the three-day journey to Grand Terre. Moreover, as early as 1812 the site was occupied (Cable 1886; DeGrummond 1961). The Temple was eventually leveled for its shell resources.

Orleans Daily Picayune 1856). Without the *Star's* superstructure firmly trapped in the sand, more would have perished. Initial newspaper narratives claimed from 260 to 300 people died (Ellis n.d.). Entire families were swept off of the island, but as more survivors were located, the final death toll was reduced to about 140. Property losses were estimated at more than $100,000, well over two million dollars in 2009 (Ludlum 1963). At the center of the island, one small hut survived, along with numerous head of cattle (Cole 1892). Otherwise, the Isles Dernières were in a shambles (Deutschman 1949).

This tragic story quickly became a synthesis of fact and fiction, for, over time, numerous imaginary embellishments were added to the Last Island legend, crystallized by the writings of Louisiana journalist/author Lafcadio Hearn's *Chita*. After this disaster, no attempt was made to rebuild the Last Island resort (Deutschman 1949). It simply became part of South Louisiana's folk history and a contemporary anchor point for a few camps and houseboats called "Millionaire's Row."

Last Island never regained its lost glory as a resort, but in the marsh north of the island, many citizens of Houma and its environs built recreational dwellings in the community of Seabreeze—which also boasted a shrimp-drying platform, as well as oyster shucking and packing sheds (Hansen 1971). The 1909 storm devastated this site, but, by 1915, it was again a thriving community with an annual July fourth regatta attracting more than seventy boats (Races attract great 1915). In addition, the *Hilda* was chartered for trips to Timbalier Island (Boutwell and Folse 1997). Contemporary maps shows the site once occupied by Seabreeze as open water—another example of land loss in coastal Louisiana.

Grand Isle: A Potpourri of Uses

Sixty-two miles due south of New Orleans lies Grand Isle. . . [I]t is a century removed from the Louisiana metropolis in point of atmosphere and traditions. There is no telephone, no telegraph, no radio communication save the United States Coast Guard's receiving set for storm warnings; mail comes only every other day (Graves 1930:410).

Further, islanders consciously sought to maintain their dissimilarity by preserving their own set of values and traditions. They purposely promulgated a distinct dialect and touted their ecologically-sound and aesthetically-pleasing 'lifestyle' set 'amid the trees, in spot as fertile and as beautifully flower-covered as any on earth,' . . . Islander desires were aided by the island's physical location distinct from competing centers of population (by 1900 the closest village was thirty miles away) and the singularity of its historical development (Stielow 1986:185).

Spanish land grants, issued in 1781, mark the beginning of Grand Isle's colonization. François Anfrey subsequently established a plantation and cattle operation before selling the island. The property then changed hands several times before Barataria Plantation was eventually established there. Barataria became a major, self-sufficient agricultural complex, typical of an antebellum Louisiana plantation. This sugar operation did very well for a number of years, but it ultimately failed because the barrier island's natural environment proved hostile to the production of a large staple crop.

Consequently, by the early 1800s, subsistence farming and fishing dominated the local economic landscape, but with the arrival of Jean Lafitte's polyglot band of privateers the island's economy took a decided upturn. From about 1800 to 1812, Grand Isle and its sister island, Grand Terre, became part of the Lafitte's "Kingdom of Barataria." The island's isolation worked to the advantage of these buccaneers, who were raiding

> **An Early Grand Isle Hotel**
>
> As a result of the Panic of 1873, the Grand Isle Hotel went bankrupt. The property was purchased by John F. Krantz and advertised as "The Grandest and the Best—the finest beach, most delicious surf and safest sea water bathing in the country. Eight hours from the city, with daily mail and passenger accommodations" (Stielow 1982:244).

One of the buccaneers who protected Jean Lafitte's encampment. (Image from Schoonover 1911.)

Spanish ships sailing off Louisiana's coast. The goods and slaves they "captured" moved freely from Grand Isle through New Orleans' underground economy making "The Terror of the Gulf of Mexico" enterprise quite profitable. This smuggling operation was in direct violation of the revenue laws, but the intricate network of waterways that constitute the Barataria Basin made it impossible to capture this illegal contraband. New Orleans elite benefitted from the fine goods brought into the city, and Lafitte had an accessible market for his "captured" valuables, making many of the local merchants quite wealthy. Grand Isle became part of this conduit, as it was, along with Grande Terre, one of the transfer depots.

Grand Isle's buccaneering days ended after Lafitte's assistance in the Battle of New Orleans during the War of 1812. Lafitte's lucrative enterprise along Louisiana's southeastern coast was terminated and the sizeable pirate population abandoned their fortifications and moved west to the Neutral Strip and then to Galveston. When this out migration occurred, the island lost a good deal of its population; as a result, an early nineteenth-century census reveals Grand Isle had a permanent French-speaking, Creole population of sixty-three residents, which was distinct from its "Cajun" neighbors (Stielow 1986). These impoverished individuals were getting by on the fish and oysters they harvested, the crops they grew, and the fish oil they made (Reeves 1985:110). And, living on the edge of the Gulf without the benefit of the spoils of Jean Lafitte's army of brigands, the island nearly reverted to its uninhabitable state.

For nearly a half-century Grand Isle's small enclave of residents was out-of-the-way and largely forgotten, as the inhabitants were living a subsistence lifestyle in near complete isolation. Although the island's residents were for a time involved in the

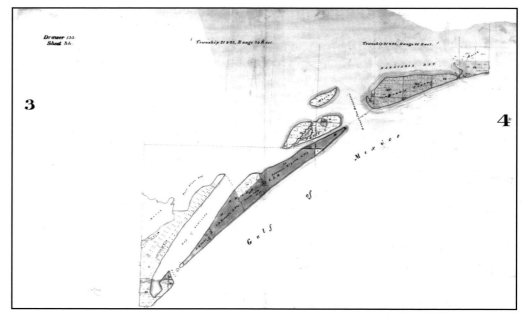

In 1843, Grand Isle and environs were surveyed. (Image courtesy of the National Archives and Records Administration, Division of Maps, Record Group 77, Drawer 133, Sheet 34, December 1843.)

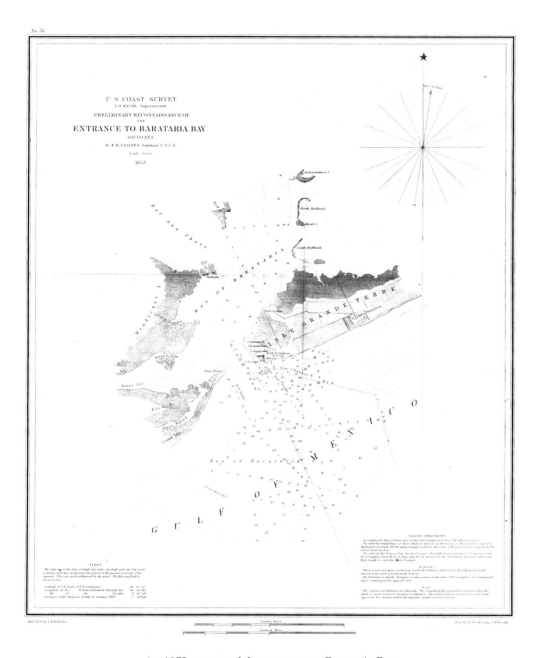

An 1853 survey of the entrance to Barataria Bay.

sugar business, they also managed several large cattle herds and operated, with the aid of slave labor, numerous fishing operations (Reeves 1985). The success of these endeavors eventually attracted outside investors, who were convinced the island could be transformed into destination point for tourist.

As a result, after the Civil War, Col. Joseph Hale Harvey—a canal and steamboat operator—and Swiss hotel manager Benjamin Margot purchased the defunct Barataria Plantation and converted it into a resort. Using the plantation's footprint, Harvey and Margot's Grand Isle Hotel included the sugar refining shed. This building was converted into a dining and dancing parlor that also held "the hotel's offices, a bar, gambling tables, billiard rooms, and quarters for a hundred servants" (Stielow 1982:243). Vigorously promoting the property, these entrepreneurs went to great lengths to attract "a wealthy, family-oriented clientele from among the businessmen and aristocrats of New Orleans" (Stielow 1982:243).

As a result of the Depression of 1873, the Grand Isle Hotel went bankrupt. The property was purchased by John F. Krantz. Krantz advertised his inn as "The Grandest and the Best—the finest beach, most delicious surf and safest sea water bathing in the country. Eight hours from the city, with daily mail and passenger accommodations" (Stielow 1982:244). With this type of hard sell, Grand Isle became a mecca for recreational activities and a center for fishing and truck farming. Even so, success of the island's tourism industry hinged upon its accessibility. Excursions from New Orleans were planned aboard numerous steamboats. For $7.50 (more than $160 in 2009) one could reserve a room on an overnight steam packet traveling to the resort (Grand Isle excursion 1866; Meyer-Arendt 1985; Meyer-Arendt n.d.). By 1861, there was daily packet service, and by 1878 a post office (A freebootin porter 1891).

The Krantz Hotel's row cottages prior to the hurricane of 1893. (Photo courtesy of The Historic New Orleans Collection, accession no. 1981.238.18.)

Getting to Grand Isle was difficult, expensive, and for the Crescent City's elite, the journey could take twelve or more hours, often requiring sleeping aboard the steamboat. Many sternwheelers and luggers made the New Orleans-Grand Isle run once or twice a week. The *Joe Webre, Tulane, Hazel, Nevada, J.S. & B.*, and many others carried shrimp, dried shrimp, shrimp bran, crabs, fish, diamond-back terrapin (*Malacoclemmys palustris*), game, cucumbers, squash, beans, tomatoes, ice, oysters, corn, furs, general freight, and passengers to and from the island, as Grand Isle made the transition into a highly diversified developed community. All of these boats did considerable business in the summer months, when "outsiders" were traveling to the island to take advantage of the well-advertised beach-oriented recreational activities.

The trip was shortened to five hours when the New Orleans, Fort Jackson, and Grand Island Railroad—known to the regulars as the Orange Blossom Route—was extended to Socola's Canal in Plaquemines Parish, where passengers were off-loaded onto a steamboat (Ross 1889; Stielow 1982; Jackson 1993). The railroad operated from 1888 to 1911. Like many railroads of the period, this "road" was the most efficient, quickest, and most cost-effective way to move goods and people. It was in direct competition with steamboats, but once the Orange Blossom Route was completed to Socola's Canal, the time difference made the railroad the most efficient way to start the first part for the journey to Grand Isle. This link meant that passengers had a relatively comfortable journey. Because the travel time was now reduced by more than half, a well-established pattern of summer visitations to Grand Isle evolved. Several notable writers, including Lafcadio Hearn (1884, 1889), George Washington Cable (1886), Kate Chopin (1899), and Frenchman Le Mercier du Quenay retreated to "The Island" to write and enjoy the quiet surroundings (Meyer-Arendt n.d.).

The second segment of the trip terminated at a dock served by a mule-powered tram that transported passengers to the Krantz Hotel (also known as the Grand Isle Hotel). The Krantz facility offered travelers standard rooms as well as thirty-eight former slave cabins that had been transformed into guest cottages. Aligned in parallel rows, the cabins designated "Bachelors Row" and "Widow's Row" were assigned on the basis of gender and marital status. According to one observer, the hotel also featured a large, low one-story dining-room, where everybody eats. Then, there is a dancing hall that was once an old plantation home, and here is where the evenings are spent. Mr. Krantz . . . seems to have overlooked the fact that people at a summer resort desire to be close to the sea. The Krantz place is considerable over a half a mile from the beach and is only frequented during bathing hours (Ross 1889B:6).

The tram took guests to the beach three times a day—5:00 in the morning, noon, and 6:00 in the evening.

If you drop in at the hotel you will find families there who have come each season for years and years, and you will get from each the same testimony of the pleasure each trip has given them. The visitors [are] cosmopolitan and the yearly gathering of guests embrace persons who are bend on rest and recreation and frolic. The crowds are southern and the customs sensible. There is none of the glitter and tinsel and sham and shoddiness of the more pretentious resorts of the north. You won't find here spider legged dudes in patent leather and high neck collars. You don't find people decked out in extravagantly rich dresses and jewels at dinner. You find an absence of the scandals that make the life at other big resorts. These accessories of other places are wanting. But the life here is just as pleasant and just as great (Ross 1889:5).

Grand Isle's other "resort" was the Ocean Club, built for an estimated $100,000— the equivalent of more than two million dollars in 2009. The Club was broadside to the Gulf and designed to rival or surpasses the resort hotels at Newport, Saratoga, and Niagara Falls (Barataria La., items 1866; Stielow 1982). The two-storied building was configured in the shape of a large letter "E" with all rooms facing the Gulf (Grand Isle: an excursion 1891). Supported by nearly 300 pilings, the hotel included 160 bedrooms, two parlors, two dining halls, a billiard hall, a card room, a reading room, pantries, a kitchen, and a laundry. One dining hall alone was designed to accommodate 250 guests (A seaside san souci 1891). The large facility was lit by 320 gas lights. Unfortunately, the Hurricane of 1893 severely damaged the hotel, and it was never restored to its original grandeur. The Krantz Hotel was also badly

Ruins of the Ocean Club Hotel on Grand Isle after passage of the 1893 hurricane, ca. 1894. (Photo courtesy of George François Mugnier Photograph Collection, Louisiana Division, New Orleans Public Library.)

damaged. Twelve hotel employees lost their lives, but the village, sheltered by a grove of oaks, sustained only minor damage (Fall 1893; Forrest n.d.; Van Pelt 1943). After the 1893 hurricane, outside business interested disappeared and Grand Isle's "participation in the unprecedented growth of tourism . . . effectively ended" (Stielow 1982:256). For twenty-seven years "The Island" served as a spa resort and redefined the local work ethic, as "the prospect of leisure became an acceptable goal" of the wealthy and Grand Isle was an important destination (Stielow 1982:257).

Jean Lafitte's privateers leaving the island and the destruction from the 1893 storm were economic benchmark events, but in both cases the island's full-time population reverted to small-scale commercial fishing and row-crop farming activities. This bucolic lifestyle was what appealed to the residents. Gusts did materialize periodically, but the island depended on the region's renewable resource for their primary livelihood.

By 1935, the Oleander Hotel and Grand Isle Inn provided island guests lodging, but these were not grand resorts. Tourists continued to find their way to the island, thereby aiding the local economy, but the local "Grand Islanders" had a rather low

Grand Isle before the modern recreation era of second home development. (Photo courtesy of the *Jefferson Parish Yearly Review*, 1939.)

opinion of visitors. They tolerated these "guests" because they brought money into the economy in the form of guide fees, boat rentals, and the sale of food, drink, and other necessities. The country was in the middle of the Great Depression. This economic slump had national repercussions, but for the inhabitants on Grand Isle, who were accustomed to living within their means, feared debt, had no bank accounts or stock portfolios, and were largely self-employed, the impact of the Depression was minimal. Even so, locals suffered, and many had to sell their small plots to outside investors.

Beyond the tourist-oriented beach, the island's center served the local farm community that was an essential part of the island's culture for generations. Tourists rarely saw this part of the island, where small orange groves—along with plots devoted to blackberries, melons, beans, eggplants, peppers, squash, cucumbers, cauliflower, and other commodities—were being produced for sale off the island (Barataria Bay 1917). In fact, at the 1915 Pan-American Exposition, one grower won a gold medal for cauliflower and an honorable mention for cucumbers, but no reference is made as to the location of this event (Kammer 1941).

Island-based truck farming posed distinctive challenges. For example, the soil could not be cultivated properly with traditional techniques, so John (Vic) Ludwig, popularly known as "King John," began using oversized hills with deep furrows to insure proper drainage. To utilize this technique, the islanders built a new levee on Grand Isle's bayside and repaired those that had been damaged by storms. In addition, flood gates were installed to keep out salt water.

The mild climate and availability of "bran" or shrimp dust to fertilize the new fields offset many of the local agricultural problems (Thompson 1944; Swanson 1975). It is thus hardly surprising these farms were successful. Grand Isle's truck farmers annually shipped to Northern markets between 35,000 and 50,000 bushels (forty-eight pounds per bushel) of cucumbers a year (Graves 1930; Thompson 1944). These vegetables beat the Florida crop by several weeks, with the resulting premium prices providing islanders with a lucrative income.

A hurricane in 1915 ruined the island's fall vegetable crop, destroyed local livestock, and caused thousands of dollars in damages. The island was covered with six feet of water; no one died on the island (Barataria Bay 1917). The destruction was so extensive the local population was reluctant to return to farming. Much of the land subsequently lay fallow. Although there were some excellent trapping property close to the island, only four or five trappers lived on Grand Isle in the late 1930s (Kammer 1941; Ramsey 1957). Instead, fishing became the principal local occupation.

One distinctive Island occupation was a large diamondback terrapin/turtle farm (Barataria Bay1917). Fishermen caught in their nets these salt-tolerant reptiles, but the market required a more dependable supply. John Ludwig developed a turtle farm—"three low barns, separated by a road, . . . [that] look almost identical with the barns of a well-appointed race track" (Housley 1913:1)—that solved the supply issue, thereby giving birth to Grand Isle's turtle business. The 1915 storm did considerable damage to this operation, but it recovered quickly (Tulian 1916). A similar business was thriving on Deer Island off the coast of Mississippi, where one dealer kept 5,000 turtles (Sheffield and Nicovich 1979) and at Beaufort, North Carolina, where one company kept more than 25,000 newly hatched terrapin (Radcliffe 1914; Coker 1920).

A photograph of a terrapin farm probably owned by John Ludwig, ca. 1900. (Photo courtesy of Fred Dunham.)

This industry was not limited to the Gulf Coast or Eastern Seaboard. In the late 1880s, about 600 "sea-turtles" were annually brought to San Francisco from Mexico. The average turtle weighted 175 pounds and sold for $4 (Jordan 1887). Coker (1920) reported that males or "bulls" sold for $10 to $12 a dozen, while "half count" females measuring between five and six inches, would bring double this price. A dozen six-inch terrapins had a market value of from $36 to $40, while seven-inch turtles could be sold for $60 to $70 a dozen, a dozen eight-inch terrapin sold for up to $125. These were wholesale prices; at retail the cost would be substantially higher. To food connoisseurs, the taste and flavor of properly prepared terrapin justified the premium expenditure.

Prior to World War I, the terrapin industry generated at least $150,000 to the "catchers" and "dealers" (Viosca 1920). Diamondback terrapin were captured by trappers and fishermen, bred, and raised in great pens for the restaurant trade—prior to the storm of 1893, this was the case on Last Island (True 1884). Some of these turtles were shipped to Grand Isle by "trappers from as far west as Brownsville, Texas and as far east as Savannah, Georgia" (Graves 1930:411). Besides breeding local turtles, Ludwig kept terrapins shipped from other wholesalers. Dealers in New York and Philadelphia shipped their turtles to the South to winter, as the cold Northern winters were too cold (Coker 1920). To "beat" these winters, a barrel of turtles could be "stabled" at Ludwig's farm for ten dollars a season (Housley 1913). On the return trip north, one or more of the Southern turtles was probably mixed in with the scarcer, but better quality, Chesapeake Bay terrapins.

The Island served as the major source for terrapin, and the market was an exclusive one. Direct sales of Grand-Isle-raised diamondbacks came from a network of customers in New York, Baltimore, Washington, D. C., and Boston. From the middle of September to the middle of April, Ludwig's farm delivered 30,000 to 50,000 terrapins annually to these wholesale and retail outlets (True 1884; Housley 1913; Graves 1930; Ramsey 1957). To feed this "herd" required one to one-and-a-half tons of fresh seafood daily. Although not reported in the literature, the thirty to forty-five tons of food needed monthly was substantial. Bycatch may have been the primary source of this food supply, or Ludwig may have had a number of fishermen working for him to provide the necessary "feed." Regardless, delivering a continuous supply of food was a full-time job that added to the operation's overhead.

With arrival of Prohibition between 1913 and 1933, this industry suffered dramatically, as most recipes required sherry. Without this ingredient, demand for turtle soup declined. Turtles were being harvested and sold, but the market was limited. In 1932, 275 dozen turtles were transported out of state. The following year, after repeal of the 18th Amendment, 2,431 dozen were distributed. The industry was reborn, as it was now possible to enjoy turtle with wine or sherry (Dauenhauer 1934).

Although the island was recognized for its terrapin and fishing fleet, few people were involved in harvesting oysters. The oysters that came to Grand Isle were used

solely for home consumption. As a result, the production of oysters from the "back-side" of the island was very small. This industry was left to the "luggermen" of La-fourche, Plaquemines, and St. Bernard parishes. Grand Islanders were not oystermen. Yet the region was, according to Moore (1899), actively engaged in the business, but it appears Grand Islanders were not directly involved in fishing for these bivalves.

A dish-washing shelf was common in many Acadian homes, ca. 1946. (Photo courtesy of the Standard Oil Collection, University of Louisville, negative no. 44761.)

Even without the income derived from the harvest of oysters, the local standard of living remained comparable to other fishing communities along the Louisiana coast. Like their counterparts elsewhere, Grand Islanders lived in wood-frame cottages, without electricity, modern plumbing, and evening newspapers. These structures were, nevertheless, considered quite comfortable by their occupants. They were highly functional, simple folk houses which frequently featured an open-air *tablette à chaudière*, or "dish-washing shelf," an extension of the window sill. While washing the dishes, this appendage gave *maman* the opportunity to keep her eye on everything that was going on in the yard and "on the road."

Grand Islanders "were bound together by similar kinship patterns, which centered upon networks of extended and nuclear families linked to their near neighbors through marriage" (Stielow 1986:184). They were also bound together by a common religion. On property in the center of the island, Capt. Horace Harvey built a foundation for a chapel. The local population completed and dedicated "Our Lady of the Isle" in 1918. Even with a designated place of worship, a "circuit priest" visited the island only once a year and sometimes even less frequently (Cheniere Hurricane Centennal 1994). Nonetheless, the Grand Islanders stayed true to their Catholic roots, particularly on All Saints' (Souls') Day, when the graves were decorated with flowers, the tombs painted white, and the cemetery was given a general cleaning. By 1929, a priest visited the island every week throughout the summer and once a month during the winter (Kammer 1941). As was the case throughout South Louisiana.

By 1929, "Grand Isle had emerged as a distinct *gemeinshaft* society—one united by an intricate web of familial, geographic, historical, linguistic, and religious ties into a community that my informants could fondly describe as a 'family'" (Stielow 1986:185). Further, with construction in 1931 of the bridge to Chênière Caminada, and completion of a road to the island in 1934, Grand Isle was united to the mainland for the first time in its history (Meyer-Arendt 1985; Meyer-Arendt n.d.).

Sweeping changes began. Access was no longer an issue, for the automobile helped change the Islanders' concept about space and time. In the process, enhanced access altered the established settlement patterns and island's geography. Buildings were oriented toward the roads, not according to the island's physical and climatic conditions. People began to modify their modes of existence, which led to the demise of the weekly practice of baking French bread in outdoor bake ovens (a long established element of rural South Louisiana's material culture), washing dishes in window stands, outside toilets, and the labor-intensive process of hand-washing clothes, which contributed to the breakdown of the island's culture (Stielow 1977; Stielow 1986).

Moreover, the economic downturn in the 1930s forced many islanders to sell their landholdings. As a result, "a single land speculator took control of a majority of Grand Isle property; his subdivisions and sales to the oil industry precipitated a revolution in

Bread, an important dietary staple, was baked daily in outdoor ovens, ca. 1890. (Photo courtesy of the National Archives and Records Administration, Still Picture Records Section, Special Media Archives Service Division, negative no. 22-FCD-37.)

the economy, and broke down the old agrarian patterns shaped by isolation" (Reeves 1985:108). After speculators purchased vast tracts of property from financially troubled farmers, the island's system of truck-garden farms disappeared. Traditional patterns of life began to change. Grand Isle began the initial phase of modernization and Americanization—innovations in transportation (for instance the Grand Isle Airways, Inc.), communication, and education were introduced to the island's inhabitants.

This retreat from their traditional values was further accelerated during World War II. Japan's sudden attack on Pearl Harbor resulted in a national mobilization that touched every fabric of American life. National defense became a critical issue, and the people of the wetlands responded by organizing watch teams looking for submarines, or for spies landing by sea. Civil Air Patrol towers were erected and manned constantly by locals—called the "Swamp Angels." This network assisted the Houma-based U. S. Navy blimp fleet to better patrol the northern Gulf of Mexico (Cheniere Hurricane Centennal 1995; Campbell 1999). Further, because of Grand Isle's strategic location, the Army Air Corps, Navy, Coast Guard, and Civilian Air Patrol were stationed there. These groups helped introduce a flood of new goods and the extension of electrical power lines to the island community (Stielow 1977).

On the *Chênière* Plain, the Swamp Angels' fifty-foot towers were spaced approximately every twelve miles; each was equipped with their own barracks and kennel. Volunteers patrolled the coast on horseback or stood watch in a tower. Many spoke only French, but they knew the coast, the marsh, and all of the associated inlets well and were ready for any invaders (Christ 2001). With the conclusion of World War II in 1945, the Swamp Angels were disbanded, and the pace of change across the coastal plain was accelerated. The "old ways" were beginning to be replaced quickly with a new lifestyle.

On Grand Isle, change was precipitated by the discovery of oil offshore in 1948.

(Left) Part of the Houma-based Navy blimp fleet. (Right) The "Swamp Angels" and others celebrating VJ Day, 1945. (Photos from Cheniere Hurricane Centennal 1995.)

To meet the needs of their offshore workforce, the Humble Oil Company, now ExxonMobil went into the housing business on the island's eastern end. Since Grand Isle lacked adequate corporate/industrial lodging, Humble built 150 residences for its employees so they would be close to their offshore job sites. In the process, the island's eastern end became one of many company-supported base camps used to support the exploration and development of the region's oil and gas resources. At its zenith, the camp supported nearly 500 employees. The structures built by Humble may have been Sears catalog houses. Nothing in the written record, or from local informants, suggests this was the source for the camps, but Standard Oil had used these catalogue homes at other locations. In Carlinville, Illinois, for example, Standard Oil of Indiana (Stanolind) built nine blocks of Sears's houses, the largest concentration of such structures in the county. The dwellings constituted a $1 million order placed in 1918, and they certainly could have been a model for the "camps" built at Grand Isle (Hastings 2007).

As the oil industry moved into deeper water, the travel time to and from the rigs became excessive. The industry began to build offshore structures identified as hotel/factories that provided the work crews all necessary amenities. They did not have to commute home every night. As a result, the Grand Isle site became less important. The camps were eventually sold; surviving structures can still be found as recreation cottages throughout the island (Alberstadt 1975). Further, with the conclusion of World War II, beachfront cottages became the focal point of new construction. Their appearance represents the "take off" phase of Grand Isle's growth in permanent and recreational housing (Meyer-Arendt 1985; Meyer-Arendt n.d.).

During the short span from the Great Depression to the 1950s, the island was completely transformed. As Frederick Stielow (1986:193-194) observes:

> it can be seen how the very fabric of life on Grand Isle was altered to the point
> that its formerly distinctive culture was all but invisible to the casual visitor.
> Instead of a small, French-speaking village in the center of the island, a tour-
> ist in the late fifties would have encountered state parks at either end of the
> island, a large oil company compound and receiving station, and an almost
> continuous line of summer houses blocking the view of the previous settle-
> ment. Through a complex process of internal and external forces—including
> the effects of mass communications, national trends, outside developers, oil
> companies, and educational measures—the natives came to accept and em-

brace the propriety of the 'American way of life.' In the process the younger generation also lost much of their ethnicity. While some of the changes that occurred redounded to the economic and physical benefit of the islanders, my own nostalgic opinion joins with the assessments given by my older informants: 'That is Grand Isle, no more.'

With attention focusing on the beach, the public—particularly real estate investors—wanted a stabilized shoreline. Private and public erosion control became critical concerns, but most of these endeavors have proven ineffective. Beach fill has helped, but accelerated beachfront deterioration is evident at many points along the island's exposed shoreline. Like many beach-oriented recreation-based communities, Grand Isle will need a constant supply of sand to maintain its beach. Beach nourishment may be the key to the community's survival, although as the island narrows, two or more hurricane-induced breaches, or passes, through the island could also do irrevocable damage. Hurricanes Katrina, Rita, Gustav, and Ike did not breach Grand Isle, yet many dwellings were severely damaged and the transient beach had to be rebuilt and reengineered. Some residents did not return, and many more were skeptical about the future, but new homes nevertheless appeared as recreationalists were attracted to the island and bought many of the ruined properties. New camps have replaced many lost in the 2005 and 2008 hurricane seasons.

Ambrose Besson noted to a *Thibodaux Daily Comet* reporter that: "if another Katrina or Rita comes, he worries that the island's population may never recover. Then again, he adds, 'where are you goonna go? This is home' and 'If I can't hear the ocean every morning,' he explained, 'I get lonesome'" (Bahr 2006).

Grand Terre, Jean Lafitte, and the First Major Wetland Settlement

On these islands, as well as on the numerous smaller ones which intersperse the bay, are vast deposits of a kind of clam shell, placed there by the processes of nature, large quantities of which have been shipped away in recent years to be used as paving material in various cities. Between Grand Isle and Grand Terre is Grand Pass, and at the western end of the former there is also a channel which connects with Caminada bay, from which a passage is found connecting with Bayous Lafourche and Terre Bonne. Barataria bay is also connected with the interior through Bayou St. Denis, Little Lake, Bayou Perot and Lake Salvador, thence via Bayou des Allemands and the lake of the same name almost to the Mississippi above New Orleans . . . During the early years of the nineteenth century considerable history was made in the vicinity of Barataria bay, by reason of a band of smugglers, commanded by Jean Lafitte, who had established their headquarters on the island of Grand Terre, and who had their stronghold in the midst of a group of the shell-mounds above referred to on one of the islands of the bay . . . (Fortier 1909:71).

Louisiana's coastal lowlands were ideally suited for smugglers, as they were nearly perfect for the storage and movement of illicit foreign merchandise. The land was not adequately mapped. Government agents, who were unfamiliar with the Barataria Bay water system, promptly became lost. A skilled smuggler could easily outmaneuver his pursuers, whether they were pirates loyal to Jean Lafitte, or rum-runners. In addition, secluded ridges or Indian middens were ideally suited to the off-loading of illegal contraband (Maygarden, et al. 1995). The estuary met all of the needs of these nefarious thieves and the barrier islands served as a near perfect base of operations.

Recognizing the geographical position of the barrier islands, privateer Jean Lafitte and his crew of Frenchmen, Italians, Portuguese, and Spaniards established a base, or *entrepôt*, on Grand Terre, with an outlying fortification on Grand Isle and elsewhere.

The "first smugglers' convention [was] held there [Grand Terre] in 1805" (DeGrummond 1961:4), and, as early as 1810, more than thirty buccaneer captains called Cat Island/Grand Terre/Grand Isle/Chênière Caminada their home (Gilbert 1814). Moreover, New Orleans newspapers reported these brigands had captured a "richly laden" Spanish ship. They removed her gun and built a shore battery to protect their base of operations" (Expedition to Barataria 1814). These seafaring bandits moved their merchandise to market through the Barataria and Lafourche waters and also through Bayou Teche into the Attakapas region (Kammer 1941). They were unmolested and had the "run" of the coast.

Because his 120- to 130-ton brigs and schooners were manned by crews of ninety to 200 men, Jean Lafitte's "navy" might be estimated conservatively at 500 sailors, with an equal number of men unloading goods, storing it in warehouses, and moving the contraband to distribution centers. The hub of this illicit trade could easily have employed up to 3,000 individuals living in isolation. In September 1814, Commodore Daniel T. Patterson learned of the existence of 1,000 buccaneers at Grand Terre alone (DeGrummond 1961).

Island-based privateers accumulated great quantities of captured merchandise. As the English closed the French-controlled Caribbean ports, more contraband was shipped to Grand Terre and then distributed to Donaldsonville, New Orleans, or other markets. To accommodate the expansion of this illicit trade, the pirates of Grand Terre built forty warehouses, along with slave pens (*barracoons*), living quarters, a hospital, and an improved fort (DeGrummond 196; Maygarden, et al. 1995). The store-houses were regularly filled with valuable "captured" merchandise that attracted merchants and traders who bought these goods for pennies on the dollar (Expedition to Barataria 1814; Jackson and New Orleans 1854). At times, the only prudent means of disposing of their contraband was to hold a public auction (Gilbert 1814). Large fortunes were made overnight through this trade in "legal pillage" with Louisiana's privateers.

In 1814, the United States Navy sent an expedition to capture all of the privateers' buildings. This successful campaign effectively terminated the storage and transshipment of illicit foreign merchandise along the Louisiana coast until Prohibition, but the trade was an important part of wetland's history for more than a decade.

Grand Terre's Sugar Plantation

Less than ten years after the Grand Terre pirates moved their operation west, Jean-Baptiste Moussier, who owned sixty-nine slaves, had established a working sugar plantation on the island. Valued in 1823 at $38,000, the plantation included a sugar house, draining house, steam engine, dwelling house, slave cabins, and other outbuildings (Chamberlain 1942). In 1831, a hurricane inundated the site with salt water twenty-feet deep. Two sugarhouses and the sugarcane in the field were blown down, the corn crop was destroyed, and the island's residents were forced to seek shelter in "their boats and canoes" (*New Orleans Daily Picayune* 1893:3).

The Moussier family subsequently sold the island, but retained most of the western tip—the future site of Fort Livingston. By the mid-nineteenth century, Grand Terre's eastern two-thirds were under the control of Felix J. and Louis E. Forstall. In 1845, this property produced 300,000 pounds of sugar. After the Civil War, the estate was abandoned, for cheap field hands were no longer available (Earth Search 1995).

Although the island was primarily devoted to agriculture, private fishing interests recognized Grand Terre's value to their operations. As a result, in 1867 the Dunbar family established the island's first commercial shrimp "canning" operation. This was early, since the shrimp-packing industry did not begin in earnest until the late 1800s. Prior to that time, a crew of twenty-five men or more harvested shrimp with

The west end of Grand Terre has put Fort Livingston in a precarious position as the shore face migrates, ca. 1930. (Photo courtesy of the State Library of Louisiana.)

seines that had a half-inch mesh size and varied in length from 100 to 3,000 feet. With seine crews, probably living on Grand Terre or Grand Isle, working off of the island, the Dunbar family had positioned themselves perfectly. Shrimp were seined and packaged within sight of the harvesting grounds. Grand Isle's steamboat fleet easily transferred the catch to the New Orleans' market.

After the Civil War, Jose Llulla—famous duelist in nineteenth century New Orleans—bought most of the island, and we can assume the Dunbar family leased property from him, but the literature is not clear on this point. Until his death in 1888, Llulla lived a quiet life, raising cattle on the island's grasslands.

With the success of Grand Isle's hotels, several businessmen were convinced that they could convert Jean Lafitte's former home into a tourist attraction. They bought the Llulla estate for $2,500 intending "to divide it up into building sites for themselves and hold the remainder" (*New Orleans Times-Democrat* 1893:9). These investors believed that "if the railroad extends seven miles toward the bay . . . they will have a small bonanza" (*New Orleans Times-Democrat* 1893:9). The railroad was never built, no

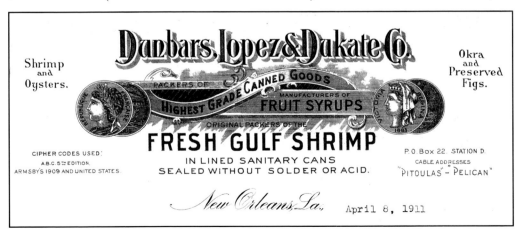

The canning industry changed permanently the dynamics of shipping a perishable commodity, 1911. (Image courtesy of the Morgan City Archives.)

An ethnically diverse shrimp seine crew of nearly thirty men was common, ca. 1900. (Photo from Cheniere Hurricane Centennal 1995.)

hotel was constructed. The 1893 hurricane washed over Grand Terre, and the island reverted to its original form. Cattle became the island's primary inhabitants, and they continue to be a conspicuous part of Grand Terre's landscape.

In 2008, some of the highest erosion rates in Louisiana's coastal system were recorded at Grand Terre. In the first decade of the twenty-first century, Gulf-side erosion rates were calculated in excess of fifty-feet per year. If this continues, the calculations suggest the island will disappear by the year 2050. Grand Terre's eastern end was reduced from 3.5 square miles in 1884 to one square mile in 1998. However, various restoration/rehabilitation projects are currently underway to protect the island (http://www.gulfbase.org).

A Scrapbook of Human Occupancy: Marsh and Fringe Settlements

> On the left bank of this Bayou Bienvenue, a mile and a half from its entrance into Lake Borgne, there was a little village of Spanish and Italian fishermen, who [would] . . . bring fish in their boats for the market of New Orleans . . . knowing that the British were hovering on Lake Borgne, . . . a squad of nine white men, two mulattoes, and one negro, to the village of the fishermen, for the purpose of ascertaining the movements of the enemy. Unfortunately these fishermen had been bribed by the British, to whom they used to carry all the information they could pick up in New Orleans, where they permitted to come daily and without suspicion to sell their fish . . . (Kammer 1941:17).

This description of a fishing community near Lake Borgne, in which the residents became mercenary spies for the British in the War of 1812, is one of the earliest references to fishermen living and working in the marshes east of New Orleans. *The Journal of John Landreth* reported a New Orleans' businessman underwriting in 1819 a fish and turtle harvesting enterprise on the Isles Dernières, with the catch being transported to the New Orleans' French Market (Landreth 1819). From these accounts, it is clear the coastal marsh's settlement history traces its origin back to the beginning of the nineteenth century. Successful marsh communities evolved into noteworthy communities, while those that did not have definite purpose were lost to history. They were simply not important enough to be accurately recorded in the historical record;

they are a forgotten part of the history of Louisiana's wetlands.

A pre-1930 marsh community consisted simply of a cluster of unpretentious homes or boats. Originally, humble huts within these settlement clusters were made of timbers placed vertically in the ground (*poteaux en terre*), or with upright planks (*pieux debout*), a French settlement custom that by 1820 was fading (Landreth 1819; Edwards 1988). Later, the simple, ephemeral, homes consisted of three rooms—a living room, a bedroom, a kitchen, and a covered front porch or "gallery." The home was the center of daily life and the focal point of all activity. "Not long ago an old man said: 'Nowadays people are born in hospitals, get married in hotels, buried from the undertaker's. All they use their homes for is a place to change clothes" (Davis 1959:277). To many in South Louisiana, the home is the epicenter of their individual worlds. These homes are not part of suburban American, but rural or near-rural dwellings that serve an important purpose; they keep the family together and grounded in their individual heritage and culture.

Since gambling was an important part of a Cajun male's leisure-time activities, neighbors gathered on porches on warm nights to play the Cajun-devised card game of *bourré*. Where high ground was available, horse racing was common on Sunday afternoons (Cheniere Hurricane Centennal 1994). Cockfights, legal in Louisiana until 2008, were also part of the region's gaming tradition and regional heritage (Fuller 2002/2003).

If there were no screens, beds were protected with a canopy of mosquito netting, and windows were covered with wooden shutters, as there were no glass windows. The walls were covered by beaded boards about four inches wide. Plaster was not used because the boards were easy to put up, required little maintenance, and could be painted. In the summer, a kerosene stove, later replaced by a "bottled gas" unit, was used for cooking, while in the winter a wood stove provided heat, and cooked meals. Properly seasoned, the cast iron skillet and Dutch oven were perfect for preparing jambalaya, simmering a gumbo seasoned with ground up sassafras leaves (*filé*), frying a "mess" of duck, *poules d'eau*, marsh hen, rabbits, squirrels, frog legs, or fish, or baking biscuits or corn bread (Pitre 1993).

As was the case in some areas of the United States, cooking was not considered a chore. The women and girl cooks took pride in their menus, and the meals were considered "a delight to the palate" (Kammer 1941:35). A small ice box eventually was part of the kitchen. Every-other-day ice was delivered by a truck vendor or ice boats (*glacier*), which added another level of convenience to the home or to the shrimper working in the inland waters, as the *glacier* was a floating wholesaler and grocery delivery service (Pitre 1993; Falgoux 2007). Further, there were no bathrooms, and baths were taken in a galvanized round or oval wash-tub. The toilet sat in an outhouse, like most toilets of early twentieth-century rural America. Potable water was supplied by a cypress cistern that collected rain water from the home's roof—the marshdwellers were completely dependent on cisterns for their drinking water. A storage shed stood to the back of the property and a rough-hewn wharf often extended into the bayou.

Land holdings were small, and since the communities were near sea level and flooding was a problem, there were no kitchen gardens. Supplies were provided by the family's trips to "town," the local grocery boats (*marchand-caboteur*), or, in the case of Bayou Lafourche, a truck (*marchand-*

Before air conditioning, French doors were opened to provide cross-ventilation, 1973. (Photo by the author.)

A large number of vendors provided the population with cisterns of various sizes. (Image from the *Louisiana Sugar Bowl*, September 1880.)

Arable land was limited, so farms were small. (Image from *Picturesque America,* 1872.)

charrette) or bus (Parenton 1938; Cheniere Hurricane Centennal 1994). These peddlers, floating merchants, and rolling stores were regional institutions that carried a wide variety of dry goods, groceries, kerosene, *bebelles* (toys), and other staples. Their shelves were lined with "store-bought" items—suits, shoes, hats, fish nets, push-poles, boots, anchor chains, putt-putt engine parts, medicines, candles, candy, brooms, mops, black cast-iron cooking pots and pans—all of the necessities a marshdweller needed.

If the truck or trading boat did not have a required item, the article was delivered on the next trip. It was an economical and convenient system. If the customer had little money, the storekeeper or boat captain would accept furs, fish, ducks, poultry, cured meat, vegetables, and other products in payment for groceries and supplies (Davis 1959; Ramsey 1957). Since chickens and eggs were popular items of trade, the *marchand-caboteur* were frequently referred to as chicken thieves. In fact, it seems these *caboteur* merchants were blamed for every missing chicken along their route (Butler 1985). In the 1930s and 1940s, general mercantile stores operated school-bus-type vehicles. These rolling stores brought to bayou communities the convenience of department store shopping in the isolated Acadians' front yard. There were at least four such vendors along Bayou Lafourche and an equal number in Terrebonne Parish (Pitre 1993).

A boat made deliveries in the marsh, as boats were the one material element that was common and universal in all communities. In the marshdwellers' folk life, a boat was mandatory. In this regard, boys were essential. They were helpful in painting, tinkering with the engines, scrubbing the deck, cleaning the cabin, and unloading the shrimp or other fish from the hold before they spoiled. Sons, who learned from their fathers, were engaged in some activity constantly. Trawling and shrimping was hard work, so the young boys were not involved in these activities until they were physically able to handle the nets, or participate in the back-breaking labor associated with tonging oysters (Payne 1916).

Trawl boats and oyster luggers went out whenever the weather permitted and were gone for several days. They returned to unload their catch and to take on supplies; after that, they went back once more to their fishing grounds and repeated their routines. The crews, often a son or nephew, lost all sense of time; the only thing that mattered was the harvest.

A practice that is almost universal throughout Louisiana's fishing area is the annual blessing of the fishing fleets—a ceremony brought from France and celebrated in many communities (Hansen 1971; Reeves and Alario 1996). For days in advance of this event, boats are overhauled, completely painted, and decorated. The local priest stands on a wharf, near the church, and as a processional of up to 200 boats goes slowly past, each one is sprinkled with holy water. A definite symbolic event showing the importance placed on the harvest (Kammer 1941). In Terrebonne Parish, the first blessing of the fleet occurred at Boudreaux Canal about 1927 (Terrebonne parish 1953; Boutwell and Folse 1997). Unlike in Scotland, where religious beliefs and legal statutes forbid fishing on the Sabbath, South Louisiana's marshdwellers were quite happy to fish, trap, or hunt on Sundays, and they suffered no apparent ill-effects as a result (Hallowell 1979).

If you were old enough to operate the tongs, you were "fishing" oysters, ca. 1855. (Image from *Gleason's Pictorial Weekly.*)

In these inaccessible, marsh-oriented communities, a young man of eighteen, or even younger, could earn a good living by hunting, fishing, tonging oysters, trapping, and—during Prohibition—rum-running. There was no economic reason why such a person should not become married. Marshdwellers married young and had big families, and every community expanded with each new marriage (Kammer 1941).

In these hamlets, the bilingual males made contacts with the "outside world," while the females, depending on locality, generally could speak only French, Spanish, Italian, or any one of a number of "foreign" languages. The males did all of the bartering for their alligator hides, furs, crabs, oysters, and shrimp. Women were expected to stay at home, largely because of the absence of employment opportunities. If work was available, it was in an oyster or shrimp cannery/shed, where they shucked and cleaned oysters or beheaded and deveined shrimp. When cleaned, sorted, and canned, refrigerator trucks and trailers took these products to markets in New York, Chicago, Philadelphia, Baltimore, Los Angeles, San Francisco, and other cities whose populations craved fresh fish products. This improved transportation element was largely the result of Huey Long's road and bridge-building campaign. When completed, the network of roads and bridges permitted regional social change.

Whereas in New Orleans, Italians were fish-buyers, in San Franciso, they were the fishermen. (Image from *Harper's Weekly,* April 1889.)

These renewable resources are a well documented feature of the coastal plain. The scientific and popular literature is replete with material related to oysters, shrimp, muskrat, nutria, alligator, ducks, and geese. What is missing in this abundant and highly-diverse collection of literature is Louisiana's early commitment to understanding the biological importance of the *marais*.

* * *

Using a point of high grass to hide me, I pushed the pirogue silently ahead, then, toward the three *canard noir*. I got so close I could almost strike them with the pole. I fired high, so only a few pellets would strike them in their heads. All three were dead in one shot. It was not sporting, but I was not hunting. I was gathering meat, and there is a difference (Segura 1982:22).

In fact,

A man using a gun there [south of Bayou Teche] does not have to bother about blinds, for nature has provided them. He does not have to worry about heavy underclothing and waterproof trousers, and a coat that will 'break the wind,' for nature has obviated all of that too. In the severest weather he will need clothing of no greater weight than is worn North in the fall. He will not have to worry about decoys, for he can always kill a duck or two, and, setting them out on the water, with sharp sticks under their chins to keep their heads up, he can kill more (Canfield 1903:417).

The Gulf Biologic Station: The State's Forgotten Research Facility

Act 182 of the General Assembly of 1898, authorized creation and establishment of a biological research station on the Gulf of Mexico. In 1900, Act 163 clarified a number of issues and gave the personnel at the station the right:

> to fish unmolested in any public waters of the State with dredging apparatus, seines, trawls, nets, surface trawls, and other instruments and apparatus for the sole purpose of obtaining the materials needed in pursuing the purposes and investigations in the direction of the scientific objects of which the Station is established, as set forth in the original Act; and generally, all power and authority necessary to carry out the purposes and objects of said Act in investigating the Fauna and Flora of the Gulf of Mexico, and the waters adjacent thereto (Morgan 1902:5).

Limited appropriations in 1900 delayed construction of the Gulf Biologic Station until the spring 1901. The laboratory and ancillary facilities were built south of Cameron—two years after a fisheries laboratory was established in a rented building in Beaufort, North Carolina. In the summer of 1901, a small research program was initiated with oysters being the first research topic on the agenda—a subject that continues to garner research support more than 100 years after the 1903 ribbon cutting ceremony.

The United States Commission of Fish and Fisheries, the National Museum, the National Geodetic Survey, and Smithsonian Institution provided reference material for the station's library. The United States Department of Agriculture gave the research facility a weather station that allowed the researchers to forecast "storms two days in advance," providing advance warnings to the parishes of Southwest Louisiana (Morgan 1902:7).

Although the research structure was completed, it was underfunded and needed $11,398 to purchase the necessary boats, laboratory equipment, and expendables to

Located south of Cameron, the Gulf Biologic Station was the first Louisiana research facility to study the marine environment. (Photo from *Gulf Biologic Station, Bulletin* no. 1, 1902.)

become fully functional. In July 1903, the facility was formally opened. The previous year, the station released its first bulletin outlining its status, goals, and objectives.

The second bulletin, dated May 1903, reported that the facility was investigating "the conditions for oyster culture at Calcasieu Pass." This work was being conducted by O. C. Glaser of John Hopkins University, Baltimore, Maryland. In addition, Glaser, along with J. C. Smith, R. S. Cocks, E. Foster, H. H. Kopman (all from New Orleans), and J. S. Hine from the University of Ohio were compiling preliminary lists of the fauna and flora of the Gulf, with annotation. By 1910, the station had produced fifteen bulletins. Few libraries have the complete collection; therefore, rarely are these early works quoted in the scholarly literature. This site laid the foundation for wetland science, but the facility simply disappeared. Although active for at least a decade, the material linked to the Gulf Biologic Station is a scientific artifact that has no legacy, yet these early studies may be important baseline data for current scientific inquiry on oysters and other issues published in the Station's bulletins. Scientific descriptions that are more than 100 years old should not be dismissed, but somehow the work of this pioneer research laboratory has gone unnoticed and unreported.

No.	Date	Articles
1	1902	First report of the director of the Gulf Biologic Station, organization and condition.
2	1904	Second report of the Gulf Biologic Station, Part I. The conditions for oyster culture at Calcasieu Pass; Part II. An incomplete list of the marine fauna of Cameron, Louisiana; Part III. Report to the flora in the vicinity of the Gulf Biologic Station; Part IV. A contribution to the entomology of the region of the Gulf Biologic Station; Part V. Notes on free-swimming copepods of the waters in the vicinity of the Gulf Biologic Station, Louisiana; Part VI. Report on the conditions of bird-life as noted at the Gulf Biologic Station; Part VII. Insects injurious to stock in the vicinity of the Gulf Biologic Station; and Part VIII. Some economic considerations with reference to the *tabanidae*.
3	1905	Notes on marine food mollusks of Louisiana.
4	1906	The conditions for oyster culture in the waters of the parishes of Vermilion and Iberia, Louisiana.
5	1906	A preliminary report on the horseflies of Louisiana with a discussion of remedies and natural enemies.
6	1906	Further studies on the oyster at Calcasieu Pass; A preliminary report on the distribution of the scallops and clams in the Chandeleur Islands region, Louisiana; A preliminary report on the oysters in Chandeleur Sound; A contribution to the fauna of the coast of Louisiana; The leaves and salt-secreting sells of *spartina stricta*; and A second contribution to the entomology of the region of the Gulf Biologic Station.
7	1907	The flora of the Gulf Biologic Station.
8	1907	The cultivation of oysters in Louisiana.

No.	Date	Articles
9	1907	A preliminary study of the conditions for oyster culture in the waters of Terrebonne Parish, Louisiana.
10	1908	Annotated catalogue of grasses growing without cultivation in Louisiana.
11	1908	Preliminary report on the life history and habits of the '"lake shrimp."
12	1909	Further contributions to the marine fauna of the Louisiana coast.
13	1909	Motile leaves of *erythrina herbacea.*
14	1909	Habits, life history, and economic value of doves; and the raising of young waxwings, *ampeles cedrorum.*
15	1910	A few notes on oyster culture in Louisiana.

The Gulf Biologic Station and others (like the Louisiana Universities Marine Consortium and Turtle Cove) along with all of the state, federal, and private refuges and wildlife sanctuaries, are not only vital for the science and stewardship roles they play in the preservation of Louisiana's natural resources, but they also represent isolated marsh comminutes or compounds. Whether at Grand Terre, or the resident keeper's camps at Audubon Rainey Wildlife Sanctuary, Bird Island Bayou, Marsh Island, Red Fish Point, the State Wild Life Refuge, Rockefeller, Pass-a-Loutre, the Game Farm on Avery Island, the Chef Menteur and Rigolets lighthouses and other sites, should not be overlooked as settlement nodes and important sites for temporary trapping and oyster communities.

The settlement function of many of these sites is more than 100 years old, and they should not be allowed to disappear, as they are important elements in the wetlands' human landscape. On Marsh Island, for example, an "alligator lottery" permits a small number of trappers annually to remove 1,500 or more gators from this property. Indirectly, the refuge is continuing to allow marshdwellers an opportunity to live and work off of the land like their ancestors on a site that at one time had a school and a full-time maintenance crew.

Established in the beginning of the twentieth century, the Gulf Biologic Station at Cameron was short-lived. Even so, its proximity to the beach face was reflected in others, largely recreationalists that also were attracted to the ebb and flow of the waves along the shore. Their cottages have been repeatedly destroyed, but they continue to be pulled back to the seashore.

Holly Beach: The Cajun Riviera

Despite the length of Louisiana's coastline, there are only a few points that have developed into true beach-oriented communities. Unlike recreational sites that boast of an oceanfront spa, lavish amenities, meeting facilities, and challenging golf courses, Holly Beach offered a site for camp development only. There were no luxuries; the site was a "Poor Man's Paradise on the Gulf" (Stanley n.d.). Located in southwest Louisiana's *Chênière* Plain, at the junction of Highways 82 and 27, the location's "recreation-shed" included a large part of the Cajun triangle (Meyer-Arendt 1982). Most of the initial occupants were from small prairie communities between Lake Charles and

Lafayette. The space morphed into an Acadiana beach resort.

Settlers on the *chênière* ridges developed a healthy economy based on cotton, fruit, and cattle. They were not interested in the low-lying marsh and never thought about owning any of the *marais*. Although surveyed, this property was not immediately sold. This real estate was eventually acquired by Jabez B. Watkins, who successfully transformed southwest Louisiana from a cattle province to one that was dotted with Anglo-Saxon migrants familiar with farming the country's plain states. Watkins was unsuccessful in quickly developing his Holly Beach real estate. The problem was easy access. Although trails and wagon roads connected several *chênières*, no public roads connected all the *chênière* ridges, and there were no north south access roads. Consequently, until the 1930s travel to this part of Louisiana was by schooner (Meyer-Arendt 1981; Meyer-Arendt 1982).

After creation of Cameron Parish (from Calcasieu and Vermilion parishes in 1870), the community of Cameron developed into the regional service center. It had one Catholic, Methodist, and Baptist church—perhaps an indicator of its diverse ethnicity (Harris 1881). By 1900, three beach-front hotels operated south of the city and one opened just south of Creole (Carter 1968). Since travel was so difficult, just as at Grand Isle, guests would arrive by mail schooner from Lake Charles, and would be delivered to their hotels by surrey. A visit to the area involved a stay of two to three weeks (Meyer-Arendt 1982).

Without roads, a journey to the *chênière* beaches was an ordeal. The problem was that in the early 1920s Louisiana had the worst highway system in the United States. There were only 331 miles of paved roads and three bridges statewide—none over the Mississippi River. This was the pattern until the 1930s, when Huey Long began to fulfill his campaign pledge to immediately begin road and bridge construction in order to help the state's infrastructure, employ thousands of poor, and "build a political following that used patronage to perpetuate it" (Jeansonne 1994:8). Highway 27 was built from Lake Charles to Holly Beach, connecting to the partially completed Highway 82 that was not completed to Texas and Abbeville until the 1950s. By the end of

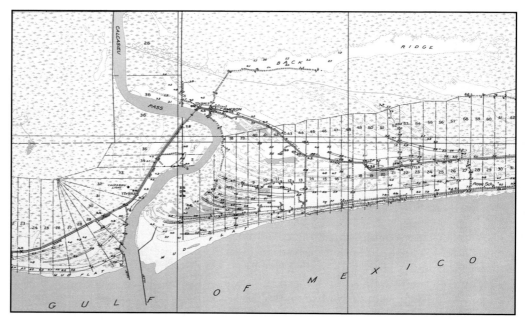

Map of long-lots. Map along Holly Beach. (Image from USGS Cameron fifteen minute quaderangle, 1935.)

the 1980s, this was "Louisiana's Eroding Highway."

With the completion of Highway 27, Watkins' Holly Beach property had a north-south link into "Cajun Country." The acreage was subdivided, lots sold (some as coastal long lots), and Holly Beach emerged as a recreational appendage to the coastal *chênières*. The highway connections gave birth to the community that was subsequently surveyed in the conventional township-and-range fashion, where the landscape appears as a checkerboard (Meyer-Arendt 1981; Meyer-Arendt 1982). The geometry is made up of right angles and the associated surveyed features follow nearly laser straight routes.

By 1934, 21 structures appeared on the first topographic map of the area. Two of these were hunting clubs, half a dozen were cabins for rent, and the remainder were private recreational camps. Most of the buildings were elevated on stilts, a style not characteristic of the Chênière Plain and previously used only as oil field camp housing in marsh areas (within this part of the state) (Myer-Arendt 1982:6).

Like Chênière au Tigre to the east, beach access and the therapeutic value of the beach environment were promoted. Busloads of Acadiana health-seekers were transported to Holly Beach. Many of these fun-seekers eventually became property owners, with the first camps being built by farmers from Kaplan and Iowa, Louisiana. When one family or group bought property, others followed. This process was repeated throughout prairie communities. Eventually, the site was populated by inter-related individuals or friends, who were part of a greater kinship group. Holly Beach was like one large extended family.

Examination of lot sales records during the 1930s and 1940s reveal over 90% French surnames and Acadiana origins. Despite periodic storm surges that caused damage to several camps, 250 structures were built between 1932 and 1957 . . . , including a Catholic church, the first in the immediate area. (Several miles to the west, the smaller resort of Peveto Beach catered to Anglo recreationalists . . . and was even nicknamed 'Texas Beach') (Myer-Arendt 1982:6).

Despite hurricanes and beachfront erosion—the dominate geologic process affecting the region—Holly Beach grew from a modest cluster of camps in the early 1930s to more than 600 in the 1980s, when there appears to have been a leveling off of these recreation sites. The Holly Beach "camps," as well as other nodes in the coastal zone, can be divided into three types: 1) permanently-occupied residences; 2) seasonally-occupied recreational dwellings; and 3) cabins for rent. Many of these structures were on vertical beams six-to-eight feet above the beach surface, driven to a depth of six to eight feet, with each post tethered to all of the others by a web of cross-members. Others were on slabs. Whether above-ground or on-the-ground, these camps according to Meyer-Arendt (1980:8) ran the gambit "from crude to innovative to semi-elaborate" in style.

Although electricity dates to 1950, piped-in water did not become available until the summer of 1980. Outdoor cisterns are characteristic of most of the older camps. The most recent camp type . . . is the mobile home. . . . (Meyer-Arendt 1980:8).

In the 1980s, the community's full-time population was estimated at less than 100. In the summer, the population exploded, with more than 10,000 recreationalists crowded on the beach for the Fourth of July weekend. The social life revolved around the nuclear family, the extended family, friends and "passing" a good time. On weekends one of the local lounges would bring in a Cajun band. Dances were common and popular with prairie Cajuns.

The beach-oriented community expanded, largely because of the absence of hurricanes, but that changed with Audrey (1957), Carla (1961), Rita (2005), and Ike (2008). These storms variously damaged or leveled the community. As one Audrey survivor noted: "It was a clean sweep across Cameron Parish. Nothing was left" (Shelton 1987B:14A). And it happened again in 2005 (Rita's wrath strikes 2005) and yet again in 2008. But after Audrey and Carla, the evacuees were anxious to rebuild, and, although the rate of construction was slow, the community was eventually reconstructed. This was not the case in the first decade of the twenty-first century.

Holly Beach: Hurricanes Audrey (1957), Rita (2005), and Ike (2008)

> As much as she would like to, she cannot forget the nightmare which began for her and other residents of Cameron Parish in the early morning hours of Thursday, June 27, 1957. For some, . . . , the memories are vivid and the hurt burns deeply 30 years later (Shelton 1987B:1A).

Like many coastal communities, beach erosion is a problem that one must simply accept for the luxury of living "on" the beach. This was certainly true for Holly Beach, where nearly two blocks of the community were lost to shoreline erosion. Most of this loss is attributed directly to hurricanes, with Audrey (1957) serving as the benchmark storm until Rita's landfall forty-eight years later. Audrey's twelve-foot storm surge and 150-miles-per-hour winds flattened the community and resulted in shoreline retreat from 100 to 120 feet. In 2005, Hurricane Rita completely leveled Holly Beach again—nothing was left but the water tower. For the second time in nearly fifty years, Holly Beach was completely destroyed, and then with arrival of Ike, three years later, the community was again inundated. The "lady" and "gentlemen" are locally referred to by a battery of impolite and expletive deleted words and phrases. Even so, they will, like Audrey, never be forgotten. Like all other storms, human stories identified with these weather events will be repeated by successive generations.

For nearly fifty years the people living on the beach felt safe. Audrey was just a memory and the community flourished, but Rita and Ike changed the tranquility. These storms left many emotional scars. People are resilient, flexible, and tough and when their second homes were damaged, or destroyed, they simply went about the task of rebuilding. They wanted to be close to the sea and were willing to live with the danger.

After Ike, the residents' resilience was challenged, simply because of the rules, regulations and costs associated with rebuilding according to bank and federal guidelines and regulations. The financial and regulatory landscape has changed dramatically since Audrey. Nineteen fifty-seven was only twelve years after World War II and the recreationalists living at Holly Beach, probably did not have a house note, insurance, or any building regulations or guidelines from local, state and/or federal authorizes. Times have changed, and borrowing money is a fact of life and the banks loaning these funds have rules and regulations that were not in the reconstruction equation after Audrey. That is not the case with Rita and Ike.

Hurricanes Rita and Ike

On September 25, 2005, twenty-seven days after Katrina came ashore in southeast Louisiana, Hurricane Rita made landfall along the Texas/Louisiana border. The storm prompted a massive diaspora—more than one million people were evacuated from Houston, the country's fourth largest city. The traffic was snarled, but damage in east Texas was minimal compared to neighboring coastal Louisiana.

Just weeks after Katrina, Louisiana had to respond to another major storm. Rita was the second-most powerful hurricane of the season (behind Wilma) and the fourth most intense hurricane ever in the Atlantic Basin. The storm's northeast quadrant passed right over Holly Beach, Cameron, and all of the *chênière* communities to the east. Rita's surge pushed inland at least twenty miles and blanketed the *marais* with a thick layer of rack—any material that flies in a high wind. Salt water drowned rice and sugarcane fields, along with cattle pastures. Immediately after the storm, rescuers pulled stranded residents out on skiffs, and Army helicopters searched for thousands of cattle feared drowned.

The survivors fared better than the region's structures. Houses were reduced to rubble. In most cases, only the slab remained, the remainder of a home's building material being scattered across the marsh. The devastation was complete; nearly every home, camp, school, hospital, and church on the *chênières* was damaged severely or destroyed. Holly Beach was but a memory; there was nothing left but the slabs and debris from the direct impact of Rita's storm surge and winds. A visit to the site after the storm was disheartening. Stop signs survived on roads covered with debris. Cars left on the beach were metal sculptures. American flags flew over properties that had been transformed into debris piles. The site was surreal, a visual canvas that expressed nature's devastation.

After Audrey, the Holly Beach community had remade itself. The same rebuilding effort was initiated following Rita. Three years later Ike made landfall west of Holly Beach. The storm's north east quadrant hit the rebuilt recreation site hard and the reconstruction process began again. It is clear that because the beach-front com-

The tenacity of the camp owners at Holly Beach is exemplified by their willingness to rebuild after the hurricanes of 2005 and 2008, 2009. (Photo by Carl A. Brasseaux.)

munity is a fine place to recreate, there is a strong incentive to rebuild. Hence, the people who are restoring their camps will take their chances with another hurricane.

To promote a more orderly community, the state health code, initiated after Rita, requires a new subdivision with more than 125 lots to build a community sewerage system. The rule applies to Holly Beach. However, because of the small lots and high density of homes and camps, the state has barred the residents from rebuilding until a $2 million community sewer system is constructed. State lawmakers convinced the state to issue a waiver on lots greater than 5,000 square feet. Since most property owners' lots are between 500 and 1,500 square feet, they are being forced to buy adjacent lots before they can rebuild or even install a travel trailer (Residents say wastewater 2006). Despite these impediments to reconstruction, new camps were on the site in 2008, prior to the passage of Hurricane Ike. Clearly, the rebuilding/reconstruction process continues, as new camps are again being layout along this stretch of Louisiana's coast.

Chênière au Tigre: *Tiger Island or Cougar Chênière*

The first reference to Chênière au Tigre comes from the Spanish explorer, José de Evia, who in 1785 drafted a map of the region from Vermilion Bay westward. In 1819, while looking for naval stores, Col. James Cathcart explored Chênière au Tigre and left accounts in his diary (Landreth 1819). This is one of the country's largest, inaccessible, and remote, *chênière* ridges.

The *chênière* parallels the Gulf in the southeastern corner of Vermilion Parish. It is sheltered from the mainland by marsh and is from 200 feet to nearly a quarter of a mile wide. The ridge extends about five miles in length from east to west, and at its highest point, it is more than six feet above sea level. Hackberry (*bois bouton*) and live oak (*chêne vert*) dominate the landscape.

During the Texas Revolution of 1835-1836, the *chênières* were a training base for the American colonists willing to fight for Texas's independence. For about six months soldiers loyal to the Lone Star State lived on the ridges and explored the surrounding marsh landscape. Some of these recruits would later return with their families. Also, during the Civil War, thousands of Louisianians sought refuge in the marshlands and the prairies lying between the Mermentau and Calcasieu rivers. An estimated 8,000 deserters were at large within this region. Some were no doubt hiding on the *chênières* (Hanks 1988). The first permanent settlers—the Dyson family—arrived on the *chênières* in the mid 1840s. They were later joined by the Whites, Sagreras (who settled on Chênière au Tigre), Rodriques, and Choates.

Travel was by boat and since Chênière au Tigre never got a road, it remained cut off and is still accessible only by water. By the beginning of the twentieth century, there were between twenty-five and thirty families living at Chênière au Tigre—cattlemen, hunters, trappers, and small farmers—many descendents of Dr. Raphael Sagrera, who was one of the island's pioneers (Hanks 1988; Bradshaw 1997). The farms grew oranges, cantaloupes, watermelon, peaches, plums, persimmons, pears, and other seasonal crops. Wild

At Chênière au Tigre, and elsewhere on the *chênières*, trappers often ran their trap lines on their Creole ponies. (Photo from *Outing Magazine*, April 1910-September 1910.)

Chênière au Tigre, although a relatively small community, supported a one-room schoolhouse. This commitment to education can be found in many of the isolated *chênière* communities, no date. (Photo from Hanks 1988.)

For more than forty years, the resort at Chênière au Tigre served a variety of guests, no date. (Images from Hanks 1988.)

OFF TO THE GULF COAST

Bathing–Fishing–Dancing–Good Eating
Horse Back Riding–Tennis

CHENIERE AU TIGRE SUMMER RESORT

Opens Saturday, June 13

RATES PER DAY—BOARD AND LODGING

Adults _____ $1.50
Children _____ .75

RATES PER WEEK—BOARD AND LODGING

grapes were abundant, which were purged periodically because the vines choked the valuable island oaks—some of which were more than twenty-five feet in circumference (Segura 1973).

The secluded ridge, which was home to a relatively large population, had a one-room school house, a church (St. Francis Chapel, administered from the St. John Church at Henry), a cemetery, a post office, numerous homes, a doctor (Douglas Duperier), and a hotel complex that frequently had from seventy-five to 100 guests. This site was considered by many as a "delightful" hideaway. From 1913 to 1958, Semmes Sagrera owned and operated Sagrera Health Resort, also called a hotel, where guests came to bathe in the Gulf of Mexico and pray.

> The hotel consisted of two wings with a screened porch facing the Gulf. Each wing held eight rooms with two double beds each. Each room had a dressing table, chairs, a kerosene lamp (in 1926 replaced by a one-bulb electric light powered by a generator), bowl and pitcher, as well as a covered chamber pot. There were five cottages not attached to the hotel, a dancehall, and a pier extending into the Gulf (Bradshaw 1997B:6).

On Saturday night, the dancehall hosted as many as 400 people who enjoyed Cajun music and danced the Cajun two-step to a washboard-like rhythm. Many of these dancers "rented sleeping space on the dance floor, and had to move their bedrolls and belongings to the rafters until the dancing was done" (Bradshaw 1997B:6).

For forty years, Chênière au Tigre served as a recreation site with a wide-variety of boats carrying passengers and cargo to the Chênière. These vessels—the *Della D, Miss Abbeville, Harvey Lee,* and *Wild West*—made regular trips to the ridge community and charged from fifty cents to one dollar passage. Once at the landing, visitors were met by wagons pulled by oxen or mules to carry baggage and supplies, later a Model T truck or car provided transportation. Supplies were delivered by schooners, such as the *Martha White* or *Etta* (Vermilion Historical Society 1983).

Visitors to the hotel paid one dollar a day for room and board, or they could rent an unfurnished camp for seven dollars per week (Hanks 1988). The hotel's menu was based on home-grown produce and freshly caught shrimp, fish, crabs, and oysters. Every morning, a 600-foot, ox-drawn seine hauled in the day's requirement of shrimp, fish, and crabs—a modification of this beach seine is found in many parts of the world. Croaker, flounder, redfish, drum, speckled trout, and alligator gar were also caught on long lines. This catch was necessary since the hotel regularly had 100 guests (Bradshaw 1997B).

Hogs were raised for ham and sausage, preserved in large tins filled with grease or cured in the Sagrera Hotel's smokehouse. Quilts were made from wool obtained from the region's sheep. Dairy cattle provided milk. Fresh oysters were culled by hand from reefs at Rollover Bayou. All of this food was necessary, for year-round residents and the guests at the hotel.

With time the resort lost its attractiveness, the population declined, children left the Chênière, and the Sagreras closed the resort. All inhabitants had left the site by the mid-1960s, but they continued their cowboy tradition by using this high ground to graze livestock, as the property has been privately owned in the original settler's families since before the Civil War (Vermilion Historical Society 1983). The site was overrun with sea water in the hurricane season of 2005 and 2008, but the century old grazing tradition continues.

Brashear City/Morgan City

In 1875 there were in Morgan City 800 houses, five churches, five schools, one Masonic lodge, two fire companies, two newspapers, one social club, one moss factory, one sash, door, and blind factory, four steam sawmills, one ice house, one custom house, three drug stores, fifty wholesale or retail stores, fifteen coffee shops, five billiard rooms, three bakeries, and seventeen vessels in active operation between Morgan City and Texas, New York, Havana, Cuba, and ports in Mexico and Central America (Broussard 1977).

Brashear City—named after Dr. Walter Brashear who owned the Tiger Island sugar plantation and who was also an early settler on the Belle Isle salt dome—was originally part of the Attakapas District of French and Spanish colonial Louisiana. In 1857, with real estate speculation booming, Brashear City was laid out beside the recently completed New Orleans Opelousas, and Great Western Railroad (NOO&GW)—an eighty-mile "Texas Gauge" (five-foot six-inches) route from Algiers on the west bank of New Orleans to Berwick Bay. This rail line was built on railroad ties milled at Gibson or Donner in the Chacahoula swamp (A sketch of 1910; Millet 1983).

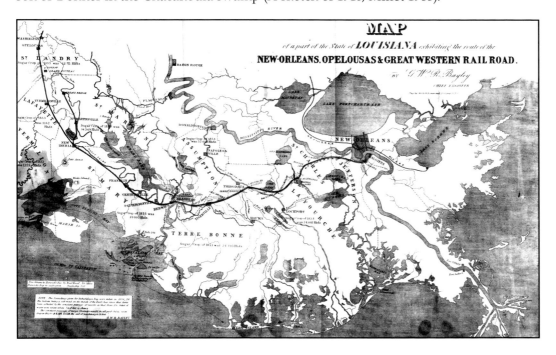

In effect, the railroad shortened the distance from New Orleans to Galveston, Texas by 160 miles and twenty-four hours over the water-only route. Shippers could now bypass the Mississippi River's unpredictable sailing conditions, while avoiding the high property taxes and port fees charged by New Orleans. In addition, the Federal government's generous allocation of land for railroad construction helped promote settlement and encouraged the railroad industry's rapid growth across the country.

When the NOO&GW was completed, land values along the line increased from $5 to $35 an acre (Millet 1983). Incorporated in 1860 as Brashear City, the town served as the railroad's western terminus (Leeper 1976; Broussard 1977; Gibson, et al. 1978). With arrival of the railroad, plantation owners had a fast and efficient way to transport their commodities to market. Along with sugar, the fish shipping business was regional economic activity that benefitted from the improved rail route as well (Fisher 1931). Local fish dealers took advantage of the three trains a day that served the city. Crabs, oysters, shrimp, catfish, gaspergoo (freshwater drum), and buffalo (*Ictiobus*) were the principal fishery products moved to markets east and west of Brashear City.

As might be expected, the NOO&GW became the preferred method of transport. To use the system successfully, planters manufactured cypress boxes to haul their sugar products to market. Small sugar mills on individual plantations were forced to consolidate, or be abandoned. They could not compete with the few sugar refineries with railroad sidings that were aggressively forming manufacturing units to maximize their refining and shipping capacities (Foscue and Troth 1936).

To serve passengers wanting to travel further west, the NOO&GW entered an agreement with Cornelius Vanderbilt for steamer service between the railroad terminus and Galveston, Texas. The side-wheeler *Galveston* was placed in service in April 1857, and a second vessel, *Opelousas*, was added the following month—four years before the start of the Civil War (Broussard 1977). During the War much of the railroad's equipment was commandeered by Confederate forces. In 1869, the railroad was sold to steamship operator Charles Morgan, who renamed the line Morgan's Louisiana and Texas Railroad and Steamship Company. In 1885, the road was acquired by the Southern Pacific Railroad. As a result of the ready availability of rapid and reliable rail service, Brashear City began to mature into a regional transportation hub.

By 1859, there were forty homes on the town site. During the Civil War, the region witnessed a number of battles, skirmishes, and, along with the entire state, the longest military occupation in the South—fifteen years. This transportation crossroads was considered important both as an infantry and a marine base, supporting Union forces involved in the Texas campaign and as a bulwark against Confederate efforts in the Teche and Atchafalaya military districts (Gibson, et al. 1978).

After the War, a way of life ended, and a new era emerged, but there were problems. In 1865 and 1867, floods caused by breaks in the Mississippi levees retarded Brashear's development. With these floods came an outbreak of yellow fever—a problem compounded by the fact the town had no cemetery. Berwick's cemetery served the town, but it was quarantined and could not be used by Brashear City's mortuaries. Consequently, land was purchased for a cemetery (Broussard 1977).

By 1875, the community's name was changed to Morgan City. The town received a new charter of incorporation under that name. Charles Morgan's transportation-oriented businesses had transformed the region, and the city was renamed in his honor. In conjunction with his steamship operation, Morgan dredged in 1872, at his own expense, the 100-foot wide, twelve-foot deep Atchafalaya Bay Channel, along with the Houston Ship Channel in 1874 that evolved into a major water-based transportation corridor.

The supporters of the Atchafalaya Bay ship channel are listed on the letterhead above, ca. 1900. (Image courtesy of the Morgan City Archives.)

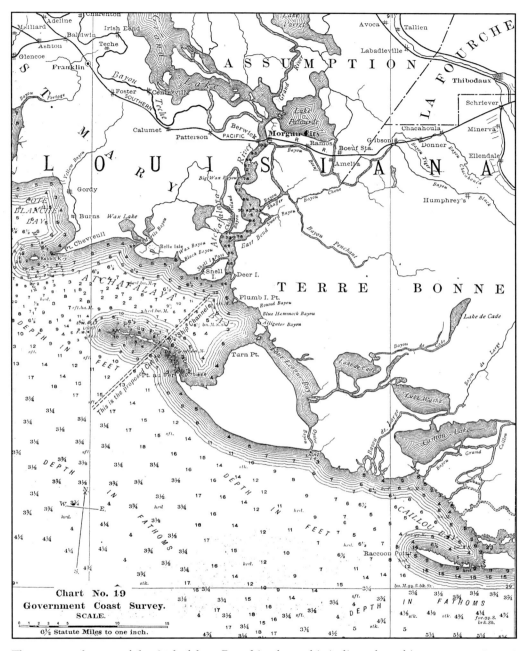

The proposed route of the Atchafalaya Bay ship channel is indicated on this government coast survey chart of Atchafalaya Bay, also known as Berwick Bay, ca. 1900.

The Atchafalaya Channel stimulated an era of major economic development and expansion, as water was vital to the region's international markets. It was a key element in Morgan's decision to make the region the hub of his steamboat operation, which functioned in close coordination with his Louisiana and Texas Railroad. Well-organized rail and water access routes, coupled with reliable service, served as the nucleus for new industrial investment, initially from the emerging cypress lumber business. As a result, sawmills were established along the rail route and in Morgan City's sister communities of Berwick, Patterson, and at sites scattered sites along Bayou Teche. The cypress processing centers provided railroad cross-ties, along with

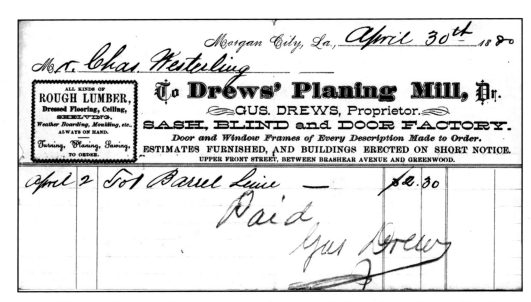

This 1880 receipt illustrates the importance of the logging industry in south-central Louisiana, ca. 1880. (Image courtesy of the Morgan City Archives.)

lumber for construction of box cars, rail terminal facilities, wharves and docks, homes for settlers, and commercial buildings (Cypress, wood eternal 1991). Cross-ties were, in fact, so important that Morgan City's cypress industry turned out millions of them. They were "the economical means of building so cheaply the great railroads from [Morgan City] to the Lone Star State" (Harris 1881:218).

Along with the logging industry, the industrial landscape was distinguished by boat- and shipbuilding, seafood processing, fur-trapping, moss picking and processing, and shell-crushing plants (Perrin 189; Broussard 1977; Gibson, et al.). Local records show that in the first quarter of the twentieth century large quantities of fish and turtles were shipped to New Orleans and Northern markets. Small sail-powered fishing smacks and trappers' wooden dinghies unloaded their marsh and Atchafalaya Basin harvest at one of the trading post that faced the Atchafalaya River, such as the Berwick Bay Fish Company and numerous others buyers whose fish houses lined the city's wharf (Ramsey 1957).

Further, during the peak of immigration through the Ellis Island Immigration Station, and because of Morgan City's importance as an inland port and a commercial fishing center, the district attracted a highly diverse population. Norwegians, Swedes, Poles, Greeks, Italians, Portuguese, Lebanese, and some Filipinos became part of the city and region's fishing, lumber, shipwright, and dry goods culture.

Since Morgan City was at the end of the 135-mile course of the Atchafalaya River that traverses the country's largest swamp, a houseboat community—called the Borrow Pit—consisting of a flotilla of 200 "shanty-boats" developed along the Atchafalaya's east-bank levee near Morgan City. This floating village was made up of a kaleidoscopic mix of water dwellers that gave the barge-based neighborhood a cosmopolitan atmosphere. The folks that lived in this eclectic community of arks and houseboats made their living as freshwater-swamp fishermen, crab and/or shrimp fishermen, moss gatherers, trappers, or oystermen. Some worked in Morgan City, and elsewhere, as tinkers, tinsmiths, basket weavers, or cobblers (Ramsey 1957). After 1882, houseboats became common sight along the Mississippi River. After 1880, they began to appear in the Atchafalaya Basin and served as the home for many unlawful tenants/squatters. Houseboats were generally simple floating cottages that measured about

While logging interests were harvesting cypress, trade boats were serving swamp communities, ca. 1900. (Images courtesy of the Morgan City Archives.)

Houseboats (above) were a part of the borrow pit community. With the discovery of "jumbo" shrimp, the economy of Morgan City changed, no date. (Photos courtesy of the Morgan City Archives.)

ten-feet wide and thirty-five-feet long and were made of thick cypress planking and could be wrenched onto the bank and anchored easily (Comeaux 1972).

Between 1865 and 1920, Morgan City's population had grown from approximately 500 to more than 5,400. After 1920, the city faced the demise of the timber industry and changes in the region's oyster business. These were difficult times. However, with establishment in 1937 of Morgan City's "jumbo" shrimp industry, the economy began to change. Local cypress mills provided milled lumber to build shrimp trawlers and wooden crates used to distribute seafood products by rail and truck directly to eastern seaboard markets. In addition, the Texas Company had a shook mill near the city. The mill built the sides of boxes that could be shipped flat to the company's Port Arthur refinery. At the refinery, the sides were assembled into sturdy wooden containers used in the shipment of five-gallon cans of motor oil or kerosene (the farmer's fuel) to overseas markets. By 1940, Morgan City was showing signs of recovery with development of the deep-water shrimping fishery.

Throughout World Wars I and II, sawmills supplied Morgan City shipyards and dry-docks with material to build United States Naval ships and refurbishing a wide-range of smaller watercraft. These mills also converted nearly every available piece of land they owned into war gardens for their employees (The War Garden . . . 2007). Also, Morgan City was the site of a defense plant charged with building "huge floating dry docks for the U. S. Navy" (Broussard 1977:97). Although a welcome addition to the local economy, the influx of people employed in this enterprise taxed the local housing market and public facilities. Morgan City responded by improving its municipal power plant, water and transmission lines, garbage and trash disposal, gas utility system, and recreation program.

In order to continue to expand its industrial base, the city needed to improve Morgan's navigation channel. This task was completed about the time the city began to recognize the importance of the area's oil and gas resources. In the first three decades of the twentieth century, oil was extracted and marketed from the marshes and swamps of South Louisiana and from fields that relied on logistic support from Morgan City. Just before World War II, the exploration frontier was pushed to the Gulf of Mexico's land/water interface. Many oil company pioneers were convinced there was oil trapped in reservoirs below the Gulf, but this was an alien environment, well beyond their drilling "comfort zone." They had to rethink and adjust their exploration and development models to accommodate aquatic drilling.

There were no guidelines for drilling in open water, and early attempts at oil exploration along the coast involved a trial-and-error process. In 1933, the first attempt was made to complete a well in the Gulf of Mexico. Four years later, the Pure Oil and Superior Oil companies completed a prospect 6,000 feet south of Creole in fourteen feet of water. World War II interrupted this activity, but in 1947 Kerr-McGee, at that time an Oklahoma independent, successfully completed the world's first oil well out-of-sight of land. The well, located 10.5 miles from shore in Ship Shoal Block 32, gave birth to a new industry—drilling for hydrocarbons in open ocean conditions (Barnes and McCaslin 1948; Landenberg 1972; Broussard 1977; Mathews 1977; Gramling 1996).

Prior to 1940, Morgan City's petroleum industry was largely overlooked, but, during the 1940s, by virtue of its proximity to the Gulf of Mexico's new petroleum exploration and development programs, Morgan City began to emerge as "the Gateway to the Tidelands and Hub of the Inland Waterways." (The town was already known as the "home of the Jumbo Shrimp Industry.") In the process, international attention was focused on the region, since it served as home port and supply base for the "gamble" and "unknowns" associated with exploration and production in open water.

With Kerr-McGee's success, an unprecedented stampede took place as major oil

From the Texas Company's Morgan City shook mill (above) the sides of boxes (below) were manufactured and used in the shipment of kerosene around the world, ca. 1910. (Photo [above] courtesy of the Catherine Dilsaver Collection, Morgan City and [below] image courtesy of the Morgan City Archives.)

The Case-Oil Trade

"In April 1888 the Standard trust had organized a wholly-owned British subsidiary, The Anglo-American Petroleum Company, Limited. This firm initially developed storage tank facilities in Britain but soon entered into the business of acquiring and building sailing ships to transport kerosene" (Maine Maritime Museum 1996). These vessels were used in the case-oil trade that involved two five-gallon cans packed side-by-side in a wooden box called a "case," the sides were called shook. In the early 1900s, The Texas Company refinery at Port Arthur employed more than 1,000 people who worked in the Can and Casing Plants, shook mill, box factory, canning factory, and filling rooms to meet the demand for lubricating oil, kerosene, and naphtha. More than two million units were shipped annually. (Gish 2010).

With development of the offshore oil industry, the Morgan City-Berwick-Patterson area witnessed an economic boom, 1956. (Photo courtesy of the Morgan City Archives.)

companies expressed an interest in operating offshore. The resulting "boom" greatly benefitted the Morgan City-Berwick-Patterson area. Because of Kerr-McGee's venture, much of the early technology employed offshore was invented in the greater Morgan City industrial zone (Mathews 1977; Gramling 1996).

By 1957, the region was described: as "one of the country's most promising frontiers for exploration" (Williams 1957:142). New businesses were established; old businesses found new markets; and the region prospered. Vendors found their niche, and Morgan City benefitted. For example in 1953, J. Ray McDermott constructed the first fabrication yard to be built solely for the offshore industry's fixed-steel structures; local fabricators eventually built nearly 5,500 of them (Le Blanc 1997).

The industry began to expand its geographic footprint across the coastal plain. The regional economy boomed and municipal governments in parishes with significant oil and gas activity were doing well. For thirty years, oil was the backbone of the economy. In the 1980s, the prosperity bubble burst. For the first time since the Great Depression, unemployment lines increased. Pink slips were common. The regional catchphrases were: "Stay Alive until '85" which was followed by "Chapter 11 in '87."

The economic forecasts were bad, as companies went bankrupt, cut back, furloughed, and laid off their employees. Anger, resentment, and frustration were the rule among those unemployed. Individuals fortunate to have a job knew that as long as they were working offshore they were safe. No one was ever laid off when they were at "work" in the Gulf of Mexico. The angst was so acute that when the industry rebounded in the 1990s, the oil industry had lost some of its best "hands," and these individuals were no longer the industry's best recruiters. They were now telling their families to not get involved in the industry, even though the work in the new and expanding deepwater province paid well and was an exciting an innovative oil industry frontier.

Deepwater became the industry's savior and Louisiana was given another chance to manage its oil revenues in a manner that would serve its long-term interests. Consequently, with discoveries of reservoirs containing at least 100 million barrels of oil or more, and prices in the late 1990s, increasing from $19 to $30 a barrel, the Gulf of Mexico quickly became one of the hottest drilling prospects in the world (Wilen 2007). Demand for drilling rigs (a colloquialism for a drilling derrick) outstripped available supply (Le Blanc 1997). By the late 1990s, virtually every fabrication facility in Louisiana, and along the Gulf Coast, was working at or near capacity. All of this industrial activity improved the regional job market. Some fabricators doubled their workforce in less than a year. Welders and shipfitters were being trained day and night to meet demand, but the memory of the 1980s was not helping potential employers fill the available jobs.

In Morgan City and elsewhere, the locals were dubious, as they could never remember any member of their families being unemployed. This was particularly true of the marshdwellers. They could always make a living off the region's natural resources. Unemployment was not part of their vocabulary, and they were not comfortable with the anxiety and social stresses associated with the industry's economic slump. Working in the marsh was not as stressful as working for wages; they liked their former lifestyles, but could not return.

The landscape and habitats had changed. Change is inevitable, and this was the case in Morgan City and other towns and villages along the marsh boundary. The coastal plain's citizens had to rethink their jobs and learn to deal with unemployment unknowns. Many simply refused to go back to work in the "oil patch." Although newspapers, billboards, and hand-lettered signs proclaimed "Help Wanted," they wanted no part of this business. They had been betrayed by their local commitment to their employers. Since they were laid off once it could happen again, so they looked for alternate employment and the industry lost a large part of its "regional memory."

The high demand for jobs prompted many shipyards to initiate outreach programs to high schools and technical schools to help train students for the expanding job market. J. Ray McDermott even visited trade schools in Pennsylvania and Ohio, but did not get any new hires (Judice and Jackson 1997). With unemployment at about 5 percent, there were few workers willing to relocate, so foreign workers began filling the void (Furlow 1997; Labor pains 1997). In 1995, as a result of deepwater activity, nearly 2,200 oil and gas based jobs were added to Louisiana payrolls. As more welders and fitters were lured to the higher wages of the offshore industry, mainland shipyards were looking hard to fill their vacancies. This trend continued into the early twenty-first century, as demand for workers remained high.

It was a worker's market, even as Louisiana was losing business to Gulf Coast competitors. Work was plentiful, and numerous contracts for platforms and boats were being awarded. Unfortunately, without the required labor force, Louisiana's fabricators could not bid on many jobs that could have generated several million man hours of work. As a result, Morgan City felt the regional fabrication downturn and the industry began to realize that the loss of their institutional memory in the 1980s was going to have long-term repercussions. In truth, many former oil "hands" went back into the marsh. Others migrated slowly back into the oil patch, an ancillary services. The money and benefits were good, but many learned well how quickly supply and demand can change and how the domino effect can have a direct effect on their ability to make a living. Caution permanently replaced their economic *laissez fare* attitude.

Why a Barrel of Oil?

Back in 1859, when American oil was first discovered near Titusville, Pa., it was put into whatever was handy—even whiskey or wine barrels—but that was not an exact measurement. Early oilmen decided to follow the 42-gallon barrel established in 1482 by Britain's King Edward IV. In 1866, that measure was further standardized by the Standard Oil Company, as its blue-painted barrels were considered the most precise. That's why "bbl" for "blue barrel" is still used as its abbreviation.

Houma: On the Edge of the Marsh

Before 1765, few European settlers lived in what is now Terrebonne Parish (Weinstein and Kelley 1992). Those who entered the area were explorers, hunters, trappers, and fishermen from settlements along the Mississippi River. Soon English, French, Acadian, and Creole farmers followed and created scattered communities along the bayous in areas not frequently flooded, particularly Bayous Black, Petit Caillou, and Terrebonne. Many of these settlements were established on French or Spanish land grants and each fronted on a navigable bayou.

These farmers also migrated from the Mississippi River's German and Acadian Coasts. Another group of Acadians arrived later from Saint-Domingue on the island of Hispañiola. They also settled in what is now northern Terrebonne Parish. After 1790, French refugees from the West Indies arrived in New Orleans and moved gradually into Terrebonne (Lyle, et al. 1960). This culture group became farmers, laborers, oystermen, shrimpers, trappers, and truck farmers. The descendants of these European farmers continue to raise traditional row crops; consequently, the original economic/cultural imprint survives.

In 1822, the areas' 1,000 inhabitants were scattered along the principal *chênieres, coteauxs*, hammocks, islands, and natural levees. Following the natural levee's crest, long-lot settlement forms emerged. These bayou-oriented communities were considered a single entity with varying degrees of continuity. Further, outside well-defined community settlement nodes, the population is locally considered rural. Therefore, there is, a continuous line of houses beside the highways that parallel the major streams. Through the entire length of the parish this pattern is repeated on all bayous. A second settlement type occurs on the parish's many plantations. These industrial villages include from ten to more than thirty dwellings, as well as a general store and may be either linear or block communities. Today, they are relics of an earlier pre-mechanization period (Rehder 1971). The third form is the compact urban settlement with associated settlement outliers or subdivisions.

By the late 1800s, the natural levees in Houma and south of the city developed into oyster and shrimp processing sites. The Houma Fish and Oyster Company is one example. (Photo from the author's collection.)

This simple model of settlement types encapsulates the natural levee-based communities that beginning in the late 1930s began to experience rapid economic growth and development. Much of this expansion is a result of hydrocarbon exploitation onshore and, more recently, offshore. Oil and gas represent a multibillion dollar industry. Agriculture, seafood, trapping, and recreation are multimillion dollar businesses. The shift in economic emphasis from agriculture to water or marsh-oriented occupations is centered on Houma—the parish seat which is directly or indirectly tied to the economics of the wetlands.

Although the parish was created in March 1822, Houma served as an administrative center as early as 1834; it was not incorporated until 1848 (Lyle, et al. 1960). For more than 175 years the city that bears the name of an Indian tribe has served Terrebonne's fishermen, trappers, farmers, oil-field workers, and entrepreneurs. At times it appears that Houma has an identity problem. It is nearly invisible in most discussions of the wetlands. However, being at the junction between a series of natural levees, the marsh, and the swamp, Houma has played a pivotal role in developing in the late nineteenth century the timber, fur, alligator, and fishing industries. This was followed in the post-World War II era with oil, natural gas, and the associated ancillary services that supported the municipality's expansion.

By 2010 more than 100,000 people resided in the parish, with about one-third of this number living in Houma. Along with an increase in population, the economy has changed from one centered on sugarcane, timber, fishing, and trapping to one based primarily on oil-related industries and marine transportation. The region's complex cultural milieu continues to absorb newcomers into the social fabric without too much disruption. However, with Houma setting on the boundary between the upland swamps and natural levees and the near sea-level marshes, it is aware of the environmental subtitles that may dictate its future.

Like most of the deltaic plain's biophysical components, the *Paroisse de la Fourche Intérieure*—the old Lafourche Interior consisting of Lafourche, Terrebonne, and parts of surrounding parishes—are well studied and documented. The region is an abandoned sub-delta composed of barrier islands, alluvial ridges, shell beaches, marsh, swamps, and water surfaces. Within the district's southern section, accretion has been replaced by subsidence and erosion resulting in the deterioration of the coastal lowlands and the partial to complete destruction of the protective barrier island complex.

A number of engineering endeavors have largely unintentionally upset the sedimentation balance, influenced saltwater intrusion, and disrupted flow regimes within the central coast (Gagliano, Kwon and Van Beek 1973). Further, as Louisiana's barrier islands and marshes deteriorate, the buffer zone between the Gulf of Mexico and the region's historic and contemporary coastal settlements narrows. For the people of south-central Louisiana, the marsh serves as a buffer against a hurricane's storm surge. When this barrier has eroded away, the province is in a most precarious situation; it has no engineered defenses that can compare to the marsh. Levees help, but they are not designed to retard all hurricane-induced storm surges. They have their limits. Therefore, with many parts of the region less than three feet above sea level, mean water flooding is a constant problem. Even though the area is drained, the natural system is superseded by an artificial one outlined by levees, flood gates, and residential/commercial/industrial activity. All are new additions to the landscape, since there is no record of leveeing the district's marshes in the 1800s (Nesbit 1885).

Soil compaction further complicates the regional environmental concerns. Therefore, when subsidence is combined with sea level rise, it has been determined relative sea level rates could range from up to nine feet over the next century (Gagliano and Van Beek 1970; Penland, et al. 1988). These critical problems are indications of the nature of the coast and its changing geometry. As a result, Terrebonne Parish includes one of the largest continuous expanses of coastal freshwater marsh in the state (Wicker et al 1980). Clearly, most of the *Paroisse de la Fourche Intérieure* is losing both land and vital parts of its productive estuarine environments. Although much of this change is attributed to natural processes, humans have had a direct impact through reclamation, levees, forced drainage, industrial expansion, and dredging activity.

Like all of coastal Louisiana, Terrebonne Parish's natural levees are a product of periodic overbank flooding and the deposition of sands, silts, and clays. Levee heights decrease from approximately sixteen feet above mean sea level in the parish's northern section to near sea level south of Houma. Along the transition zone, where levee deposits blend into the interdistributary area, elevations are from two to three feet above mean sea level. Natural-levee soils, for the most part, have been cleared for settlement and agriculture—a relatively easy process that is visible through the

(Image courtesy of the Center for Louisiana Studies, University of Louisiana at Lafayette.)

system of interlocking plantations.

Historically, sugarcane has been the commodity of choice, but string beans, Irish potatoes, sweet corn, shallots, cabbage, sweet potatoes, pecans, and tomatoes have also been grown. Add to the list cattle, swine, citrus, pond crawfish, and alligator farms and the parish is moderately diversified in its agricultural endeavors. Although the largest in land area, Terrebonne ranks among the smaller parishes in land devoted to crops. Even so, agricultural activities have occupied an important position in the area's social and economic environment. Wealth gained from hydrocarbons, commercial fishing and trapping, industrial development, and tourism do not overshadow the value of agricultural products from a historical point of view. From a spatial perspective, sugarcane, like parts of Lafourche and St. Mary parishes, has been a continuous part of the local economy for more than two centuries.

By the 1860s more than eighty-five sugarhouses were operating within the parish; sugarcane had successfully superseded cotton to become the major crop (Lytle, et al. 1960). With expansion of their agriculture land, the plantation community became increasingly aware of floods and the general and specific problems associated with uncontrolled water. To be a successful agriculturalist, it was imperative that levees be built to prevent or partial impede flooding events. Like the citizens of New Orleans and along the Mississippi River, it was clear that levees, pumps, canals, and drainage programs would have to be approved and built to guarantee natural levee land would not flood. Water would have to be managed to help expand the ten percent of the parish used for crops and pasture (Lytle, et al. 1960). These poorly drained lands, unless reclaimed through a system of levees and pumps, flood frequently. In these areas, a pattern of agricultural land use has evolved that is dependent on parish-supported forced drainage programs and reclamation efforts (Lytle, et al. 1960).

One of the best early examples of land reclamation is the Louisiana Land Reclamation Company's (chartered in 1878) system of canals, levees, and dikes designed to reclaim 13,000 acres in the western marshes of Terrebonne Parish. The tract was broken up by steam cable plows for the production of rice, jute, and vegetables. Even though this reclaimed real estate was producing agricultural commodities, the general belief was that "marshes have no value" (Nesbit 1885:183). The danger of floods prevented capitalists from investing more heavily in these endeavors, particularly after the flood of 1882 that was responsible for putting up to nine feet of water on the region's cultivated fields. New drains were necessary; they were built and remain a part of the modern landscape. Although the Louisiana Land Reclamation Company's polder failed, the canal pattern's orderly geometry survives and outlines the project's boundaries. Like so many of these projects, canals are historical artifacts of an unsuccessful reclamation endeavor.

Yet, canals built in response to the flooding problem largely worked. Regrettably, as the system expanded, these engineered water channels played a role in altering the natural hydrology; thereby, modifying natural sedimentation processes and the historical patterns of freshwater flow. With more than 140 named bayous and canals transecting the landscape, altered hydrology is a concern, since these watercourses carry and distribute runoff generated by local precipitation, or rainfall from the northern swamps (T. Baker Smith & Son, Inc. 1979). In terms of water storage capacity, Bayous Grand Caillou, du Large, Terrebonne, and Petit Caillou are the most noteworthy. Moreover, their natural levees sustain the most cultural development.

These waterways, and others, are distinguished by their general north-south orientation. Accordingly, they carry water from the higher elevations in the parish's northern swamps towards the near sea-level coastal marshes. A notable exception is the east-west trending Gulf Intracoastal Waterway that effectively partitions the parish into two distinct north and south zones. Approximately 75 percent of the parish is south of this waterway. Further, the channel exerts a significant influence on the local hydrological regime, acting as it does as a type of manifold, receiving much of the water from the upstream catchment basin at one point and distributing this water to various bayous that intersect along its length. However, as a unidirectional canal, connected to the Houma Navigation Canal, the watercourse also serves as a conduit for saltwater. Since the parish's main water plant siphons water from the Intracoastal Canal, drinking water contaminated with sodium chloride is a long-term dilemma that is being addressed by the parish (Gagliano, Kwon and Van Beek 1973; Curry and Leemann 1978).

South of Houma, the natural levee ridges decrease in height and width. With this landscape transformation, traditional occupations change from agriculture to harvesting the marsh's aquatic and terrestrial resources. Shrimp, oysters, crab, menhaden, muskrat, nutria, and alligators are the renewable quarry, often harvested and processed at end-of-the-road communities, or just "up the bayou" from these sites. Agriculture is not abandoned entirely, since some areas within the coastal marshes are suitable for seasonal grazing, and, until the second half of the twentieth century, lands were farmed. With the exception of the development of the parish's hydrocarbon and sulphur resources, the local economy continues to reflect the past. Levee agriculture and the exploitation of fish, shellfish, and other wildlife in the swamps, marshes, lakes, bays, and bayous are still evident among the visual paraphernalia that fisher folks accumulated in their yards. In some cases, these elements of material culture are reminders of when the population lived in isolated encampments, or were part of their transient hunting, fishing, and trapping activities.

Throughout the coastal lowlands and—particularly in the southcentral areas—the marshdwellers aquatic-based harvest provided the impetus to build and maintain the roads that parallel all of the zone's bayous. As these resources were promoted beyond the markets accessible by water, roads and railroads became critical. In response to this need, these transportation arteries were constructed to connect the bayou fishing communities to nationwide markets, with Houma serving as the intermodal or hub city.

In the analysis of the region's post-World War II financial base, the principal economic resources are related directly and indirectly to the petroleum industry. This sector of the economy is buttressed by a regional commitment to agriculture and the harvest of the estuarine-dependent aquatic life. Although all of these industries are vital, they are, with few exceptions, overshadowed by the production of raw materials. Employment, therefore in the production of raw materials is quite high. Most of this production is exported; hence the region does not benefit directly from any value-added endeavors. The economic mainstay revolves around the petroleum industry. Consequently, almost every basic economic activity can be traced to the petroleum, natural gas, and other mineral reserves, the estuarine system, the fertile soils, or the navigable waterways.

With discovery of easily marketable hydrocarbons, Houma developed rapidly into a regional logistic-support center. Petroleum- and marine-related industries have become the region's economic mainstays. In light of the demand that this growth and development has placed on the region's resources, the parish is faced with three key concerns: 1) the effects of continued population growth and industrial development patterns on land that is threatened by serious erosion and subsidence problems; 2) the growth-spurred demand for leisure time activities in an environment that is changing rapidly; and 3) the ability of the parish to provide needed services to an expanding population, when some of these communities are going to require extensive flood and drainage control measures that have directly and indirectly contributed to the region's environmental problems.

Regardless of the future needs of the Houma metropolitan area, the marshdwellers of the parish have endured, sacrificed, and suffered numerous hardships. The one constant is their resilience and determination to live along the bayou, but work in "their" marsh. This is shown by their continued commitment to "fishing oysters," shrimping, and crabbing. Their cultural heritage is also tied to trapping "rats," "neutrals," and alligators. They thrived in encampments that served as shrimp boat rendezvous sites and brought their catch to isolated shrimp-drying platforms. They were survivors, who were tough, durable, and above all optimists. These characteristics were part of *grand-mère* and *grand-père*'s cultural heritage and may serve as the historical human model on how to live and work in a hostile and ever-changing environment. Their will is too strong to give up, so they adapt. This trait may be the key to survival in the changing coastal plain. For to the people living south of Houma and elsewhere in the coastal lowlands, they may have to move. They have done it before, and they can do it again, but up the bayou may be unacceptable. In their mind, a move is measured in one or two miles, no further. To some, Houma may be safe and secure, but it is too far removed from looking out their windows and seeing the uninterrupted landscape of the marsh. In some ways, just like their ancestors, this view is what they live for, and without it they are lost. City life is not in their bloodlines and any ordered retreat will have be done carefully with one eye always on the locals' culture history, as it is the key driver in most of their decisions.

Trapping as an Economic Engine

The Oct. 31, 1925, *The Houma Courier* reported that Louisiana trappers had taken more than six and a half million furs during the 1924-25 season. "Local residents of that day were already aware that the dollar a pelt being paid for good adult muskrat skins was responsible for a winter migration to the coastal marshes of whole families who would stay on the trapping grounds until February, forcing a change in some school schedules and resulting in Christmas celebrations postponed until spring or summer."

The *Courier* published the following on Nov. 14, 1925, "Trappers Prepare For Big Catch This Season; Many Houseboats Are Seen Headed For Trapping Grounds." "On the Terrebonne (bayou) dozens of houseboats, carrying provisions and trapper's complete outfits, are seen daily headed for the trapping grounds in the lower part of Terrebonne, in order to be on the ground when the trapping season opens, Nov. 15. Terrebonne leads all of the Louisiana parishes in the production of furs, which means that Terrebonne Parish is at the head of the list of counties in the United States in fur production, as Louisiana leads the United States and Canada, too." Further, "Trapping furnishes a livelihood to hundreds of families in this parish. The average trapper will earn from $2,000 to $4,000 in a season, and fortunes have been made by the middle man."

The Dec. 5, 1925, *Courier* detailed the economic impact of the season already under way in a story headlined "Big Fur Catch Is Expected This Season." "A fair idea of the magnitude of the fur industry of Terrebonne Parish can be drawn from the volume of drafts handled by Houma Banks last week for fur dealers,'" editors wrote. "Something over $350,000 passed through the three Houma banks last week for the purchase of furs, breaking the record for any one week. It is believed that the fur catch in Terrebonne Parish this season will exceed that of any past year. It is probable that the total value of furs caught in Terrebonne this winter will exceed $2,000,000" (Ellzey 2006).

Isle de Jean Charles

During the four years I passed in Montégut, I went repeatedly to Jean-Charles. This humble community has been a new experience in my priestly life, an experience I will never forget. I found at Jean-Charles an entirely different world, different in scenery, different in language, different in its way of life. It was a way of life abundant in contrasts, a life shrouded in mystery and melancholy, a life of serenity and disillusion [*sic*], a life of isolation and deep fraternity, a life of hte [*sic*] past solidly anchored in ancestral traditions (Pelletier 1972).

In South Louisiana's wetlands, many distributary ridges/levees—or in a few cases, hummocks—have partially subsided. The isolated remnant remains as "high" ground surrounded by a green fringe. Called islands, these ridges are easily identified by the presence of trees.

The Isle de Jean Charles community occupies one of these linear features, elevated only inches above the *marais'* surface. This ribbon settlement exists along each bank of the narrow Bayou Jean Charles, and, in the early 1970s, it was distinguished by rows of houses, all of wood construction and painted white or cream, though a few are covered with brick veneer. Many residences are surrounded by a picket fence with low shrubbery in front. Chickens abound, and a few pigs and a cow may also be noted on the property. These homes are simple, neat and orderly, furnished originally with home-made tables, chairs, cabinets, and armoires (Pelletier 1972).

Three families settled the "island" in the early 1800s—Walker Lorvin, Jean Charles and Jean Marie Naquin (Guidry n.d.). According to oral history accounts recorded by Ramsey (1957), Jean Charles Naquin and his brother Jean Marie came from France and settled the island in the late 1700s. Regardless of the date of initial settlement, the occupation of this small, narrow, strip of land, barely above the marsh grass, had to be a difficult an arduous task. Migration to this property resulted in the birth of Louisiana's most solitary, remote, and inaccessible continuously occupied coastal communities.

Early in its existence, Isle de Jean Charles was a farming community, but, as the following quotation makes clear, environmental changes in the early twentieth century forced the inhabitants to adapt to radically different circumstances:

Old Adolphe had mentioned that, years ago, when he was a young man, they had large crops of rice and corn from Isle Jean-Charles as far as Lake Tambour, but that the hurricane of 1909, followed by a terrible tidal wave, had swept away all the arable soils, and since then, the population has turned to the sea for a living (Pelletier 1972:18).

The island's inhabitants subsequently derived their living from the sea, harvesting oysters, crabs, fish, and shrimp. However, their small boats, would only allow them to harvest the resources from the waters close to the community.

Until the early 1950s, Isle de Jean Charles was completely cut off, with only limited outside contacts afforded by gas boats or *pirogues*. The community's physical isolation ended in 1953, when spoil extracted from a "borrow" canal became the foundation for a road connecting the island to the mainland at Lower Pointe au Chien. With the road came electricity, telephone connections, television, and the automobile (Pelletier 1972). Like so many South Louisiana communities, "the pave" changed Isle de Jean-Charles's character. But the language of choice remained French. Unfortunately, the French-speakers' illiteracy was an impediment to the Jean-Charles community in its negotiations regarding property and mineral rights with oil company attorneys after World War II, which was the case throughout the coastal plain. Problems with clear titles became the foundation for numerous court cases. Property litigation continues, as boundary issues became more continuous with discovery of marketable hydrocarbons (Rushton 1979).

Prior to construction of the first roadway, everything on the island had to be hauled through the natural waterways, canals, or *traînasse*. To attend their Montégut church, parishioners from the ridge took their boats through Lake Felicity, Lake Barré, Terrebonne Bay, and up Bayou Terrebonne, a distance of twenty miles (Pelletier 1972). The community's physical isolation was compounded by its social segregation, stemming primarily from the inhabitants' multi-racial background:

> Here [Isle de Jean Charles] lived a group that the French people of Houma called 'Sabines,' that other Louisianians called Indians. . . . Their group was a tragic one . . . since they were accepted as belonging neither to the white race nor to the red or the black. Schools they seldom had, as they could not go with the white people and would not go with the black (Ramsey 1957:44).

It is thus hardly surprising the Isle de Jean Charles' residents seldom left their island.

The only "outsider" to visit regularly was the priest, who came every three to four weeks. He regularly married one or more couples (Boutwell and Folse 1997). Although the wedding ceremony was important, the people of the island would often *sauter balai,* or "jump-the-broomstick," to formalize a couple's decision to live together; they jumped into matrimony and were "saluted as man and wife by the assembled witnesses" (Crété 1981:280). Before a priest began to make regular visits to the island, this was the island's marriage tradition and often recorded by the Terrebonne Parish clerk of court, who also made periodic trips to the village (Kane 1944). To christen their babies, the Isle de Jean Charles' dwellers needed to "have the water poured," so a lugger would set out with as many "as a dozen babies, and also fathers, mothers, godfathers, and godmothers. The journey might take a full day each way . . ." (Kane 1944:89). After the ceremony everyone returned to the marsh settlement.

In at least one case, the priest brought the church to his out-of-the-way parishioners by means of his boat, the *St. Thomas*. The arrival of the priest meant Mass was said on the spot (Kane 1944).

> . . . they were all there, some seventy-five to eighty of them, men, women, and children, some seated, but most of them standing along the rear wall, all in silence. Their priest had come to see them and they were all there. They had not gone fishing for that day. . . . [T]hey were independent. . . . [T]hey were their own boss, . . . [T]hey worked only when they wanted to (Pelletier 1972:16).

This was a communal society that remained inaccessible, ignored, and unmolested until oil exploration and a public road opened the community to the outside (Pelletier 1972). At one time, farmland and pastures existed behind the community's homes. These farmlands have succumbed to subsidence and erosion. Water is now closer to the island hamlet, and the residents consequently must always keep a vigilant eye on the weather and the landscape, as both are a challenge to their survival.

> It may be easy for others to write off Isle de Jean Charles. 'But it not easy when it is your home,' Naquin says. 'My grandpa, when he was alive, saw it growing. My father and uncle saw it when it was about at its peak. Now that I am chief, I am watching it wash away' (Knapp and Dunne 2005:86).

The island's future is thus uncertain at best. A new hurricane protection system does not include the island, and this resulting exposure "will leave them [the citizens] to the mercy of the weather." Yet, the island's longtime residents nevertheless have expressed great reluctance to leave (McKnight 2005). This is home, and has been for perhaps more than 200 years.

Other marshland sites were settled, but have not endured as well. They were abandoned. Only a few of the deserted, ephemeral, and weather-worn artifacts remain. These relic features are ghostly reminders the site was something more than a topographic curiosity—a remainder of a once-prevalent riparian lifestyle.

Mauvais Bois

Like Isle de Jean Charles, Mauvais Bois was also settled on an abandoned distributary ridge. This natural-levee-farming-community never supported more than eight families, who drew their subsistence from agriculture and seasonal fishing and trapping. Dispersed farmsteads fronting on the bayou averaged five *arpents* in width, with a maximum depth of two-and-a-half *arpents*. The people of Mauvais Bois cultivated corn and sugarcane, while also maintaining vegetable gardens. At the base of the levee, these farmers grew rice—one of the few places, outside the *chênière* plain and Chênière Caminada, where rice was cultivated in isolation (Detro and Davis 1974).

Unlike some inaccessible wetland communities, Mauvais Bois and Isle de Jean Charles did not have a school, store, or church. They were too small or too insignificant. So, like many wetland communities, if children went to school, they traveled there by boat. In some instances, the parish provided the remote ridge with a "school boat" to guarantee that the children had access to an education. In some cases the children were home schooled (Krammer 1941). Even so, illiteracy was high, largely because of the unavailability of teachers and language difficulties, which was common in many places in the United States (Shanabruch 1977).

Because of their remoteness, many of these kinship-based hamlets were unattractive to qualified educators who were not accustomed to the monotony of living in a cluster of homes "at the end of the road," or on a levee remnant, or even in the middle of the marsh. Few schoolteachers consequently applied for vacancies in marshland schools. Furthermore, students had to learn English before they could learn anything else. Whether at Mauvais Bois, Isle de Jean Charles, or hundreds of other tight-knit marsh communities, English was a "foreign" language. Many young people either became discouraged and dropped out of school, or they became frustrated at being punished for using French in school. These Francophile students were severely punished for using the only language they knew and understood.

Another problem was that Louisiana traditionally lagged behind other states in education. In 1920, the state had the nation's largest number of illiterates over ten years of age, and school absenteeism was quite high, so why get an education when the marshdweller, like the Mennonites, Hutterities, and Amish, valued the simplicity of life and the group's oral rules and traditions concerning the discipline of work (Din 1988). To the marshdweller, an education met learning the ways of the wetlands and so the residents of Mauvais Bois and elsewhere may have gone to school, but only occasionally.

In the 1930s, school was important, but not as important as working the land. Hence, local educational opportunities were limited. For example, students who finished elementary school on the Deltaic Plain could attend only four high schools. Along the Mississippi River south of New Orleans, Buras, Braithwaite, and Port Sulphur were available, but along Bayou Lafourche, south of the Intracoastal Canal, only Golden Meadow had a high school. There were no high schools south of Houma, so the children living at Mauvais Bois and at sites east and west of Bayou Lafourche had limited access to a "formal" education, but they knew the marsh and how to plant and

Children Were Often Home Schooled

"At the mouth of Bayou Perot on the shore of Lake Salvador there are six families with twelve children of school age. They live too far from school to send the children, and their only means of transportation is by boat. . . . All were taught to read and write by their parents. Twice within the past few years a school teacher was hired for three months during the summer to teach the children" (Kammer 1941:66).

For the children of the marsh, the local bayous were the highways to their "end-of-the-road" schools. (Photos [left] from Butler 1980 and [right] courtesy of the Standard Oil Collection, University of Louisville, negative no., 30306, 1945.)

harvest sugarcane.

At Mauvais Bois, sugarcane was produced on the ridge. As a result, a small syrup mill was constructed to process the crop. Also, each resident fenced their small farm plot and allowed their cattle to range in the open marsh. Supplies for the community were obtained through a series of bayous, lakes, and hand-dug *traînasse*. Trips for supplies, recreation, and church attendance were made about every three to four weeks. Prior to arrival of the small marine engine, this trip required a full day of poling a *pirogue* through a near invisible path. After powered skiffs were introduced, the time required for the round trip was shortened, and the need for basic subsistence food crops disappeared. The community's economy consequently shifted from subsistence to commercial activities.

In 1925, the first family departed Mauvais Bois; it was no longer necessary to live at this site. Gasoline-powered boats made access easy. There was, therefore, a gradual migration from the ridge to the hamlets along lower Bayou du Large. By 1935, the out-migration was almost complete. Only one family remained, and they left in 1940 (Detro and Davis 1974).

Powered skiffs, rural electrification, and shell roads marked the demise of this formerly permanent community. The residents moved closer to desired amenities, and, as a result, the community has been transformed. It is no longer a permanent settlement, but it has not lost its usefulness, as many people still use the ridge for a variety of recreational pursuits.

A Generic Description of the Bayous Ribbon Settlements;
Bayou Lafourche, A Former Mississippi River Distributary

From Donaldsonville to Lockport, Bayou Lafourche is almost as populously settled as St. Charles Avenue. Not an acre goes to waste, nor an arpent lies idle. Great fields of corn and cane roll away three and four miles deep, and between these are the forest groves, in which the plantation homes are placed . . . (Cole 1892:12).

Bayou Lafourche—"the longest village street in the world"—is perhaps one of the most densely populated "rural" areas in North America (Ditto 1980:1). From Donaldsonville to Golden Meadow, there is an almost uninterrupted string of buildings. Settlement succession progresses from sugarcane plantations, to linear villages, to "nearly" inaccessible fishing and trapping communities. The settlement sequence also represented a strict hierarchy of social classes. This pattern is evident along the five major bayous south of Houma—Bayous du Large, Grand Caillou, Petit Caillou,

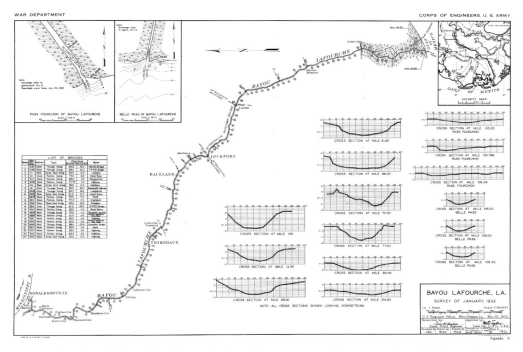

In 1937, the 107-mile length of Bayou Lafourche was crossed by twenty-four bridges—a bridge approximately every 4.5 miles.

Terrebonne, and Pointe aux Chien as well. These rural bayous have the appearance of long, densely populated thoroughfares. The houses lie in a single line, fronting on the bayou, with windows facing the street or bayou. Further, "an important consideration is the remarkable fluidity of traffic and movement along any [of these] bayous" (Knipmeyer 1956:38).

These linear villages may be described as agriculture, urban (which replaced agriculture villages), fishing, trapping, marsh, swamp, and combinations of these. Such patterns of land occupation were not devised to suit South Louisiana's bayous; they have discernable European roots. The linear settlement model was fixed in the colonial period. Subsequent expansion has followed this initial form throughout southeastern Louisiana. Bayou communities typify the complexity of linear settlement types. In a sense, each bayou is a homogeneous unit of interrelated inhabitants. The local *habitant* or *petit paysan*, therefore, consider a bayou community, regardless of length, a single entity with varying degrees of continuity.

Even with the presence of plantations, there are along all of the bayous that penetrate into the *marais*, numerous small farms. Large garden plots occupy the property between the road and the bayou. In local parlance, this is called the *batture*—a site selected for the moderating climatic influences of the watercourse. According to local custom, by the first of November, All Saints' Day, all crops had to be harvested and this is the case on Bayou Lafourche and elsewhere (Post 1962).

These occupancy patterns and other material cultural elements are visible culture traits that have been passed from generation to generation. Small farms are more numerous than plantation nodes and comprise the greater portion of the bayous' settlement morphology. Since Bayou Lafourche is more than 100 miles in length, these ribbon farms are distinguished by their dwellings, outbuildings, and cultivated fields. They occupy a narrow strip of land whose length is many times its width. Dwellings are on "the front" with the cultivated land behind the farmstead. As one travels "down the bayou," the farm's contours narrow to conform to the reduced size of the natural levee. This is true whether on Bayou Lafourche or along one of the bayous south of Houma.

In all cases, the last housing clusters are the homes of trappers and fishermen. The *marais* is at their backdoor and these are the dominant economic activities. This settlement type is not always restricted to land unsuited for any other use, but in general it occupies very narrow slivers of land that are only slightly above sea level. Any small change in water levels results in flooding. Although all flooding is important, even that associated with south winds. But the real issue is a hurricane-induced storm surge, which was evident in all of the storms in 2005 and 2008 and caused considerable "end-of-road" property damage.

In the lower reaches of these bayous there may be marsh available for livestock grazing. If so, the animals usually belong to farmers "up the bayou" who lease the grazing land, but this occupation is of little interest to the trapper-fisher folk who live at the end of the road or natural levee. Although land may be available for a small vegetable garden, gardens are rare—unlike the *habitations* "up the bayou." "Down the bayou" natives prefer fishing and trapping. Within these communities, the houses are smaller, more closely spaced, and closer to the bayou. The yards have a general chaotic look and are not well organized or in some cases well kept. Outbuildings are few, and fenced enclosures are absent. In these fishing and trapping villages, piers, boats, and related equipment replace farm machinery.

Regardless of the inhabitants' social position, the bayous of South Louisiana were—and remain—the foci of these linear communities. Each waterway was the main artery of commerce, and everyone depended upon the bayou. As in the past, each house has a boat of some type docked in front, attesting to the bayou's importance. Trade is essential so boats and waterways are a necessity.

Evolution of Bayou Lafourche's Line Settlement

By 1770, at least fourteen Acadian families had migrated into the upper Lafourche Valley. They established their riparian farms on the west bank of Bayou Lafourche between the modern communities of Donaldsonville and Labadieville in a province later known as *Paroissse de la Fourche Intérieure*. These *émigrés* chose to live on the west bank because it was not flooded as frequently as its eastern counterpart. Other disenchanted Acadians drifted into the Lafourche wilderness as well.

The Spanish monarchy in 1785 granted a large number of Francophile refugees the opportunity to select their own home sites. Six hundred built farms along Bayou Lafourche, between modern-day Labadieville and Lafourche Crossing. By 1788, these bayou Acadians constituted 61 percent of the populace (Brasseaux 1985). Further, because of the fertile soils on the vacant land, Creoles, Gallicized Germans, Portuguese, Spanish, Chinese, Americans, British, and Italians were also attracted to the area.

These immigrants adopted many of the customs, mores, core traditions, and values of the established French-speaking residents. They also embraced the Cajun identity (Perrin 1985). In general, Bayou Lafourche's west bank is always more densely settled than its eastern counterpart, mirroring the pattern established by 1770 on the bayou's upper reaches (Knipmeyer 1956; Newton 1972; Davis and Detro 1975).

The approximate dates to 1900 of the immigrant groups who migrated to Louisiana
(from Brasseaux 1996)

Date	Immigrant group	Date	Immigrant group	Date	Immigrant group
1699	French	1795	Spanish	1865	Chinese
1700 & 1809	French Creoles	1803	Anglo-American	1850	Italian
1719	African	1700 & 1809	West Indian	1880	Sicilian
1720 & 1850	Germans	1803 & 1830	Irish	1890	Lebanese
1764-1785	French Acadian	1820 & 1870	Yugoslavian	1900	Hungarian

By 1812, all culture groups now represented (with the exception of the new additions from Vietnam) were present. The process of gallicization, rather than hispanization, was well advanced, since schools, newspapers, and officials employed, openly embraced, and used the French language. Many Spanish surnames were altered; for example, Caballero became Chevalier, Placencia turned into Plaisance, and Dominguez, Rodrigues, and Acosta were Gallicized into Dominque, Rodrique, and Acoste or D'Acoste respectively. Because of settlers' reticent nature and physical isolation, French remained the dominate language until the Civil War (Din 1988). Material culture was French from the outset.

The local collective identity evolved into "Cajun"—a term rarely heard prior to the 1970s (Ancelet 1999). Today, virtually all Bayou Lafourche residents proudly claim and relish Cajun. And those that live in the tight-knit communities south of the Intracoastal Waterway remember the stories, all of the stories of storms that are now benchmark events in their cultures. These are the narrative accounts of hurricanes and the villages of Leeville, Carmadelle, and Chênière Caminada—the forgotten village of ridge dwellers.

Chênière Caminada: Caminadaville

Across the narrow pass the island village of the Cheniere Caminada lifts its comb of roof and gray gable and soft-colored adobe chimneys from out of the clumps and clouds of the chinaberry tree. . . . Years ago the island was a long oak forest, but this has all been cut away to make room for the orchards and homes of the islanders . . . The island has a distinct front and back door. On the front facing the gulf . . . , all the houses are built. They are a long row of little gray, pleasant homes, set close together for space is precious, and before each is a grassy yard where zinnias and marigolds grow and orange trees pelt their splitting globes of fruit into the long grass. In the corner of nearly every yard will be a shed, where luggers are lying bottom up, out of the sun, or where a new boat is being beautifully built. . . . The fences are made of drift wood stuck into the ground just as it floated ashore. . . . In the bayou . . . are luggers, schooners and pirogues. . . . The pirogues look like that bit of foot gear known as a Creole slipper. . . . There is the smell of tar and paint in the air as the fishermen are busy getting ready to sail off to the winter fishing grounds. . . . Along the shores in the water shallows the fishermen have hung their long seines to dry (Cole 1892:12).

At the west end of Grand Isle, less than a mile across the bay, is the *"Isle of Chênière"* or "Island of Chetimachas" (On a claim 1836), later named for Francisco Caminada—a New Orleans merchant and landowner during the Spanish regime (Place names of 1971). The island, valued at nearly $20,000 and home to nearly fifty slaves in 1836, was a working plantation, the ownership roots of which go back to 1763 (On a claim 1836; Swanson 1975). By 1890, Chênière Caminada—translated as a roadway through an oak grove—was a quiet, sail-boat and seine-fishing community of nearly 1,500—probably the most densely populated village along Louisiana's Gulf shore (Ramsey 1957). It was a close-knit, multiethnic, encampment of row houses.

The inhabitants of the *chênière* were mobile, dispersed, and represented a shifting collage of operating groups, focusing on one fishing area, then another, creating a daily rhythm of activities. Nearly an endless procession of boats harvested one or two areas. The efficiency of these watermen resulted in the annual harvest of thousands of pounds of fish that were sold in New Orleans' French Market through two dealers—Bartholomew, Tallon, and Company or Felisado and Company (Sterns 1887).

This 1891 photo of a palmetto house at Chênière Caminada provides the earliest visual evidence of African Americans working in the wetlands as full-time fishermen. (Photo courtesy of the National Archives and Records Administration, Still Picture Records Section, Special Media Archives Service Division, negative no. 22-FCD-4.)

In the 1880 census, 15 percent of the surnames were Terrebonne and 10 percent were descended from Alex Lefort. The Sicilians—Angelettes, Valences, Alarios, and Picciolas—settled on the ridge in the 1870s and learned French from their wives (Reeves and Alario 1996).

The enclave was a thriving hamlet whose wharves were lined with working sail boats. Palmettos covered *bousillage* folk houses were stretched side-by-side in two long lines. Space was precious, so homes were set close together. The *chênière*'s cosmopolitan population was made up of Frenchmen, Austrians, Italians/Sicilians, Chinese, Malays, Portuguese, and African Americans (Sampsell 1893). It is claimed, but not verified, that many villagers were descents of Jean Lafitte's buccaneers. This ethnic mosaic of trapper-farmer-fisher folk practiced their seasonal occupations in virtual isolation. It was a community that was practically unknown to the outside world, and it was recorded in narrative accounts by only a few visitors (Kammer 1941).

These ridge dwellers' homes were spartan, but neat, with sand-scrubbed or painted brick-dust-floors and large fireplaces. The smell of *café noir* or *café au lait* was al-

After the 1893 hurricane, Chênière Caminada community was reestablished as an oyster and shrimping village, no date. (Photo courtesy of Louisiana Department of Wildlife and Fisheries.)

ways in the air—"black as sin, hot as the hinges of hell, and strong as revival religion" (Frost 1939:76). Good coffee was dark, omnipresent, made in a drip coffee pot (*grègue*), served in a tiny demitasse cup, and prepared very carefully to insure the water neither boiled nor had a chance to get cold. Coffee was more than a drink; it was the basis for socializing. A pot was always on the stove, whether in the home or on a lugger, as it was considered bad manners not to offer a guest a cup of *café*. This ritual was almost a religious experience and common throughout the communities in the coastal plain.

Unlike on the prairie region, where *pieux* fences were common, *chênière* fences were made of drift wood stuck into the ground (Cole 1892B). Behind their home, frequently in a grove of orange trees, stood a homemade earthen oven (*petit four*)—a primitive form of France's folk oven, which was shaped like a locomotive boiler, open in front, without any door. In these ovens, a women, wearing a *garde soleil* (sunbonnet) and a "crisp white apron" (Perrin 1985:85), baked huge round loaves of hot bread (*pain chaud*)—twelve to fifteen loaves at a time.

Before the bread could be baked, the earthen ovens were loaded with driftwood and allowed to burn for several hours, similar to a wood-fire pizza oven. The coals were then rearranged with a large-bladed wooden hoe made for this purpose. The temperature was determined by tossing a piece of wheat flour or paper into the *petit four*. If either browned, but did not burn, the temperature was correct for baking. Large round loaves of dough were then put on a paddle and slipped into the oven; the coals then were piled around the baking loaves. After a half-hour to an hour, when the bread was brown and crusty on top, the coals were removed. The *pain*

Throughout South Louisiana, consumption of French roast coffee was an important part of the social fabric of every household, 1946. (Photo courtesy of the Standard Oil Collection, University of Louisville, negative no. 44500.)

Trawl boards changed the shrimp industry dramatically. Seines were quickly replaced with the new technology and the associated nets, no date. (Photo courtesy of the Morgan City Archives.)

chaud was left to bake in the embers, while the oven cooled (Kniffen 1960B). The finished product, which has been described as some of the "best bread you ever ate," was a dietary stable (Lenski 1943:94).

The men of the community were seine fishermen. Their hand-woven, cotton seine and trammel nets were made by the women of the community (Davis and Posey n.d.). The trammel net resembled a chain-link fence with stretch. The net was made with three individual wall-like layers. A slack, small mesh, inner sheet of netting was sandwiched between two outer walls of woven mesh that entangled and captured fish. The net also snared the catch in bags or pockets of netting, as well. This occurred when a fish swam through one of the outer panels, hit the inner woven sheet, and passed through to the other outer section, which created a bag or pocket. At this point, escape was impossible (Reeves and Alario 1996).

Whether manhandling a trammel net or seine, a large crew was required, as a shrimp seine measured 1,500-feet in length. Twenty- to thirty-foot *canots*, each powered by a single-cylinder engine rated at three horsepower, were used to assist with managing the large net, or prior to the introduction of gas-boats, sailing smacks supported the seine fishermen (Cheniere Hurricane Centennal 1994; 1995). Once the net or seine was played out by a boat (a seiner), the crew waded in chest-deep water, managing the net, once the net felt right it was hauled ashore. The fish and shrimp were removed one-by-one—the marketable ones were saved and the undersized fish were thrown back. With no local market for their *fruits de mer,* the fishermen of the *chênière* shipped their catch to New Orleans by a weekly packet steamer. This routine was replicated daily as long as the weather allowed. The net was the key to the fishery. Therefore, seines, like those used by *chênière* fishermen have been a part of Louisiana's fishery since the 1800s, with Landreth (1819) reporting their use in 1819. Prior to 1917—the year trawl boards were introduced—state license records show 300 shrimp seines. Many of these operations were based at Chênière Caminada or the region's shrimp-drying platforms. By 1949, the historical record reports only four seine crews survived. Instead, 3,310 motorized trawls were in use (Werlla 1950).

Since this fishery required large crews, Chênière Caminada evolved into a "city" with nine grocery stores, owned by Julien Lefort, Marco Picciola, Thomas Alario, Thomas Valence, and others (Reeves and Alario 1996). These surnames indicate the ethnic diversity of this site. Among the principal items carried by these tradesmen were seines, cast nets, sails, and oil coats (Cole 1892B). As at Mauvais Bois, rice was grown on the island for local consumption, and fish were plentiful, so the diet was high in starch and protein. All other material wants were satisfied by grocery and supply boats bringing supplies to the community through the Barataria waterway system (Van Pelt 1943). A Breton priest, Father Grimeaux, built a high, narrow, brown and yellow church, midway on the island and dedicated it Our Lady of Lourdes (Cole 1892B). A school also was part of the hamlet's landscape—a rare occurrence in coastal Louisiana's secluded settlement clusters, as noted at Mauvais Bois.

When the men were not working, the *chênière* residents gathered for a Saturday-night ball, their chief form of entertainment. This affair was free, but soft drinks, gumbo, and coffee were sold, along with a regional specialty—boiled mullet or *meuil*

Unlike many marsh communities, Chênière Caminada had a church with a resident priest, ca. 1890. (Photo courtesy of the National Archives and Records Administration, Still Picture Records Section, Special Media Archives Service Division, negative no. 22-FCD-39.)

bouille (labeled the poor man's fish). Guests attending these functions were guaranteed a supper with red wine, for a fee of twenty-five cents (Cole 1892B).

Frugal though they were, marshdwellers knew how to have a good time. As a result, dancehalls, like the Tokio in Raceland, were found in every community. Saturday night was for dancing. Young women would come to the party with shoes and stockings in their hands; their bare feet on the ground, ready to enjoy the evening's festivities (Kammer 1941). The dancers worked hard five-and-a-half days a week, but they reserved the period from Saturday noon until midnight Sunday as a time of relaxation and recreation.

On Monday morning, it was time for the Chênière's marshdwellers to return to work. These inland fishermen preferred sail-driven luggers, steered with a rudder controlled by one of the Chênière's watermen (Cheniere Hurricane Centennal 1994). Piled aboard the vessel would be big, tall, bell-shaped wicker baskets filled with the day's harvest. Every family's boat was moored in front of their home; the boat was the net fisherman's car, bus, and truck. These water dwellers would sail to their winter camps, where they harvested various aquatic species. Shrimp, oysters, and crabs (*Callinectes sapidus*) were their principal quarry (Van Pelt 1943). They typically did not return home for several months.

Chênière Caminada fishermen gained some notoriety for the quality of the oysters and shrimp they removed from Barataria Bay reefs. To process these oysters, a packing plant was opened on Bayou Brulés in a building recycled from the 1884 New Orleans World Exposition. The enterprise failed, so the local harvest had to be shipped by steamer to New Orleans.

The community routinely moved tons of fish to New Orleans. The village was alive with activity, until October 1893. Thirty-seven years after the *Isles Dernières* storm, Chênière Caminada was destroyed and largely forgotten by an unannounced hurricane and its associated tidal surge. Not enough well-to-do people were killed, the site was too remote, secluded, and inaccessible, the damage was to riparian ridge dwellers, and the fisherfolk affected were considered by some as social outcasts. Therefore, the demographics did not warrant much news coverage. People died and two narrative and picture accounts recorded the event—*The Story of the Storm in Louisiana* by R. Fall (1893) and M. Forrest (n.d.) *Wasted by Wind and Water: a Historical and Pictorial Sketch of the Gulf Disaster*. Otherwise there are only a few extant newspaper accounts that acknowledged the event.

The 1893 Hurricane

With an angry roar the winds rose, shifted direction, and bore down upon the island with a 125-mile-per-hour blast. Gargantuan tidal waves poured in one after another and swept over sands, fish docks, village streets, and over homes and people. In fifteen minutes the island was covered with five feet of water; in half an hour, with eight feet.

Chaos came with the waves. Their homes and boats splintered around them, men, women and children were swept into the sea, grasping for something to cling to, finding nothing. Some clutched at rooftops, found a temporary raft to float on, then felt it smash beneath them and spew them like spray into the sea. Clinging to bits of scattered wreckage, mothers knew the agony of babies snatched from their arms, oldsters saw their grandchildren sink and drown within their reach (Ramsey 1957:119).

Chênière Caminada was totally destroyed by the 1893 hurricane. With little notice from the outside world, the storm passed between New Orleans and Port Eads on

The 1893 Hurricane on the Mississippi and Louisiana coasts. (Image from *Harper's Weekly*, October 1893.)

Isolated oystermen's camps were vulnerable to hurricanes and other weather events, 1938. (Photo courtesy of the Morgan City Archives.)

October 1. For all intents and purposes, the land was swept clean. Indeed, one study of the storm notes that "where buildings once stood, there were merely foundations to mark their locations" (Plaisance 1973:182). Only four homes remained (Cheniere's priest tells 1893; Forrest n.d.). Of the island's fishing schooners and red-sail luggers, only the *Good Mother* and *Counter* survived (*The Daily Picayune* 1893).

More than half of the population was lost. The death toll reports varied from 779 to 822, and although these numbers are impressive, an exact count was never tabulated (Cheniere's priest tell 1893; Plaisance 1973). Many of the fatalities occurred when even the sturdiest homes disintegrated. For example, seventy-eight people sought refuge in one home. At the height of the storm, the house collapsed, and seventy-four persons were killed (A graphic picture 1893). Corpses were strewn everywhere. ". . . [A]fter the storm a brave woman was seen, . . . , slowly and painfully making her way through the morass. Clenched between her teeth were the ends of a sheet within which rested a tiny baby, still alive; while another was carried under each arm. By a truly remarkable exhibition of daring courage and endurance she had saved all three of her children" (Forrest n.d.:17).

Only 696 persons survived, most clustered in the Caminada's four remaining homes. As suggested above, survivors saved themselves by holding onto any type of floating debris—including timber, roofs, doors. Some of the survivors drifted nearly eighty miles across the Gulf to Southwest Pass.

The storm also took its toll on Grand Isle and on many shrimp platforms and oyster camps west of the Mississippi River. Rescue boats from New Orleans brought supplies, and relief workers were startled by the destruction (Van Pelt 1943). Water was in short supply, so relief boats brought ice to the survivors, but found it melted quickly.

Coffins were unavailable, and separate graves were impractical; bodies were buried where they were found. There were so many dead that the graves of those who were recognizable were aligned like rows in a plowed field (Sampsell 1893; A graphic picture 1893). Difficult decisions had to be made. But the central issue is one pondered every hurricane, whether to move or return an start all over and deal with the risk and uncertainty of another hurricane. A few of the original residents returned.

> Men of fortitude have gone back to the Cheniere and have brought their wives and families. They're an industrious group—these people and have know that it is economically sound to use Cheniere Caminada as the base of operations for their prosperous fishing business. Like the trappers, the fishermen's life requires long hours of work. It is only natural that a fisherman likes to spend his all too few leisure hours in his home, with his family. And so, the wives have returned with their hard-working husbands—and have helped to make the many homes that now dot the ridge of Caminada. These women have endured hardships in rebuilding their community and they deserve a great deal of credit for their pioneering, courageous spirit. Once again, families are getting a firm foothold here—and this time a foothold that they believe will become deep-rooted in a prosperous future (Baker 1946:117).

The returning settlers' high expectations were unwarranted, for their new community was destroyed by a 1915 hurricane (Baker 1946). To the east in Plaquemines Parish, Venice and Boothville were destroyed completely. Olga, Fort St. Philip, and Buras sustained extensive damage as well. Empire, Zibilich, Illyrica, Louisa, and Nairn were under water, along with the communities of Nichols, Doullut's Canal, Metcalf, Bowers, Sunrise, Bay Adams, and Bayou Cook (Wires down 1915).

Olga, like all lower Mississippi River communities, was battered repeatedly by hurricanes, but the population repeatedly rebuilt. (Image from the author's collection.)

As the Chênière Caminada experience makes plain, living on the Gulf's edge is, at best, a gamble, for hurricanes are always a threat. Many marshdwellers who survived the 1893 storm moved to the Bayou Lafourche community of Leeville (originally called Orange City). Residents felt safer there and established a "comfortable community with a school, a church and a grocery . . ." (Ditto 1980:68). This feeling of well-being did not last long.

The retreating waters from the 1909 storm left a six-foot water mark on the homes that endured the surge. Numerous survivors were rescued by boats owned by the state's Oyster Commission and the Texas Oil Company. Another ordeal sixteen years after the Caminada storm and the marshdwellers again had to make a hard decision. Should they leave? Should they stay? Some stayed and others chose to retreat and relocate at sites inland. Many moved to a number of communities on the west bank of the Mississippi across from New Orleans (Place names of 1971). A few refugees relocated to the small community of Salaville, situated at the locks along the Westwego canal, where lots were available for forty dollars (Reeves and Alario 1996).

Those who decided they did not want to leave, because fishing was too much a part of their life, began to rebuild straight away. Further, since the hurricane made landfall during the oyster and shrimp seasons, fishermen took their boats and resumed their harvesting activities. They were down and needed to return to the sea. Throughout the coastal lowland this was the prevailing attitude. A hurricane was a nuisance that had to be dealt with, but boats, water, sea spray, fish, crabs, oysters, and shrimp were their livelihood, so they lived with the threat of storms and persevered.

Carmadelle (Comardelle)

Prior to abandonment, Carmadelle was an unassuming small natural levee village southeast of Des Allemands. The site between 1915 and 1925 was home to twenty-five families. The first Euroamerican inhabitants arrived in the 1880s. Early families lived in homes constructed from hand-sawed cypress, covered with palmetto fronds and insulated with Spanish moss, perfect for this rather detached and rugged environment.

By 1920, Carmadelle had attracted itinerant fishermen from riparian hamlets along the north shore of Lake Salvador. These marshdwellers seined the lake for a freshwater fish known as buffalo—a member of the "sucker" family. Although buffalo has numerous small bones, its good flavor made it one of the more valuable of the non-game freshwater fish. As a result, the harvest was shipped to market aboard freighters operating between Carmadelle and Westwego. Freight boats enabled fishermen to stay out much longer pulling their seines, running their trot lines, along with checking their hoopnets, trammel nets, and wooden slat traps. They might be away from their marsh homes for nearly a month at a time thanks to general cargo vessels that ran a ferry service. In some cases, fish cars were used that kept the catch alive.

Fish cars allowed a coastal dweller to ship live product to market, ca. 1890. (Photo courtesy of the National Archives and Records Administration, Still Picture Records Section, Special Media Archives Service Division, negative no. 22-FCD-10.)

Sometimes, the watermen would take their catch directly to either Westwego or a stretch of the Barataria and Lafourche canal known locally as the "French Market"—a hamlet consisting of a cluster of sheds operated by New Orleans vendors, who came to the canal to buy seafood (Reeves and Alario 1996). This market was vital to the fishermen in the Barataria Basin, as it funneled fish products into New Orleans. By the early twentieth century, luggers from the dispersed home sites scattered throughout the Barataria region were lining the canal to offload their products. By unloading on the west bank, the captains and boat owners avoided the lock fee required to enter the river. Eventually, a number of canning companies lined the canal, and they prospered from the estuarine fishery exploited by fishermen from Carmadelle and elsewhere in the Basin.

At Carmadelle, the natural levee's width produced a line settlement with "common" land reserved between the bayou-fronting lots. At this site, and elsewhere, a sizeable part of the population lived in houseboats that were anchored in slips or cuts excavated in the bank of the common property (Cheniere Hurricane Centennal 1994). In the case, houseboats were pulled up on land and were used as semi-permanent residences. When the owner left the village, it was easy to refloat the home and move it to a new site. Marshdwellers living in a shotgun home would dismantle the structure and barge it to a new site, where it was reassembled as a camp (Detro and Davis 1974; Newton 1985).

A sizeable number of the families living along the Carmadelle ridge switched in the fall from fishing to market hunting and guiding duck hunters. This was a lucrative business, as the region's numerous lakes were "favorite resting places for the immense flocks of *poule d'eau* and ducks that come down from the colder climes of the North" (Harris 1881:169). Since the area was close to New Orleans and thus accessible to urban sportsmen, the large number of birds that wintered in the marsh provided the Carmadelle inhabitants with a livelihood at a time when the fishing was slow and crabs were not in season.

Marc Alcide Camardelle was a market hunter, guide, trapper, fishermen, and decoy carver who lived at the village. Like many marshdwellers, his avocation was carving decoys. His trademark style included a crooked neck tilted to the back of the bird. This design made for a compact decoy (Cheramie 1997). Years of observing ducks in their natural habitat helped Camardelle insure a decoy that was correct in every detail.

Families began to leave Carmadelle after a series of early twentieth century storms leveled the village. By 1925, most of the surviving inhabitants had moved to Bayou Gauche—the "last jumping-off point to the marsh around Black Prince Island, Simoneaux Pond, and Lake Salvador"—all important waterfowling sites" (Cheramie 1997:106). Bayou Gauche stretched along Bayou des Allemands and was the home of trappers and fishermen, whose camps and boats dotted the banks of the bayou. The site bordered the southern edge of the Sunset Drainage District and had road access. In that sense, it was an "end-of-the road community."

The former village residents who did not move to Bayou Gauche settled in Gheens, Lockport, Des Allemands, Luling, Raceland, and New Orleans. Many of these folks continued to support themselves through seasonal fishing and trapping. By 1938, Carmadelle was abandoned. After local fishermen installed small inboard engines in their skiffs and *pirogues*, they no longer needed to live in this vulnerable community.

St. Malo and Fisherman's Village

Of the 13 or 14 picturesque buildings nearly all have dried fish hanging from the roof, with chickens and pigs beneath the planking. They are lighted by lamps in which fish oil is used. The reason so little is known of the settlement is due to the peculiar reticence of the inhabitants, its isolated location, and the fact that they trade almost entirely with Chinese or Malays who live in out of the way places in New Orleans (Fortier 1909:307).

During the Spanish colonial period, planters considered runaway slaves (*cimarrones*) to be a serious problem. The St. Malo band of *cimarrones* roamed and terrorized the region east of New Orleans in the early 1780s. Because the band had acquired "a notorious reputation for its misdeeds" (Din 1980:247), the Spanish government unsuccessfully attempted to destroy the fugitives' communities on the lakes bordering Lake

This woodcut depicts the buildings of the all-male community of St. Malo. (Image from *Harper's Weekly* March 1883.)

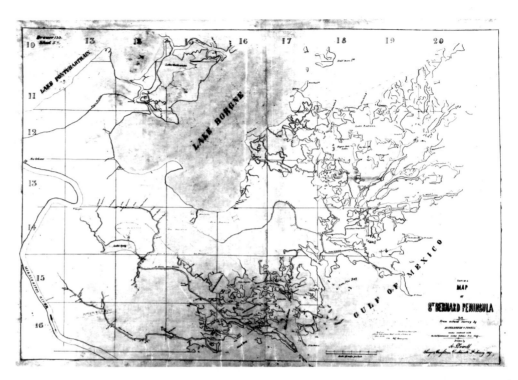

As early as 1847, the community of St. Malo was significant enough to appear on government maps.

Borgne east of New Orleans.

The lacustrine village of St. Malo—perhaps named for the runaways' leader—may have been one of the oldest known marsh communities. In all probably it was the home/hiding place for these *cimarrones*, although "the band occupied all the bayous that led to Lake Borgne, from Chef Menteur to the Duprés plantation" (Din 1980:248). Clearly, as early as the 1780s, runaway slaves discovered the marshes and swamps and used these environments to their advantage. Many slave fugitives were eventually apprehended, captured, jailed, and sentenced; most were hanged or banished permanently from the colony, although the fate of the St. Malo band is not known (Din 1980).

At the time of the *cimarrones*, or perhaps later, a group of Manila men—*Tagalos* from the Philippine Islands—lived at St. Malo in post-supported homes only inches above the surrounding marsh muck. These wooden dwellings were erected in true Philippine style with large eaves and balconies. The people spoke Spanish, *Cebuano*, and *Tagalog* (Espina 1988). The village's vernacular architecture was intended to withstand the region's violent climate. Traditional palmetto and woven-cane structures were inadequate.

St. Malo, like most of Louisiana's marsh communities, was characterized by a relatively small population. The Filipinos of St. Malo were semi-Spanish in culture and outlook and were some of the pioneers in the state's coastal fisheries (Reinecke 1985). The community differed little from the *barangays* in the Philippines, which were kinship units of from thirty to 100 families. Wherever the Filipinos settled they set up voluntary benevolent associations, like the *Sociedad de Beneficencia de los hispano Filipinas,* established in 1870 at St. Malo, to compensate "for the familial kinship loss due to immigration" (Espina 1988:77).

The primary difference between the Louisiana settlement and its Philippine counterpart was that St. Malo was a community of men (Espina 1988).

> No women are allowed in the colony and if a man has a family they must be kept elsewhere. The life of the colony is connected with New Orleans, where the headquarters of their benevolent society is maintained, and when a fisherman dies his remains are finally interred in one of the cemeteries in New Orleans (Fortier 1909:307).

Of the ethnic groups that worked in Louisiana's wetlands, the Filipinos are well documented in the work of Espina and Din. Blacks and East Asians are the least know groups; they are the forgotten minority, absorbed into the mainstream. They are scarcely mentioned in the historical record, which magnifies the importance of the following eyewitness description of the Filipinos at St. Malo, an observation that may also have applied to the area's East Asians.

> Out of the shuddering reeds . . . on either side rise the fantastic houses of the Malay fishermen, poised upon slender supports above the marsh, . . . Hard by the slimy mouth of the bayou extends a strange wharf. . . . Odd craft huddle together beside it, fishing nets make cobwebby drapery about the skeleton timber-work. Green are the banks, green the water is, green also with fungi every beam and plank and board and shingle of the houses upon stilts. All are built in true Manila style, with immense hat-shaped eaves and balconies, but in wood; for it had been found that palmetto and woven cane could not withstand the violence of the climate.
>
> They speak the Spanish language . . . and communication is still kept up with Manila, and money often sent there to aid friends in emigrating. Such emigrants usually ship as seamen on board some Spanish vessel bound for American ports, and desert at the first opportunity. It is said that the colony was founded by deserters . . . (Hearn 1883:196).

Louisiana's Filipinos were actively involved in the state's coastal fisheries. As a seafaring people, the Filipino immigrants were constantly searching for productive fishing grounds. The waters from Lake Borgne to Breton Sound met their criteria, as well as numerous areas in Barataria Bay, where they were also participants in the shrimp fishery (Espina 1988).

It appears that the community of Fisherman's Village, along Bayou Bienvenue about a mile-and-a-half from Lake Borgne, was similar and in close proximity to St. Malo. This site was used by the British invasion fleet in 1814. The riparian community "consisted of twelve large cabins made of stakes with thatched palmetto-frond roofs. The enemy soldiers surprised the village and captured the residents and the small military detachment" (Din 1988:91). The site is now underwater and largely forgotten—another example of a 200 year old community lost to time and tide.

Delacroix Island

Historian Gilbert C. Din (1988) reports that a number of writers visited "*la isla*" and described as late as 1894 a landscape dominated by palmetto huts and bare-headed, bare-footed children playing in the yards. The settlement's economy was based on hunting and fishing. The women fished in the bayou, and the men fished in the Gulf and hunted in the surrounding marshes. They brought back "immense quantities of fish and ducks, which [were] sent to Olivier railroad station, ten or twelve miles [away] . . . , in small carts drawn by oxen, yoked Spanish fashion, by the horns" (Din 1988:127).

Immigrant Benevolent Groups

Germans, Italians, Yugoslavians, and other ethnic groups, like the Philippine immigrants, also organized benevolent societies. These organizations "combined the function of insurance societies and aids for assisting unemployed and disabled workers" (Lovrich 1967:155). In addition, these benevolent groups supported the newly-arrived immigrants by finding them permanent homes with members of their nationality. Other charitable gestures included assisting the immigrants in finding jobs and how to deal with day-to-day issues of living in their "adopted" home (Lovrich 1967; Williams 1974; Magnaghi 1986; Merrill 2003, 2005; Margavio and Salomon 2002-2003).

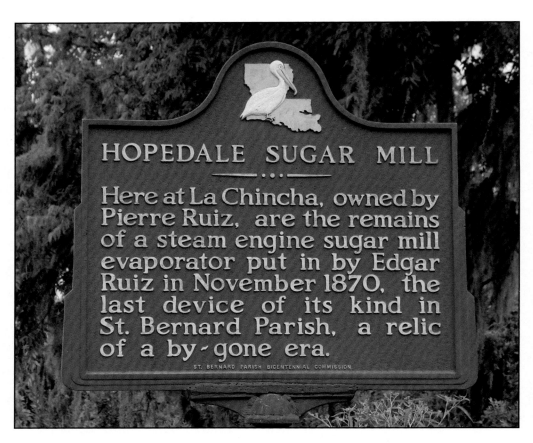

Spanish-speakers created plantations along Terre aux Boeufs in the eighteenth century, 2005. (Photo by the author.)

It was also reported that not one of these citizens could read. Accordingly, their folk traditions were recorded in songs, locally called *décimas*. The songs chronicled their way of life, and the Isleños of Delacroix Islanders clung tenaciously to their lifestyle, because they knew no other. Unlike other coastal communities, the storm of 1893 flooded the island and caused some damage, but no one died. A storm in 1901 hit the parish and "everything in its path . . . was swept away and few . . . inhabitants were left to tell the tale" (Din 1988:129). In 1909, another storm inundated the parish. Residents of Shell Beach, Alluvial City, Yscloskey (originally Proctorville), Bencheque, and Delacroix had to find high ground. The 1915 storm killed 50 inhabitants. Many Delacroix residents were displaced by storms in 1919 and 1920. An unnamed 1947 hurricane and Flossy (1956) severely damaged Shell Beach. Betsy (1965) left only six homes standing of the nearly 600 in Delacroix. In 2005, Katrina mimicked the 1909 storm by leveling or severely damaging Reggio, Yscloskey, Shell Beach, Hopedale, and Delacroix. But life goes on and has since the 1780s.

In Delacroix, the Spanish language—mixed with a Creole *patois*—was used extensively. This pattern prevailed up to World War II. After the war, the younger generation made little effort to speak Spanish. In fact, in the 1980s, less than 500 people in St. Bernard Parish spoke Spanish.

These marshdwellers lived off the land. Even though economic activity accelerated in the twentieth century, with construction of a local cypress mill, a cannery at Delacroix, and a plant that substituted palmetto for moss in mattresses, saddles, and cushions, the people of Delacroix were still physically detached from the "outside"

(Din 1988). In the late 1930s, approximately 1,000 Delacroix Island residents were still trappers, fishermen, and rum-runners. Their skill with boats made it easy to move contraband ashore through the maze of largely uncharted coastal waters.

The Delacroix Islanders were just one of many involved in this illegal trade, because during Prohibition, Louisiana's coastal lowlands were a haven for bootleggers and moonshiners. Prior to Prohibition's repeal, rum-running was the sole occupation of many Delacroix inhabitants, as well as others along the forbidding coast (Jeansonne 1995). Their ability to speak Spanish made them ideally suited to transport illegal alcohol offloaded from "mother" ships from ports in Cuba, Central America, and the West Indies. Further, the delta offered a climate suitable for year-round smuggling, and the region's numerous small islands, lakes, bays, and passes made close surveillance impossible. The government could not dedicate an adequate patrol fleet that in the words of one marshdweller "would have taken a nice piece of the United States Navy" (Kane 1944:180). As a result, Prohibition smuggling became a part of the region's unwritten history.

Many "locals" benefitted from the illegal alcohol that moved through the wetlands' maze of waterways, and they reveled in the illicit activity for they had a love of danger and a cavalier attitude toward governmental regulations. Bootlegging was considered by many to be an honorable means of augmenting the family's yearly income (Jeansonne 1995), and, indeed, money never came so quickly or easily to the marshdweller. Otherwise honest men were simply involved in an illegal profession that did not interfere with their "moral compass."

Marshdwellers offloaded mother ships from the Bahamas, Cuba, Mexico, and British Honduras in international waters, and smaller fishing boats relayed the cargo to rendezvous points onshore. These contraband operations were quite resourceful. For example, boats were frequently hired as decoys to lure the Coast Guard away from the main fleet of rum-runners (Kammer 1941), and private radio and commercial radio stations would broadcast codes telling smugglers where and when the mother ship would arrive (Kane 1944). As long as the "mothers" remained outside American coastal waters, they were safe, and the watermen's skill at night navigation made it easy to slip past patrol vessels with their holds filled with illegal alcohol off loaded from schooners that could transport more than 300,000 cases (Segura 1973).

Smuggling was a rewarding business, as marshdwellers were paid a minimum fee of $100 to $500 to transfer the contraband to an inland point from off-loading sites, usually off the Chandeleurs or Breton Island or elsewhere west of the Mississippi delta. Once loaded onto a small boat, the illegal alcohol was destined for New Orleans—"never a place that embraced or even comprehended the law against liquor" (Kane 1944:180). Federal law enforcement agencies, however, wanted the marshdwellers' clandestine smuggling stopped, and, as a result, "a whole army of agents was called in; in one day a series of raids brought forth a million dollars of liquor. Federal warehouses could not hold all of it." In fact, "an agent from Maine exclaimed in bewilderment: 'I never *thought* there was that much anywhere'" (Kane 1944:184).

Interception by federal authorities was not the only threat faced by smugglers. Once the smuggled goods were onshore, hijacking became an issue. Hijackers "became so bold that they once stole 1,500 quarts of impounded liquor from the St. Bernard Parish jail" (Jeansonne 1995:23). The "authorities" did not overlook the bootleggers who were violating the law, but considered the hijackers much more dangerous. Hijackers were also the target—literally and figuratively—of bootleggers, for gunfire was frequently exchanged during hijackings. Outraged bootleggers/rum-runners also went to court to prosecute hijackers. In short, it was considered alright to bootleg, but not to hijack. This was not a moral conundrum.

Even with bootleggers and hijackers, Delacroix survived and preserved its fishing

---

The Ballot and Patronage

For years, the ballot in St. Bernard Parish was in Spanish, but because of high illiteracy rates most people voted the rooster (also on the ballot), which was the symbol of the Democratic Party. In 1930, "St. Bernard had a registration of 2,454; when it went to the polls, it recorded itself as 3,979 for Huey P. Long and 9 for his opponent" (Kane 1944:201).

Further, with discovery of oil and gas in the delta local governments prospered and "it became difficult to find a family or a branch without a connection to the public payroll" (Kane 1944:204). Patronage from loyal campaign workers meant jobs. Often more jobs were promised than were available.

and trapping traditions; however, more formidable challenges were ahead. A succession of storms—including an unnamed 1947 hurricane, along with Hurricanes Flossy (1956), Betsy (1965), Camille (1996), Georges (1998), and Katrina (2005)—destroyed nearly all of Delacroix. Prior to 2005, "those who returned to the island continue[d] with a sense of nineteenth-century stoicism, accepting the ravages of nature as their fate" (Din 1988:198). But after 2005, many Delacroix Island inhabitants have been particularly critical of the United States Army Corps of Engineers for the construction of both the Mississippi River's levees and the Mississippi River Gulf Outlet (MRGO).

The outlet destroyed thousands of acres of marshland, and the levees stopped the annual deposits of sediments that are an essential element in the delta building process. MRGO, which greatly increased the storm surge damage associated with Katrina, has been a political issue in St. Bernard Parish for decades because the environmental impact of this channel detrimentally affected the natural landscape that the Isleños use to make their living. In 2009, the channel was closed. The champions of this closure won, but it took decades and a hurricane to stop what was clearly a mistake.

The future of local trapping and fishing as a profitable enterprise is difficult to predict. Decline seems inevitable, and indeed it has started. The *décima* proclaims: *"Ya la Isla no es la Isla como era de primero"*—"The Island is no longer the island as it was in the beginning" (Din 1988:194). That was certainly the case after Katrina left Delacroix in ruin.

Shell Beach/Alluvial City

> In St. Bernard Parish two settlements have distinctive characteristics. The first of these is Shell Beach, a wind-blown little place of about twenty families living along both sides of Bayou Yscloskey where it empties into Lake Borgne. The residents here are strikingly like those on Grand Isle. They show little or no ambition; their houses are ramshackle, though very clean. The driving force here—is a woman, who is a native of New Orleans. She prides herself on having the ear of the sheriff, the most important personage in the Parish, an influence gained by her seeing that all the eligible voters of Shell Beach cast their ballots for him in a close election. She feigns annoyance as being bothered by her neighbors who want favors from the sheriff. To be fair, she did heroic work when the worst storm since the 1915 hurricane struck Louisiana last August and the residents of Shell Beach had to be evacuated. When they returned, she saw that they received clothing and enough food to tide them over until the shrimp season began (Kammer 1941:88).

Shell Beach, like Yscloskey and Hopedale, developed as support centers for the fishermen and trappers who harvested the region's renewable resources. Like many "end-of-the-road" communities—like Delacroix, Venice, Lafitte, Bayou Gauche, Cocodrie, Port Fourchon, Pointe au Chien, Dulac, Four Point, Lower Bayou du Large, Cypremort Point (also known as Cypremort Prairie), and Intracoastal City—Shell Beach metamorphosed from a small fishing and trapping community into one that supports charter fishermen and recreational boaters. These places also emerged as anchor points for medium to very large recreation dwellings.

The "outsiders" occupying these recreational dwellings were not always welcomed, for the locals were quite willing to fight threats to their livelihoods. In the 1980s, Terre aux Boeufs commercial fishermen formed a roadblock to prevent sport fishermen from accessing "their" local fishing grounds. They felt that their livelihood was being threatened by individuals who did not fully understand their way of life (Gowland 2003).

This concern may still be important, but the economics of recreational activities are now co-mingled with those of commercial fishermen. Boat launches and marinas easily identify the recreational importance of this site. Quick access to Lake Borgne and an easy drive from New Orleans are two contributing factors to the site's recreational growth.

Hurricane Katrina devastated Shell Beach and many other "end-of-the-road" access points across southeast Louisiana. These sites welcomed the economic benefits of recreational sportsmen, but their orderly routines have been disrupted. In the aftermath of storms in 2005 and 2008 the question is: "Will these sites be reinvigorated?" In the last fifty years, the region has been damaged and/or destroyed repeatedly by Hurricanes Betsy (1965), Camille (1969), Katrina (2005), and Gustav (2008). After any hurricane, recovery is always an issue, but Shell Beach and the other Terre aux Boeufs communities have rebuilt in the past, and there is no apparent reasons for them not to do so again, for the residents, like most of those born or raised in the wetlands, accept the risk of living close to the edge of the marsh and water.

With more leisure time and surplus income, urban dwellers increasingly avail themselves of charter services and marinas across the coastal lowlands, 2009. (Photo by the author.)

Fort Balize: The Wickedest City in Louisiana

Mr. Hutton and myself went on shore to the Balize[;] this is one of the most miserable looking places I ever saw for human beings to live upon there is not high ground enough to build their houses upon and not a sport for a garden it is an intire [*sic*] marsh . . . (Landreth 1819:155).

The French wanted to build a harbor in the Mississippi River's delta to guide ships across the dangerous sand bars at the mouth of the Mississippi. Bienville assigned Pierre Le Blond de la Tour the task of creating an outpost in the delta "that consisted of a small island of river deposits jutting out of the waters. Mud dredged from the pass was used to form a larger and firmer foundation and floating logs were retrieved from the waters to be used to construct the barracks. Soon a chapel with a steeple that doubled as a lighthouse had been completed" (The Balize 1992:8). Balize (from the French word *balise*, meaning "beacon") had thus been established of the river's Northeast Pass.

Located on the sea's edge, Balize was not a place of comfort, for it was remote and vulnerable to hurricanes and enemy warships. When the French first occupied the post in 1722, it was a little flat island called Toulouse by the locals (Roland 1740; Casey 1983). To build the fort, "planks, beams and eight hundred piles were brought from New Orleans and the Tchoupitoulas swamp near the city. Many of the piles were used to try to stop erosion of the island" (Casey 1983:7). Building the fort was a slow process; in fact, as late as 1742, engineers were still trying to complete the project (Robinson 1977). One problem was all of the pilings needed to build the fort had to be hauled to the site by ships, for large cypress rafts were inefficient and broke apart before they reached the Balize (Moore 1983B).

The fortification was established to serve as a defensive outpost at the mouth of the river, aid in trade with the Spanish, and assistance in guiding ships into the Mississippi. Over time, the outpost became an important community (Surrey 1916; Rob-

The Balize was the first European settlement site in the Mississippi's birdfoot delta, 1819.

inson 1977). Warehouse facilities eventually were provided to offload cargo for the "coasting trade," so bigger ships would not have to make the difficult ascent to New Orleans (Kniffen 1990). As early as 1728, sailing craft used this sixteen-foot channel to gain access into the Mississippi River. In fact, vessels regularly had to wait for months for a favorable wind to carry them upstream (Kniffen 1990). New Orleans was the meeting place for the respective cargos of ocean-going vessels and Mississippi River boats, and Balize was the portal to the economic bounty of the Mississippi drainage basin.

By the beginning of the Spanish era, the fort contained a small battery composed of three or four cannons (The Balize 1992). The Balize was so secluded that everything had to be imported. Moreover, the settlement strip was so narrow there was no room to cultivate a garden. As a result, locals were compelled to purchase goods that were inflated three to four times their normal retail price.

When Antonio de Ulloa, Louisiana's first Spanish governor, arrived at the Balize in 1766, the post needed revitalization. While awaiting his fiancée's arrival, Ulloa lived at the site for seven months, thereby making the Balize the de facto capital of the new Spanish colony. Because Balize Bayou was silting up and becoming un-navigable, Spanish officials relocated the Balize near the entry to Southeast Pass, which was becoming the main channel for ships entering and leaving the Mississippi River. The Spanish spent more than 20,000 pounds sterling to build a new stronghold that was used for approximately 150 years (Tombs only testify 1921). Balize "eventually . . . included a warehouse, powder magazine, chapel, and two barracks large enough to house 50 soldiers" (Buras 1996:31). Using material from the Spanish Balize—dubbed Fuerte Réal Catolica—the old French Balize was restored (The Balize 1992).

After the Louisiana Purchase, the Americans took over the fort. Without adequate maintenance funds, the remote fortress deteriorated, but the ancillary support community survived (Casey 1983):

. . . the settlements on the various passes, particularly the American Balize at the head of Balize Bayou where it entered Southeast Pass, were the habitat of

This 1776 French map shows the pass to the Balize, which was the principal route into the Mississippi Valley.

river pilots, boatmen, fishermen, and a host of others who supplied the skills for the Balize to flourish. Approximately five hundred persons were living in these settlements by the end of the 1850s, with most of them at the Balize (Jackson 1993:8).

As the Mississippi River became an increasingly important American commercial artery, the Balize became an important supply center (Buras 1996). Yet the Balize was so secluded it became a hangout for shady characters—"men who had deserted military posts, been expelled from the military for wrongdoings, or who had jumped ships" (Buras 1996:45). "Riots and brawls" were common, and "low revelry and debauchery the pastimes of the night" (Tombs only testify. . . 1921:12). Over time, the community became known as the "the most wretched village" in the country (Buras 1996:45), and it was considered a dangerous place to visit.

This dire situation changed when river pilots began to use the site as their base of operations. With formation of the Pilots Association and the discontinued usage of common sailors "picked up in the city" as pilots, married men were attracted to the out-of-the-way village. The pilots closed the "resorts," and the community's riotous disorder gave way to a more tranquil way of life. The village, whose population increased to 800, became the supply and labor center for incoming ships.

In the 1860 census, branch pilots were listed from such foreign locales as Denmark, Sweden, England, Wales, Ireland, and France. Others came from within the United States—from Maine, Connecticut, Massachusetts, New York, New Jersey, Pennsylvania, Virginia, and of course, Louisiana. A cook at the Balize was from the Philippines, and the schoolmaster was a German from Hanover. There was a lighthouse keeper from Holland, a bookkeeper from Norway, and a gun-shop proprietor from Italy. The three carpenters mentioned in the 1860 census were from Louisiana, Illinois, and Holland. Several seamstresses living at the Balize came from New York and Pennsylvania, and there was a Spanish tailor from Florida. Fishermen listed included natives of such diverse places as Turkey, Denmark, England, Scotland, Austria, Ireland, Portugal, and Sicily, as well as Louisiana (Jackson 1993:8-9).

Balize, like all of the inaccessible communities along the coast, had to endure the hardships of hurricanes, as evidenced by the following 1860 headlines from the New Orleans *Delta Crescent*: "Hurricane strikes Balize; worst storm ever; buildings destroyed;" and "every house at the Balize blows down." Hurricanes were simply a fact of life and, because of its physical location, the Balize was the first settlement to feel the winds and waves preceding approaching storms.

The river posed another environmental risk. Over time, Southwest Pass became the deeper channel, and the local bar pilots were forced to relocate their base of operations. They moved to Pilottown Bayou (also known as Pilot Bayou and Pilotsville) on Southwest Pass, the principal access channel to the Mississippi where their services were required. In the 1830s, this garrison of pilots consisted of about seventy residents, and, by 1861, there were thirty houses, "at least seven of them impressive two-story dwellings. . . . But it . . . was in ruins by 1914" (Jackson 1993:73).

Meanwhile, the Balize had become the home of a few hunters and trappers who used the site until a yellow fever epidemic in 1888 forced the survivors to relocate. After this exodus, the Balize was deserted completely—except for a few oyster camps established in the small bay immediately west of the mouth of Southeast Pass (Moore 1899). By the 1930s, the old defensive station had subsided, and the town hall, church, school, shell road, homes, and tombs fell below sea level and were captured by the Gulf of Mexico (Meyer 1981; Buras 1996). However, as late as the early 1970s, hunters reported finding the tombstones of the Balize's cemetery (The Balize 1992), the only remaining artifacts of Louisiana's first coastal fortification. The site is now lost, but the community's legacy survives as a place name in the Mississippi's bird-foot delta (Walker and Davis 2002).

Pilottown or South East Balize and Port Eads

On both sides of the bayou on the lower east bank of Southeast Pass—Pilottown Bayou—more than two dozen beautiful homes had risen. And besides the Bar Pilots who lived there with their families, there were also the many boatmen, watchmen, and general help, so that quite a thriving community had built up (Buras 1996:70).

In addition,

a few of its people dwell upon the 'chenieres' and ridges that rise above the sea marsh or upon the low sand islands of the coast (Harris 1881:182).

Prior to the Civil War, sediment accumulation at the mouth of the Mississippi River hampered river commerce and threatened commercial activity at the New Orleans' port. In fact, in 1859, New Orleans was "virtually under a mud blockade. . . . [F]orty-two outward bound vessels carrying over 10,000 bales of cotton (several million dollars worth) were prevented from passing into the Gulf" (Clark 1967:127). Clearly, New Orleans' business community was held hostage by the Mississippi. Alternate routes away from New Orleans were being considered, since the water corridor was frequently too shallow. When the river stage was low, towboat owners charged exorbitant fees to pull vessels over the sand bars. This was an unexpected cost that altered

(Left) Ten years before the hurricane of 1893, Port Eads was a thriving community that met the needs of the shipping industry. (Image from *Harper's Weekly,* February 1884.)

(Bottom left) A late nineteenth-century trade token used at Port Eads.

(Below) The *Essayons* dredging the bar at the mouth of the Mississippi River. (Image from *Harper's Weekly,* June 1871.)

the shipper's profit margin. With earnings being affected by the sand/mud bar across any primary shipping channel into the Mississippi, the business community called for a resolution to this annual problem.

James Buchanan Eads, a self-made engineer, had an engineering solution he was willing to fund privately—with one condition. If he was successful in solving the shoaling issue, the Federal government would reimburse his costs. He envisioned solving the shoaling issue by building a jetty system at the river's mouth. Congress allowed Eads to implement his jetty plan, which proved a great success. The completed jetty provided a thirty-foot channel, which opened New Orleans to the largest vessels then afloat (Nau 1958; Lowrey 1964; Cowdrey 1977; Walker and Davis 2002).

After the endeavor was completed in 1879, Eadsport—or Port Eads, which had grown up with the construction effort—remained a viable community, like the later construction communities of Boulder City, Nevada and Page, Arizona. At Port Eads locals could find construction work, and the cooks, preparing meals for the construction crew, were reliable consumers of the local oystermen's harvest. Over the four years required to complete the jetties and dredge the channel, Port Eads expanded to include: a school, a wood-frame hotel that provided living quarters for many of the crew, a brick and metal lighthouse that served as a refuge during hurricanes, and about twenty-two rather weather-worn homes. According to historian Joy J. Jackson (1993:51), the community eventually "expanded to about 32 houses and other

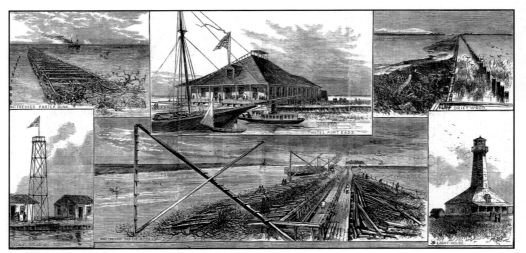

The Mississippi River at Port Eads. (Image from *Harper's Weekly*, March 1878.)

buildings." The Customs and Quarantine Services personnel lived in some of these structures, as they inspected incoming crews and passengers at the Port of Entry.

In fact,

> The white walled, red-roofed settlement [Quarantine Station] was set out on a broad lawn at the edge of the river [and] opened on May 1, 1892, with 24 employees. A hospital, offices, barracks, and other buildings at the station were designed and constructed to withstand tropical storms. Two large rows of oak trees planted parallel with the river formed an impressive oak alley leading to the settlement. The alley was destroyed by Hurricane Betsy in 1965. . . . (Buras 1996:158).

To meet the general merchandise needs of this modest government-service base, the local store carried grocery and hardware items transported from New Orleans. Needles and thread, dress materials, ready-made clothes, shoes, and jewelry were occasionally also brought to the community by itinerant merchants, who went from house to house hawking their goods (Jackson 1993). The village's church had no regular services by any single denomination. Protestant ministers and Catholic priests took turns descending the Mississippi "to minister to the spiritual needs of the river

(Right) The Quarantine Station at the mouth of the Mississippi River. (Photo from Buras 1996.)

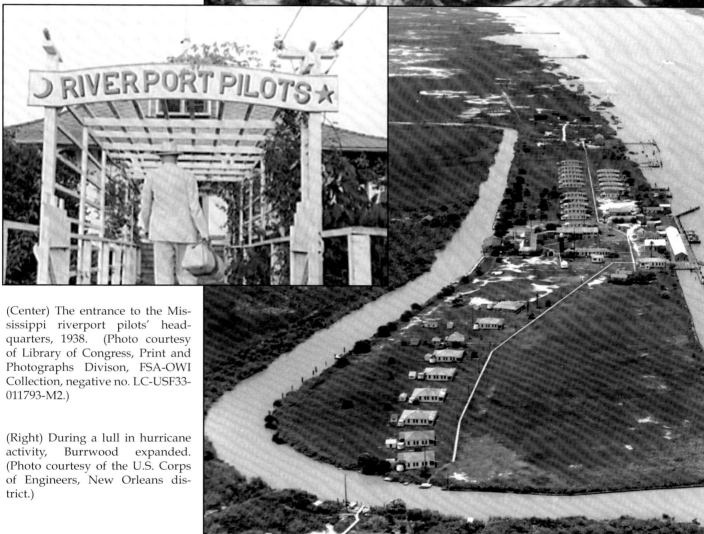

(Center) The entrance to the Mississippi riverport pilots' headquarters, 1938. (Photo courtesy of Library of Congress, Print and Photographs Divison, FSA-OWI Collection, negative no. LC-USF33-011793-M2.)

(Right) During a lull in hurricane activity, Burrwood expanded. (Photo courtesy of the U.S. Corps of Engineers, New Orleans district.)

"At the mouth of South Pass lay Port Eads, a remote way station for bar pilots, oyster fishermen, trappers, and government employees engaged in keeping the pass navigable for oceangoing ships" (Jackson 1993:2).

village" (Jackson 1993:26). At Port Eads, weekly dances were also an important part of the community. People would dance until one or two in the morning to the tunes the Port Eads Brass Band (Voorhies 1978; Eads: the men . . . 1992).

All of the linear village's buildings were raised on beams above the marsh with wooden sidewalks connecting each home to one-another and to the river's levee. By the end of the nineteenth century, the now complete village served three functions: as the primary maintenance site for the jetties; as a staging area for the dredges used to maintain South Pass; and as a government coaling facility for the Army Corps of Engineers' vessels (Jackson 1993).

From the 1870s to 1903, the Eads family owned this land, and, from 1881 to 1901, they held a contract to maintain the channel, jetties, and auxiliary works at South Pass. The contract expired on January 18, 1901. As a result, Port Eads became the home of Army Corps of Engineers personnel and the labor force required to operate "one tug, one steam launch, one pile driver, one derrick boat, eight barges, and five skiffs" (Jackson 1993:54). After World War II, Southwest Pass replaced South Pass. As a result, jetty maintenance crews were moved to Burrwood/Hollywood on Southwest Pass, where twenty to thirty white buildings with well-mowed lawns and concrete sidewalks dotted the site. This community was constructed to support the families and diverse crews required to keep open the main passage in and out of the river. Also, the site served as the primary storage facility for a wide assortment of government supplies (Kane 1944; Cowdrey 1977; Buras 1996).

Even though the Port Eads community was abandoned after World War II, fishermen continued to dock their boats at the Port Eads' piers. Over time, sports fishermen flocked to the community to take advantage of the numerous game fish accessible close to the site. To accommodate the needs of these sportsmen, Plaquemine Parish invested in a marina. This facility was frequented in the summer months by well-to-do New Orleans businessmen, including many members of the New Orleans Big Game Fishing Club (Hays 1980).

Burrwood/Hollywood

The Corps of Engineers' coal facility formed the nucleus of the Burrwood community, which became the coaling and refurbishing center for the dredges that maintained Southwest Pass. Shortly before the United States entered World War II,

A *Harper's Weekly* image (December 1861) showing views of the Mississippi River at Southwest Pass.

the Navy began building a base on the lower portion of the Burrwood reservation. Only a barbed-wire fence separated the base from the civilian housing section of Burrwood. Among the numerous buildings constructed for the modest base were the administration building, a barracks, officers' quarters, a mess hall, a storehouse, and a heating plant. The base also had a 100,000-gallon water tank with an observation tower and signaling platform, four fuel-storage buildings, and a fire pump stored in another building. Five buildings were constructed to hold ammunition and explosives. Two of them were large bunkers—one of which was a high-explosives magazine. This latter group of structures was located on the lower edge of the base as far from the Burrwood population as possible. A sentry box was placed at the lower end of the Navy post, and a gun battery was installed near the mouth of Southwest Pass with a wide range of fire.

The station was supposed to help in antisubmarine warfare, but it never had the fast, powerful boats or the aerial backup necessary to make this objective a reality. Nor were the gun battery at Southwest Pass and a similar one placed at the mouth of South Pass of much practical value in fighting the terrible submarine menace in the Gulf in 1942 (Jackson 1993:204).

By 1985, Burrwood, like Port Eads, was a ghost town, "sinking fast into the mud" (Jackson 1993:247). These humble, utilitarian outposts that were once small, unassuming communities were dead. Like nearly all of the wetlands' communities, they were a casualty of time.

Pilottown: Too Tough to Die until Hurricane Katrina Destroyed It

In 1867, the village of Pilottown Bayou was established. The modest strip community was strung out along the Mississippi's main channel. The houses and walks, like those at Port Eads, were supported by piles from half-a-foot to two-and-a-half feet above the marsh muck. As was the case in many bayou-oriented villages, wharfs connected to each home. Although Pilottown's primary function was to meet the needs of the river's bar pilots, a boarding house and school were also a part to the "built" landscape.

The community grew rapidly, and, by 1880, Pilottown Bayou benefitted from jetty

> **Some of the First Pilots**
>
> South Slavic immigrants were one of the first ethnic groups to get involved in the business of piloting vessels into the Mississippi River. Using small boats with oars and sails, these pilots would sail out into the Gulf of Mexico and wait to meet the incoming ships. Before the creation of a pilot organization, to regulate who worked on these vessels, the first man to reach a ship got the job of piloting her "over the bar" and into the Mississippi's main channel (Vujnovich 1974).

construction on South Pass and expanded accordingly. As the number of workers needed on Ead's jetties and the associated maintenance crews were reduced, the Pilottown Bayou village was eventually abandoned. Many of the site's buildings were moved to other locations along the river.

However, Pilottown was not lost to history, for it was rebuilt around 1900 on the Mississippi River near Head of Passes. Postal records indicate the community had a permanent population of about 100 (Bowler 2008). One hundred years later the community consisted of a conglomeration of crude one-story buildings on the river's east bank (Buras 1996). An elementary school existed at the site, but children who wanted an education beyond the elementary grades had to cross the Mississippi and take a bus to a school at Boothville or Buras.

The pre-Katrina site was selected because of an agreement with the river pilots, who handled all traffic above the community, and the bar pilots, who were responsible for all traffic below Pilottown. The aforementioned professional groups are cooperatives. The pilots own shares in their respective professional groups, and their membership fees go into a pool. After expenses are paid, earnings are divided among the pilots according to hours worked.

Pilottown served both groups well, and Head of Passes residents boasted in 1970 that they had no cars, crime, drugs, pollution, or congestion (Buras 1996). Those individuals who did not work for, or with, one of the pilot associations fished, trapped, or worked for one of the delta oil companies.

Hurricanes Betsy (1965), Camille (1969), and Katrina (2005) adversely impacted the Head of Passes community. Camille's winds destroyed more than thirty structures; in fact, only four or five remained standing after the storm (Buras 1996). Katrina sealed the site's fate, for it left Pilottown in complete ruin, and pilots scrambling to get traffic moving again on the Mississippi were forced to hire helicopters to get to their posts.

In Katrina's aftermath, the Associated Branch Pilots, or Bar Pilots, voted not to rebuild their old station and to abandon the town's two dozen structures—many more than a century old (Burdeau 2006). They subsequently moved to Venice. According to some accounts the pilots had had enough. The Associated Branch Pilots set up a permanent base in Venice. The Crescent River Port Pilots decided to rebuild Pilottown in grand fashion in order to pilot ships up and down the 106 miles of the Mississippi River between Pilottown and New Orleans.

> . . . when you have a home somewhere for a hundred years, you just live with it [the elements]. Once Katrina came through, I knew we would have to do something different (Bowler 2008:44).

Even so,

> if Pilottown's future seems uncertain, with all of its permanent residents resettled elsewhere, that's because it is (Bowler 2008:45).

Lighthouses and Military Settlement Sites

When the French first occupied the Balize in 1722, they realized the importance of providing navigational aids at the Mississippi River's mouth. Four years after establishment of New Orleans, men began to inhabit lonely, out-of-the-way pilot stations to help move commerce through the numerous watercourses with access to the Gulf of Mexico. A few months after the Louisiana Purchase, Congress authorized construction of a lighthouse, originally called the Mississippi River lighthouse, on Frank's Island. Designed by Benjamin Latrobe, the architect of the United States capitol, this brick and iron lighthouse was intended to withstand the rigors of direct exposure to the Gulf. The substructure was raised using material delivered from Boston. The structure's "brick and mortar" cost $85,707. Once completed, the structure was described "as a Gothic Revival palace complete with a circular dwelling, stone piazza and 8,000 tons of materials heaped on a foundation of inverted arches" (Burst 2005:22).

As might be expected, the structure was the most expensive lighthouse the government had constructed to that time. The cost reflects the difficulty of building on the delta's soft sediments. In clear weather, the light was visible for up to eighteen miles. When lighthouses were built at South and Southwest passes, the installation's name was changed to Frank's Island Lighthouse. The site was abandoned in 1856 and allowed to sink into Blind Bay. By the early 1940s, it was reported the light had subsided three and a half feet in 100 years (Lighthouses: beacons of 1992). Even while subsiding, the "high-ground" around the lighthouse served for a half-century as a near inconspicuous settlement site.

Other early nineteenth-century lighthouses were soon established along Louisiana's coast. These often unpretentious installations varied in size from "lights" occupied by one person to the Chandeleur Islands Quarantine Station and a lighthouse that was part of a "compound made up of five buildings—a hospital, boathouse, and individual quarters for the commander, steward and seamen, along with women employees" (Chandeleur Island completely 1893:1). In every case, the lighthouse and the surrounding property served three functions: 1) it met the local maritime needs; 2) it often served as a rendezvous point for local fishermen; and 3) was a de-facto settlement node that added to the individual mystic of each light and their collective histories.

(Left) Delivering a note to a Louisiana lighthouse. (Image from *Harper's Weekly*, January 1877.) (Right) Newly constructed Timbalier Lighthouse, June 1920. (Photo from Randolph A. Bazet Collection, Archives & Special Collections, Nicholls State University.)

THE MISSISSIPPI RIVER.

THE "Father of Waters" is not only the greatest and grandest, but also the most peculiar of rivers; and his ways, though not past finding out, are certainly very queer and singular and mysterious. It was only the other day that either he or one of his tributaries, having no respect for State lines, suddenly indulged in an extensive crevasse, and transferred one of the most enterprising towns of Iowa to the State of Wisconsin. Along the upper Mississippi the soil consists of sand deposits, without cohesiveness, "and is cut," says RICHARDSON, in his admirable book *Beyond the Mississippi*, "by the water like sawdust. The shifting channel sometimes moves forty or fifty yards in a single week." "Its water will deposit a sediment an eighth of an inch thick upon the bottom of a tumbler in five minutes." "Navigating the Missouri" (or upper Mississippi) "at low-water, is like putting a steamer upon dry land and sending a boy ahead with a sprinkling pot." This is on the upper Mississippi; more than thirty thousand miles of large rivers are collected to form the volume of the Mississippi, and this mighty current below the mouth of the Ohio is less in width, but increased in depth and volume, and rushes with a greater velocity than above that point, thus naturally producing another character of country. And in this is displayed one of its greatest peculiarities. One would imagine that it would require a mountainous country to confine this volume of water to proper limits, while the fact is that the Southern country through which it passes is almost entirely level. Sir Charles LYELL

records that an old Mississippi pilot pointed out to him an island in the Delta of the Mississippi which he described as "*very high land*," and explained, in answer to a second query, that by high land he meant "3 or 4 feet above the sea." "In all Louisiana there is not," says PARTON, in his *Life of Jackson*, "a hill 200 feet high." The streets of New Orleans are only 9 feet above the level of the Gulf of Mexico, and are actually below that of the levees which confine the river to restricted limits. "The Mississippi," says PARTON in the work from which we have just quoted, "is apparently the most irresolute of rivers; the bed upon which it lies can not long hold it in its soft embrace. Wearing away the concave side of its numberless bends, rushing through new channels, slicing off acres in an hour, leaving lakes where it found forests, holding dissolved in its yellow tide land enough for a plantation, and carrying down in one season more trees than the Black Forest can boast, it reaches at last the Delta—that cess-pool and general emptying-place for half a continent. Arriving there with its deep, narrow volume of waters—two hundred rivers in one—it can no longer contain itself, but breaks into several channels, and pushes its way through the black ooze of its own depositing, in a manner which looks helpless and sprawling, but which is in reality the shortest and directest way by which that prodigious torrent could find its way to the deep waters of the Gulf. There are so many streams, bayous, lagoons, and branches of the great river in the Delta, that it looks on the map like a damaged spider's web, with New Orleans in the midst thereof representing the spider."

THE DELTA OF THE MISSISSIPPI—SCENE AT SOUTHWEST BAR.—[SKETCHED BY B. F. ORSON.]

THE DELTA OF THE MISSISSIPPI—TELEGRAPH STATION AT SOUTHWEST BAR. [SKETCHED BY B. F. ORSON.]

(Top left) Lighthouse and approaches to New Orleans. (Image from *Harper's Weekly*, November 1867.) (Top right) Southwest Pass Lighthouse, ca. 1890. (Above) Chandeleur Lighthouse, ca. 1945. (Right) South Pass Lighthouse, ca. 1890. (Photos courtesy of the National Archives and Records Administration, Still Picture Records Section, Special Media Archives Service Division, negative no. 26-LG-37-34; 26-S-153; 26-LG-39-14.)

Marsh and coastal lighthouses
(From: List of lighthouses 1866; Cipra 1976; Burst 2005; Burst 2005B)

Lighthouse Name	Date of Installation	Description
Chandeleur Islands	1848	The lighthouse was designed to help guide vessels to the Ship and Cat Island anchorages. The structure was fifty-five feet above sea level and visible fourteen miles at sea. Destroyed and damaged by numerous hurricanes the light has always been rebuilt. After serving as a beacon for generations of mariners, the 110-year old structure was destroyed by Hurricane Katrina on August 29, 2005. A year later, a team of investigators found no trace of the lighthouse (see http://www.lighthousefriends.com/light.asp?ID=810 for a discussion of the history of this facility and others along the Louisiana coast).
Proctorsville (also Procterville and Proctorville)	1850	Located near Fort Proctor, this tiny light was authorized at a cost of $500 and built in 1850. It was destroyed by fire in 1853. Congress authorized another light, which was completed in 1858 and destroyed by the 1859 hurricane. It was not reconstructed.
East Rigolets	1831	Located sixty-five feet above sea level and visible for thirteen miles, the East Rigolets light was across from the mouth of the West Pearl River and was discontinued in 1874.
Pass Manchac	1837	Pass Manchac is a narrow neck of water that connects western Lake Pontchartrain to Lake Manchac and is the southern boundary of Tangipahoa Parish. Part of this line divided the Isle of Orleans from the Florida parishes and was also the boundary between British West Florida and Spanish Louisiana, 1763-1783; Spanish West Florida and French Louisiana, 1803; and the United States and Spanish West Florida, 1803-1810. The site was damaged during the Civil War, but the Manchac light was rebuilt and became automated in 1941. The light keeper's home was razed in 1952.
Tchefuncte River	1837-1838	The light, like all of the lighthouses in South Louisiana, was destroyed either by the Civil War or hurricanes. Even so, the Tchefuncte River light was operated by a keeper until 1935. In 1952, it became fully automated and continues to provide a light to the entrance to the Tchefuncte River. In 1999, Congress transferred the property to the community of Madisonville and a multi-phase project, managed by the Lake Pontchartrain Basin Maritime Museum, has been initiated to restore the station to its original design and protect the site from continued erosion. Battered by Hurricane Katrina, the lighthouse continues to aid boaters entering the Tchefuncte River (Anderson 2008).
New Canal	1838	New Canal was a route from downtown New Orleans to Lake Pontchartrain. The lighthouse was discontinued in 1890 and replaced with a lantern hung from a pole. Later, the New Canal light was reactivated and served the New Orleans' sailing and powerboat community until Katrina severely damaged the structure. If the necessary funds can be obtained, the building will be rebuilt and operated by the Lake Pontchartrain Basin Foundation as the New Canal Lighthouse Education Center.

Port Pontchartrain	1838	Referred to as the Milneburg Lighthouse, this edifice was part of Pontchartrain Beach Amusement Park and is preserved on the campus of the University of New Orleans. The light was authorized in 1834, built in 1838, and decommissioned in 1929. Built in two feet of water, the light was "high and dry" as a result of a reclamation project started in 1926 on the south shore of Lake Pontchartrain. When the University of New Orleans purchased the property from the New Orleans Levee District in 1991, the light morphed into a university landmark.
Bayou Bonfouca	1848	Destroyed during the Civil War and never rebuilt, this lighthouse was an important reference point for vessels moving through the eastern half of Lake Pontchartrain.
West Rigolets	1854-1855	Located on the south bank of the Rigolets, the West Rigolets light was in 1869 damaged, rebuilt, and raised in 1917 and later abandoned and left in disrepair. In 1945, the lighthouse was discontinued and sold to a private owner. The light has the distinction of being the only lighthouse to have its keeper killed during a war. The remains of the relic structure were destroyed by Hurricane Katrina on August 29, 2005.
Point Aux Herbes	1875	Built as a landmark between the Rigolets and Milneburg, the Point aux Herbes light was destroyed in the Civil War and reopened in 1875. The foundation was plagued by subsidence issues that were not fully corrected. Decommissioned after World War II, the site was destroyed in the 1950s by a fire.
The Balize	1716	The Balize may be the first lighthouse built in North America (although the Boston Lighthouse built in 1716 claims that distinction). Originally constructed by the French as a guide into the Mississippi River, the lighthouse became the centerpiece of Louisiana's first out-of-the-way community—the Balize.
Frank's Island	1818	This was the first coastal lighthouse authorized after the Louisiana Purchase. Located near the Mississippi's Northeast Pass, in Blind Bay, and commonly referred to as "The Mississippi River Light." The eighty-one-foot brick tower's light could be seen eighteen miles offshore in good weather. The light was discontinued in 1856, and it then began to sink into the marsh. In 2002, it succumbed to the elements leaving behind a mere pile of rubble (Burst 2005B).
South Pass	1831	The sixty-five-foot brick South Pass light, which was visible for twenty miles, became the anchor point for a buoy and coal depot at Port Eads. A storm in 1840 destroyed the structure. It was rebuilt in 1848 (Lighthouses: beacons of 1992). This was the first light seen by vessels approaching the Mississippi River from the east. "The two-story keeper cottage circled the base with a central cylinder spinning its way to the black lantern tower" (Burst 2005B:23). The lighthouse was automated in 1971, but it is no longer in service (Burst 2005B).
Southwest Pass (frequently called the Old Spanish Lighthouse)	1831	The Southwest Pass light collapsed seven years after its construction. Foundation problems plagued the structure until it was rebuilt as an iron tower, supported by 185 support posts, four-feet apart, driven thirty-three feet deep, and surrounded by concrete. In 1871, the industrial age brought the octagonal pyramid design to this lighthouse. The iron superstructure, unaffected by erosion, was discontinued in 1953; it is now "a prisoner of the marsh" (Burst 2005B:23). Even so, ships still pass the relic brick tower, an iron skeleton, and a modern tower positioned near the entrance to Southwest Pass.

Southwest Pass Jetty	1962	This "modern platform holds a cylindrical steel tower on a two-story concrete keeper quarter mounted on piles" (Burst 2005B:23). The United States Coast Guard maintains the facility, which was supported on posts in the water just off the jetties. In 2007, the complex was demolished and replaced by a three-legged piling-supported structure.
Pass-a-Loutre	1855	The only tower on the Gulf of Mexico to sport spiral bands, the Pass-a-Loutre lighthouse, originally located at Head of Passes, immediately began to sink into the marsh muck. By 1868, the light keeper's house had settled three feet leaving the sills only eighteen inches above the marsh surface. In 1934, the state took ownership. "The marsh continues to suffocate the eighty-five-foot lighthouse dwarfing it to a mere fifty feet" (Burst 2005B:23). The lantern room, damaged by Hurricane Katrina, toppled off the rusted cylindrical structure.
Barataria Bay	1856	Erected to mark Grand Pass, the Barataria Bay light was active for thirty years until damaged by the 1893 hurricane and never rebuilt.
Lake Salvador	1910 (?)	The Lake Salvador lighthouse was built and maintained by Harvey Canal Land and Improvement Company, but it was nevertheless under the "charge of the United States Government" (A sketch of 1910:63). The closure of this light is unknown.
Timbalier Bay	1856	Located on a barrier island, the Timbalier Bay light was plagued by erosion problems. The light was reported as the least stable on the Gulf Coast. Designed to guide vessels between the Ship Shoal and Atchafalaya Lighthouses, the light had numerous problems. The third light was completed in 1917. The station was discontinued in 1934. In 1939, the light was reestablished as an unmanned facility. It was abandoned in the 1950s. In 1985, Hurricane Juan destroyed the station, and it was not resurrected.
Ship Shoal	1859	Ship Shoal's 125-foot-iron-skeleton tower was supported on screw piles located in fifteen feet of water. It was commissioned after the 1856 Last Island hurricane. The tower was built in Philadelphia, then dismantled and shipped to Louisiana, "where eight, 30-foot screw piles were driven 15 feet into the shoal. The tower stood 125 feet with a two-story, cylindrical keeper dwelling at the base" (Burst 2005B:240). After its completion, lighthouse keepers became sick and paralyzed as a result of the red-lead paint used on the structure. Erosion became a major concern in the early 1870s. This was a continuous issue until granite blocks were employed to stabilize the structure in 1896. The light was decommissioned in 1965. The town of Berwick has publicized plans to relocate this lighthouse to the Berry Lighthouse Park adjacent to the Atchafalaya, close to the Southwest Reef light moved to the park in 1987. Hopefully, this restoration effort will also be a success.
Point au Fer	1827	Also known as the Racquet Pass Lighthouse, the light was constructed at the mouth of Bayou Teche. It was located seventy feet above sea level and replaced eventually by the Southwest Reef Lighthouse.
Vermilion Bay	1839	The fifty-four-foot tower was visible for sixteen miles and was apparently destroyed by a storm and replaced by the Shell Keys Lighthouse.
Southwest Reef	1858	The light in this tower was elevated forty-nine feet above sea level. In 1916, the light was replaced by the Point au Fer Reef Lighthouse. Thanks to a local restoration effort, the light now sits on the Berwick waterfront in the Berry Lighthouse Park and has been placed on the National Register of Historic Places.

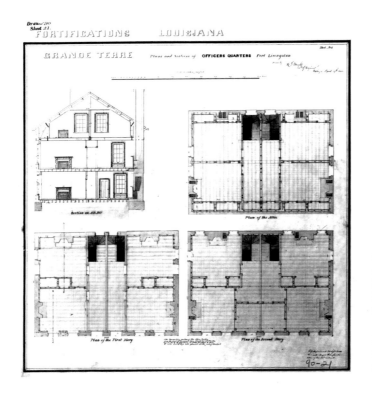

(Left) Architectural drawings of military housing at Fort Livingston, ca. 1862. (Image courtesy of National Archives and Records Administration, Division of Maps, Record Group 77, Drawer 90, Sheet 21, April 1842.)

(Below) The Civil War in The U.S. Bombardment of Forts Jackson and St. Philip, ca. 1865. (Image from the author's collection.)

(Right) Plan of Fort Burton, the only fortification within the Atchafalaya Basin, April 1863. (Image courtesy of Division of Maps, Library of Congress, G4.14.F5971863.U5CW233.)

(Below) Civil War fortifications on the approaches to New Orleans, February 1863.

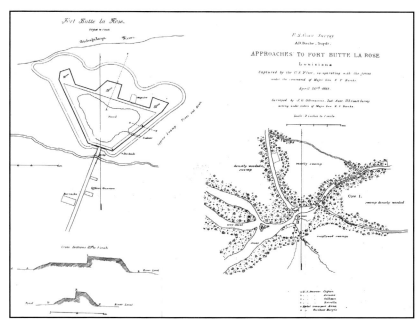

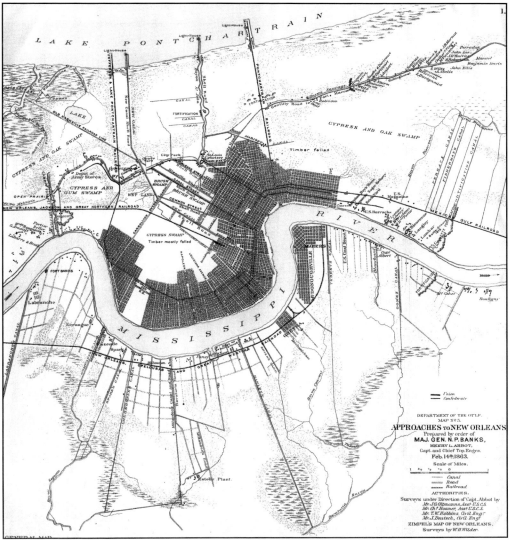

Shell Keys	1859	This iron screw-pile structure's light was seventy-one feet above sea level. Before its destruction by a hurricane, the light was an important marker for the steamer trade between New Orleans and Galveston. Trinity Shoal light replaced the light at Shell Keys.
Trinity Shoal	1871	Trinity Shoal light was twenty miles from shore and was a challenge to build; even so, the structure was completed in October 1873 and destroyed by a hurricane the following month. The lighthouse was replaced with a lightship.
Oyster Bayou	1903	The entrance to Atchafalaya Bay was used by more than 300 vessels that frequently missed the entrance. Establishment of the Oyster Bayou light and associated dwelling provided a beacon into the Bay.
Point au Fer	1916	This light replaced the Southwest Reef Lighthouse and included a main building seventeen feet above high water and a light visible for thirteen miles. The quarters were large enough for three keepers and were deactivated in 1975. Later the surviving building was destroyed.
Sabine Pass	1856	The Sabine Pass light was located on the east side of the Sabine River. Constructed of New Jersey brick, the light's white tower—buttressed by eight fins—put the light at eighty-five feet above sea level and could be seen for sixteen miles at sea. After retiring in 1952, light keeper Steve Purley went on a successful mission to rescue the light. In 2001, the Cameron Preservation Alliance acquired the light's title and worked to raise money to refurbish and save this light. Hurricanes Rita and Ike put this effort on hold.
Sabine Bank	1906	The foundation for this structure was fabricated onshore and towed to its location fifteen miles offshore. Its foundation was dug by workmen underwater in a pressurized chamber. The end result was the only caisson-foundation lighthouse on the Gulf of Mexico. The 1915 hurricane damaged the structure, but the foundation remained intact. The light is still operating.
Calcasieu River	1876	The light was a square pyramidal tower sheathed in iron. The structure, outbuildings, and boathouse were damaged in an 1887 hurricane, but the light was not extinguished. Although the lens was fifty feet above sea level, there were times that the lens was so blanketed with insects that the light was probably only visible for two-to-three miles. The site was deactivated about 1940.

Even though lighthouses were established to aid mariners, the navigational beacons evidently confused ship captains. For example, in the 1800s, the Chandeleurs were littered with the wreckage of sailing ships. Rather than decreasing the number of shipwrecks, the light's installation actually resulted in more accidents, for it appears sea captains mistook the Chandeleur light for the light off Mobile Bay and consequently sailed directly into the island.

Although primary function of these thirty lights was to serve the variety of maritime interests that required navigational aids, their secondary function was to serve as modest settlement nodes. Since many of the early structures had light keepers, the property became more than an aid to navigation, but a piece of property that served many of the local inhabitants as well. Fishermen, trappers, and others were aware of each light in their respective regions and knew that the site afforded them some comfort in a storm or access to general merchandise. They were nuclei for the community of marshdwellers living and working in the shadow of each beacon.

The Military and Their Temporary Encampments

After the Louisiana Purchase, the United States military constructed a number of unassuming fortifications of varying sizes to protect the various strategic marine approaches to the Mississippi River and New Orleans. In fact, for the first century of its history, New Orleans was a militarized town, with Jackson Square (originally *Place d'Armes*) serving as a parade ground for troops garrisoned in the city. After the 1788 fire, the Spanish planned to construct five forts at New Orleans-area sites, including Bayou St. John, English Turn, and Plaquemines Bend. These unpretentious fortifications and their barracks served as wetland settlement points (Robinson 1977; Heller 2003). These were modest sites, which were, nonetheless, vital pieces of Louisiana's coastal settlement history, as nearly each fortification saw additional development after the Louisiana Purchase.

A survey conducted by Capt. James Gadsden constituted the first attempt to chart Louisiana's coastline accurately, as a prelude to the national government's effort to fortify Louisiana's coast. Although Gadsden's analysis was well received, it was eventually superseded by that of a French military engineer—Simon Bernard. The year-long survey and detailed drawings by Bernard led Congress to approve the necessary funds to lay the groundwork for a regional network of defensive structures in Louisiana. These fortifications, like the unassuming lighthouses, added new, although modest, settlement clusters at Rigolets Pass (Fort Pike), Chef Menteur Pass (Fort Wood, later named Fort Macomb), Grand Terre (Fort Livingston), Bayou Bienvenue (Battery Bienvenue), Tower Dupré; and on the Mississippi River south of New Orleans at Forts Jackson, and St. Philip. The cost of these defensive positions exceeded $1.5 million, largely because the War Department determined all of these bulwarks should be permanent masonry structures, making these defensive strongholds the country's most expensive (Robinson 1977).

South Louisiana's military installations
(From Casey 1983 and Parkerson 1990)

Installation Name	Date of Construction	Description
Fort de la Boulaye or Fort du Mississippi	1699	This was the first European settlement in present-day Louisiana. The garrison was built by Bienville in 1699 to prevent the British from seizing the Mississippi Valley. With establishment of New Orleans in 1718, the Fort de la Boulaye was abandoned. The site is also identified as Fort on the Mississippi, Fort Louisiana, Fort Iberville, or Vieux Fort.
Fort Bayougoula or Fort Iberville	1706	This outpost was an enlargement of the original Fort de la Boulaye which included an unpresumptuous collection of huts, along with a chapel, and a forge.
Fort de la Balize	1723	Bienville selected the Mississippi River's Southeast Pass as the deepest entrance into the Mississippi. To protect the site, Bienville had a small garrison housed at the fort. During the Spanish regime, the modest fortress was renamed Fort Réal Catolica. When the Pass silted up, the site was abandoned.
Fort St. John	1740	This mud and log structure, located on Lake Pontchartrain at the mouth of Bayou St. John, was designed to protect New Orleans (Heller 2003). Under the Spanish regime, the humble fort was enlarged to prevent smuggling with the English colonies north of the lake.

Fort San Felipe de Placaminas/ Fort St. Philip	1792	Spanish colonialists established a post at Plaquemines about seventy miles south of New Orleans, since enemy ships would be vulnerable to cannon fire as they maneuvered the bend. The post could also support the garrison at Balize. The Fort at Plaquemine was replaced by Fort St. Philip which was built across from Fort Jackson. The arrangement of bunkers "allowed for the maximum field of fire upon any enemy ship in the river" (Parkerson 1990:104). The stronghold was the site of a twelve-day siege in April 1862 and surrendered to Union forces allowing David Farragut—the United States Navy's first rear admiral, vice admiral, and full admiral—to take New Orleans. The citadel was decommissioned in 1923 and is privately owned and in need of repairs.
Fort Petit Coquilles	1793	French explorers named the shell midden at the Rigolets—*Petit Coquilles*. Since the Rigolets was a natural waterway connecting Lake Borgne and Lake Pontchartrain, it was prudent to fortify the pass. The Spanish built the fort and the American's occupied the site during the War of 1812. Fort Pike replaced Fort Petit Coquilles and was decommissioned in the nineteenth century and was damaged by Hurricane Katrina's storm surge.
Lafitte House	1800	Located on the western tip of Grand Terre, Lafitte House was the headquarters of Jean Lafitte. "The base consisted of wharves, housing, warehouses and subsidiary buildings, and was fortified with several cannons planted in the sand on the beach" (Parkerson 1990:35). In 1850, Congress authorized construction of Fort Livingston on this site.
Camp Sabine	1806	With about "six hundred infantry and artillery," this camp was established to negotiate "boundary questions with the commander of the Spanish troops across the river. . . . While in this camp [Gen. James] Wilkinson negotiated an agreement whereby neither country would occupy a neutral strip between the Sabine River and the Rio Hondo pending the settlement of the location of the boundary by the respective governments" (Casey 1983:188).
Fort Wilkinson	1813	This garrison was built at the Balize and abandoned. The site was designed to protect New Orleans from an attack using the Mississippi River. The British captured the site and remained there until after their unsuccessful attack on Fort St. Philip.
Chef Menteur	1814	Gen. Andrew Jackson ordered a battery constructed at the junction of Chef Menteur Pass and Bayou Sauvage, since "the Chef Menteur road began where Bayou Sauvage entered the pass and followed the bayou to the city. This was the only dry land access to New Orleans" (Parkerson 1990:37). Without this fortification, shallow-draft boats could easily reach Bayou St. John—the back-door route into New Orleans.
Temple Battery/Little Temple Battery	1814	Gen. Andrew Jackson ordered construction of a battery at this site because it offered a high, dry, and commanding location. With the attack of the British at Chalmette, the site was abandoned.
English Turn/*Tour d'Anglais*	1814	In 1746, the French fortified this strategic point by constructing Fort St. Leon on the Mississippi's west bank and Fort Ste. Marie on the east (Heller 2003). "The Spanish had neglected these French forts, choosing instead to build Fort St. Philip at Plaquemines. . . ." (Parkerson 1990:54). Gen. Andrew Jackson ordered Fort Ste. Marie reactivated. In addition, earthworks at Terre aux Boeufs and Phillippon's Canal were also constructed.

Fort Darby	1815	Along with the earthworks at English Turn, Fort Darby—named after geographer W. O. Darby—was constructed at the confluence of Bayou Terre aux Boeufs and Lake Lery. It was fortified with a battery.
Fort Pike	1819	This brick fortification was constructed to protect the Rigolets and New Orleans from a naval attack. The site was abandoned after the Civil War. This rampart, now a state historic monument, was damaged by Hurricane Katrina.
Fort Wood/Fort Macomb	1820	The brick Fort Wood was built in the vicinity of the fort at Chef Menteur. Like Fort Pike, it surrendered to Confederate sympathizers in January 1861. The post was renamed Fort Macomb in 1851. Owned by the state, the property was open to limited tourism in the late twentieth century. The bulwarks' decaying condition was judged unsafe and hazardous for public use and the site consequently was closed. Located within the city limits of New Orleans, Katrina caused considerable damage to this property.
Fort Jackson	1822	After the War of 1812, Fort Jackson, about seventy miles south of New Orleans, was constructed on the western bank of the Mississippi River. This pentagonal shape and five bastions structure was built in the style of French military engineer Bernard du Vauban. In January 1861, the fortification was taken over by the Louisiana militia. Fort Jackson was restored to some extent in 1898. The modest remodel was in response to the diplomatic tension between Spain and the United States. The site was reactivated and used as a training center in World War I. After the conclusion of this conflict, Fort Jackson was abandoned about 1920. The fortification has been owned by Plaquemines Parish since 1962 and declared a National Historic Landmark in 1960. The site was damaged by Hurricane Katrina's storm surge.
Battery Dupré/Tower Dupré	1828	Louisiana's "Martello" tower was built to mimic the small defensive structures constructed in several countries of the British Empire. Battery Dupré was one of seven of these modest fortifications built along the Eastern Seaboard and the Gulf of Mexico. Located on the shore of Lake Borgne, the hexagonal fortification was designed to protect New Orleans. The tower was built between 1830 and 1840. It was captured and manned by Confederate troops. At the time of its construction, it was on land; shoreline erosion has resulted in the tower being well offshore, and Hurricane Katrina damaged the structure severely.
Battery Bienvenue	1828	This battery, constructed to protect New Orleans from the British army in the War of 1812, was a rectangular brick fort. During the Civil War, a small detachment was kept at this site.
Fort Livingston	1841	Fort Livingston was built to guard against an invasion force gaining access to Louisiana through Barataria Bay. Occupied by more than 300 Confederate soldiers, the garrison's guns saw no action. The walled structure is now deteriorating from age, neglect, shoreline erosion, and damage from Hurricanes Katrina, Gustav, and Ike.

Fort Proctor	1846	"Fort Proctor was located on the south shore of Lake Borgne near Yscloskey in St. Bernard Parish about thirty miles from New Orleans" (Parkerson 1990:81). The defensive site never saw action. Like Tower Dupré, this modest structure is surrounded by water. On some maps the site is identified as "Old Fort Beauregard" (Casey 1983:179).
Little Temple Battery	1861	The Little Temple Battery was planned for the Little Temple Mound site. Jefferson Parish Police Jury voted the necessary construction funds, but there is no evidence the earthwork was completed.
Fort Berwick and Fort Chêne	1861	These earthen Confederate forts were declared "Guardians of the Attakapas." They were designed to protect the entrance to the Atchafalaya in order to prevent a water assault on Louisiana through the lower Atchafalaya River and its associated watercourses.
North Pass	1861	After the surrender of New Orleans in April 1862, some Confederate troops were sheltered in simple fortifications at North Pass and Pass Manchac. Federal gunboats captured these two sites in June 1862.
Pass Manchac	1861	The Confederate army built this earthwork on the north side of Pass Manchac. It was subsequently captured by the Union Army. The structure's three-foot-thick brick walls supported a light forty-five feet above Lake Pontchartrain. "This lighthouse sits in a watery grave more than 1,000 feet from shore as coastal erosion has stolen precious property that just 100 years earlier boasted a thriving garden and small farm" (Burst 2005:6).

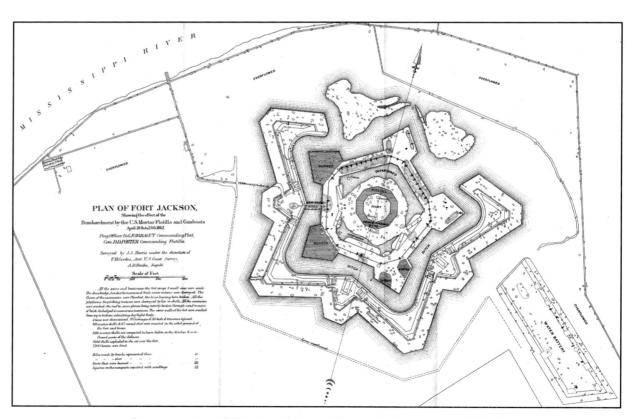

(Image courtesy of Division of Maps, Library of Congress, April 1862.)

Although sporadically occupied for brief periods of time, the twenty-five fore-going fortifications provided the impetus for settlements located at, or near, each of these fortified points. All evidence of many of the most modest and unpretentious sites have vanished. Others are preserved as historical parks and recreational venues. All of the surviving fortifications are visual reminders of the military's interest in coastal defense, which continued into the twentieth century.

Holmwood: A World War I Pilot Training Site

Gerstner Field was a large World War I aviation training camp that operated be-tween 1917 and 1921 about fifteen miles southeast of Lake Charles, near the modern village of Holmwood. During its short existence, the airfield encompassed several thousand acres and consisted of twenty-four hangars and nearly 100 ancillary build-ings. Although the airbase operated only five years, it graduated 499 fighter pilots and aviation instructors. Holmwood housed more than 2,000 military personnel involved in training the pilots, maintaining the aircraft and providing the daily necessities that kept the fliers and airplanes going.

During its single year of service, the Signal Corps put tremendous pressure upon the field's commanders to produce trained pilots in a hurry. But accelerated train-ing, combined with fragile aircraft, meant a high number of accidents, and the loss of many lives. Other problems included wartime equipment shortages, localized flood-ing at the camp, the 1918 global Spanish flu epidemic, and the strong, unexpected hurricane of August 6, 1918, which killed two soldiers, battered barracks, destroyed hangars, and mangled 100 airplanes. The pilots who trained at the facility and flew over the marshes provided many Southwest Louisiana residents with their first glimpses of aircrafts. The site closed and was dismantled in 1921. The only easily identified re-minders of this important airbase are highway signs: Gerstner Memorial Drive and Old Camp Road (Gerstner Field 2007).

Although at the marsh's northern margins, Gerstner Field's proximity to the wet-lands suggests pilots had a training route over the *marais*. Part of a pilot's training was over an environment that was not a perfect surface to land a troubled aircraft, but the surface had enough buoyancy to give the pilot a better chance of surviving any mishap. The site also represents one of the numerous "forgotten" communities that played a directly or indirectly role in the perception, knowledge, and use of Louisi-ana's marshes.

Although the main navigation channel of the Mississippi River was a natural settlement node, shrimpers, oystermen, and trappers built transient settlements. (Image from *Harper's Weekly*, January 1885.)

Chapter 7
TRANSIENT SETTLEMENTS

Forms of economic endeavor (i.e. fishing or agriculture or lumbering or moss-gathering) seem to be the rallying points around which settlement complexes gather (Kniffen 1978C:65).

Shrimp Fishery: From Drying to Freezer Packing

Shrimp are marketed with heads on or headless, peeled, frozen, dried, or canned. It is interesting, that before the Second World War began shrimp from New Orleans were actually shipped in the frozen condition to markets as distant as Shanghai and Tokyo (Robson 1956:117).

Shrimp is by far the state's most important fishery resource by dollar value. Although the harvest fluctuates wildly, the catch generally has a value in excess of $200 million (Keithly 1991). Commercial and recreational fishermen harvest two species—white and brown (*Penaeus setiferus* and *P. aztecus*). Both spawn offshore, the white from spring through fall and the brown in March and April and again in September and October. The tiny almost invisible shrimp eggs hatch within a few hours after being released into the waters of the Gulf of Mexico. In three to five weeks, the post-larvae migrate into Louisiana's estuary nursery ground.

The economic viability of the shrimp fishery is, therefore, estuary dependent. Survival rates are determined by salinity conditions, water temperature, rainfall, and river discharge (White 1975). Once in the estuary, a wide tolerance to salinity and temperature enables the shrimp to spread over a range of environments (Kutkuhn 1966; Barrett and Gillespie 1973). In Louisiana, the ecosystem preferred by this mainly ocean-dwelling crustacean is confined to the central and eastern portions of the coast. Although there are shrimpers along the western part of the Louisiana coast, the primary fishery is east of Vermilion Bay. At the western edge of this boundary, docks, icehouses, and other ancillary services at Intracoastal City and Delcambre sustain the fleet trawling the central segment of the coasts "inside" water.

Before development of canneries, shrimp docks and shed, and a fleet of mechanized fishermen trawling for the elusive *crevette*, shrimp were harvested by hand, without ice, and delivered to an out-of-the-way shrimp-drying platform. The product was highly perishable, valuable, and required strong seine crews, based close to the harvesting sites, to capture marketable shrimp. To overcome the perishable issue, sun-drying platforms were constructed to improve the product's shelf life and weight. The finished product could be easily packaged in barrels and moved to market.

Shrimp used in the original sun-drying process predate the industry's mechanization. Seine crews operated in the states "inside" waters particularly: Barataria, Timbalier, Terrebonne, Caillou, Atchafalaya bays, and Breton and Chandeleur sounds. In the late 1800s to the early 1900s, these geographic regions were the foundation of Louisiana's shrimp industry (Adkins 1973). Since seine crews were the backbone of the fishery, and were represented by a multitude of water-oriented culture groups, these estuarine or

The development of commercial ice helped revolutionize development of the shrimp industry as the product guaranteed fishermen could keep the holds of their boats cold and their product fresh. This led to the demise of the shrimp-drying industry, ca. 1950. (Photo courtesy of the Standard Oil Collection, University of Louisville, negative no. 67535.)

estuarine-like areas became notable settlement sites, because prior to the availability of ice and modern-freezing techniques, shrimp caught in these fishing grounds were taken to one of the numerous "Chinese" platforms to be dried, packaged, and moved to market. Informants note that "these platforms were everywhere" (Guidry 2007, pers. comm.).

An abandoned shrimp platform near Lake de Cade. Note the A-frame supports. In inclement weather, drying shrimp were raked under the frame and covered with a tarp, 1974. (Photo by the author.)

Up to fifteen seasonal seine crews, and a year-round work force of about 100, contributed to a maximum of 300 to 500 people living on any one platform. The term "platform" has two meanings, one references the undulating, wooden drying area and the other includes this structure as well as the associated support buildings. When active, each shrimp camp was an unpretentious, resource-specific, factory-like village built on pillars, suspended above the marsh.

The shrimp-drying platform at Dog Lake, ca. 1900. (Image courtesy of Blum & Bergeron, Inc., Houma, La.)

Blum and Bergeron, the state's largest distributor of dried shrimp, owned platform in Terrebonne Parish that were at least three acres in size at Sister Lake, Dog Lake, and Lake Felicity. Other "shrimp camps" in the parish included Philobruce, Coon Roads, Seabreeze, Redfish Bay, Robinson Canal, Grand Pass, Lake Mechant, Bayou Sevin, Blue Hammock, Lake Barré, Oyster Bayou, Bayou Gireau, Dulac, Cocodrie, Pellegrin, and Petit Caillou. The money required to build each platform was not readily available. In one case, the entire capitalization of a Terrebonne Parish bank, $10,000, was loaned to Blum and Bergeron to build one of their platforms (Blum 2009, pers. comm.). Since entrepreneurs in the industry could not obtain the necessary financing to build their respective businesses, the number of platforms constructed was in direct proportion to the financing available. Remote and cut-off from the "outside" world, these sites were vulnerable to hurricanes. As a result, hurricanes in 1893, 1915, and 1926 destroyed many of these business enterprises. Prior to these storm events, a relatively small number of companies owned most of the platforms. After the hurricanes, these firms were split into smaller units to reduce their risk and insurance premiums.

Although the dried shrimp product has always had a market, the introduction of canning technology transformed the shrimp industry by vastly expanding the market and the demand for the product. In 1917, 138 large shrimp schooners were licensed to operate in Louisiana's waters. Of these boats, nine were fishing for Louisiana canneries. The remaining vessels were shrimping for Biloxi, Bay St. Louis, Pass Christian, and Lake Shore canneries. Seines also were being used by fifty-six licensed gasoline boats, small schooners, and luggers. It was estimated there were probably about eighty to 100 other small, non-licensed fishing craft pulling seines. These were mostly owned by Lafourche and Terrebonne Parish fishermen. In addition, seven gas boats had obtained a license to use otter-trawls introduced in 1917. The otter-trawl diffused to Louisiana from the Atlantic fisheries, where it was first tested in the early twentieth century, is still in use (Tulian 1918).

In 1918, seventeen fishermen were using otter-trawls—only one of whom was working for a Louisiana-based cannery. There were 144 shrimp schooners engaged in the fishery—all but fourteen were contracted to Mississippi canneries. However, nearly all of the small-vessel-dominated seine fleet fished for Louisiana-based businesses, and a large percentage of them delivered their product to the state's shrimp-drying communities (Tulian 1918).

Over the years, an increasing portion of the catch was delivered to canneries. In some cases, shrimp-canning factories were built on barges and anchored near seine-fishing grounds. These facilities could buy shrimp, pack them into cans made with a special lining to help prevent spoilage, and quickly ship the canned product to market (Rushton 1979; Falgoux 2007).

Outside of Birmingham, Alabama, the South never had a steel-making tradition; it is highly likely that these cans came from mills in Baltimore or Pittsburgh. The number of four ounce cans would have numbered in the millions, and the canning process allowed the business to evolve from a fresh or dry trade to one based on tin-can packaging. At this point, the market became the world.

Cans expanded the oyster industry's market, but needed to be hand-soldered. (Image from *Harper's Weekly,* March 1872.)

This is an essential factor in the industry's evolution and although cans were readily available, the lids were soldered by hand until the early 1900s. This was a labor-intensive process and is well documented in the Chesapeake oyster industry. However, no records have been uncovered to suggest Louisiana's canneries employed teams of solderers to seal their products. It was not until the 1920s that improved can linings made of zinc compounds were developed to lengthen the shelf life of the contents and "crimping" lids became the norm, thus improving the marketability of shrimp products.

As a result of these technological improvements, shrimp fishermen no longer had to sell their catch to a platform. They relied on "ice boats" that delivered "manufactured" ice that preserved their catch. These "company" boats were also floating shellfish wholesalers and grocery delivery vessels that were equipped to pick up the catch and deliver it to a cannery. In many cases, these "specialty" boats worked for a specific cannery to make sure the catch was transported in a timely manner and the fishermen were continuously re-supplied. This work plan assured the cannery's fishing fleet could stay out longer, thereby maximizing the harvest. These cannery-owned boats were larger than an ordinary trawl boat. They shuttled back and forth from the fishing grounds to the factories, taking the catch quickly to their processing facilities and leaving the fishermen to fish in the "inside" waters. This efficient system was used throughout Louisiana's commercial shrimp harvest areas (World's largest shrimp 1938). Further, within the natural levee communities, canaries and ice-houses dotted the landscape and attested to the value of Louisiana's shrimp harvest.

Fishermen organized their vessels into a fleet. Each boat in the fleet carried a distinctive flag, which enabled the ice boats to pick out the vessels that they serviced. By being a member of such a fleet, shrimpers were assured ice, so they did not carry ice that could weigh more than a ton in their hold. Using this innovate process, the local watermen did not have to shuttle back and forth into port to replenish their ice and food supplies. By not having to go to port regularly, the typical shrimper's income improved to an average of about $150 per month in 1940 (Kammer 1941).

During the first four decades of the twentieth century, Louisiana's shrimp fishery was limited to the state's inland and coastal waters—that is within the three-mile limit. In 1937, "jumbo" shrimp were reported in the Gulf's deeper waters. This discovery changed the industry. At this time, these "outside" waters could be fished between the end of the June harvest and the beginning of the August seasons, thereby providing canneries with another source of product.

In the canning factory or shrimp shed—like the Morgan City Processing and Canning Company plant and the Isaac Griffin's shrimp shed on Bayou Lafourche—the shrimp were stored on ice, not only to preserve the meat, but also to make peeling easier (Cheniere Hurricane Centennal 1995). The peeling was done by hand by as many as 100 laborers, including children. The workers were paid a penny a pound, and the best peelers made about two dollars and fifty cents a day. Once peeled, the shrimp were washed, boiled in salt water, cooled, graded, and hand-packed into cans.

By 1930, Louisiana's shrimp canning factories led the nation in production. Indeed, South Louisiana plants produced nearly four times as much as any other state, canned more than half the total of all other states, and twice as much as the entire East Coast. The region's canneries sustained their productivity throughout the Great Depression, and, while much of the county languished economically, several coastal communities became shrimp boom towns.

The rapid expansion of the Louisiana shrimp industry created growing pains. As the industry's focus shifted offshore, Louisiana's fishermen discovered their boats, which were designed to work in the protected waters of the state's estuaries, were not seaworthy enough to trawl in the Gulf of Mexico. In addition to boat design problems, Bayou Lafourche fishermen could not easily navigate the bar at Belle Pass. As a consequence, the offshore shrimp industry was initially developed by outside interests that operated bigger boats designed for open-water conditions and run by captains familiar with south Atlantic and Florida ports. Fleets of these vessels began to harvest the offshore waters, but Louisiana fishermen quickly responded with their own class of large vessels (Padgett 1969).

Consequently,

changes and introductions have occurred principally where expansion of the industry has resulted from increased market demand, and where distance to grounds have prevented the employment of traditional vessels and gear. Additional cost of new, more efficient gear has also limited the number of fishermen participating in the offshore shrimping. It must be emphasized that much of the relatively low-cost gear are satisfactory for pursuit of the shell-

Shrimp Trawlers Company Identification Flags

Researched by Leroy J. Dantin
Summer 2002

Early in the 20th century, local fisherman in the bayou area began working together in groups called companies. In most cases, well respected & wise individuals started these companies. Many companies were formed within a very short period of time and had a strong economic impact on the area while they were in existence. The company system started when small boats started installing engines in their boats and began to disband by the end of the war in 1945.

Once a company was formed, a flag was designed to identify each boat participating in the company. Companies consisted of three main boats, called mother boats, along with 20-50 smaller trawling boats that would sell their shrimp to the mother boats. A boat crew usually consisted of two people, a captain, and a deckhand. All the boats of the company would fly the company flag. Since there was no radio communication at that time, the flags served as an identification system.

During the early years, steamboats traveling to our community would bring ice to an acceptable location. The trawling company's mother boat would travel to this convenient location to get their loads of ice. Periodically, the trawling company would transport their shrimp to the New Orleans market place to be sold.

It was some time later when the first shrimp sheds, icehouses, and shrimp canning factories were built in the bayou area. Area residents remember three ice houses, three canning companies, and many shrimp sheds along the bayou.

The first shrimp season of the year opens in mid-May and lasts for approximately 40-45 days. Another season reopens again in mid-August and lasts until sometime in November.

During these seasons, two of the three mother boats would be loaded with crushed ice, while the one would remain empty. While the smaller trawler would be shrimping, two of the mother boats, one with ice and one empty, would anchor and remain ready to receive the shrimp caught. These mother boats were lifesavers for the smaller boats because most of them were not rigged to carry ice.

On the first day of a season, it would not be uncommon for the first mother boat to be loaded by that afternoon and on its way to deliver the load to a shrimp shed. This would leave two mother boats out, one empty and one with ice. The process would be repeated. Another load would be on its way to deliver its load, while the first boat would return loaded with ice. This process would be continually repeated through the season.

The trip to the shrimp sheds usually took from five to ten hours from the trawling area. However, the total turn around time could take twenty-four hours or more. Once the shrimp had been sold and the boat reloaded with ice and fuel, the boat would hurry back out to the trawling areas. By the time the mother boat had returned to a trawling area the rest of the company may have moved to another area. In most cases, while searching for their boats, the mother boat would meet boats from other companies and would get assistance in locating their boats.

There were both advantages and disadvantages to the company system for both the mother boats and the individual trawlers. One advantage the men on the mother boats had was the ability to see their families when they were getting their shrimp unloaded at the sheds, even if it was only for a very short period of time.

The smaller boats of the company carried drums of gas or diesel in order to be able to stay out for longer periods of time. This allowed them to have longer trawling time with the opportunity to catch more shrimp, therefore, making more money. It was not uncommon for these boats to stay out for four to six weeks at a time. Most of the boats had a 20-40 horsepower engine and pulled 25-45 foot nets. Everything was lifted by hand, no wenches.

While the smaller boats had the advantage of not having to transport their catch to the sheds, this meant that they had no opportunities to see their families. The long separation was a hardship for the crews

and their families during the season that these boats were out.

These boats were supplied with the basic necessities for meals. They had coffee, sugar, oil, flour, and canned goods. Except for salt meat, they did not have other meat on board. They had many opportunities to sample their catch during their meals. Occasionally, a boat would need additional supplies and the mother boat would pick them up while unloading the catch and deliver them to the other boats when they returned to the trawling area.

After all of the days work was done, most of the boat would tie along side of each other. At dinnertime all of the food pots would be put on the deck of one boat and shared between the captains and crews of all the boats. Deckhands have reported that some of their most memorable meals of their life came from these boat meals.

Some captains were known to lord over their deckhands after these meals. The chore of cleaning up after themselves after dinner would have meant bending over the side of the boat to wash their plate and spoon in the bay water. Instead, they would call their deckhand to pick up and wash their dirty dishes for them.

Another disadvantage for the mother boats was their inability to do their own trawling while they were out because they

had to be ready to take on shrimp from the smaller boats. The exception to this was when all three of the mother boats were out at the same time. At that time, the third in line would be able to spend some time trawling.

On a normal day, weather permitting, the mother boat would be at anchor in the work area ready to buy shrimp. If the weather were a little rough, the mother boat would anchor behind an island for protection.

When the smaller boats had their catch, they would unload onto the mother boat. The mother boat would buy the shrimp by the basket, not by weight. Half filled or the overflow in a basket would be given to the mother boat. The trawler would receive a receipt from the mother boat for their shrimp. Boats from one company were not restricted from selling their shrimp to a different company's mother boat if they wanted to. Shrimp from the trawlers were usually unloaded onto the mother boats at approximately 10:00 or 11:00 am and again an hour before sundown.

Because of the tremendous number of mosquitoes, the crews could only enjoy free time before sundown. At dusk and after sundown, they would either have to be in their cabins or under a mosquito net. The mosquitoes were not only a problem for the

humans, but also for the animals. The cattle on the islands would go into the water and stay submerged most of the night to get away from the mosquitoes.

Unloading the shrimp at the sheds was done by independent laborers, not the boat crews or workers from the shed. These laborers shoveled the shrimp onto conveyors from the boat. They were paid by the number of barrels the mother boat had noted from the boat purchases. The person unloading the boat would get paid 4-5 cents per barrel. A barrel weighed 210 lbs. Because of this pay scale structure, the mother boat was able to save 25-30% on the off loading fee they had to pay the laborers.

The price that the mother boat paid the trawler for his baskets of shrimp was the same price he got from the shed. These larger boats made their money by the weight. In most cases, the mother boat had a 25-30% gain plus the shed may have given them $.50-$1.00 per barrel on the side. Each mother boat could take on 15000-20000 pounds of iced shrimp.

The mother boats had the ultimate responsibility for the safe hauling of their product. They had to make sure the shrimp was iced down well. The state of Louisiana had inspectors to inspect the shrimp loads. If the inspector found that some of the shrimp had begun to turn red, which meant they had been too warm, he may make the boat throw the whole load overboard.

The company system broke down at the end of the war. People were able to buy better boats and engines. The coming of the high speed and high powered Lafitte Skiff made it possible for the trawlers to leave home early in the morning and was back by midday. The rest of the boats started to carry their own ice. This was the end of a very interesting part of the Cajun way of life and Cajun history.

ALIDORE DELGRANDILE

CLAIRBORNE BOUDREAUX

EDISON TERREBONNE (TEE MAL)

GASPARD BROTHERS (GATIN, GALOUP)

MARCIAL CALLAIS

ALCIDE JAMBON

LOUIS GRIFFIN

ETIENNE PERRIN

PITRE BROTHERS (TEE DERDER)

THERIOT BROTHERS (TEE NONAN)

ARAMISE MARTIN

HUBERT LAFONT

TEMPLET BROTHER (SCAB)

DR. DESCRAMCY (TERRE LAFONT)

EUNICE VINET

Price Comparison of Shrimp from 1946 to 2002

Size of Shrimp	1946 Price for 210#	2002 Price for 210#
80/100 count	$6.00	$105.00
40/50 count	$16.00	$315.00
10/15 count	$28.00	$630.00
	$50.00	$1050.00

These prices show an increase in the price received for shrimp to be over 20 times more now than in 1946.

(Researched and produced by Leroy Dantin.)

fish resources in the areas of greatest abundance—the near-shore and inside waters of the delta (the offshore shrimp grounds are an exception). Low-cost gear and operations are more suitable for shellfish capture and this industry, owing to the nature of the gear, and generally abundant distribution of the resource, favors scattered fishing communities and relatively large number of fishermen, many of whom can participate on a part-time basis (Padgett 1969:491-492).

During the shrimp season fishermen were relentless, because when their boats were not working, they had no income. Whether shrimping or trapping, the marsh-dwellers were always aware of the importance of working at a constant and steady pace in tracking down their seasonal resources. They knew their business and resented the Federal government's early efforts to tell them what to do, when to do it, and where they could do it. When federal inspectors rejected a boatload of shrimp as being unfit for human consumption, shrimpers were particularly outraged. Over time, however, marshdwellers began to appreciate the beneficial nature of harvesting restrictions and their enforcement, which ultimately enhanced the wetlands' productivity. In the process, personal liberties had to be sacrificed so that the environment could continue to provide them a living, as insolvency was unacceptable (Kammer 1941).

The marshdwellers' adaptation to federal regulations reveals their pragmatism and business acumen. Most of these watermen were illiterate, but not simple-minded; they were good businessmen and proud of their accomplishments. They may not have been able to read or write, but in their own way they knew how to add, subtract, and multiply. When they bought gasoline or supplies or sold their catch, they knew what they should pay or how much they should receive for their catch. Storekeepers and fur buyers quickly learned that "they may not know how to read or write, but you can't gyp them that way" (Kammer 1941:62).

In the pre-industrialization of the shellfish industry, bartering was the norm. Money played a role in the economy. However, in the state's first organized harvesting enterprise, fishermen worked on remote shrimp-drying platforms. They performed yeoman service in a segment of the industry that served as the "platform" for the modern shrimp fishery. Shrimp drying is a nearly forgotten part of the evolution of the modern shrimp fishery, but its importance should not be overlooked or understated, as it opened the local industry to world-wide markets, well before the successful canning of shrimp.

The terms isolated, remote, secluded, and out-of-the-way best describe these villages of laborers, who worked in the harsh sun, pulling seines, drying shrimp, repairing the platform, often using "oar" or sail boats to transport the catch to the platform, offloading the catch, repairing seines, and loading the dried product all for minimal wages. In the late 1800s and early 1900s, thousands of people were directly and indirectly employed in this business, with perhaps as many as 5,000 people living on the platforms year around—about 20 percent of the 1900 population of Terrebonne Parish. The seasonal population could escalate to more than 20,000, with in at least one instance nearly 1,000 laborers living and working for one camp. Yet, little is written on this segment of the fishery and particularly quiet and unassuming role of the Chinese in developing, nurturing, and promoting the enterprise. An activity responsible for colonizing the wetlands with a montage of ethnic minorities, who lived together, in close quarters, in apparently segregated conditions in pursuit of one objective, *crevette*.

(Image courtesy of
J. L. Riseden, Jr.)

Shrimp-Drying is an Ancient Chinese Art

And as we drew nearer there spread before our eyes a great fleet of sailing-boats with red sails drying in the sun; dugouts, painted green and red, were tied to a long wharf that ran back to a huge platform upon which seemed to be spread something red. Facing this platform and extending back along a narrow bayou were twenty or more houses, all raised high above the water upon posts of cypress . . . long ladders led from the porches to the water craft moored below. It was for all the world like a miniature Venice (Schoonover 1911:81).

Shrimp-drying, rooted in Asia, diffused to Louisiana by Chinese immigrants who disappeared from the historical record and became an inconspicuous and forgotten minority (Cohen 1984). In all likelihood, the route of diffusion was through San Francisco Bay, where the industry started in the mid-1860s (Jordan 1887; Bonnot 1932; Adkins 1973; Muir 2001). In 1871, Chinese immigrants began harvesting San Francisco Bay shrimp. From the start, the Bay's Chinese fishermen dried the bulk of their catch for the Oriental export trade, where it sold for one to one-and-a-half cents a pound. The industry expanded quickly into a major enterprise, as San Francisco's and Oakland's Chinatowns were the major markets. To maximize the harvest, fishing was carried on at many shrimp camps on the shores of San Francisco Bay, with a version of the Chinese "junk" serving as the vessel of choice in the harvesting process. (China Camp, one of the largest of these villages, is now a unit of the California State Park

The Chinese captain of one of the state's early shrimp-drying platforms. (Photo from *Report of the Conservation Commission of Louisiana, September 1, 1912-April 1, 1914*.)

This postcard is the only extant evidence that shrimp drying was practiced in Texas, no date. (Image from the author's collection.)

New York's China-town sells Louisiana dried shrimp. The oriental market was critical to the success of the industry, 2009. (Photo by the author.)

A red-sail lugger bringing fresh shrimp to a drying facility. (Image from Schoonover 1911.)

System and a California State Historical Landmark [China Camp 2006]).

By 1873, less than ten years after the conclusion of the Civil War, Chinese settlers from California had introduced the lucrative sun-dried-shrimp industry into Louisiana's inland waters. These *émigrés* hoped to duplicate the business achievement they attained in San Francisco Bay (Jordan 1887; Scofield 1919; Bonnot 1932; The mysterious but . . . 1937; Padgett 1960). As a result of this unrecorded movement into the wetlands, one observer notes at Bassa Bassa—a Tagalog word that translates as "wet wet"—the entire village was made up of "Chinamen" or perhaps Filipinos, who, dressed in wide flopping trousers and loose shirts, moved effortlessly on the platform (Schoonover 1911).

The Chinese clearly recognized the value of coastal Louisiana's estuarine bays. Therefore, in the late nineteenth century these waters served as an attractive venue for establishment of shrimp harvesting villages and their attendant drying platforms. These low cypress platforms often covered up to three acres. One of these sizeable platforms required about thirty linear miles of twelve-inch-wide lumber to cover the surface. In addition, the laborers typically needed about 3,750 pilings eight to ten-feet long. These posts buttressed the three-acre surface. Since the eight-to-ten inch supports were driven by hand, on about six-foot centers, constructing one of these elevated villages was a difficult and time-consuming feat of carpentering and engineering.

All of this lumber had to be ferried to the site via sail or steam-powered vessels. When one considers that there were reportedly eighty of these structures, most an acre in size, logistic support was quite an achievement, as the total building material necessary would equal 800 linear miles—about the distance from Baton Rouge, Louisiana to Chicago, Illinois—and 100,000 poles up to ten feet in length, or nearly 189 linear miles. In addition, nails were required. Hand-forged nails were not used, but platform carpenters hammered cut nails until about 1910. After that date, mechanized wire, round nails were available. The number and weight of this freight is

A shrimp village on the edge of San Francisco Bay with drying fields in background. (Photo courtesy of San Francisco Maritime National Historical Park, National Archives, Fish and Wild Life Photo Collection, B11.16.013.)

Chinese fishermen, perhaps in Louisiana. (Photo from the author's collection.)

not known. The product represents another element in the supplies required to build the state's shrimp camps. None of these short-lived structures endured, but many of the support pillars are still visible, as they were anchored well into the marsh muck.

Before the advent of ice and modern freezing techniques, shrimp caught in Louisiana's inland waters were taken to one of the "shrimp camps" to be dried, packaged, and sold. These villages were manned by Acadians, Germans, Italians, Spanish, Portuguese, Filipinos, Chinese, American Indians, and African Americans. However, segregation existed in these polyglot communities, where French was the common spoken language, and very few of these workmen could read, write, or speak English. Each cultural group had to stay with their "own kind" in order to communicate.

Conflicting reports credit Lee Yeun, Chen Kee, Yee Foo [Fo], and Lee Yim with introducing the Chinese technique of sun-drying shrimp into San Francisco Bay and later into Louisiana (Jordan 1887; Terrebonne Parish 1953; Adkins 1973; China Camp 2006). There is consensus, however, regarding the location of the first crude drying platform, which reportedly was built on the "south side of the mouth of Grand Bayou in Bara-

This Barataria Bay piling-supported shrimp village is one example of the many industrial communities in the coastal zone. (Photo from *Report of the Conservation Commission of Louisiana, September 1, 1912-April 1, 1914*.)

taria Bay, at a site later to be Cabinash (Cavenash). This camp was originally used in an effort to sun-dry oysters, but when this proved . . . impractical the men began to dry shrimp" (Padgett 1960:142). This "camp" and three others, each boasting about 100 residents, were established along Bayou Rigaud and at Fisher's Settlement. When not engaged in drying shrimp, the inhabitants, depending on the season, were fishing oysters, seining for fresh or saltwater fish that might be dried, or trapping (Barataria Bay 1917).

In the early 1880s, according to Louisiana Land Office records, East Asian immigrants purchased—at a cost of twenty-five cents an acre—several small islands in Barataria Bay to be utilized as platform sites (Adkins 1973). By 1885, the industry was well established when "Yee Fo was issued Patent Number 310,811 (January 13, 1885) for a process to sun-dry shrimp. Actually, the Chinese [had] used this method for preserving shrimp and other animal foods for centuries, but the patent made the process an established method of food preservation" (Love 1967:58). According to Blum (n.d.), the first man to dry shrimp in Louisiana was called Ting-Ting, which may be a nickname.

Many of the men working at these sites were smuggled into the wetlands, where they typically remained. Because they were in this country illegally, they did not leave their secluded communities. If the "runner" smuggling Chinese immigrants into Louisiana was being chased by the Coast Guard, his human cargo, sealed in barrels full of holes, was unceremoniously dumped overboard to remove all evidence of this illegal, but lucrative, activity (Kane 1944). This practice was not condoned by most marshdwellers, and many informants consequently refuse to talk about this practice. In their words: "That was bad times."

Shrimp-Drying Platform Communities

It is variously estimated that dried shrimp will keep from one to six years, but the odor which permeates a factory suggests the wisdom of the slogan: 'The sooner eaten the better,' if pungency increases with age (Graves 1930:427).

Like their counterparts on San Francisco Bay, Louisiana's shrimp camps were established to preserve shrimp for shipment to out-of-state markets (Chung Fat platform 2006; Guidry 2006, pers. comm.; Pellegrin 2006, pers. comm.; Quong Son platform 2006; Blum 2008, pers. comm.). Because a sizeable number of platforms were destroyed by hurricanes in 1893, 1915, and 1926, an accurate tally was never compiled; however, at the dried-shrimp industry's zenith, an estimated eighty "camps" were operational (Pillsbury 1964; Blum 2009, pers. comm.). The local canning and packing

(Left) The Chung Fat platform, ca. 1895. (Photo courtesy of the Alexander Allison Photographic Collection, Louisiana Division, New Orleans Public Library.)
(Right) The Quong Sun platform, ca. 1895. (From the Mayer-Engelbach Collection, Louisiana Division, New Orleans Public Library.)

factories were also hard hit, and the fishing fleet was decimated by these hurricanes. Even so, shrimpers continued to market their catch to the region's surviving shrimp-drying communities.

Seventy-nine of the known named platforms
(From the records of Blum and Bergeron)

Bassa Bassa	Bayou Brouilleau	Bayou Du Large - St. Martin Co.	Bayou Gireau or Goreau	Bayou Rigaud	Bayou Sevin – Grand Caillou Packing Co (3 Platforms)
Blue Hammock - Henry Marmande	Blanchard Cabinash	Camp Dewey	Chênière Caminada – Calvin Authement	Chenier Dufon	China Town
Chong Song	Chung Fat	Cocodrie – Linton White	Cocodrie – Constant Henry	Cocodrie – "Black" Murphy	Cocodrie – Clarence and Albert Scott
Cocodrie -Percy and Houston Foret (2 Platforms)	Coon Roads	Dog Lake	Dulac	Fifi Island	Grand Bay
Grand Caillou – Ellis Lottinger	Grand Caillou – Octave Lapeyrouse	Grand Isle – Bob Collins	Grand Pass	L & G	Lake Barré – Alidore Mahler
Lake Barré – Céleste Hebert	Lake Barré – Tones Foret	Lake Barré – O'Neil Sevin, Horace Authement, and Alvin Nelton	Lake Felicity	Lake Mechant – Calise X. Henry	Lake Mechant – Henry Marmande, Sr.

Lake Mechant – Cyprien Voisin	Petit Caillou - St. Martin Co. and Blum and Bergeron	Petit Caillou/ Price Robichaux	Petit Caillou - Octave Lapeyrouse	Petit Caillou - The Price family	Petit Caillou - The Picou family
Petit Caillou/ Magnus and Noland Blanchard	Petit Caillou - Philogean Engeron	Petit Temple - Daize Cheramie	Manila Village	Oyster Bayou – Alidore Mahler	Oyster Bayou – Paul Voisin
Oyster Bayou – Claude Boudreaux	Oyster Bayou – Alphonse Authement	Oyster Bayou – Harry Bourg	Oyster Bayou – Aubin Buquet	Oyster Bayou – Horace Authement	Oyster Bayou – Ivy Authement
Oyster Bayou – Wiltz LaBlanc	Oyster Bayou – Calvin Blanchard	Oyster Bayou – Aaron	Oyster Bayou – Norris Price	Pellegrin Periac	Philobruce
Point au Fer	Proveausal Bay	Proveausal Bayou	Quong Sun	Redfish Bay	Redfish Bay – Ernest Voisin
Redfish Bay – Nicholas White	Redfish Bay – Thaddeus Pellegrin	Rogers	Robinson Canal – Lapeyrouse	Robinson Canal – Macon Stringer	Robinson Canal – Lester Dubois and Anatole Trahan
Seabreeze	Sister Lake	Taylor's Bayou			

The structures that survived the late nineteenth and early twentieth-century hurricanes, served various world markets. Pacific Coast Asian communities were the primary retail outlets, with each camp shipping an estimated $100,000 ($2.1 million in 2009) worth of dried products annually. Conceivably, the total value of the late nineteenth century harvest approached eight million dollars (based on eighty camps)—a noteworthy figure in 1890 (and equal to $174 million in 2009) (Cole 1892).

As production increased, distribution expanded, largely through the marketing efforts of Blum and Bergeron in Houma, to include most of the Far East, particularly China, the Philippines, and Hawaii. Other markets were included the West Indies, Cuba, Panama, the Guianas, Peru, and Bolivia, along with other Central and South American countries—United Fruit Company was a major market, as the dried shrimp were rehydrated and used in the diet of the local banana pickers (Werlla 1950; Blum n.d.). In addition to Blum and Bergeron, the Quong Sun (later Gulf Seafood Company) and H. T. Cottam companies served as the principal shipping agents (Blum n.d.). The production of dried shrimp reached its peak in 1929, when about five million pounds were brought to the camps.

Barrels of dried shrimp destined for an international market, 1926. (Photo courtesy of Blum & Bergeron, Inc., Houma, La.)

Barrel templates used by Blum and Bergeron to market their exports, ca. 1920. (Images courtesy of Blum & Bergeron, Inc., Houma, La.)

The 1914 shrimp-drying harvest from Barataria Bay (Barataria Bay 1917)

Product	Value	Adjusted 2009 dollars
131,224 sacks of oysters	$118,100	$2,525,639
7,502 baskets of shrimp	$ 46,385	$ 991,971
7,152 hands (four inches) of fish	$ 14,309	$ 305,899
2,328 barrels of dried shrimp	$113,490	$2,427,051
127 tons of shrimp bran	$ 2,540	$ 54,319
Combined shipment	$294,819	$6,304,881

The Gear Required

Before introduction of the otter or shrimp trawl (also known as "boards" or "doors"), almost the entire shrimp catch was taken by haul seines as long as a third of a mile (Gomez 1998; Landry 1999). In the fishing grounds most convenient to local markets, all favorable seining "flats" were obtained by fishermen or fishing firms. These companies build houses and wharves at these sites to solidify their hold on the flats and protect them from others (Stearns 1887B). From these locations, seining crews harvested a variety of fish, including bluefish, pompano, Spanish mackerel and a variety of "bottom fish" (Sterns 1887). Working on shares, the crews placed themselves between the catch and deep water and pushed their way inland. Usually standing chest deep, with nothing but their heads visible, the process was repeated over and over with the crews dragging the net ashore. At this point, "the net, the schooner, and the men seem to come together in one struggling mass" (Schoonover 1911). With better boats and markets supported by shrimp-drying platforms, this method of fishing declined rapidly, although seine crews provided the earliest platforms with their product. The idea, however, of protecting fishing grounds with outbuildings and wharves proliferated.

Barataria seines, used in the shrimp-drying business, were considered some of the largest in the world. To maneuver this net, a single boat's crew of from eight to twenty men was essential to man-handle the weight of the harvested shrimp (Cole 1892; Johnson and Lindner 1934). While a crew sailed the lugger, men in small skiffs played out the seine by rowing away from the lugger, then circling back.

> The lead, or weighted, edge of the net dragged along the bottom, forcing the shrimp and fish to collect in the wider, pouch-like central part of the seine. The shrimp were then dipped out of the net, placed in the boat's holds and kept cool with dampened palmetto leaves (Landry 1999:2).

Using this method, a good seine crew could catch up to one ton of shrimp and miscellaneous other fish per day. At times, the catch was so plentiful that shrimp camps would operate around-the-clock to keep up with their crews.

> the haul seine could be used only in shallow waters, requiring a large crew. It could be operated for only a limited time during the summer and fall . . . [;] the otter trawl was adaptable for use over a much greater range, could be operated with fewer men, yielded a greater production per man, and was a much more efficient type of gear. With its introduction, entirely new fishing grounds were opened up and a rapid expansion of the fishery followed (Padgett 1960:147).

Even though the seine was replaced by the otter-trawl, fishermen were using the seine as late as 1930, when the Louisiana Department of Conservation issued seventy-four saltwater seine licenses (Leovy 1930). As the otter-trawl diffused throughout the region, new boats needed to be designed to accommodate the nets and the larger catches. Sailboats, skiffs, "oar" boats, luggers, and other non-powered vessels were no longer acceptable. The state's watermen needed powerboats that had the horsepower to pull the otter-trawls fast enough through the water to force the boards to spread the nets and winches powerful enough to lift the heavy "bags" on deck (Lindner 1936).

Seines were efficient, but the otter-trawl revolutionized shrimping and allowed marshdwellers to harvest shrimp year-round, scooping up an unparalleled harvest. By 1930, there were nearly 2,400 otter-trawls operating in the Southern states, except in Louisiana, where a considerable portion of the shrimp harvest continued to be cap-

Part of Louisiana's wooden fishing fleet, 2009. (Photo by the author.)

tured using old-fashioned seines (Higgins 1934). Eventually, Louisiana's fishermen began to use "doors" as well. Even with the addition of new arrangements of weights and floats, the otter-trawl used in the twenty-first century is essentially identical to the nets used in the second decade of the twentieth century.

Louisiana shrimpers now commonly pull a trawl that consists of a bag made of netting spread by a pair of otter boards into a wing configuration designed to direct shrimp into the net (Lindner 1936; The mysterious but . . . 1937). The otter boards are at the extreme end of each wing to hold the net open; tow lines are attached to the boards and secured to the vessel. When the net reaches the bottom, it extends out from the back of the boat ninety to 100 feet, but it has only a tiny six-foot-wide opening. Moving at about three-miles per hour, the boat's forward motion keeps the bag open. Depending on what is caught in the "try net," a single drag might last from forty minutes to three hours. If the net is full, wenches pull the net off the bottom. The shrimp are then dumped on deck to be sorted, iced, and stored in the boat's hold.

Sometimes less than ten drags are required to fill a boat's hold. At other times, a captain may crisscross a bay or lake fifty times and return to port empty. Schooling shrimp swim fast in tight formation, so one boat's trawl may fill completely, while thirty-to-forty feet away a boat may come up empty. It is an unpredictable fishery that is dependent on a crustacean with a one-year life-cycle.

Powerboats expanded the range of the state's shrimp fleet. Fishermen were no longer limited to the shallow lakes and bay bottoms. As a result, marshdwellers benefitted from a dramatic increase in their catch. By the 1930s, the annual harvest was more than 30 million pounds, nearly twice as great as the preceding year (Padgett 1960). Catch statistics normally fluctuate, but this increase is attributed directly to the acceptance and use of the otter-trawl, the availability of ice, and the near complete transformation from sail to powerboats.

These changes were initiated and accelerated by rapid technological innovations that improved the economy, altered the regional social order, and changed the typical marsh-dweller's relationship with the lowland landscape (Kniffen 1978C).

Poupier: The Easy Way to "Catch Shrimps"

A butterfly net, or night trawl (in French *poupier*), was invented to supply smaller and cheaper *crevette* to the sun-drying industry. The *poupier*—a low maintenance, stand-alone device that does not require a crew—represents one element in the pattern of landscape use introduced into the marsh-dweller's harvesting culture by technological change and innovation.

Mounted on a boat, barge, or supported on posts with access from the shore, the *poupier* is rigged on an iron-pipe frame. The frame's size varies from seven-square-feet to twelve-square-feet. Attached to this structure is a small, three-quarter-mesh bag about fifteen-feet long. The butterfly net is lowered into the water, left unattended and checked periodically. The rig provided an easy way to catch shrimp, as there no major reoccurring costs involved.

Generally used at night, the *poupier* is deployed in about three feet of water. When not mounted on a barge, the rig is pulled by eighteen-to-twenty-five foot Lafitte skiffs.

Barge mounted *poupier*, 2006. (Photo by the author.)

Xipe/Chopstick

Vietnamese fishermen introduced the *xipe* or chopstick net into Louisiana in the early 1980s. These immigrants were resettled in this country by the Catholic Church following the American military withdrawal from Vietnam. Like the Chinese and Filipinos, they are a largely forgotten minority, but they may account for more than one in every twenty Louisiana fishermen (Kilbourne 1999).

The chopstick, similar to the butterfly net, was attached to a rigid frame. The frame was mounted to a boat's bow, attached to a pair of skids, and fished by using the boat's engines to push the net along the bottom. The device's advantage, like the butterfly net, allowed the fishermen to dump the catch without raising the complete net out of the water.

If an otter-trawl was used, the entire net had to be pulled out of the water and re-set after the harvest was unloaded—a time consuming and repetitive process. In 1984, the chopstick-beam-trawl was designated illegal in Louisiana's inshore and offshore waters (Hein 2006).

Skimmer/Bay Sweeper

The "skimmer" or "bay sweeper" is the latest shrimp harvesting gear utilized in coastal Louisiana. In the early 1980s, shrimpers in the Barataria basin began to experiment with this new technique. The skimmer was developed primarily to catch white shrimp. When using traditional shrimp harvesting equipment, shrimpers noted that as they trawled in shallow water, white shrimp would jump over the cork line. They were lost so through experimentation the bay sweeper was introduced into the fishery.

This gear requires the fishing vessel to "possess some style of A-frame or super-structure to which the net frames are secured, generally in the vessel's forward one-third to one-half. A short shaft capable of swiveling up and down is located at the base of the A-frame onto which the net frames slide and are secured by a bolt or pin. Net frames are raised and lowered by winches and pulleys and folded against the vessel fore or aft for transit" (Hein 2006:3).

The skimmer net's frame is designed to be elevated above the waterline; as a result, white shrimp cannot escape over the net's top. The nets were so successful that, in 1989, the Louisiana legislature made an unsuccessful attempt to ban their usage. This gear initially was not widely used, for many fishermen believed this net arrangement would be banned and declared illegal, like the chopstick nets (Hein 2006).

In September 1991, however, the Louisiana Legislature in House Bill 533 legalized skimmer nets and defined them as 'a net attached on two sides to a triangular frame and suspended from or attached to the sides of a boat, with one corner attached to the side of the boat and one corner resting on the water bottom. A ski and one end of the lead line are attached to the corner of the frame that rests on the water bottom and the other end of the lead line attached to a weight which is suspended from the bow of the boat' (Hein 2006:2).

Since adoption of this legislation, the number of skimmer licenses issued by the Department of Wildlife and Fisheries has increased, while butterfly net and trawl licenses have decreased. In fact, once the gear was accepted by Barataria Bay fishermen, the gear expanded west into the fishing communities south of Houma. By the early 1990s, skimmers were being used throughout southeastern Louisiana and as far east as North Carolina. Such quick acceptance occurred because skimmers were out-catching traditional trawls by a ratio of three-to-one (Hein 2006).

Shrimp Camps were Thriving Communities on Stilts
and the Growth of the Industry

Each island is a sort of factory where the catch is brought and prepared for the world outside. And the factory is a simple affair. It consists of two huge iron caldrons in which the shrimp are boiled and [an] immense platform a hundred to two hundred feet square upon which they are dried. These platforms dominate the entire island—everything centers about them. From their huge size the island and the others near by [sic] obtain their names, for they are known as 'platforms.' Sometimes the name of the owner is attached; again, the name of the bayou and perhaps a word in addition is pictured upon a board in rough lettering that gives one an inkling of the island's earlier life. Such is the case with this one, which is known as 'Manila Village'; about the platform in front of us were many of the dark-skinned Filipinos (Schoonover 1911:81).

Fisher Bros., composed of Messrs, Isadore and J. G. Fisher, is the leading firm down in the Barataria Country engaged in the shipping of fresh and dried shrimp. These gentlemen take a keen interest in the improvement of the South Louisiana Waterways. Their shrimping plant is located on Barataria Bay and is known as the Manilla [sic] Village. In connection with this business they operate fourteen fishing smacks. Besides catching, drying and packing shrimp they ship through the firms of Dunbar, Lopez & Dukate [also spelled DuKate] and H. T. Cottam & Company These shrimp are shipped throughout the United States, Cuba, Porto Rico [sic] even as far as the Hawain [sic] Islands. They also ship salt water fish, oysters and game and are large dealers in hides

Manila Village was the epicenter of shrimp drying in Barataria Bay. (Image from Barataria Bay, La.,. . . . 1917.)

and furs, they conduct two large mercantile establishments one on Bayou Barataria and one on Barataria Bay at their shrimp plant (A sketch 1910:68).

Located in Barataria Bay, Manila Village and its sister platforms—Chong Song, Bassa Bassa, and Rogers—served lugger crews and later Lafitte skiff fishermen. A newspaper account (Franz 1937) suggests Manila Village was a Spanish colony established about 1770. With a permanent population of from 200 to 300 "Manilamen," the site was first used for sun-drying purposes in about 1873; twelve years before a shrimp-drying patent was issued (Barataria Bay 1917; Espina 1988). Prior to that time, the site was a rendezvous point for pirates.

The seasonal population, during the peak of the sun-drying season, could involve as many as 500 to 700 men. These laborers pulled seines and operated the shuttle boats required to move the harvest to the platform/factory. When gas boats were readily available, forty to fifty of these vessels operated out of Manila Village. Other platforms had similar labor and boats requirements as well (Higgins 1934).

Manila Village. (Photo from the *Jefferson Parish Yearly Review*, 1938.)

Large-scale shrimp-drying communities—like Manila Village, Bassa Bassa, Chong Song, Rogers, and Bayou Rigaud—were morphologically distinct, but rather simple in their layout and design. They contained a group of small, rude shacks of rough, unpainted cypress boards that served as warehouse, storehouse, and living quarters. The platform was encircled by narrow plank-built foot bridges raised above the marsh that connected the platform to the homes, boat-landings, and ancillary buildings, like the fishermen's bunkhouse (Schoonover 1911).

Along these wooden paths were poorly constructed wooden shanties. Like at St. Malo, the more picturesque "Malay" hut—with a thatched roof and sides covered with palmetto—was also present (Cole 1892). All buildings at Manila Village and the other platforms were of frame construction and rectangular, ranging in size from the typical shotgun to a large general store. The structures were positioned so the occupants could fish right in front of their doors.

Small vegetable gardens at Manila Village and elsewhere were raised in wooden containers, wash tubs, or rotting *pirogues* filled with marsh soil—rich in nutrients, night soil, and bran—a by-product of the drying process. These gardens supplemented and enriched the diets of the platform's population. These buildings and the wharf, used to unload the newly arrived unprocessed shrimp, were built over the shallow water on hand-driven support columns. Pillars supported the community's dominant feature—the cypress platform utilized in the cooking, drying/dehydration, and threshing procedures. The drying areas varied with each site; the average was about one acre—a football field—with a capacity of 1,000 hand-woven, tall, China baskets used for weighing purposes.

Each basket held about 105 pounds or half a barrel (locally called a *chinee* and pronounced "shinnee")—although some shrimpers realized that a full basket bulged in the middle and probably contained more than the stipulated 105 pounds. One thousand *"chinee"* baskets represented about fifty-two tons of unprocessed shrimp that arrived unannounced at the platform, stretching the workforce to the utmost to preserve the catch. Only the deftness and speed of the operation guaranteed the catch would be properly preserved for market.

Fishermen unloading shrimp into *"chinnee"* baskets. (Photo from *Jefferson Parish Yearly Review*, 1944.)

A smaller hand-woven wooden basket, referred to as "champagne," held seventy pounds and was utilized by shrimpers to sort their catch. By the 1940s, wire baskets began to be appear on the boats, and, by the 1950s, plastic champagne baskets entered the business. Regardless of the basket type, the trawler captain kept count of the filled baskets and thereby had a good estimate of how many pounds of shrimp were in the vessel's hold. Dockside, a wire basket called a half-barrel is now used to unload and weigh shrimp in 100-pound quantities (Sea Grant Program . . . 2000). Historically, shrimp were packaged in barrels for shipment. Barrels were not used on-board a shrimp vessel; they were too heavy and cumbersome to be on the deck of the small boats used in the fishery. In the shrimp-drying business, however, barrels were the preferred method to export the dried shrimp product. In at least one case, the barrels were assembled at the wholesaler's business to ensure a constant supply (Blum 2008, pers. comm.).

Manila Village's platform's cypress decking followed the pattern of all shrimp camps. The exposed board floor was constructed from four to perhaps ten feet above the marsh—to facilitate the free passage of air under the deck thereby aiding the curing process. The platform's surface was not level, but undulated with an ocean-wave effect. The ridges or humps were about three-to-four feet high, five feet wide, with a distance of up to thirty feet from crest to crest. A-shaped frames, placed along the ridge crest, supported tarpaulins that could be tied along the base of each stand (Pillsbury 1964). When rain threatened, the drying shrimp were raked to the top of the wooden waves and covered, to prevent the absorption of moisture. At night, they were covered for protection from dew. This covering remained open at each end to provide ventilation and prevent spoilage.

Frequently processors used small sea bob (*Xiphopanaeus kroyeri*), which is an English corruption of the Cajuns' *sept barbes*, or "seven beards," because of their distinctive whiskers (Viosca 1962; Rushton 1979). These "green" shrimp (also called raw shrimp) were carried in *chinee* baskets to wood-fired, oblong, brick-lined boiling vats, where they were boiled, in super-saline water, just long enough to ensure the shell could be removed easily after drying—about fifteen-to-twenty minutes (Kammer 1941).

The quantity of wood required by these boilers has not been determined. Wood or "cord" boats delivered the required fuel. The quantity to firewood carried by each vessel is not know, but a full cord measures four-feet high by four-feet wide by eight-feet long and has a volume of 128 cubic feet. Depending on boat size, from 25 to

(Top left and right) Raking shrimp and dancing the product. (Images from Schoonover 1911.)

(Right) The model for the patent of a mechanical shrimp huller, 2009. (Photo by the author.)

(Below) After boiling, the shrimp are placed in wheelbarrows for delivery to platforms, ca. 1920. (Photo from the author's collection.)

perhaps 40 cords (including the deck) could be carried per load. The schedules or number of boats employed in this service, along with the sources of this fuel, have not been determined, but it is highly likely most platforms had their own boats meeting their needs. With perhaps as many as eighty platforms in the business, the accumulative fuel needs would be impressive.

If each platform required a minimum of five cords a day, four hundred cords would be necessary to maintain the boiling vats. If the season is half a year, 72,000 cords (about 110 million linear feet, or nearly 21,000 miles—3,000 miles short of going around the world at the equator) were needed to keep the platforms operating. Without this fuel, the industry would have collapsed, so firewood was the lynch-pin to success; yet there is nothing in the record to indicate how this supply chain operated or the costs involved in maintaining the required supply.

After boiling, the crustaceans were removed from the super-saline brine tanks, placed in wooden wheelbarrows, left to drain, and then spread evenly on the cypress-drying surface. While exposed to the sun, the saturated shrimp were turned with wooden rakes to insure uniform dehydration. About eighteen hours of sunshine was required to dry the shrimp properly.

When the shrimp were thoroughly dried, the heads and shells had to be removed. Prior to invention of the "shrimp shelling machine"—patented (Number 1,493,425) by Fred Chauvin and Shelly J. Bergeron of Houma in May of 1924—that removed the shell, heads, and tails (Love 1967), laborers wrapped their shoes in cloth or sacks and "danced the shrimp" or did the "shrimp step" by shuffling on the dried product (Dauenhauer 1938). They crunched and ground the claws and armor-like shell into small fragments. In some cases, small batches would be flailed with a bundle of branches or a large homemade "flyswatter."

Once the shrimp were "danced" or "flailed," loose hulls were removed by shaking the *crevette* on a hardware-cloth frame or winnowing by throwing them in the air during a brisk wind (Love 1967). The inedible outer layer was called "bran" or "shrimp dust." Found to be rich in protein, this by-product was sold as a fertilizer or supplementary feed for livestock and poultry. In the 1930s, Germany was the principal foreign market for shrimp bran (The mysterious but . . . 1937). After the First World War, the Germans were limited in their ability to produce munitions. Bran, being high in nitrogen, was used by the Germans to make gunpowder (Blum 2009 pers. comm.). This bran-infused gunpowder was used against the Allies in World War II.

The mechanical shelling machine revolutionized the business, for it enabled great quantities of shrimp meat to be separated from the shell without hand labor. Such equipment—and a bank loan—allowed Blum and Bergeron to become the largest early twentieth-century business in Terrebonne Parish. Other local inventors further improved the shelling process (Blum n.d.). In 1960, Louis L. Blum invented and developed a cleaning and grading machine (Patent Number 2,921,382) that refined the shrimp-drying process further.

At Blum and Bergeron, the dried shrimp meats were packed in paper-lined barrels for export. In the drying process, a 210-pound basket of green shrimp would yield between fifteen-to-thirty pounds of dried product and thirteen

An early label for dried shrimp. (Image courtesy of Blum & Bergeron, Inc., Houma, La.)

pounds of bran (Kammer 1941; Blum n.d.). The shrimp sold for from fifty cents to one dollar and twenty-five cents a pound. The bran retailed at about seventy-five dollars a ton. The fishermen were paid, depending on the market, about thirty-five dollars a barrel (Blum n.d.).

The finished product was packed in barrels averaging 225 pounds and sent to New Orleans for distribution. Like the shrimp dried along San Francisco Bay, and through an exclusive license with China, a large proportion of Blum and Bergeron's product was exported to China and America's Chinatowns. Through the services of Henry Loose of San Francisco, Louisiana's dried shrimp found a ready market in East Asia. At its high point, the company distributed more than two million pounds of dried product annually.

In the 1920s and 1930s, Blum and Bergeron employees would annually ship hundreds of barrels of dried shrimp to China (Blum n.d.; Terrebonne parish 1953; Boutwell and Folse 1997; China Camp 2006). In the 1960s, the market was expanded through the cellophane packaging of dried shrimp. A. M. Angelette of Raceland and C. J. Authement of Dulac were two of the pioneers in this type of "card" packaging (Blum n.d.). This convenient food snack continues to be sold as a finger food in Louisiana taverns and grocery stores.

Several platforms also dried speckled and white trout. These fish were caught with a pole and line or in a seine. The gills were removed, which also removed the entrails. Once "cleaned," the fish were washed, placed in brine barrels, and, depending on the size of the fish, soaked from one-to-three days. They were then placed on long drying tables and allowed to dry. Depending on the weather, drying time entailed one-to-three days. Once dried, the whole fish was packed in dry-barrels and shipped to market (Werlla 1950).

Along with drying shrimp, some platforms also dried fish, largely for the Asian market, 1966. (Photo from the author's collection.)

Although never a primary industry, the sun-drying business played a key role, albeit a largely forgotten one, in nurturing Louisiana's estuarine fisheries. Depending of the platform's size, the season, and resident population, these shrimp villages may have had a resident population that totaled eight to perhaps ten thousand people. The "faces" of these camps were highly diverse and largely unrecorded. Platform settlements clearly show that since the late 1800s fishermen vigorously exploited the wetlands' resources and harvested extensively the estuary-dependent shrimp.

During Hurricane Betsy (1965), the last remnant of Manila Village was lost. Like so many of these early settlement sites, it is now a memory with only a few exposed posts remaining that indicate something once occupied the space. Platforms were short-lived features. They were phased out of the industry because of increasing operating costs, competition from fresh, frozen, and canned shrimp, as well as dried imports entering the market from San Francisco. Consequently, Louisiana's shrimp-drying platforms were replaced gradually by dockside canneries and packing plants.

As these new facilities began to multiply, the old remote, largely inaccessible, humble, and modest drying platforms and *chinee* baskets simply disappeared. They became archeological relics on the marsh landscape, but during their time, they were vital to the shrimp business and extremely important settlement sites. Their trail-blazing operations have metamorphosed into the modern shrimp industry, with a small number of individuals using natural-gas-fired aluminum vats to boil shrimp in commercial "sea salt," purchased in fifty-pound bags. Once the boiling process is complete, the shrimp are placed in elevated "shrimp boxes," enclosed in a shrimp shed that may house up to twenty-five drying boxes. The shrimp are dried with large natural gas heaters and associated hot-air blowers. The process can take up to twelve hours to insure the product's shelf life is stable and safe. The finished product is marketed by a regional wholesaler—Blum and Bergeron, Dried Shrimp International, and High Seas—to a world-wide market. Besides America's Chinatowns, the dried product continues to be sold in a number of Mexican border communities, California, and Hawaii (Boutwell and Folse 1997).

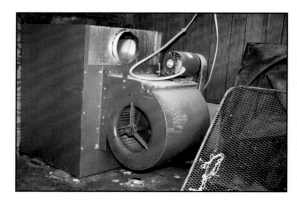

Contemporary drying operations rely on blowers to quicken the drying process from out of doors to covered sheds, 2009. (Photo by the author.)

Even though only a small segment of the shrimp industry, the dried shrimp business continues to have a viable market. In New York's Chinatown and in several Asian specialty stores in the San Francisco Bay area, Louisiana's dried shrimp retailed in 2009 between twenty and twenty-five dollars a pound. Shark fins sell for more than five hundred dollars, while fresh shrimp retail from $2.29 to nearly eight dollars a pound depending on size and source.

Louisiana's Shrimp Industry

The Lafitte skiff and the Florida trawler are the two classic shrimping craft, but Louisianans by no means restrict themselves to classic forms. The opening of the season brings out any number of nautical concoctions, which constitute a motley parade down the bayous to the shrimping grounds. The only pieces of standardized equipment are the trawls and the door board, two squares of weighted wood that force the jaws of the trawl open as it scrapes across the bottom (Hallowell 1979:129).

Historically, shrimp is Louisiana's most important seafood product, but habitat degradation, exorbitant operational costs, low landings, fluctuating shrimp prices, overseas shrimp ponds, and other globalization issues regulate the number of people pulling trawls. Habitat degradation is particularly critical. If wetland loss continues at its current rate, in the next seventy-five years "brown shrimp catches may fall to near zero" (Tidwell 2003:267).

Although habitat issues are important globally, shrimp provides a livelihood for fishermen from the waters off India, China, Ecuador, Mexico, Thailand, and Vietnam to the northern waters off Norway, Labrador, and Alaska. Imported shrimp are becoming more and more prevalent. In the process, North American shrimpers are losing critical market share. "Eat Louisiana Shrimp" now appears on billboards, advertising literature, and in the media. Shrimpers are looking for some protection against foreign competition—often from countries that are producing shrimp as a form of aquaculture. These over-seas operations are not restrained by the stringent environmental regulations and labor costs that limits this activity in the United States. This competition is adversely affecting the economy and culture of seafood; as a result, the shrimpers protesting on the steps of the state capitol the prices they are being paid compared to the price paid in the supermarket. In August 2009, shrimpers were being paid sixty cents a pound. At this price, they cannot afford to start their boats. The issue is intractable, and it has resulted in many watermen's decision to tie up their boats.

The Growth of the Modern, Boat-oriented Shrimp Industry

This fishery was built around the independent fishermen, who operated from a single, small, dispersed, port and generally worked for only one buyer throughout the season. Fishing grounds constituted those areas that could be reached within a reasonable length of time. Without refrigeration, fresh shrimp, crabs, and oysters spoiled easily. Before the development of ice plants, drying camps preserved the product. If an individual wanted shrimp for a gumbo, they were caught, but the enterprise was entirely a subsistence occupation.

Refrigeration and transportation were of great significance. These innovations allowed individual fishermen to become self-employed and provided others outside

For many fishermen, the Southern Shellfish Cannery at Harvey, considered in its heyday one of the largest shrimp packing facilities in the United States, was the ultimate destination for their shrimp, 1936. (Photo from the *Thirteenth Bienniel Report of the Louisiana Department of Conservation, 1936-1937*.)

of the immediate area to enjoy fresh seafood. Consequently, with improved boats and equipment, the industry expanded from its shrimp-drying roots. Numerous packing houses began to process Louisiana's catch. In fact, in the late 1930s, the Southern Shellfish Company was the largest shrimp cannery in the United States. During the season, more than 100 vessels provided this Harvey, Louisiana plant with as much as 1,500 barrels of shrimp a day (Dauenhauer 1938; World's largest shrimp 1938).

In the 1930s, observers estimated that about one-half of the shrimp catch was utilized in the canning industry; hence, throughout the coastal zone, canneries had become the industry's primary market. This part of the industry's roots date to 1867, when G. W. Dunbar's Sons of New Orleans made the first attempt to can Louisiana shrimp (Fiedler 1932; Clay 1938; Dauenhauer 1938). It was not until they devised the bag lining for cans in 1875 that Dunbar was successful. By 1880, the canner was producing 700,000 cans of shrimp annually. Twenty years later, the Biloxi–based Lopez, Dunbar's Sons Company, shipped 525 carloads of shrimp and oysters—twenty-six trainloads of twenty cars each to railroad accessible markets (Fountain 1966). This is only one canning operation. The total number of operations has not been determined, as a portion of these operations disappeared annually.

Extent of the wholesale oyster trade and the canning
of oysters and shrimp in Louisiana, 1890
(From Collins and Smith, 1893)

Number of firms	12
Number of employees	335
Value of property	$108,750
Wages Paid	$67,900
Oysters handled in barrels	189,895
Value paid	$250,701
Value of oysters sold fresh	$342,164
Number of oyster cans prepared	287,336
Value received	$34,699
Shrimp handled in pounds	1,153,469
Value paid	$34,604
Number of shrimp cans prepared	447,738
Value received	$77,538
Enhancement in value of products	$169,096

Without any knowledge of the total number of canning facilities, it is difficult to determine the number of cans required by the season. However, if one considers that Lopez and Dunbar may have been producing more product than most canners, then 500,000 tin containers per operation may be plausible. If there were ten canneries, which probably is not unreasonable assumption, these processors would need at least five million tin cans annually. Without these containers, the industry's market would have been restricted. Metal containers like the firewood used in the shrimp-drying business, were critical to expanding the market; yet invoice records, and names of suppliers, of this critical component in the industry are not reported in the literature.

With development of a tin can lining, a new industry was born and the raw and package shrimp industry evolved into a crucial part of the wetlands' economy. Canneries provided employment for shrimp pickers, who individually could clean up to 180 pounds of product a day. Each plant employed up to 200 pickers, paying these women and children a fixed rate per pail or cup of shrimp meat processed. Wage

A bucket used by cannery workers for their pealed product. (Photo courtesy of Lou Anna and Roland Guidry, 2007.)

scales varied considerably by region.

Once picked, the shrimp were washed, blanched or boiled in brine, cooled, re-picked for refuse, and graded by hand or mechanical graders as small, medium, fancy, extra fancy, or jumbo. Once graded the shrimp were packed in cans, glass containers, or boxes, and recooked/heated to 250°F for up to fifty-three minutes, depending on the type of processing being used to ensure a safe product (The mysterious but . . . 1937; Dauenhauer 1938). This hand operation was eventually replaced by mechanical shrimp processing machines, which sped up the procedure, but displaced many workers in the process. The end result is the market has expanded, demand has increased, and Louisiana's *crevette* are now a well-received seafood product.

However, prior to World War II shrimp were practically unknown on the average American household's table. As a culinary item, *crevettes* were strictly a part of the coastal fishermen's diet and a component of associated regional markets. With the growth and expansion of tin-can technology, refrigeration, transportation, and fast-food restaurants, national demand for shrimp increased dramatically.

Once these *fruits de mer* became part of the country's gastronomic lifestyle, consumers were willing to pay a premium price for the crustacean. Whether boiled, fried, barbequed, or grilled, shrimp are now on the menus of many national and regional food-chains. *Crevette* may be the country's most popular *fruits de mer*, but South Louisiana's shrimpers are struggling to make a living. Even so, industry growth and the expansion of markets resulted in shrimp becoming Louisiana's most valuable fishery. In the early part of the twenty-first century, the industry generated nearly $140 million in revenue (National Marine Fishery Service Landings Query Results. Louisiana shrimp 2006).

As the shrimp market began to expand, Louisiana's fishermen prepared carefully for the first day of the season. They made sure their boats were painted, gasoline or diesel engines were in good running order, winches were greased and tested, nets prepared, and all mechanical components checked and rechecked. They all realized that if their boats did not run properly, they could not make a living, and the season would be over before they launched operations. As a result, every fisherman was a small-engine mechanic, carpenter, painter, electrician, and cook. When the shrimp season was about to open, and if the "shrimps" were "runnin'" it meant boom times for everyone involved in the industry

Sorting shrimp in a Morgan City packing facility, no date. (Photo courtesy of the Morgan City Archives.)

At every platform, boat maintenance was a constant issue, ca. 1935. (Photo from the author's collection.)

(Ramsey 1957). At this time of year, there was a great deal of excitement in communities supported by this fishery. Merchants stocked their shelves. Bartenders and nightclub owners made ready for big business, by ordering as much beer as they could store. Ice houses turned out carloads of ice. Net and trawl board shop employees worked long hours. Gas stations were busy fueling the tanks of the fishing fleet, as Louisiana's shrimpers were counting the days to the start of the harvest, but these boatmen were also worried about their operating expenses and imports.

The present problem is a glut of imported pond-raised shrimp. These *crevettes* are undercutting the value of the wild catch produced domestically. Further the market price has not changed significantly, but the dockside value has decreased dramatically. Between 2000 and 2003, the average wholesale price for Gulf of Mexico frozen shrimp decreased from $6.25 a pound to $4, but major seafood restaurants nevertheless increased prices on their shrimp menu items. To the independent fishermen this is not fair, as they do the work, but it appears middlemen and end-users are making the profits. As a result, in the first decade of the twenty-first century hundreds of shrimp boats and thousands of shrimpers, deckhands, and "factories" have left the fishery (Degraff and Gresham 2002; Burdeau 2004). This process may be further accelerated from boat and infrastructure damages inflicted on the business by Hurricanes Katrina, Rita, Gustav, and Ike.

If the fishermen do not return, the end result will be the loss of an entire sector of the state's commercial fishing community. If this happens, a valuable part of Louisiana's heritage may be in jeopardy, permanently changing the coastal plain's cultural landscape. (For an in-depth look at the shrimp fishery from the North Carolina perspective, see Maiolo 2004). As one shrimper lamented: "I'm surviving but I am not making a living. . . . I don't feel happy that a lot of the older people are being put out of business. The government people tell us we should be happy 'cause we are the survivors, but I can't feel happy if the traditional people are out of work" (Hallowell 2001:99).

Oystermen's Wetland Communities

Like his brothers who had set up their households along the banks of South Pass, Monroe found a suitable place. It was a stretch of west-bank land bordering on Whale Bay [that eventually became the site of the community of Oysterville]. This site was about seven miles from the Gulf and about five miles above Port Eads. He acquired a lease from the state of Louisiana to seed the bay with oyster beds. . . . Monroe, with the help of his father and brothers, built a camp on an island in the bay. The island had sparse vegetation, with only a few trees near the water's edge. The lumber for the camp was salvaged from a discarded coal barge brought downriver to supply government boats. It was cheaper to demolish the barges than to haul them back upriver, and many structures on the lower river were built from such remnants. . . . Most of Monroe and Eliza's children were born in the island cabin. . . . (Jackson 1993:22).

During the early days of the Louisiana oyster industry, free-ranging fishermen waded in waist-deep water to scrape up by hand any easily accessible bivalves from the state's oyster reefs. They collected seed oysters (*huîtres*), placed them on skiffs, and rowed or sailed to favorable bedding sites. Once in a promising area, they transplanted the oysters one by one with enough space in between to allow the bivalves room to grow. It was a painstaking, labor-intensive process. In the 1880s, tongs were introduced and used by the largely foreign-born oystermen (*ostrigari*) to remove oysters from deeper waters. With this tool, the industry began to thrive, and by 1890 Louisiana ranked first among Gulf States in the number of individuals involved in the fishery. In addition, there were more foreigners fishing in Louisiana than in any other Gulf state (Collins and Smith 1893).

In all, an estimated 4,000 people worked in and around the reefs: the Chandeleur Islands, Bayou Cook, Grand Bayou, Bayou Lachuto, Timbalier Bay, Last Island, Barataria Bay, Wine Island Lake, Vermilion Bay, and Calcasieu Lake (Sterns 1887; Collins and Smith 1893; Moore 1899; Zacharie 1898). The aforementioned waterbodies and others were fringed by the distinctive, one-room, elevated camps of the oystermen. An assemblage of these structures could be loosely described as a community, like the village of Oysterville that became a major point for packing and shipping oysters raised on leases from Breton Sound to Barataria Bay. At this site's shucking shed, oysters were opened, packed in cans, iced down in wooden boxes, and shipped to New Orleans. Other than references to operation in Chesapeake Bay, there is no record of the source, quantity, and sealing techniques used in the oyster canning process. Based on the harvest, undoubtedly the number of containers required by the industry was impressive.

Once the cargo reached New Orleans, the oysters were re-iced and shipped by rail to out-of-state markets (Buras 1996). Using a fleet of freight boats, wholesalers initially

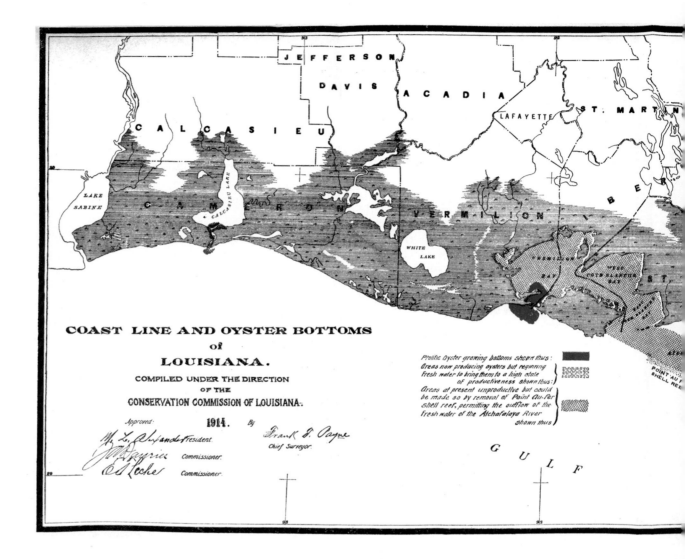

COAST LINE AND OYSTER BOTTOMS
of
LOUISIANA.

COMPILED UNDER THE DIRECTION
OF THE
CONSERVATION COMMISSION OF LOUISIANA.

Approved   **1914.**   *By*

purchased 100-pound barrels from these "rude camps" (Moore 1899:71) and, later, 600 to 700 sacks of *huîtres* at forty cents a sack. The accumulated load approached the maximum shipment a lugger, schooner, or steamboat could handle and operate with a safe freeboard.

During the last decade of the nineteenth century, many of these marketable oysters were drawn from West Karako Bay, which was widely used by luggers working for Louisiana and Mississippi "steaming" canneries (Moore 1899). In this type of operation, a schooner or steamboat served as the mother ship, and a number of smaller boats gathered the bivalves and shuttled them to the schooner or steamboat. This fleet of transfer vessels would rendezvous at a predetermined site to offload their catch. Three-Mile Bay and other sites were easily accessible to the New Orleans' market and the cities along Mississippi Sound, so these were prime gathering sites.

The mother ships carried from ten to nearly fifteen tons (200 to 300 barrels, based on twenty barrels to the ton) of product for the cannery trade. Depending on conditions, a full load could either be completed quickly or take from ten to seventeen days (Moore 1899). In addition to the operations immediately east and west of the river, Grand Isle's shallow-draft fleet delivered from 50,000 to 125,000 barrels (from

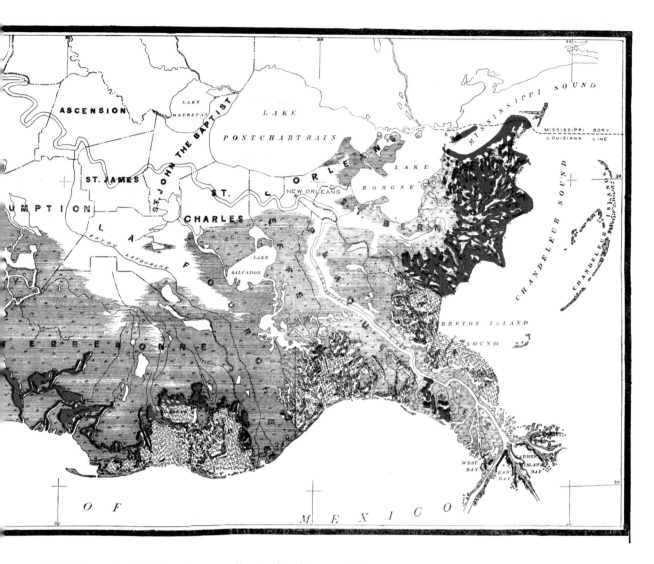

2,500 tons to 6,250 tons) annually to the Crescent City, largely for the restaurant, and counter trade. When the sack became the "official" unit of measure, Grand Isle steamboats handled an estimated 14,000 sacks of oysters a week—representing 18,000 dozen. A sacks like a barrel, was estimated to weigh 100 pounds.

　　This ferry system was an efficient means of moving *huîtres* from the region's oyster camps or from reefs to mother ships. The shuttle craft allowed the *ostrigari* to work their reefs nearly continuously, without stopping for the time-consuming trip to New Orleans. This field production system was established in the late 1800s and continued into the twentieth century. By 1932, a fleet of eighty-three boats ferried the annual crop to market (Fiedler 1932). In this way, small lease holders remained at work. It was a good arrangement for all involved.

　　The foregoing system, however, was not perfect, for

Whether used by oystermen or trappers, palmetto-covered camps were common, ca. 1905. (Photo from Gates 1910.)

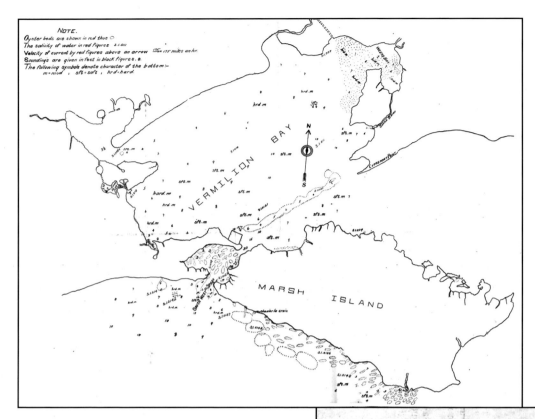

(Right) The oyster ferry system was vital to the New Orleans market. (Photo from *Report of the Conservation Commision of Louisiana, September 1, 1912-April 1, 1914*.)

(Left) The motor launch *Baton Rouge* patrolling Louisiana's coastal waters, ca. 1910. (Photo from *Report of the Conservation Commission of Louisiana, September 1, 1912-April 1, 1914*.)

not all boats culled their catch properly. Small oysters, used in the cannery trade, were mixed in with those going to the restaurant counter trade, so there were also issues concerning size and quality of the harvest. But these were minor problems, since the oyster business was booming in the 1890s and early 1900s.

Factories and shucking houses were thriving from Biloxi, Mississippi (then billed the Seafood Capital of the World) to Morgan City, Louisiana—where oysters were peddled in the streets for ten cents a dozen or bought directly off the luggers for thirty cents a hundred (Harris 1881; Sheffield and Nicovich 1979; Gutierrez 1988). Competition between Louisiana's and Mississippi's lugger fleets over oyster reefs east of the Mississippi River, became so keen that each side accused the other of pirating oysters. The issue became a heated one. In 1905, armed boats patrolled the state boundary to insure that only licensed fishermen were exploiting Louisiana's prolific oyster beds (Report of Conservation 1915; Fountain 1985). However, no one knew the precise location of the boundary between the neighboring states, so stakes were set to mark the state line, but on "dark nights they were mysteriously moved back and forth" (Fountain 1966:5). A seafood conflict seemed imminent, not unlike the oyster wars of Chesapeake Bay, but without any gunfire or oyster-police-cruisers outfitted with machine guns (Wennersten 1981). However, by 1913, the state did have at least one patrol boat—the *Baton Rouge*—equipped with a bow-mounted machine gun to discourage oyster piracy and undoubtedly visually illustrate the state's interest in protecting its aquatic resource (Payne 1914).

To settle the boundary dispute, both states agreed to drop a whiskey barrel overboard at the mouth of the Pearl River and accept its "wayward drift as the state line" (Fountain 1966:5; 20). Louisiana's side of the "barrel boundary" was determined by a west wind that carried the bobbing container east into the open Gulf through Cat Island Pass. The boundary dispute was settled. Therefore, to take advantage of the oyster grounds east of the Mississippi River and to exert some control over the seafood market, some Biloxi operators established satellite plants in Louisiana; in this way they did not have to worry about the boundary between Mississippi and Louisiana (Fountain 1966).

Natural reefs were concentrated in the adjoining states' brackish water estuaries, sites ideally suited for reef development. As the industry became more efficient, the question emerged as to how to manage the state-owned water bottoms, because by the early twentieth century, the once almost inexhaustible reefs were nearly depleted. Faced with their own "tragedy of the commons," oystermen formed gangs and battled over the available reefs. This battle was not just against the "oyster pirates" of Mississippi. The "locals" engaged in this practice as well. Ownership was a serious issue that needed a statewide solution.

To restore order, a lease plan was devised to encourage oystermen to become farmers of the sea, rather than plunderers (Kuriloff 2006). When state officials privatized the state's water bottoms, as opposed to a public or common property system, they restored order to this important fishery. For a lease fee of two dollars per acre, per year, individual oystermen were guaranteed a tonging ground.

Leases were obtained originally from parish police juries (Payne 1920). This changed permanently when the Louisiana Oyster Commission (predecessor to the Louisiana Department of Wildlife and Fisheries) was formed in 1902, and oystermen began "renting" directly from the state. The record indicates that by 1913 almost 17,500 acres (27.3 square miles) of bedding grounds were under contract (Hart 1913). An important by-product of this process is the leases helped promote establishment of additional communities built solely to manage and watch the leases to insure poachers would not raid these tonging sites. By the late twentieth century, about 80 percent of the marketable oysters were taken from these private leased water bottoms, but the number of communities devoted exclusively to oysters had declined substantially (Ancelet 1994).

The first official lease was granted to J. R. Brown of Port Eads, who obtained water bottoms on the west side of the Mississippi River in what was once Whale Bay. From this fee-based process, a partnership between the state and private oystermen was formed to promote the use of publicly controlled seed grounds and privately leased state water bottoms (Louisiana oyster industry 2006). Oystermen could "fish oysters" on land they "rented," but they still needed a well-defined season.

According to the historic record, the oyster season was first established by Act 18 in 1870, which set the season from September 16 through March 31 of the following year. In 1871, Act 91 shortened the season by one month (Payne 1920; Wicker 1979; Noland 2001). Through time there have been some refinements to the season, based on health concerns, fears of premature harvesting, or protection of recently attached oyster larvae or "spat" (Wicker 1979; Ancelet 1994). In general, the fishery begins at sunrise on the first Wednesday after Labor Day in September and ends at sundown on April 1 of the following year. Fishermen now had a well-defined season and an accurate survey of their individual beds. They could now focus on "fishing oysters,"

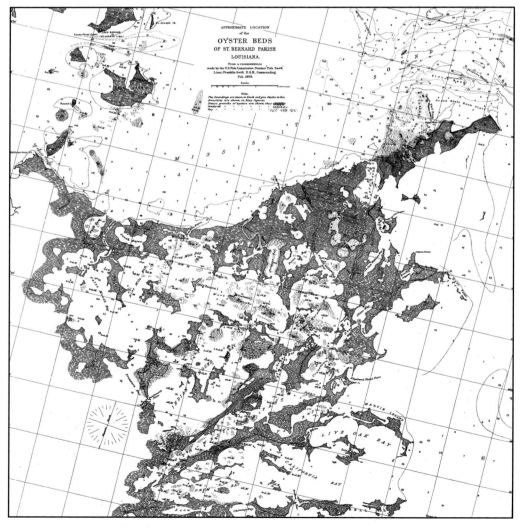

Once oyster beds had been surveyed, systematic leasing could begin, as was the case in St. Bernard Parish in 1898.

and they did.

For eight months oystermen were busy "fishing" their leases, but before a lease could be profitable, the beds had to be prepared to encourage oyster growth. This was accomplished by putting a layer of recycled oyster shells on the lease's bottom. In

Since the 1840s, Louisiana oystermen have encouraged the formation of new oyster beds by placing a layer of recycled oyster shells on estuary floors. (Photo from the *Jefferson Parish Yearly Review*, 1946.)

1844, old shells were used for the first time in Louisiana to encourage spat development and the formation of new oyster beds. To build new reefs, thousands of shells were pitched over the sides of schooners, or oyster luggers, until the entire bottom of a lease's surface was covered. To further enhance productivity, each packing plant, beginning in 1929, had to return to the state's water bottoms 10 percent of the shells normally discarded in the shucking process. Over time, this 10 percent rule resulted in hundreds of thousands of tons of oyster shell being reintroduced into the state's water bottoms—a process that helped preserve the state's natural reefs and expanded the industry dramatically (Yearly planting of . . . 1929).

Without oyster shells, or some other hard substrate, oyster larvae settle into the silty, soft, bottom sediments, where they are easily silted over and smothered. The hard surface allows the spat to develop. When the spat reaches a size of one inch, it is identified as a seed oyster. Once a *huître* measures three inches, it is considered saleable. Depending on a number of variables, an oyster may go from spat to marketable stock in a period ranging from five months to two years (McConnell 1932; McConnell 1950; Friedrichs 1962; Treadaway 1971).

In most cases, public seed grounds, like California and Quarantine Bays east of the Mississippi River, provided the juvenile oysters that were dredged, transported to a lease, and washed overboard by large water hoses, or simply pushed off the deck manually to enhance the "new" reef's productivity (A brief history . . . n.d.). Oystermen

Bedding oysters was an integral part of an oysterman's yearly routine. (Image from *Ninth Biennial Report of the Department of Conservation of the State of Louisiana*, 1929.)

maximized loads of seed oysters removed from state-owned beds east of the river. The weight of the load resulted in nearly no freeboard. As a result, when these oyster-laden vessels went through the Ostrica locks into the Mississippi River's fresh water, the deck would be awash, because of the density difference between fresh and salt water. Once across the river, and through the Empire locks, the water's salinity increased. The lugger's self-elevated and again had a bit of freeboard (Guidry 2007, pers. comm.).

These locks were not free. As part of their overhead, oystermen had to pay tolls to use Empire's Doullut's Canal and Ostrica's Quarantine Bay Canal. A fee of one dollar per month was collected for each boat using these channels and an additional penny a sack was assessed on all oysters brought through the lock—the same toll, or something similar, may have been charged for barrels, but no documentation of these fees has been discovered. By the 1930s, more than 200 vessels used these canals. Some oystermen made a trip nearly every other week (McConnell 1932). These surcharges were part of the business. Fishermen paid the tolls because the route allowed them to live on the river's west bank and "fish oysters" east of the Mississippi, without traveling down the Mississippi, through one of the River's eastern passes and then north to the seed grounds. Recognizing the high fixed costs related to obtained seed oysters, the state purchased both canals in 1932 for $55,000. The channels were immediately made toll free (McConnell 1936).

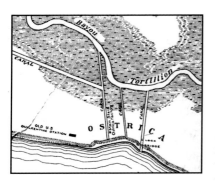

(Image from *Report of Conservation Commission of Louisiana April 1, 1914 to April 1, 1916.*)

Toll Charges to use Empire's Doullut's Canal and Ostrica's Quarantine Canal
(from McConnell 1932)

For boats under 30 feet	$3.25 at each lock
For boats even 30 feet	$3.75 at each lock
For boats over 30 feet	$3.75 plus ¢.15/each additional foot

Besides tolls, oystermen paid a three cents privilege tax—for the "privilege of engaging in the business—on every barrel of oysters taken from Louisiana's waters. A license tax of fifty cents per ton, or fraction of a ton, was also levied on luggers or schooners with a cargo capacity of one ton (twenty barrels) or more. Other taxes were collected on all vessels purchasing oysters for resale to factories canning oysters in Louisiana, as well (Campbell 1914). These costs were part of doing business, but the industry's underpinnings were seed oysters taken from the state's public grounds, and the "raw" trade and cannery markets.

Since oysters were considered one of the state's most valuable natural resources, shell piles blanketed the shore fronts of many coastal communities. For example, in the waters east and west of Bayou Lafourche, "approximately 60,000 barrels [about 3,000 tons] of the bi-value were harvested annually for canneries, like Pelican Lake Oyster and Packing Company; Last Island Cove Oysters; The Baltimore Packing Company; American Oyster Depot; Daigle Oyster Company; R. J. Younger; and St. Martin Oyster Company in Houma and other sites around New Orleans" (Tyler 1932:25). Because several canneries had direct access to rail service, oysters were shipped quickly to United States and European wholesalers, further expanding the market and the demand. Many canning companies also provided their laborers with living quarters, described by some as "being cozy, clean and well kept" (A sketch of . . 1910:13). Regrettably, this was not the case with all cannery-owned living quarters. These facilities were provided to the labor force (with employees frequently as young as eight to ten years old), because oysters were plentiful, the market was expanding, and people could make a living from the harvest, but it was a backbreaking business that added to the wide variety of settlement types associated with the wetlands.

About the time the state established its lease policy, a barrel of oysters commonly sold for $2 to $3.50. With most luggers capable of delivering at least 100 barrels, each load was worth, at these prices, from $200 to $350. Considering the number of boats that lined the New Orleans waterfront in the oyster supply chain, the income generated, collectively, was sizeable for the period. This was good money, but tonging oysters was labor-intensive, time consuming, and not very efficient. Since the beds harvested were limited by the length of the tongs, oysters in deep water were untouched. Tongs were replaced eventually by the oyster dredge, but recreational toning continued until 2004. In that year the state sold sixty-two resident oyster tong licenses. Historically, commercial oyster harvest in Calcasieu and Sabine Lakes was restricted to tonging only. Legislative changes in 2004 now allow a hand-dredge (36" and less in width) to be used for commercial oyster harvest in these lakes (Louisiana Department of . . . 2006).

Introduced in 1905, the oyster dredge allowed oystermen to retrieve *huîtres* at much greater depths and thus increase their yields (Sheffield and Nicovich 1979; Louisiana oyster industry 2006). The first dredge was installed on a boat owned by L. Taliancich. The device consisted of "V-shaped iron frames with ring-mesh sac-like enclosures, usually about three to four feet in length . . . connected to the oyster boat or lugger by chains attached at the head of the frame" (Van Sickle, et al. 1976:10). A deck-mounted manual winch was a refinement that made it easier to haul the catch onto the deck. For eight years this was the standard practice, until two brothers, John and Anthony Zegura, installed on their lugger the first power-operated dredge. Also during this same time frame, traditional sailing luggers were being replaced, or converted, into gasoline-powered boats. By 1920, the sail-powered, commercial-oyster-fleet had nearly disappeared.

Dredges, winches, and power boats revolutionized the industry. These improvements along with increased speed, refrigeration, and cargo capacity made a difference in each boat's efficiency, but no noteworthy changes occurred in the actual harvesting process. Oystermen would get up at four or four thirty in the morning and motor to

A load of dredged oysters, 2003. (Photo by the author.)

Culling and cleaning the oyster harvest was a tedious, backbreaking enterprise, ca. 1925. (Photo from *Ninth Biennial Report of the Department of Conservation of the State of Louisiana*, 1929.)

their lease. When over their tract, the iron frame was lowered into the water. It was then dragged slowly in a circular pattern over the reef. When the sac-like enclosure was perceived to be full, it was winched on deck, offloaded, and lowered into the water and the process was repeated.

While the boat continued its circular path across the reef, the oysters on the deck were culled, or cleaned, a process that involved breaking the harvested clusters apart. To separate these clumps, a small, culling hatchet was employed. The goal was a single oyster or a clump of two. The small, non-marketable oysters and shells would be thrown overboard at sites the oystermen wanted to use for future production (Jackson 1993:27). It would take hours to "clean" the harvest.

By the late 1930s, the barrel was no longer the standard of measurement, so, if necessary, the harvested oysters had to be shoveled into sacks, although bushels were used to describe the harvest as well (Guillot, et al. 1936). Each sack consisted of fourteen dozen oysters, and sold for fifty cents—three-and-a-half cents a dozen. Six hundred sacks, or more, were considered a full shipment. This cargo was worth about $300. With this kind of shipment, the lugger's freeboard was awash.

If the boat was going to a cannery, the oysters were not sacked. They were offloaded directly onto the company's conveyor belt, which fed the load into the shucking house or shed. If the load was delivered to a dealer's truck, or the docks in New Orleans, the oysters were sacked (sacks were provided by the dealers for twenty-five cents each) and arranged on deck in a large symmetrical pile. The exception was during Easter and Christmas, when many *ostrigari* tied their oyster boat to their dock and sold directly to consumers, who would use them to make oyster stuffing, oyster stew, or eat them raw.

Mechanization transformed the effectiveness of the over-water end of the business. In addition, oystermen no longer had to live on or near their leases. As a re-

The oyster fleet sailing to their individual oyster leases. (Image from *The Century Magazine*, November 1900.)

Measuring and sacking into standard-size wire baskets. (Photo courtesy of the National Archives and Records Administration, 8A23673R.)

sult, their marsh communities died. These communities became ghostly reminders of their importance to the oyster trade, or evolved into camp clusters supporting recreational endeavors. Power-assisted boats allowed these watermen to travel more than 180 miles to dredge prime reefs (Van Sickle, et al. 1976). With this transformation and enhanced dredging activity, Louisiana and Mississippi became leaders in American oyster (*Crassostrea virginica*) production. By 1940, using the technologies introduced in the previous three decades, an oystermen could gross about $5,000 (Kammer 1941).

Business was good and oyster fishermen began to expand their leases, but it was a slow process. By 1950, only 23,000 acres were under lease—a relatively small increase in nearly forty years. By 1970, leased acreage was reported at 120,000 acres and almost doubled to 230,000 acres by 1980. In 1988, more than 328,000 acres were leased (Keithly, et al. 1992). By 2005, the acreage had increased to 397,000 acres (620 square miles, slightly less than the geographic size of Dallas-Fort Worth), involving 8,300 leases—on average 47.8 acres (Louisiana Department of . . . 2006B). This areal expansion is directly linked to the industry-wide practice of not using all property simultaneously. This custom permits leases to recover naturally from oyster dredging operations. Also, oystermen report that harvesting the same lease twice a year reduces the number of predators.

A snapshot of oyster producing regions, 1914 and 1920
(From Campbell 1914; Payne 1920)

Parish	*Description from 1914 to 1920*
St. Bernard	This is the most easterly of the oyster-producing parishes. In the 1915 to 1920 time period there were 146,500 acres (nearly 229 square miles) of oyster-producing bottoms. The tracts being harvested were considered the most prolific water bottoms in the state. Most of the oysters were used principally for the steam packing trade. Number of acres under lease　　6,926.32 Number of active leases　　45.00 Average size of a lease in acres　　153.90
Plaquemine	Since the 1870s, oysters have been produced in this parish. Bayou Cook and Cyprian Bay *huîtres* were renowned for their flavor and excellence. Plaquemines Parish possessed some of the best oyster grounds, but the beds were seriously distressed by storms and too much salt water. The storm-disturbed reefs were: California Bay, Quarantine Bay, Salt Works on the east side of the Mississippi, and Bayou Cook, Bastian Bay, Grand Bayou, and adjacent waters on the west side. Due to these causes, many leases were abandoned and their former owners quit the business. As a result, the harvested acreage was reduced greatly. Number of acres under lease　　2,698.65 Number of active leases　　357.00 Average size of a lease in acres　　7.56
Jefferson	At one time, the waters of Jefferson Parish contained large natural reefs. However, by the second decade of the twentieth century they were extinct/dead. Salt water appears to have been the destructive agents, as the water became too salty. This inhibited the setting of spat. Prior to 1905, no oysters were planted or cultivated in the parish. In 1906, the state planted sixty barrels (three tons) of unculled oysters on about five acres. The experiment was a success and resulted in the rehabilitation of the parish's oyster industry. Number of acres under lease　　444.42 Number of active leases　　46.00 Average size of a lease in acres　　9.66

Parish	*Description from 1914 to 1920*
Lafourche	The oyster region in Lafourche Parish includes a portion of Caminada Bay, Lake Raccourci, Timbalier Bay, and several tributary channels. By 1920, Bay Leau Douce, China Bay, Bay Creux, Bay Canard Gris, and adjacent waters had been added to the parish's list of productive beds. The industry encompasses about 3,000 acres (3.1 square miles). Number of acres under lease　　　1,203.59 Number of active leases　　　95.00 Average size of a lease in acres　　　12.61
Terrebonne	The oyster producing bottoms of Terrebonne extended from the west shore of Timbalier Bay on the east, to Atchafalaya Bay, including Point au Fer, on the parish's western edge. Approximately 122,000 acres (190 square miles) were involved. By 1920, legislation set aside Bay Junop and Sister Lake as seed grounds. These waterbodies were not subject to lease (Payne 1920). Number of acres under lease　　　7,808.24 Number of active leases　　　606.00 Average size of a lease in acres　　　12.87 Oysters in Atchafalaya Bay never reached maturity. The annual input of fresh water from the Atchafalaya basin destroyed their growth and development. Each year a new crop grew on dead shells and the following spring the next generation were killed. Over time, the cycle created a reef between Point au Fer and Marsh Island. This reef was an effective barrier to the waters of the Gulf of Mexico. An estimated 50 million cubic yards of oyster shells buttressed this reef complex (Payne 1920).
St. Mary, Iberia, Vermilion	In 1914, these parishes were classed as oyster producing, but were not actively involved in the industry. The problem was that he available oysters were destroyed annually by the fresh water emptying into the Gulf from the Atchafalaya River. In 1914, there were five leases involving 267.37 acres—less than one square mile—in Vermilion Parish.

Parish	Description from 1914 to 1920
Iberia	By 1920, the oyster-producing regions of Iberia Parish were closely identified with Marsh Island, along with the bayous leading into the island. An estimated 4,000 acres of oyster bottoms were available. Until about 1916, few oysters were taken from these reefs. With construction of the "Ship Channel" through the Point au Fer reef, the salinity changed dramatically. The fresh water impounded in the region was mixed with more saline water. The change in hydrology allowed oysters to grow; it was no longer too fresh. Oysters harvested in these waters were taken to local markets in Lafayette, Abbeville, Lake Charles, and the towns and residents along Bayou Teche. Some were marketed in Morgan City (Payne 1920). The industry was small, as less than one square mile total of leased beds were being tonged. Number of acres under lease 565.00 Number of active leases 15.00 Average size of a lease in acres 37.67
Vermilion	In 1906, an investigation of the oyster reefs in Vermilion Bay revealed a large reef that extended northeast from just inside the entrance to Southwest Pass to about two miles southwest of Cypremort Point. The reef was from 600 to 1,200 feet wide and submerged under three to six feet of water. Numerous other reefs were recorded in Southwest Pass and fringing the Gulf side of Marsh Island. Due to excessive fishing, the half-mile wide "Little Hills" reef, located four miles west of the entrance of Southwest Pass was reduced to a few tong fishermen (Cary 1906). By 1920, the principal oyster grounds were in Vermilion Bay, Hell Hole Bay, Bayou Fearman, Southwest Pass, and the Gulf of Mexico, near Southwest Pass. The fishery "labored under the same disadvantages as Iberia Parish due to the waters of the Atchafalaya River" (Payne 1920:139). With the "Ship Channel's" completion, oyster-growing conditions improved, but the fishery, as in Iberia Parish, involved less than one square mile. Number of acres under lease 391.75 Number of active leases 5.00 Average size of a lease in acres 78.35

* In 1914, Louisiana had more oyster bottoms than all of the other oyster producing states combined. More importantly, Louisiana's oysters matured in twenty months. In northern waters, it took up to five years to obtain the same results. With this cycle, two crops could be produced in Louisiana, compared to only one in northern environments (Campbell 1914).

** "Unfortunately, the past administrations have been too liberal in their discretion, and exercising the authority given them by Legislative enactments. As a consequence, the State's industry, and its allied industries involving the culture of oysters and leasing of water bottoms, have been, to some extent, abused. The granting of long leases covering large acreage has brought about a condition of an apparent monopoly, meanwhile affecting vary materially the revenues of the Department" (Maestri 1930:18).

Louisiana's Oystermen

Oysters were the craze of the day: they were in great demand in New Orleans, where rich and poor alike devoured them at all hours of the day or night. Oysters were served raw, fried, or boiled; in stews or chowders; with coffee, tafia, or whiskey. The best were to be found in 'Mussel Valley,' a broad expanse of flatland between La Balize and Fort Plaquemines, when they were transported to New Orleans. According to the Baron de Montlezun, 'pirogues loaded with forty thousand oysters were sold for a total of forty gourdes [one gourde was the equivalent of one piastre [the original French word for the United States dollar], and sometime more' (Crété 1981:283).

The first Europeans to become actively involved in Louisiana's oyster fishery were Slovenians from the Adriatic Sea. These South Slavic, or Balkan, immigrants typically made several trips to various American ports before they made the decision to jump ship. Many settled in the port cities of San Francisco, Baltimore, Mobile, New York, and New Orleans seeking freedom and fortune. Most of the early New Orleans settlers found employment on the docks, where they felt welcome and comfortable, or in the oyster industry (Vujnovich 1974). These were not illiterate peasants. As seafarers, they learned a number of languages, and they adjusted quickly to the social or occupational patterns they encountered in New Orleans.

Immigrants from Dalmatia, who initially came to Louisiana in the 1820s, were drawn primarily from the communities of Duba, Sucura, and Split (Lovrich 1967; Ware 1999). By 1864, some of the nearly 500 South Slavs who immigrated to New Orleans between 1850 and 1860 had settled in Plaquemines Parish. With surnames like Brocadovich, Cognovich, Franovich, Iancovich, Jurivich, Millanovich, Tosich, Ubirichich, and Zibilich, members of this "second wave" of immigrants were more likely to be fishermen than career sailors. In time, these Dalmatian *émigrés* were joined by newcomers from Serbia, Montenegro, Greece, and Albania, who also became permanently identified with Louisiana's delta oyster industry. Raised on the shores of the Adriatic, and trained from an early age in the art of fishing and handling a small craft, these settlers had no problems adapting to Louisiana's inland and open waters. They soon became expert saltwater fishermen, trappers, and oystermen, but few were shrimpers, as this form of fishing was not wide spread among the state's Dalmatians.

Of the three above mentioned occupations, oystering proved to be the most dependable and profitable; hence, it soon became their principal profession. Many sought only to make a few hundred dollars and then return home. Using the community of Buras (a misspelling of the local Burat surname) as their jumping-off point, these "Lower Coast" settlers gained access to some of the state's richest oyster beds (Ramsey 1957; Jackson 1993). This type of work required no special skills other than the ability to handle a boat, which was already part of their cultural baggage. They did not speak English. When working with their fellow countrymen, they conversed in their native Croatian. Their social lives consequently were limited to interacting with others employed in the oyster business. As bachelors, with no local family obligations, they worked seven days a week from remote oyster camps (Vujnovich 1974).

Driven by this strong work ethic, these immigrants developed the art of cultivating oysters to a science. They discovered an abundance of natural brackish water reefs east of the Mississippi River. Here, the oysters grew so fast they exhausted the available food supply, so the *ostrigari* thinned out the beds. In the process, they developed a cross-river culture. By trial and error, early oystermen discovered when these east-side oysters were to be moved west of the Mississippi, where the water salinity was nearly perfect. In these waters, the replanted oysters "acquired the tangy taste for which this type of oysters soon became famous" (Vujnovich 1974:101).

What Did It Cost to Become an Oystermen in 1930?
(McConnell 1931:13)

Equipment	Initial Cost	Depreciation	Maintenance
1 52 foot gas boat fully equipped	$7,500.00	10%	$750.00
2 oyster skiffs	450.00	10%	45.00
1 cabin and equipment	500.00	10%	50.00
Miscellaneous tools, tongs, etc	100.00	100%	100.00
Fencing, 9 rolls heavy galvanized wire @ $14.50 per roll	128.50	100%	128.50
Posts	50.00	50%	25.00

Operating Costs	
Salary—3 men for 8 months @ $120.00 per month	$2,880.00
Food and tobacco—3 men for 8 months @ $75.00 per month	600.00
Fuel—for 20 trips to natural reefs for seed oysters	480.00
Canal fees for 20 trips to natural reefs for seed oysters	520.00
Insurance—fire, tornado, and liability	200.00
Survey of bed by state for lease	11.00
Rental from state @ $1.00 per acre	8.00
Tonnage license from State	3.50
Dredging license from State	50.00
Total	5,851.00
Production 15,000 sacks @ $1.00 per sack on bedding ground	15,000.00
Net Profit	$9,149.00
*Net Profits adjusted for inflation to 2009	$116,448

This activity marked the beginning of the modern oyster industry and the development of natural reefs that provided *huîtres* for cooking, canning, and for the raw or oysters-on-the-half-shell market. Cultivated oysters were soon in great demand among New Orleans' restaurants, steamboat lounges, oyster bars, and hotels. Neighborhood restaurants served raw oysters, along with fried shrimp, oysters, or trout. These items came as po-boy (or poor-boy) sandwiches or plates (Mizell-Nelson 2009), but to the true oyster connoisseur, there is nothing better than eating an oyster only minutes after it was dredged from a perfect underwater habitat. To many, this was the perfect natural culinary treat—to be enjoyed for its excellence in taste.

To harvest oysters, many South Slavs scattered into the marshes and lived in isolation on boats or in camp clusters of no more than ten to twenty residences crowded along a bayou (Ware 1999). They settled at Grand Bay, Bayou Cook, Bayou Creek, Bayou Chutte, Shell Island, Adams Bay, and elsewhere. If there were oyster reefs, the *ostrigari* lived on or near them in small, one-room shanties that may have been stand-alone palmetto-covered huts. The oystermen built unpretentious one-room hovels upon four corner pilings. Their floors were raised about six feet above the marsh surface for protection from hurricanes and wind-driven tides. Also, a raised structure was drier and cooler than if placed on the moist marsh ground. These lumber-covered huts contained "only beds, ropes, clothes hanging from the rafters, and tins of food" (Kane 1944:96) and olive oil, lots of olive oil.

As a rule, these oyster camps were not agglomerated into a community. They were scattered throughout the lower delta's brackish water habitats to guarantee an oysterman could protect his beds from poachers and predatory marine animals (Padgett 1966). Living in these small surveillance structures was a lonely life, but such a solitary existence was necessary, for the oystermen's daily job was labor-intensive, and he needed to be close to his reefs.

When guests visited, the *ostrigari* greeted them with the expression: "*Kako ste's?*" ("How are you?"). The odd syllables amused French visitors, who began calling the new-comers "*Kako ste's,*" which evolved into "Tocko" (also spelled "Tacko"), a phonetic approximation of the Slovenian greeting (Ramsey 1957). However, folklorist Nicholas R. Spitzer (1985) suggests the term is derived from the Isleño word for Austrian—*Austrico*. Regardless of its origin, one can still, on occasion, hear "Tocko" used by elderly fishermen along the Mississippi, where the Legendre, Robichaux, and Bourgeois families lived alongside the Zibiliches, Jurisiches, and Popiches; in fact, to the local French "if it don't got an 'itch,' it ain' Tocko" (Kane 1944:97).

(Photo courtesy of Carl A. Brasseaux, 2009.)

The "iches" dominated the regional oyster industry. In fact, as early as 1893, there were more than 400 South Slavs living in the Louisiana delta, and their camps were scattered throughout the oyster-producing habitats. Freight boats initially bought oysters directly from these Dalmatian fishermen camps. Under this arrangement, the waterman never left his lease. In later years, the *ostrigari* typically met cargo vessels at a Mississippi River landing near a small canal—particularly the Socola, Jurjevich, Valer, and Nestor canals—dug by *ostrigari* to permit transportation of their oysters as near the river as possible (Harris 1881). Usually at the end of the canal there was a "large shed where the oysters were unloaded and carried in baskets of a particular size—so that a tally could be kept by the captain—over the levee to the waiting lug-gers" (Vujnovich 1974:118). Delivery of the fresh product was a multi-step process, which made the oystermen uncomfortable.

The *ostrigari's* harvest was handled through market agents. These wholesalers presented the oystermen with a number of issues, largely related to shipping efficiency and how to fairly quantifying loose oysters to assure proper payment. Commercial freight boat captains wanted to haul oysters in bulk, as this was a quick and easy method of handling the product, but such means of conveyance made assessing proper payment difficult. In the first decade of the twentieth century, wholesalers convinced oystermen to package their harvest in sacks. Oysters were no longer sold loose and measured by the barrel; they were sold by the sack. After the state defined and legalized the sack measure, recycled, burlap coffee sacks were preferred. Even though legal, dealers were not comfortable with the sack as a measure of production. They made oystermen sew the sack's tops shut, rather than simply tying them. Eventually, dealers agreed to provide the sacks and allowed the oysters to be delivered in sacks that were tied, not sewn shut—a much more cost- and time-effective process.

All this new shipping technology accelerated the process of oyster production and delivery. As a result, more *huîtres* were delivered than the market required. The resulting imbalance dramatically affected the stability of the commodities market price. In 1906, an *ostrigari* received forty-five cents to fifty cents per sack, but by 1923, the price had dropped to twenty-two and-a-half-cents (Vujnovich 1974). By the early 1930s, however, the price had increased to $1 (McConnell 1930).

The coffee sacks evolved into the standard measure of oysters. This may represent the earliest example of mandated recycling, 2009. (Left) Each sack, once full, contained a bushel and a half of the bivalves. (Photo [left] from McConnell and Kavanagh, 1941; Photo [right] by the author.)

Despite such price fluctuations and other issues, these fishermen enjoyed their independence, and the camaraderie they shared with their comrades, also living in remote sites near their oyster gathering grounds. Physical isolation was the rule, but these farmers of the sea loved their occupation. By 1930, they had been actively involved in the fishery for more than eighty years, enduring numerous hardships. By the late 1800s, camp clusters were scattered throughout the "Oyster Salinity Belt." This changed in 1893. For example, at Bayou Cook, the camps were organized into a substantial community (estimated at between 300 to 500 people) that was destroyed completely in the hurricane of that year.

> The loss of life here was terrible. After the storm it looked as if none of the fishermen nor their families in Bayou Cook and vicinity survived to tell about the hurricane and its destruction of everything. . . . There is not a family of our countrymen that has not lost one or more of its members. Some families are wiped out completely. . . . No words will describe the horrors of death and destruction. There is not a camp that is not destroyed and most of them were carried away by the water (Vujnovich 1974:135).

Further,

> at this time two men arrived from some oyster stations near the lower coast bearing information that overwhelmed with grief the Austrian colony in the city and added to the general consternation. They had come from what is known, or rather, what was known, as the Bayou Cook settlement. Bayou Cook had owned a population of five hundred, all fishermen, most of whom possessed families and comprised a thrifty community which had been drawn together in the various homes that eventful Sunday night . . . Luggers, smacks and fishing boats of many varieties were anchored along the picturesque edge of the sluggish bayou and the evening lamps in the one-storied houses of which the village was composed were extinguished one by one as families retire to their slumbers for the night . . . the water of the bayou [Cook] suddenly rose, covered the adjacent swamp and spread quickly over the inhabited portion as well. Gale [winds] and waves fought for victims, bringing down the strongly built cottages like pieces of crumbling dirt . . . (Mayfield 1896:4).

After the hurricane, many oystermen migrated out of the delta to New Orleans or returned to their ancestral villages along the Adriatic. Some remained in the industry. Despite countless hardships, they reestablished their orange orchards, built better camps, and acquired boats with the financial support of the Dalmatian community's benevolent society (Lovrich 1967).

These *ostrigari* ultimately prospered; some saved their money and, after ten or fifteen years, visited the old country. They often married their childhood sweethearts and then returned to Louisiana (Lovrich 1967; Vujnovich 1974). Others, once a year, would tie up their boats and leave for their native Adriatic villages, where they typically spent the summer months with their families, tending their vineyards or olive groves. In September, the travelers returned to Plaquemines Parish to work their oyster beds. This type of commuting was commonplace from about 1880 to the beginning of World War I (Vujnovich 1974).

Most of these Croatian-Americans maintained a strong identification with the village in which they or their parents were born. Each village had a patron saint and although the saint's day celebration was not particularly formal, it was nevertheless an important cultural event. Even in their secluded oyster communities, Sts. John, Kuzma, Damien, Anthony, and Joseph, as well as the Blessed Mother remained part of the religious tradition these *émigrés* brought to Louisiana, as folklorist Carolyn Ware indicates below:

> [M]en and women in their sixties and seventies remember building bonfires at their fishing camps on their patron saints' day. Peter Vujnovich ... recalls that when he was a boy living with his father in a Plaquemines Parish fishing camp, people would gather at one of the camps on holidays like Saint Anthony's Day. They would kill a few chickens for a good meal, the women made cakes, and people played cards. The Vujnovichs' neighbors came to their camp for St. Anthony's Day, and the family would visit other camps on their respective saints' day (Ware 1999:5).

Over time, the St. Anthony's Day celebration was eclipsed by the St. John's Day observance:

> Milos Vujnovich says that earlier this century [the twentieth], St. John somehow became [the fishermen's] 'patron saint.' On St. John's Day (June 24), the oystermen put their tools and paintbrushes away and took a holiday ... boats tied up alongside each other . . . The day was spent in feasting, drinking, swimming, singing, and romancing, the latter under the watchful eyes of the elders. In addition to the wide variety of seafood—oysters, shrimp, and fish—a lamb or a side of beef was barbecued on a spit, Dalmatian style (Vujnovich 1974:65).

The oystermen's solidarity was visible during St. John's Day observances and at other times of the year. Their camps were gathering sites, and no one was ever forgotten, for each member of the group supported everyone else; it was a communal life. The small, modest camps represented the occupants' singled-minded focus on harvesting oysters. However, once married, the typical former *ostrigari* bachelor embarked upon a home-improvement campaign, usually building a kitchen, a bedroom or two, and a front porch across the entire length of the enlarged structure. These dwellings were no longer huts, shacks, or raised-sheds, but well built and maintained properties. Even so, one-room water-worn oyster camps, elevated on stilts above a blanket of oyster shells in the middle of the oyster "bedding grounds" were still part of the local landscape. No grass, no flowers, and no non-functional items were found in the yard. The camp's simplicity matched its utilitarian purpose, as laborers quarters.

Yugoslavians are Generally not Shrimpers

Shrimping has never been as wide-spread among Croatian-Americans as oyster fishing. Some did trawl for shrimp, but most lived as commercial oystermen (Ware 1999).

Before the building was lost to a hurricane, the Bay Junop Oyster Company had a visible presence. The namesake of this company was the primary source of seed oysters west of the Mississippi. The site saved oystermen considerable travel time, for they no longer had to obtain their oysters from beds east of the river, 1997. (Photo by the author.)

At Bayou Cook, Adams Bay, and Bayou Chutte, these South Slavic oystermen built their camps near each other and formed a community. Children were born and raised at these sites, and, at Bayou Cook, a one-room school intermittently provided classes (Vujnovich 1974).

Despite the dearth of various amenities, particularly the sporadic availability of educational resources, these coastal families enjoyed an untroubled existence, and, the state's brackish water oyster reefs were home to a sizeable, but unrecorded, population until the 1893 storm disrupted their nearly idyllic lifestyle. Prior to the storm, there were nearly seventy identified oyster beds. If each reef were the home of ten to twelve people, these sites supported from 700 to nearly 850 *ostrigari*—another example of how the marsh-estuarine environment was being utilized by a group that were ignored in the census and the literature of the period. They were forgotten.

After the storm, many South Slavic oystermen sent their families to New Orleans. They decided an education would permit their children to start a new life in a less vulnerable area. Once combustion engines became the industry norm, many oystermen transported their oysters directly to the New Orleans market. These trips to the oyster docks permitted married *ostrigari* to visit their families. Such commuting was commonplace for eight or nine months a year, but, during the summer, the typical *ostrigari* family would close their New Orleans home and move to their wetlands oyster camps (Vujnovich 1974).

Names of designated oyster beds in 1899
Plaquemines, Lafourche, and Terrebonne parishes
(From Moore 1899; Louisiana State Board . . . 1907)

August Bayou	Banana Bayou	Barataria Bay	Bastian Bay	Bay Adam
Bay Canard Gris	Bayou Cook	Bay Coquette	Bay Creux	Bay des Islettes
Bay Devise	Bay Jocko	Bay Joyeuse	Bay Junop	Bay Leau Douce
Bay Voisin	Bayou du Large	Bayou Grand Caillou	Bayou Cook	Bayou Lachuto

Bayou Landry	Bayou Provencal	Big Bay Genope	Blue Hammock Bayou	Calcasieu Lake
California Bay	Caminada Bay	Camp Malnommé	Cat Bay	Chandeleur Islands
Champagne Bay	Chi Charas Bay	China Bay	Cyprian Bay	Lake Felicity
Four League Bayou	Grand Bayou	Grand Bayou du Large	Hatchet Bayou	Indiana Bay
Jack's Camp	Jack Stout Bayou	King Lake	Krakao Bay	Lake Barré
Lake Chien	Lake Felicity	Lake Raccourci	Lake Washa	Last Island
Little Bay Genope	Little Lake Pass	Mozambique Point	Mud Bayou	Muddy Bayou
Northern Timbalier	Oyster Bayou	Pass des Isles	Pelican Lake	Pelto Bay
Point au Fer	Quarantine Bay	Sister Lake	Tambour Bay	Taylor Bayou
Timbalier Bay	Vermilion Bay	Wilson Bay	Wine Island Lake	

*In the 1890s, Terrebonne Parish contained the state's most important oyster-grounds, and Sister Lake became an important source of seed oysters by 1918. There were 600 boats licensed to fish within the parish's borders.

**There were about 200 boats licensed to harvest the natural reefs of Lafourche Parish.

In the hot, humid summer months, oyster sales came to a standstill. This was a perfect time for oystermen to spend quality time with their families. These brackish-water fishermen did not look for another source of income. Alternative employment was not part of their work culture; instead, they reconditioned their luggers and skiffs, hauled soil to the rear of their camps, and made a garden. The wives tended to the garden and made sure flowers filled the long wooden troughs lining their front porches, a visual reminder of the flowers that framed their native villages. The site may have been remote, but the home was well maintained and did not lack for color. The children, who spent much of the year in New Orleans, had a prolonged country vacation.

This summer migratory pattern continued through World War II and into the 1970s. As the oyster trade expanded, the delta's Yugoslavians were thrown into contact with others. Even so, they maintained their cohesiveness and identity as Dalmatians and resisted assimilation. They, therefore, "maintained their ethnic identity and to a very large degree their old ways of life" (Lovrich 1967:164), and, although they lived in the midst of a distinctly French culture, they preserved their own cultural patterns. As with the Cajuns, a stranger was always well received. Their hospitality was proverbial. Their culture was important to them, and they preserved their language through the only foreign language newspapers in the wetlands: the *Hrvaski List-Danica Hrvaska, Yugoslavia,* and *Hrvatski Svijet*—two of which were published in New York, one in Chicago (Kammer 1941; Vujnovich 1974).

A well-maintained cluster of oyster camps and associated outbuildings, ca. 1970. (Photo from Vujnovich 1974.)

These Dalmatians cultivated citrus groves (as early as 1885 near the community of Triumph), operated wineries, became truck farmers, and established oyster camps. As a result, they were too busy to pursue a formal education. Like their French counterparts, the *ostrigari* learned English, but it remained for members of the second and third generations to move toward the cultural mainstream. Educated descendants of these South Slavic immigrants became business executives, lawyers, engineers, restaurateurs, clergymen, physicians, dentists, and educators, not *ostrigari* (Lovrich 1967; Vujnovich 1974).

For those individuals who did not move into the white-collar sector of the regional economy, oyster fishing remained the profession of choice. In the twentieth century, oystermen chose to congregate in communities along the Mississippi that provided marsh access. These villages included, but were not limited to Buras, Grand Bayou, Home Place, Empire, Boothville, Venice, Port Eads/Burrwood/Hollywood, Happy Jack, Ostrica, Pilottown, Burrwood, Oysterville, and Olga.

As in most marsh-oriented communities, the priest, or priests in very large parishes, met the people's spiritual needs. Mass was held every Sunday or, in remote communities, biweekly, sometimes bimonthly. Most of these ecclesiastical visits involved tedious boat excursions. Grand Bayou, for example, required a two-hour boat ride. Because mosquitoes, deer flies, sand flies, green heads, "no-see-ums," and other nuisance insects are always present, Sunday Mass and other services were a trying endeavor for everyone involved during the summer months.

Such trips were usually undertaken in vessels built locally. From shipyards in Olga and Empire, Slovenian shipwrights built low-decked, shallow-draft, and wide-beamed boats, with deep holds for extended stays over their fishing grounds. These one-masted, lateen-rigged sailboats were from thirty to forty feet long (Kane 1944). Some of the larger "rigs" carried up to twenty tons—400 barrels.

To maneuver this watercraft around an oyster bed, oars, sails, and push-poles were commonly used. Narrow walkways framed both sides of the vessel, so the *ostrigari* could walk from bow to stern pushing the poles and moving the boat forward. This watercraft did not have much equipment and could be purchased for $300 to $500. Because of the vessels' affordability, oystermen usually quickly accumulated enough money to own their own luggers (Vujnovich 1974). They required a crew of two—typically consisting of brothers, cousins, or other close relatives. Over time, the boats grew bigger and faster as the horsepower increased.

Like watermen on Chesapeake Bay, Louisiana's oystermen originally harvested beds with a pair of tongs that resembled two long-handled rakes, tied together with their teeth facing each other. Leaning over the lugger's side, the six-foot-to-twelve-foot tongs were thrust into a shallow reef to loosen and retrieve an oyster clutch. This

(Image from *Report of Conservation Commission of Louisiana April 1, 1914 to April 1, 1916.*)

procedure was repeated continuously until the boat was full, the catch proved disappointing, it grew dark, or bad weather forced a return to camp. To handle the oysters on deck, oystermen utilized a shovel. At first the shovel was employed only to unload and load the shells spread on a bay bottom. Because it was believed a shovel would damage the bivalves and reduce their value, oysters were culled by hand. Eventually, the myth about shovel damage was refuted, and the shovel became the tool of choice to unload *huîtres* from the decks of luggers and skiffs and to transfer the bivalves to freight boats and canneries (Vujnovich 1974).

A snapshot of the floating equipment used in the oyster industry, 1913, 1914, and 1918 (From: Report of Conservation 1915:113; Third Biennial Report 1918:164)

	1913	1914	1918
Power Dredges	7	15	
Sail Dredges	41	83	
Flats/bateaux	35	10	
Schooners	276	235	223
Gasoline Boats	342	291	263
Luggers	415	367	159
Skiffs	61	25	6
Cat Rigs/sailboat		18	2
Sloops		34	16
Barges			11
Total	1,177	1,078	640

Outfitted with a false deck and temporary sides, a lugger's deck became an extension of the small harvest vessel's hold. In the mid-to-late 1800s, this smaller watercraft could carry up to eighty barrels—8,000 pounds (Prindiville 1955). Locally, these barrels were called "bank measures" (Zacharie 1898). It took two bank measure barrels to yield three barrels sold in the New Orleans' market.

The bivalves were offloaded from a small fleet of luggers, which in 1878 numbered 120. By 1887, the oyster trade was well established in coastal Louisiana, with about 200 large luggers delivering product to New Orleans (Collins and Smith 1893). This fishing fleet employed a work force of at least 600. At docks on Lugger Bay (also known as the Picayune Pier), the Old Basin Canal, and Bayou St. John, as well as the Dumaine Street wharf, oystermen delivered their cargoes to wholesalers and retailers (Sterns 1887; Vujnovich 1974; Cheniere Hurricane Centennal 1994). Sicilian and Italian stevedores, known locally as *descareadores*, controlled the crews working on the docks. Even so, oyster boats docked, shucked sacks of oysters at the wharf, and sold them for six dollars a thousand (Job 1910).

After World War I, the city's remaining oyster dock was moved from the foot of Dumaine to the foot of Barracks Street. This pier was closed during the early 1950s. Individual boats had been making the trip to New Orleans for more than 100 years. With closure of the Barracks Street wharf, dealers' trucks began to meet the oystermen's boats at points along the coast. This simple, straightforward, and time-saving operation improved the oysterman's efficiency and reduced spoilage of his product.

If the oyster market was depressed, the *ostrigari* would not ship their catch to New Orleans or Mississippi. Instead, they would offload their harvest in temporary beds near their camps, where the oysters could not be stolen. When the market improved, these "new" beds would be re-tonged. The harvest was then sent to market to take advantage of better prices (Moore 1899).

"Lugger Bay" was the destination for New Orleans oysters, ca. 1890. (Photo from the author's collection.)

The *descarieadores* controlled the unloading of Louisiana's oyster luggers, 1891. (Photo courtesy of the National Archives and Records Administration, Still Picture Records Section, Special Media Archives Service Division, negative no. 22-FCD-265.)

Although it took nearly fifty years of operating with middlemen, the Dalmatian oystermen organized in the 1930s their own oyster association. The Louisiana Oyster Dealers and Growers Association was established to improve the price fishermen received for their harvest. They felt the dealers "had been sapping the profits in the oyster game, neither working nor cultivating, but only taking the oysters from the landing on and delivering them to the shops" (Lovrich 1967:161).

To show their resolve, the *ostrigari* refused to sell any oysters to New Orleans' dealers. The *huîtres* war was on and the stubborn, inflexible, uncompromising, and independent nature of the state's oystermen became apparent. Wholesalers eventually capitulated and gave these farmers of the sea a fair price. The incident served to intensify distrust of non-Yugoslavs. It was not long after this "war" that the association went into the wholesale business. Overall, the business improved after World War II, when new refrigeration methods, quick freezing, truck transport, and air express made fresh oysters readily available throughout the country.

Although business was good, predators were a constant problem. An oystermen could lose from thirty to forty barrels of bedded oysters per day to oyster drills (*Thais haemostoma*) (known locally as conches) and boring snails (*Thais floridana*). In addition to these predators, oystermen faced threats from boring sponges (*Cliona*), boring clams (*Martesia*), saltwater drum (*Pogonias cromis*), Sheepshead (*Aplodinotus grunniers*), large rays (*Batoidei*), and the devil-fish (*Manta birostris*) (Gates 1910; McConnell 1934; McConnell and Kavanagh 1941; Schlesselman 1955; Waldo 1957; Van Sickle, et al. 1976; Dugas 1977).

All of the new technology introduced into the industry could not safeguard an oyster bed from these marauders. To protect their beds, the oystermen employed three strategies. For drum, sheepshead, rays, and devil fish, they encircled their beds with old seines supported on pickets, or hardware cloth. Later, underwater galvanized wire-mesh fences, supported by large poles, were used as a barricade against these swimming predators. Such primitive, but efficient, barriers protected the beds from schools of drum and sheepshead, whose insatiable collective appetite could destroy a reef in less than twenty-four hours (Van Sickle, et al. 1976).

Protective fencing was used to prevent aquatic marauders from raiding oyster beds. (Image from McConnell and Kavanagh 1941.)

To protect against conch depredations, stakes with bunches of palmetto leaves wired to them were placed throughout a lease. Conch, during the breeding period, has a tendency to climb as high as possible. The palmetto-based traps captured the animal as it ascended towards the surface. Periodically, the traps were removed and shaken over the bottom of the collector's boat. Using this technique, thousands of conch and millions of eggs were removed from a reef as small as 100 yards square (Burkenroad 1931).

The other boring animals were another problem entirely, since they had the capacity to drill or bore a smooth round hole through the shell and extract the meat (Chapman 1959; Van Sickle, et al. 1976). The oyster has no natural defense against these deadly marauders, other than their ability to survive in low salinity waters. Salinity, therefore, became the oysterman's natural defense against these predators, because when oyster beds were located in low salinity waterbodies, drills were not a serious problem (Burkenroad 1931; Galtsoff 1964).

Oyster Camps and the Market

In the late 1800s, Timbalier Bay's oyster reefs, in Terrebonne Parish, were the focus of intense activity, particularly in the vicinity of Jack's Camp, Camp Malnommé, and Bayou Landry. At each of these sites, but especially at the first, there were small villages made up of camps built slightly above the marsh's water level. In the immediate neighborhood, the oystermen had bedding grounds where their harvest was stockpiled. This site was separate from their major beds and allowed the *ostrigari* to accumulate a catch large enough to warrant a trip to the New Orleans market (Moore 1899:71). Further, reefs in Lake Felicity, Bay Jocko, and Lake Barré—as well as those at Mud Bayou, Hatchet Bayou, and Muddy Bayou—were also dredged or tonged with remarkable efficiency (Moore 1899). In some ways these were new bedding grounds, because in the mid-1800s, there were no marketable oysters north of Bayou Lagraisse. Nor were oysters available in some of the small bayous that feed into Lake Barré. Oysters were, however, present in these areas in the late 1800s. Drainage projects initiated by the logging industry changed the regional hydrology. As a result, oysters flourished, and transient oyster communities began to appear in the literature.

On Bayou du Large in the late 1800s, there were at least twenty camps between the Gulf of Mexico and Sister Lake. Oyster camps also fringed Pelican Lake. With a relatively small fleet harvesting the beds, oystermen took four to eight barrels per day (400 to 800 pounds) from Sister Lake's reefs alone. Because the reefs were initially ignored, numerous boats began in 1898 to tong the water bottoms for Morgan City canneries (Moore 1899). It is a reef complex that continues to serve the oyster industry well. In addition, seed oysters were obtained from Sister Lake and Bay Junop and used in bedding grounds throughout the region (Payne 1920; McConnell 1932). These seed *huîtres* were critical, as the natural reefs were nearly exhausted. This dilemma was noted in 1907 by the Gulf Biologic Station, which urged the industry to abandon its dependence upon natural reefs.

After reviewing production records extending over a decade, the Station's scientists concluded that several natural reefs had no living oysters on them. In addition, the living reefs would be viable for only five to ten years (Louisiana State Board . . . 1907). The state needed to safeguard its natural reefs and help the bivalves build their own new, living reefs. In May 1917, Louisiana planted 16,238 barrels—about 812 tons—of shells in Sister Lake and 5,075 barrels about 254 tons—on St. Bernard Parish's Cabbage Reef to help enhance the region's output (Payne 1918). As late as 1945, the state was continuing its effort to expand the Sister Lake Oyster Reservation (Payne 1918; McConnell 1946).

With a dependable source of seed oysters on both sides of the Mississippi River, oystermen focuses their reef building efforts within the band of brackish marsh considered ideal for oyster production. In the process, they paid particular attention to salinity conditions. With development of new oyster producing grounds, communities based on the bivalve came into existence on both sides of the Mississippi River, generally south of Phoenix and Myrtle Grove. In addition, there were oyster and trapping communities along Bayou Terre aux Boeufs, at Delacroix, parallel to Bayou Lafourche south of Cut Off, down all of the bayous south of Houma, and in scattered locations between Morgan City and the Sabine River. Between 1913 and 1914, 1,664 lessees were tonging oysters from 21,206.77 acres. Each *ostrigari* controlled, on average, 12.75 acres (Report of Conservation . . . 1915). From base camps in St. Bernard, Plaquemines, Jefferson, Lafourche, Terrebonne and Vermilion parishes, oystermen "fished oysters" for the over-the-counter (raw-shop) trade and for canneries.

"Man, there is nothing better in life, than a dredge full of salty oysters. . . . Pop them open and swallow 'em, an' you think yer in heaven" (Hallowell 2001:4).

Leased water bottoms for oyster production by parish in 1913 and 1914
(From Report of Conservation . . . 1915:124)

Parish	Number of Leases	Acreage in Leases
St. Bernard	44	4,825.6
Plaquemines	840	6,415.41
Jefferson	74	686.56
Lafourche	95	1,203.59
Terrebonne	606	7,808.24
Vermilion	5	267.37
Total	1,664	21,206.77

Raw-shop, or counter-trade, oysters were usually taken from natural reefs. This consumer-oriented business demanded an oyster uniform in size, saltiness, and fat. *Huîtres* meeting these standards were considered to be of premium quality. Some of the finest oysters were shucked and sold in bulk to the café trade. Oysters for this market were cultivated on leased bedding grounds, but great care was taken in harvesting the reefs to produce the quality demanded by the restaurant business.

Along with the raw-shop trade, a great deal of the harvest was steam-canned. The steam-canned industry involved independent *ostrigari* and cannery crews. These individuals brought their harvest to packing houses—a more or less open shed, build near the shore end of a long pier. These plants paid the independent oystermen fifty cents a barrel (100 pounds). When their oyster schooners or luggers arrived at the dock, the oyster pile was offloaded. A mechanical shovel dumped the load into latticed steel crates, or cars, mounted on wheels. These "steam cars" were used to pass the oysters through a steam box, where they were heated, under pressure, for about five minutes. This process caused the shells to open, making it easier to remove the meat. From the steam box, the cars ran along tracks into a shed, where shuckers— usually women and children—opened the shells, cut out the meat, and dropped the half shells on the floor.

The oyster meat was placed in a large metal pail. When full, the metal bucket was taken to a weighing station. The shucker was paid according to the number of pounds in their shucking pail. A woman and child typically could shuck between 1,500 to 2,000 oysters a day. They rarely received cash, as company tokens or script was the currency of choice (Child labor . . . 1922).

Once weighed, the oyster meats were washed and hand-packed into half-gallon and gallon tin cans that were numbered to identify the source. The full containers were placed on a belt that carried them through a "briner" that added salt water to each tin. By the mid-1920s the containers were mechanically sealed, put into large wire baskets, lifted into a kettle of boiling water, and heated to 240°F for no more than fifteen minutes. After processing, the canned oysters were immediately cooled, packed in wooden boxes, labeled, and sent to market (Paradise 1922; Fiedler 1932).

Following the introduction of refrigerated trucks and rail cars, the market expanded "all over the world" (Ditto 1980:39). In the early 1930s, Biloxi, Mississippi was home to seventeen canning plants and the center of this industry.

In Biloxi, and elsewhere along the coast, labor camps consisting of long rows of shotgun-type homes. In Biloxi, these homes were occupied by transient "Bohemians" from Baltimore. These workers were the canning company's oyster shuckers or, in some cases, shrimp peelers. Until just before World War I, these itinerant workers came to Biloxi by the "trainloads." With the start of the War, the demand for Biloxi-processed seafood declined. The need, therefore, for imported labor was terminated (Fountain 1966; Sheffield and Nicovich 1979; Bergeron 1981).

As might be expected, the cannery trade annually handled vast quantities of oys-

Shrimp and oyster cans are highly coveted by collectors. For example, in July 2009, a Louisiana oyster can sold at auction for $2,275. (Photos from the author's collection.)

"About two-thirds of the oysters packed are cooked. These are brought to the docks in pungies, raw. They are then put into iron lattice-work cars, holding about 25 bushels of oysters in the shell each. These cars are run into a number of furnaces, each furnace holding two cars, where they are left about ten minutes, till the oysters are steamed, or the shells begin to open. Then the cars are taken out, and immediately the shuckers gather around, and begin to open the oysters. The oysters are then put into round cans and sealed, and the cans put in hot water in large boilers.

In capping the can before it is put into the hot water, a small perforation is left in the centre of the top. From this little hole all the air is forced out by the action of the hot water, and the tinker with his soldering material soon closes that, and puts an end to the process of hermetically sealing. One firm, used $100,000 worth of tin in one year. The number of cans used in Baltimore is estimated at twenty million per annum." (*Frank Leslie's Illustrated Newspaper* 1873).

"The oyster trade of Baltimore." (Quotation and images from *Frank Leslie's Illustrated Newspaper*, October 11, 1873.)

To meet the demand for oysters, women worked in the oyster sheds. (Image from *Harper's Weekly,* March 1872.)

Children were also widely used in the oyster shucking business. (Photo courtesy of the National Archives and Records Administration, Still Picture Records Section, Special Media Archives Service Division, description identifier 102-LH-2061.)

Louisiana's Post-World War II Yugoslavians

"Since World War II, hundred of Yugoslavs have been added to the population of Louisiana. Most of these new arrivals were seafaring men, who had been sailing with various lines in the Western Hemisphere, helping the war effort through their maritime skills. When the war ended, they refused to return to devastated Yugoslavia and made their way to Louisiana where they had friends and relatives or knew of the Yugoslav concentrations in the state. Other immigrants were displaced persons who had suffered not only at the hands of the Nazis, but also at the hands of the Communists in their homeland" (Lovrich 1967:150).

ters. Since 1899, Louisiana has maintained oyster landing documentation. This record indicates the state's shucking houses processed more than ten million pounds of meat annually (Moore 1899, Van Sickle, et al. 1976). This is the equivalent to 5,000 tons, or for comparison purposes 181 gold ingots weighing 27.5 pounds each. Mississippi oystermen were also actively engaged in the industry, but they delivered their Louisiana-grown crop to Biloxi, so the quantity of meat packaged annually was certainly much higher than the reported totals.

At the turn of the twentieth century, Golden Meadow oyster canning factories were active in the trade as well, as were canning plants as far north as Lockport. Around 1930, Houma was considered the "hub of this phase of the industry and [was] known from coast to coast as the Oyster City of the South" (McConnell 1934:34). At this time, the industry was flourishing, with catch statistics revealing a progressive increase in local production after 1900.

Yet, market fluctuations did occur. About 1910, the first major decline occurred. Demand increased in the 1920s and remained stable into the mid-1930s. As the harvest increased, health concerns became an issue. As a result, in the late 1930s, the United States Public Health Service required oystermen to sack and tag all oysters at the bedding grounds (Clay 1938) as a means of identifying the product's source—a technique that is still in use. All oysters must be tagged, whether in containers or sacks. Any untagged or improperly tagged container or sack is considered a health hazard. Further, "oysters must be kept in the container in which they were received until they are used, except that retailers may place them in a display container" (Horst, et al. 2003:1).

Unshucked oysters must be tagged as well, with the harvester's name, address, license number, area harvested, and the harvest date. Further, containers of shucked oysters must be dated and have the name and address of the original processor, shucker-packer or repacker, and the Louisiana certification number to allay concerns regarding health issues.

These refinements reduced the problems associated with contaminated oysters. As a result, the industry continued to expand, peaking in 1985 when oystermen harvested more than thirteen million pounds (Keithly 1991). With the globalization of a number of industries, the oyster business has felt the pressure of foreign completion. By the early 1980s, most of Louisiana's oyster canning firms had disappeared—victims of competing imports from South Korea and Japan (Wirth 2004). Only the over-the-counter trade remains viable.

The Industry Has Changed Very Little from Its Late Nineteenth-Century Roots

Oyster landings are highly variable in terms of volume. For example, in 1988, Louisiana was responsible for 83 percent of the Gulf's oyster landings, but, by 1991, the catch had dwindled to 53 percent (Ancelet 1994). Landings generally range from 4,000 to 6,000 tons. Even so, landings of greater than 6,100 tons are not uncommon (Keithly, et al. 1992). This figure has remained constant for more than twenty years. Only severe environmental catastrophes, such as fecal coliform loading, *vibro vulnificus*, hurricanes, or the opening of the Bonnet Carré Spillway influence the harvest dramatically. (The Bonnet Carré has been opened nine times over the course of its existence.) Oyster production is particularly affected when the Spillway's sediment-laden waters flow directly into Lake Pontchartrain (Engle 1948; Dugas 1977). After the initial shock, growth rates, however, increase, and production ultimately improves.

In the early part of the twenty-first century, based on almost fourteen million pounds of oysters processed, the industry generated nearly $35 million in revenue, (NMFS Landings Query Results. Louisiana oysters 2006). Yet, plagued periodically by bacterium, Louisiana's oysters are often labeled tainted or bad, but better handling and monitoring have reduced problems associated with the most common *vibrio* bacteria. *Vibro vulnificus* affects a small portion of the human population, but can be deadly. The industry responded to this concern by employing two post-harvest-treating-methods—either a warm water bath, followed by an ice-cold shock bath, or high-pressure processing equipment to reduce dramatically the number of pathogens.

The later technique involves almost no heat transfer and results in no change to the natural taste or texture of the oyster. The 2001 patented (Number 6,217,435 B1) procedure uses hydrostatic pressure, up to 40,000 pounds per square inch for 15 minutes, which automatically shucks the oyster by causing the detachment of the adductor muscle from the shell. Thousands of oysters are processed daily, but the meat is not removed from the shell. The two-halves are held together by a large flexible, detachable band and appropriately marketed as "Gold Band." Since the oysters are pre-shucked, no skilled shuckers are required. Any restaurants, with the proper refrigeration equipment can serve oysters on the half shell, as no oyster knives are required. The wait staff only has to remove the band, and present the product, or the product can be shipped frozen on the half shell by means of utilizing cryogenic freezing technology. In short, a chef needs only thaw, serve, and watch a patron enjoy. Further, the process has been proven to reduce *vibrio vulnificus* to non-detectable levels. The end result is Louisiana's oysters continue to do well in the national market (Horst 1997; Wirth 2004; Horst, et al. 2003).

Although the aftermath of Hurricanes Katrina, Rita, Gustav, and Ike played havoc with the state's primary oyster beds, the industry is recovering slowly. Even so, environmental problems are nearly an annual occurrence. Harvesting restrictions, which have become part of the business, are occasionally widespread. The ever stoic oysterman has learned to live with these adversities. Even though the oyster industry has to deal with bad press, predators, industrial wastes, and other environmental issues, the harvest continues to be a vital integral component of the commercial fishing industry.

In 1913, over 1,700 persons were involved in the fishery (Hart 1913), and, as late as 2005, oyster dredging licenses consistently exceeded 1,000. But the industry's future is presently in doubt. The fishery's future will depend, in part, on the environmental changes taking place along the coast. Salinity-dependent, healthy, oyster beds are confined generally to polyhaline zones, with salinities that range from eighteen to thirty parts per thousand (Van Sickle, et al. 1976; Dugas 1977). Sea-level rise, subsidence, and other factors are contributing to salinity increases that may have an adverse affect on the continued viability of Louisiana's oldest fishery (Barrett 1970; Morgan 1972).

Even with these environmental issues on the horizon, many of the state's older oystermen lament they have only one regret—they are too old to work their oyster beds anymore. Their cultural heritage is water based, because

> When a man's worked the water all his life, he'll keep coming back, even if it's just to sit around the dock. . . .' 'Here on the water, now we all know each other and we all care about one another. Guess that's why I decided to stay a waterman (Whitehead 1979:n.p.).

Although this statement describes Chesapeake Bay watermen, it applies equally well to Louisiana's *ostrigari*.

Trapping: A Three-Month Exile in the Marsh

> . . . Grandpère stood there in long hip boots and leather jacket, a corduroy cap perched jauntily on his white mop of hair. He held his shotgun in hand. As he raised it and pointed it skyward, he winked gaily at me. Then the blast nearly knocked me off the boat. Grandpère lowered his gun, smacked his lips with satisfaction, and called to Camille: 'Oui, bien merci . . . another season!' (Ramsey 1957:159).

Louisiana's fur industry dates to the 1700s, but the state did not become a significant fur producer until the twentieth century. From the early 1900s through the 1980s, Louisiana led the nation in the production of wild fur pelts. At its height, when the price of fur skyrocketed, the trapping industry provided employment for 30,000 people (Daspit 1944). In fact, by 1912 trapping was so commonplace the legislature imposed trapping season dates and required trappers to be licensed. What is often overlooked is that these 30,000 people were frequently in the marsh with their families.

It is, therefore, highly probable that more than 120,000 individuals (considering a family of four) were directly engaged in this industry—one-fourth of the population of New Orleans in 1930. From the Sabine to the Pearl rivers, trappers "homesteaded" yearly their trapping grounds. In the process, they established small, short-lived, inconspicuous, and largely forgotten, water-based communities. Considering the number of individuals involved, this may be the largest, continuous, non-farm, annual, regional migration in the country. These transient laborers collectively constitute one of the faces of the wetlands. More importantly, their cumulative numbers were large and unreported, as they were harvesting furs from sites in an environment that was viewed unsympathetically by the general population.

A trapper walking through the marsh, checking his trap line. (Photo courtesy of Library of Congress, Print and Photographs Division, FSA-OWI Collection, LC-USF34-056864-D.)

They nevertheless transformed Louisiana's alluvial lowlands into the country's preeminent fur-producing region in less than fifty years. Still, few people presently recognize Louisiana was a major hide-and fur-producer. To many people, the jobs and income this seasonal occupation provided was inconsequential. It was not an important part of mainstream life, yet millions were made in the industry and proved the marsh's value went beyond aquatic species—crustaceans and bivalves. Four-legged animals were part of the living matrix as well and were responsible for a yearly human exodus that was stunning in its scale. The trapper's footprint was small, but hardly insignificant.

The state's subtropical marshes had been ignored by trappers (*piégeurs*) until the 1800s, when alligator, mink (*Mustela vison*), otter (*Lutra canadensis*), and raccoon (*Procyon lotor*) were recognized as valuable hide-and fur-bearing animals. In the early 1900s, trappers and their families headed for the *marais*, since all of these animals could be processed into fine furs or tanned into durable leather. These trappers, in turn, were supported by up to 1,000 fur buyers and dealers (Louisiana Fur and Alligator 2004). Prior to the assassination, in 1914, of Archduke Franz Ferdinand, heir to the Austro-Hungarian throne, and the subsequent outbreak of World War I, Louisiana fur prices were quite high and the market was stable. However, with the outbreak of the "European War," prices plummeted, and the market nearly collapsed.

This situation lasted for only two years. By 1916, the price for raw pelts had recovered, reaching its highest point ever (Report on fur-bearing . . . 1918). Twelve years later, trappers harvested 5,909,546 muskrat (*rats musqués*) pelts, valued at $8,526,740 (when adjusted for inflation, this figure equates to more than $168 million in 2009). These pelts were often dyed and marketed as: Hudson Seal; French Seal; River Sable; Water Mink; Southern Mink; and Lutrinae (Commercial value . . . 1929; O'Neil 1968).

In 1951, fur labeling laws removed these romantic names. The garment had to read "muskrat." Dyed raccoon lost its name—Laskin Sabelin. The Back Marten had to return to its common name, opossum. Promotional material also had to reflect these changes. As a result of this truth in advertising, sales quickly declined (O'Neil 1968). However, for more than half a century, consumers were buying fur products through a naming convention that led them to believe these were exotic furs and not "rats," possum, or raccoon from Louisiana. The names used by marketers did not bother the trappers. Chances are they had no idea the market dedicated a name change. They were making money and did not care what a "*rat musqué*" was called in the market place, as long as they got a fair price for their harvest.

Between 1914 and 1920, a typical trapper could earn in excess of $3,000 in a five to six month season—nearly three times the average household earnings in 1920. There was clearly primary and secondary value to the wetlands, and, for the first, time "outsiders" began to appreciate the wetland's intrinsic value. Prior to the flapper era typified by young, short-skirted women, speakeasies, and muskrat-coated college students, no one considered owning marshlands. But garment trends changed this mindset.

When muskrat pelts (the poor man's mink) became a valuable commodity, ownership issues and back taxes became controversial topics throughout the coastal lowlands. The state legislature passed a law allowing lands to be removed from delinquent tax rolls by simply paying overdue taxes. As a result, "the legislative loophole brought about a surreptitious land rush that kept the clerks of court in Plaquemines and St. Bernard parishes busy recording redemptions. By 1926, some marshland exceeded dry land in value" (Gowland 2003:424).

The fur trade's spectacular growth was a result of the local inhabitants' exploitation of muskrat and later nutria (*ragondin*). Although muskrats are native to Louisiana's marshes, Arthur (1931) and O'Neil (1949) were unable to discover any documents suggesting that their pelts were included in the early French fur trade because colonial fur buyers regarded the muskrat as worthless. It remained undesirable until 1914, when muskrat pelts began to appear on the fur market (Chatterton 1944). In a relatively short period, the *rat musqués* was destined to become Louisiana's most important fur-bearer—a title it ultimately relinquished to the *ragondin*. This aquatic, marsh dwelling rodent was first introduced in southern California in 1899 and later into Louisiana. Worldwide it is known as: South American beaver, swamp beaver, beaver rat, and coypu (Kammer 2001).

(Top) A Louisiana muskrat, ca. 1945. (Photo courtesy of the Louisiana Department of Wildlife and Fisheries.)

(Bottom) A St. Bernard Parish woman showing off part of her family's harvest, 1941. (Photo courtesy of Library of Congress, Print and Photographs Division, FSA-OWI Collection, LC-USF34-057019-E DLC.)

Prices Paid to Trappers, 1915 to 1918
(From *Report on Fur-Bearing . . .* 1918:82)

Animal	1915-1916 Average price	1915-1916 Value	1916-1917 Average price	1916-1917 Value	1917-1918 Average price	1917-1918 Value
Muskrat	$0.08	$280,033	$0.15	$318,750	$0.80	$346,805
Raccoon	1.25	665,600	1.25	848,547	3.00	440,220
Opossum	0.30	58,092	0.35	80,122	0.90	84,075
Mink	1.33	154,737	1.45	177,596	3.00	106,800
Skunk	0.20	4,734	1.15	29,467	2.50	18,907
Otter	6.00	21,240	6.00	41,640	13.00	15,880
Other animals	1.00	6,740	1.00	8,980	2.00	4,650
Total		1,191,176		1,505,102		1,017,337
Adjusted for inflation to 2009						14,371,221

The rising economic significance of the muskrat trapping industry prompted Louisiana's government to mount an effort to develop and conserve this natural resource. To better understand muskrat behavior, the Louisiana Department of Conservation in the late 1920s set up muskrat plots on their experimental fur-farm on Avoca Island (also known as Cowpen Island). Each plot encompassed about one-tenth of an acre. Shortly after the farm was established, the experiment was abandoned. Following the state's led, entrepreneurs set up "rat farms" at a number of sites in the marsh. Canals were cut to gain access to these *"rat musqué"* properties and serve as the "farm's" legacy, as these channels are visible reminders of this forgotten enterprise. These "rat farms" were a landscape novelty. The real "ranch" encompassed the entire marsh and the individual trappers that managed the environment and harvested its resources.

Trapping Is Part of the Marshdweller's Heritage

The job of running a trap line in the marshes is not an easy one, even with the use of a pirogue. The pirogue is paddled a short distance up the *traînasse* with its load of traps, and the trapper must then trudge through mud and ooze, oftentimes thigh deep, to set them. He then returns to the pirogue, paddles a little farther, and repeats the operation. After the traps have been set, they must be visited daily. . . . As soon as the line has been run, the trapper returns with the catch to his camp where the animals must be immediately skinned. This job is usually done by his wife and daughters. After the animals have been skinned, the pelt is run through an ordinary clothes wringer to remove moisture and any bits of flesh that may still be clinging to the hide. It is then placed on a stretcher to dry (Kammer 1941:105).

For nine months, the typical marsh denizen caught shrimp, crabs, frogs, or gathered moss, but in the winter they became vagabond *piégeurs*. The annual trapping migration "is so deeply instilled that many people in South Louisiana regard it as instinctive" (Hallowell 1979:4). In the winter, a large number of itinerant trappers happily entered into voluntary exile. Indeed, there was an excitement associated with the trapping season. When families arrived at their trapping sites, the community bonded together by building camps, digging and/or cleaning out their narrow *traînasses* and preparing their lease by monitoring water levels, and if necessary burning the marsh.

Curing a trapper's harvest, 1933. (Photo from the *Louisiana Conservationist,* vol. 7, 1933.)

To exploit the marshland's fur resources, *piégeurs* relied upon comfortable floating homes, "gas boats," rowboats, and *pirogues.* Five- and six-family houseboat/campboat communities often lined a bayou's banks, providing shelter and a sense of camaraderie during the trapping season. As a result, temporary encampments of full-time trappers were scattered widely throughout all the marsh's navigable waterways. In these transient villages the residents displayed the best aspects of the regional culture—families helped families, and everyone benefitted from the fur harvest. The food, the

Burning the marsh, 1982. (Photo by the author.)

A rendezvous site in the marsh, 1920. (Photo from Cheniere Hurricane Centennal 1994.)

sense of community, and the camaraderie were part of the season. Food came from the bayous, bays, and marshes and was turned into bouillabaisse, gumbo, and other dishes. To many, this was a great life (Falgoux 2007).

In the early twentieth century, Louisiana's annual fur and hide harvest was greater than those of Alaska and Canada combined (Daspit 1949). The animals responsible for this spectacular output were the muskrat and nutria. Louisiana's wetlands were teaming with fur-bearing animals, but demand was limited. In the nineteenth century, Europe was the major market for all types of furs, but sales were confined to the elite and moneyed classes. These individuals preferred more prestigious furs than those of the *"rat musqué"* used by many furriers. As styles changed in the first two decades of the twentieth century, fur-coats became fashionable. By 1950, a muskrat coat, depending on quality, could cost from $1,000 to $4,000. Nutria coats, depending on the fabric with it was paired, could cost from $1,500 to $6,000 (Price schedule n.d.). Fifty years later, the pelt was nearly worthless.

Muskrat and Nutria

> I think the quality of muskrat and nutria pelts was better in the old days than it is today, because we had better marsh, better vegetation then. The marsh has changed so much, with canals, erosion, salt water intrusion (Gomez 1998:157).

Muskrats build homes (*buttes des rats musqués*) of woven-marsh grass, plastered with mud and rising about two to three feet above the marsh surface. They also build canals and intricate apartment houses in the marsh muck. These mounds constitute a base from which the animals can forage in the surrounding terrain. Since the mud heaps identify the muskrat's brackish-water habitats, trappers use mound density as an indicator of a region's productive value and set their traps accordingly. *Musqués* are primarily vegetarians. They prefer stems, roots, and tubers and are voracious eaters. Their normal dietary intake is often as much as one-third of their body weight a day (Murchison 1978). Because they are constant foragers, these rodents were traditionally caught in unbaited traps, which were often marked with rags that fluttered in the wind (Job 1910).

To improve the commercial harvest, marshdwellers burn the paludal surface, removing less desirable vegetation—which is a common marsh management technique throughout the country (Lynch 1941; O'Neil 1965; Schmeltzer, et al. 1991; Nyman and Chabreck 1995). Marsh conflagrations were rare before 1910, but, by the 1920s, burning was a well-established practice, and it remains commonplace. From the trappers' perspective, these fires promoted the growth of three-cornered grass (*Scirpus olneyi* also *Schoenoplectus americana*)—the muskrat's preferred vegetation. Although *scirpus olneyi* appeared to send up more new stalks following burns (Arthur 1931), Lynch (1941) and Hess (1970) reported plant growth was actually accelerated by removal of the marsh-hay cordgrass (*Spartina patens*), which gave an edge to the three-cornered grass. Regardless of the science behind the phenomena, a trapper usually burned marshgrass in the fall to aid in poling for alligators and to make muskrat trails more visible, which helped him place his traps.

Unlike the indigenous muskrat, the nutria is an invasive species. E. A. McIlhenny has been held responsible for many years for introducing nutria to Louisiana. This is not the case. Company papers show he "was at least the third nutria farmer in the state and at least the second to set loose nutria into the wild on purpose. Furthermore, E. A. McIlhenny never imported nutria to Louisiana, as often claimed, but purchased his original nutria from one of the pre-existing nutria farms in St. Bernard Parish . . ." (McIlhenny Company delays . . . 2006: internet site). Like most nutria farm owners in the 1930s and 1940s, E. A. McIlhenny eventually released a large number of nutria into the wetlands. This was a conscious act and not the result of a hurricane, as has often been reported in the popular literature.

A nutria, 1984. (Photo by the author.)

After these *ragondin* were released, this Argentine rodent expanded its range quickly (Daspit 1946). In the late 1940s, the semi-aquatic nutria was promoted by state officials as a biological agent for controlling aquatic weeds, primarily water hyacinth—waterborne kudzu—and alligator weed (*Alternanthera philoxeroides*). The animal was consequently transplanted throughout southeastern Louisiana to control this non-native perennial plant. The reasoning behind the effort was to utilize the nutria's grazing ability to control problem plants and to optimizing the harvest. The first well-established nutria colony was located near White Lake in southwest Louisiana.

In 1942-43 season 436 Louisiana nutria pelts reached the market. They had an average value of fifty cents. Four years later, 8,784 pelts were sold at $5 each. Rapid population growth followed for several years thereafter (Nutria population dynamics . . . 2003). By the early 1950s, fur and land operators, throughout the coastal zone, were purchasing nutria from the Vermilion Parish area for transplanting into their respective marshes. In the 1950-51 season 78,422 pelts were marketed at $4.65 each—six times the seventy-five cent minimum wage. This was great money, but not altogether easily earned, for skinning, fleshing, and stretching nutria skins was hard work (Tompkins 2006). Even so, as early as 1948, some individuals were predicting the garment industry's demand for nutria pelts would assure its future (First nutria fur . . . 1948).

While Louisiana was a primary producer of fur and alligator skins, a majority of the state's pelts and hides were baled and sent to New York, Europe, Asia, and Japan. Buyers in these regions tanned the product and benefitted from the value added, as they had the necessary expertise to manufacture fur and leather goods. Manufacturers in these markets were highly dissatisfied with the industry's quality controls; as a result, trappers were not benefitting from the best possible prices (Dozier and

E. A. McILHENNY

SPECIALTIES:
CAMELLIAS
AZALEAS
IRIS
WISTERIA
EVERGREENS

"PLANTS FOR THE SOUTH"

SPECIALIZING IN LANDSCAPE SERVICE

AVERY ISLAND. LA.

Jan. 10, 1949.

SALES YARD AT:
WESTHEIMER & POST OAK RD.
HOUSTON, TEXAS.

EXPRESS
FREIGHT
MAIL ⎱AVERY ISLAND, LA.
TELEGRAPH
TELEPHONE

Mr. J. Cornelius Rathborne,
Harvey, La.

Dear Mr. Rathborne:-

Your letter of January 6th. regarding nutria and addressed to Mr. Walter McIlhenny, has been turned over to me for answering. Shipment of nutria can be made immediately by express collect.

The Nutria I have originally came from South America and are natural color - about the color of a dark muskrat. I can ship you any age animal from a year and one-half down to four months. There is no difference in price for the age. Since my Nutrias are on large open range, it would be impossible to state whether any females I might ship are bred or not. My prices are:

Females	. . . .	$ 20.00 each
Males	. . . .	15.00 each
Crating charge	. . . . .	7.50 the crate

cash in advance. However, crating charges are refundable upon the return of the crate or crates as the case may be.

These animals can be grown very easily in pens and thrive on any kind of grain or garden truck or garden tubers, with the exception of white potatoes. They like beets, sweet potatoes, carrots, cabbage, turnips and grain of all kinds. They pasture where they can get sufficient green grass. They need no other food; they eat the same food the year round. It is not necessary for them to have water to swim in, and I have never given my animals scratch food.

If you desire, you may obtain a book entitled, "Nutria Raising", from the Fur Farms Publishing Co., 33 Winston Bldg., Utica 2, N.Y.

Trusting I may serve you,

Very truly yours,
E.A. MC ILHENNY

BY: *Polly McIlhenny Simmons*
MRS. F.E. SIMMONS

PMS/id

Correspondence from the E. A. McIlhenny Company Concerning the Sale of Nutria, 1949. (Image courtesy of Rathborne Commercial & Industrial Properties, Harvey, La.)

Ashbrook 1950; Washburn 1951). This did not bode well for the state's trappers, who were clearly at a disadvantage in the international fur market—a market dominated and controlled by foreigners. The result was low prices to the trappers, buyers, and dealers, but high prices for finished goods sold to American fur and leather consumers (Shelton 1987).

Trappers had to rethink how they cleaned, skinned, and dried their pelts. Western Louisiana's nutria pelts were the catalyst in this reeducation process. These pelts were of fine quality and color, and were in demand. After dressing these late 1940s pelts were worth between five and six dollars a pelt. Although valuable, the industry had to solve a wide array of problems before this "new" fur animal could meet the needs of the highly discriminating fashion-fur business (O'Neil 1968). By teaching trappers how to handle their furs, advertising the quality of the state's raw pelts, and encouraging competitive bids through the auction process, trappers began to get a better return on their marketable pelts.

A better return was essential to Louisiana trappers, because the prolific small, beaver-like, nutria quickly began to replace the muskrat. *Ragondin* are ready to reproduce after four to six months of age. Moreover, females can breed within twenty-four hours of giving birth. Hence, the population is, without help from a major disease, nearly impossible to deplete.

Myocastor coypus's nocturnal habits make them visible in the early morning and late afternoon. Weighing from ten to nearly thirty pounds, the rodent was originally considered a nuisance because they were heavy to carry out of the marsh, difficult to skin, and confined to a single area (Daspit 1949; Waldo 1958; Dozier and Ashbrook 1950). A trapper could handle 100 to 125 muskrats in the time, expense, and effort it took to trap and process twenty-five nutria. As a consequence, the huge rodents were considered a liability, but attitudes eventually changed (Daspit 1948; Daspit 1950).

A trapper preparing to lay out his trap line. (Photo from the *Louisiana Conservationist*, vol. 10, 1958.)

European fur demand kept prices relatively stable through the mid-1950s. In 1955, supply overcame demand, and nutria prices dropped precipitously. As a result, there was an over-abundance of the animal, and their destructive effect on crops and marshlands was quickly felt. To rectify this situation, the Louisiana Department of Wildlife and Fisheries searched for new markets, but their efforts were successful. By the mid-1960s, the German fur market began importing annually more than one million nutria hides (Louisiana Fur Industry . . . 2003). In 1976, Louisiana trappers sold an estimated 1.8 million skins. During the 1980s, pelt prices peaked at near eight dollars, but shortly thereafter the fur industry declined, prices dropped, and it was no longer economically feasible to trap nutria. As a result, almost no one is currently trapping this big mammal (Tompkins 2006).

The problems now faced by Louisiana trappers are compounded by the persistent foreign domination of the vertical market. Even in flush times, the state lacked the processing and manufacturing capabilities to handle, dress, and improve the value of raw fur. As a supplier of raw materials, Louisiana essentially had a colonial economy, with most of the industry's profits going to out-of-state or foreign participants. The end result is a foreign-controlled market that often leads to low prices to the trappers, buyers, and dealers, but high prices for American consumers.

To counteract this trend, the state legislature approved Act 455 in 1986, which established the Louisiana Fur and Alligator Public Education and Marketing Fund. The Act was designed to identify consumers of Louisiana furs and hides, develop fur and alligator markets, and implement an international advertising campaign promoting fur and alligator products. The Act was supposed to promote the fur industry and encourage the establishment of processing facilities in the state. Marketing is, in fact, the key to this industry. Even so, trapping is on the decline. It is simply no longer profitable to "walk the marsh," and a centuries-old tradition is fading into history.

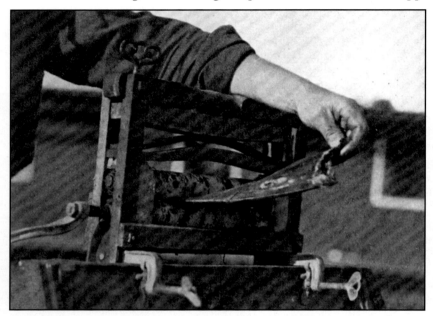

A clothes ringer cleaning muskrat pelts, ca. 1925. (Photo from the *Seventh Biennial Report of the Department of Conservation, 1924-1926.*)

Trapping seemed to have peaked in the 1976-1977 season when the industry was worth about $25 million. Prices for nutria that season averaged $7.80; dropped to $4.21 in '78-'79; peaked at $8.19 in '80-'81; and bottomed out at $2.80 in '82-'84. In the 2004-2005 season nutria sold for $1.50 and was valued at $55,657. Muskrat sold for $0.77 and was valued at $1,814 (Comparative take 2005).

With the decline of the nutria market, the rodent population exploded. As a result, sugarcane fields were damaged, and large eat-outs began to appear in southeast Louisiana marshes. The invasive rodent feeds on the roots of marsh plants and destroys them in a process described as an "eat-out" (O'Neil 1965). The consumed plants were necessary to help hold the marsh together and protect it against erosion, while also providing valuable habitat for a wide-variety of aquatic and avian species. These voracious vegetarians typically consume daily 25 percent of their ten-to-thirty pound body weight (Tompkins 2006). With this kind of appetite, nutria can quickly destroy large tracts of valuable wetland habitat," in the process, "jerking the habitat rug out from under other species" (Schultz 1997:6A).

Two of the most intensely trapped and managed properties, one tract of 150,000 acres in Vermilion Parish and a tract of 155,000 acres in Cameron Parish, were completely leveled by nutria, with peak takes of marketable pelts in the 60,000 to 70,000 figure, after which came sharp drops in production accompanied by poor pelt quality due to the lack of food supply.

The active Mississippi River Delta, comprising of about 350,000 acres with unprecedented growing seasons, also went to pieces by 1956-57, as a result of the 250 nutria transplanted there in 1951. There was a gradual rise from 1951 to the peak in the 1955-56 season, when nutria were everywhere with vegetative cover still standing. By the following season, only the pass banks appeared to be holding the delta together (O'Neil 1968:11).

Without proper management, the over-grazing nutria and muskrats completely denude a region's vegetation. Because they are so prolific, their populations expand rapidly with dire environmental consequences. As early as 1845, land survey crews described a Deltaic Plain eat-out, indicating clearly that muskrats have destroyed portions of their habitat periodically for more than 160 years (Managing the mysterious . . . 1956). At times, the problem has been extremely critical. In 1923, almost all of the *Chênière* Plain's marsh was eaten out. Eight years earlier, practically all of the region's muskrats had been killed by a deadly hurricane, but they rebounded quickly and overran the marsh (O'Neil 1949). Eaten-out areas frequently never recover completely from overpopulation pressure. Consequently, years may be needed for impacted habitats to produce even a small muskrat harvest (O'Neil and Linscombe 1975).

When an exploding population eats all of the existing vegetation, including the root mass, the end result is a "rotten wasteland" (Murchison 1978:5). In many cases, ranging nutrias are the catalyst for accelerated marsh losses. Eat-outs have turned many sections of marsh into a closely cropped lawn, which, in turn, helped transform marshes into open water. Sometimes these animals eat the entire plant, making it difficult for the vegetation to reestablish itself naturally (Saving our good 1995). Muskrats and nutria can cause a great deal of damage and have contributed directly and indirectly to the state's deteriorating wetlands. Because muskrats and nutria combined have helped destroy the marsh in Louisiana, Texas, and parts of Chesapeake Bay, these marshes are no longer a part of these state's natural storm protection system (Blakenship 1999).

"Herbivory" is the term used to describe this form of marsh destruction. Evans (1970) suggests it can take up to a decade for an eat-out area to recover. In 1998, the first coast-wide-nutria survey determined 23,960 acres had been destroyed by this grazing rodent. An April 2005 aerial survey revealed an additional 53,000 acres of marsh—an area slightly larger than the District of Columbia—damaged by nutria (Roach 2005). Several months after this survey, Hurricanes Katrina, Rita, Gustav, and Ike hit Louisiana. Every blade of grass devoured be nutria could have helped reduced the massive storm surges, but the rodent's habit of eating everything in sight reduced some of the marsh's ability to absorb the storms' impacts.

Hurricanes Katrina, Rita, Gustav, and Ike temporarily set back the nutria population, but given the animals' prolific nature, their recovery is certain. As a result, these mammals will continue to be an environmental issue. They can be controlled—nutria were wiped out in Britain during the 1980s—but without proper financial incentives, it is highly unlikely that the animal will be eradicated completely (Blankenship 1999).

To help manage the overgrazing problem, Louisiana initiated in the 2002-2003 trapping season a four dollars-per-tail "incentive payment" on nutria through the Coastwide Nutria Control Program (Louisiana Coastwide Nutria . . . 2006). By 2007, the program had paid more than six million dollars in incentive payments. A coastwide survey in 2009 showed the program is working, with a year-to-year consistent decrease in the acres lost to the voracious eating habits of the nutria. Prior to establishment of this control strategy, the state had 871 trappers, down from an average of 11,059 between 1977 and 1985 (Louisiana number of . . . 2005). The eat-out issue was of minimal concern when the fur market was strong, and trappers were annually harvesting 400,000 nutria.

In the new millennium, furriers are paying only $1.50 to $1.75 per animal. Their carcasses were worth about eighty cents apiece to alligator farmers. By 2009, with the downturn in the world economy, demand for nutria pelts was essentially dead. The market had virtually, vanished with perhaps only one businessman continuing to buy and sell nutria fur (Buskey 2009; Buskey 2009B).

Pelt Prices are on the Decline

"Trapping seemed to have peaked in the 1976-1977 season when the industry was worth about $25 million. Prices for nutria that season averaged $7.80; dropped to $4.21 in '78-'79; peaked at $8.19 in '80-'81; and bottomed out at $2.80 in '82-'84. In the 2004-2005 season, nutria sold for $1.50 and was valued at $55,657. Muskrat sold for $0.77 and was valued at $1,814" (Comparative take . . . 2005).

The coast-wide nutria control program
(From: Herbivory damage and . . . 2007)

Year	Nutria Tail's Harvested	Value of Harvest
2002-2003	308,160	1,232,640
2003-2004	332,596	1,330,384
2004-2005	297,535	1,190,140
2005-2006	168,596	675,371
2006-2007	375,683	1,878,415
Total	1,482,570	$6,306,950

The federally sponsored coast-wide nutria-control plan has reduced considerably wetland damage from the nutria population. Further, the strategy is not only exterminating more nutria, but it is also providing commercial watermen with a source of income during the winter off-season. Sharpshooters, hunters, and trappers are paid $5 for each nutria tail harvested. The goal of placing a bounty on the non-native species is designed to reduce the number of nutria to the carrying capacity of the landscape and in the process limit the destruction of the state's wetlands by these free-range grazing animals. The program, by mid-2009, appeared to be working, as surveys revealed the number of acres affected by foraging nutria has declined (Burdeau 200). Even with all of its myriad current problems, the state's fur harvest still generates about two million dollars annually from a dedicated trapping culture in north and South Louisiana (Louisiana Department of Wildlife 2004).

Nutria-induced wetland damage
(From Herbivory damage 2007; Wetland damage 2009)

Year	Acreage	Year	Acreage	Year	Acreage
1998	23,960	2002	21,185	2006	12,315
1999	27,356	2003	21,888	2007	9,244
2000	25,939	2004	19,906	2008	6,171
2001	22,139	2005	14,260	Total	198,192 or 319.31 square miles

The American Alligator

They hunt alligators during the hot months. They live far up from the gulf, in rude palmetto-roofed shanties and huts made of split cypress boards, on the banks and bordering shell mounds of Lake Salvador, Bayous des Allemands, St. Denis, Dupont, and Barataria, and numerous other sluggish tidal streams and lakes in the great tidewater wilderness of Louisiana (Wilkinson 1892:407).

Before there was a legal season, we used to hunt alligators every day, except in winter . . . I used to love to hunt them at night, with a light on my head. We used carbide lights at first, then switched to battery-powered. When the light passed over an alligator in the water, its eyes would shine like a taillight on a car. . . If the [eyes] were red [and close together], it was a small alligator; if they were real light [and far apart], it was a big one" (Gomez 1998:78).

First described in Louisiana in 1718, *Alligator mississippiensis* has survived more than two centuries of intensive hunting. Alligator oil was used as an engine lubricant during the steamboat period, and its hide has periodically met the needs of the world's fashion houses. But even after extensive exploitation to meet the Civil War demand for shoe leather and meat, the marshes supported an immense alligator population (Wilkinson 1892; Johnson 1969).

In his *History of Louisiana*, Le Page du Pratz recalls killing a twenty-foot alligator, whose head was three-feet-long and at least thirty-inches wide (Waldo 1957). In the late 1800s, fifteen-to eighteen-foot alligators were so commonplace that they attracted little attention. Indeed, the giant reptiles were so abundant they were a nuisance (True 1884; Wilkinson 1892). *Alligator mississippiensis* consequently have been hunted commercially since the mid-1800s, and "as late as 1890 some 280,000 alligator skins were being processed annually in the United States" (Waldo 1957:12). In New Orleans, the market value of alligator hides was quoted in the daily commercial reports of the local papers (Wilkinson 1892). Unfortunately, between 1880 and 1904 hide hunters' indiscriminate harvesting routines, radically reduced the species' breeding stock largely because the animal is rather docile and easy to harvest when using rather simple techniques.

Hunters developed three methods to track alligator: "shining" at night with a "bull-eye" lantern, using baited lines, or daytime "polling."

An alligator hunter "shining" for the eyes of his quarry. (Image from *The Century Magazine,* January 1892.)

When shining, a hunter poled his *pirogue* along a watercourse while throwing a beam of light from one bank to the other. Since alligators are nocturnal, a "bull-eye" lantern was used to spot the luminous eyes of an unsuspecting alligator. As long as the light is trained on an alligator's eyes, the animal will not move. The hunter could then kill the reptile with a gun at close range. The dead animal was then either pulled into the boat or dragged ashore to be skinned the next morning.

Before there was a legal season, we used to hunt alligators every day, except in winter. . . . I used to love to hunt them at night, with a light on my head. We used carbide lights at first, then switched to battery-powered. When the light passed over an alligator in the water, its eyes would shine like a taillight on a car. . . . If the [eyes] were red [and close together], it was a small alligator; if they were real light [and far apart], it was a big one (Gomez 1998:78).

Baited hooks suspended from a forked pole hung over a waterway were also quite efficient in capturing alligators. After the alligator swallowed the bait, the hook was ingested and the animal was caught. As soon as the trapper found the baited line in the water, he pulled it up carefully, and, as the alligator surfaced, shot the reptile between the eyes with a small bore gun, which killed it. After the animal was dragged to shore or loaded into a boat, an axe blow severed the spine to prevent the tail from moving (Comeaux 1972). The process was repeated until all of the baited lines were checked. If an alligator was too small, the trapper cut the line and the animal's digestive juices dissolved the hook.

Poling involved the use of a seven-to-eight-foot pole "of two-inch dressed pine with an iron hook at one end" (Report on fur-bearing 1918:96). Once an alligator hole was located, the hunter would call a reptile by mimicking its cry. Generally, an alligator would respond by crawling out of its hole. As the head surfaced, the hunter would hit the gator between the eyes with a sharp, heavy axe. If the axe blow failed to either stun or kill the animal, the reptile retreated into its cave. The trapper had to dig into the cave and prod the reptile with the pole and iron hook. Once the animal was hooked, the trapper pulled it out of its hole and finished killing it. Depending on the reptile's size, this could be a formidable task.

> It is said by experienced alligator hunters that the pole method is the only proper method as commercial-sized alligators can be secured in this manner while in shooting at night all sizes particularly small ones, of not much commercial value are killed. Skins from 4 to 8 feet are considered best by hide buyers and smaller or larger ones are not wanted (Report on fur-bearing 1918:96).

Value of alligators hides in 1916 and 1917

(Alligators were graded according to size—measured from the tip of the jaw to the tip of the tail. A skin six feet, eleven inches would be sold as a six-foot skin).
(From: Report on fur-bearing 1918:96)

Size	1916	1917	Percent change
7 foot	$0.90	$1.35	50%
6 foot	$0.60	$0.90	50%
5 foot	$0.40	$0.65	63%
4 foot	$0.20	$0.45	125%
3 foot	$0.10	$0.25	150%
2 foot	$0.05	$1.05	200%

Historically, hides greater than seven feet brought the same price, no matter the length. This is no longer the case—the bigger the gator, the higher the price. Despite a continuous decline in the reptile's population, the government took no protective measures until 1960, when a five-foot size limit and sixty-day season were established. At that time, a hide brought about twenty dollars. By 1981, alligator hides sold for $125 (Palmisano 1972; Breaux 1983).

The Alligator is Put on the Endangered Species List

In the twentieth century, illegal hunting and the interstate shipment of the illicit hides became a serious problem. As a result, alligator hunting was limited from mid-April to mid-June in 1960 and 1961. In 1962, with the prices for skins at three dollars per linear foot, buyers, dealers, and trappers lobbied for relaxed size restrictions, because the marsh's supply of large gators had been depleted. Their efforts failed. The state government closed the season, and the Federal Game Reserves followed Louisiana's lead shortly thereafter. Closing the season, along with landowner cooperation,

Dave Hall, a member of the "samurai class of the conservation movement," reported that Kraemer just west of Lac Des Allemands, was next to the Florida Everglades, the alligator-poaching capital of the United States (Reisner 1991).

enforcement activity, and sympathetic courts contributed to the return of a viable alligator population in South Louisiana's marshes (Reisner 1991:15).

To assist in the management effort, the alligator was placed on the federal list of rare and endangered species in 1966. This proved to be an ineffective deterrent to poachers who could make "$4,500 for one night's outlawin'." The result was a very active underground economy in which "game laws were violated more than the speed limit" (Reisner 1991:33). Using 220-horsepower airboats, with a top speed of over sixty-miles per hour, the "outlaws" could run circles around the game warden's fifty-horsepower bass boats. The poachers were winning. In fact, one Atlanta, Georgia buyer—Q. C. Plott Raw Fur and Ginseng Company—marketed in three years more than 127,000 alligator skins, which were shipped primarily overseas. In New York, one dealer exported in three years "a quarter of America's surviving alligators. . . . Most were doused with fragrant oil to camouflage the smell and packed in wooden boxes labeled 'machine parts'" (Reisner 1991:53).

To halt this illegal enterprise, federal laws in 1970 were enacted to prohibit the interstate shipment of alligators trapped illegally. Under the terms of the Endangered Species Act and an amendment to the Lacey Act of 1906, persons dealing in alligator pelts could be imprisoned. Throughout the southeastern United States, aggressive enforcement of this legislation allowed the reptile to survive (Nichols, et al. 1976). These legal measures were supplemented by habitat preservation measures and an aggressive research program at Rockefeller Refuge that allowed the alligator to be managed as a renewable resource, with a controlled annual harvest based on habitat quality. These events set the stage for the season to be reopened over a limited geographical range. By 1975, the Federal government had delisted the reptile in Cameron, Calcasieu, and Vermilion parishes. In 1976, the state's controlled harvest consisted of 4,300 hides selling for $510,840 (O'Neil and Linscombe 1975).

The hunt area was gradually expanded until 1981, when the September season was opened statewide. Since 1981, the state has used tags to regulate the number of alligators that can be harvested. The tag includes the state's abbreviation, the year, a serial number, and a locking mechanism to keep the tag attached to the reptile's tail. The label stays with the animal from point of capture to the tannery. Since only tagged hides can be legally bought and sold, the temptation to "outlaw" has been eliminated. The end result is that the American alligator has made a dramatic recovery in coastal Louisiana (Gomez 1998). In the 1999 season, depending on size and quality, the price per foot ranged from six dollars to twenty-four dollars. At these prices, a good alligator hunter could clear in the month-long season between $5,000 and $10,000—depending on the number of alligator tags he was allocated (Hallowell 2001). By all measures, the program has been a success, with each hunter being awarded alligator tags based on habitat quality and other variables.

When the alligator went on the endangered species list an important source of income to Louisiana's trappers vanished, 1954. (Photo courtesy of Louisiana Wildlife and Fisheries.)

Alligator Farms

Because the season is short and demand for alligator products is high, more than 100 commercial alligator farms supply hides to the global market in the first decade of the twenty-first century, turning this prehistoric creature into a cash crop. Alligator farms are, however, a complex and costly business. Along with the expenses linked to building alligator houses and setting up temperature units within the structures, farmers must maintain drainage systems in order to promote good alligator hygiene, and buy, freeze, and use tens of thousands of pounds of feed—primarily nutria meat—that can cost as much as $20,000 a week. They must also pay the high utility expenses associated with keeping the enclosures at the correct temperature and pay to skin and ship the skins to overseas markets. If they have a breeding program, a pond is fenced in that contains alligators in the eight to ten-year-old range. Since alligators do not normally successfully hatch eggs until they are ten-years old, farmers must buy eggs from approved suppliers/landowners until their breeding program produces an appropriate supply.

The "farming" operation, therefore, begins with the harvesting of eggs. Since the eggs are initially collected in the wild, the harvest can earn the landowner from two dollars to five dollars per egg. To maintain the wild stock, farmers must return a percentage of the farmed alligators four feet or longer to the marsh (Gomez 1998; Elsey 2005). This percentage varies, but is consistent with the natural survival rate. Replenishing the wild stock from farm-raised alligators ensures the reptile will continue to be a part of Louisiana's wetland landscape for many years to come.

A normal release season for farm-raised alligators begins in mid-March and continues into late August. Louisiana Department of Wildlife and Fisheries personnel measure, mark, tag, and sack between 40,000 and 50,000 alligators that must be released into their wetlands of origin. Since alligator farms are scattered from Cut Off to Winnsboro to Hackberry and West Monroe, the release program is a labor-intensive and time-consuming process, but, under ideal conditions, a crew can work with from 800 to 1,000 alligators a day (Elsey 2005).

Proliferation of alligator farms reduced alligator skin prices and affected the local trapping economy. It will take time to estimate the overall influence of these commercial enterprises on the indigenous trappers, but the industry is accustomed to fluctuations. Even with market problems and a decline in the price of skins, alligators continue to generate revenue for trappers as well as farmers. In 2004, the value of hides and meat was about $36 million (Elsey 2005).

Before the downturn in the economy in late 2008 and 2009, a hard-working and dedicated alligator farmer would sell between 120,000 to 150,000 skins a year. Demand was so high, that it was difficult for farmers to fill all of their orders. One farmer noted in 2008, he sold 50,000 skins; in July 2009, he had not sold a hide. The demand for luxury goods has declined dramatically. With the demand down for high-end alligator products, there is no market; as a result, the state's alligator farms are hurting and cutting costs or closing their operations. Consumers are simply not buying purses, belts, shoes, and watch bands made from the tanned alligator skins. In order for these farms to survive, the market has to improve, for overhead expenses are constant and some are just barely making ends meet (Ward 2009).

The Trapping Industry

When trapping time comes, or a friend reports that the alligators are more plentiful than usual, some grow restless on the jobs. With high oyster prices, they can expect two months or more of bonanza pay on a lugger; an especially good season with the rats, and a man can bring home more in a day than a steady job will net in six months. Some of the [oil] companies have worked out a compromise. As trapping opens, for instance, a man takes a leave of absence. He returns satisfied, comparatively enriched, a happier Deltan. Deny him this, and he will fidget, swear at his Yankee overseer, and quit for the marsh (Kane 1944:259).

Like many businesses, good and bad years are part of the trapping industry's natural economic cycle. Throughout its history, the industry has had economic problems. Low prices, competition from synthetic fibers, the closure of trapping areas, the anti-fur campaign of animal rights advocates, and other factors contribute to the industry's yearly success or failure. Trapping is not an attractive employment option for many young people. To others it is a significant part of their winter employment cycle; trapping is in their genes (Bertrand and Beale 1965; Shelton 1987). Yet many young people are unwilling to become *piégeurs*. They prefer to seek better-paying jobs in the area's extensive oil economy. Jobs as deck hands, roughnecks, derrick men up on the monkey board, roustabouts, and welders offer a steady income and the promise of high wages. Although pelt prices were not particularly high, in the pre- and post-World II eras, the additional income was welcomed by many South Louisiana households. During this period, the proceeds from a trap line employing from fifty to 250 traps was an important buffer against economic hardships.

Many people go into the marsh because they enjoy the out-of-doors; for them, trapping is a form of recreation or therapy. At times, the pursuit can be quite profitable, for in 1977 *Chênière* Plain trappers received $9 or better for nutria pelts (Trapping ends in . . . 1977)—a considerable increase over the fifty cents paid in the 1943-1944 season, when 436 pelts were harvested. In the early 1940s, there was no market for nutria fur, but that changed quickly. In addition, outboard engines and faster boats changed the industry.

A *piégeur* no longer had to live in the marsh. Their homes could be on the edge of the marsh. They pulled their boat to a public landing, or kept it at the marina, and ran their trap lines on a daily basis. The outboard made it easy. Before the outboard, a trapper had to live in the marsh. They had to trap their lease from houseboats or rustic camps, often made of palmetto or scrap lumber. Houseboats were preferred, as they were part of the trapper's lifestyle and easily moved. All other structures were simple one-room shacks that served as living quarters and drying shed. The odor could be dreadful, the flies formidable, and the labor hard and intense, but such was the life of a *piégeur*.

A remote trapper's camp. (Photo from *Louisiana Conservationists*, vol. 20, no. 9-10, 1968.)

The Trappers Temporary Encampments

Suddenly we rounded the point, and there, almost hidden by the hanging moss, was a shelter for some nomad of the swamp, a hut, palmetto-thatched and raised high above the water on great posts of cypress. A dugout rested against the roughly fashioned steps. The still wet blade of a paddle glistened in the light. Traps hung from a railing of a small platform that served as a porch. And through a square hole that answered for a window came an impression of swarthy skin, straight, black hair, a sport of red a few beads— then a twist of the bayou and it was gone. But it was life and gave promise of something more beyond (Schoonover 1911:90).

Before 1914 to 1922, a period that witnessed an increase from eight cents to fifty cents per muskrat pelt (Branan 1938; Chatterton 1944), hunting was more profitable than trapping, with a brace of ducks selling for twenty-five cents. But, with the 500 percent increase in fur prices, locals quickly changed their winter subsistence occupation from hunting to trapping. From late fall to early winter, Louisiana's *piégeurs* spent every day from sunup to sundown making the rounds of their traps. By 1916, muskrat was the mainstay of the trapping industry.

Ten years later, approximately 20,000 people were engaged in trapping in Louisiana's coastal wetlands. In the 1920s, muskrat pelts were made into coats, and suddenly housewives and working girls could afford a fur coat. The garment industry did not waste any part of a muskrat pelt, the dark brownish-black back, the reddish or golden hued sides and the white or silver "bellies." During this "flapper era," muskrat pelts were dyed to resemble sable and mink, while the trimmings were used to make felt hats (Daspit 1948).

In the wake of the resulting regional economic boom, the state's marshes were considered worthy of protection, and landowners began to realize that their wetland tracts were natural "rat ranches" where they "could maximize muskrat production by regulating trapping and initiating habitat management" (Gomez 1998:159). By the 1925-26 season, trappers were harvesting pelts worth $1.30 apiece. Louisianians had found wealth and prosperity in the marshes many previously had considered worthless. Financially, trappers were doing well, as three pelts were collectively worth more than the country's average daily wage.

By 1930, entrepreneurs developed 170,000 acres in Cameron Parish as a mammoth muskrat ranch. A contemporary observed that "ninety-five miles of canals, sixteen-feet-wide and six-feet deep have been dug here, providing easy access, by water, to every part of the marsh, which has a maximum length of twenty-nine miles, a width of fourteen miles, and a frontage of five miles on the Gulf" (Graves 1930:409). Permanent male-only camps were built for the trappers, who could make "good money" in the seventy-to-seventy-five-day trapping season. One trapper recalled:

I'd walk that marsh every day. It ain't nothing to skinning a muskrat. You don't use your knife but twice to do it. I'd find one in a trap, kill it with a club I carried, take it out, reset the trap, then walk to the next one. I could skin one before I got to the next trap, throw the carcass away, and put the skin in my pack. I'd be so tired, I'd say, 'Oh, Lord, don't let there be one in this next trap' Them wet hides in that pack were heavy . . . Its an awful lot of work, but there's good cash money in trapping. We made six thousand dollars two years running once, and that's in only forty-five days . . . It use to be a lot of good money in that ol' marsh, but the big shots have taken it all over now. Soon as a man gets to making a lot of money, these big wheels come along (Jones 2007:150).

Before World War II, entire families migrated into the marsh. Collectively, this transient population annually could have easily exceeded 100,000 people, ca. 1936. (Photo from the author's collection.)

With the record high prices for pelts, outsiders, or *chivos* (goats) descended in such numbers that, by the end of the 1926 season, a *piégeur* was lucky to catch thirty-to-fifty animals a day. The industry was essentially uncontrolled. Even so, a good trapper could earn from $3,000 to $4,000 in the two-and-half month season—when the national average was about $1,200 a year. During this period, in Plaquemines Parish alone, pelt sales were collectively worth several million dollars. Trappers were flush with cash, but unaccustomed to handling this kind of easy money, the marshdweller was an easy mark for charlatans, hucksters, and other slick-talking salesmen (Jeansonne 1995).

These *piégeurs* set from 250 to as many as 400 traps on any available land that was crisscrossed by meandering muskrat "runs." No one was concerned about property ownership, only the land's productivity. The marshdwellers trapped where they wished. Their right to roam and harvest the land at will was never questioned, until the boom years. Suddenly, land that was considered worthless now had value. But because the coastal marshlands had been devalued, land titles were poorly defined.

Under the Swamp Land Acts of 1849 and 1850, the Federal government had transferred thousands of wetland acres to the states (Cowdrey 1977). Louisiana had sold much of this land for next to nothing, but since it was considered unfit for human habitation, many landowners—who were often illiterate—had neglected to pay their property taxes, and the land's ownership reverted to the state. When the property's perceived value increased, landowners clamored to reclaim their

A conservation agent removing a trap set too close to a muskrat house, ca. 1924. (Photo from the *Seventeenth Biannual Report of the Department of Conservation, 1924-1926.*)

property, and the state responded by enacting legislation that permitted the original titleholders to pay their back taxes and reclaim their properties. Where

> land was not claimed by individual owners, it was gobbled up by land companies, many organized solely to exploit the fur trade. Titles and leases to trapping lands were obtained by means both foul and fair: through purchase and redemption and through chicanery and liaison with corrupt officials and judges. By 1926, some marshland was worth more than dry land" (Jeansonne 1995:34)

The new landowners made trappers pay for the right to work land they previously trapped for free. As a result, the local trappers were confused. "They had no understanding of titles, rents, leases, or rights. They could not read the No Trespassing signs" (Jeansonne 1995:34). Even so, several communities in St. Bernard Parish, for example, owed their origins to the Isleños and Spanish land grants. Bencheque, Reggio, Violet, Shell Beach/Alluvial City, and Hopedale (*La Chinche*) trace their roots back to the early nineteenth century. The communities' elders probably had land claims that predated the Swamp Land Acts, but their illiteracy prevented them from understanding what they owned and their rights of ownership (Din 1988). Locally, these remote lands, termed "down below," were the haunts of the region's trappers and were always considered free for everyone's use (Gowland 2003).

Prior to the land boom, taxes, and other matters settled by attorneys, a *piégeurs* most important investment was his double steel-jawed traps—the first to catch the foot of the animal and the second to crush and hold the animal so it could not escape—and the time required to walk the marsh laying out his trap line (Graves 1930). Each "set" involved an unbaited trap intentionally positioned along a muskrat or nutria run. The trap was attached to a chain with a ring positioned back in the marsh grass and anchored into the ground with a cane pole.

The traps were sold in barrels containing 156 traps, which cost from sixty-five dollars to eighty-five dollars. For an investment of under $200, a man could become a professional trapper (Kammer 1941). Although the law specifically permitted only 250 traps to be set in a day, it was impossible for law enforcement officials to locate and count every trap set, and some trappers took full advantage of this fact.

To work the land, trappers went into the *marais* with their entire family, for everyone was involved in the industry. Women and children worked with the men, walking the trap lines and cleaning and stretching the skins. The adults were joined by their inevitably large broods. Among *les petit habitants*, seven or eight children were the norm. Ten or more was considered a sign of God's benevolence, and the children's names often all began with the same letter, such as Odile, Odalia, Olive, Olivier, Olivia, Octavia, Olite, and Otta or Valmir, Valmor, Valsin, Valcourt, and Valérien (Ramsey 1957; Crété 1981). Five to ten children improved the work force and instilled in each child an appreciation for the land and an unrelenting and tireless work ethic.

Marsh Access and Ownership "Misunderstandings"

Marshdwellers brought order to what could have been chaos by using cane poles to mark their trapping areas (Daspit 1948B). Once staked out, individual plots were respected. *Traînasses* were cut to gain marsh access. Since a *piégeur* often made several runs a day to check his traps, these shallow ditches allowed the trapper access to his snares and the means to transport the trapped animals back to his camp. These watercourse locations frequently had to be changed, as water movement along the narrow route often widened the channel. Trappers did not utilize these enlarged channels, so they constantly moved their *traînasses* to protect their trapping lands (Kammer 1941).

They managed "their" property carefully and were instrumental in making sure their ditches did not become permanent features. They wanted a "pirogue trail," not a twenty-five-foot-wide canal.

It was understood a *traînasse* crossing a claim could be used as a water route to another trapper's property, but traps were never set on someone else's land (Davis 1976). Folk law dictated a person's trapping ground was always to be honored. When fur prices escalated and landowners demanded trappers pay for the right to trap, they refused. They could not understand why they had to pay for something that was always free. *Chivos* were recruited to put the locals out of work, and the marshdwellers responded by firing upon and otherwise harassing their replacements (Jeansonne 1995). These outsiders competed for the choice trapping areas. Their blatant disregard for individual trapping rights culminated in the St. Bernard and Plaquemines Parish Trapper's War, a tumultuous time when land company guards and deputies patrolled the area (Washburn 1951). The trappers may have been "confused" on land issues and legal "mumbo-jumbo," but they knew "their" land and were willing to fight for "their" trapping rights. After all, they walked the land and were keenly aware of every nuisance. They were comfortable in their sea-level habitat and were not going to move or be intimidated by others.

The Deltaic Plain Trapper's War

What do you think, Mr. Easton (then *Courier* publisher Tris Easton), those Americans are going to do? Why do you think they have one office in Houma? It is for collecting rent on those marsh and prairie lands for trapping the muskrat.

You and me, and our fathers and our grandfathers have lived here for one hundred and fifty years without paying rent for trapping on the marsh, and after all that time, they want us to pay one hundred dollars for a half mile of land, even if there are no muskrats there.

You see the object of that rent? It is for keeping the Creoles poor. Ah, I see their design. And when Telesse Bodouin sees, he sees well. And when those Yankees, represented here by Alidore Picou, try to make the poor Creoles more poor than he is, Telesse will be there to protect the people.

What are we going to do if there is no more land for trapping, and how are we going to live?

You think we are going to allow ourselves to be starved, me and my father? No! They will never collect that rent. What do I care about those Yankees? I didn't ask them to come to this parish. What was good for my father is good for me. He traps muskrat on those marsh lands; I trap muskrats there too. He goes to Dupont's (A. M. and J. C. Dupont's big general merchandise store then in downtown Houma) to buy his traps and provisions for the winter. I go there too. He passes by the barroom and drinks his toddy. I make my own liqueur since prohibition.

No, my friend, we will never consent to pay those rents to trap muskrats on the marsh. It is an imposition.

They tell us that because those Yankees bought those marshes for fifteen cents an arpent (a little more than an acre), and don't pay taxes, they believe they are going to run this parish. Now is the time for you and me and our friends to make the Yankee understand they have no say in this matter.

For some time, they have had their foot on our heads, but now is the time for Telesse Bodouin; we are going to fix this parish to suit ourselves. If we say there is going to free trapping on the marsh lands and prairies, there is no use for them to kick, there is going to be free trapping, that's all.

You read the newspapers? I don't read English, but my brother Alphonse reads the *Houma Courier* to me every day.

I think the papers say the best thing they have ever said when they say this is not a question of sentiment. That's just what I say.

I say to you again, that I see very plainly what the Yankees have their eye on. They want to deprive the poor Creole of his bread, but we are better informed than they think. How are we going to buy automobiles if we consent to pay the rent for trapping? You are going to see hard times in this parish if the people don't do something.

The muskrat is the back-bone of the prosperity. Ask the banks in Houma. If it were not for muskrat money, where would they find cash to advance to other people? It is muskrat money that keeps Houma going economically.

Separate from any rental issues, by the early 1930s muskrat coat popularity had waned, and the prices paid local trappers for the skins had dropped dramatically.

The locals knew the marsh well and continued to trap, regardless of who was supposed to own "their" trapping land. When they heard the putt-putt of a landowner's patrol boat, they would disappear into the labyrinth of marsh waterways. Eventually, 150 delta trappers were cited with contempt of court for trapping land they considered theirs. In 1924, Judge Leander Perez intervened and helped organize the St. Bernard Trappers' Association and the Plaquemines Parish Protective Association. For a one-time investment of $100 a trapper acquired one share in the association. This assured this share-holder could trap land that was originally his. An annual fee of fifty dollars was assessed by the association for a lease. The *piégeur*s liked the arrangement, but since many were illiterate and often spoke only Spanish, they did not understand "the legal chants and spells that permitted them to tend their traps unmolested" (Jeansonne 1995:36). These individuals thought they could trap in their "back yards" forever, for in their minds the marsh was free for everyone's use (Nunez 1979).

Because the price of fur had reached an unprecedented height, the St. Bernard Trappers' Association leases were transferred through a bit of chicanery to J. Walter Michel. The trappers were led to believe this new arrangement would allow them to exchange a one-year lease for an eight-year lease. This was not the case. Lease prices were tripled, and those that knew a little arithmetic were suspicious, particularly since potential lessees had to be "personally acceptable" to Michel who could, in reality, lease to anyone willing to pay the inflated price.

An attorney working for the Association explained the scheme to approximately 800 trappers, who grew angry and responded by filing a lawsuit to annul the agreement. Because the trappers were misled by Judge Perez, he was considered the most hated man in St. Bernard Parish. In fact, the *piégeurs* had sworn to kill him. The ensuing trial featured courtroom fistfights, charges and counter-charges, mysterious land transfers, suspicious bookkeeping, questionable board of directors meetings, family alliances, hostilities, arrests, beatings, libelous allegations, conspiracies, contempt citations, bizarre legal complications and strategies, that eventually led to a decision annulling the leases. The trappers were ecstatic. Perez announced he would appeal and his cousin, John R. Perez, went into the land business (Jeansonne 1995; Din 1988).

Within weeks after the decision, John R. Perez paid $600,000 to the Phillips Land Company of New Orleans for 100,000 acres. The company's legacy may be the Phillips canals in St. Mary and Lafourche parishes. The Chicago meat-packing Swift family sold an additional 10,000 acres, described as the richest area in the delta, for $125,000. He also bought eight square miles known as the Finkle lands and an additional 15,000 acres of the Schwab lands. In a short period, John Perez had assembled "one of the greatest trapping empires in the world" (Jeansonne 1995:51). More than 200 square miles of marsh in Plaquemines and St. Bernard parishes were under his control for an investment of nearly $1,000,000 (adjusted for inflation about twelve million dollars in 2009).

John Perez subleased the land to E. P. Brady, who represented the Delaware-Louisiana Fur Trading Company (Gowland 2003). The company owned or leased well over a million acres of marshland that was subdivided into smaller tracts, ranging from 125 acres to 1,000 and 2,000 acre parcels, and sometimes more. These parcels were leased to trappers for a flat rental fee for at least three years. In the lease, the trapper was responsible for "ditching, building of levees and the planting or seeding of known muskrat food grasses" (Arthur 1927:107). Terrebonne Parish's Brady Canal is one indicator of Brady's fur interest.

Landowners gradually began to demand rent to use their land. Trappers protested, and the matter ended in the Louisiana Supreme Court. The Court decided trappers must obtain permission and pay a fee to the landowner for the right to trap. This decision did not settle the issue, for trappers maintained the marshes were a free area where they could trap as they pleased (Kammer 1941). They were confused as to who controlled the right to trap on what land. Without a clear understanding of ownership, these trappers felt they had a "free" right of use.

John R. Perez accused the *piégeurs* of trespassing on his land and then began to destroy the locals' camps. In addition, E. P. Brady demanded payment from the Isleños for the right to trap on the Perez tract. Trespassing signs began to appear on land the *piégeurs* had "used unencumbered for generations." *Piégeurs* "now had to pay for the right to trap or risk arrest and prosecution for poaching" (Gowland 2003:424). The trappers were enraged. This feeling of betrayal was further enhanced when the Louisiana Supreme Court reversed the decision that annulled their leases and refused to lease any part of what was described as "the greatest trapping empires in the world." They were mad, and sporadic violence broke out, intensifying when the Perezes hired *chivos* to trap their land.

One week before the opening of the 1926 season, the "Trappers War" (sometimes called the War of the *Tejanos*), broke out when a small raiding party of Perez guards aboard the oyster lugger *Dolores* attacked Delacroix Island trappers. About 400 armed *piégeurs* outgunned the men aboard the *Dolores* and quickly won the fight. Within hours, the trappers predicted they "would have a thousand armed men to fight the company guards and sheriff's deputies" (Jeansonne 1995:58). All roads leading into Delacroix and all of the marsh lands were under their control; trees were then cut down to block access to Delacroix. Company guards and outsiders abandoned their camps and left the region quickly to escape the enraged Isleños. The next day, the trappers also went home. When the governor drove into Delacroix to assess the damage, he found no firearms or evidence of the previous day's battle. "The town was quiet and almost abandoned" (Jeansonne 1995:59).

Shortly after the siege, Perez found himself without any imported trappers to lease his land; hence, there were no funds to cover the cost of the land purchases. The trapping empire was in disarray. As a result, John R. Perez sold the Phillips and Swift lands to Manuel Molero, who purchased the properties on behalf of the local

Manuel Molero versus Leander Perez

Manuel Molero was probably the wealthiest Isleño in Louisiana. He invested in a variety of businesses. Gowland (2003:422) remarks that Molero owned a grocery store in Delacroix "and a fleet of produce delivery trucks that doubled as bootlegging vehicles." He was, indeed, an "extraordinary man" and along with his attorney, Oliver Livaudais, sided with the Isleño trappers against the power of Leander Perez.

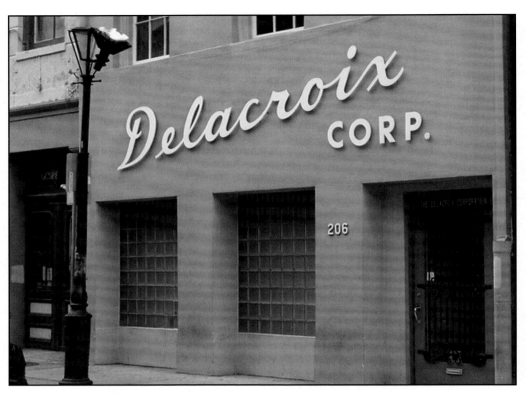

The Delacroix Corporation's French Quarter office, 2009. (Photo by the author.)

marshdwellers. This purchase on November 23, 1926 ended the Trappers' War. Molero subsequently formed the Acme Land Company—the predecessor of the Delacroix Corporation (Gowland 2003).

The *piégeur*s agreed to pay for use of the land by pledging a percentage of each year's catch to retire the $800,000 purchase price for these tracts. The 1926-27 trapping season was outstanding. Everyone was making money. Molero's marshland was generating a profit. In the flood of 1927, a group of New Orleans businessmen paid $1.5 million to Molero to allow the levee at Caernarvon to be dynamited to divert water out of the Mississippi as a means of protecting New Orleans. After the 1927 flood, the fur fad ended. When the Depression hit in the 1930s, the industry collapsed, in the process deepening the already entrenched poverty within the wetlands.

The Depression, World War II, and the Trapping Industry

Between 1928 and 1933, the price of a muskrat pelt declined from a dollar forty-two to nineteen cents. Trappers, now "little better off than the animals they hunt[ed]," found it harder and harder to pay off the land they had bought (Jeansonne 1995:60). Many went to work for the Delacroix Corporation, and some began working on shares. In this system, a trapper kept 50 to 65 percent of his catch. The remainder went to the landowner (Din 1988).

Many Isleño and Acadian trappers persisted in believing the *marais* was free. Their ancestors had trapped these lands, and they felt they needed neither the owner's permission nor a state license to trap. This widespread belief led to poaching, trespassing, and an occasional flare-up of violence (Din 1988).

Pres. Franklin Roosevelt's New Deal helped restore optimism and promote modernization in the country and in some wetland communities. The Works Progress

Counting and packing furs at a Marsh Island camp, ca. 1948. (Photo from the *Third Biennial Report of the Louisiana Department of Wild Life and Fisheries, 1948-1949*)

Grading pelts at a New Orleans wholesaler's warehouse (Photo from the *Jefferson Parish Yearly Review*, 1939.)

This sign is a reminder of the WPA's importance, 2009. (Photo courtesy of Carl A. Brasseaux.)

Administration (WPA) provided employment and assisted the Isleños and others through these hard times, when almost a quarter of all Americans were out of work. The St. Bernard Parish courthouse was built with WPA assistance, while Cameron, Iberia, and Terrebonne parishes also constructed new courthouses with WPA funding. New Orleans' Sewerage and Water Board also upgraded the city's drainage system by installing nine new pumps with the ability to drain one billion gallons water a day (Vileisis 1997; Leighninger 2000; Means 2003). In addition, the WPA travel guides provided a literary journey through Louisiana that focused on virtually every aspect of the state's regional cultures, while also fostering readers' opinions that were often distorted, for they did not report on the economic hardships and associated social problems that accompanied the Depression (Means 2003).

Additionally, trapping began to recover. By the early 1940s, thanks to a dramatic increase in wartime prices for furs and skins, prices had stabilized at about five dollars. For a time, tons of meat were shipped to Northern markets and sold as "marsh rabbit," or disguised as terrapin. This created an additional income stream for the formerly economically beleaguered trappers (Frost 1939).

Because of the trapping industry's fluctuating economic fortunes, the state intervened. A season was established, and pelts were graded for the first time. Landowners allocated parcels of land to individual *piégeurs*. By designating property to licensed trappers, poaching on choice trapping grounds was terminated (Washburn 1951).

Arrangements with landowners varied. A trapper had to lease trapping rights, and, in Terrebonne Parish, a seasonal lease was as much as $800 (Graves 1930). On the other hand, the landowner may have leased the land to the highest bidder. Or, the trapper may have leased the land on shares. In general, a *piégeur* worked on a 50-50 basis. When furs were scarce, a 65-35 share was negotiated, with the trapper receiving 65 percent (Frost 1939). These ratios have changed over time. Even so, over the past half-century, a trapper often paid as much as 35-to-40 percent in cash or skins to the landowners (Shelton 1987).

To take advantage of a sudden change in fur prices, a trapper would hide some of his choicest furs from his primary fur buyer. He sold these "bootlegged" furs to another buyer or entrusted them with another *piégeur*, who would arrange the sale. In at least one case, these bootlegged furs were concealed in a wooden coffin (Ramsey 1957).

Trappers who hid their skins were probably evading one of the New Orleans' fur companies, such as Steinberg Fur, or Houma's independent fur dealers—Blum and Bergeron or Mahler Fur. These companies purchased fur based on five grades: 1) tops; 2) seconds; 3) mediums; 4) kits and damaged; and 5) mice. Even though others were engaged in the fur business, the New Orleans' fur dealers were critical to the industry's success. These professional buyers often purchased more pelts than they could sell. This practice ensured that they always had a backlog and thus could hedge the market. The Mirandona, Mares, J. F. Landry, Decatur Fur, William E Voelkel, and Steinberg firms also had sufficient money to keep ahead of the market. This practice was also good for the trapper in the field. In addition, their efforts helped promote the industry (Frost 1939; Gomez 1998). These dealers were part of a network that averaged between 1928 and 1950 forty wholesalers. These dealers obtained their furs from approximately 200 buyers (Sale of fur 1950). In the second half of the twentieth century, the industry began to decline, and the last New Orleans fur dealership closed its doors in 1989.

Landowners, as well as their agents and lessees, patrolled their respective lands before and after the season to prevent poaching. This was necessary because, prior to the opening of the season, a poacher, working at night, typically set from fifty to

---

Did the Trapper get Fair Market Value for His/Her Pelts?

"If the market price for muskrat is, say, fifty cents, the landlord will set his price at forty cents, take his 35 per cent of the latter price, and give the trapper his 65 per cent. In this way, the landlord is actually making almost 50 per cent, instead of the stimulated 35 per cent" (Kammer 1941:102). It is difficult to determine how widespread this practice was among landowners.

seventy-five traps per outing—enough to have a significant impact on the number of pelts taken legally at the beginning of the season. Since there was no way of detecting a skin taken from an animal caught out of season, poaching proved a highly profitable enterprise (Kammer 1941).

Poaching was only one of many human threats to the trappers' arduous way of life. To maximize income, *piégeurs* lived in camps on land they reluctantly rented for trapping purposes. Since many, if not most trappers were not well educated, they were at the mercy of fur buyers and landlords, who persuaded them to put their marks on what they believed was a bill of sale for trapping lands. The *piégeur*, under such circumstances, was completely at the mercy of the landowner, so much so that the landowner often determined where the trapper could trap. In addition, trapping leases usually included a clause that the trapper had to sell all of his catch to the landowner or his agent on unfavorable terms. It was the *piégeur's* word against a signed document. Such "misunderstandings" were particularly commonplace in St. Bernard and Plaquemines parishes. In these parishes, trapping land could only be leased if the trapper supported the landowner's candidate for political office (Kammer 1941).

Because of the resulting financial hardships, many trappers turned to the Farm Security Administration for loans. In the late 1930s, 261 St. Bernard and Plaquemines Parish lease-holding trappers borrowed nearly $110,000—the equivalent of $1.4 million in inflation adjusted 2009 dollars. Statewide, 185 trappers borrowed nearly $480,000—the equivalent of $6.1 million in 2009 dollars. These funds were used to purchase 23,409 acres. On average, each *piégeur* paid twenty dollars and fifty cents an acre to trap on 125 acres. These loans were repaid on the basis of 35 to 50 percent of the catch. The trappers were good risks, since only 3 percent were delinquent in their repayments.

Through this arrangement trappers could, for the first time, own their own land; they were no longer "share trappers." For those trappers who did not participate in this plan, they had to continue to lease land. This leasing changed in 1940, when state legislation was passed that mandated an individual lease could not exceed 640 acres, no lessee could own more than one lease at a time, and land leased from the state could not be sub-leased. This legislation effectively removed speculators, who would lease large tracts from the state at a nominal fee and then sub-lease to the trappers at a substantial profit (Kammer 1941; Din 1988).

Whether they owned their land, or worked as a share trapper, during the late fall and early winter trapping season, the entire family moved from their home to their marsh camp or houseboat. Trappers often a one- or two-room, dilapidated, wooden or palmetto-covered huts initially developed by local Native Americans as their "camps" (Daspit 1948B; Cheniere Hurricane Centennial 1994). These crude, temporary dwellings were later built with scrap materials, the occupants believing that they did not merit improvement since the structures were utilized only a few months per year. In some cases, the camps were torn down at the end of the season, and the materials were moved to another location to be set up for the next season. To provide easy access for fur buyers and the trappers, these modest dwellings, or crude houseboats were located on the banks of a bayou or lake (Daspit 1948B).

The trapper's boat was used to run his lines and go to the nearest store for supplies. In some cases, grocery boats served this floating, semi-permanent population. The entire family crowded into the hut's one or two small rooms. Often three or four children shared the same bed. They slept on homemade mattresses, often with heated bricks laid at their feet to keep them warm. The top mattress was made of corn shucks stuffed between sheets of ticking sewn together. The second mattress was stuffed with Spanish moss, while the third was made of feathers (Pitre 1993). Since air readily permeated a moss mattress, it was desirable in the summer. In the winter, paper was placed under the mattress and extra blankets on top (Martinez 1959).

A wood or kerosene stove was used both for heating and cooking; no one went hungry with shrimp, crabs, oysters, and fish abundantly at hand. Rows and rows of skins stretched to dry on frames hanging from the ceiling or outside. When the grocery boat made a "pass," a portion of the catch was hidden so the boat owner could not talk to others about the size of their catch. This floating store was a link to the outside world, and it served as a miniature market. Its arrival was a "thrilling sight for the isolated families" (Ramsey 1957:176). The motorized barge *Glenwild* was one of the wholesale grocery boats serving several of these transient communities (Wilby 1991).

A house or campboat was merely a hut built on a small barge that could be towed to a *piégeur's* lease and tied to a slip dug into the bayou's bank (Cheniere Hurricane

(Left) Bad or inclement weather required trappers to improvise by drying their pelts indoors, 1941. (Photo courtesy of the Library of Congress, Print and Photographs Division, FSA-OWI Collection, LC-USF34-056801-D.)

(Right) A St. Bernard Parish trapping family, 1941. (Photo courtesy of the Library of Congress, Print and Photographs Division, FSA-OWI Collection, LC-USF34-056855-D DLC.)

Centennal 1994). Prior to the "big day," trappers outfitted and repaired their campboats—animals and pets were confined to their cages, and then kerosene, groceries, canned goods, cases of beer, and other provisions, often for as many as six families, were properly stored on board, along with fishing tackle, oyster tongs, muskrat traps, clothes wringers, carpenter's tools, and a vast assortment of other utilitarian items.

Each campboat had its own towboat, and all of the smaller gas boats, skiffs, and *pirogues* were tied together and lashed to the stern. Once the waterborne caravan was underway, the trapper's winter homes were moved to their trapping lands. Such processions encountered other caravans, or luggers loaded to the gunwales with mattresses, bedsprings, blankets, pots, pans, and other household necessities stacked together atop the vessel moved slowly into the marsh. This migration was an annual event. Many campboats clustered together into a makeshift "community," whose galleries served as meeting places where trappers and their families gossiped or scolded their children good-naturedly. At these sites, chicken coops and a hog pen had to be built. A place for the family cow had to be created. Wooden racks for drying muskrat pelts had to be laid out and assembled, so rows of wire hangers (or adjustable spring frames) used in stretching the pelts could be hung from nails attached to the drying frame (Dozier and Ashbrook 1950). Platforms for the wringers used to squeeze out the skins had to be made as well.

In some cases, campboat communities were established to permit the residents to trap a specific site and were, in effect, mobile encampments. Boats and huts lined up on each side of a bayou, creating what R. A. Graves (1930:407) described as a "Venetian slums main street." Regardless, large boats provided camp access, while gasoline-powered *pirogues* and mudboats, as well as eighteen-foot-skiffs powered by small engines allowed trappers to increase their trapping lines from 150 to 400 traps. The skiffs often featured power plants lifted from automobiles and placed amidships, as well as propellers designed to push the boats through channels that were half-water and half-mud (Kammer 1941; Ramsey 1957; O'Neil and Linscombe 1975; Hallowell 1979).

From November to the first of February during the trapping season, the marsh teamed with activity. In a typical trapper family, the husband and boys set out the traps and then ran the lines. They placed their traps near muskrat houses. These traps could not legally be within ten feet of these igloo-like, mud- and grass-covered mounds (Daspit 1930). In some cases, traps were set below the water's surface, so the trapped muskrat drowned. Or, the sets were placed along the run. Once an animal was caught, it was killed with a blow to the head. Unlike Northern trappers who could depend on the death of their animals by freezing, marsh trappers had to check their traps regularly, usually once a day.

Constructed of three-corner grass, a muskrat house provided some protection from rising water during tidal events. They also constituted a visual guide for trappers, ca. 1945. (Photo from O'Neil 1949.)

When the day's catch was brought home, the women and girls skinned the animals and then fleshed, washed, and stretched the pelts, placing them in the sun to dry for three or four days. After drying, the hide was removed from the stretching board or wire frame and packed in a burlap sack to be sent to a fur broker. Local fur buyers often visited *piégeurs'* camps to buy the pelts, which prevented trappers from having to leave the marsh periodically (Hansen 1971).

The routine was interrupted only when the trappers returned to a "ridge" settlement to celebrate Christmas or during the rare day off to buy supplies at the nearest store. When the boys could run their own traps, they worked for a share of the season's catch. Upon reaching the ages of eighteen to twenty-one, sons became full partners with their fathers—a partnership that often lasted a lifetime.

The method employed in trapping and handling the fur has changed little since the invention of the steel trap by Sewell Newhouse in the mid-1800s (O'Neil 1969). Prior to the availability of reliable traps, marshdwellers achieved only uncertain results from nets, snares, and dead falls. Reliability is significant because trapping is a labor-intensive industry. *Piégeurs* must walk their land to make a living, and they originally had to live near their trapping territories. "Marsh walking" was not easy, for it involved moving from grass tuft to grass tuft. Sure-footedness was required, for one false step would find a trapper knee-deep in the Deltaic Plain's *flotant* (Cottman 1939). In the *Chênière* Plain, the marsh surface was firm and easier to walk than on the marshes further east.

Since the 1970s, the industry has changed. Many coastal resource users have been forced to seek employment in the oil and gas industry or elsewhere, and it is questionable whether they will ever return to trapping. During the 2001-02 trapping season, fewer than 1,000 trapping licenses were sold statewide.

The Crab Industry Added to the Marshdweller's Income Base

Although the crab industry has been an important fishery in Europe for centuries, North America's commercial industry only began in 1875, when the first soft-shell crabs were shipped from Maryland. Crabmeat was not a known commodity; therefore, it took time for the population to understand and appreciate its cooking properties. Once crabmeat became an accepted food item, the fishery expanded beyond its regional core. By the 1880s, New Orleans hotels, restaurants, and steamboat operators had collectively become an important blue-crab market. Stalls in the French Market were lined with the local harvest of this bottom-dwelling predator, as marshdwellers added another income stream to their seasonal harvesting activities (Sterns 1887; Jaworski 1972). In 1908, crabmeat produced in Louisiana was valued at only $21,000, but thirty years later, Louisiana ranked third in the nation in crab harvest.

When the trapping and shrimp seasons were closed, marshdwellers turned to crabbing, using a trotline (*drague*), which was simply a long line with a series of baited drop lines hanging in the water. The line was anchored at each end by tying it to a tree or large stake in the region's lakes, bays, and bayous. Fishermen using a skiff or *pirogue* pulled themselves along the line, retrieved the baited lines, and caught blue crabs hanging on the bait in a scoop net (Kammer 1941). The crabs were kept alive in bushel baskets that sold to a wholesaler for fifty cents to a dollar each in the 1940s.

The wholesale trade began in Morgan City with establishment of the first crabmeat plant in 1924. By 1930, there were eight crab processing facilities in the Morgan City-Berwick area. These wholesalers employed at least 600 people. Pickers averaged about $1.50 per day, although the more proficient pickers could earn as much as four dollars a day (Fisher 1931; Jaworski 1972). The one-to-five pound containers used in the industry were hand-picked and graded into three classes, the "lump" meat from the back fins, the "white" or "flake" meat from the smaller muscles, and the "claw" meat. Since the industry generated considerable waste, shells, together with other refuse, were dried and ground into animal feed and fertilizers which brought the processor about twenty-five dollars to thirty dollars a ton (Clay 1938).

Once the fishery had a large-scale wholesale and distribution network, marshdwellers began to rethink their harvesting methods. The industry, consequently, began to expand and prosper with development and adoption of a simple, small "U"-shaped roller attached to one side of the bow of the watermen's boat. The crabber idled his engine until it slowly pushed the boat along the buoyed-marked crab line. As the boat advanced, the line was lifted over the roller. The blue crabs clinging to the bait were caught in a small dip net and placed in a basket. The process was repeated at every drop line until the entire *drague* was harvested.

In the 1950s, a mechanized crab cage was developed. This basket-like net was placed just below and behind the rollers, at water level, so as the line passed between the rollers the crabs were knocked off the bait and swept back into the net by the boat's forward motion (Jaworski 1972). With this device, a crabber could use longer lines and more of them to improve his harvest.

Crabs caught in this manner were brought into the boat and covered with "green" moss. Transfer boats were used to unload the catch and transport the harvest to crab sheds at unloading docks. A crabber had three ways to sell his or her product: 1) directly to the consumer; 2) to a seafood dealer; and 3) to a specialized crab buyer.

Between 1950 and 1960, following the introduction of crab traps, or pots, more and more crabs were taken with this method, and the trotline-net fishery was largely abandoned (Gowanloch 1952). The crab cage is

A Jefferson Parish crab-processing facility. (Photo from the *Jefferson Parish Yearly Review,* 1946.)

made of welded chicken wire or a similar high-grade welded wire wrapped in a vinyl protective coating. The cage is designed to be baited with an opening for crabs. Once inside, a crab cannot exit the metal enclosure. Using plastic milk jugs or painted corks as floats, the traps are marked for easy recovery by a crab fisherman. The crabber pulls the line attached to the cage up from the bottom and dumps the captured crabs into a box or basket—now provided by the dock. This process is repeated until the entire line of "jugs" is checked and harvested (Kammer 1941; Adkins 1972).

In the past, the daily crab harvest was sold by weight to buyers who took the catch to a processing facility. At the factory, the crabs were placed in circular, iron-framework baskets. These containers were about three feet in diameter and sixteen inches deep. Once filled, the vat was hoisted into a slightly wider cylindrical-metal-tank and cooked for about twenty-five minutes. Once cooked, the crabs were dumped onto picking tables, where the back shells were removed. Using a sharp knife, "pickers" removed the meat from crabs' bodies. These workers were paid, as in the oyster and shrimp fisheries, according to the weight of the meat harvested. An experienced packer could process sixty to seventy pounds of meat per day. The meat was packed in one-pound cans, sealed, and placed in cold storage (Leovy 1930; Fisher 1931).

The soft-shell crab was a particularly important delicacy. Upon attaining adult status, each crab sheds its shell approximately fifteen times. For two hours after molting, *callinectes sapidus* becomes a soft-shell crab that is unable to defend itself. During this process the crab is helpless and seeks shelter instinctively (Adkins 1972). Knowing this, crabbers provide a artificial shelter—"*seria*" (the colloquialism for the French "*ceriser*" or "cherry tree")—for shedding crabs by tying foliage to

A box of crabs ready for the retail market. (Photo from *Louisiana Conservation Review,* vol. 6, no., 1, 1953.)

their hand lines. They also used a trotline "baited" with *seria* or waxy myrtle (*myrca cerifera*) bunches.

To prepare a "bush," crabbers assemble six-to-seven fresh branches about three feet in length and bind them together. The bushes are re-tied to a line about fifteen feet apart. This formed a bush line. "A soft-shell crab fisherman [originally] used about 200 bushes, but in the 1970s the fishermen were using from 500 to 1,000 bushes" (Jaworski 1972:46-47). With 500 bushes, a fisherman could anticipate catching about 150 "green" crabs or "busters" a day. To improve the soft-shell harvest, Louisiana crab fisherman developed a crab scraper or dredge that allowed them to harvest crabs in grassy shedding areas by using gear that rolls the crabs up unharmed from the dead grass (Gowanloch 1952).

Empty crab-shedding cars, ca. 1970. (Photo from Jaworski 1972.)

The crabber hauled in these lines and removed the soft-shell crabs (Frost 1939B). Also, the fisherman would examine their catch to see if any hard-shell *callinectes sapidus* had developed a crack along the shell's underside. If a crack was visible, these "busters" were placed in "boxes"—approximately seven-feet long, five-feet wide, and two-feet deep—that were partially submerged in the bayou to keep the crabs alive before marketing. Larger "shedding cars," about eight-feet wide, twelve-feet long and three-to-four feet deep were used to keep from 250 to 500 live "peelers." When the busters emerged from their old exoskeletons, they are soft shell crabs ready for the market (Viosca and Gresham 1953; Jaworski 1972). To optimize their productivity, marshdwellers often established houseboat communities near harvest sites. One of these communities was "Crabtown."

In "Crabtown," the crabbers' transient houseboat community on Bayou Villars (know to the locals as "Bia Willa") connecting Lake Salvador with Big and Little Bayou Barataria, floating boxes, or crab or shedding cars were established (Frost 1939B; Viosca and Gresham 1953). At this site and others along the banks of a number of bayous, the boxes could be raised and lowered mechanically to see if any crabs had shed their shells. It some cases, each crabber could have from thirty to 100 floating boxes that were tied to stakes and physically checked. Soft-shell crabs were removed, put on ice, or packed in wet moss to be sold to a buyer, who paid a much higher price for these crabs than the hard-shell variety.

Time was critical, since after only two hours the soft-shell crab morphs into a "paper shell" of lesser value (Kammer 1941). Crab-buyers, using fast boats equipped with refrigeration compartments, bought these crabs for cash and delivered them to packing sheds where they were frozen "so hard you can drive a nail with them" and sold to out-of-state markets in California and New York (Frost 1939). By 1950, Louisiana marketed more than 600,000 soft-shell crabs (Werlla 1950). A half century later jumbo soft-shell crabs—over six inches across the back—sold for nearly $70 a dozen from a Chesapeake Bay distributor (http://www.crabplace.com 2007).

Crabbing is an activity that is not only important to commercial fishermen, but it is also enjoyed by a large number of recreational sportsmen. Using an inexpensive, lightweight, and easily obtained wire-rimmed drop-net, a recreational crabber can catch up to twelve dozen "beautiful swimmers" per person per day. If traps are used, the recreationalists can use up to ten traps, but they must first obtain a recreational crab-trap license, in addition to a basic fishing license—eleven or more traps legally qualifies a fisherman as a commercial crabber (Burke 2002). The easiest way to collect crabs is to use a dip net. The sport's accessibility to everyone makes crabbing a popular roadside activity.

In warm weather, with abundant available food, a crab can mature in about twelve months. While crabbing is a near year-round activity, concentrated fishing corresponds to the summer and spring shrimp season. In both periods, fishermen harvest hard- and soft-shelled blue-point crabs. In the commercial fishery, a minimum of five inches in width from point to point is required for harvesting. There is no size limit in the recreational fishery, but these part-time crabbers can only have in their possession no more than twelve dozen crabs (Burke 2002). Regardless of who is involved in this fishery, crabbing is an important asset to the state's economy, often accounting for more than 70 percent of the total Gulf of Mexico production, but it is a difficult industry to forecast (Burke 2002).

Optimal conditions for blue crabs include shallow water, mud and/or mud-shell bottoms, detrital matter, tidal fluctuation, warm temperatures, and mid-to-low salinities (Adkins 1972). If any of these variables are changed, the industry will be affected. The number of individuals working in this fishery also depends on a number of variables. But, because a crabber can harvest blue crabs for a relatively small investment, crabbing is a fall-back economic pursuit during hard times. In the late 1980s and early 1990s, the number of crabbers increased noticeably, primarily because of the large number of displaced oil industry personnel who began to make their living fishing.

Eventually, the state found itself facing a serious dilemma—there were too many fishermen and too many cages in an overcapitalized fishery. As a result, the catch-per-trap decreased drastically. To compensate for declining market prices, fishermen used more traps, which reduced the catch-per-trap still further. Even so, Louisiana still produced between 50 to 70 percent of the Gulf region's annual harvest of blue crabs. Further, the state was responsible for 15 to 25 percent of the nation's annual harvest. As a result, the dockside value of this fishery is about $20 and $30 million annually (The Louisiana blue . . . n.d.; NMFS Landings Query Results. Louisiana crabs 2006). With discovery of oil in deep water, and the after effects of Hurricanes Katrina, Rita, Gustav, and Ike, the number of individuals involved in this industry has changed.

The industry's material legacy, however, has endured, Because of the large number of durable vinyl-coated traps used in the industry; they often become "lost." When these traps are "misplaced" they are known as "ghost traps." Because of their

Early twenty-first century crab traps, 2005. (Photo by the author.)

longevity, these cages are now part of the region's growing assortment of marine debris (Guillory 1993; Guillory, et al. 2001; Farren 2003; Guillory 2005).

With more than 3,000 crabbers, each using 250 to 270 traps, it is easy to see how the number of ghost traps could become a problem. According to the Gulf States Marine Fisheries Commission, a million blue crab traps are set in Gulf inshore waters each year. One-fourth of these are lost, but they continue to capture and kill crabs.

Roadside signs advertising fishery products are a common sight in South Louisiana, 2007. (Photo courtesy of J. Walker.)

Moreover, the "bycatch" mortality is quite high. In Louisiana, each ghost trap kills an average of twenty-five crabs per trap per year. In fact, Louisiana ghost traps collectively could be responsible for the loss of between four to ten million blue crabs annually (Guillory 1993; Farren 2003).

Considered personal property protected by law, these traps once could not be removed without the respective owner's permission. In fact, during coastal cleanup programs, volunteers are told to ignore traps, even those that may have washed ashore. However, legislation was passed in 2003 (Act 48) giving Louisiana the legal authority for a trap removal program, and, as a result of the 2003 legislation, Louisiana initiated a derelict trap cleanup initiative. Using nearly 140 volunteer boats, the state's Department of Wildlife and Fisheries picked up slightly more than 11,500 ghost traps in 2004 and 2005 (Guillory 2005).

Market Hunting

Here come four ducks—three by herself and one in a bunch (Graves 1930:406).

For the dedicated waterfowler, the marsh offers marvelous hunting opportunities; it was the marshdweller's outdoor supermarket, as the marsh is an ideal habitat for migratory waterfowl. Duck hunting also became an important recreational pursuit as the abundance of waterfowl proved irresistible to the recreational sportsmen. Because of the resulting demand for ducks, marshdwellers discovered another source of winter income and began to fill barrels with ducks instead of oysters. "Ducking" became as much a part of these folks' life as crabbing, "tonging," "dredging," shrimping, or trapping. Along with trapping, the winter months were devoted to hunting, regulated only by common agreements among villages to limit the time allotted to this activity. The hunt usually had to end by noon. If this rule was ignored, the community's elder confiscated the firearms used. It was folk law.

The men and women of the marsh were born to hunt. In the vernacular of professional waterfowl hunters, Louisiana's watermen were first and foremost "gunners." This adjunct to their "regular" wages was almost wholly dependent on their firearms and their skill at shooting birds in flight. In Louisiana, more ducks were killed by more hunters, for a longer period of time, than in any other part of the country. These waterfowlers hunted with grim efficiency. In some cases, they added eleven-shot extensions to their shotguns or *fusils*. Their mantra was simple: "No duck—no dinner." Natural conservation laws were unknown. The marsh was free for everyone to use, and it provided abundant game. In some cases, trappers encouraged hunting and allowed hunters to stay at their camps, so they would reduce the birds

Well before the popularization of recreational activities, Louisiana sportsmen patronized marketers of guns, rifles, fishing poles, and other sporting gear. (Image from *Louisiana Sugar Bowl* [New Iberia], 1880.)

2,000 ducks awaiting shipment from a marsh camp to Lake Arthur. (Photo from *Louisiana Conservationist*, vol. 54, 2002.)

that were "destroying" their muskrat habitats (Kramer 1974).

Until the imposition of a ten dollar "Market Hunter's License" in 1908, the only limiting factor was the weight of the ducks that had to be carried out of the marsh. As early as the 1870s, "during the winter season several thousand dollars' worth of wild-duck are killed on the lower Lafourche and shipped to New Orleans" (Talfor 1874:768). Tens of thousands of waterfowl were killed during the market hunting era from the mid-1800s to 1920. By the early 1900s, some conservation-minded individuals were beginning to question the long-term ramification of market hunting. In this regard, Louisiana in 1912 initiated a 115-day season—nearly four months—with a bag limit of twenty-five. Market hunting was still allowed, and for many marshdwellers, this was a good way to make extra money. By 1918, the season had been reduced to ninety days and market hunting was declared illegal. A ninety-day season and twenty-five-bird-bag-limit remained in effect until a reduction in the migratory bird population brought about Federal control in 1932-33 (St. Amant 1959).

At the beginning of the twentieth century, a nearly endless hunting season enabled a successful professional waterfowl hunter to often shoot more ducks than he could carry. In the late 1800s and early 1900s, a successful Louisiana market gunner used wooden decoys, live goose or duck decoys (called a toller in Chesapeake Bay) tethered in front of a blind that were available through mail-order supply houses (Walsh 1971), baited fields, a *pirogue* or "sneak" skiff, push-pole, a *pagaille* or sneak paddle, a kerosene lamp (or "bull-eye") for night shooting, a wooden shell case with 200 rounds of black powder shells, and a good repeating shotgun. To be successful, all of these elements were used as efficiently as a well-oiled machine. All 200 rounds often were fired in a day (Lacaze 2002) and in some cases there were so many birds that decoys were not needed (Kramer 1974).

> The technique of flock shooting with an automatic shotgun and the judicious use of corn constitute the deadliest method of duck destruction ever devised. The tremendous power of this tool (bait or corn) to concentrate waterfowl is well known. Given enough room and bait, all the waterfowl in one region, or even a so-called flyway, could be concentrated into one area. A poor habitat can be converted into a prime area with its holding or carrying capacity almost unlimited (Walsh 1971:29).

Decoys were essential to the success of the commercial hunting business. (Undated advertisement.)

A successful hunt, therefore, depended on a blind, decoys, and bait. The blind was crucial and the pattern of decoys was determined by the direction of the wind. With the wind in the hunter's face, big spreads (also called rigs) of decoys were grouped close to shore and the blind. When the wind was at the hunter's back, the decoys were located close to the blind to draw the birds closer to the waterfowler (Walsh 1971; Frank 1985). Decoys were essential and had to be well-designed, sea-worthy, and stable. High quality decoys were crucial to the hunt's success, for a large spread could involve hundreds of these artificial lures. The gunner could not manage such a spread if the decoys were not designed to float properly (Kimball and Kimball 1969). Corn was the bait of choice.

In the 1880s, at the height of commercial waterfowl hunting, market hunters used large-bore, canon-like "punt" guns that fired a massive charge of shot. These big guns—having a 2-inch bore, extending eight- to nearly ten-feet in length, and weighing in excess of 100 pounds—were quite popular. For example, on Chesapeake Bay's Smith Island, professional hunters used perhaps twenty-five of these big weapons. Once these big guns were fired, the gunner "could expect a good ride in reverse" (Kimball and Kimball 1969:25), as nearly two pounds of shot were hurdled towards the unsuspecting assemblage of ducks.

These weapons were employed by market hunters on Chesapeake Bay, in Illinois, and in other areas, but they were not common in South Louisiana (Walsh 1971). Big-gun hunters often worked in groups of eight-to-ten boats that would coordinate their "firing" to harvest entire flocks of birds with a single volley. The gun was mounted on long, square-ended, flat-hulled, boats called punts. By lining up their boats, these professional waterfowlers would often harvest 500 or more, birds in a single day. It was a deadly, efficient system of market hunting.

Very few, if any, of Louisiana's market hunters used these cannons or cannon-like devices; instead, they did well with a standard, often modified, shotgun. Unlike the coordinated fire power of eight-to-ten boats used by East Coast waterfowlers, Louisiana hunters considered "thirty ducks and eight to ten geese . . . a good shot" (Walsh 1971:89). In the local vernacular, when a hunter killed many birds with one shot, it was called a *caramlade*.

To get "top-dollar" for the birds killed, hunters were obliged to move the game to market quickly. Before refrigeration, when ice was quite expensive, these birds were field dressed, often stuffed with Spanish moss, placed in ventilated barrels (approximately 100 ducks per barrel), packed between layers of salt, covered, and shipped by boat to the nearest rail station. At the station, the barrels were iced down and then sent by train to New Orleans. To improve the distribution of game being delivered to Lake Arthur, south of Jennings, the railroad built a spur line from Lake Charles to Lake Arthur. "Man, in the migration season those trains were carrying carloads of ducks. They didn't even bother with geese because they were too much trouble, and they got almost as much money for ducks. Thirty-five cents a pair" (Reisner 1991:17). Hunters also sometimes shipped ducks from Venice by packet boats.

Waterfowl sent to the Crescent City were often sold to commercial buyers in the French Market, where butchers and other vendors ran their own concessions (Cheramie 1997). Meat could not be brought to the market before 2 a.m. or after 5 a.m. In order to keep the waterfowl, and other exposed meat products, cool, the market shut down by noon—10 a.m. during the summer. Ice and electricity changed the market's hours and pattern of operation (Reeves 2007).

Even so, for the market hunter, delivery in the early morning was ideal. In fact, the entire process of killing, packing, and delivering waterfowl to market often took less than eight hours. This daily routine lasted three months of the year (Frank 1985; Cheramie 1997; Lacaze 2002).

If the game were not packed and shipped immediately after being killed, the birds would be unsalable when they reached the French Quarter. With development of large freezers and refrigerator railroad cars, market hunters in Illinois, Minnesota, and elsewhere could ship their harvest to Northern markets year-round, thereby increasing their profits. Prior to this development, these Northern professional gunners could only distribute their harvest to a very limited area, for the expense of ice packing often was greater than their monetary return on game (Kimball and Kimball 1969).

Louisiana's market hunters were much more fortunate, for they had a market that was less than a day from the marsh, and rail connections were close to their hunting camps.

> During the 1880s and '90s, with improving communication, the old market at New Orleans did a thriving business, taking almost as many ducks, geese, or other game as the Deltans could provide. Some had their first direct contact with the city in supplying this demand. As one recalled from his youth, 'We went out to take whatever number we wanted—two hundred, three hundred in a day.' Gutting the birds quickly, leaving the feathers on, they kept an appointment with the captain of a freight boat or a man along the railroad track (Kane 1944:83).

Before bag limits were established, market hunters clearly could make a good living by shipping game birds by rail, truck, or boat to New Orleans restaurants, where they were prized fare. Market hunters earned twenty-five cents per mallard pair; pintail brought twenty cents, teal fifteen cents (more if they were plucked). No other species were desired or purchased for the market (Lacaze 2002).

Stories abound of huge duck harvests by market hunters around 1900. Cheramie (1997) reports it was not uncommon for a team of market hunters to kill more than 1,500 ducks a day. If the average price was twenty-five cents, and there were 750 pairs, a day's income ca. 1913 was $187.50; adjusted for inflation that would be more than $4,000 in 2009. Although the income was shared, this return was quite good, since the overhead was limited, and the marksmen's abilities were "dead" on.

If the hunt was in the marshes south of New Orleans, luggers would transport the harvest to the French Market, the kill hanging from the boat's sides. Wild duck became gourmet fare, and duck orange, bloody duck, and French-duck soup appeared on many menus (Cheramie 1997) because it was cheaper for local cooks to buy "wild" game at the market, than to personally hunt them in the marsh.

During the 1917-18 season, prices increased dramatically for wild ducks. The South was in the second year of an unprecedented drought, and crucial feeding grounds, lagoons, puddles, shallow lakes all exhibited the effects of a rainless season. The wintering ducks had to take to open waters, making it difficult for market hunters and sportsmen to approach within shotgun range. Hence, there were more ducks and more hunters in the marshes, but fewer ducks were killed. When market hunting opened on December 15, the drought was at its worst, and ducks were difficult to shoot. By the close of the season—on February 15—"ducks in the market were at a premium and the price of ducks reached the highest prices ever known in the New Orleans market" (McIlhenny 1918:70). Yet, at the same time, persons in the food business were encouraging people to buy ducks, geese, and other game birds to "relieve the food shortage and complained that by allowing sportsmen to hunt from November 1st—these individuals were taking most of the duck and putting the market hunter at a disadvantage" (McIlhenny 1918:71).

Waterfowl prices paid to market hunters, 1917-1918
(From: McIlhenny 1918:70)

Bird	Average in past years	Highest	Average Price in 1917-1918
Mallard	$0.85 a pair	$1.75	$1.50
Pintail	$0.65 a pair	$1.25	$1.00
Teal	$0.50 a pair	$0.90	$0.90
Ring-neck (black)	$0.85 a pair	$1.50	$1.25
Canvasback	$0.85 a pair	$1.50	$1.25
Spoonbill	$0.83 a pair	$0.60	$0.60
Scaup (*dos-gris*)	$0.40 a pair	$0.60	$0.55
Coot (*Poule d'eau*)	$0.15 a pair	$0.40	$0.30
Geese	$2.00 a pair	$2.50	$2.25
Snipe	$3.00 a doz.	$4.00	$3.50

Since New Orleans was Louisiana's primary market for wild game, and since the price was at an all time high, the Game Division had to be ever-vigilant for ducks and other waterfowl that were smuggled into the city, as hunter's daily limit was nearly impossible to assess and manage. If caught with more birds than the law allowed, prosecuting the offenders was difficult, with courts friendly to the waterfowlers.

Most of the illicit trade into New Orleans originated in the parishes of St. Bernard and Plaquemines.

> By constant night and day watchfulness, . . . agents were able to throw a line around the lower part of the city and apprehend those endeavoring to run the blockade with illicit shipments of game. In this manner, over 5,000 ducks were confiscated and distributed to charitable organizations in New Orleans. A few lots of ducks got past [the blockade] and were peddled about the streets[,] but none were sold openly"

> . . . it was impossible for us to stop this illicit market gunning on the hunting grounds. Not only were there physical difficulties to overcome, but as each hunter found in the marshes had his proper amateur dollar hunting license we had no way of knowing whether or not he was intending to sell his game (McIlhenny 1918:71).

In order to keep track of the ducks being sold by market hunters, the state's Game Division developed a tagging system to help regulate the shipping of game allowed to be sold in the market. These "Market Hunter's Shipping Tags" recorded each hunter's kill and helped developed a statistical profile of the harvest.

Market hunters harvest, from 1913-1914 to 1917-1918
(From: McIlhenny 1918:73)

Birds	1913-1914	1914-1915	1915-1916	1916-1917	1917-1918
Mallards	117,843	99,613	92,252	126,552	105,708
Pintails	27,955	17,963	71,486	22,140	7,466
Ring-neck (Black)	13,532	8,260	26,544	7,903	1,798
Gadwall (Gray)	15,620	6,419	20,652	22,688	2,540
Canvasback	1,037	1,522	5,448	2,723	1,646
Redhead	798	496	516	Coupled with Canvasback	1,006
Shoveler (Spoonbill)	36,864	14,471	22,908	19,851	12,156
Teal	30,276	21,378	16,159	33,891	4,210
Scaup (*dos-gris*)	38,560	6,432	13,067	13,524	2,138
Coot (*Poule d'eau*)	39,114	28,260	14,636	36,108	17,824
Wood duck (*Branchu*)	850	Non-marketed	492	Non-marketed	Non-marketed
Geese	2,315	1,652	494	3,233	1,762
Snipe	46,790	73,031	11,913	39,267	12,348
Total	371,554	279,497	296,567	327,880	170,602

The Business of Market Hunting

There was a time when wild waterfowl kept a lot of southern Louisiana housed and clothed and fed. During the heyday of the market-hunting era—from 1880 to about 1915—the surface of Catahoula Lake, in late November, was covered by three, four, or five million ducks. Another million or two were on Lake Arthur. The two Grand Lakes and White Lake, with a combined surface area larger than Tahoe but depths more accurately measured in inches than feet—an explosively productive habitat for ducks—held millions more. The marshes in between held millions. There were more ducks wintering in southern Louisiana than survive on the continent today. . . . There was no other spectacle like it in America (Reisner 1991:19-20).

In southwest Louisiana, near Lake Misère (south of Lake Arthur—known as the duck-market-hunting capital of the world), was the "Dudley Camp"—a commercial duck hunting operation owned by Fred Dudley.

Dudley purchased 10,000 acres [15.6 square miles] of marsh at $2.00 per acre and set up the most efficient market hunting operation ever. A flotilla of cypress shanty boats provided in-season homes for the families of the hunters; tutors provided schooling for the children; and a bookkeeper tallied the daily score and extended credits for groceries and other staples, even shotgun shells at $10 per case (Lacaze 2003:16).

A load of Dudley Camp ducks en route to the rail depot at Lake Charles, ca. 1910. (Photo from the *Louisiana Conservationist*, vol. 54, 2002.)

Market hunting was a lucrative business, with Camp Dudley providing the New Orleans market with 2,000 birds per day. At from twenty cents to $1,25 a pair for mallards, the corporation could earn $2,500 in less than a week. Based on the period between 1913 and 2009, the Dudley enterprise, adjusted for inflation, was generating more than $53,848.

Often the birds were not plucked, since New Orleans' buyers wanted them with their feathers on—it made them more attractive when displayed in New Orleans' markets.

The hunters built houseboats and towed em out in the marshes and moved the whole family in—kids, wives, Grandma. The men hunted and the women and kids gutted the birds. They put them on ice in barrels and shipped them to New Orleans. If everything went right, they got there in eight hours. The freshest-killed ducks, they shipped them on as far away as Chicago! New York, too. They went to Nashville, Memphis, Mobile, Atlanta, Saint Louis. If you took a steamboat up or down the Mississippi, you ate nothing but crab and crawfish and viande de chevreuil and venison and wild duck. . . . May, they must have thought it would never end (Reisner 1991:17).

In addition to ducks, waterfowlers killed a variety of other feathered game, because at the turn of the twentieth century, stylish women wore hats with the latest feather-topped design from Paris, New York, and other fashion centers. Millinery houses in Europe and America traded internationally and indiscriminately for birds and bird feathers, like the feathers from the once common red-breasted herons, which were widely harvested around Bayou Petit Caillou, near Chauvin (Rushton 1979). The more exotic or unique the hat design and feather display, the larger the sales (Doughty 1975).

According to Bénard de La Harpe (1971), cardinals (*Cardinalis cardinalis*) were introduced into Louisiana by the Spanish and their plumage was greatly admired by the Europeans; hence, the sale of feathers may date back to the Spanish colonial period. To meet the demand for feathers as well as for food, plume hunters were killing many of the most unique and colorful birds. In fact, they killed so many waterfowl that their uncontrolled and unregulated slaughter had a direct impact on the Mississippi Flyway's migratory bird population.

Federal laws—primarily the 1900 Lacey Act and the 1918 Migratory Bird Treaty Act—banned punt guns and market hunting. These initiatives were enacted to protect the continent's bird population (Cheramie 1997; Vileisis 1997). Following passage of this legislation—over the aggressive lobbying of the millinery industry—approximately 1,000 Louisiana market hunters found themselves unemployed, but for nearly forty years they had sustained this lucrative business.

Illegal harvest of game was a constant concern of Louisiana Wildlife and Fisheries agents, ca. 1945. (Photo courtesy of Louisiana Department of Wildlife and Fisheries.)

One of the first federal attempts to enforce the Lacey Act resulted in the seizure of 2,600 gulls at a Baltimore millinery firm. The confiscated birds had been shipped from Morgan City to Maryland. This case of interstate transfer of plumage in violation of the Lacey Act resulted in a $100 fine. More importantly, the raid forced millinery houses in Boston, New York, and Philadelphia to inventory their stocks for illegal plumage. As law enforcement agents began to seize shorebird plumes, intended for the out-of-state millinery industry, unlawful sales in seabird plumage dropped immediately (Doughty 1975).

The demand for feathers, like market hunting, contributed to the decimation of a wild bird population that had endured decades of over-hunting. The trade in feathers was terminated in the 1920s, and when coupled with the Lacey Act's affect on market hunting, migratory waterfowl began to make a comeback (Doughty 1975).

Market hunting had ended, but wealthy recreational sportsmen needed guides, camp caretakers, and decoys to meet their needs. The marshdweller provided all

of these services. Moreover, as the country's standard-of-living increased, and with a larger middle-class emerged, many men and women discovered the unique waterfowling experience offered in Louisiana's wetlands, and a passionate love of recreational duck hunting was born. Further, several national sports hunting periodicals were established reflecting the growing popular interest in hunting. Articles frequently decried the overharvesting of waterfowl and encouraged sportsmen to practice harvesting techniques that would protect their wild game. Consequently, "the journals created a sense of fraternity among sport hunters nationwide, which spurred the formation of sportsmen's clubs. During the winter of 1874-1875, nearly 100 sportsmen's organizations were founded. . . ." (Vileisis 1997:152).

With the demise of market hunting, many former commercial hunters became guides. (Photo from *Louisiana Conservationist,* vol. 54, 2002.)

By serving as guides and surrogate hunters, Louisiana's marshdwellers profited from the emergence of these new sportsmen. It was a rare day when the hunting gentry went home without their limit, because at times the sky was black with ducks. Consequently, during the late 1920 and the 1930s, well-to-do sportsmen joined or founded private hunting clubs, such as the Little Lake Club south of Lafitte, the Tally-Ho Club in New Orleans East, the Fish-A-Bit Lodge at Delacroix, Delta Duck Club (which became the Avoca Island Duck Club), and many others. (The Tally-Ho, formed in 1815 on Bayou Sauvage, close to its junction with Chef Menteur Pass, may be the oldest continuously used formal hunting club in the United States [Capooth 2006]).

These clubs paid the state five dollars for a special hunting club permit and license. Once established and populated by gentlemen hunters, the clubs hired local marshdwellers as their guides and camp caretakers. They also filed reports with the state on all game killed by their members.

The guides often used a wooden kidney boat, with a pointed bow and stern, and covered with canvas and sev-

Located along Chef Menteur, the Tally-Ho Club may be the oldest continuously used sporting facility in North America, 1940. (Photo from the *Louisiana Conservation Review,* vol. 10, 1941.)

eral layers of paint. (The boats were named after Dan Kidney of DePere, Wisconsin.) Or, they used "Delta Duck Boats"—the favorite of many club members (Cheramie 1997:226)—that were easily identified by the vertical tube extended from the front deck through the hull. The pipe allowed the boat to be staked with a push-pole so the boat could easily rise and fall in tidal ponds. When secured in this configuration, the delta duck boat provided a very stable gun platform and was an efficient method of duck hunting. As long as the ducks were flying south, the duck clubs were in business, sportsmen were happy, and guides were busy. Floods, the dust bowl, and the Great Depression changed the harmonious relationship between the recreational hunter, his or her gun, and a day on the marsh.

The 1927 flood and the 1930s dust bowl respectively flooded the wetlands and dried up the country's agricultural heartland. Habitat was lost, and the Mississippi Flyway's waterfowl population declined, which adversely affected the hunting business and the guides who "put them [members of the hunting gentry] on birds." Because of the declining demand for their "escort" services, many former gunners returned to the now illegal business of market hunting to generate additional income to feed their families during the economic slump (Lacaze 2002).

After the Depression and the return of the migratory bird population, duck hunting was again an important recreational or commercial activity for the people of the marshes and marsh fringe. With the advent of better roads, automobiles, gasoline-powered boats, and cheap guns and ammunition, access to the marsh was no longer limited to the marshdweller. The marshes became available to members of all economic classes, with a bit of spare time. Sports hunting was no longer the domain of the wealthy. These elements, coupled with an abundance of ducks, added to the recreation use of the marshes, not only in Louisiana, but nationwide (Rochester 1994).

In the marshdweller's annual use-cycle, market hunting was replaced by recreational hunting. With time, the locals provided escorted hunts that included a guide, accommodations, meals, and the services of duck pluckers who would clean the day's harvest. Hunting had become another element in the economics of the marsh, joining fishing, crabbing, and trapping as a means to enhance the financial well-being of those who made their living off of Louisiana's marshes (Gomez 1998).

> "Clustered in the middle of a field . . . , just beyond rifle range, were four or five thousand geese. Four or five thousand geese. The density of birds—a thousand on a tennis court was a passable guess—was such as I had never seen. Most were blue-snow geese, . . . huddled defiantly in their last little winter redoubt, a rice field on the edge of a wildlife refuge" (Reisner 1991:11).

Duck Camps of the Market Hunter

Louisiana was ducks. Ducks, ducks, and more ducks. It was like the buffalo on the plains. Only we had our ducks a century after the buffalo were gone. I killed thousands and I'm ashamed of it. But we had millions and millions and millions (Reisner 1991:291).

To guarantee that French Quarter merchants had plenty of ducks, hunting camps were established in prime habitat. Local marshdwellers were employed to hunt waterfowl. "Gunners" typically worked for lodging, meals, and payment based on each pair of ducks killed. Hunting from an hour before sunrise until after dark, the professional gunners provided local markets with thousands of ducks annually. For example, during the 1913-14 season, 371,654 birds were reportedly killed by Louisiana market hunters. If the average price was twenty-five cents a bird, the year's hunt generated $92,973.50. When adjusted for inflation to 2009 values, the enterprise produced more than two million dollars. This assessment, based upon a count of market receipts, is only an estimate, and it is highly likely that the actual number of birds killed was much greater (Conservation of Wild . . . 1914).

I personally knew two market hunters who had their camp in the marsh north of White Lake, Vermilion Parish, whose average daily kill of mallard ducks was 200. They had a 2000-pound ice box stored at their camp to accommodate their daily kill. When this box was full the contents were loaded on sleds drawn by oxen and dragged to high land and conveyed to Gueydan for shipment to market (McPherson 1951:16).

The money generated by this industry is speculated, at best, as there are no records on the exact quantity of birds harvested. Assuming that at least twenty-four million *canards* were harvested between 1880 and 1920 and that the New Orleans market paid an average of twenty-five cents each, the industry generated at least $150,000 a year. In 2009 dollars, that equates to $3.2 million. With this type of return, it is no wonder this industry flourished, and at times the cannon-like volleys sounded like a raging battle to the camp-based Cajun market hunters (Gomez 1998). Harvests of this magnitude, whether common or rare, led to legislation and regulations banning this type of hunting. Even so, market hunting remained a respected profession.

Recreational Hunting

Nationwide, millions of migratory waterfowl use several North American (Mississippi and Central) corridors to make the annual trip south. Many of these birds winter in Louisiana's marshes. Ducks that follow these primary migratory routes into Louisiana, the terminus of their primary migratory corridor, can annually approach five million, while geese can exceed one million. The state's wetland habitats, fertile soils, semitropical weather, long growing season, abundant annual rainfall, and more than 500,000 acres of row-crops at the marshland fringe constitute the attractions that make South Louisiana a "duck mecca" (Helm 2000:15). The appeal of these habitats to waterfowlers dates from the late nineteenth century, well before the proliferation of exclusive, high-dollar hunting clubs.

For example, New Orleans' hunters in the early 1900s took the train to the La Branche railroad station where they had easy access to wetland hunting sites. Since the roads in South Louisiana, at that time, needed improvement, travel by rail was an accepted means of transporting sportsmen to their hunting leases. As a result, in the early 1920s, New Orleans fishermen caught the 3:45 a.m. L&N fisherman's special for Michoud, Chef Menteur, Lake Catherine, or the Rigolets. At the end of the day, they caught the return train back to New Orleans often loaded down with their kill and their shotguns, breach open, resting on their shoulders (Deutsch 1968).

Railroad travel was generally faster than the automobile, particularly if the hunter was traveling south of New Orleans. During the period around 1930, trains left Algiers daily at 8:00 a.m. for Buras. A mail-boat met the train in Buras, and after lunch, took guests to Pilottown, arriving at 4:30 in the afternoon. Here the sportsmen would be met by a Louisiana Department of Conservation boat. A half-hour later, they were at the Pass à Loutre Public Shooting Club. The round-trip train fare was four dollars. The mail-boat charged a dollar each way and the daily fee to use the club was twelve dollars and fifty cents. "This covers services of guide, duck boat, decoys, breakfast, lunch, dinner, and lodging. Sportsmen must bring their own guns, but shells for standard 12, 16, and 20-gauge guns can be purchased at the club house at retail prices" (Get your limit 1931:145). Due to stringent trespass laws, no open hunting was available except at sites like the Pass à Loutre Public Shooting Club, which was designated open to the public.

Since the post-World War II era, practically all

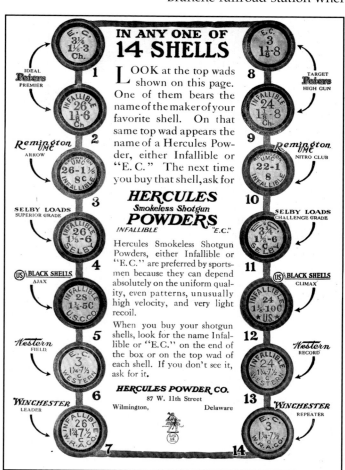

1918 advertisement for shotgun shells.

Get Your Limit on Ducks!

THE Department of Conservation, of the State of Louisiana, cordially invites you to visit the Pass a Loutre Public Shooting club under its direction, at the mouth of the Mississippi River, during the season of 1930-1931, November 1 to January 31.

The club house is adequately appointed for the entertainment of guests, being supplied with a comfortable dormitory, a light plant, a water supply system furnishing hot and cold water, and a cuisine under the management of competent help.

The many ponds have been opened with trails leading from the main passes; the equipment, such as duck boats, decoys, and blinds, has been put in proper shape for the season.

The hunting of wild waterfowl is permitted only from a half hour before sunrise to noon. This gives the ducks a half-day rest for feeding in the ponds.

The Pass a Loutre Club is located near the mouth of the Mississippi, on one of the passes of the river, 90 miles from the City of New Orleans.

Trains leave New Orleans (Algiers side) daily at 8:00 a. m. for Buras, where the mail-boat meets the train and, after lunch, conveys the guests to Pilot Town, arriving at 4:30 p. m. Here the sportsman is met by a department boat and a half hour later is at the club house.

The train fare is $4.30 the round trip. The mail-boat charges $1.00 each way.

At the club house the daily charge is $12.50. This covers services of guide, duckboat, decoys, breakfast, lunch, dinner, and lodgings. Sportsmen must bring their own guns, but shells for standard 12, 16, and 20-gauge guns can be purchased at the club house at retail prices.

Sportsmen desiring to visit the club must register, either in person or by mail, at the office of the Department of Conservation, 126 N. O. Court Building, New Orleans. A registration fee of $5.00 is required, which is accepted by the club manager as part payment on the guest's account. Failure to avail oneself of the registration forfeits the fee.

For full information relative to registration and accommodations, apply to

DEPARTMENT OF CONSERVATION

126 N. O. Court Building   **New Orleans**

Pass a Loutre Public Shooting Club House

Advertisement for the Passe à L'Outre Hunting Club, managed by the Louisiana Department of Conservation. Note the kidney boats in the foreground. (Image from the *Louisiana Conservation Review,* 1941.)

(Photos [left] 2009 and right [1997] by the author.)

hunting up to the 1960s was controlled by either commercial or private hunting clubs. After 1960, an aggressive land acquisition program by Louisiana's Department of Wildlife and Fisheries and the opening of a number of Federal Refuges increased the property available for public hunting. Also, high quality duck and goose shooting causes the area to attract a large seasonal influx of tourists, who expend large sums to enjoy the local water-fowling experience.

On some private leases, gamekeepers work throughout the year to ensure that the best possible conditions exist for the annual migratory game bird migration. The first day of the season is like "The Glorious Twelfth" in England, or "Elk Day" in a number of western states—the blinds have been made ready, boats have been serviced, guns, boots, shotgun shells, and other outdoor equipment are ready—the wait is over, it is time to hunt. To many, bagging the limit is not always the issue, it is, instead, being out-of-doors enjoying a quiet sunrise. The excellent hunting provides seasonal employment to the local population. These individuals work as guides and cooks. Local women often will clean the day's limit. It is not uncommon on the *chênières* to see signs proclaiming: "We Clean Ducks." The marshdweller's hunting expertise continues and a wide array of sportsmen have learned, what the marsh resident has always known, that Louisiana is a sportsman's paradise.

Decoys and the Carvers

When asked what the primary center of decoy carving was in days gone by, Frank said, 'it centers just short of Grand Isle up to Thibodaux with Bayou Lafourche as the axis. I think that if you go much farther north in this area the decoy carving becomes less of an art. Essentially Bayou Lafourche was the axis of carving. I feel that the reason for this is that the rice fields to the north were much more attractive to large concentrations of migratory ducks than our open marsh. We needed good decoys to help us in South Louisiana' (Duffy 1973:6).

Waterfowlers, such as Andrew "Tan" Brunet, Sidney Foret, George Frederick, Jr., Charles Numa Joefrau, Laurent Verdin, Remi Ange Rouselle, Jr., Dewey Foret, Mitchel LaFrance, Nicole Vidacovich, Clovis "Cadice" Vizier, Odee "Bee" Vizier, and Mark McCool Whipple used their knowledge of a duck's size, feather pattern, and color to carve realistic decoys (Frank 1991; Cheramie 1997). These "hatchet sculptures" were used to improve the chances of a successful hunt for the sportsmen they escorted into the marsh. For some carvers, decoys—as folk art—eventually became an important source of revenue. To supplement their income, carvers sold their decoys to recreational hunters for eighteen dollars to twenty-five dollars a dozen (Frank 1985; Frank 1991; Cheramie 1997). Across the coastal zone, each hunting region had its own distinct style, and these items of folk art, to the trained eye, became regional identifiers.

Carvers were originally motivated by necessity, not financial reward. However, as the demand for decoys increased in New Orleans' markets, bayou folk artists took their hand-made decoys to New Orleans' French Market and hardware stores for sale. Indeed, prior to the tourist gentrification of New Orleans' French Quarter, the DeLuca Hardware store was always well stocked with handmade decoys, which were eventually replaced by factory-made models sold at Sears and Roebuck or Montgomery Ward (Cheramie 1997).

Louisiana had more decoy carvers than any other state (More than 300 documented). With time, their work was prized increasingly for its beauty rather than its functionality. As one New Orleans carver lamented: "In the old days we used to catch birds with decoys, nowadays we mostly catch men" (Spitzer 1985:135).

Decoy carving eventually became many waterfowlers' principal profession.

Decoy carving became part of Louisiana's folk art repertoire. (Photo from the *Louisiana Conservationist,* vol. 10, 1958.)

Carvers' standards for design and quality were established very early, and the art form has persisted with few deviations (Wildlife carving 1998). The decoys' realistic designs worked, and there was no reason to change, as many sold before the paint was dry. George Viavant's early twentieth century watercolors captured the essence of the marsh's birds, fish, and small game (Jordan 2004), but a piece of wood became the waterfowler's canvas. The end product is valuable, cherished, highly collectable, expensive, and an example of the artistic talent of the wetland carvers.

Decoys are now generally made of plastic, cork, and inflatable rubber. Some modern battery-powered decoys are designed to look like a duck, swim like a duck, and flap wings like a duck. These modern-day robo-ducks are the latest in decoy tools used by hunters to lure real ducks into shooting range. These "faux fowl" are so realistic that they have been banned by a number of states. A "rig" of wooden decoys is history, but some carvers continue the cultural tradition. Collectors constitute the current market for these hand-carved decoys, not the serious hunter who used wooden decoys well before the invention and marketing of rubber, plastic, or cork imitators.

Various carving styles are found in Louisiana. Those following the older tradition carve ducks in a style and manner not intended to be realistic. Many are sleek without individual feathers indicated, and either have a natural finish or are painted in certain color combinations. More recently, carvers have begun creating more realistic images of a wider variety of wildfowl. Some carve or burn each feather and paint the decoys realistically. Today, native and exotic water fowl, shorebirds, birds of prey, songbirds, and hummingbirds are carved in life-size, half-size, and miniature replicas. Full-size carvings may be in groupings, or placed in carefully researched habitats. The miniatures may be used as jewelry, and come complete with stand which both protects the delicate items and creates an appropriate habitat. Some carvers also carve Louisiana's saltwater and freshwater fish, crawfish, other animals native to Louisiana, and exotic tropical fish. Native Louisiana tupelo gum and cypress are the most frequently used woods although basswood and other hardwoods are occasionally preferred (Wildlife Carving 1998).

Menhaden-Based Communities

The earliest American pioneers settling the East Coast sought menhaden after they were taught by native Indians that the fish made excellent fertilizer. The name, in fact, came originally from an Indian word 'Munnawhatteaug' meaning 'fertilizer' or 'that which manures.' Originally, menhaden were spread directly on planted fields (McSherry 1980:10).

Along with the popular shrimp, oyster, and crab fisheries, Louisiana's coast also supports the economically important Gulf menhaden purse-seine fishery. In fact, as early as 1930 the state was supporting research on the menhaden's commercial importance (Harrison and Pottinger 1931). During the harvest of this industrial herring-like fish (also known as hard-head, bunkers, bony-fish, moss-bunker, alewife, water witches, shiner, pogeyhaden, and herring), crews are housed at the processing site or nearby, creating a small fishery community. In this regard, the menhaden industrial operation is like that of the earliest coal camps, which often consisted of a boarding house for the male employees. Housing for the transient employees—many from Virginia's Northern Neck who worked the Atlantic and Gulf fisheries—was either aboard the fishing vessels, in rooms that were part of the processing plant, or in trailers.

The crews live in these facilities during the six-month season (from mid-April through mid-October). They return home to their families for the winter, when menhaden fishing is forbidden by law (Fritchey 2001). In the fall, the migration process starts again. The relocation of these fishermen resembles that of the first Dalmatians who returned to their Adriatic villages each year (Spitzer 1985). As a general rule, menhaden boat captains, mates, and pilots were white, while Afro-Americans constituted most of the crewmen who handled the nets and stored the catch (Moore 1996).

One of the impressive nets used in the menhaden industry, 1947. (Photo courtesy of the Standard Oil Collection, University of Louisville, negative no. 50053.)

The menhaden industry was traditionally centered on a land-based factory, typically employing nearly 100 laborers for its respective fleet. Each fishing vessel (steamer) included a crew of from twenty to twenty-six individuals. The number employed depended on the size of the pogie fleet. Work in the fishery, like any Louisiana fishery, was hard, requiring a concentrated effort, and long days under extreme conditions (Cramer 2006). Indeed, the work was intense. Each laborer worked on shares, while the captains were paid with fish. Even so, the bonus and pay could be quite substantial. Although originally concentrated in New England, and dating back to the 1800s, because of labor, fuel, and property costs, the fishery gradually migrated to the South (Frye 1978).

It is highly likely that the Gulf Coast fishery dates back to the late nineteenth century, but the location of plants, catch statistics, and types of boats involved were not recorded. In all probability, menhaden were by-catch and used as crab or tarpon bait (Frye 1978). In 1880, less than 1,000 pounds of menhaden were landed, but from this small beginning, the industry has experienced considerable growth.

The Gulf's menhaden industry recognized its potential in the 1930s, but it took nearly twenty years before this purse-seine fishery was firmly established along the Gulf Coast by Atlantic Coast and Chesapeake Bay fishermen. By the late 1940s, the menhaden industry was operating from plants along Louisiana's coast, thanks to the efforts of Wallace Quinn and the Smith brothers. Quinn entered the Gulf of Mexico fishery near Pascagoula, Mississippi in 1939. In 1949, he built his biggest plant at Empire, Louisiana—near primary fishing grounds in Breton Sound and west of the delta beyond Grand Isle (Frye 1978). Because Hurricane Audrey (1957) damaged his Texas operation, he built a facility at Dulac that could process 100 tons an hour. Meanwhile, the Smith brothers—Harvey, Otis, and Gilbert—established their operation at Monkey

Island, near Cameron; in 1977, this plant processed 306.7 million pounds. They also owned operations at Morgan City, bought in 1957 from the Guarasco family, and built a plant at Intracoastal City in 1965.

Despite variability in the catch record, landings generally have increased steadily since the 1950s (Christmas and Etzold 1977). The production curve reached its peak in 1971, when Gulf of Mexico ports processed 1.6 million pounds. Thirty-three years later the nation harvested 1.4 billion pounds, with Louisiana providing 60 percent of the total catch. Between 1950 and 2006, Louisiana's "pogie" fleet has averaged nearly 450,000 tons annually, with a cumulative value of $1.8 billion (NMFS Landings Query Results 2006). Menhaden was second in 2004 to Alaskan pollack (*Theragra Chacogramma*) in terms of pounds landed (Pritchard 2005).

Even with such impressive production, the number of companies, plants, and steamers involved has declined since the 1970s (Vaughan, et al. 2000). Consequently, at the beginning of the twenty-first century, only about forty vessels—with a capacity of nearly 1 million fish each—were involved in this fishery, down from a previous high of ninety-two (Vaughan, et al. 2000). Most of the fish caught by these steamers are harvested in the waters along the fringes of the Louisiana coast; a particularly productive area is located in and around the Mississippi delta. All of the fishing is done offshore, with the exception of Breton and Chandeleur sounds.

The fishery has blossomed into a major industry, because when processed the oil and fertilizer meal are highly marketable (Perret 1968). The fish's oil, high in Omega-3 fatty acids, is an ingredient of enriched foods. The oil is also mixed with other elements for: cooking oils and shortening, marine lubricants, plasticizers, alkyd resins, and oils for paint and lipstick. Menhaden oil has been popular for many years in Europe as a health food supplement and as a primary ingredient in margarine.

Brevoortia meal is a high-protein blend of nutrients used in feeds for swine, poultry, and cattle. Less than 5 percent of the catch is used as bait for blue crab, crawfish, and other fisheries. Although the dollar value for shrimp remains unsurpassed in Louisiana fisheries, the menhaden fishery easily exceeds it in terms of volume. By the early 1970s, menhaden caught off Louisiana's waters had become the single largest industrial fishery, by weight, in the lower forty-eight states. In the 1970s, more than one billion pounds were harvested annually (Frye 1978).

Much of the catch was taken by steamers owned by John Santos Carinhas. Carinhas, from St. Augustine, Florida, owned shrimp and menhaden interests that were eventually intertwined. In the late 1930s, he left St. Augustine to take part in the Gulf's white shrimp industry by reestablishing his fleet and business at Patterson. At his Patterson shipyard, the family constructed shrimp and menhaden vessels for their own interest and for others. John Santos noted: "I had to build my own boats if I was going to stay in business" (Frye 1978:158). Although Carinhas never owned a menhaden plant, his fleet of menhaden vessels, by the early 1950s, included:

John Santos Carinhas, of Portuguese ancestry, was active in the menhaden and shrimp processing industries, 2008. (Photo by the author.)

Eight wooden boats, the largest the 137-foot Admiral, the smallest the seventy-five-foot Freedom. And there were six steel boats, including the Captain Wes Robinson. The newest then was the 114-foot Jose E. Carinhas, built and named for his younger son, . . . (Frye 1978:158).

The menhaden industry's roots are in the Eastern Seaboard. The examples above and below are from Albermarle Sound. (Images from *Harper's Weekly,* August 10, 1889.)

As a result, processors did not have to own a fleet of pogey boats. They could obtain their boats from Carinhas. In 1952, his pogey feet produced 230 million pounds of menhaden—nearly the entire Gulf of Mexico harvest. Being of Portuguese descent, John Santos remembered his roots and always tried to make sure he had Portuguese working for him. Many net menders at the Empire Menhaden Company were from Portugal, as well as at Carinhas operations in Patterson (Frye 1978).

The Portuguese are another ethnic group that is a forgotten part of Louisiana's ethnic history. They are lost in the historical record, yet the Gulf Coast has many Portuguese names attached to its fisheries. This small contingent of fishermen, many of whom were transients, constitutes an important part of the wetland settlement story.

Processing plants, or fish factories, were located originally in Empire, Dulac (closed in 1996), Morgan City, Intracoastal City, and Cameron. The menhaden catch made these ports some of the most important in the country, with the collective harvest valued at slightly more than $33 million annually (NMFS Landings Query Results 2006). Ownership of these facilities has changed over time, but the nation's three largest menhaden processors—Zapata Haynie Corporation, Seacoast Products Incorporated, and Standard Products Company once were involved in Louisiana's pogey business. About the size of a sardine, the small *brevoortia* travel in large schools that feed in estuarine environments and appear in the Gulf from April to November (Vaughan, et al. 2000). Prior to the 1950s, these schools were located by spotters in the steamer's crow's nest. This was an effective technique, but the industry subsequently began to use airplanes to locate the fish, and fleet efficiency increased significantly. Pilots now notice the tell tale "whip"—formed by little individual fish splashes. From these signs the pilot can direct the harvesting procedures from the air.

The actual fishing operation involves a 170-foot-long ship that maneuvers close enough to the school to launch, from the stern, two forty-foot-long seine or "purse" boats. Once these small boats slide off the stern, one-half of the 600-foot long, nylon, purse-seine is dropped from behind each boat. Once overboard, floats hold the top of the seine at the surface. To set the net, the purse boats separate and begin immediately to circle the school. They follow a half-circle course, come together, and close the net's bottom. At this point, the purse boats are "made fast" at one end next to the steamer (Fritchey 2001). Once the net is in position, the crew "scraps" or "brails" the menhaden aboard with a large dip net capable of offloading 1,000 pounds at a time. With the advent of hydraulic pumps and suction hoses, a crew can discharge 20,000 fish a minute into a refrigerated hold. Approximately a million fish constitute a full load (Cramer 2006).

Purse boats were vital to the menhaden harvest, 1982. (Photo by the author.)

It can take up to twenty sets to make up a load. "The action is quick and fast, competition between boats is fierce, and all hands share in the profits" (Fritchey 2001:6). Once the boats are at capacity, there is a dash to the processing plants. The plants can only pump out three boats, before they must begin to process the catch. The fourth boat to arrive at the dock loses a workday, because they have to wait to be off-loaded. Toward the end of the day, the competitive captains begin to watch each other, as it is a cutthroat business to be one of the first three boats to reach the dock. On a good day, a crewman can make better than $300. For a variety of reasons, the fleet shuts down for the weekends to give the crews and the fish a rest.

Environmental factors have increasingly played a role in the harvest. In late 1995, for example, the large Dulac-Chauvin menhaden processing facility south of Houma

Hydraulic and suction hoses dramatically increased a crew's ability to remove menhaden from the purse seine, 1982. (Photo by the author.)

reportedly closed because of the "dead zone" in the Gulf of Mexico—a condition in which there is too little oxygen in the water for anything to live, also known as hypoxia. Closure of this plant affected the local economy and the status of the region's fish processing.

The health of the region's estuarine environments, upon which the menhaden fishery is based, is also of great concern to the industry. Young *brevoortia* use the estuaries in the early stages of their development. Since the juveniles are primarily herbivores, it is imperative that the estuary be relatively free from pollutants. If not, this critical developmental stage could be detrimentally impacted to the point of destroying the multi-million dollar fishery. Further, the habitat changes that will result from land loss will mean Louisiana's position as one of the nation's largest seafood processors will vanish. In addition, the jobs directly and indirectly associated with this renewable resource will also disappear.

The lynch pin of this change may not be the perennial dead zone problem, but the aftermath of Hurricanes Katrina, Rita, Gustav, and Ike. These storms severely impacted Louisiana's menhaden industry and steamer fleet. In Plaquemines Parish, one menhaden plant was flooded with several feet of water and eleven boats were beached. The plant accounted for about one-third of the total Gulf menhaden landings. If it were to close, the Department of Wildlife and Fisheries estimates the lost to the state's economy would be nearly $160 million. However, the industry may bounce back. Regardless, the short- and long-term impacts are not trivial (Burke 2005), for the menhaden catch was valued in 2005 at $22 million, down from a record $68 million harvest in 2000.

The industry may be at a "tipping" point, and only time will tell if this significant fishery will rebound.

Chapter 8
SULPHUR, OIL, AND NATURAL WETLAND TRANSIENT COMMUNITIES

Sulphur in Louisiana

The American brimstone industry was founded on sulphur associated with salt domes. In spite of the salt's value, these geologic anomalies are presently more important for their petroleum and, in some cases, sulphur. Along the Gulf coast, by 1935, more than sixty salt domes were producing oil at an aggregate rate in excess of fifty million barrels per year. Nine produced commercial grade brimstone, but sulphur-producing domes are rare (Cunningham 1935). Less than 10 percent of those salt formations fringing the Gulf of Mexico contain commercially recoverable sulphur.

The nation's first sulphur mine based on the Frasch process was developed at what is today known as Sulphur, but identified as Sulphur City in 1899. (Image from Harris, et al. 1899.)

In mining sulphur, the cap rock, absent on some domes, contains the recoverable sulphur. Sulphur from this zone was first extracted from Louisiana's "sulphur mine" near the town named after the deposit. As a result of Herman Frasch's hot-water extraction process, this feature was for many years the world's greatest sulphur producer. The "sulphur mine" established Louisiana as a dominant force in the sulphur industry. Production from this first dome began a new era in sulphur mining and the creation of semi-permanent

When sulphur companies expanded into the marsh, survey crews faced a formidable challenge, 1932. (Photo courtesy of Waldemar S. Nelson and Company.)

407

industrial communities in the state's marshlands (Davis and Detro 1992). Fourteen mines were established in Louisiana; the largest—Grande Écaille—was in the marshes west of the Mississippi River and north-northeast of Grande Terre.

Louisiana's sulphur mines

Mine	*Date Established*	*Location/Environment*
Bay Ste. Elaine	1952	In open water marshes in Terrebonne Parish
Bully Camp	1968	In open water marshes in Lafourche Parish
Caminada Pass	1968	Offshore, southwest of Grand Isle
Chacahoula	1967	In the swamp in Lafourche Parish
Caillou Island	1980	In open water marshes
Garden Island Bay	1953	In open water marshes in Plaquemines Parish
Grande Écaille	1933	In the marsh in Plaquemines Parish
Grand Isle Block 18	1960	Offshore, west of the delta and southeast of Grand Terre
Lake Hermitage	1968	In open water marshes Plaquemines Parish
Lake Peigneur/ Jefferson Island	1928	On the prairie in Iberia Parish
Lake Pelto	1960	In open water marshes in Terrebonne Parish
Main Pass Block 299		Offshore, east of the delta's Main Pass
Starks Dome	1951	On the prairie in Calcasieu Parish
Sulphur Mine	1894	On the prairie in Calcasieu Parish

Grande Écaille: An Industry on Stilts

The Grande Écaille salt dome is in Plaquemines Parish, Louisiana, 10 miles west of the right descending bank of the Mississippi, 45 miles below New Orleans, and within four miles of the Gulf of Mexico. The terrain is a low, flat, uninhabited area of marsh land, intersected by innumerable shallow lakes and bayous. Except for salt grasses, the region is devoid of vegetation and presents an unobstructed expanse to the vagaries of the winds (Burns 1938:69).

Grande Écaille (tarpon in French) was nothing but marsh—no highways, railroads or fresh water—only tides, hurricanes, and *maringouins* in an environment best described as subaqueous organic ooze, rather than high-load-bearing soils. These above-ground conditions presented an unusual number of obstacles and problems; the most important of these was constructing support facilities and their associated foundations in an alluvial wetland. An industrial city, weighing approximately 326,000 tons, needed literally to be suspended in air (Burns 1938). When completed, Grande Écaille was supported by 35,854 pilings, (enough to stretch from New Orleans

View of the construction of Grande Écaille's power plant, 1933. (Photo courtesy of Waldemar S. and Nelson Company.)

to Houston that if placed end-to-end). Most of the pilings varied in length from forty to eighty feet (Burns 1938) and were anchored by their skin friction with the marsh soils.

Part of the industrial complex that made up Grande Écaille, 1933. (Photo from the *Eleventh Biennial Report, Louisiana Department of Conservation, 1932-1933.*)

These supports are the foundation of what developed into the oldest producing sulphur mine in Louisiana and the second largest in the world (Wilder 1954; Netzeband, et al. 1964). Grande Écaille represented an expenditure of millions to place mining equipment in a geographic location that was more water than land. It was a difficult environment to establish an industrial complex.

In February 1932, Freeport Sulphur (a Texas Company incorporated in 1912 and was the Lone Star state's first sulphur producer) acquired the sulphur rights to Grande Écaille, in order to help the firm rebound from its depleted supplies at Bryan Mound, Texas. Because of the urgent need to find new reserves, Freeport began to exploit Grande Écaille immediately. Exploratory wells indicated the dome possessed large quantities of recoverable sulphur, but there was no way of knowing whether the deposit could be mined at a profit. Freeport would have to speculate millions—eventually more than $6 million ($93 million inflated for 2009)—before it could be determined whether sulphur could be produced in commercial quantities. Almost immediately after Freeport executives decided to challenge the logic of working in a marsh, actual construction got underway. Freeport engineers, and engineering consultants from New Orleans and New York, decided that the foundation for power plant and auxiliary buildings would consist of heavy reinforced concrete mats supported by pilings. They were going to build a sulphur mine on stilts.

Before the construction of Grande Écaille, test borings were taken to see what engineering difficulties lay ahead, ca. 1930. (Photo courtesy of Waldemar S. Nelson and Company.)

Less than a year after the sulphur rights were secured, eighteen wells were drilled and sampled (Lundy 1934). In fact, drilling activity was continuous. Some wells were phenomenal in their productive life. Well No. 643, for example, produced for more than 800 days—prompting the Grande Écaille sulphur men to dub it "Old Faithful" ('Old Faithful' has 1946). By the end of 1932, more than 200 acres of the dome's 1,100-acre sulphur-bearing zone had been surveyed. The survey proved that the company's experiment was a success (Grande Ecaille's success 1958). The deposit was large, valuable, and an economic boom in the depths of the Great Depression.

Pile drivers walked across the marsh, elevating board walks to be used by mine workers, 1933. (Photo courtesy of Waldemar S. Nelson and Company.)

Building Grande Écaille

"Men worked up to their chests in quagmires, sometimes slipping over their heads; and the mosquitoes and other pests became so bad that they could not continue until engineers devised 'blowers'—automobile engines with airplane propellers attached—to drive off the insects" (Kane 1944:257).

Indeed, Grande Écaille quickly proved a bonanza, eventually producing 1,200 tons of marketable sulphur a day.

The mine's bog-like terrain, required everything to be moved over board roads. Originally, these boardwalks were simply laid in the mud, and the soil under the boards often became waterlogged; hence, the road sank and became impassable. To correct this problem, wooden sills—structural members consisting of continuous horizontal timbers forming the lowest members of a framework or supporting structure—were incorporated into the board-road design to elevate the surface, promoting drainage and permitting the ground to air dry. Even with these precautions, torrential rains would flood the site.

To overcome terrain problems, the company utilized drilling rigs erected on steel barges specially built for drilling in the unconsolidated marsh sediments. Within the first ten years, drilling crews completed 270 wells (Those Grande Ecaille 1943). Drilling was a cumbersome operation. In the early days, heavy wooden sills were used to support the derrick, and each sill had to be moved with each derrick. This grueling, labor-intensive operation required boards and rollers over which the derrick was moved by means of block and tackle. Eventually, a permanent steel sub-base was attached to the derrick; thus the drilling rig could be skidded across the field by tractor. The derrick then became a portable unit.

As construction progressed, major logistic problems had to be addressed and solved. To alleviate the transportation issue, Freeport selected and purchased a site on the Mississippi River, accessible by the New Orleans and Lower Coast Railroad and Louisiana Hwy 23. The site, initially named "Grandeporte," was later called "Port Sulphur."

Providing rapid and economical transportation from the Mississippi to the mine required dredging a 100-foot wide, nine-foot deep, ten-mile long canal—identified on maps as the: Freeport Sulphur Company Canal. The project involved the movement of two million cubic yards of alluvium, with the spoil serving as the bed for a roadway

Grandeporte, later named Port Sulphur, was one of Louisiana's first industrial cities. It is pictured here in 1933. (Photo courtesy of Waldemar S. Nelson and Company.)

parallel to the channel (Burns 1938). Once completed, the canal served as the mine's logistic-lifeline.

> Through this channel piling totaling 2,126,301 linear feet, or 403 miles, was shipped in; and other shipments included 4 million board feet of lumber; 200,000 linear feet of pipe four inches in diameter; ten miles of 33,000-volt power line; five miles of 2,300-volt; 15 miles of telephone line; 9,102 tons of structural steel; 586 tons of roofing, siding sashes, and doors; 5,832 tons of material and machinery; 19,206 tons of concrete; and 6,757 tons of wooden buildings (Burns 1938:70).

The construction schedule required precise timing, since there were no storage facilities at the mining site. Each item had to be set in place as it was unloaded. Freeport could not afford any down-time. Any delays had to be corrected immediately in order to avoid the congestion of materials at the handling facilities. The volume of material required by the project was too great to be stockpiled; everything had to move according to a strict time table (Thirty-two years 1935). To meet this schedule, a terminal was established at Harvey, across the Mississippi River from New Orleans. The terminal was required to bypass some of the congestion that occurred at Port Sulphur and to provide adequate storage space for pipe and other materials required at Grande Écaille. Using two retrofitted Landing Craft Tanks (LCTs), a ferry service was established to Grande Écaille through its back door by way of Barataria Bay (Long trail to 1947). These vessels, which could move from 150 tons to 175 tons of material per trip, became an important part of the mine's logistics supply chain (The Harvey terminal 1947; Long trial to 1947).

As the marsh would not support large loads, the mining area was filled to a height of four to eight feet. To counteract subsidence, hydraulic fill was provided by the cutter head dredges *Ballard*, *Chert*, and *Louisiana* (New lands to 1944; Field 'sinking' a 1960). For 32 years, dredges were used to fill subsidence cavities with mud. By 1962, a total of 39.4 million cubic yards—enough to fill a canal thirty-feet wide by ten-feet deep for

Building the foundation for Grande Écaille was a tedious, labor-intensive process. Pilings were crucial to the mine's operation, so the engineers designed the structure around "a floating foundation," 1933. (Photos courtesy of Waldemar S. Nelson and Company.)

a distance of 672 miles—had been dredged and pumped onto the mine. Often a hole forty- to fifty-feet deep had to be dredged to obtain suitable fill material; as a result, one area subsided from six-feet above sea level to seventeen-feet below—a difference of twenty-three feet. Some sections recorded subsidence rates of thirty-three feet.

The sinking is the byproduct of the mining operation. It happens because a void is created when the sulphur-bearing caprock is liquefied. When the top collapses from the weight of the overburden, the surface sinks, settles or subsides (Field 'sinking' a 1960). To correct the problem, levees were built around the subsiding areas, and new fill was added. Conversely, the area selected for building the storage vats had to be raised by fill to a height of twelve feet (Lundy 1934; Lundy 1934B).

The job at that time concerned designing a piling-supported foundation that would carry the mine's support buildings with minimum subsidence. No stratum was discovered that would support 1,200 pounds per square foot. To compensate for the low load-bearing consistency of the marsh muck, it was determined that seventy-five-foot pilings were the correct length for use under the primary structure (Lundy 1934; Lundy 1934B). Nearly thirty years after the first pile was driven, more than 200,000 had been hammered into the marsh—representing an investment of nearly $11 million. These pilings supported an industrial community ultimately weighing more than 325,000 tons, including the mine's power plant, shops, warehouses, crew quarters, sulphur vats, water, oil and bleed water tanks, water, booster lines, and the sulphur docks (Burns 1938).

Cooling vats were used to contain the mined liquid sulphur, no date. (Photo courtesy of Fred Dunham.)

The first pile was driven on February 5, 1933. On that day, the pioneer crew had to stand on a plank in hip boots and hand-hammer a pile into the marsh muck to support

Part of the vast assortment of pipelines required to liquify and transport sulphur at Grande Écaille, 1933. (Photo courtesy of Waldemar S. Nelson and Company.)

their lunch boxes. From this beginning, Grande Écaille began to evolve. Freeport successfully built an industrial plant ten miles from fresh water and fuel, exposed to the full force of Gulf storms, on a surface described as *"prairie tremblant,"* and under engineering conditions that continuously challenged the management decision to build over this subsurface salt dome. With all of these issues, not the least of which were the insects that added to the discomfort of the men working on this project, Grande Écaille began producing sulphur on December 9, 1933—less than a year after the first lunch-box was supported on a piling driven in the barren marsh (Burns 1934; Haynes 1934).

The power plant and all permanent buildings were constructed of steel frames designed to withstand 125-mile per hour winds. The structure's floor was twelve-feet above mean Gulf tide. That was considered ample to protect the mine's support buildings during storm-induced high water: "the piling was cut off about 1 foot above the marsh, capped with thick concrete mats and piers constructed to support the plant floor and equipment" (Lundy 1934). In addition to untreated and cut-off piling, about 40 percent of the piles used were cypress and treated piles (Burns 1934).

To reduce subsidence problems, the power plant was located approximately one mile from the mining operation. The superheated water (325°F) required to melt the sulphur had to be moved on a timber trestle to the mine site. The pipes required by the mine were welded together on site and divided by their purpose: conveying hot water, compressed air, or steam. The challenge was moving the liquid sulphur to the storage vats. This could be accomplished by either a steam jacket or an inner line. On a long line, a "gut" or inner steam line was used to maintain the desired temperature. At Grande Écaille, the "gut line" was a two-inch galvanized pipeline that "floated" in the main line, since no effort was made to center this line in the larger pipe (McLaughlin 1938).

Sulphur mining requires enormous quantities of water, and Freeport's engineers determined the Mississippi River provided the only water sufficiently free of encrusting contaminants to be used by the facility. To accommodate the three million gallons of water per day that was necessary to keep the out-of-the-way mine in operation, a fifty million gallon (a fifteen-day supply) reservoir was constructed for settling the turbid water at Port Sulphur (Grande Ecaille: Louisiana 1933). From this reservoir, a ten-mile, welded-pipeline was constructed to carry water to the power plant. The line was

As the essential elevated board road was constructed at Grande Écaille, trucks were off-loaded from barges to provide access, 1933. (Photo courtesy of Waldemar S. Nelson and Company.)

designed originally to transport 4.2 million gallons per day, but its capacity was later increased to handle 7.8 million gallons—more than the power plant's eventual capacity (Blackstone 1949). Cement lined pipe was also used to reduce the corrosion problem. Along the trestle's right-of-way, utility poles were erected, since power generated in the plant was carried on a 33,000 volt high line to Port Sulphur. The electricity was used in loading the sulphur ships, pumping water into the reservoir, and in the homes built by Freeport at Port Sulphur (Blackstone 1949).

A two million gallon storage reservoir was built at the plant. This engineer-designed basin was necessary to insure continuous operation in the event that the main reservoir, pumping equipment, or pipeline needed to be repaired. Once constructed, the plant's water supply was guaranteed (Lundy 1934). This reserve was only large enough to meet the power plant's daily process-water requirement. Subsequent expansion and improvements resulted in an increased demand for water. Eventually, the plant had a capacity of 6.2 million gallons per day. With these improvements, the reservoirs at the mine and Port Sulphur were enlarged to impound a total of 400 million gallons—a 200-day supply—taken from the Mississippi during periods of low salinity (Netzeband, et al. 1964; Blackstone 1949).

To fire the boilers, Freeport opted to use fuel oil delivered by tanker to Port Sulphur and stored in three 55,000 barrel tanks. The fuel oil was moved to the plant by barges operating through the firm's canal and discharged into storage tanks. Natural gas was also a critical part of the mine's operation. A long-term contract signed with the Texas Company in 1936 guaranteed delivery. The natural gas was routed to Grande Écaille through an eight-inch, twenty-five-mile-long pipeline from the Texas Company's Lafitte oil and gas field in Terrebonne Parish. Gas was first used at the plant on February 1, 1937 (GE—The mine 1962). The switch from fuel oil to natural gas increased the mine's efficiency. Other improvements were added gradually to increase the mine's production. By 1960, Grande Écaille had produced

Even after its closure, Louisiana's largest marsh industrial city, Grande Écaille, maintained a ghostly presence in the coastal wetlands, 1976. (Photo by the author.)

23.2 million tons of sulphur—at a rate of nearly 900,000 tons per year. When shut down in December 1978, Grande Écaille had produced a block of almost pure sulphur (99.75 percent) one-mile square and twenty-nine feet high.

To operate this facility, a city was created in the marshes of South Louisiana. Driven by a single natural resource, inventive engineering, and risk-taking industrialists, Grande Écaille represents an industrial city that mimics any in the "Rust Belt," only on a much smaller scale. In the late 1800s, as industries expanded, capitalist needed labor, transportation, housing, power, potable water, and the other social and economic amenities that allowed them to prosper into scions of the Industrial Age.

The end result of this "organized" expansion was creation of boomtowns, which were a blessing and a curse. In Freeport's case, they controlled the laborer flow at Grande Écaille and the site was at sea-level with all large-scale permanent structures on pilings. It was an industrial city that has no counterpart anywhere. It was unique, and its population presented to the world a different group of faces from the wetlands;

Freeport built housing facilities at Grande Écaille to guarantee their labor force was on-site, 1933. (Photo courtesy of Waldemar S. Nelson and Company.)

Building Grande Écaille required an industrial labor force that transformed the marsh into an industrial city, 1932. (Photo courtesy of Waldemar S. Nelson and Company.)

these were not true "marshdwellers," but factory-men who worked a fixed schedule and commuted into the marsh to extract a non-renewable resource, not carefully harvest a renewable resource. A different group had invaded the marsh's tranquility, and they represented the first wave of industrial laborers who would permanently transform the marsh landscape. The jump-off point to Grande Écaille was at Port Sulphur—Freeport's base-camp community.

Port Sulphur

> Port Sulphur's 600 residents benefit from community facilities unknown to many larger and long-established towns. Planned by Freeport executives, the town layout is spacious; garden space is provided adjacent to each house. There is a community house, theater, library, well-run boarding house for single men, lighted tennis court, lighted baseball and soft-ball diamonds, and a modern hospital (Moresi 1939:22).

The sulphur produced at Grande Écaille, and subsequently at several other mines, was barged to Freeport's ship-loading facilities at Port Sulphur. The town, built on property owned by Freeport, served a dual role. It served as the central storage and transshipment point for Freeport's mined sulphur, and also as a hometown for many of Grande Écaille's employees.

Before construction of Port Sulphur, crews boated to Grande Écaille from Lafitte. They worked eleven days on and three off, with a work day revolving around a dawn-to-dusk and dusk-to-dawn schedule. The original living quarters were houseboats, some of which were eventually replaced by more comfortable bunk houses. Some employees considered the trip to Lafitte to be too tiresome, so they stayed at the site—

often for more than 100 days (Grande Ecaille's success 1958).

With construction of Port Sulphur, and establishment of a water-taxi-service, the commuting time was reduced to less than thirty minutes. Three years after diesel-powered boats were introduced, more than 21,000 trips had been logged by the company's navy. In that period the "total number of passenger miles traveled exceed[ed] five and a quarter million" (Salute the 'Navy' 1943:2). With this type of intensive use, the boats were taken out of the water every ninety days, so repair crews could clean and service the vessels properly. Speed and comfort were considered essential. In 1947, five new passenger boats were put into service. Built in Michigan and transported to Port Sulphur on flatcars, these fifty-passenger vessels improved the connection between Grande Écaille and Port Sulphur (Transportation gets a 1947).

Along with building the town, Freeport had to establish a private navy that was based at Port Sulphur but served the needs of their Grande Écaille mine. The company's labor crews were dependent on an efficient water transportation system, since there were no conventional roads to their job sites. Pushboats, tugboats, and speedboats were to the citizens of Port Sulphur what the railroad was to the early West. Crewboats traveled 5,000 miles (for comparison purposes this is about the distance between New York and Hawaii) a month carrying men and equipment to Grande Écaille. After the mine was completed, there was a constant stream of barges piled high with sulfur going between the mine and Port Sulphur. This was a twenty-four-hour operation, 365 days a year, as the mine never shut down (The Port Sulphur 1943).

Freeport's company town, Port Sulphur, became the focal point of their marsh operation, ca. 1937. (Photo courtesy of Waldemar S. Nelson and Company.)

Built in 1933, Port Sulphur was considered a model community and was designed to insure that the Grande Écaille workforce was comfortable. The town was planned to meet the housing needs of Freeport's employees and their families. The mine was not convenient, so it was important to develop a logistic support facility that was also the home of the company's Grande Écaille labor force, as they had to commute to the mine every work day, or stay at the marsh complex.

The town, laid out on about 1,100 acres, was designed so each house was eighty-feet apart. The structures were accessible by footpaths, and each faced a garden. Port Sulphur was described as: "probably . . . the most completely up-to-date community in the state" (By yellow magic 1937:18B) and "as folksy as a party line" (Port Sulphur: a 1950:14). The original design included three, four, and five-room homes that would be used by 125 families. Considerable thought was given to the community's collective architecture. A colonial-type structure was built, with twenty-seven distinct designs.

Although somewhat isolated, Port Sulphur evolved into a substantial Plaquemines Parish community, with homes, a hospital, and a community center, ca. 1947. (Photos courtesy of Waldemar S. Nelson and Company.)

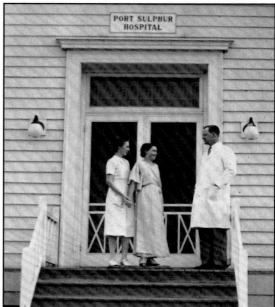

This variation broke up the visual monotony that is often found in company towns, like the redundant cottages associated with a sugar mill. A variety of house types also helped give Port Sulphur residents a sense that they were not residents of a company (Model community at 1939). There was no company-owned store or commissary. Freeport allowed the town to develop its own identity and its own self-sufficiency. A person's avocation, such as repairing shoes or cutting hair, became an important and needed community service. Several small commercial centers developed near the town-site. Surveys were taken periodically by Freeport personnel to make sure that prices at these stores were in line with those in New Orleans. Groceries, meat, clothes, and other necessities were available at these businesses; no advertising or script tokens were issued (Model community at 1939).

A major corporate goal was elimination of traffic from the town. Cul-de-sacs were incorporated into Port Sulphur's design, along with a community house large enough to hold the town's entire population. The streets had no names and the houses had no numbers, but it did not matter; it was a community of like-minded people working for a single industry (Markland 1945). A playground, two swimming pools, a nine-hole golf course, softball fields, tennis courts, a community canning kitchen, theater, library, school, and the first hospital built in Plaquemines Parish (boasting eighteen rooms) were also part of the community. For a small monthly fee ($2.50 for the head of the family and a $1.50 for each additional individual) hospital care was provided at Port Sulphur's hospital or the offices of associated doctors (Moresi 1939; Markland 1945).

Freeport furnished the services normally provided by an incorporated municipality, such as sewage and water systems and garbage collection and disposal. In 1943, civic-minded leaders organized the Port Sulphur Township Association. The nine-member board became the community's liaison between the company and other private institutions. The town did not have a mayor, city council, or city taxes, but it did have a small mimeograph sheet call *The Sulphur Dust*, that functioned as the community's newspaper.

The board also initiated a "job idea" program to provide the community's young people an opportunity to learn about various professions and trades. A youth recreation center was built to provide supervised recreation and social functions. In the 1940s and 1950s, Port Sulphur served as a node of community activity. It was difficult and time consuming to leave the area, so the township turned inward for its social and recreational needs. Company-owned property was used by the Sulphur Employee's Club for recreational pursuits—baseball games, fishing, hunting, oystering, and picnicking. For a membership fee of three dollars a year, the club improved the facilities and patrolled the land.

With 244 company-owned family dwellings and dormitories for 194 single employees, the town, by 1950, housed 1,200 people—double the size of its 1939 population and about 12 percent of the parish's 1950 population (Moresi 1939). To supplement the houses being built on site, prefabricated duplexes were barged to Port Sulphur from Orange, Texas. In addition, the original dwellings were supplemented by eighty homes barged from Kessler Air Field in Mississippi into the community of Orange Grove—a new town-site developed after World War II (Housing at Port . . . 1946; Mengis 1950). By 1937, there were 100 homes perched on 252,000 cubic yards of fill (Townsite hurdled housing 1962). By 1950, 244 houses were located in the unincorporated community of Port Sulphur—164 on the original town-site and eighty in Orange Grove (Port Sulphur: a 1950).

Port Sulphur eventually expanded from a logistic-support center for Grande Écaille into the central operating, maintenance, and administrative headquarters for Freeport's Louisiana mines. To accommodate the expanded supply of sulphur barged

The French Custom of Pre-Paying a Doctor

"It is an old French custom with the majority of the inhabitants to subscribe to the doctor's service. This is a unique characteristic which is advantageous to both parties, for it insures the physician a definite income, and on the other hand, reduces the family's doctor bill to a minimum expense. The arrangement is simple; the doctor charges a certain stimulated sum of money annually per person. This subscription rate, or *l'abonnement* as the French call it, is usually paid at the beginning of the year" (Parenton 1938:77).

to Port Sulphur as a liquid, a new storage area was built. As a result, liquid sulphur barged to Port Sulphur was unloaded into dockside tanks. From there it was pumped into a number of twenty-ton storage tanks that could be filled in eight minutes and siphoned automatically into the large sulphur bins. These storage bins were located on an eighty-acre site. Elevated about eight feet by fill and sitting on 25,000 pilings, the two thirty-foot high, 200 by 1,124-foot storage sites provided a reserve of 450,000 long tons (a long ton is equal to 2,400 pounds) of sulphur (Bartlett, et al. 1952).

The molten-sulphur tank's design insured only a thin layer of sulphur was added to the bin, a technique that ensured the layer was solidified before another sheet of sulphur film was deposited (Bartlett, et al. 1952). Aluminum sheets served as forms. They were raised and reinstalled periodically at higher positions as the bin progressed upwards. When a container was filled to a height of thirty feet, the sides were removed. These holding "tanks" were not dynamited, which was the original method of breaking pieces away from the sulphur block. At Port Sulphur, electric-power shovels removed the mineral directly from the solidified brick at a rate of at least 500 long tons per hour. From the storage site the bulk sulphur chunks were moved by a conveyor system, through a crusher to reduce their size, and then into the holds of ships or barges (Gustafson 1950; Bartlett, et al. 1952), where a special chute reduced the danger of a flash fire from the static electricity picked up by the dusty sulphur (Sulfur sparks new 1957).

Between 1959 and 1963, Freeport changed its method of delivery and established a vast distribution system capable of handling sulphur above its "freezing" point. Moving sulphur as a liquid was an extension of the company's water-born shipments, initiated in 1948 at Grande Écaille. To implement this departure from traditional methods, the Canal Barge Company built a fleet of nineteen liquid-sulphur barges. They varied in capacity from 2,000 to 4,000 long tons. The vessels loaded at Port Sulphur subsequently served Freeport's sulphur terminals, which at that time were located at Joliet, Illinois; Wellsville, Ohio; Tampa, Florida; Everett, Massachusetts; and Bucksport, Maine. To meet customer's winter demands, when ice limits barge traffic, Freeport had its own melting plant. Sulphur could be melted from a reserve stockpile of about 200,000 long tons (How sulfur flows 1967).

Before sulphur was shipped in liquid form, electric shovels handled the mined product. (Photo from the *Louisiana Conservation Review,* Summer 1939.)

At Port Sulphur, Freeport invested between three and four million dollars for tanks and loading equipment. These facilities allowed the docks to load 1.5 million long tons per year (Trend to molten 1961). Shipping the product in a liquid state reduced dust losses and handling costs, while it also increased the delivered sulphur's purity, because no airborne contaminants could accumulate in the molten sulphur. Since it was already liquid, the sulphur did not have to be melted by the consumers. As a result, the inventory was easy to monitor; this improved the economic efficiency of moving large tonnage (Doak 1963; Williams, et al. 1965). Freeport had planned by 1961 to be shipping 50 percent of its sulphur in a liquid state from terminal facilities at Port Sulphur (Grandone and Hough 1962). The company met and exceeded this forecast. In 1962, 80 percent of the elemental sulphur shipped in North America was moved in a liquid state (Babcock and Stanley 1963).

For Louisiana-produced sulphur, the largest market was centered in Tampa, Florida, where sulphur was converted to sulphuric acid used to process phosphate rock into fertilizer. Liquid sulphur demand was so great that Freeport increased its liquid storage facilities at Port Sulphur by about 50 percent (Grandone, et al. 1964). Although Tampa was the major market, 25 percent of the firm's sales went overseas. European sales increased when the Sulphur Export Corporation (Sulexo) inaugurated a new transatlantic delivery system in 1964. The route connected the Gulf Coast with storage and handling facilities at Rotterdam, Holland (Grandone, et al. 1965). Eight ships with a combined capacity of 139,300 long tons were involved in the trade. Freeport acquired a 24,000 long-ton ocean tanker, *S.S. Louisiana Brimstone*, to service the Eastern Seaboard (Ambrose 1965).

By 1970, almost all sulphur was shipped as a liquid. Sulphur from Grande Écaille and later from Bay Ste. Elaine, Garden Island Bay, Grand Isle, Lake Pelto, and Caminada could be shipped to Port Sulphur and moved to the market in a liquid state. A new trend developed in the sulphur industry. When sulphur began to move by thermos barges and suburban expansion moved towards Port Sulphur, it became apparent that a company town was no longer necessary. The amenities provided by the parent company—schools, churches, good roads, and numerous other urban refinements— were now readily available.

In 1959, Freeport began selling town-site houses to employees, eventually dismantling Port Sulphur through a company-sponsored, interest-free, home-loan program. Many homes were moved to new lots. By 1962, 146 buildings, formerly owned by Freeport, had been sold to its employees (Townsite hurdled housing 1962). Many of the community's buildings were moved or disassembled for the usable timber or were and turned into "camps." For example, the Port Sulphur interdenominational chapel was barged to Dulac, Louisiana, where it served as the sanctuary for the United Methodist Church (Little church on 1979).

After nearly twenty years of service, Port Sulphur like other true company towns, was dismantled, but the place name survives. It is a visual reminder of the importance of this community in the regional, national, and international market for elemental sulphur. Over time, the site will become an archeological artifact, like Grand Écaille, but its significance in the industrialization of the marsh cannot be understated. Unbeknownst to them, the industrial pioneers at Freeport broke new ground in revolutionizing marsh settlement history. With the advent of road-access to the outside world, Louisiana's marshdwellers had retreated from their out-of-the-way, humble, camps. But with industrialization, wage-earners went back into the marsh to work in isolation, but with quick, generally easy, and efficient boat access. The settlement cycle had gone full circle and is represented by Grand Écaille and other mines branded with Freeport's logo.

Other Mines

Garden Island Bay: Sulfur in the Delta

The Garden Island Bay Dome was discovered in 1929 by the Texas Company. The mine, located in Plaquemines Parish, is situated on Dennis Pass—a distributary of the Mississippi River. The site is about 100 miles southeast of New Orleans in the

Mississippi delta. In order to exploit this sulphur deposit, Freeport obtained the rights from Texaco in 1951. Under the terms of the agreement, the sulphur company paid Texaco half the profits it derived from the dome (Freeport breaks news 1951). The drilling barge *W. L. Russ*, a used quarterboat, and three drilling crews completed their first well in twenty-four days and produced excellent sulphur cores. The second well hit gas and blew out—burning uncontrolled for two weeks before dying a natural death (Mine at river's 1962).

The following year, Freeport announced their Garden Island Bay mine was the largest sulphur bed discovered since the Boling Dome in 1928 and Grande Écaille in 1933 (Freeport's find 1951). Normally, such an announcement went unnoticed, but *Business Week* (1951), *Newsweek* (1951) and *Time* (1951) carried articles related to the find. The timing was perfect. The 1950 record sulphur output of 6.3 million long tons could not keep up with demand. By 1951, there was a one million long ton deficit. Sulphur an essential raw material—and badly needed during the Korean conflict—was in short supply. By 1952, industrial consumers became alarmed, since above-ground stocks had dwindled to below 2.8 million long tons (Freeport breaks news 1951).

The biggest news in the Garden Island Bay strike was that when the mine became operative, it would produce 500,000 long tons of sulphur a year, enough to break the world's sulphur shortage in two years. It was decided that living facilities would be built at the mine. Operational personnel would work an off-and-on schedule. The original camp consisted of eighteen five-room cottages, a large dining hall, first-aid building, offices, and "enough cleared space to allow mine personnel to play softball or practice their putting" (Mine at river's 1962:12). A new industrial settlement layer, like that at Grande Écaille, was added to the marsh terrain, broadening the quiet and unpretentious industrialization process.

Before Garden Island Bay became fully operational, three issues had to be addressed—fresh water, sulphur storage, and sulphur transport. The mine's dome is only three miles from the Gulf of Mexico. Salt-water intrusion intensified the water supply problem, since there are two-to-six month periods when the region's water

The Garden Island Bay mine shortly after going into production, no date. (Photo courtesy of the Morgan City Archives.)

The Garden Island Bay mine nearing its last days, 1979. (Photo by the author.)

cannot be used. The company's only alternative was to construct a 600-acre reservoir capable of storing 600 million gallons of fresh water. This was enough to run the 2.7 million gallon a day plant for approximately six months, considering inevitable losses from evaporation, transpiration, and seepage. The reservoir's levees were a challenge due to the consistency of the marsh muck. To build a ten-foot levee required a number of lifts. Waiting for the soil to consolidate between each lift met the levee took about twenty months to complete. Once completed, the levee reservoir guaranteed the mine fresh water (Bartlett, et al. 1952).

The reservoir became an air-photo anomaly. The image of a large holding pond in the Mississippi delta was a peculiar geographic feature that seemed out-of-place. It was misplaced from an interpreters' point-of-view, but absolutely essential to the successful operation of the Garden Islands facility. Geography aside, it worked.

Like all sulphur mines, Garden Island Bay required continuous drilling of sulphur wells to maintain production. Surveyors laid out these new well sites carefully. If a well was inaccessible, a channel was laid out so a dredge could excavate a canal to the new location.

To retrieve the sulphur from its water repository, Freeport engineers had to rely on the work they had done at Grande Écaille to build a plant at Garden Island Bay. The company estimated the recovery plant would cost from $10 to $15 million. The initial outlay was $14 million, making this mine the most expensive sulphur mine built up to that time (Netzeband, et al. 1964).

Unlike Grande Écaille, the marshes along Dennis Pass were recent deposits and subject to flooding, but the natural levee parallel to the distributary was moderately firm, from two to four feet above sea level, and as much as 100-feet wide. Soil tests revealed the subsurface clays extended to a depth of 150 feet, but indicated seventy-five-foot wood pilings would have to be used to support the power plant. Each pile would support seven tons by skin friction and carry an area load of 1,200 pounds per square foot. This arrangement would result in nine inches of net subsidence (Bartlett, et al. 1952). The design resulted in the center of gravity and the center of buoyancy being along the same vertical line. Thus, if the area should flood, the plant would virtually float on an even keel (Freeport Sulphur Company 1978). In the first three years of operation, the power plant settled about 0.29 inches—less than planned (Swamp buggy helps 1957). Even so, subsidence at the mine required the pipe support system to be raised and or redesigned or relocated—a costly process.

In 1965, at least $400,000 was spent to raise a portion of Garden Island Bay's above ground operation. Approximately sixty hydraulic jacks—with a capacity of twenty-five to fifty tons—were used to lift the relay station and several thousand feet of pipelines. The structure had to be elevated—a few inches per day—and releveled at eight feet (Job started to 1965). All of these precautions related to subsidence were a necessary part of operating in Louisiana's wetlands and were a precursor to what the oil and gas industry had to begin to address in the last decade of the twentieth century.

On all of Freeport's marsh-oriented mine sites, subsidence and stability were critical. Pilings supported the industrial village at Grande Écaille, ca. 1935. (Photo courtesy of Waldemar S. and Nelson Company.)

The Garden Island Bay mine was also vulnerable to hurricanes. Hurricane Betsy (1965) did some damage to the property, but the power plant operated through the storm; it did not shut down. Four years later, Hurricane Camille (1969) skirted the Mississippi delta on its way to the Mississippi Gulf Coast. A nine-and-a-half-foot storm surge inundated the mine; extensive damage was reported to the power plant and dormitory buildings; the microwave shack was destroyed; two drilling rigs and one boat were lost; insulation was peeled from pipeline and tank surfaces; skylights were shattered; and corrugated metal ripped off metal sheds. The storm forced the mine to shut down, but shortly after the storm, Humble Oil crews began to supply natural gas to feed the mine's boilers and production was resumed (Camille strikes home 1969).

Three months after Camille, Hurricane Laurie approached the Louisiana coastline, forcing the evacuation and shut down all working mines—Grand Isle, Garden Island

Bay, Grande Écaille, and Lake Pelto. Laurie changed course radically and spared the mine any actual damage, but a sizeable production loss was suffered. It took about a week to bring production back to normal levels (Hurricane Laurie causes 1969). In 1974, Carmen also shut down the mine, but it missed the property by veering west-northwest.

Since the terrain and foundation conditions were better at Port Sulphur than at Garden Island Bay, management decided the dome's sulphur would be barged there, rather than stored at the Garden Island Bay site. Sulphur barges traveled forty-five miles from the mine to the unloading docks at Port Sulphur. Four barges were used to keep up with the approximate production of 1,500 long tons a day.

With completion of this mine, the United States' sulphur production increased 7 percent. The country's sulphur production in 1954 was the highest in history. Louisiana and Texas accounted for all of the Frasch sulphur produced in the United States (Rollman and Hough 1957). Sixty-three percent was produced in Texas, 36 percent in Louisiana, and the remainder came from California. Louisiana's output increased 22 percent as the Garden Island Bay mine reached capacity in February 1954 (Larson and Marks 1958). The mine closed in 1991.

Lake Peigneur: A Mine in a Lake

In December of 1928, the Jefferson Lake Oil Company began exploring for oil on the Jefferson Island salt dome in Iberia Parish. After drilling a number of dry holes on the dome's flanks, the company decided to drill a well in the middle of the lake. This well pierced a bed of sulphur at 660 feet. The deposit was locked in the caprock of a dome approximately two-miles long by one-mile wide and contained an estimated three to five million long tons (O'Donnell and Todd 1932). The bed proved to be 211 feet thick (Moresi 1934; Louisiana oil well 1929). To produce sulphur commercially, the company built a power plant capable of providing 1.5 million gallons of superheated water daily. The boilers were designed to use fuel oil, but could be adapted to gas firing, if necessary (O'Donnell and Todd 1932). The boiler house was built on the lake's shore; the 325°F water was pumped about one mile to the lake's injection well.

Two artesian wells supplied the power plant's water demands. The water was stored in a twenty-acre, fifty-million-gallon reservoir located nearby to guarantee continuous operation. Water from this reservoir was processed to insure zero hardness; a development that assured the water would be free of scale and foreign substance, a problem that plagued the Union Sulphur Company's mine at Sulphur, Louisiana (O'Donnell and Todd 1932; O'Donnell 1933). Everything worked; the well was productive and the world's first sulphur mine over water was operating.

To support the sulphur pipes, a trestle was constructed to the well. This trestle carried the weight of five pipelines: hot water, steam, cold water, air, and molten sulphur. The hot-water, steam, and sulphur lines had to be insulated. This was accomplished by using "mineral wool" delivered in a number of railroad cars—three inches of mineral wool encased in galvanized iron insulated the hot lines. The pipes also had to be equipped with large expansion joints, since the pipe would expand two feet in every 1,000 as

Before sulphur was shipped in liquid form, it had to be consolidated into large "bricks" for temporary storage, ca. 1930. (Photo from the *Louisiana Conservation Review,* 4, 1934.)

a result of the superheated water, steam, and sulphur moving along the conduit. The mine's molten sulphur was discharged into vats about 160 x 500 x 40-feet high and occupying fifty acres (Sulphur plant started 1931; O'Donnell 1933).

Once solidified, the sulphur block was blasted apart, loaded into railroad cars by means of locomotive cranes and shipped to domestic consumers or exported to France, Germany, England, South Africa, and Australia. In 1932, the mine produced 13,401 long tons; a year later production increased to 303,787—194,287 long tons over the power plant's designed capacity. The mine's design engineers estimated Lake Peigneur's production at about 200 long tons per day, but it was far greater. At times, the mine liquefied more than 1,200 long tons a day. At eighteen dollars per ton the company was making between $3,600 and $21,000 per day, which indicates a wide range of process efficiency—as might well be expected. In June 1936, the plant closed as the sulphur was depleted after 430,822 long tons, with a market value of more than $7 million ($108 million in 2009 dollars); 115,202 long tons per year had been removed from under Lake Peigneur (Hazleton 1970). Although short-lived, the Jefferson Lake Oil Company pioneered mining from beneath water; they set the stage for mining in Louisiana's marshes. Mining in a lake might have, in fact, some real advantages, since the costs associated with backfilling, as subsidence occurs, was eliminated.

In November 1980, a Texaco drilling rig, operating in the lake, punctured the mine's salt cavity and in less than one hour drained the lake dry. The incident resulted in the freshwater lake to be replaced with saltwater that had a detrimental effect on the surrounding inhabitants and the Chicot Aquifer. The inundation terminated industrial activity in Lake Peigneur for fourteen years, until Equitable Storage Co. of Pennsylvania obtained a mining lease in 1994 from the State of Louisiana to create two salt caverns for the storage of natural gas. Atlanta-based AGL Resources subsequently acquired the rights to the mine and operated the facility as the Jefferson Island Storage and Hub, LLC facility. The company charges a fee for storing natural gas for other companies (Worthy 2009).

Bay Ste. Elaine: Louisiana's First Amphibious Sulphur Mine

The Bay Ste. Elaine Dome is approximately thirty-five miles southeast of Houma and was discovered in 1927 by the Louisiana Land and Exploration Company (later Burlington Resources that was acquired in 2006 by ConocoPhillips). The first well was completed in 1929 with an initial gas production of 90 million cubic feet per day. The Texas Company discovered oil at the site and by 1955 had completed 112 wells, 111 of which were producing oil (Schneider 1959). Freeport Sulphur became interested in the dome's sulphur in 1932, but did not acquire the sulphur rights from Texaco until 1951. Developing the dome was a major pioneering effort, involving a $2 million investment on the design and construction of the world's first floating sulphur plant (Sulphur plant makes 1952).

No roads served the area and the nearest source of fresh water was thirty-five miles away. By itself, the marsh physiography posed no unfamiliar problems. The problem was the reserves. The deposit's small size and thin horizon would not justify the investment required to build a large permanent facility, because annual output was estimated at only 100,000 long tons (Seaborne plant drops 1952). Freeport's engineers worked for eight years designing a completely amphibious power plant; a technique that negated the corrosive effects of sea water (Problem: build this 1952). For the first time in the history of tidewater mining, brackish water, instead of fresh water, could be used—a first that contributed greatly to the success of the mining enterprise. As a result, the complete marine operation required little dredged fill. The mine was floated onto the site with boats taking the place of trucks and tractors (Price 1952).

Working with engineers at Waldemar Nelson and Company, Freeport built the world's first amphibious sulphur mine, ca. 1952. (Photo courtesy of Waldemar S. and Nelson Company.)

Prospecting was accomplished with the use of barge-mounted drilling rigs.

To exploit the subterranean sulphur, a specially designed steel power unit had to be built atop a 200-foot by forty-foot barge and towed to the mining property. Before the barge was anchored in place, the bottom muck had been veneered with fill. After settling, the fill was topped with sand until the water depth was about six feet. The barge was towed into place and partially sunk on the prepared bottom and began the process of liquefying sulphur (Sulphur plant makes 1952; Seaborne plant drops 1952). The amphibious plant was designed to furnish an average of 1.75 million gallons of 325°F water per day and miscellaneous steam for heating sulphur lines and equipment. The plant was designed to produce 200 long tons per day. Based on its total production of 1,131,204 long tons, the mine averaged 440 long tons per day.

The key to the operation was the sea water used in the boilers; water with up to 28 parts per million of salt could be utilized without worrying about scaling and corrosion (Frasch plant goes 1952; Price 1952). This was a radical process, as the ability to use salt water was critical. It was too expensive and inefficient to move fresh water from the Mississippi River. The process was not an immediate success. Frequent interruptions and other problems prevented favorable results. Trial and error became part of Freeport's engineer's learning curve. Brine water worked, but only after considerable experimentation (Bay Ste. Elaine 1962). In addition, the mine pioneered the use of directional drilling techniques that were required at the company's Chacahoula mine and Grand Isle property—where 108 wells were drilled from one structure (BSE a vital 1959).

The boiler house supplied enough superheated water to liquefy sulphur in six wells and produced annually in excess of 160,000 long tons. Once the water was injected into the well, the molten sulphur was air-lifted into 1,000 long ton, insulated tank barges. Since the site would

Steam, water, air, and sulphur pipelines from the power plant allowed the Bay Ste. Elaine property to produce liquid sulphur, ca. 1953. (Photo courtesy of Waldemar S. and Nelson Company.)

not support a large storage vat, the sulphur was transported in molten form to the Port Sulphur storage bins. Two barges were used in this operation, completing the 150-mile-round trip in about thirty-six hours (Price 1952).

This new type of marine mining, with its barge-based facilities, utilization of seawater, and transportation in a molten state were all firsts. These developments made it possible to mine a subaqueous sulphur lease, where conventional land-type sulphur mining methods could not be employed.

During its lifetime, Bay Ste. Elaine shut down seven times due to Gulf storms, gas fuel failures, or delivery problems. After the mine closed, the amphibious "tools" were towed to Lake Pelto and placed on a standby basis (Larson and Foley 1960). Even though the dome was depleted in seven years, the mining plant was not confined to this deposit. It was not stationary; on the contrary, it was completely mobile and needed only to be floated and towed to another "inaccessible" marsh sulphur dome. Bay Ste. Elaine represented a new chapter in the mining of sulphur and Lake Pelto was the second phase of the story.

Lake Pelto

The Lake Pelto salt dome's caprock covered about seventy acres. First discovered by Texaco, the site was later acquired by the Freeport Sulphur Company. To mine the deposit, Freeport refloated its amphibious power plant from the depleted Bay Ste. Elaine mine and towed it six miles to Lake Pelto. The Lake Pelto boilers were test fired on November 11, 1960. The tests were successful; as a result, on Thanksgiving Day, sulphur was liquefied and production began from this lease.

As at Bay Ste. Elaine, the extracted sulphur was moved by insulated barges to Port Sulphur, since there were no storage facilities at the mine's aquatic location. To accommodate the necessary ancillary structures, an artificial island was built that encased the mine's vital liquefying components (Netzeband, et al. 1964). The island-based infrastructure, including a two-story, fifty-six bedroom and four guest rooms dormitory, dining, and recreation facility, a 300,000 gallon reservoir, and domestic water treatment plant were fabricated on the island or moved onto the site (Lake Pelto gears 1960).

All of these facilities were designed to withstand hurricane-force winds and the associated storm surge. To add structural integrity to the facilities, the buildings were anchored to piling supports. The field's mile-long lateral walkway, leading from the island's base to the production area, was supported by twelve-inch steel piles, elevated twenty-feet above the water's surface (Lake Pelto development 1960). Subsidence studies revealed the movable production system should be located at least 3,500 feet from the ore-body. To meet this criteria, a small island was constructed 5,000 feet— nearly a mile—from the dome that supported the mine's relay facility (Lake Pelto 3rd 1962). Bleed water was pumped into a reservoir on the Isles Dernières—about two miles south of the Lake Pelto property. All wells were directionally drilled from the floating barge (Fifth mine taking 1957).

Construction began in September 1955, when a ring levee was placed around the island's edge. Once in place, a bucket-type dredge filled the interior, which was allowed to settle and harden, resulting in an elevation about ten-feet above the surrounding surface. Around the island's perimeter piling, mats, and rip-rap were used to further fortify the island from erosional forces (Fifth mine taking . . . 1957). Even with all of these precautions, hurricanes were a problem. Hurricanes Betsy (1965), Camille (1969), Laurie (1969 which did not make landfall), and Carmen (1974) shut down, slowed or otherwise disrupted the Lake Pelto mine. Carmen inflected the greatest damage by ripping the gas line off its piling supports, pulling siding off of buildings, and severely

Lake Pelto's distinctive pink dormitory remained a landmark for the mine site, 1988. (Photo by the author.)

damaging the mine's boat dock. Water and wind damage was evident throughout the dormitory, shell rip-rap was strewn over the island, and many of the mine's network of ancillary pipelines were destroyed or damaged (Carmen shuts down 1974).

Lake Pelto came on stream at a perfect time, as 1960 was marked by record free-world production and consumption of sulphur. An estimated 17.9 million long tons were consumed. Most of this demand was met from stocks of elemental sulphur, with the United States producing about 5 million long tons or approximately 25 percent. By 1963, Lake Pelto, along with the other Louisiana mines, became the world's largest producer of Frasch sulphur; Louisiana's production outperformed Texas for the first time in forty years (Babcock 1964).

For fifteen years, Lake Pelto produced sulphur. In September 1975, it closed after producing more than 5.6 million long tons—at an average rate of 1,000 long tons per day (Freeport opens Caillou 1980). Higher operating costs and depleted reserves prompted Freeport to terminate the mine's production. The power plant moved to Freeport's Caillou Island sulphur deposit in late 1979.

Although depleted reserves terminated the mine's productive life, it continues to serve the region by being an excellent habitat for a number of species of recreationally important fin fish and as a visual clue to navigating across Lake Pelto.

Lake Hermitage

In 1966, Jefferson Lake Sulphur Company discovered enough sulphur in the Lake Hermitage Dome in Plaquemines Parish to justify commercial operation. The property was obtained from Humble Oil and Refining Company (now ExxonMobil) and the Gulf Oil Corporation (now Chevron). The contract with these two firms stipulated they would receive a 19 percent royalty on the first 800,000 long tons and 26 percent on all other production (Lewis 1968). Jefferson Lake Sulphur decided the most economical method of mining the deposit was to use a barge-mounted power plant, similar to that employed at Bay Ste. Elaine and Lake Pelto (Jones and Hough 1967).

The plant was completed in 1967 at a cost of $5 million. Due to a sulphur shortage, the water-heating facility operated almost immediately at its designed capacity of 3 million gallons of hot water per day. A report in *The Wall Street Journal* (Occidental Petroleum plans 1966) estimated that Lake Hermitage would yield 200,000 long tons per year, nearly 550 long tons a day. The mine began producing in 1952 and closed twenty-years later.

Bully Camp: A Problem with the Availability of Natural Gas

Texasgulf Sulphur Company began as the Gulf Sulphur Company in 1909 in Matagorda County, Texas. The company owned the Boling Dome in Texas that produced elemental sulphur for more than thirty years. In 1967, the firm moved into Louisiana. The Texasgulf established a Frasch mine at Bully Camp in the waters west of Larose in Lafourche Parish. Like other over-water operations, the site required a fleet of barges to ferry the materials needed for the plant's construction. The barge-mounted plant was designed to produce at an annual rate of 300,000 long tons (Lewis 1968).

When Bully Camp opened in May 1968, Louisiana had nine mines simultaneously producing Frasch sulphur, the largest number ever to operate in the state (Eilertsen 1969). When operational, Bully Camp produced about 3 percent of the total United States Frasch sulphur (Carleton 1974).

The mine normally required 10 million cubic feet of natural gas per day to produce 820 long-ons of sulphur. United Gas Pipeline Company reduced the mine's gas supply. Since Texasgulf felt it was impossible to produce any sulphur from such a small quantity of natural gas, they asked the Federal Power Commission (FPC) to order United Gas to deliver an average of seven million cubic feet per day and no less than 1.5 million cubic feet in any single day. The FPC ruled the gas cutback would probably cause irreparable damage to the Bully Camp operation. They ordered United Gas to deliver at least 1.5 million cubic feet of gas per day (FPC high on 1972). This 85 percent gas reduction meant the mine could produce, working at full capacity, only 123 long tons of sulphur per day. This production was not enough to meet expenses, as the mine produced only 170,000 long tons per year—slightly more than half of its design capacity (Gas lack at 1973). Texasgulf contacted every available gas supplier in an effort to regain a reliable gas source. It is reported that their offer exceeded their contract price with United Gas by 100 percent (Gas lack at 1973). Yet, they were not successful; Texasgulf closed its Bully Camp mine. It was abandoned due to high operating costs, declining reserves, and increases in the cost and intermittent curtailment of their natural gas supply from the United Gas (Harrison and McGrain 1981).

The mine eventually reopened. Production rates were, however, substantially lower. By early 1973, Texasgulf had laid off 70 percent of its employees. The company charged that its gas supplier "sold more gas than it had reserves to cover" (Gas lack at 1973). This situation, coupled with higher gas prices, and a supply that was cut 85 percent, resulted in much higher operating costs, and reduced the mine's profits. The mine's marginal production made it especially vulnerable to a reduction in natural gas supply; it simply became uneconomical to operate (Sulfur mine shutdown 1978). In fact, shutting down Bully Camp was symptomatic of the decline in Frasch-produced sulphur in the United States. Although yields at the mine were below its potential capacity, it was only a part of a series of shutdowns by Frasch producers who were recognizing that it was not profitable to continue to liquefy sulphur with expensive natural gas. As a result, Frasch sulphur production dropped steadily since 1975 (Sulfur sources shift 1978).

The mine produced 1.7 million long tons, an average of 170,000 long tons per year, well below the mine's "nameplate" capacity of 300,000 long tons per year (Texasgulf closing Bully 1978). During its last year, the mine produced 129,900 long tons, only 6 percent of Texasgulf's total output (Sulphur mine to 1978).

After a decade of mining, Bully Camp was closed. The mine now serves the recreational sportsmen. Like the abandoned Lake Pelto site, Bully Camp has become, because of subsidence over the dome, an excellent "honey hole," which to the local fishermen is a superior fishing spot that contains a number of big fish.

Caillou Island

In 1979, Freeport initiated development of a small sulphur deposit in the Caillou Island area, thirty-five miles southeast of Houma. The mine became operational in 1980 and represented a complete reversal of trends, since most salt dome sulphur mines were then going out of production. Ordinarily, it would not have been possible to mine the deposit, but with the availability of Freeport's unique barge-mounted power plant, an assured fuel supply, coupled with improved sulphur prices, and the Company's need to better balance their supply with their sales, it was possible to go ahead with the project (Freeport to open 1979; Freeport opens Caillou 1980; Production of sulfur 1981).

The opening of Caillou Island meant Freeport could build up its above-ground inventories in the face of high United States demand despite, at the time, record sulphur prices. On a worldwide basis, sulphur from Poland and the Persian Gulf were diminished severely as a result of labor and shipping problems in Poland and economic chaos in Iran and Iraq. When these decreased supplies were combined with high United States demand, and reduced recovered sulphur from petroleum refining and natural gas processing, Gulf Coast inventories declined considerably. Caillou Island helped reverse this trend (Freeport opens Caillou 1980; Rangnow and Fasullo 1981).

Bringing the mine on stream cost Freeport $26 million and included housing, maintenance shops, and other support facilities for the ninety people required to exploit the deposit (Freeport commences production 1980). The mine's design included two main platforms, one measuring 180 by seventy feet and the other 230 by seventy feet, plus seven satellite structures that supported communications, water supply, sewage treatment, and auxiliary power generation equipment (Production of sulfur 1981).

To run the mine, Freeport recycled the power plant utilized at Bay Ste. Elaine (1952-1959) and Lake Pelto (1960-1975), making Caillou Island the third mine to employ the amphibious power plant. After four years of disuse, it needed a complete overhaul to make it operational (Freeport opens Caillou 1980; Sulfur mine opens 1980). The 200-foot, twenty-eight year old barge was removed from mothballs at Lake Pelto and towed eleven miles to Caillou Island. The power plant, with a steam generator large enough to power a small city, was capable of heating 2.5 million gallons of water per day to 325°F. The mine's annual capacity was estimated at 350,000 long tons.

Sulphur extracted from the dome's caprock

Although Caillou Island was a short-lived sulphur mine, the property became one of Texaco's most important coastal oilfields, 2004. (Photo by the author.)

was discharged into 2,000 long ton liquid sulphur barges and towed to Port Sulphur to help replace Freeport's substantially reduced inventories (Freeport Sulphur plans 1979; Freeport opens Caillou 1980). The costly mine only produced for four years.

Company "Towns" in the Marsh

The marsh-oriented sulphur mines' work forces typically lived and worked at the mine. These individuals were part of the industrial settlements that were an important part of the mine operation. Dormitories, cottages, baseball fields, boat docks, dining halls, and other ancillary structures were part of the industrial landscape. And, like other marsh communities, these sites were always vulnerable to hurricane winds and the associated storm surges. However, unlike oyster and shrimp-drying comminutes, these industrial sites were easily evacuated. Nevertheless, they represent one of the earliest industrial settlement forms in the marsh.

Prior to construction of Port Sulphur and Grande Écaille, the oil and gas industry was actively involved in the exploration and development of hydrocarbons from the wetlands (Shaw 1938). The wells drilled outlined fields that were often the bases of operations for a company's industrial activities. Field crews were housed in camps or quarter boats located throughout the wetlands. Although an accurate number of the camps implicated in the early development of the state's wetland fields have never been assembled, the number of people involved in the industry was fairly large.

With more than fifty fields discovered between 1901 and 1940, the associated settlements became a highly visible part of the cultural/industrial landscape. Each field represented a settlement node, generally occupied by a transient labor force that depended upon a vast array of crewboats (Falgoux 2007). In some cases, particularly on the end-points of natural levees, these sites were often well-designed and like Port Sulphur, were true industrial communities that played a vital role in transforming the marsh from a subsistence-based economy to one based on wages.

Texaco's Lafitte oilfield was one of the industrial communities that became commonplace in coastal Louisiana in the pre-World War II era. With time, these communities were associated with more than 400 oilfields, ca. 1935. (Photo from the *Louisiana Conservation Review*, 1937.)

Sulphur and oil companies became the new face of the wetlands. They did not transcend all employment activities. Fishing, trapping, and hunting continued to serve the marshdweller's monetary needs. But the corporate culture did evolve into a major force in assigning "new" value to the forgotten, devalued, and worthless marshes. They brought into the marshes an innovative approach to evaluating the landscape. Rather than assessing the marsh's economic value from the surface, they appraised value from the subsurface. This was a new beginning for how one defined Louisiana's marshes. Geographically, the coast's geomorphology was in a state of constant change. People who have lived and worked in this landscape for more than a century began to realize that their homes and property were no longer worthless. "Black Gold" revolutionized the perception and heightened awareness of the coastal landscape. The surface may go through various visible modifications, but the subsurface hydrocarbons were always there; therefore, ownership took on new meaning at all levels of government and among hoards of speculators, charlatans, and attorneys. In the process, settlements took on new purpose from a legal perspective, as they could document use and perhaps ownership.

Hydrocarbons in the Wetlands

> Perhaps no industry has affected Louisiana so profoundly as the oil business. Besides providing jobs and filling the state's coffers (at least during boom times), oil production has spurred economic development and road building in many sections of Louisiana which were previously quite isolated—especially in south central and southwestern Cajun and Creole parishes. Such development, with its accompanying influx of mainstream American culture, increased pressures to assimilate and speak English that already existed in these areas. Fortunately, however, the past 15 years have seen such ethnocentric attitudes replaced by pride. Today, Cajun/Creole language, music and folklore are finally treated as cherished cultural resources, even as their home turf has been thoroughly modernized (Sandmel 1999:1).

Seventeenth century sailors exploring the northern Gulf of Mexico shrugged off seeing an oil sheen on the water, as this tar-like substance was unimportant (Submerged regions of 1935). Although Indians used oil from natural seeps for medicines, it was largely unknown. The liquid ooze represented a small portion of the hydrocarbons trapped in a geosyncline extending along the Gulf Coast from Mississippi to Texas.

The subsurface hydrocarbons formed millions of years ago by the heat and pressure associated with successive layers of sedimentary deposits laid on top of organic refuse: plants, dinosaurs, plankton, and diatoms. This natural biological debris decayed into this nonmetallic mineral resource. During the Miocene era this organic matter was trapped in sand and along the edges of salt deposits (Seglund 1956).

Seven distinct sedimentary layers provide natural traps for pools of oil and gas. More recent layers represent organic decay during the Pleistocene era, between 10,000 and two million years ago. These deposits are closer to the earth's surface and are relatively easier to exploit than those associated with the Miocene (Wilson 1965). Within these layers, geologists located and mapped many subsurface salt domes, whose flanks served as natural reservoirs for the accumulation of hydrocarbon. These hydrocarbon pools along the outside border of the salt dome became the touchstone of 1920s Gulf Coast exploration (Bell 1924; Deussen 1923; Goodwill 1938-1939).

Louisiana's wildcatters made their first oil and gas discoveries on dry land in the older, deeper, sand deposits. But as exploration extended southward into the coastal zone, drillers tapped the newer deposits laid down in the Pleistocene. These shallow deposits were relatively easy to drill. Even so, getting the equipment in place to exploit these resources was a real challenge, as South Louisiana's wetlands were a logistic nightmare. Drillers and others working at the site had to become amphibious and work in and on an unfamiliar topography. The oil was there; the challenge was getting to their near sea-level, aquatic-based, often wet grass-covered, lease sites—where the land is almost water, and water was everywhere.

To meet this challenge, the human and physical dimensions of the coastal zone changed, as the history of hydrocarbon

As Louisiana matured as an oil province, all of the major oil companies were involved in exploration, 2003. (Photo by the author.)

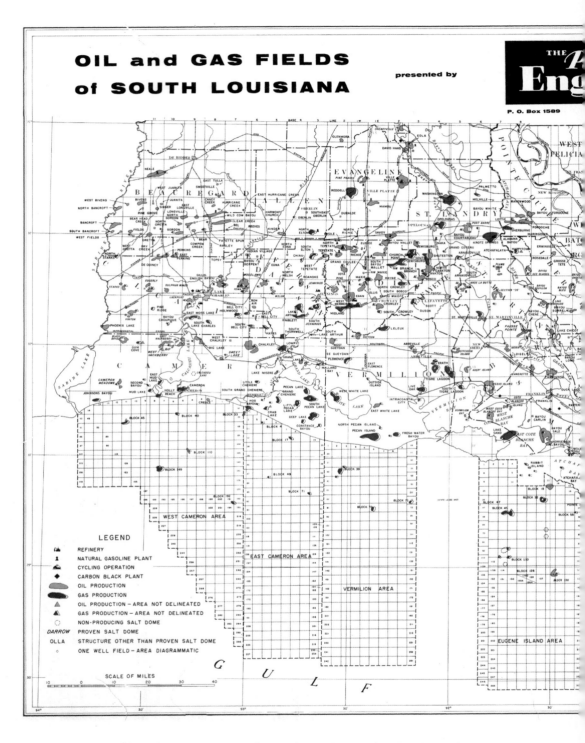

development within this area is one of interdependence of technological innovation, entrepreneurial risk-taking, resource management, judicial decisions, legislation, marketing, employee good will, infrastructure, and support services. Every move into a new geographic province, whether the swamps or marshes, involved altering the industry's operating philosophy; discovery of virgin pools necessitated altering

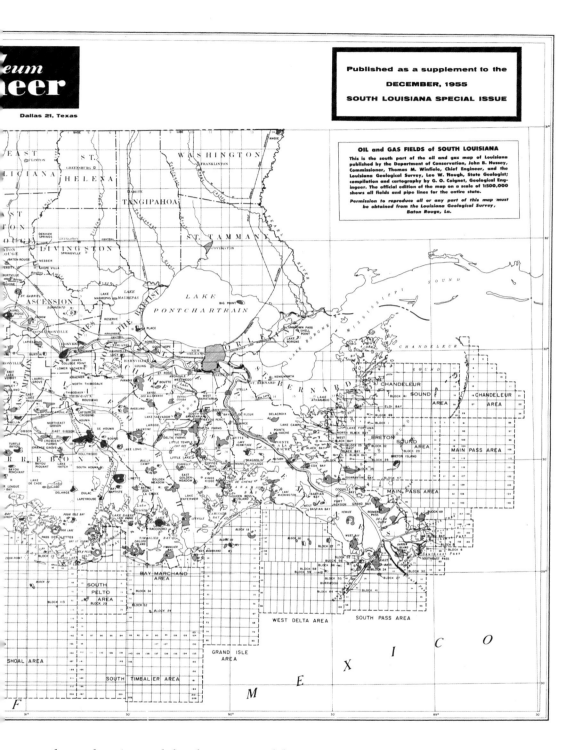

eum
eer

Dallas 21, Texas

Published as a supplement to the

DECEMBER, 1955

SOUTH LOUISIANA SPECIAL ISSUE

OIL and GAS FIELDS of SOUTH LOUISIANA

This is the south part of the oil and gas map of Louisiana published by the Department of Conservation, John B. Hussey, Commissioner, Thomas M. Winfiele, Chief Engineer, and the Louisiana Geological Survey, Leo W. Hough, State Geologist; compilation and cartography by G. O. Coignet, Geological Engineer. The official edition of the map on a scale of 1:500,000 shows all fields and pipe lines for the entire state.

Permission to reproduce all or any part of this map must be obtained from the Louisiana Geological Survey, Baton Rouge, La.

the exploration and development model.

The science necessary to maintain an aggressive exploration and development program was crucial to finding new reservoirs. As technology changed, improved, or adapted to meet the industry's needs, new exploration frontiers were methodically explored by a highly concentrated cluster of wells. With no spacing laws, these

Working in Louisiana's swamps required a network of elaborate board roads, (left) 1944, (right) 1946. (Photos courtesy of the Standard Oil Collection, University of Louisville, negative no. 1643 and 37803.)

structures were so close it was easy to walk from one drilling platform to another across the entire zone of interest.

As a result, by 1932, about 97 percent of the country's hydrocarbon production came from seven states (Interstate compact for 1932). In Louisiana the oil companies were exploring flank extension and deeper sands in old pools. The industry was entrenched in north Louisiana. South Louisiana's fields were a different matter. Drilling on the prairie tracked the exploration methods refined in north Louisiana, but looking for subsurface reservoirs in the swamps and marshes were only beginning to be moved past the hiking in the mud stage.

Accompanying the new advances in the tools necessary to explore the wetlands was an army of laborers. None of these newcomers were locals. They needed to be housed at every field—by 2000 there were 412 oil and/or gas fields in the coastal parishes. With each new field, industrial settlement sites were necessary to maintain production. The wetlands were being industrialized by a highly diverse group of independent oil interests that had no idea of the cumulative affect they were having on the wetlands' social and economic fabric. The goal was oil and industrial communities were simply a logical way to manage their field's assets.

Barge-mounted drilling rigs expanded marsh exploration, no date. (Photo courtesy of the Morgan City Archives.)

Number of Oil and/or Gas Fields by parish, to 2000

Parish	Number of fields before 2000	Percentage of the total before 2000
Terrebonne	70	16.99
Cameron	62	15.04
Plaquemine	56	13.59
Lafourche	55	13.34
Vermilion	42	10.19
St. Mary	34	08.25
Iberia	26	06.31
Jefferson	24	05.82
St. Charles	19	04.61
St. Bernard	18	04.36
Orleans	6	01.45
Total	412	99.95

Another New Form of Industrial Settlement

When extensive hydrocarbon deposits were discovered under Louisiana's waters, the event changed the coastal zone's land-use patterns permanently and cultural homogeneity completely. The economic boom that followed centered on Louisiana's wetland parishes. Change was unavoidable. Hyper urbanization—the phenomenon of boomtown growth—began straining the region's ability to provide essential services. Coastal communities were not prepared for the enormous growth and responsibilities associated with providing necessary community services. Overcrowding symbolized the shift from a village to a small town to a city.

Even so, this onshore and, later, undersea mineral province cannot function without logistic support. Unlike land-tied resource exploration, which can be supplied via federally subsidized roads and railroads, on- and offshore exploration and development firms had to create their own transport system (Davis 1990).

Promising fields were just too much trouble to exploit, as wetland exploration involves much more than a superficial knowledge of the regional geography. Boats, barges, canals, pipelines, and port facilities were the economic drivers in this physiographic province; all were alien to wetland drilling crews. These elements were available, but the scale was too small to meet the industry's needs. Exploration and development was, therefore, not practical until the 1930s, when the request support facilities were available and the industry could begin to systematically expand into the wetlands (Barton 1930). Before they could advance their exploration agenda, they had to either acquire a "brown-water" navy or contract with locals to insure they had someone on the payroll that understood the intricacies of Louisiana's waterways and was capable of keeping everything on schedule (Field operations in 1955).

The culmination of these logistic events occurred during the economic chaos of the 1930s, when

Before pipelines were developed, oil storage tanks, like these at Lake Pelto, were used in conjunction with barges to move product to market, ca. 1935. (Photo from the *Thirteenth Biennial Report, Louisiana Department of Conservation, 1936-1937*.)

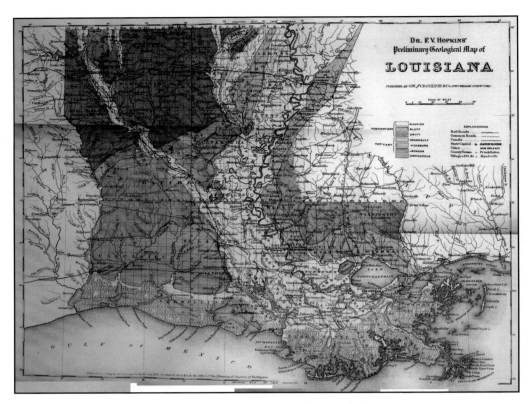

Five years after the conclusion of the Civil War, professors from Louisiana State University produced the state's first generalized geological map, 1870.

wetland inhabitants were living essentially in a barter system, at near subsistence levels, in places where there was no electricity, no telephones, no running water, heating and cooking was done on a wood or kerosene stoves, no indoor plumbing was available, clothes were hand-me-downs and often made from salt or flower sacks, and French, Spanish, or Serbian/Croatian were the languages of choice. And, the only way to access these communities was by boat or on horseback.

These marshdwellers were not accustomed to outsiders. They did not trust them, as they were not "Cadiens." They were "Texien." They spoke English, were Baptist, did not maintain their homes or iron their clothes. They ate cold sandwiches for lunch, instead of a hot meal, and would eat meat on Friday and get drunk in the middle of Lent. To the Acadians, they were hypocrites, as their religion told them not to drink alcohol or dance, but they would drink and dance with the local women every Saturday night (Falgoux 2007).

But these *maudit* Texiens and their *maudit* oilfields offered the marshdwellers an opportunity to make good money—very good money at a time when money was becoming part of the regional culture. The talents and skills of the marsh's watermen were needed in the exploration and development of new fields. Access was by boats, boats were money, and school was a nightmare. So education became secondary, as the petroleum industry needed the bayou country's boatmen to meet their needs. Just as in the cypress industry, Acadians rarely were axmen and day laborers. They were the small-boat skippers—practically an innate skill among bayou Cajuns.

This expertise, coupled with an understanding of the local geography, is what the oil industry wanted. Because they were water-based operations, transportation of personnel and equipment was a major undertaking. Mobility and flexibility was

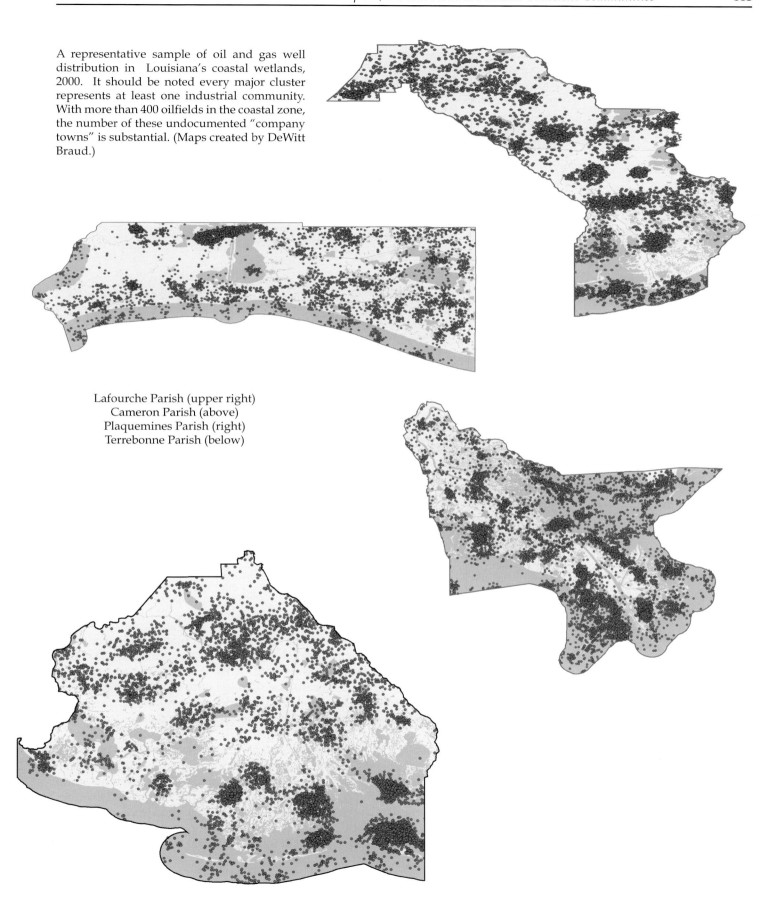

A representative sample of oil and gas well distribution in Louisiana's coastal wetlands, 2000. It should be noted every major cluster represents at least one industrial community. With more than 400 oilfields in the coastal zone, the number of these undocumented "company towns" is substantial. (Maps created by DeWitt Braud.)

Lafourche Parish (upper right)
Cameron Parish (above)
Plaquemines Parish (right)
Terrebonne Parish (below)

critical to all of these operations. Therefore, a system of luggers—later replaced by tugboats, barges, twin-engine diesel-fueled crewboats—and self-propelled oilfield-equipped units operated on a twenty-four-hour basis were vital to the success of wetland operations. Further, barge-mounted drilling rigs needed to be refloated and moved by tugboats to new locations. Trucks involved in paraffin melting and other tasks floated on barges that also had to be moved. In addition, specially designed maintenance units were housed on barges to perform any type of roustabout operations, such as laying, retrieving, and repairing small-diameter flow lines.

To operate efficiently in Louisiana's wetlands, oil-collecting facilities were scattered throughout the coastal lowlands, 1948. (Photo courtesy of the Standard Oil Collection, University of Louisville, negative no. 62216.)

These warehouse barges also provided a bathhouse, ice plant, work rooms for onboard machinists and other personnel, kitchen, bedrooms, and office space, along with any other tasks required in the expanding field. All of this activity was managed from permanent or barge-mounted field camps associated with every new field (Scott 1952; Lipari 1963). Each field evolved, therefore, into a complex system of reservoirs, wells, and installations that were often mounted on converted cargo barges to facilitate oil storage (Short 1945).

This flotilla of boats was captained by experienced watermen, who could consistently make a profit of twenty dollars a day ferrying men and equipment into the new oilfields. During the industry's infancy, this was more money than could be made shrimping, trapping, hunting, or fishing oysters. These uninvited Texiens, coupled with the knowledge and skills of the local swamp and marshdwellers, contributed to the success of the wildcatters' exploration experience. In the end, these outsiders had initiated an industrial assault that was tearing at the seams of the local culture. Over 200 years of cultural stability changed. The landscape was not the same, but the country needed and benefitted from the hydrocarbons discovered in the decade before World War II, when fossil fuels became essential to the war effort and more than 2,000 wells were completed in the coastal lowlands. Each well represented a symbol of the industrial age and the potential site for a transient community, as the wetland's subsurface geology was being unraveled

Wells Drilled Prior to World War II, by parish

Parish	Wells drilled prior to WW II
Cameron	516
Iberia	576
Lafourche	305
Terrebonne	261
Plaquemines	195
St. Mary	163
Vermilion	53
St. Charles	41
St. Bernard	35
Orleans	12
Jefferson	17
Total	2174

The wetlands were "discovered" during the beginning of the country's industrialization process. Oilmen fanned out across this broad lowland, establishing new fields that by design were settlement sites for "outsiders." Each new field was an industrial hamlet identified by a field name, such as Kelso Bayou, Caillou Island, Lake Washington, Dog Lake, Hackberry, Sweet Lake, Lake Barré, and many others. As exploration began, and development followed, the wetlands were influenced by a new "money-based" culture. Income from oil royalties, and jobs associated with the oil companies changed the region's social structure. An economic renaissance had begun to transform the marshdweller's communal lifestyle.

Through time, the industry has flourished. Admittedly, some parishes produce more hydrocarbons than others. Regardless, every coastal parish benefits in some way from the "spin-off" industries connected to this production. In the industry's infancy, timber contractors were one of the earliest groups to provide support to the drilling effort. When they operated at maximum load, boilers used to generate steam employed in the drilling process needed at least fifteen cords of wood each. This was a costly and inefficient fuel source. In less than a decade, the industry was using oil to power its derricks. Each operating derrick consumed about thirty barrels of crude oil per day. If there were 600 producing wells in a field, they required 18,000 barrels per field per day—a significant use of the field's production. Moreover, all of these early rigs were made of timber. Tens of thousands

Terrebonne Parish's Lake Barré oilfield, ca. 1930, shows the difficulty of working over water. (Photo from the *Thirteenth Biennial Report, Louisiana Department of Conservation, 1936-1937.*)

With the discovery of marketable hydrocarbons, wetlands inhabitants enjoyed additional economic options. Their barter economy changed to one based on wages. (Photo courtesy of the Standard Oil Collection, University of Louisville, negative no. 48780.)

of board feet of lumber would have been required, but like the tin cans in the shrimp and oyster businesses, and the timber used in building shrimp platforms, no records have been uncovered documenting the quantity, source, and method of moving this lumber to each new well site. Based on the wells drilled, the amount of framing timber used for construction of the rigs' exoskeletons was substantial.

The business of finding oil was a terrestrial enterprise. Therefore, in the early years of exploration, mule-drawn wagons were used to transport seismograph crews and their equipment around the marsh. Teamsters, often working for $2.50 a day, became the backbone of early exploration. Wagons were an efficient transportation tool that worked on land, but was impractical in the wetlands. Boats became the new backbone of the industry, because finding, drilling, and producing oil in a watery environment was a new experience for terrestrial drilling crews and their financial backers.

Exploration and Development

When one considers the difficulties of exploring for fossil fuels with heavy machinery on muck, or even no land at all, it is easy to understand why it took so long for oil companies to exploit Louisiana's near sea level oil and gas wealth. In 1901, W. Scott Heywood completed the first producing well in South Louisiana, near Jennings at Evangeline (Barton and Goodrich 1926; Postgate 1949; Davis and Place 1983; Lindstedt, et al. 1991; Morse n.d.). As a result, oil, and natural gas, along with sulphur, has been a vital part of Louisiana's economy for more than 100 years.

After the Heywood find, other wildcatters followed, but lost interest after struggling with the environmental constraints. Early drillers moved to north Louisiana to exploit the easily accessible Caddo and Monroe fields and their extensions; they ignored the coastal lowland's marshy terrain until 1917, when the Mansfield Gas Company completed the first natural gas well in coastal Louisiana. The Lirette No. 4, in Terrebonne Parish, was at that time the largest gas producer in the world (Metzger 1938). Shortly after the completing of this well, exploration crews began to move into the coastal lowlands. With this advancement into this uncharted terrain the drilling companies discovered each new well was an individual problem that defied upland exploration practices (Bell 1927; Moresi 1934B). By the mid-1930s, this region had become a new frontier. The landscape was sprinkled with derricks that appeared almost overnight throughout the coastal zone.

The process of finding oil involved a number of well defined steps. Based on information provided by a geologist, surface expression, or instinct, the land or lease-man was the first person to survey a potential drilling site. He secured leases from large land holders, or, in the case of the Golden Meadow field, and many others, from numerous small tracks held by a highly diversified assemblage of individuals residing within the prospective site (Williams 1939). The object was to lease a contiguous swath of property that encompassed the estimated boundaries of the subsurface field.

When all of the leases were in place, geophysical parties (usually made up of six to eight engineers and geologists) began to thoroughly explore and survey the area. These seismic vendors used torsion balance, refraction, and reflection seismography, or other geophysical instruments, coupled with a "shot" of dynamite to generate the necessary shock waves. These tools acquired valuable data throughout the prospective area. A geophysicist then evaluated the subsurface signals to obtain a "picture" of the geologic formation (Brace 1939). Further, without the benefit of roads or

Once leases were obtained, drilling was quick and efficient. There was no concern about hurricanes, sea-level rise, or subsidence, as is shown in this 1930 image of the Golden Meadow field, no date. (Photo from Cheniere Hurricane Centennal 1997.)

canals, the bug-infested wet terrain made this work difficult and time-consuming, but necessary in the assessment phase of field development.

This interpretation phase of the business prompted local interest in the geosciences. Many "doodle bugging" or seismic crews roamed across the lowlands, and the results of their surveys had a direct bearing on the importance of clear land titles—a topic of conversation throughout the coastal plain.

Depending on the size of the area being investigated, this stage of the operation could take up to a year. Teams of geologists and geophysicists would then spend additional time processing the data and interpreting potential areas to prospect, given what they have learned about the subsurface geology.

Once the data has been analyzed and a potential site selected, engineers were hired to dredge a canal or, where possible, construct a board road. Once the access route was completed, and before development of the floating drilling barge, an expensive piling foundation was erected to support the machinery used to drill the first exploration well. The purpose of this well was to prove or disprove the existence of marketable hydrocarbons.

The coastal zone's oilfields are being retrofitted to address concerns about hurricanes, sea-level rise, and subsidence, 2004. (Photo by the author.)

Prior to the general adoption of steel superstructures, derricks were erected of wooden cribbing, laid on wooden mats that had to be designed for marsh areas that would only support about 250 pounds per square foot. These mat-based foundations were critical, as the static loads of derrick, substructure, and drilling equipment could involve more than 150 tons (Hebert and Anderson 1936). It required a process of trial and error. When one considers the number of wooden derricks in some of these early fields, it is clear that the volume of timber required was large and necessary—simply an early example of the support services required to keep the wells operating at maximum efficiency. In the industry's evolution, it takes one technology to discover and produce the product, and another to move these mineral fluids to market. Both technologies developed simultaneously.

If oil was discovered in a new reservoir, then several delineation wells were required to quantify just how large the reserves were (this would be for larger fields; smaller fields drilled by independents likely did not require this step). After the reserves were assessed, development wells were methodically drilled into the formation. This component of field expansion took years and was the most labor-intensive part of the process, requiring small company enclaves within the marshes

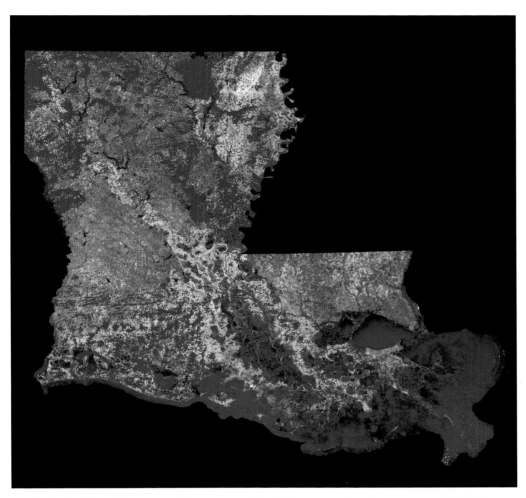

By the beginning of the twenty-first century, oil and/or gas production was associated with every Louisiana parish. This map shows the locations of at least a quarter-million oilwells, 2003. (Image courtesy of the Louisiana Department of Conservation.)

and swamps. Simultaneously, facilities would be installed (flow-lines, pipelines, additional canals, processing centers, dormitories, tank batteries, wharfs, barges, and other ancillary out buildings) to process the hydrocarbons and route them to regional distribution centers for transport to the market.

The original flow-line gathering system suffered from a general lack of planning, sound engineering, and a misunderstanding of the behavior of soft sediments. Like Topsy, the pipeline schematic just grew and expanded. Engineers were designing pipeline systems that were difficult to construct using hand labor and little equipment. It was a backbreaking exercise that required "gangs" of laborers using tongs to carry a length of pipe along a right-of-way (Williams 1936). Or, using dredges and equipment often designed on the spot to put a pipeline through the marsh.

With time, the list of pipelines in the wetlands increased, eventually replacing the region's natural waterways for transportation of oil (Pipe lines supplant 1937). The process worked and slowly lengthened like the spokes in a wheel. From each individual well, a gathering pipeline moved product into pipelines with larger diameters. These interstate pipelines were a critical component of the maize of interconnecting routes that funneled crude oil and natural gas into the intrastate distribution network that helped meet the domestic demand for hydrocarbons.

The system was adequate until World War II, when the twenty-four inch "Big Inch" and its companion project the twenty-inch "Little Inch" pipelines were constructed by the War Emergency Pipelines, Inc. These lines transported crude oil from oilfields in East Texas and refined products from the Gulf Coast to distribution points near New York City and Philadelphia. Their construction by-pass using tankers, that where were being harassed and torpedoed by German submarines. In fact, the massive demands of World War II for domestic overland transportation of crude oil and products demanded not only the construction of new large-diameter pipelines, but also the operation of existing lines at extraordinary new throughputs.

It was not, however, until after World War II that the gathering system was given preferred attention by the industry's pipeline engineers. New specifications and standardization policies brought some order to the chaos of early pipeline systems, within and without each individual field (Anderson 1946). The pre-1940 as built drawings for many of these lines, if they were ever used, are largely lost. The array of lines put in place during this early phase of development is a mystery. Their exact locations have been lost or never properly recorded, but many are still in play and moving liquids from fields that are more than fifty-years old.

As wells were drilled and facilities installed, production began. Once production was initiated, the labor force needed to oversee the field was reduced to small maintenance crews that checked on the wells and often lived in crew quarters within the field. Some locations required only an occasional check-in and were essentially stand-alone, in that they did not require much maintenance. A notable exception would be "workover" activity, an example of which could include re-completing wells in up-hole productive zones once lower reservoirs were depleted. A final step, begun in the 1960s, was site remediation after production has depleted within a given reservoir (Shaw 1938B; Guidroz 2008).

This sequence was repeated throughout coastal Louisiana and is the basic model in the search for oil. The model worked, but the initial interest in the coastal zone was slow to move; as a result, in South Louisiana between 1901 and 1923 only eight salt dome-related oilfields were discovered (Postgate 1949).

Every step in the process, but the canals noted above, were part of the industry's land-based operations, but water was an unfamiliar impediment. The industry's learning curve was a gradual process, but the one easily identifiable variable was the need for an efficient water-based supply chain. Even with this awareness, logistics associated with wetland drilling overwhelmed the industry; consequently, exploration and development of potential wetland fields was not practical until the late 1920s and early 1930s (Shaw 1938; Falgoux 2007). However, once boat transport and canal access became available, the industry flourished (Falgoux 2007). For example, Cameron Parish represents how quickly the industry moved into the region and found oil. The Sweet Lake oilfield was discovered in 1926. Other significant fields: East Hackberry (1927), West Hackberry (1901), Back Bayou (1929), and Cameron Meadows (1934) followed quickly. Many of these fields are still in production. By the end of 1935, there were seventy-field fields in Louisiana; fifty-two were discovered in the 1925-1935 period.

Early on, it was apparent the industry leaders would need to build their own infrastructure. The Texas Company, for example, discovered its own clay and fuller's earth beds, so as to be independent of suppliers of these materials essential to refining. The company made its own oil cans and acquired timberland and a lumber mill near Morgan City to produce milled lumber for its packing cases. For a while, the Texas Company made its own tank wagons. It was considered more profitable and advantageous to control every aspect of the industry, rather than outsourcing to outside vendors (Rankin 1938).

M. Frank Yount: A Successful Gulf Coast Wildcatter

Wildcatters M. Frank Yount (often called the "Godfather and Financial Gibraltar of Beaumont") and Thomas Peter Lee started Yount-Lee Oil Company at Beaumont, Texas (McKinley 2007). By 1935, the company was a highly successful independent oil producer. When adjusted for inflation, the 1935 sale of Yount-Lee to Stanolind Oil Company would be worth $711 million in 2009 dollars (Yount-Lee . . . 2007; No. 1 Texas . . . 2007).

In order to prospect for oil, the Stanolind Company (Standard Oil of Indiana) became one of the largest landowners in southwest Louisiana. (Image from the author's collection.)

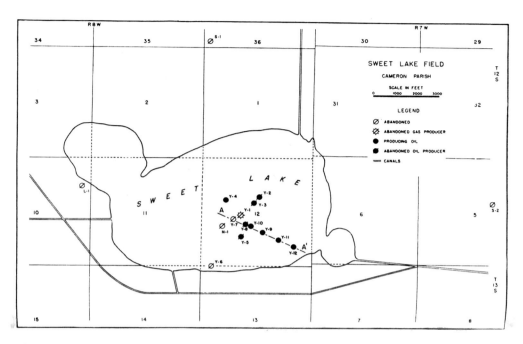

The Sweet Lake Field may be the oldest completely over-water oilfield in the coastal zone, ca. 1935. (Image from the *Louisiana Geological Bulletin,* no. 6, 1935.)

By 1936, the Cameron Meadows oilfield, operated by the Texas Company, Magnolia Oil Company, and Burton-Sutton Oil Company, was beginning to show promise. (Photo from the *Thirteenth Biennial Report, Louisiana Department of Conservation, 1936-1937.*)

Boats, however, were different. The company could own the watercraft, but needed skilled boatmen. In the beginning of their aquatic enterprises, these vessels were owned, operated, and maintained by "illiterate" men who quickly learned a boat was a valuable tool to the industry that could buy them "a ticket to almost any life" (Falgoux 2007:3). For the first time, marshdwellers were selling their skills and services; there were no tokens or script in this industry. They were not making money by harvesting the wetlands renewable resources, but from theexpertise and knowledge they acquired capturing and marketing these resources. In fact, when the

Wells Drilled in the Coastal Zone Prior to World War II
(December 7, 1941), by Operator

Operators prior to World War II	*First Well*	*Wells drilled prior to WW II*
Inactive Operator	01/01/1900	1541
The Texas Company (Texaco)	04/04/1929	346
Humble Oil and Refining Company	02/25/1923	91
Freeport Sulphur Company	08/20/1929	56
Gulf Oil Corp	01/24/1919	30
Sun Exploration and Production Company	05/10/1930	28
Texas Gulf Sulphur	07/30/1929	18
Louisiana Land and Exploration Company	08/17/1927	17
The Superior Oil Company	12/12/1936	10
Shell Oil Company	04/12/1935	8
Conoco	12/02/1939	7
Amerada Petroleum Company	5/29/1937	4
Hochendel Consultants	02/27/1935	2
Union Production Co./Union Expl. Partners	06/10/1938	2
Alltex Exploration Company	06/09/1938	1
Amoco Production Company	11/25/1938	1
C-Hawk	05/07/1938	1
Cities Service Oil	05/16/1941	1
Emerald Petroleum Corp.	10/01/1936	1
Jolly Petroleum Company	3/25/1940	1
Lyons	06/17/1939	1
Omeara Brothers	12/19/1939	1
Phillips Petroleum Company	03/24/1941	1
R. H. Parker	2/24/1940	1
Skelly Oil Company	12/01/1940	1
Target Resources	07/27/1923	1
Texas Pacific Oil Company	01/20/1940	1
W. P. Luse	11/16/1940	1
Total		2,174

support services became fully operational, fossil fuels exploration reached boom proportions across South Louisiana. Local shrimpers had learned quickly they could make good money driving their boats for the oil industry (Falgoux 2007). The price paid for shrimp or muskrat was no longer an issue. The marshdweller could not

The green "T" on a red star with the black Texaco lettering was the company's iconic logo from 1936 to 1965. In the ten years preceding World War II, the company became the dominant oil producer in coastal Louisiana, no date. (Image courtesy of Michael W. Quin.)

be ruined by depressed prices. Their services were needed, and they felt secure in having a reliable source of income. In the process, their boats became the Clydesdales of the marine-dependent oil industry. As one boatman noted "the family didn't have to invest any capital into converting their luggers into tugs; they only needed some stronger rope" (Falgoux 2007:21) and insurance—something they had never heard of before and/or needed.

Remote tracks of marsh and oilfields that depended on a fleet of support vessels became the norm. Working these fields required a full-time labor force that managed the field operation around-the-clock. Barges became living quarters. Where possible, stilt-supported bunk houses, warehouse, and out buildings appeared. The oil industry camp became the wetlands' "new" industrial settlement nodes, with each major field serving as the focal point of one of these camp clusters. With more than 1,500 wells drilled prior to World War II, these camp assemblages became the region's most important industrial hamlets. They were not recognized as communities by the census and had no post offices, but they dominated the region's economy. They were permanent, in a non-permanent sense, and gave birth to the recreation camps that migrated into the marshes and swamps in the post-World War II era.

The oil industry camp was an efficient way to turn raw materials into profits by guaranteeing that the production facilities were pumping continuously the extracted mineral fluids to market. Since the marsh was considered unimportant, there were no restrictions where these camps were built, or who built them. They were just another element on the landscape, whose form was simply a box enclosing a collection of rooms. Nonetheless, they were essential in the management of every marine-based oilfield (Falgoux 2007). In some cases, a one or two-story houseboats containing bunking quarters, a complete kitchen, dining room, and recreational facilities was the fifty to seventy man crews home away from home (Williams 1936B).

Unlike the company towns that were common in the oilfields of north Louisiana, Louisiana's coastal lowlands presented a new set of challenges. Oil was being discovered in remote regions where access was difficult. Travel time was too expensive and too long. To work in this environment, the hydrocarbon industry needed to build living quarters (camps) for their labor force. Elevated, stilt-supported camps needed to be constructed, or, where applicable, such as at Hackberry, a complete community was founded on oil. These were like Louisiana's cypress logging camps, shrimp-drying platforms, oyster shucking sheds, sulphur-mining operations, and market hunting camps—single-industry-communities housing the workers needed to extract the region's raw materials.

These communities were not like company towns in the coal, metal mines and lumber industries, or the towns associated with a steel mill, Pullman railroad cars, shoes, textiles, forest products, or Hershey's™ chocolate. These "camp" communities were transient and established so the required labor force could live and work at the job site. In some cases, the industry built schools, hospitals, recreation halls, and other community services that today are provided by municipal governments. In most cases these worker camps were associated with a particular oilfield and were dominated by some form of dormitory.

With the late arrival of adequate transportation, corridors in the coastal plain in the post-World War II era, oilfield camps were part of an "off the grid" community that served the maintenance needs of the field associated with each site (Williams 1933). Production problems often required barge-mounted compressor stations, permanent on the ground storage, or barge-based units that could be moved as the field expanded vertically into new production zones and horizontally to determine the field's subsurface boundaries. To manage the sites, barges also served as living and working quarters for the roustabouts or work gangs that consisted of a pusher

Texaco, like other oil companies working in coastal Louisiana, had a fleet of aircraft to service their isolated fields, ca. 1938. (Photo courtesy of Bernard Davis.)

and five men. Once the field was defined, more permanent quarters (dormitories for the male laborers) were built to maintain the field and the canals that connected all of the wells. In many fields, up to thirty miles of canals and also hundreds of wells needed to be monitored.

If the field was a success, these temporary camps were replaced by permanent, piling-supported structures, with boat, and later, seaplane-docking capabilities. This was the norm across coastal Louisiana's inaccessible and remote oil and gas fields. For example, within the Cameron Meadows oilfield the Magnolia Oil Company (later Mobil and now ExxonMobil) built a row of piling supported houses, interconnected with board-walks. This was a small village that was dominated by a gigantic boarding house for the men whose families did not move into these marsh-oriented industrial communities. Known locally as Fuzztown, this site and many others like it are now forgotten. They are in a sense "ghost towns." The workers were eventually relocated and the houses sold and moved (Stanley n.d.).

Eventually, Louisiana's marshes were laced with camps—reminiscent of boarding houses or barrack-like quarters—that catered to each field's labor force. All amenities were provided by the industry, and employers went to great lengths to insure that day-to-day requirements were met by developing or putting on contract a fleet of crew and supply boats (Falgoux 2007). It was a one field, one camp-cluster concept that brought Louisiana's forgotten and "useless" wetlands to the attention of a broad cross-section of individuals. The marshes became industrialized, and the camps and the jobs the industry provided played a major role in shaping the region's economy and culture. The marshes were settled by a new breed of transient laborer. When the natural resource was exhausted, the labor force moved on. Their company-owned camps became derelict, creosoted-post-supported ghostly reminders of what was once a thriving industrial node that with time simply vanished, but provided the bases for the pre-1940 revolution in drilling for oil in a wet, mosquito-invested, hot, humid, and almost land/almost water environment. A new age in oil exploration was initiated that proved the tenacity of the country's oil men in their quest to meet the nation's expanding demand for fossil fuels. It was a sudden, swift, and tenacious revolution.

The Challenge of Working in the Marsh

Exploration and development of Louisiana's fossil fuels reserves was so rapid that by the early 1930s, approximately three-quarter billion barrels of oil had been produced from shallow fields, involving approximately 150,000 acres—234 square miles—approximately the geographic footprint of Chicago (Chisholm 1929; Priest 2003). By 1939, thirty-seven parishes were involved in the industry—more than half of the state's parishes. Two new fields, on average, were being discovered in every month and from fifteen to twenty new wells every week. The industry was booming, largely because of the discoveries associated with the state's salt-dome structures (Barton 1930; Branan 1937; Shaw 1938). A geologist noted "Louisiana has one of the world's greatest petroleum reserves. . . . But we have barely scratched the surface. . . ." (Branan 1937:7). Louisiana's commissioner of the Department of Conservation, W. G. Rankin reported: "We see our marsh-land, even our water bottoms, literally dotted with derricks that have arisen almost overnight—in nearly every parish of Louisiana we see exploration followed by production; we see the income of this section swelling from oil royalties, from the labor of oil operations and related sources" (Rankin 1938:5).

The oil was there; it just had to be found and moved to market. Finding the reserves was not easy, as drilling rigs were blown up by gas explosion. They were also blown down by storms. Drill bits were broken off and lost. Clay used in "mudding" in the hole was often delivered by *pirogue* and flatboats. Canals came later. In some cases wells were abandoned. The pay-off often came after the third, fourth, or fifth dry hole (Branan 1937). It was a highly speculative environment. Perseverance paid off well for the wildcatters and others willing to take a risk. However, finding oil in the wetlands was not an easy "play," as these new discoveries were difficult to find, supply, and pay for—as the costs were described as "stupendous" (Branan 1937:6).

Unfortunately, no record exists of the frustration levels oil company engineers experienced during the pre-1940s, but it must have been high. They had to rethink their understanding of load-carrying capabilities. They were accustomed to drilling on land that supported 33,000 pounds/yd^3. Marshland peats supported only 2,600 lb/yd^3 (Herbert and Anderson 1936). To overcome this problem they tried everything that might support a load. Wooden mats, composed of layers of boards laid out in crisscross patterns, did work in some shallow water areas, but frequently rotted, split apart, or sank. In open water, pilings were used, but repeatedly sank out-of-sight. Drilling contractors discovered it too expensive and time-consuming to assemble a drilling rig, tear it down after the job, and move it to the next site.

No one had perfected an efficient, economical, floating drilling platform (Williams 1934). Crews could be moved, housed, and fed on barges and boats, but they required a stable platform to support a derrick, power supply, and drilling equipment. Activity in the wetlands was handicapped by the absence of a stable derrick support that could function in the quicksand-like soils that was a drilling crew's nightmare. If the industry was going to expand profitably in the wetlands, the soil issue was a dilemma that needed a solution. Because a spot that looked safe to walk on could "engulf a person to [their] arm-pits in seconds, and whatever land is hard enough to permit walking will quickly swallow all tracks left behind" (Pelletier 1972:13). Wetland drilling needed new technology to allow the industry to work in an environment that could not make up its mind if it was water or land.

The Floating Drilling Barge

In 1928, Louis Giliasso patented a submersible drilling barge. Four years later, the Texas Company wanted to avoid the expense and uncertainty of using piling-supported platforms or mats to develop their Louisiana leases. Searching for patents,

Texas Company officials found Giliasso's floating drilling barge and purchased the rights to the design (Texaco built first 1949; Landenberg 1972). As a result, they built the barge and put it to work; other companies followed their lead, as it was estimated that approximately $15,000 was saved per well by using the submersible drilling unit. This advancement in drilling technology resulted in the American Marine Corporation (New Orleans) building more than half of all inshore, barge-mount, drilling rigs used by the industry. The demand was so high that the company was often fabricating as many as six barges simultaneously. By 1946, the company had assembled nearly ninety drilling units, each requiring an eleven-to-twelve man crew (New Orleans firm 1960).

The Texas Company used in the fall of 1931 the *Giliasso* in their Lake Barré operation, and began a new era in petroleum exploration in wetland environments. In the Lake Barré field, one well was completed in one afternoon, and the rig then moved to another location and began drilling the following day at an estimated savings of $75,000 over the conventional piling-foundation technique. The field grew quickly, and it was described as "having produced an average of one-fourth million barrels of oil per month through the year [1932]" (Shaw 1933:7).

Texaco activities in the coastal parishes

Parish	First Well	Wells drilled prior to WW II	Total wells drilled in the parish to 2000
Cameron	04/04/1929	25	171
Vermilion	07/07/1940	2	117
Iberia	06/09/1929	38	698
St. Mary	10/17/1930	9	1,042
Terrebonne	07/31/1929	172	4,157
Lafourche	11/07/1930	40	1,200
Jefferson	07/17/1940	3	765
Plaquemines	08/11/1929	24	107
St. Bernard		No wells drilled	
St. Charles	11/25/1938	33	431
Orleans		No wells drilled	
Total		346	8,688

Once the Texas Company discovered oil at Lake Barré, crews (like their counterparts in other fields across the lower-tier of parishes) had to live in piling-support camps suspended over the marsh muck. Drilling mud was hauled thirty-five miles to the site, and above-ground storage was a problem. Everything was shipped by water (Williams 1929; Shaw 1930; Postgate 1949). Innovation was the rule; field storage for the produced oil was in three obsolete oil tankers grounded in Cat Island Pass, that were connected to an old steel schooner used as a loading dock. Without pipelines, this innovative storage technique was necessary, but the longevity of this peculiar "port" is unknown.

From "Port Texaco," oil was lightered to vessels offshore (Moresi 1935). Texaco used a similar system in the delta to move crude from their Garden Island Bay field to waiting tankers at anchor in the Gulf of Mexico (Pipe lines supplant 1937). A disadvantage of this system was that the oil often had to be handled five times before it reached the refinery. A pipeline would have helped, but such a system did not proliferate

To facilitate movement of crude oil, the Texas Company developed their Port Texaco shipping terminal, ca. 1933. (Photo from the *Louisiana Conservation Review,* 4, 1934.)

across the coast until after World War II. Seven years after the war, the Texas Pipeline Company completed a 135-mile pipeline that connected the firm's Bay Ste. Elaine, Lake Barré, Lake Pelto, and Caillou Island fields in Terrebonne Bay to Port Arthur. This solved the handling issue (Trow 1952). Further, by the mid-1960s, Texaco's Caillou Island, Lake Barré, Bay Ste. Elaine, and Lake Pelto fields "had a combined cumulative production and remaining reserves of more than 1 billion barrels" (Priest 2003:18).

With the success of the *Giliasso,* the industry flourished in South Louisiana. This event marked an innovative era in the region's infant fossil fuels industry. In the decade after the launch of the *Giliasso,* a large number of associated industries were established to meet the marine hardware needs of the industry. Using this new "floating derrick," nearly every major oil company in the country was involved in the growth of the state's energy industry. The technology came at an appropriate time, since new markets were being created as the population began to move from an agrarian lifestyle to an urban one.

The mechanization of farms after 1941, for example, was revolutionary (Maier 1952; Ferleger 1982). Farm-tractor consumption of fuel increased 100 percent. More motorists were doing more driving; more airplanes were flying longer distances; railroads had four times as many diesel engines; and hundreds of thousands of homes switched to fuel oil for heating. To meet the increased demand, the industry had to expand its exploration, development, and production schedules. Risks had to be taken and new fields needed to be developed in challenging environments. This was the case in the move offshore (Gramling 1996).

In the early 1940s, many oil firms were unsure about South Louisiana's long-term economic importance as an oil province. That attitude changed, particularly with the 1947 discovery of marketable hydrocarbons in field's out-of-sight of land in the northern Gulf of Mexico. The following year, twenty-three companies were drilling, rigging up, or building platforms to explore more than 1.8 million acres of ocean bottom off Louisiana's coast (Davis 1991). This pace continued into the 1980s, when there was a severe downturn, and things looked bleak. Oil discovered in water depths greater than 600 feet and up to 10,000 feet changed dramatically the notion that offshore Louisiana was a dying oil province and established a new era in drilling for oil world wide.

Two deepwater fixed platforms—*Cognac* and *Bullwinkle*—led off the industry's exploration of deep water in the Gulf of Mexico (Richardson, et al. 2004). Walker Ridge, Green Canyon, East Breaks, Garden Banks, Ewing Bank, Atwater Valley, Mississippi Canyon, and Viosca Knoll then became deepwater target areas as well. (See *http:// www.gomr.mms.gov/homepg/lsesale/opd2.pdf* for a lease map of these sites.) To meet the technological challenges presented by these aquatic environments, platforms with names like *Auger, Brutus, Crosby, Kings Peak, Mars, Mensa, Petronius, Thunder Horse, Troika,* and *Ursa,* along with eighty other structures, have since been installed and the number continues to increase.

Drilling and production structures operating off Louisiana pushed the limit of production into water depths from 800 feet to 1,100 feet (LeBlanc 1982; Metzler 1978). With the advent of deepwater drilling, the frontier has been pushed to 10,000 feet. To maintain this industry, a large and diverse group of people and businesses are a vital link in maintaining the industry's presence in Louisiana. Many of these small-to-medium businesses rely on this industry for their economic survival. The industry

Discovery of marketable hydrocarbons offshore required a logistic support system to meet the needs of offshore contractors, no date. (Photo courtesy of the Morgan City Archives.)

has prospered through their contributions, and their presence in many communities within the state has contributed to the economic well-being of these towns. Both benefit from the favorable geologic structures that underlie Louisiana.

The new deepwater frontier employs thousands of people, who can commute from their homes for their seven and seven shifts. They no longer have to reside in the marshes; they now live offshore, in hotel-factories exploiting the region's recoverable mineral fluids. More than 20,000 individuals are offshore on any given day, living on platforms suspended above the water's surface. These sites are aquatic villages that have pushed the concept of settlement into the Gulf of Mexico. As in early marsh and swamp settlements, the oil company field hands, do not own the land; they work the site for the convenience and efficiency of living at their job. The pattern has come full circle, from watermen living at their harvesting sites, to oil drilling and production professionals doing the same thing more than 200 years after the first marshdwellers established their secluded communities. The "community's" stilts are longer, but the results are the same—the efficient production of the region's natural resources.

Since the first successful oil well at Jennings/Evangeline, Louisianians have benefitted from the jobs associated with the oil business. There was a downturn in the 1980s, and many left the business. This changed with deepwater discoveries, because for thirty-five years prior to the slump, the drilling community was optimistic about Louisiana's onshore future. The area had proved itself. Decline is inevitable, but the fields discovered offshore had reinvigorated the province's falling onshore production.

In tandem with new developments offshore after World War II, the industry unilaterally enlarged its pipeline web to meet the needs of an expanding market.

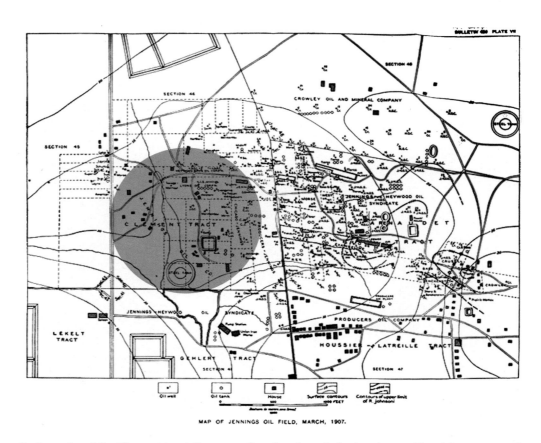

MAP OF JENNINGS OIL FIELD, MARCH, 1907.

In the wake of the Clement tract discovery, the oil and gas industry changed Louisiana economic and cultural landscapes, 1910. (Image from United States Geological Survey, Bulletin 429.)

In St. Mary, Terrebonne, and Lafourche parishes the marshland pipeline network increased to sixty miles. Another 300 miles stretched along the region's natural levees. With each new field extension, the pipeline system followed (Davis and Place 1983; Gramling 1996; Turner and Streever 2002). Currently, the coastal lowlands are a maze of overlapping and interconnecting pipelines, many of them sharing the same rights-of-way. In the twenty-first century, the entangled web continues to proliferate, as the industry moves recovered fossil fuels from its offshore fields to distribution hubs onshore.

Drilling offshore has become the new "workhorse" of oil and gas production, while onshore independent oil companies have replaced the majors in re-working old fields that began to show they were reaching the end of their productive life in the 1960s and 1970s (Lindstedt, et al. 1991). During this time period, the onshore province had reached a mature state. Major new discoveries were rare. Although in a period of sustained decline, more than 580,000 acres—906 square miles—was used to support the petroleum industry's activities (Davis and Place 1983; Lindstedt, et al. 1991). Because of this fact, company camps were closed or manned sporadically, as most fields could be serviced easily from end-of-the-road facilities using fast supply boats (Falgoux 2007). The need to have a resident labor force in the field was no longer necessary.

Also during this time frame, approximately 75 percent of the exploratory wells and about 35 percent of the development wells went dry (Edred and Johnson 1965; Hurley, et al. 1973). In 1973, only six new fields were discovered, and the only significant activity was extending existing fields. By 1974, onshore leases had declined

15 percent (Stevens and Callahan 1974). Several wetland fields had reached the end of their usefulness (Lindstedt, et al. 1991). Their infrastructure was also slightly weather worn. Since most of the equipment associated with these fields predated environmental concerns and regulations, and was designed to maximize oil and gas production, there were clean-up and other environmental matters. Prior to World War II, there were no concerns regarding infrastructure longevity in oilfields across the country, or the environmental consequences associated with a sixty or seventy-year productive life. Maintenance was critical, but often delayed until something went wrong. The old axiom—if it ain't broke, don't fix it—often prevailed.

In the wetlands, the industry had to deal with many problems that were beyond their general expertise. Salt spray was a variable that was not an issue with upland drillers. Sodium chloride is largely responsible for the relentless corrosion of metallic objects near the coast. Every metal object was at risk, but preventative maintenance was expensive and often put off. Further, many of these depleted reservoirs were linked to fields that were designed to operate in shallow estuarine waters. They were never intended to survive open Gulf conditions.

As erosion, subsidence, and sea level rise change the land/water ratios, many wetland fields will be subjected to wave and energy conditions well beyond their design limits. Some examples are beginning to emerge. Wells and infrastructure in these fields represent the earliest signs of problems associated with this aging infrastructure. Can these wells and associated infrastructure withstand this type of environmental pressure? If they cannot, it is time to retrofit those fields at risk, or prepare for the environmental consequences, because many wells may not survive.

Wells Drilled by parish to 2000

Parish	Wells Drilled to 2000	Percentage of the Total to 2000
Plaquemines	16,732	27.48
Terrebonne	9,577	15.56
Lafourche	9,020	14.65
Cameron	6,988	11.35
St. Mary	5,464	08.88
Vermilion	4,513	07.33
Iberia	3,735	06.07
Jefferson	2,831	04.60
St. Bernard	1,554	02.52
St. Charles	979	01.59
Orleans	137	00.22
Total	61,530	100.25

A Louisiana swamper. (Image from the *Illustrated London News,* October 1858.)

Chapter 9
SETTLEMENTS WITHIN THE SWAMPS

Only one informant (Kramer, May 15, 1958) reported working in the time-honored pre-industrial manner on a seasonal basis as an independent swamper, and trapping and farming at other seasons. Kramer, his brothers, and friends worked together in a group of seven. One stayed at the camp to hunt, fish, and cook while others girdled and felled trees. A rotation system was used whereby one day was spent at the camp as cook, fisherman, and hunter, and six days in the woods. For shelter the swampers built a cabin, usually of board-and-batten construction, but occasionally of palmetto. They took in enough coffee, sugar, flour, rice, beans, and condiments, but no whiskey, to last several weeks. Two-or-three-days' supply of meat was brought in, but afterwards the cook was depended upon to supply the group with fish, squirrels, ducks, alligators, and other wildlife as meat. At the time of the spring flood, the logs were floated out and sold to a sawmill . . . (Mancil 1972:234).

Swamps, or "wet forests," extend from Texas to Delaware, occupying the humid climatic zone of the southeastern United States. These *cyprières* exist where the soil is saturated for one or more months of the growing season, with water not too deep to prevent germination or to drown year-old plants. These wet forests are best developed within the region's floodplains, which provide an ideal habitat for two dominant plant species—baldcypress and tupelo gum. In the late 1800s and early 1900s, these trees became important marketable commodities from a forest type formally perceived as wicked, impenetrable, mysterious, and the home of a wide-variety of folk monsters, including the Cajun *loup garou*. Writings, drawings, paintings, and sketches in popular books and magazines, such as, *Ballou's Pictorial Drawing Companion, Frank Leslie Illustrated Newspaper* and *Harper's Weekly* were responsible for the notion swamps were dark, evil, and nefarious environments that they were best avoided (Hall and Penfound 1939; Conner and Day 1976; Vileisis 1997).

Even with these labels, red cypress, oak, tupelo-gum, and other trees were utilized by early settlers. Swamp timber was readily available and an ideal construction material for small cottages, boats, fences, furniture, cisterns, silos, plantation manor houses and out buildings, sugar mills, and associated structures. Milled cypress, in particular, is perfect for Louisiana's climate, as it is nearly indestructible. Because of this quality, *Taxodium distichum* quickly became a sought-after commodity. It was milled into beams, planks, boards, shingles, laths, railroad cross-ties, molding, boxes, and other products used by manufacturers.

Since shingles were one of the principal products of the cypress industry, shingle machines, like the one pictured above, operated continuously, 2006. (Photo by the author.)

Cypress shingles were the principal product marketed in the 1880s to 1890s, with some mills fabricating more than 150,000 a day (Prophit 1982; Castay 2006). Working at full capacity, one cypress mill could easily manufacture up to one million shingles a week. In communities with up to five lumber mills operating simultaneously, the weekly output was a staggering 4.5 million shingles. In its heyday, the Louisiana Cypress Lumber Company mill in Harvey made a million shingles a day, along with a variety of other cypress products that were shipped by barge up the Mississippi River to St. Louis to be distributed throughout the Midwest

HARPER'S WEEKLY.

JOURNAL OF CIVILIZATION.

VOL. XXXII.—No. 1656.
Copyright, 1888, by HARPER & BROTHERS.
All Rights Reserved.

NEW YORK, SATURDAY, SEPTEMBER 15, 1888.

TEN CENTS A COPY.
WITH A SUPPLEMENT.

THE U. S. M. MISSISSIPPI PASSENGER STEAMER.—Drawn by Charles Graham.—[See Poem, Page 694.]

(Oral history interview 1960). At that rate, the supply barely kept up with the demand. In addition, as railroads moved west and expanded their reach into western, eastern, and southern markets, demand for cross-ties developed into a significant early market as well.

Rotary, circular, and bandsaws, new and improved methods of tree harvesting and removal, coupled with an expanding market attracted lumbermen/entrepreneurs and their sawmills to Baldwin, Berwick, Bowie, Donner, Franklin, Frenier, Gibson, Houma, Centerville, Patterson, Plaquemine, Ponchatoula, Reserve/Garyville, Ruddock, Morgan City, New Iberia, White Castle, and other swamp-accessible villages, towns, and cities on the east and west sides of the Mississippi River.

Sawmills in these communities, and others like them, were located on the region's waterways and railroads. These transportation arteries could easily furnish the fuel required by the wood-burning steam engines used by river boats and railroads. In addition, the Southern Cypress Lumber Selling Company began an aggressive campaign to promote the superior rot-resistant qualities of cypress, which was now seen as more than a boiler fuel. Later organized as the Louisiana Red Cypress Company, the group's salesmen promoted the "wood eternal" throughout the country and sales to Eastern cities increased dramatically. By the beginning of the twentieth century, profits were enormous. New mills were built, logging expanded, and sawmills operated continuously, as a fleet of steamboats, and later gas boats, provided an around-the-clock supply of cut timber (Vileisis 1997). In addition, in the late 1800s and early 1900s, schooners and steamboats were operating throughout the coastal zone carrying a wide assortment of wood products to East Coast destinations.

The *Frances, Hilda,* and *Burdin,* for example, were used to tow logs from the Catahoula swamp to mills on Bayou Teche and the *Antonia Wilbert, Carrie B. Schwing, Sewanee, M.E. Norman, Amy Hewes, Jennie Louise, Nettie Verret,* and *Black Prince* worked throughout the Atchafalaya. In some cases, moving cypress from the harvesting site to the lumber yard often took three weeks. Although the distance between some harvested tracts and a logging firm's sawmill was relatively short, the water route frequently extended more than 100 miles, particularly when the logs were harvested in the Catahoula Swamp and towed up the Teche to St. Martinville (Looney 1974). Even so, the bayous and ancillary waterbodies served as the swamp's streets and roadways and the logging industry used them well.

In the 1870s, the Pharr-Williams Company established a cypress mill at Patterson. The firm was renamed the F. B. Williams Cypress Company and their on-the-ground operation became the largest lumber mill west of the Atchafalaya. Williams owned more than 60,000 acres

(Images courtesy of the Morgan City Archives and Rathborne Commercial & Industrial Properties, Harvey, La.)

The Wilbert Lumber Company's Big Jim sawmill in Plaquemine, La.—like all cypress mills—required water access, ca. 1915. (Photo courtesy of the A. Wilbert's Sons Lumber and Shingle Company, Plaquemine, La.)

(ninety-three square miles) of timber lands containing about 1.5 billion board feet of lumber. Other lumber companies in the area included Berwick, Gates, Albert Hanson, May Brothers, Coon Cypress Silo, Trellue, Red Cypress, Riggs, Cypress Tank and Manufacturing, Brownell and Moore, Thorgusons, Hanson-Tevis, Col. Pease-Smith, George Vinson Shingle mill, Kyle-Taylor, Baldwin, Jeanerette, Norgress-Menefee, Brownell and Drews, Cotton Brothers, Ramos, and Waddell-Williams, that in 1922 became Norman-Breaux (Cypress, wood eternal 1991).

In Terrebonne Parish during the early 1900s, there were numerous cypress mills as well—some larger than others. Parish-wide the companies involved included C. P. Smith, C. M. Boudreaux and Sons, Farquhard Guidry, Bonvillain Brothers, Dibert, Stark and Brown, F. E. Shepherd, Goodland, L. S. Boudreaux, Gibson, Caillou, and Dulac (A sketch 1910; Wurzlow 1976B). By 1906, cypress lumber, called "forest gold," was the second largest industry in Terrebonne Parish—sugar was number one—with the Parish's largest sawmills producing from 30,000 to 40,000 feet of lumber a day, or about 12,000,000 feet annually—about 2,272 linear miles (A sketch 1910; Wurzlow 1976).

By the late 1800s, lumbering on the western fringe of the Atchafalaya was the single most important industry in Iberia Parish. Three mills in New Iberia could not keep up with the demand for milled cypress, oak, ash, magnolia, sweet gum, hackberry, and other varieties. The same was true for other communities within the region. The cypress timber industry dominated local business interests between 1880 and 1920. As a result, many mill owners supported improved transportation systems. These modified or new channels were considered essential in their efforts to expand their market (Fisk 1890).

The hectic lumber production schedule lasted until the mid-1920s, when nearly all remaining old-growth trees were cut. Norman-Breaux was the last cypress mill in Morgan City, and by 1925 it was the largest producer of cypress products in the

United States—though the Hebardville mill processing Okefenokee cypress from southeast Georgia also claims this title. The Norman-Breaux operation shut down in the 1950s—about thirty years after most of the competition had dismantled their facilities. While in operation, Norman-Breaux shipped boxcar orders of cypress to clients in thirty-six states (Cypress, wood eternal 1991).

The economic benefits of the industry lasted only as long as the resource was available. In the end, more than 1.6 million acres (2,500 square miles—about the size of the state of Delaware) of cypress bottom lands were harvested: "The natural riches that had taken hundreds of years to create vanished" (Vileisis 1997:122). The industry's legacy may be the large number of items built from cypress that survive today as reminders of the industrial age of cypress logging. At its high point, the region's sawmills turned out cypress in quantity. Further, this was a product recognized for its quality as well. Because of the value of each cypress board, there was relatively little waste; pieces as small as three or four inches wide were used to make buckets, tubs, washing machines, and small vats—all beneficiaries of advertising proclaiming that "Cypress Defies Decay" (Horn 1943).

After the record harvests of the late 1920s, the colossal industry was on the decline. In many swamps, the trees were harvested completely by 1925, and large-scale logging was largely dead throughout coastal Louisiana and the other Southern tidewater cypress regions. With the demise of this industry, most sawmill towns suffered, as hundreds of workers and their families moved to other areas to seek employment (Maygarden and Yakubik 1999).

Ponchatoula was one of the towns that endured considerable economic hardship. With construction in the early 1920s of two large cypress mills—F. B. Williams and Joseph Rathborne—the city flourished. Hundreds of workers were hired, who with their families increased the city's population. New businesses followed the lumber companies, as the expanding population needed additional services. A new city hall and fire station were added to the city's profile, as well as a high school, Movie

Cypress logs being milled in a small Rathborne facility at Choctaw, La. Such small mills, which rarely appear in records, are usually documented only in photographs, such as the one above, no date. (Photo courtesy of Rathborne Commercial & Industrial Properties, Harvey, La.)

The oil industry constituted an early market for cypress timber which was used for board roads, 1944. (Photo courtesy of the Morgan City Archives.)

Theater, train depot and other structures. In 1929, less than ten years after their construction, both mills closed and the labor forced began to migrate elsewhere.

Loss of the mills and the associated jobs, coupled with the Great Depression, further contributed to the city's severe economic decline. In 1936, the Louisiana Cypress Company, operating from the old Rathborne mill site, began cutting cypress trees from a new section of the swamps south of Ponchatoula. The mill was operational until 1956. For several years prior to its closing, this facility processed mahogany logs imported from Honduras. The city was eventually reborn, but not all of the cypress-based communities were so lucky.

Gibson, Donner, Timberton, and Garden City, for example, today show no signs of the enormous sawmill and lumber yard that dominated the geographic foot-print of these communities. Like so many things in the coastal zone, they are lost to history. In many cases they are simply a footnote, but were vital in documented the people that gave the region its meaning.

In looking back, major industrial exploitation of cypress began quickly, expanded rapidly, initiated hydrologic changes in the swamp landscape, and concluded about thirty-five years after its birth. The gigantic mills had cut out the mammoth tracts of timber. The end result is a clear example of how efficient economies of scale can be in a single industry. Although the industry collapsed, royalties from hydrocarbon reserves have allowed many of these pioneering lumber firms to continue to prosper.

Lumber companies oil wells to 2000 in descending order
(If a company did not use their name in the well name,
it does not appear in the database.)

Lumber Company	*Total wells in the forested wet lands*
A. Wilbert's Sons Lumber and Shingle Company	988
Schwing Lumber and Shingle Company	538
Williams, Inc.	315
Lutcher Moore Lumber Company	153
Baist Cooperage and Lumber Company	130
Dibert, Stark, and Brown or some derivation on the names	116
Jeanerette Lumber Company	103
Norman-Breaux Lumber Company or some derivation thereof	91
Rathborne Land and Lumber Company	86
Brownell-Kidd Lumber Company (Brownell and Drews)	70
South Coast Company	66
Bowie Lumber Company	65
Industrial Lumber Company	47
Natalbany Lumber Company	42
Powell Lumber Company	36
J. A. Provost Lumber Company or some derivation on the names	30

Lumber Company	Total wells in the forested wet lands
Morley Cypress Company	30
White Castle Lumber and Shingle Company	30
Edgewood Land and Lumber Company	27
Cypress, Inc.	23
Ramos Investments, Inc.	22
Baldwin Lumber Company	21
Opdenweyer-Alcus Cypress Company	20
Krause and Managan Lumber Company	14
Cotton Brothers or some derivative of the name	12
Grief Brothers Cooperage Corporation	12
Iberville Manufacturing Company (Iberville Land Company)	12
Koonce, Inc.	10
Miles Timber Company	9
Planters Lumber Company	9
Burton-Swartz Land Corporation	8
Gates Lumber Company	4
Williams Cypress Company	3
Acme Land and Timber Company	2
Allan Land and Lumber Company	2
Boise Southern Lumber Company	2
Kyle Lumber Company or some derivation on the name	2
Lotham Cypress Company	2
White and Friant Lumber Company	2
J. L. Stebbins Lumber Company	1
New Orleans, Texas & Mexico Railroad Company	1
Total	3,156

In the industry's heyday, forest ingress and timber removal were of paramount concern. Access problems were resolved by excavating thirty-to-fifty-foot-wide, and six-to-eight-foot-deep canals to the logging sites at a cost of about $10,000 per mile—railroad logging cost as much as $15,000 per mile (Watson 1906; Mancil 1960; Mancil 1972). To maintain a watercourse, the timber company had a full-time maintenance crew cleaning the invasive water hyacinth (*Eichhornia crassipes*) from the waterways. This alien species introduced into Louisiana at the World's Industrial and Cotton Centennial Exposition of 1884-1885 was considered one of the world's worst weeds—aquatic or terrestrial (A sketch of 1910). As a result, the largest timber companies owned a fleet of dredges and pullboats, and, where practical, their own standard-gauge logging railroads, but it took a good stand of timber to justify the expense of maintaining rail access to their timber stands.

The girdling technique, which dates back to at least 1725, was used extensively by these professional loggers. Because "green" cypress would sink, axmen would cut a three- or four-inch ring into the bark completely around the trunk. Once girdled in the fall, the tree naturally drained its sap and became more buoyant. Timing the return of the logging crew was critical, as the tree was dying. It was essential that the tree be harvested before it became bug infested and lost some of its market value.

With discovery of marketable hydrocarbons in the swamp, many lumber companies became lessors, 2007. (Photo by the author.)

The ringed trees were cut with axes and hand saws. For his efforts, a logger was paid by the number of feet of marketable lumber in the trees they felled—totalling approximately twenty to twenty-five cents an hour (Wilt 2005). As in other labor-intensive industries, lumbermen were often paid in tokens—redeemable only in a company town in a company store. In the Florida cypress industry, these tokens were called borozeems. And, as elsewhere in the alluvial wetlands, hard work was rewarded with small pay. Common laborers made from one dollar to two dollars a day. A foreman would make slightly more. The highest paid job was that of the pullboat operator, who would make five dollars a day. In the swamps, owner/operators appeared to have forgone payment in script. All records indicate they paid workers in cash, which was not the case in many upland operations.

Once a tree was cut, an auger was used to bore a small hole in each log, and then these logs were "chain-dogged" together into a small raft that was pulled to a collection point—a bay or slip. Once assembled in the slip, the little rafts were lashed together into "double-spliced rafts" or "cribs"—made up of ten trees abreast—and taken to the sawmill by narrow-bodied steamboats following the region's "float roads" (Moore 1967; Mancil 1972; Moore 1983). Later, small, narrow, one- or two-man gas boats would move the log rafts; on occasion these rafts could exceed 500 feet. Barges were seldom used.

In the rafting operation, many logs were lost. If the log did not float properly, it would begin to sink and act as an anchor. These logs were cut out of the tow and allowed to sink. They were often quickly buried in the bottom sediments and when recovered were identified as "sinkers." A small cottage industry developed in conjunction with the discovery and removal of this buried timber. This timber tends to be of the highest quality and brings the salvager a good return on his time and investment. Accompanying the raft were "pushers" who walked along the raft with long poles and helped direct the raft through curves and around channel debris. They were also responsible for cutting out the logs that were not floating properly.

A variation of the field girdling technique was used by the Rathborne Lumber Company. The firm used four-and-a-half-to-five foot high levees, locks, and pumps

(Left) Swampers had to survey, girdle, and prepare cypress trees for harvesting, no date. (Photo courtesy of Commercial & Industrial Properties, Harvey, La.)

(Below) Once cut, cypress was transported along the floating railroad, 1946. (Photo courtesy of Standard Oil Collection, University of Louisville, negative no. 44710.)

(Left) From staging areas, cypress as hauled to the mill, 1946. (Photo courtesy of Standard Oil Collection, University of Louisville, negative no. 44710.)

(Left) One of the water control structures used by the Rathborne Lumber Company, no date. (Photo courtesy of Rathborne Commercial & Industrial Properties, Harvey, La.)

(Right) The Rathborne Lumber Company would flood a leveed portion of the swamp to improve access into an area to be logged , no date. (Photo courtesy of Rathborne Commercial & Industrial Properties, Harvey, La.)

(Left) Small motorboat pulling a string of logs to the mill, no date. (Photo courtesy of Rathborne Commercial & Industrial Properties, Harvey, La.)

(Right) Grading logs before they were sent to the mill, no date. (Photo courtesy of Rathborne Commercial & Industrial Properties, Harvey, La.)

(Left) A large tow being moved to the Norman-Breaux mill site near Morgan City, ca. 1900. (Photo courtesy of Catherine B. Dilsaver.)

(Right) The lumberyard for the Louisiana Red Cypress Lumber Company at Ponchatoula, 1948. (Photo courtesy of Standard Oil Collection, University of Louisville, negative no. 62253.)

to construct a 1,200-acre artificial impoundment, up to thirty-six inches deep, at cost of $25,000 each. Once the pond was leveed, it took about a month of flood the area to the required depth before lumberjacks could begin cutting timber. No pullboat was needed, as the cut logs were simply floated into the locks, where they were scaled, weighed, locked, and floated into the central canal, where they were loaded, towed, and delivered to Rathborne's mill at Harvey (Kerr 1953; Lucas 1957; Swanson 1975). Other companies, like the Cotton Brothers, also used this method. Their ponds impounded up to 2,500 acres—nearly four square miles.

On other property, removal of the cut timber was accomplished by using pullboat-mounted steam engines that methodically dragged logs into a dredged channel (Cypress, wood eternal 1991). If a pullboat was not used, an overhead skidder, introduced in 1883, moved the harvested timber. Working in conjunction with a railroad constructed into the swamp, the skidder consisted of a cable stretched between two high, or spar, trees that allowed the logs to be dragged by the overhead cable slightly above ground to the rail line (Comeaux 1972).

Working from quarter boats and temporary camps, field crews systematically harvested cypress, 1948. (Photo courtesy of the Standard Oil Collection, University of Louisville, negative no. 62329.)

At the lumber yard, there were graders, sawyers, and scalers who would calculate just how much lumber could be cut from each log. Wide lumber brought better prices, but this required big logs. Most of the timber was cut into shingles, laths, railroad cross-ties, and staves used to make molasses barrels, cisterns, and tanks. If a planning mill was part of the operations—fence pickets, banisters, window panes, doors, and a wide variety of fancy millwork would be added to the inventory of material curing in the company's lumberyard (A sketch of 1910; Wurzlow 1976). During the Vietnam era, cypress cisterns were used by the United States' armed services. When shot, the tanks did not drain, they self-sealed, and the soldiers' water supply was not lost (Sheets 2009, pers. comm.).

The earliest lumbermen were either former slaves or poor whites who were glad to be employed. These locals were joined later by axmen recruited from the forests of the North and West. Regardless of their origins, these day-laborers worked in waist-deep water to guarantee the lumber yards a constant supply of cypress. Labor was crucial; therefore, "nationwide advertising campaigns promised workers the highest wages in the timber industry, company housing, stores, schools, and full reimbursement of travel costs. Although the folklore of logging generally depicts loggers as independent bachelors following seasonal work opportunities, the Southern climate allowed year-round work which, in turn, enabled 'skidder' towns "to be set up" (Vileisis 1997:119-120). Potential new employees flocked to the swamps to harvest cypress and tupelo. It was hard, back-breaking, wet, and redundant work. Some did not make it. Those who stayed learned to insert a platform into the base of a tree from which they cut down the target species. Other hardy and reckless loggers used their balance and precision axe cuts to fell trees while standing in a *pirogues* or *bateaux* (Moore 1983).

> A large part of the time they must be hip deep in the water. They must girdle or deaden these trees several months ahead of the choppers otherwise the logs will not float. At the proper time, these trees, sometimes six and seven feet through, with tremendous swell butts, must be felled and sawed into proper lengths. Then they are ready for the pullboat or skidder and are yanked by powerful steam appliances from hundreds of feet away into the canal or alongside the railroad (Watson 1906:44).

With arrival of an appropriate labor force, full-service "skidder" towns were established. These moveable settlement clusters were centered on frame houses mounted on barges known as quarterboats. Few resident loggers, known as "swampers," lived permanently in these one- or two-story quarterboat-based communities (Mancil 1960; Mancil 1972; Case 1973). These facilities served as the transient crew's dormitories and mess halls, where squirrel or stewed chicken, white beans and salt meal, vegetables, pie, cornbread, biscuits, and coffee were waiting at the end of the day. A crew would go into the woods on Monday and return on Friday, after putting in fifty hours per week.

> My father only made 25 cents an hour cutting trees down in the basin . . . The tree were so big that a man could fit lying down inside the trunk (Wilt 2005:40).

Forest Products Producers in the coastal lowlands forested wet lands (swamps) – 1932 (From Sonderegger, V. H. Department of Conservation, Division of Forestry, Classification and Uses of Agricultural and Forest Lands in the State of Louisiana and the Parishes. Bulletin No. 24, Vol. VIII 1939)

Company	City	Parish or Parishes of Operation
Abraham & Kahn	Raceland	Lafourche, Terrebonne
Acme Veneer Company		St. Martin
A. H. Koonce		Calcasieu
A. J. Evans	New Orleans	Jefferson, Plaquemines, St. Bernard, St. Charles, St. James, St. John the Baptist, Terrebonne
Albert Ardone		Lafourche

Company	City	Parish or Parishes of Operation
Albert Vicnair		Assumption
A. Wilbert & Sons Company	Plaquemine	Iberville
Bass-Horless Lumber Company	Lake Charles	Calcasieu, Vermilion
Bayard Lumber Company	New Iberia	St. Martin
B. E. Causey	Luling	St. Charles, St. James, St. John the Baptist
C. A. Lutz	West Lake	Calcasieu
Charles Sigler	West Lake	Calcasieu
D. D. Johnson		Iberia
D. E. Hillyer		Iberville
Eagle Lumber and Supply Company	Morgan City	Assumption, Iberia, St. Martin, St. Mary
Ernest Pitre		St. Martin
Eunice Band Mill Company	Eunice	Iberville, Terrebonne, Vermilion, West Baton Rouge
Everton Johnson		Iberia
F. D. Foote Lumber Company	Alexandria	Iberia
Fred Brenner Lumber Company	Alexandria	Iberville
Frost Lumber Industries, Inc	Shreveport	Lafourche
Gantt Nicholson		St. Martin
Gibson Lumber Company		Terrebonne
Hillyer-Deutsch-Edwards Lumber Company	Oakdale	Iberia
Home Lumber Company, Inc	Lake Arthur	Vermilion
Iberville Manufacturing Corporation		Assumption, Iberville, West Baton Rouge
Jack Cormier		Calcasieu
James Phelps	Port Allen	Iberville, West Baton Rouge
J. H. Lugging	Abbeville	Vermilion
J. B. Herrod Lumber Company		Iberville
J. B. Norgress	Thibodaux	Lafourche, Terrebonne
J. F. Ellis Lumber Company	Vinton	Calcasieu
Jos. A. Provost Lumber & Shingle Company	Jeanerette, La.	Iberia, St. Martin, St. Mary
Joseph Rathborne Land Company	Harvey	Jefferson, Lafourche, St. Charles, St. James
Kellogg Lumber Company	Alexandria	Iberia, Iberville, St. Charles, West Baton Rouge
Kirby Lumber Company	Houston, Tex.	Iberia
Kyle Lumber Company		Iberia, Iberville, St. Martin, St. Mary
Lapeyrouse & Aubert		Terrebonne
Léonce Angelle	New Iberia	St. Martin

Company	City	Parish or Parishes of Operation
L. M. LeGendre	Thibodaux	Lafourche
Long-Bell Lumber Company, Inc.	Kansas City, Mo.	Calcasieu
Louisiana & Arkansas Railway Company	Shreveport	St. John the Baptist
Louisiana Box & Lumber Company	Baton Rouge	St. Charles
Louisiana Box Company	Kenner	Jefferson
Louisiana Cooperage Company	Bunkie	Iberville
Louisiana Hoop Company	Bunkie	Iberia
Louisiana Tie Company		St. John the Baptist
Louisville Cooperage Company	Monroe	Iberville
Ludeau & Guillory	Ville Platte	Iberia
Lutcher-Moore Cypress Company	Orange, Tex.	St. James
Martin Veneer Company	Ponchatoula	St. John the Baptist
May Brothers	Memphis, Tenn.	Iberia, Iberville, St. Martin, St. Mary, Terrebonne, West Baton Rouge
Mengel Company	Baton Rouge	Iberville, St. Charles, West Baton Rouge
M. F. Tucker		St. John the Baptist
M. H. McClelland	Allemands	Lafourche
Middle Bayou Lumber Company	New Orleans	St. John the Baptist
Moorman Oar company	Plaquemine	Iberville
National Box Company	Natchez, Miss.	Terrebonne
National Lumber & Tie Company	New Orleans	Plaquemines, St. Charles
New Orleans, Texas & Mexican Railway Company	Houston, Tex.	Calcasieu, Iberia
Norman-Breaux Lumber Company		Assumption, Iberia, St. Martin, St. Mary, Terrebonne
Nick Chiara		Assumption, Lafourche
O. A. Hargrove		Vermilion
Oesterland & Knight Company	Oakdale	Calcasieu, St. John the Baptist
Peavey-Moore Lumber Company	Shreveport	Calcasieu
P. H. Kenny		St. Mary, Terrebonne
Powell Lumber Company	Lake Charles	Calcasieu
Ramoneda Brothers	New Orleans	Iberville
R. G. Garland	Ville Platte	Iberia
Riverside Lumber Company		St. John the Baptist
Roy O. Martin Lumber Company	Alexandria	Iberville
Sam Marcelli		Lafourche

Company	City	Parish or Parishes of Operation
Schwing Lumber & Shingle Company	Plaquemine	Assumption, Iberia, Iberville, St. Martin, West Baton Rouge
S. G. Johnson		Iberia
Shreveport Creosote Company	Shreveport	St. Charles
South Coast Corporation	New Orleans	Lafourche, Terrebonne
Southern Lumber Company	Lake Charles	Calcasieu
S. T. Alcus Lumber Company		Iberville, St. Charles, St. John the Baptist
Standard Box Company	Baton Rouge	West Baton Rouge
The Veneer Company	Plaquemine	Iberville
Thistlethwaite Lumber Company	Opelousas	Vermilion
Texas Company	Port Arthur, Tex.	Calcasieu, Vermilion
Turner Brothers Lumber Company	Opelousas	West Baton Rouge
Varice Clark	Starks	Calcasieu
Verret Lumber Company		Terrebonne
W. Breaux Company		Iberville
W. J. Bentley		St. John the Baptist

Although Louisiana's cypress/tupelo swamps were harvested completely, the mineral rights associated with these lands allowed many of these early logging companies to continue to prosper exploiting hydrocarbons and managing their lands for recreational purposes.

The Swampers

> While in the swamps, Acadians constructed homes similar to those on the natural levee lands, using a heavy framework of timbers and filling the intervening spaces with nogging of mud and moss. However, as floods destroyed many of these homes, few were rebuilt, and with time the art of home construction declined, resulting in houses resembling camps. Those homes were built around a framework of trunks of cypress saplings with split cypress clapboards and shakes (*merrains*) . . . (Comeaux 1972:14).

"Swampers" who settled in swamp communities made their living as subsistence farmers; working in the logging business or by harvesting the region's wild game and Spanish moss (also known as: long moss; black moss; Florida moss; and New Orleans moss) (Browne 1977). Removal of timber was, in fact, the oldest economic activity practiced by swampers. Swamp communities were established at modern day Bayou Boeuf, Bowie, Choctaw, Donner, Gibson, Kraemer, Pierre Part, Indian Village, Timberton, and numerous other communities that are included in, or border, the region's swamps.

At Pierre Part and other swamp communities, moss pickers would go into the swamp between November and April to harvest the moss. A skilled picker, could gather from 800 to 1,000 pounds a day. These villages of fishermen, trappers, and moss gatherers were out-of-the-way and difficult to access. They were self-sufficient, kinship-based, communities. A few were established as mill towns and had levees around them to protect against flooding (Mancil 1972). Boats were the principal mode

1. Entrance to Atchafalaya River.　　2. A "Swamper's" House on the Atchafalaya.　　3. A Swamper.　　4. Steamer running the Rapids of the Atchafalaya.
5. Red River Landing.　　6. Castle on the Atchafalaya.　　7. Little Whiskey Bayou.　　8. A Swamper's Garden (in a Canoe).　　9. The Ash Cabin, Atchafalaya.
10. Map showing Changes in the Mississippi's Current.

A TRIP ON THE ATCHAFALAYA RIVER.—Drawn by J. O. Davidson.—[See Page 235.]

of transport, as roads and automobiles did not arrive until the late 1930s or early 1940s. For example, a nine-mile road was completed from Bayou Corne to Pierre Part in 1933 (Jacobi 1937).

Frogs and the Swamper

Between late February and early June, frogs (*grenouilles*) were another source of income for marsh- and swampdwellers. Catching these nocturnal animals was part of the swampers' income base (Hansen 1971). Using a carbide "bull-eye" lantern attached to a cap with a band of leather, a hunter could easily see the *grenouille* and capture it by hand, and shove it into a frog box attached to a burlap bag (Wilkinson 1892). A frog placed in the box would jump almost immediately into the bag. The catch was sold in New Orleans and shipped out-of-state to Cleveland, Chicago, Cincinnati, Pittsburgh, and Los Angeles. The size and abundance of bullfrogs (*Rana catesbeiana*) and pig frogs (*Rana grylio*) in the mid-twentieth century made Louisiana the foremost frog-catching state.

The industry began in Morgan City by 1916. Shortly after the trade was founded, more than a million frogs were shipped out of Louisiana annually. New Orleans consumed more than 100,000 annually. At that time, the winter price was from one dollar to a dollar-fifty a dozen. The summer price declined to fifty cents to seventy-five cents a dozen (Tulian 1918; Viosca 1918). At the industry's height, some buyers were handling about a 1,000 a day (Comeaux 1972). Frog shippers had purchasing agents throughout the coastal zone, who would buy frogs from local frog catchers. The catchers were paid prices based on market conditions.

A good night's work for catchers would often yield as many as 100 frogs—a little more than 8 dozen. About 400,000 "dressed" frogs were shipped in a season (Dauenhauer 1934). In 1939, for example, the state produced more than two million pounds with an average weight of about one pound and collectively worth slightly

Although considered a *lagniappe* crop, Louisiana's frog harvest had a national market. (Image from Broel 1937.)

more than $225,000 (Louisiana's bull-frog 1940). Ten years later, Louisiana exported only 200,000 pounds. The entire catch was exported, as the supply could not meet the demand. Since frog legs were considered a delicacy, Northern and Eastern markets were paying top dollar for Louisiana frogs (Werlla 1950). By the 1970s, dealers in St. Martinville, Des Allemands, and Rayne reported one recreational frogger might take 100 pounds in a night. Frogs for the restaurant trade were being imported from Japan and India, as native frogs could not meet the demand (Soileau 1977).

Collecting Spanish Moss

Swampers were part of a collecting economy. Spanish moss (which is not a parasite, but an epiphyte related to the pineapple family) was ginned, like cotton, into a clean product that was incorporated into a variety of finished goods, including the stuffing in Model T seats, fine Victorian furniture, mattresses, mulch, cushions in airplanes and railroad cars, and as a packing material. In Louisiana, the commercial industry started shortly after the Civil War. However, throughout the War one of the most obscure items issued by the Confederate Ordnance Department was the Spanish moss saddle blanket. Tens of thousands of these coverlets were manufactured and issued to the cavalry (Knopp 2001).

Moss fibers could also be spun on a small Cajun spinning wheel to produce *tarabi*—a rope-like material—utilized in hand-made horse blankets, horse collars, and bridles (Saxon 1942; Browne 1977; Rushton 1979; Din 1988). In 1927, approximately 1,200 railroad cars of moss were shipped to markets outside of Louisiana to be used largely by upholsterers. Because of its resiliency and insect resistance, this product was used only in the finest and most expensive furniture or cushions (Martinez 1959). Moss gins were found throughout the region, but as the industry declined so did the number of gins.

To the swamper, moss was considered a "*lagniappe* crop" that provided periodic or regular employment to many *habitants*. Picking privileges were generally gratuitous; however, some landowners wanted a small fee, while some logging companies wanted half the cured harvest from moss removed from felled trees (Aldrich, et al. 1943). In at least one instance in the Manchac Swamp, the lumber company allowed the moss pickers to ride their logging trains into the swamp to harvest moss. At the end of the day, each moss gatherer would load their sacks of black moss, similar to cotton sacks, on the train and ride out of the swamp (Carroll 2008, pers. comm.). Collecting moss in late fall or winter, the moss-gathers used a long pole with a hook or "double barb" on the end to pull or tear the green moss loose from its perch. The "swamper" moved throughout the region gathering the green moss, often using a standing skiff outfitted with a *jourg* (also *joug*).

The *jourg* or yoke elevated the oars above the gunnels, allowing the swamper "greater leverage while rowing in a standing position" (Comeaux 1972:41) facing the boat's bow. Also known as a standing skiff, this is the only boat in North America of this type. Modifications of this type of skiff and all others used in the swamps and marsh changed with development of affordable diesel and gasoline engines. Oars were discarded quickly. Boat designs incorporated marine plywood and sheet aluminum instead of traditional cypress planks (Brassieur

Collecting moss, no date. (Photo courtesy of the Morgan City Archives.)

A standing skiff was used to transport moss to the dock, 1946. (Photo courtesy of the Standard Oil Collection, University of Louisville, negative no. 44462.)

1999). With better power, special barges equipped with pole towers extending up to fifteen feet were used to pull the moss from the highest points on the trees. It was not unusual for a swamper to collect several hundred pounds of green moss per trip. When necessary, climbing spikes, used by telephone lineman, were adapted to extend a gatherer's reach. On occasion, moss was harvested directly off the ground (Aldrich, et al. 1943; Shoemaker 1957).

Once collected, the moss was brought to a yard and piled up in small conical shapes. To promoted decay of the outer coating and to reduce or prevent spontaneous combustion, this drying moss had to be turned regularly. This procedure was known as "working the moss," which subsequently deteriorated into a deep brown (Jacobi 1937). At this stage, the stringy mass was hung along fences to dry. After it dried out, the black moss was cleaned of twigs and leaves and gathered in piles. The curing process was necessary to remove the moss's outer layer and expose the inner fiber. At this point in the curing process, the moss has lost about two-thirds of its original weight and bulk—a ton of green moss would yield only about 500 to 700 pounds of cured moss that is quite resilient, resistant to insects, and slow to rot.

Properly cured moss was black in color, so the darker the color the higher the grade. Moss that was not cured properly was brownish-black (Shoemaker 1957; Simmons 1940). After proper treatment, the moss's inner fibrous portion resembled horsehair and was very resilient and durable. When the curing process was completed, the moss was sent to a gin where it was graded, cleaned, and baled. Before 1929, a man was paid from four-cents to five-cents a pound. During 1933, the price dropped to ½-cent a pound but, by the late 1930s, the price had stabilized at three-cents a pound. A good picker made about $350 a year (Jacobi 1937).

In World Wars I and II, when cotton was very expensive, moss became the product of choice. It was a money crop for those individuals who inhabited the swamplands. During World War II, the price stabilized at five-cents a pound. The price was good,

After moss was cured, it was ginned like cotton to remove miscellaneous particles, no date. (Photo courtesy of the Morgan City Archives.)

the supply plentiful, and some entrepreneurs made up to $2,000 a month (Aldrich, et al. 1943; Saxon 1942).

A picker could gather about 500 pounds a day and it took about 144 moss pickers to keep a gin running at maximum capacity (Sonderegger 1930). In 1941, there were twenty-six active moss gins operating in Louisiana that ginned moss like cotton. The gin removed twigs, trash, and other foreign matter from the moss and separated the outer covering from the fiber (Aldrich, et al. 1943; Reeves and Alario 1996). The cured moss was marketed in 125-pound bales through dealers in Louisiana, as well as in Chicago, North Carolina, and Florida. The annual output per gin varied from one to fifty railroad carloads, with an average production of about twenty carloads, with a ten-ton carload valued at $2,000 (Aldrich, et al. 1943). In the 1940s, when foam rubber and imported fibers began to replace moss in the upholstery market, demand declined quickly, as moss had to compete eventually with excelsior, cotton, kapok, hair, and down/feathers (Martinez 1959).

By 1975, only one gin remained in the state, perhaps the last in the United States (Treadway 1975). When the logging industry eliminated virgin hardwood forests, qualitatively and quantitatively the best moss sites, the period of easy moss exploitation was over. It was a short-lived industry, but an important *lagniappe* crop to the people of south-central Louisiana's wetlands.

Prior to World War II, when demand for Spanish moss was high, changes were taking place in the swamper's life. Gasoline-powered electric generators for lights, coal oil-kerosene-powered refrigerators, tin roofs, and radios were added to the swampdweller's homes. Their standard of living was improving, and they were no longer as isolated. These new amenities, however, allowed them to continue to live debt-free in the dense, dreadful, bug-ridden, reptile-infested, mysterious, tree-blanketed, neither water nor land *cyprière*. This was the swampdweller's home and they built communities accordingly.

Partial List of Louisiana Moss Gins
(From: Sonderegger 1930)

Company	Location	Company	Location
Standard Moss Factory	Red Cross	Richard Wilhelm Moss Gin	Rosedale
J. I. Pisonnat Moss Gin	Livonia	Angelloz Moss Gin	Maringouin
Schwing Moss Company	Plaquemine	L. J. Russ Moss Company	New Roads
Luke B. Babin Moss Company	White Castle	Opelousas Ginnery	Opelousas
Stevens & Case	Plaquemine	Joe Saladino	Plaquemine
Evangeline Moss Manufacturing Company	St. Martinsville	Peoples Moss Gin Company	Palmetto
Louisiana Moss Products Company, Inc	Patterson	E. P. Blanchard	Plaquemine
Rosson Moss Company	Morgan City	Bach David & Company	New Orleans
Crescent City Moss Ginnery	New Orleans	Kohlman Moss & Cotton Felt Manufacturing Company	New Orleans

Leading dealers handling Louisiana's ginned moss, ca. 1930
(From: Sonderegger 1930)

Company	Location	Company	Location
Borgwardt & Ernest Company	Chicago, Ill.	Forfeich & Company	Morgan City
Geo. Giles & Company	Ocala, Fla.	Louis Kohlman	New Orleans
Geo. D. Luce	New Orleans	Phoenix Furniture Company	Charleston, S.C.
E. Schloss	Baton Rouge	Septime L. Theard	New Orleans
Morley Cypress Company	Morley, La.		

Milling the Moss

At the Mill

Moss Press.

Gathering Moss

W. P. Snyder

THE MOSS INDUSTRY IN THE SOUTH.—Drawn by W. P. Snyder.—[See Page 551.]

Swamp Villages: A Cluster of Camps

Swampers' "picker" camps were located on whatever elevated land they could find and would often include a small garden, pigs, and chickens. With the cash they received for their moss and other swamp-related products, these Atchafalaya-based swampers were fairly independent. Each swamp community's economic identity varies with the topography, but material culture elements are duplicated. Swamp villages and bayou-natural-levee agriculture villages vary with economic opportunities.

Along the swamp bayou's natural levees, the principal house types are the shotgun, camps, and an occasional *Créole* cottage (*maison carré*), complemented by a generous sprinkling of houseboats or campboats moored in small *poches*, or pockets, cut into the bayou banks (Jacobi 1937). Swamp villages are different from bayou settlements in that they appear crowded and cluttered, and the homes were often built on land belonging to lumber companies or "outsiders." On these lands, the setters were thus squatters (Jacobi 1937). Outbuildings, such as small sheds and barns, boxes for raising turtles, pens for hogs, lath boxes for keeping live turtles and fish, trammel nets, basket traps, hoop nets, and crawfish traps cluttered the stream banks and house sites. There were cypress *pieux* fenced-enclosures for livestock. In front of each house was a wharf and various types of boats; these include the *pirogue*, skiff, and, later, outboard or inboard engine-powered wood or aluminum boats (Comeaux 1978).

Hoop nets were widely used by swampers in the Atchafalaya Basin, no date. (Photo courtesy of the Morgan City Archives.)

> The housing conditions are atrocious. It is not uncommon to find a family of ten and twelve living in a two-room shack. The homes are built of lumber roughly prepared by hand. The walls and floors are full of cracks. There are no window panes, and on rainy days when the solid windows and doors have to be closed, the family has to light a lamp by which to see. Their chimneys are built of pounded brick and clay. There are no screens. The water supply is gotten from open kettles, and there are few sanitary pit-privies in the community (Jacobi 1937:25-26).

Further,

> The order and cleanliness of most of the homes are striking. The floors of the front porch and rooms are scrubbed regularly and thoroughly, as evidenced by their color—a clear, golden yellow. No dust is to be found on any of the furniture. The housewives pride themselves on the immaculate smoothness of their bedspreads. The pastor explained that even though a family might have only two changes of bed-linens these were washed every other day to keep them always clean (Jacobi 1937:25-26).

A priest, using a small towboat called the *St. Francis Xavier* pulled a houseboat—the floating chapel boat *Our Lady Star of the Sea*—to isolated parishioners from Pierre Part (Jacobi 1937; Ramsey 1957). The chapel could seat about eighty-five people, and an additional forty could be crowded into the aisle and rear of the chapel. As a rule, the priest spent two days at each of the most distant swamp communities (Jacobi 1937). Later, two Protestant churches, the Baptists and the Seventh Day Adventists, were active in the Atchafalaya as well. The Baptists used a floating chapel to conduct their services, while the Seventh Day Adventists constructed a church on Bayou Crook Chêne, a site on the fringe of the Atchafalaya Basin that was one of numerous cluster communities to "appear" after the 1927 flood, which caused extensive damage to Mississippi River floodplain communities.

To protect settlements, the Corps of Engineers built an extensive Atchafalaya Basin levee system—designed to provide an outlet for floodwater. The spillway construction, coupled with increased managed flow from the area's natural waterbodies, forced "swampers" to abandon their interior swamp communities. They migrated to the swamp's outer edge, where their descendants live today (Comeaux 1972). Consequently, displacement resulted in new strip communities along the guide levees and associated service roads in Verret and Fausse Pointe. In their migration, English-speakers moved out of the Atchafalaya basin to Bayou Sorrel, Morgan City, or abandoned their swamp life to find employment in other surrounding towns and cities. French-speakers settled in Bayou Pigeon, Belle River, Pierre Part, Stephenville, Henderson, or Bayou Benoit. Most of these folks continued to make their living in the swamp.

> It is true all has vanished, and the Cajuns live outside the levees, but they and others—operating from the most part alone or in pairs—go into the swamp and take twenty-five million dollars' worth of protein out of the water in any given year. The fish alone can average a thousand pounds an acre, and that . . . is . . . two and a half times as productive as the Everglades (McPhee 1989:70).

Due to the change in emphasis from farming to trapping-fishing-hunting, little land was needed. The trapper-fisher-swamper landscape had two settlement forms—the line village, and the remote dwelling. The village was the most important, and remnants survive throughout the region's swamp forests. Isolated dwellings were the seasonal residents of the *piégeur*; today they survive as camps or recreational dwellings. Trapping was so profitable that swampers would leave their homes to maximize their income base.

With the advent of good roads and automobiles, many swamp residents continued to live near the *cyprière*, though they have become well-trained pipefitters, welders, and carpenters—earning their living outside the wet forests, but living as close to the "trees" as possible. Often these forests are just beyond their back doors—in their minds, an ideal situation. In this way, they are guaranteed the opportunity to hunt and fish in the swamp easily. Fishing is often no longer their primary source of income, but an important avocation.

Bayou Chêne: An Atchafalaya Basin Swamp Community

In the late-1820s and early 1830s, a growing demand for agricultural land prompted widespread surveys of the swamps. Land was subdivided and sold. Even though plantations were in the basin, many subsistence farmers hunted, fished, collected Spanish moss, and cut timber. By 1841, there were at least sixteen planters homesteading within the Atchafalaya basin. Bayou Chêne, Bayou Crook Chêne, Bloody Bayou, and Bayou dePlomb were the centers for these plantations.

Sugar production in hogsheads (about 1,000 pounds)
From 1849 and 1850 from these swamp plantations
(From: Case 1973:43)

Plantation Owner	Location	Production in hogshead
Bell and Leaky	Bloody Bayou	26
Godfrey Carline	Bayou Chêne	37
Urban Carline and Company	Bayou Chêne	46
P. C. Bethel	Bayou Chêne	30
Henry C. Dwight	Blood Bayou	30
A. G. LaFontain	Big Bayou dePlomb	41
J. B. Angers	Beau Bayou	25
Henry Rentrop	Not Recorded	33

Using horse-powered cane mills, these planters raised sugarcane on small parcels of land. After the Civil War, a few planters had steam-powered mills, but they used open kettles to boil the sugar instead of vacuum pans (Maygarden and Yakubik 1999).

The Civil War was not kind to the region. As a result of direct military action in the Basin, many boats, sugarhouses, and stores of sugar were destroyed by Union troops. Because of a levee break on Grand River, the region went under water. The Bayou Chêne post office was forced to close in 1866, though it reopened ten years later. Of these communities, Bayou Chêne descendants lived at the site for over a century. Many of these folks settled in the area after the Civil War, since land could be purchased for as little as twenty-five cents an acre. By 1870, there were 277 people living in the community making a living cutting timber, hunting, fishing, or raising livestock. Most were Anglo-American and only a few were of French descent (Maygarden and Yakubik 1999). The region had a frontier character and as long as newcomers behaved themselves they were accepted. Even so, the lumberjacks and others could be a "rough crowd" (Maygarden and Yakubik 1999:11).

In the period between the introduction of the gasoline-fueled, single-cylinder, two-horsepower internal combustion boat engine and the disastrous 1927 flood, Bayou Chêne served as the nodal point for individuals working in the swamp forests. The community had a church, school, general store, numerous structures built in the late-nineteenth or turn-of-the-twentieth century style, and a post office. In addition, nearby on Bayou LaRompe "houseboats and shantyboats lined the banks for miles" (Case 1973:26).

> Acadian-style houses and shotguns raised on wood blocks were common. Some residents resided in houseboats. . . . Only a few families had brick fireplaces and chimneys; some had traditional stick and mud chimneys. . . . The favorite heating and cooking wood was ash, which had a low market value and could be cut freely anywhere (Maygarden and Yakubik 1999:14).

Food was plentiful. Along with the readily available wild game, beef, pork, poultry, and beans were part of the daily diet. According to local folklore, "a man could put a pot on to boil, leave the house with his gun, and return with a pot full of squirrels before the water was boiling" (Maygarden and Yakubik 1999:21).

Bayou Chêne began to decline soon after the flood of 1927, and this was accelerated three years later by the Great Depression. In its heyday, the community had a population of some 500, with the combination bar/grocery being the center of the community. Like many settlements in South Louisiana, "people enjoyed dancing until the sun rose in the morning," and "the fiddlers and accordion players never seemed to mind the long-lasting parties and had as much fun as anyone there" (Case 1973:153). The saloon contributed to the rough-and-tumble behavior, but "this was probably no more common here than anywhere else in rural South Louisiana at the time" (Maygarden and Yakubik 1999:17). In 1952, the Bayou Chêne post office closed and this swamp community symbolically came to an end. Virtually all remaining residents left the village soon afterward.

The Swampers Boats

Often a swamper would tie up his houseboat, along with others, at a logging site. Boats were essential since they provided commerce, access to work, travel, and pleasure. *Pirogues*, blank boats—a poor man's *pirogue*—skiffs, and flatboats were part of the swamp landscape. Around 1915, "gazzoleen"-powered "Jo-Boats" (also called putt-putts) were added to the vessels traversing the basin. These boats increased the distances traveled daily by swampers or independent loggers and enabled more children from a wider area to attend the Bayou Chene school. The school boat operated year round. Mail was carried along Marine Route No 2, Morgan City, Louisiana to people living along Bayou Chêne (Hubbard 1990).

In the late 1800s, these folk boats brought the swamp villages supplies and traded these goods for "fish, fur, alligator hides, frogs and anything else they could use. . . . They brought ice, too, in which to pack the perishable items" (Case 1973:91). Access to the outside marked the beginning of the modern period of commercial exploitation for the swampdweller, who began marketing a variety of freshwater fish. Establishment of an ice plant in New Orleans in 1883 met "fresh fish could be . . . frozen and kept perfect for any desired length of time" (Comeaux 1972:34).

Atchafalaya Basin School Boat, 1945. (Photo courtesy of the Standard Oil Collection, University of Louisville, negative no. 67905.)

Access to the "outside" was provided by fish- or trading-boats with the fish dealer becoming an important part of the swamper gatherer's life (Comeaux 1972). Among swampdwellers, fish-boats, whose holds were used to bring the catch to market, were tied up along the bayou. Floating fish-cars were tied to stakes and used to keep their catch alive (Comeaux 1978B). These "cars" were:

> built in the shape of a flat-bottomed skiff, sharp at each end, the sides, top and bottom being formed of slats, with space between each slat for the free circulation of water. They range in length from, eighteen to thirty feet and about five feet in width. At each end there is a watertight compartment with about forty gallons capacity, and by emptying or filling these compartments with water the buoyancy of the car may be regulated (Comeaux 1972:31).

When full, fish-cars (also known as well-cars or live-cars) were towed to market or offloaded onto a fish-boat. This transfer procedure began in Morgan City in 1873—the same year the first experimental transport of fish by rail—and helped establish the state's commercial fishing industry. Using this technique, fish could be delivered fresh to the railhead and successfully shepherded safely by railcar across the nation

Trading boats were as essential to the swampdwellers as the "rolling stores" were to the marshdweller, no date. (Photo courtesy of the Morgan City Archives.)

(Comeaux 1978B; Comeaux 1985).

The fish industry began to expand. By 1912, there were twenty-one gasoline boats capable of carrying from two to three tons of fish from the Atchafalaya basin to markets in Morgan City, Plaquemine, and Melville. Three years later, the number of boats involved in this trade was twelve. Not quite half of the fleet was gone, but the record indicated that these boats served approximately 500 fishermen.

In the summer, catfish had to be kept alive in fish-cars until the fishermen caught enough to deliver directly to the dealer. In hot weather, fish remained in the live-car for no more than two to three days. If a dealer's boat was late, fish in these boxes often died. When this happened a fisherman might lose up to 50 percent of his harvest.

With time, other swamp products were marketed as well (Comeaux 1978). When it was time to move, the swamper's houseboat was towed or allowed to drift to a new site. High land was plentiful, so establishing a new village on the waters of the *cyprière* was relatively easy.

Moving Out of the Swamp

. . . in a sense the community [of Bayou Chêne] still lives; proud of its past, and grateful for the legacy it can give its descendants (Maygarden and Yakubik 1999:27).

Leaving the swamp, 1946. (Photo courtesy of the Standard Oil Collection, University of Louisville, negative no. 44743.)

Kinship played an important role in resettlement. Members of an extended family tended to relocate in the same vicinity; as a result, former residents clustered in New Iberia and St. Martinville to the west and Bayou Sorrel and Plaquemine to the east, and in other small villages, like Bayou Benoit located on the Atchafalaya Basin's western protection levee in St. Martin Parish (King 1977). These sites provided the former swamp residents with access to their traditional fishing grounds, electricity, schools, and roads leading to "civilization."

Since many of these former swamp residents could not afford to purchase land, and renting was unavailable, they simply "settled" as close to the levee as possible. They were, in effect, squatters. After all, no one questioned their right to "settle" where they wanted in the swamp. Why would it be any different on the swamp's fringe? But it was. With the upgrading of the Atchafalaya's protection levee, the residents of Bayou Benoit were forced to relocate through the process of eminent domain. For fifty-one years they had lived on the levee at Bayou Benoit. A conflict arose from a small group of levee dwellers attempting to live and make a living in an area needed to protect hundreds of thousands of homes from a possible flood. They did not move easily, as the fight was fierce. These "folks" now live in Coteau Holmes and Portage and recall the "past sadly, . . . , but look to the future with optimism and security" (King 1977:50).

Cypress Mill Towns: Bowie, Frenier, Ruddock, and Timberland

A two-story barracks for single workers rose against the western tree line, and in front of it, . . . ran two rows of shotgun houses, paintless, screenless, not a shutter on a single one of them. South of this row by a hundred yards he spotted the manager's house, a square, porched, steep-roofed structure of raw, pink-tinged weatherboard, to the rear of it a cabin and tiny stable, then a short crude fence of cypress bats, and beyond that a wide canal, . . . Between the house and the mill was a looming commissary . . . and a good distance behind it was the low saloon, carelessly built and rangy, sagging back from a wide gallery bearing a dozed scattered hide-bottomed chairs. To the rear of the saloon three cabins and a line of privies perched at odd angles on the berm of the canal. On the other side of a soaring mill was a longer double row of forty shacks without porches or steps—the black section, he supposed —and two more of the featureless, rain-streaked barracks . . . he could see a line of low houses with screened windows and blistered porches facing south.

In the middle of the clearing roared the mill itself. Out of every metal roof rose jetting exhaust vents or hundred-foot black iron smokestacks streaming flags of wood smoke (Gautreaux 2003/2004:80-81).

Although Tim Gautreaux is writing fiction, his portrayal of a logging village is probably quite close to accurate.

Near Raceland was the real community of Bowie that probably mirrored Gautreaux's narrative. In 1895, William Cameron bought about 25,000 acres (thirty-nine square miles) of swamp from Leon Godchaux—a large Mississippi River sugar planter and entrepreneur—and worked out a deal with George M. Bowie to build a sawmill on the land. It was a paternalistic company that needed to extend maximum control over its labor force, so it developed its own sawmill town. Bowie needed a labor force willing to work "from can, to can't" six days a week. With this concept as the driving force, the company provided nearly all of its employees needs. Like nearly all lumber company towns, Bowie was made up of several basic divisions—the land office, the lumber camp and tree-cutting operation, the railroad and/or boat division, the sawmill, and the ancillary facilities, or services.

With construction of the Bowie Lumber Company mill, about 1,500 people moved into the community. The community, called "Bowie Boom Town," was developed with a definite geographic footprint/plan that represented the ethnic groups that made up the logging crews. The town-site's layout included Michigan City, Italian Settlement, Cuban Settlement, Free Town, and the Puerto Rican Settlement. The site was held together by a network of standard gauge railroad tracks. Along with the mill, the town included: a slaughterhouse; a school; a Catholic and Presbyterian church; a bakery; a drug store; general store; a hotel; boarding house; and an entertainment center (Cortez and Rybiski 1980). With time, the village contributed immeasurably to the local economy.

Bowie's mill was said to be the largest in the world with a wood yard curing lumber, shingles, laths, and railroad cross-ties (Cortez and Rybiski 1980). In fact, "thousands of railroad cross-ties [were] made from the cypress in the Lafourche swamps" (Harris 1881:170). There were "enough cross-ties to build a railroad from Raceland to San Francisco" (Cortez and Rybiski 1980:49). When the mill burned in 1917, more than fifty-five million board feet of wood fueled the blaze. The town essentially died after this event and second fire in 1924 that coincided closely with the demise of Louisiana's

(Left) The F. B. Williams cypress mill in Patterson, no date. (Photo courtesy of the Morgan City Archives.)

(Below) Bowie General Store, no date. (Photo from Cortez and Rybiski 1980.)

(Above) The F. B. Williams commissary, no date. (Photo courtesy of the Morgan City Archives.)

(Right) Women swimming in mill pool at the F. B. Williams company town, no date. (Photo courtesy of the Morgan City Archives.)

cypress logging industry.

In this time period, other companies were expanded as well. East of the Mississippi River Charles H. Ruddock along with William L. Burton established the Ruddock Cypress Company (later to become the Ruddock-Orleans Cypress Company), headquartered at Ruddock, on the western edge of Lake Pontchartrain, in 1892. The company was established to harvest cypress from the Manchac Swamp; Burton estimated in 1888 that the area held about four million linear feet of cypress. The Main, Ruddock, and Galva Canals were cut to move the company's pullboats into the swamp (Kemp 1997). Further, by 1894, Landry (1996:2) reports these two logging firms "had become the two largest suppliers of cypress timber in Southeast Louisiana. In that same year Ruddock-Orleans replaced pullboat/canal logging with railroads that hauled logs to their mill" (Louisiana Cypress #2 2006). As a result of this change in logging technique, the company, along with several others, were always building and removing their track; it was a constant process. In 1954, the last of the Manchac swamp's track was removed (Carroll 2008, pers. comm.).

The Ruddock Company specialized in car-roofing and siding for the Pullman Palace Car Company and filled orders that required fifty railroad cars to complete. Burton eventually sold his interest in the firm. His retirement was short-lived. In 1904, he organized the Burton-Swartz Cypress Company at Burton in St. James Parish that operated until 1919, when all of the available and easy harvestable, cypress had been removed (Harrington 1983).

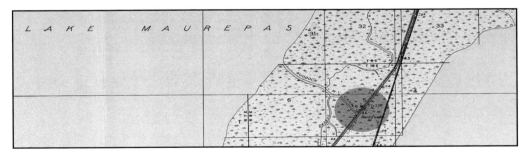

Located between Lake Maurepas and Lake Pontchartrain, Ruddock serviced the cypress logging industry. (Image from the USGS Ruddock fifteen minute quadrangle, 1936.)

The communities of Frenier and Ruddock were similar to Bowie in that they were company towns built to support their parent company's swamp-based operations. Consequently,

> At the height of its prosperity, Ruddock was a progressive, booming community built on stilts above the black waters of the swamp. Stilt-supported wooden sidewalks ran the length of the village with walkways branching out to two-story houses on each side. Most of the structures, particularly those located track-side, were painted "railroad" gray. The village also boasted a community center, a blacksmith shop, a locomotive repair shop, an office and commissary for the Ruddock Cypress Lumber Company, a one-room school house, the Holy Cross Catholic Church, and a railroad depot with a two-story rooming house attached. The Owl Saloon, specializing in men's entertainment, was discretely located about a half-mile south and down the line from the town.

> At Frenier and the other small communities the economy centered on manufacturing barrel staves and cabbage farming. The prized vegetables were harvested, packed in locally made barrels, and then shipped via the railroad to Chicago, Illinois and other northern cities. Most of the residents in these villages prospered and were able to live comfortable lives. Like other

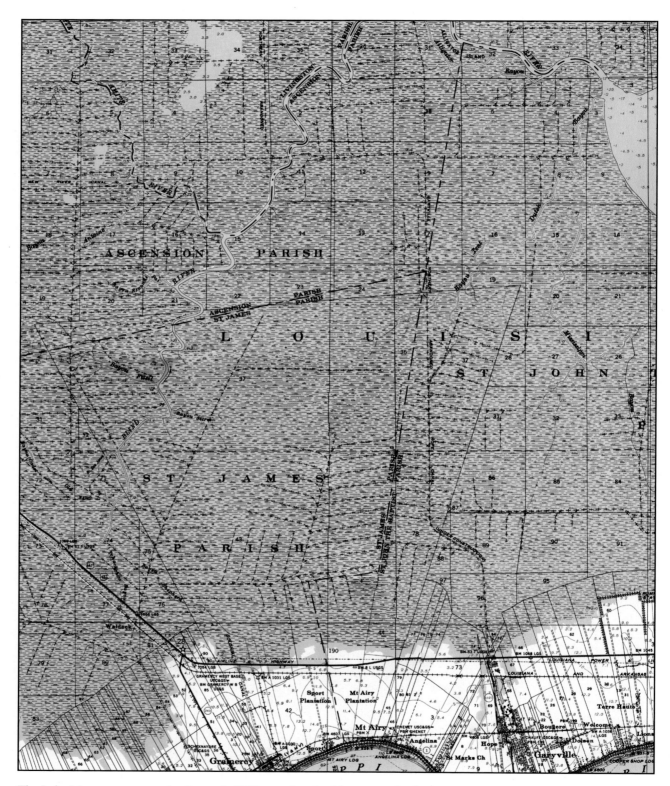

The Lake Maurepas swamp by the early 1930s was laced with a network of narrow gauge railroads transporting cypress to various mills. (Image from USGS Mt. Airy fifteen minute quadrangle, 1939.)

farming communities, because of the hot, humid climate, workers came in from the fields at lunch time and returned to their work at three o'clock in the afternoon. There were no grocery stores, and housewives would stand track-side to wait for the daily train to New Orleans. The train would stop, and the housewives would give their grocery lists and money to the engineer who would drop them off in New Orleans. The engineer would then pick up the orders and deliver the groceries by train a few days later (Landry 1996:3).

When lumbermen living in Frenier and Ruddock were not cutting trees or milling lumber, they fished, trapped, and gathered moss. Although fishing, trapping and gathering moss added to a family's income, these were logging boomtowns. By 1915, Frenier had a resident population of 200. Ruddock's population was estimated at more than 700. The 1915 hurricane destroyed both sites, along with the village of La Branche, south and west of Frenier (Dunne 2006). After the storm passed, the death toll was 275. These once thriving logging-base industrial sites were never rebuilt. The only reminder that Ruddock and Frenier existed is the place names that survive on a number of maps and the recreational camps an associated amenities that have located at, or near, these former company towns (Kemp 1997; Landry 1996).

Dr. Carl A. Brasseaux, professor of history and director of the Center for Louisiana Studies at the University of Louisiana at Lafayette, has asserted that "Louisiana has been an economic colony for the United States since the Civil War. Generation after generation, we have seen companies move in from elsewhere in the nation to exploit resources here, destroy the environment, and move on. The cypress industry has created this paradigm" (Wilt 2005:38).

Preserving the History of Logging

In Louisiana, there are two museums devoted to the forest products industry. The Southern Forest Heritage Museum in Long Leaf Louisiana is on a fifty-seven acre site that displays rare, one-of-a-kind, equipment and buildings dating back to the early 1900s. The site represents one of the sawmill towns that flourished throughout the South and offers a glimpse at the importance of the forest in Southern heritage and culture. In Patterson, the Patterson Cypress Sawmill Collection documents the history of the cypress lumber industry with a focus on Patterson—home, according to some, to the largest cypress sawmill in the world.

Derelict logging engine near Lake Verret, 1975. (Photo by the author.)

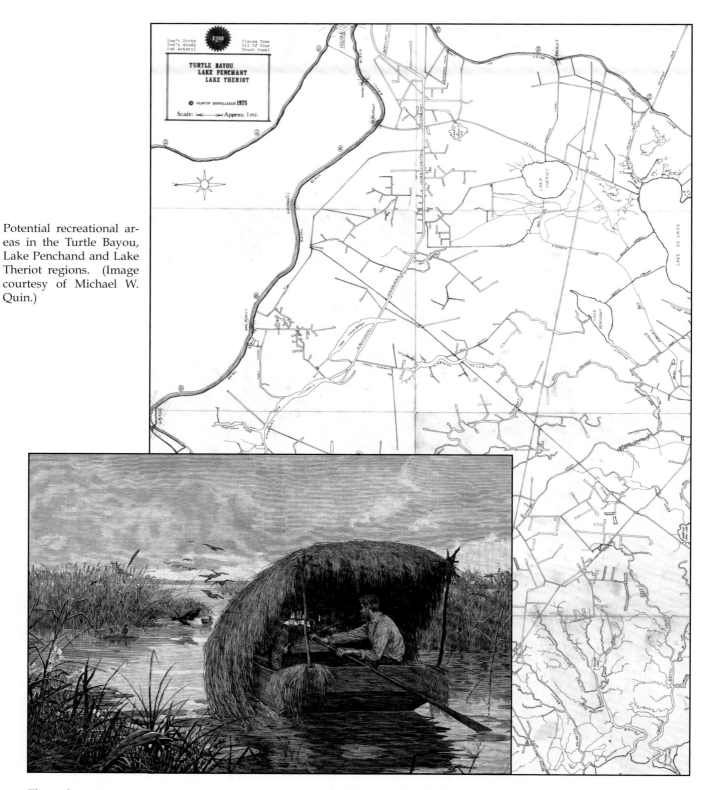

Potential recreational areas in the Turtle Bayou, Lake Penchand and Lake Theriot regions. (Image courtesy of Michael W. Quin.)

Throughout America, recreation and professional hunters took advantage of waterfowl concentrations in the wetlands in the late nineteenth century. This activity has become an important recreational pursuit for the common folk, albeit at significant cost. (Image from *Harper's Weekly*, November 1885.)

Chapter 10
RECREATION CAMPS: THE MODERN FORM OF SETTLEMENTS

On that day, something seemed right about Louisiana. All the opinions and perceptions, whether pessimistic or overly confident about the well being of Louisiana's natural resources were dispelled. We felt fortunate to pass through an ongoing seam of life that rises boldly and recedes quietly like the tide. It happens every day . . . somewhere on our mystical coast (Holm 1999:11).

South Louisiana's climate provides the recreational enthusiast with nearly ideal weather conditions. Warm summers and mild winters are the generalized weather conditions. Since precipitation falls all year, there is rarely a dry period. In spite of nearly ideal weather and lengthy coastline, beach-oriented recreation is limited (Gary and Davis 1978; Gary and Davis 1979; Davis and Detro 1975). There are few accessible beaches within the coastal lowlands; Holly Beach, Constance Beach, Cypremort Point, Johnson Bayou, Rutherford Beach, Grand Isle, Elmer's Island, and Fourchon are the exceptions. Day trips are a common recreational endeavor, but for the most part, Louisiana's outdoor recreationalists prefer to build "camps" that are used as away-from-home bases for hunting, boating, and fishing.

Increased leisure-time has resulted in a wetlands landscape dotted with seasonally-occupied camps, either as remote structures often in open water, or clustered on the beach face, the area's secluded ridges, narrow spoil banks, marsh sites, or natural levees. Most of these structures are self-contained buildings, providing sportsmen with a summer site for fishing and a winter base for hunting and trapping.

Whether for a day trip or longer, live bait is critical, 2008. (Photo by the author.)

Camps

Before the 1920s, and the acceptance of small gasoline engine-powered boats, permanent home-type dwellings were built in the marsh. With the advent of gasoline-powered boats, the need to reside near habitats for aquatic and avian species was eliminated. Many of these former homes became the coastal marshes' first wide-spread camps—a utilitarian week-end retreat, not to be confused with a New England forest lodge, a Florida beach house, or a Colorado chalet. Marsh camp distribution is a consequence of long-term interaction between numerous biophysical and cultural factors.

There are at least 10,000 wetlands camps in coastal Louisiana. These recreational dwellings come in all shapes, sizes, styles, and designs. Whether built on pilings above marsh mucks or on a slab anchored to a natural levee, *chênière*, or beach, the dwellings include roughhewn tar-paper rustic eyesores, piling-

In the immediate aftermath of the Civil War, the residents of New Orleans took advantage of the Lake Pontchartrain lakefront, with the establishment of the camp-based community of Milneville, later Milneburg. (Image from *Frank Leslie's Illustrated Newspaper*, September 1867.)

495

supported mobile homes suspended as much as fifteen-feet above the ground, simple bungalows, elaborate second homes, and a multitude of other architectural gems. On account of their dilapidated status, many are described as "Tilted Hiltons" and are without question "man space." They have no designer touches. Swimming pools, glass-enclosed verandas, and enough rooms and beds to accommodate twenty guests comfortably are normal for luxurious camps that are homes away from homes. Some two-storied units are equipped with outside elevators. Others are one-room "houses" built for only the most rugged and determined individual and are simply a modern reincarnation of the original palmetto hut used by the earliest marshdwellers. Whatever design and costs are involved, camps are constructed to meet their owner's leisure-time needs, since all camps can be considered multi-functional and seasonal. Based on utilitarian function, two types emerge—hunting and fishing.

Hunting camps are utilized mainly during the fall and winter hunting season, with the exception of the *Chênière* Plain, where hunting camps are well maintained and highly functional. Conversely, on the Deltaic Plain hunting camps tend to be flimsy frame shacks located in fresh and brackish marshes, sites preferred by wintering waterfowl. In contrast, an extended family's sport fishing camps are used year-round and are generally more elaborate than those used for hunting. Several hundred barge-mounted camps are used for saltwater angling behind the barrier islands during summer and transported to more inland sites for the hunting season. Since game fish and certain shellfish are found in almost all wetland habitats, fishing camps are located throughout the marsh.

Most of these structures are located near the state's larger cities and communities. Those adjacent to highways are better built, and public utilities are often available. Structures accessible only by water are self-contained units often equipped with batteries, generators, butane tanks, ice machines, and ingenious cisterns to make

Camps evolved from functional trapper and oystermen homes to weekend recreational retreats, ca. 1910. (Image courtesy of Fred Dunham.)

them a bit more comfortable. Although lacking the amenities of the near lodge-like structures with direct highway access, isolated camps—a phenomenon found almost exclusively in the southeastern marshes—have the advantage of being closer to the habitats preferred by sportsmen.

Regardless of location, camps—or pontoon-supported houseboats—provide sportsmen with a summer site for fishing and a winter base for hunting and occasionally trapping. Because of their proximity to the Gulf, many have felt the effects of repeated hurricane-induced storm surges. They are quite vulnerable and were either damaged or destroyed by Hurricanes Katrina, Rita, Gustav, and Ike in 2005 and 2008 respectively. As a result, revised construction guidelines are requiring new camps to meet strict height requirements. This has changed the visual landscape to one dominated by elevated structures incorporating sacrificial first floors, designed to be blown out by the associated forces of a hurricane, and suspended on pilings often from ten to fifteen feet in the air.

Without the wetlands, there would be no need for these structures. Many game species would still be available, but there would be no anchor points to locate a camp, unless it would be over water or on a barge, as was the case of some shanty towns in the marsh and, in at least one case, in the early oyster industry. People would certainly continue to enjoy the out-of-doors, but species composition and the spatial distribution of these species would be altered. Also, individual willingness to pay for recreational activity would change, as it currently depends on the quantity of marsh acreage available for their recreational enjoyment.

When this wetland habitat is gone, the recreationalists' willingness to pay will also depend upon their experience—the number of fish caught, aesthetics, recreational preferences, and individual income. If the experience is not pleasant, rewarded by the size and number of fish caught or ducks harvested, they may not participate in this endeavor. The user is only willing to pay so much per year for this activity. If the catch or harvest is limited, then the willingness to pay will be reduced as well. Other variables may change, but by the time 80 to 90 percent of the wetlands have disappeared, the recreationalists' willingness to pay for the experience may have disappeared as well (Farber 1996).

The loss of the marshlands means economic activities associated with these lowlands will either no longer be possible or will require expensive substitutes. Usage rates will be modified and perhaps approach zero, and recreational behavior will change as well (Farber 1996). Even with the reality of a person's willingness to pay, recreation is an important part of the regional culture; it is hard to accept that sportsmen will no longer have an interest in spending time on or in the water. They may change their focus, but the coast will still attract users—the environment/landscape may have changed dramatically, but the desire to be out-of-doors is still the overriding force determining the use of these "new" habitats.

The Organized Hunting Camp

The marshlands serve as a winter feeding ground for many species of waterfowl as well as for marsh and shore birds (Chabreck 1988). Sportsmen take advantage of the birds' migratory cycles and utilize the region as a major waterfowl hunting locale, bagging more than one million waterfowl annually. Traditional harvest statistics reveal how valuable the marshes are to the sporting community; moreover, the state has initiated a point system to control the harvest of selected species. The daily bag limit is 100 points. Also, one should emphasize that because of the duality of recreational activities in the wetlands, persons frequently engage in hunting and fishing on the same day. Recreational endeavors totaling millions of man-days annually take place

Hunting For Sport

"During the winter season this section of the State [Iberia Parish] offers rare inducements to sportsmen, and many persons are in the habit of coming here from the Northern States to amuse themselves at the expense of the wild animals that abound in the dense forests and the fish and water fowl that may be found in unlimited quantity and variety along the various lakes and water courses" (Harris 1881:162).

SEA DUCK.

STARTING FOR THE

CLUB DUCK

POT HUNTERS.

For more than 150 years sportsmen have engaged in recreational duck hunting.

ING GROUNDS.

FRESH WATER DUCK.

ROUNDS.

THE BRUSH BLIND.

(Image from *Harper's Weekly*, November 1868.)

in the waterlogged lowlands, often from private hunting clubs and the state's wildlife refuges (Kramer 1974).

At the turn of the century, hunting clubs catering to wealthy, usually Northern waterfowlers organized to take advantage of the land they leased from large land-holding syndicates. In some cases, these clubs managed extensive hunting tracts. Other clubs controlled smaller plots. Regardless of the size of lease-holding organizations, hunting space was guaranteed in Louisiana.

On club property, facilities range from spartan to spacious. Some club members pay an initial fee ranging from $1,000 to more than $5,000 as well as yearly dues of as much as several thousands of dollars. In such surroundings, the only thing a member does is pull the trigger. All arrangements, including providing a guide, boat, supplies, accommodations, and cook are made to insure a successful hunt. Often club employees kill the game, so members do not need to leave the clubhouse. And, in at least one club—Oak Grove Club on Grand Chênière—"promptly at 5 P.M. the staff appears from the kitchen dressed in tuxedos to serve hors d'oeuvres to members and their guests" (Kemp and Sims 2004:10).

Many of these clubs have hosted hunters from all over the world; industrialists, like Henry Ford, and famed test-pilot Chuck Yeager have enjoyed hunting in Louisiana's marshes (Kemp and Sims 2004). The Oak Grove Club has only nine members, but it supports a full-time household staff of eight and eighteen guides who use the club's 9,600 acres (fifteen square miles)—leased from the Miami Corporation, who holds one of the club's nine membership slots. To insure the best hunt possible the staff of some clubs, such as the Avoca Island Club, build and remove their blinds daily. In some cases, a cook or cooks meticulously prepare meals, guides clean all guns, and return boots and boats to the club's inventory. At least one club has an ATM machine on site, just in case additional funds are needed for the evening poker game (Kemp and Sims 2004). These facilities have evolved over time. Many are more than eighty years old and are serving as hunting sites for a fourth generation of users.

> . . . W. L. "Cub" Wulff, who for 62 years has found waterfowling pleasure throughout the region's vast coastal marshes [south of Lake Charles]. At 87, he is recognized as the oldest local gunner on the water—still hunting from a boat blind, up to four days a week.

> 'I've hunted every year since 1926, except for three years when I was in the army,' Wulff says. His introduction to Louisiana duck hunting was memorable. The first stop was a commercial club.

> 'The road was muddy, and I was the only hunter who showed up. We used double-end pirogues, and those guys must have pushed me three or four miles. I couldn't talk to them, because they spoke French. There were plenty of ducks,' Wulff says, 'and I could pretty much shoot what I wanted.'

> Wulff's first pirogue was purchased from the late Miller Faulk, who was recognized as the finest at his craft. 'I asked him how much and he said $3. I told him I wanted a really nice one and was going to pay $5,' Wulff says. 'That pirogue was tidewater cypress, and it lasted forever. . . . .'

> Waterfowl have been wintering here by the millions for eons, and while residents relied on ducks, geese, and other marsh critters for survival (including sales to the market), sport hunters were quick to partake of the incredible shooting opportunities.

> Among the immediate region's oldest duck clubs were the Oak Grove and the

Coastal. Shortly after retiring from a career as a manufacturer's rep, Wulff for four years managed the Chateau Charles Hunting Club.'

'We'd get people from all over the country,' Wulff says. 'We hunted as many as 3,000 hunters a year. We had 40 guides and 30,000 acres leased. It was a labor of love.'

In his more than six decades of waterfowl hunting, Wulff has raised and trained 58 Labrador retrievers. He has also made his own duck calls and carved decorative decoys. . . .

'The coastal marsh doesn't look like it used to at all,' Wulff says. 'Saltwater came in and killed a lot of the grass; you don't see the bullwhips, the cattails, and other stuff we used to have. The number of ducks . . . there's no comparison to what it used to be. Waterfowl have changed their habits. The snow and blue goose used to be birds of the marsh' (Koehler 2005).

One Example of a Hunting Club

One example of these early hunting clubs is the Louisiana Coast Land Company, originally established by E. A. McIlhenny and later called the Vermilion Corporation. This club has a ninety-nine-year lease on more than 125,000 acres (195 square miles), more than 70 percent of which are classified as wetlands. Slightly more than half of the Corporation's property is arable and used by tenant rice and crawfish farmers; the remainder of the land consists of marsh and swamp. The Corporation manages this property, which was deeded to its corporate predecessor—The Orange Land Company—by the Department of State from public land holdings within Vermilion Parish in 1849. Hunting was the primary objective of the well-to-do persons interested in this club and others scattered across Louisiana's wetlands.

A thirty-five-page brochure titled *America's Last Great Hunting Ground*, prepared by the Gulf Coast Club, described the property's wildlife in order to attract wealthy sportsmen to purchase Club memberships. The Club's objectives were twofold: 1) the members wanted to develop a profitable recreational facility; and 2) to preserve the property's environmental integrity. The Club's 1925 subscription list provides an indication of the money individuals paid to hunt ducks in Louisiana's western marshes. For this privilege, sportsman in 1925 paid hunting dues of $10,000 (Knapp 1991)—adjusted for inflation the fee in 2009 would exceed $121,000.

Partial List of Subscribers to the Stock of Louisiana Coast Land Company, ca. 1925
(From: Knapp 1991)

Name	No. of Shares @ $2,000 each*	Residence	Occupation/Position
Adams, Walter	5	St. Louis	Pres. Adams New & Twine Company
Bell, James F.	5	Minneapolis	V. P. Washbum-Crosby Company
Billings, Frank	1	Chicago	Physician
Clement, Allan	5	Chicago	Pres. Clement, Curtis & Company
Dickinson, B. M.	5	Pittsburgh	Physician

Name	No. of Shares @ $2,000 each*	Residence	Occupation/Position
Hammers, Morgan	5	Chicago	Pres. Nokol Company
Hedges, M. M.	5	Chattanooga	Pres. Casey-Hedges Company
Johnson, E. R.	5	Camden, NJ	Pres. Victor Talking Machine Company
Joyce, E. J.	5	Chicago	Pres. Joyce Filing Company
Knight, Harry F.	5	St. Louis	Pres. Knight, Gamble, Goddard
LaBahn, Paul O.	5	Chicago	Hallbauer-LaBahn, Inc.
Marland, E. W.**	33	Ponca City, OK	Pres. Marland Oil Company
Meechan, G. F.	5	Chattanooga	Pres. Ross-Meehan Foundries
Moller, A. W.	5	New York City	Pres. The Duz Company
Morton, Joy	5	Chicago	Pres. Morton Salt Company
McCally, J. C.	5	Chicago	Attorney
McCormick, Cyrus H.	3	Chicago	McCormick Harvester Company
McFadden, W. H. **	34	Ponca City, OK	V.P. Marland Oil Company
McIlhenny, E. A.	20	Avery Is., LA	Pres. McIlhenny Company
Mills, W.	1	New York City	Pres. Central Union Trust Company
Penton, John A.	5	Cleveland	Pres. Penton Publishing Company
Playfair, James	1	Midland, Canada	Pres. Great Lakes Trans. Ltd.
Probasco, Scott, L.	N.A.	Chattanooga	Pres. Amer. Bank & Trust Company
Smith, Z. E.	5	Chicago	Architect
Steedman, Edwin H.	5	St. Louis	Pres. Curtis Manuf. Company
Warrick, W. E.	5	Chicago	V.P. Standard Oil of Indiana
Watkins, Horton	5	St. Louis	V.P. International Shoe Company
Wright, Warren	5	St. Louis	Pres. Calumet Baking Powder Company

* The 193 memberships in 1925 was worth $386,000, in 2009 these individuals/ companies would pay in excess of $4.5 million

** In 2009 the fee the Marland Company paid would exceed $1.6 million.

The Club failed, but it did attract about fifty wealthy individuals who continued their interest in the property for hunting and economic development. The Gulf Coast Club's successor, Coast Land, also failed to find the capital to purchase this tract from the owner, the Land and Mining Company. Perhaps the important legacy of this piece of real estate is the successor corporations: Furs, Inc., Furs Corporation, and The Vermilion Corporation (Knapp 1991).

Furs, Inc. incorporated in late 1927, was later changed to Furs Corporation, Inc., which was eventually dissolved and acquired by the Humble Oil Company in 1958. At that time, Humble agreed to the retention of the ninety-nine-year surface lease to Vermilion, which was organized and incorporated in 1958 as part of the terms of the act of sale (Knapp 1991). From 1927 to 1958, the defunct Coast Land operated as Furs, Inc. and later as Furs Corporation in order to trap, cure, and transport pelts and alligator skins to New York City. The company had two income streams—fur and pelt sales and mineral leases. Later rice, cattle, and hunting leases were added to the company's revenue base. The Vermilion lease maintained that the surface would be for the "the sole purpose of hunting migratory water fowl, trapping, and otherwise capturing fur bearing animals and alligators, and for farming and pasturing" (Knapp 1991:40). The surface rights to 44,000 acres (sixty-eight square miles) were subleased to the not-for-profit Bayou Corp Hunting Club.

As is the case with many marsh landowners, the surface is managed for aquatic and avian species, while the subsurface mineral rights are often under the control of a different owner—profits from this income source are not necessarily used to maintain the land surface. The rewards of owning such land must be weighed against the risk and liabilities associated with managing the surface, where operating costs often exceed profits, which is a real dilemma.

Along with the Vermilion Corporation, other clubs (most notable of which are associated with the *Chênière* Plain) also own hunting rights to large tracts—often greater than 40,000 acres (sixty-two square miles). Other clubs control smaller plots. Regardless of club size, hunting space is guaranteed. On these smaller clubs, colorful placards identify camps as "Les Deux Ponts," "Tropical Gardens Gun Club," The Scrip 'N Scrounge Duck Club," "Carlton's Folly," or "Florence Hunting Club." Louisiana's French heritage is reflected in camps called *"C'est Notre Plasir," "Chateau de Bateau," "Lagniappe,"* and *"C'est La Vie."* Whatever whimsical name was employed, these dwellings were staging points for recreational activities (Davis and Detro 1975).

> **Membership Varies by Club**
>
> "In some cases, membership lists are long; others have fewer than a dozen names. Some clubs have no members at all, just invited guests" (Kemp and Sims 2004:10).

Other Clubs Followed the Vermilion Corporation's Lead

Every chartered, or unchartered hunting club, or association, in Louisiana having more than three regular members and occupying a club house, club-boat, or camp, apply to the Department of Wildlife and Fisheries for a special hunting club permit and license. As a result, by 1930 there were forty-three licensed hunting clubs in the state.

Report of Licensed Louisiana Hunting Clubs 1927-1930
(From: Arthur 1929; Ninth Biennial Report . . .1930; Hunting in Louisiana 1931)

Club Name	Licensed Hunters	Club Name	Licensed Hunters
Alligator Club	6	Savoie Club	57
Buck Horn Club	6	Galva Club	4
Coastal Club	561	Florence Club	64

Club Name	Licensed Hunters	Club Name	Licensed Hunters
Delta Duck Club	674	C. A. Savoy Club	84
Lake Arthur Club	93	Crescent Gun and Rod Club	13
Crowley, Louisiana Club	158	Lafitte Gun and Rod Club	10
Daigle Hunting Club	196	Orange-Cameron Land Co. Club	47
Star Hunting Club	338	Mount Forest Club	8
E. L. Pratt Club	228	The Rigolets Club	3
Little Lake Club	28	Manchac Hunting Club	17
Pass-à-la Loutre Club	253	Ruddock Gun and Rod Club	9
Savanne Neuvelle Club	37	Lake Catherine Club	5
Norbert Duhon Hunting Camp	N/R	Lake Charles Hunting and Fishing Club	N/R
Stella Duck Club	22	E. M. Percy Club	8
Netherlands Gun Club	12	Grand Chenier Club	N/R
Dixie Delta Club	132	Seven Ponds Club	7
Lake Charles Club	66	Sweeney Hunting Club	N/R
Barmore Hunting Club	5	Manning Club	52
Pine Hills Club	36	Rigolets Club	2
Pine Island	17	Eulies Benoits Hunting Camp	N/R
Pete Buras Hunting Camp	N/R	Burnside Hunting Club	N/R
Venice Hunting Club	N/R		

N/R = No Record

The Florence Club

One of the state's oldest hunting clubs, with a membership of sixty-four in the late 1920s and a location on the *Chênière* Plain south of Gueydan, was established by Edward Arpin and named after his daughter, Florence. In addition, Arpin established the small community of Florence. After the Depression, the village was abandoned, but the town's hotel, built in 1911, became the Florence Club—often labeled the "Duck Capital of the World." This club does not have any members; just family and guests of current owner—William W. ("Billy") Rucks IV— have access to the clubhouse, boats, *pirogues*, guides, a kennel, an airstrip, and 5,100 acres (about eight square miles) of ma rsh. This exclusive property provides its guests with everything a waterfowler might need for a successful hunt. Property access has been simplified by a series of canals, dug at four-and-a-half mile intervals across the organizations nearly four square miles of marshland and represents the visible artifact of the sites original reclamation endeavors (Hanks 1988).

The Delta Duck, Chateau Canard (Duck Castle), and Other Hunting Clubs

The Delta Duck Club

On the Deltaic Plain in the Mississippi Delta, John Dymond, Jr. purchased 30,000 acres (forty-six square miles) that became the Delta Duck Club. Members from throughout the county took advantage of the excellent hunting and fishing offered within minutes of the club's lodge on Octave Pass. Guides' houses, boats, and storage buildings were part of this complex (Buras 1996). On the delta's East Fork Pass, the Leiter Chateau Canard Hunting Club was built by multi-millionaire Joe Leiter—a Chicago financier—around 1900. It is reported by Buras (1996) that the building and its furnishings cost nearly $50,000—more than $1.2 million in 2009.

Leiter Chateau Canard Hunting Preserve

In 1935, the Delta Duck Club and the Leiter Chateau Canard Hunting Preserve were purchased by the Federal government so the general public could hunt in the region without paying for the privilege. The property was the foundational element in the creation of the Delta Wildlife Refuge—the country's fist state-owned public shooting grounds (Daspit 1930).

Contemporary Duck Clubs
(From: Kemp and Sims 2004:7)

Avoca Duck Club	Bayou Club	Cajun Way Hunting Lodge	Cherry Ridge Hunting Camp
Coastal Club	Dupont Cutoff Fishing and Hunting Club	Florence Club	4 Square Duck Club
Goose Lake Camp	Grosse Savanne Lodge	Hackberry Hunting Lodge	Hackberry Rod & Gun
K&J Hunting and Fishing Lodge	Lacassine Lodge	Lake Arthur Club	Le Camp Canard
Little Lake Hunting Club	Little Pecan Island Preserve	Lulu's Hunting Club	McGowan Brake Club
Oak Grove Club	Pecan Brake Lodge	Savanne Neuvelle	Section 14 Club
Whitehall Plantation	White Lake Hunting Club		

Florence Hunting Club, south of Gueydan, 2006. (Photo by the author.)

(Middle, left) The Delta Duck Club's kidney boats. (Photo from Cheramie 1997.)

(Middle, right) Ace Hunting Club, south of Kaplan, 1997. (Photo by the author.)

(Bottom) Polo Hunting Club, ca. 1915. (Photo from Cheramie 1997.)

Other Contemporary Clubs

The White Lake Hunting Club and others

In most cases, these organizations control the land around the club site. For example, the White Lake Hunting Club was once the private hunting reserve of the Stanolind Oil Company. The property's clubhouse was the Stark Headquarters of the Orange-Cameron Land Company that was acquired by Stanolind. Through time and a series of acquisitions, British Petroleum became the owner of record. This site involves 70,965 acres—equal to the incorporated area of Tampa, Florida—and was donated in 2004 to the state of Louisiana. This tract, now known as the White Lake Wetlands Conservation Area, is considered by many as "one of the best overall hunting spots for waterfowl in North America" (White Lake Wetlands 2006).

The property that became the Orange-Cameron Land Company was purchased by Lutcher Stark from the Texas Company for one dollar and seventy-five cents an acre in 1918; part of this property became the Sabine National Wildlife Refuge in 1937. In addition, the company owned the traps, drying racks, and built a number of "rat camps" composed of fur house, bunk houses, kitchen, and mess hall—permanent housing for trappers who paid one dollar a day for board. At the Stark Headquarters camp, they stored about 50,000 traps and maintained the central fur house and pelt processing facility. The Company sold the annual harvest and gave the trappers a percentage (Arthur 1927; Block 2007). "By 1925 the value of the annual fur catch marketed by Lutcher Stark exceeded $1,000,000" (Block 2007)—slightly more than twelve million dollars in 2009.

Typical drying rack often associated with a "rat camp," ca. 1920. (Photo from the *Seventh Biennial Report of the Louisiana Department of Conservation, 1924-1926*.)

(Photo by the author, 2006.)

Part of this property became the White Lake Wetlands Conservation Area in 2004. Ownership records show the connectivity between this land and harvesting the region's renewable and non-renewable resources. Originally, the marshland was set up as a "Rat Ranch." Stanolind Oil Company—Standard Oil Company of Indiana (later to become the American Oil Company or Amoco and then part of British Petroleum)—obtained the property from Wright Morrow in 1935. This sale included all of the property acquired by the Yount-Lee Oil Company (by 1935 the largest independent oil producer in the South with 283,000 acres of oil lands and leases in Texas and Louisiana) from P. L. Lawrence in 1931. Further, a portion of the White Lake property was acquired in 1929 by M. F. Yount from Elizabeth M. Watkins—part of the 157,060-acre tract obtained by J. B. Watkins under the Swamp Land Acts—in 1929 (Hunting Conservation Area 2006). Stanolind purchased the Yount-Lee Oil Company in 1935 for forty-six million dollars ($723 million in 2009), which at the time was the third largest financial transaction in American business history (Yount-Lee 2007; No. 1 Texas 2007). This purchase assured Stanolind an adequate supply of crude oil for its Texas refiner's subsidiary, Pan American Petroleum and Transport.

The Watkins property was originally purchased for ten-cents an acre. In 1904, the land was sold to the John Deere Plow Company for sixty-cents an acre; nine years later the Texas Company bought the land for about one dollar an acre. In 1918, Lutcher Stark bought the Orange Land Company tract for one dollar and seventy-five cents—the price of one muskrat pelt (Block 2006).

At the Little Pecan Island Preserve, the 14,000 acres (twenty-one square miles) utilized by guests is either owned by a private corporation or leased from the Miami Corporation—a major Chicago-based landholding company. At this club, guests are escorted to their blinds by a small flotilla of guides and their retrievers.

The Coastal Club was founded in 1928 by lumber executives from Alexandria, Louisiana. Members can hunt on 12,000 acres (eighteen square miles); they own 6,000 and lease an additional 6,000 from the Miami Corporation. Eighty-seven waterfowlers own stock in the Club and "if a share of stock comes up for sale, there's never a lack of people who would like to have one, . . . Some people have waited fifteen or twenty years" to become a member of the Coastal Club (Kemp and Sims 2004:15).

The Grosse Savanne Waterfowl and Wildlife Lodge is owned by Mr. and Mrs. Buddy Leach and the Sweetlake Land and

Entrance to the Grosse Savanne lodge, 2008. (Photo by the author.)

Oil Company. The clubhouse sits on 5,000 acres (nearly eight square miles) of marsh, with access to an additional 50,000 acres (seventy-eight square miles) of privately managed property. Grosse Savanne has received from the Orvis Company, America's oldest catalog company, the "Wing Shooting Lodge Award of the Year." The Lodge can accommodate eighteen guests in nine bedrooms, with all of the conveniences and comforts of home, including daily linen and turn-down service. Professional guides and retrievers are available. Exclusive use of the facility by corporation and others for one, two, or three nights is available for a fee. After the waterfowl hunting season, the site serves as a bed and breakfast and has available overnight packages for anglers, alligator hunters, and bird watchers. In September, Grosse Savanne offers morning hunts and afternoon fishing as a "blast and cast" event.

As a general rule, if a marsh hunter chooses not to become a member of a private club, a hunting or deer lease must be obtained from one of the landowners who allow hunting on their property. Costs vary depending on location, acreage, number of ponds, and the tract's hunting potential. As a standard rule, the better the hunting the greater the lease fee. For those who cannot afford a lease or club membership, state operated wildlife management areas are free (Duffy and Hoffpauer 1966).

Refuges

Since the state obtained its first marsh tract, a vigorous land acquisition program has helped protect numerous avian and aquatic species. On wildlife refuges hunting is not permitted, since they are important as nesting and/or resting sites for recreationally important species. As a result, more than 1.4 million people visit Louisiana's national wildlife refuges annually (Curry 2003). In addition, in several of the state's wildlife management areas, it is possible in a day to make a successful combination hunting/ fishing trip. A direct result of early twentieth century efforts to protect and manage wildlife habitats for use by the state's citizens and others interested in the out-of-door.

Breton National Wildlife Refuge, the second oldest refuge in the country—after Florida's Pelican Island, turned 100 years old on October 4, 2004. In 1904, Pres. Theodore Roosevelt heard about the destruction of birds for millinery trade and the collection of eggs, as many as 50,000 yearly, on Old Harbor, Freemason, Chandeleur,

Conservation agent's house and lookout on state wildlife refuge, ca. 1915. (Photo from the *Fourth Biennial Report of the Louisiana Department of Conservation, 1918-1920.*)

and Breton islands. Soon afterwards, Roosevelt created Breton National Wildlife Refuge. He visited the site in June 1915. At that time, several families and a school were located on Breton Island. A hurricane that year destroyed the community, and it was never rebuilt (Barry 1979; McNamara 2004/2005; Cipra 1976). Since creation of this refuge, at least 239 bird species have been documented using the Breton Refuge (Mathews 2003).

Louisiana's first wildlife management area was established in 1911. E. A. McIlhenny, along with W. Ward, purchased from the Orange Land Company 54,000 acres (eighty-four square miles) on the west side of Vermilion Bay. On November 4, 1911, these philanthropists donated 13,000 acres (twenty square miles) to Louisiana that became the Louisiana State Wild Life Sanctuary. The donation created the first wildlife refuge in the world privately funded for the public good (McIlhenny 1930).

Family enjoying the freshwater well on the Marsh Island Refuge, ca. 1945. (Photo from *Third Biennial Report, Louisiana Department of Wildlife and Fisheries, 1948-1949*.)

While this tract was going through the acceptance process, McIlhenny quietly got together options on Marsh Island. This process was not easy, since all of the people who owned property on the island had to be willing to sell their land holdings. Further, all titles had to be researched, and a registered survey had to be completed. In order to complete the acquisition, McIlhenny needed to finance the sale. Working with a number of intermediaries, the proposed refuge came to the attention of Mrs. R. Sage—widely considered one of America's greatest philanthropist—who paid $168,980—more than $3.6 million in 2009—for the land that would become the Marsh Island Refuge. The title was put in E. McIlhenny's name.

In 1913, the real estate was placed under the control of the State of Louisiana (McIlhenny 1930). As a result, the 82,000-acre (128 square miles) Marsh Island Refuge has developed into "one of the most important wildlife areas on the North American Continent, particular from the standpoint of migratory waterfowl. . . ." (Yancey 1962:14). Not only did Mrs. Sage underwrite the cost of Marsh Island, she eventually deeded more than forty square miles of marshland for the establishment of additional refuges.

The Louisiana State Wild Life Sanctuary and Russell Sage refuges represent some of the earliest American efforts to provide wildlife habitat designed to promote

To inspect oysters destined for Louisiana markets, the state maintained a port of entry site at Grand Pass, ca. 1945. (Photo from *Second Biennial Report, Louisiana Department of Wildlife and Fisheries, 1946-1947.*)

waterfowl hunting on a restricted basis. At the time, these properties were being developed, sportsmen and conservationists were encouraged by the passage of the Migratory Bird Law of 1913 and the Migratory Bird Treaty Act of 1918. Under the provisions of this legislation, spring shooting and market hunting were abolished—a move considered a major step in the conservation of migratory waterfowl. Since the purchase of Marsh Island and the creation of the Russell Sage Refuge, other properties have been purchased by the public as resting areas for migratory waterfowl.

In addition, the state's wildlife refuges in the first half of the twentieth century—coupled with the Department of Wildlife and Fisheries laboratories at Grand Terre, the Port of Entry at Grand Pass, and oyster camps at Bay Gardene, Sister Lake, and Lake Felicity—also served as important settlement nodes. These sites were well kept, manned, and, although remote, provided the state with continuous oversight of its renewable natural resources (McConnell 1952).

One of the last sites added to the state's inventory of refuges is the Atchafalaya Delta Wildlife Management Area, immediately east of the Russell Sage property. In the state's annual aerial survey of wildlife within this management area, surveyors "look down and actually see water churning brown from rafts of pintails rooting in the duck potato"—prime duck fodder (Fontova 1997B:14). The Delta covers 137,000 acres (2,114 square miles); most of this acreage is water. Only about 30,000 acres (forty-six square miles) are vegetated. Even so, from 200,000 to 300,000 ducks utilize this habitat; and as a result, each hunter bags an average of two to three ducks per trip (Fontova 1997B).

Louisiana is part of the Mississippi Flyway. It is one link in the North American Flyway management areas that help alleviate heavy shooting pressure on waterfowl. Often funds required to buy this land came from oil royalties from property under the control of the Louisiana Wildlife and Fisheries Commission. Reduced hydrocarbon production in recent years has unfortunately slowed the land acquisition program. Even so, the state has a fair number of hunting sites available for the general public in the marsh. Louisiana Department of Wildlife and Fisheries operates and manages more than thirty wildlife areas encompassing nearly one million acres (1,562 square miles—about the size of Rhode Island). Nearly half of this land is in the marshes.

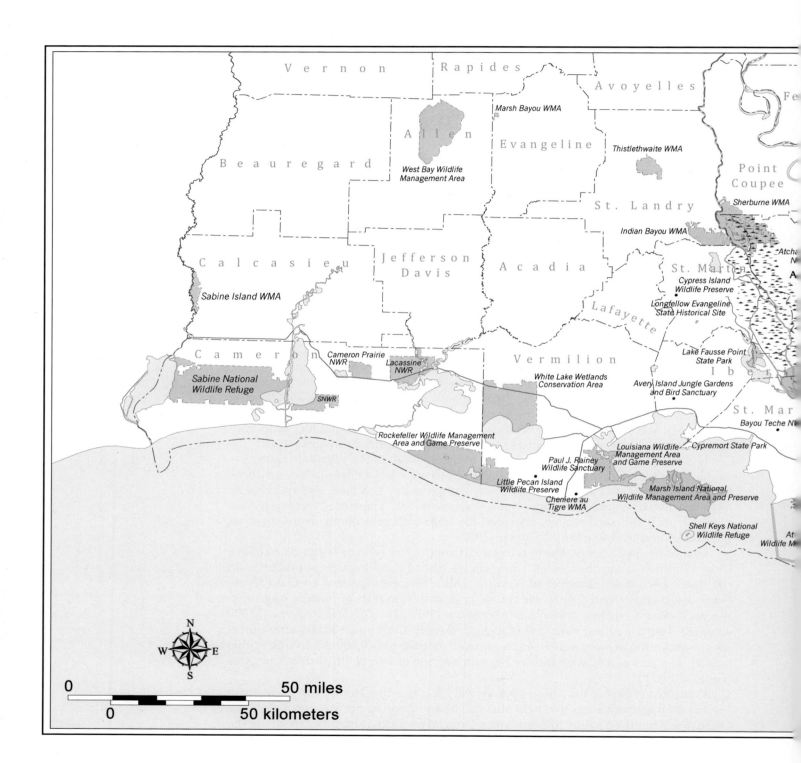

(Map courtesy of the Louisiana Geological Survey, 2010.)

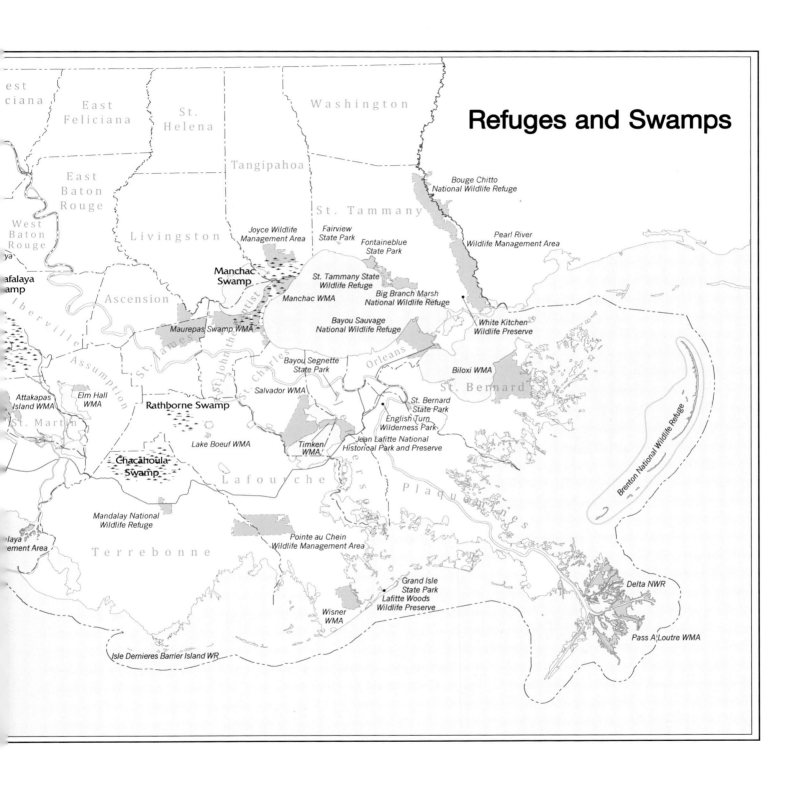

Refuges and Swamps

est
ciana

East
Feliciana

St.
Helena

Washington

Tangipahoa

East
Baton
Rouge

St. Tammany

West
Baton
Rouge
ya

Livingston

Joyce Wildlife
Management Area

Fairview
State Park

Fontainebleu
State Park

Bouge Chitto
National Wildlife Refuge

Pearl River
Wildlife Management Area

afalaya
amp

**Manchac
Swamp**

Ascension

St. Tammany State
Wildlife Refuge

Manchac WMA

Big Branch Marsh
National Wildlife Refuge

berville

Maurepas Swamp WMA

Bayou Sauvage
National Wildlife Refuge

White Kitchen
Wildlife Preserve

Assumption

Elm Hall
WMA

Bayou Segnette
State Park

Orleans

Biloxi WMA

St. Bernard

Brenton National Wildlife Refuge

Attakapas
Island WMA

St. Martin

Salvador WMA

Rathborne Swamp

St. Bernard
State Park

English Turn
Wilderness Park

Lake Boeuf WMA

Timken
WMA

Jean Lafitte National
Historical Park and Preserve

**Chacahoula
Swamp**

Lafourche

Plaqu

laya
ement Area

Mandalay National
Wildlife Refuge

Pointe au Chein
Wildlife Management Area

T e r r e b o n n e

Delta NWR

Grand Isle
State Park

Lafitte Woods
Wildlife Preserve

Wisner
WMA

Pass A Loutre WMA

Isle Dernieres Barrier Island WR

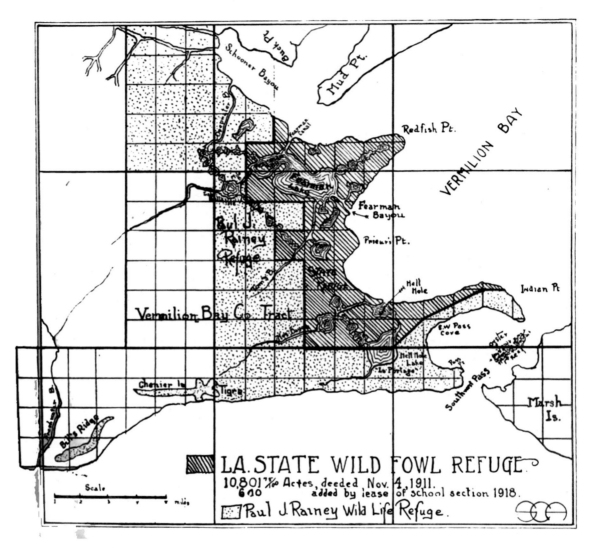

(Image from *Seventh Biennial Report, Louisiana Department of Conservation, 1924-1926.*)

South Louisiana Wildlife Management Areas

Atchafalaya	Delta Manchac	Timken
Attakapas	Maurepas Swamp	White Lake
Biloxi	Pass a Loutre	Wisner
Elm Hall	Pearl River	
Joyce	Pointe Au Chene	
Lake Boeuf	Salvador	

National and State Wildlife Refuges

Atchafalaya	Cameron Prairie	Rockefeller
Bayou Sauvage	Delta	Sabine Wildlife
Bayou Teche	Elmer's Island	Shell Keys Mandalay
Big Branch Marsh	Isles Dernières	State Wild Fowl
Bogue Chitto	Lacassine	
Breton	Marsh Island	

State and National Parks

Jean Lafitte National Historical Park and Preserve
Longfellow-Evangeline
Bayou Segnette
Chênière au Tigre
Cypremort Point

Fairview Riverside
Fontainebleau
Grand Isle
Lake Fausse Pointe
St. Bernard

Nature Conservancy, National Audubon Society and Others

Avery Island Jungle Gardens and Bird Sanctuary
English Turn Wilderness Park
Little Pecan Island
White Kitchen

Cypress Island
Lafitte Woods
Paul J. Rainey

Principal Recreational Activities

Hunting

Winter recreation endeavors focus on hunting. Licensed hunters can be divided into two categories: those who hunt waterfowl and those who hunt quadrupeds, principally white-tailed deer, squirrel (*Sciurus carolinensis carolinensis* and *S. c. fuliginosus*), and swamp rabbit (*Sylvilagus acquaticus*).

South Louisiana's marshes, swamps and waterbodies constitute one of the nation's most important waterfowl wintering habitats; millions of birds rest and feed in the coastal zone before flying to their wintering grounds in Central and South America. During their winter stay, the migratory populations seem to prefer fresh to intermediate marshes, although some species can tolerate brackish conditions. They make hunting an extremely important and popular pastime, generating considerable income from the sale of licenses as well as the paraphernalia associated with the sport. Managing this resource is accomplished by regulating hunting pressure within breeding, migration, and wintering.

Fishing

Wham! Water erupted in frothy fury as another big-mouthed beast devoured the bait. This fish happened to be a 2-pound largemouth bass. On another cast, it might have been an 8-pound redfish . . .

On one cast, you can catch a redfish. On the next cast, you can catch a bass. On the third cast, you can catch a speckled trout. That happens to me all the time. . . . (Felsher 1997:17).

The large variety of fresh and salt water species in Louisiana make fishing the marsh's largest recreational activity. The sport is a year-round pastime that varies with the breeding cycle, water levels, fishing pressure, and aquatic-life productivity. Thousands of miles of wetland shoreline provide the fisherman with extensive recreational opportunities and to some degree it is all used. If a boat can get into the aquatic habitat, it will be utilized by the state's fishing enthusiasts. In fact, specialized boats, like the "Go-Devil™" and a variety of air boats are particularly useful in gaining access to sites inaccessible with other boat types. If these boats will not work, kayaks and canoes are used.

Heavy-use periods are during the summer months. There are times when so

For more than a century, tarpon have provided sportsmen with a challenge.

(Image from *Harper's Weekly,* May 1890.)

One of a number of charter services in the coastal zone, 2007. (Photo by the author.)

many people seek marsh access that 100 or more automobiles, or trucks with boat trailers, can be counted at public launching sites. To meet public demand for launching facilities, boat ramps dot the landscape. There are more than 1,000 launching ramps with about one-third available for public use. As might be expected, these sites range from small roadside ramps, able to accommodate five to ten automobiles, to private marinas with as many as four launching ramps or hoists. At many of these facilities, charter boats take small groups of fishermen offshore to troll, or bottom fish for larger species. In some cases, marinas also support a growing group of guides who take fishing parties into the state's inland waters. Inland fishing guides, like their offshore charter boat counterparts, are often booked for more than 200 days a year.

In addition, these launching sites provide not only a place to put a boat into the water, but they furnish weekend crabbers and cane-pole fishermen with recreational space. Such persons do not use boats; they take advantage of the fishing in the vicinity of the launching facilities. In the warm months, these recreational enthusiast line the roads. When land fishermen are combined with boat-oriented sportsmen, the launch sites and roadsides become highly congested. In addition, camps are in constant use and, to the uninitiated, the isolated and uninhabited marshland appears heavily trafficked.

Once their boats are in the water, the recreationists can go after fresh or salt water species. Travel is easy, as the region is laced by an intricate system of natural and artificial waterways. These routes supply the connectivity necessary to exploit marshland resources. In many places, it is difficult to find a "pond" or "location canal" that is not being utilized because along the coast sixty fish species are associated with the estuarine or marine environment. As a result, fishermen measure their catch by the ice chest, not stringer. In salt water, a two-ice-chest day is considered a success.

Freshwater fishermen seek a diversity of fish species, especially: largemouth bass, catfish, "sac-a-lait" (or crappie), and bluegill (or bream). The black bass (largemouth bass) is considered the state's most sought-after game fish. In freshwater marshes, the fishermen's quarry is a five pound or better largemouth bass. When caught in brackish water, a largemouth bass was probably foraging for food. They prefer freshwater and are often caught around water hyacinth (*Eichornia crassipes*), among trees and stumps that have fallen into and across the region's waterways, in the cuts that connect marsh ponds, or in pipeline and location canals associated with the inland petroleum industry. Bass are difficult to catch, and it takes "bass savvy fishermen" to land them consistently.

Saltwater fishermen primarily catch spotted trout or "specs," the most sought-after salt water species. Found in shallow waters, "specs" average from one to five pounds or better and represent about 40 percent of the daily saltwater catch in Louisiana's coastal waters. Maximum trout catches occur in October and November, but they are caught year-round.

The saltwater angler understands that the favorite habitats of speckled trout are warm shallow bays, cuts, passes, bayous, and lagoons; rarely do they venture more than a mile offshore. When schooling, "specs" are plentiful, fight well, and provide considerable excitement during the "catch." With the right tackle or "spec rig," it is not uncommon to hook two trout at a time—filling an ice chest with the twenty-five limit per person quickly.

Atlantic croaker is one of the most abundant commercial fish along the Gulf Coast, but it is not considered an important game fish. Although an industrialized species, it appears to be underutilized by the recreational sector. However, redfish sometimes referred to as "bull" or "rat" reds, along with black drum, are considered worthy adversaries for the state's anglers. When the big ten-pound-or-better "reds" are "turned on," a fisherman can boat the five-per-person limit quickly, so it often becomes a process of deciding which fish to keep. Only one can be over twenty-seven inches long, which on a really good day can be a problem.

Along the Gulf Coast, gigging flounder along the beach face at night is a popular recreational sport. This endeavor is a favorite pastime for those recreationalists who have camps on the barrier islands and other points along the coast. Usually, an outing is deemed a success when ten flounder (the daily limit) are gigged. Then again, some people are happy to get only one, as founders are considered a delicacy when covered or stuffed with lump crabmeat or shrimp.

In Louisiana's offshore waters, more than 4,000 oil platforms are anchored to the floor of the Gulf of Mexico. Until hydrocarbon exploration and production was well established offshore: pompano (*Alectic ciliaris*), sheepshead (*Archosargus probatocephalus*) king mackerel, (*Scomberomorus cavalla*), Atlantic croaker (*Micropogonias undulatus*), jack crevalle (*Caranx hippos*), and red snapper (*Lutjanus campechanus*) were rarely caught. The offshore rigs changed fishing in Louisiana's coastal waters. The industry's production platforms became, in effect, artificial reefs. As new platforms were added, they enhanced the saltwater species feeding ground. Each of these structures serves as an artificial reef for recreational fish stock. With time, these "reefs" became some of the world's finest offshore fishing provinces (Ditton and Auyong 1984; Reggio 1987; Wilson, et al. n.d.). Now, with many of these structures no longer in production, they are being recycled as artificial reefs in designated dumping areas off the coast. In this manner, the rigs continue to serve as underwater habitat for a variety of offshore species.

To take advantage of the clustering of fish around the platforms, a fleet of charter boats ferries saltwater anglers to these sites. These charter boat marinas are located at Empire, Buras, Venice, Grand Isle, Cocodrie, Intracoastal City, Cameron, and a number of other sites with relatively easy access to the Gulf of Mexico. The captains of these twenty-eight-to-fifty-foot boats know the "rigs" that yield the highest catches. This knowledge often ensures the fishing party will limit out in a variety of species. Fishing the "rigs" is considered by many to be some of the best fishing in the world and it attracts sportsmen from well beyond Louisiana's boundaries.

Often organized into clubs, fresh- and saltwater anglers have added new meaning to the word "rodeo." In 1928, a group of New Orleans' sportsmen organized the Grand Isle Tarpon Rodeo—one of the earliest sporting events in coastal Louisiana. In that year, eight tarpon were "brought to gaff" (Durand 1933:13). In South Louisiana, therefore, a fishing rodeo means a fishing contest that draws large numbers of entrants. These organized fishing tournaments will often attract more than 50,000 spectators and participants. Size records are regularly broken by the participating anglers. These records are broken because the estuarine-marsh-swamp system's nursery ground guarantees an abundant seafood supply. In fact, more than 90 percent of the Gulf's fin fish spend part of their life-cycle within the coastal zone. Although most species are commercially exploited, recreational enthusiasts contribute more than $400 million to the local economy, with more than half a million people involved in this leisure-time activity. Besides rod and reel and/or fly-fishing, four additional activities are important—crabbing, shrimping, frogging, and crawfishing.

A successful 1936 fishing trip in lower Terrebonne Parish. (Photo courtesy of the Randolph A. Bazet Collection, Archives & Special Collections, Nicholls State University.)

Crabbing

The blue crab is one of the more abundant macro invertebrates in Louisiana's coastal waters. The species occupies almost all available aquatic habitats and uses a highly diverse food supply. Optimum conditions include shallow water, mud and/ or mud-shell bottoms, mollusk beds, tidal exchange, warm temperatures, and mid-to- low salinities (Adkins 1972).

The blue crab is sensitive to changes in salinity and temperature. The greatest numbers are caught in waters of oligohaline to mesohaline salinity and warm temperatures (Jaworski 1972). Highest catches occur in winter and early spring because the crabs tend to concentrate in the tidal channels, especially near oyster beds. Summer months are considered the favored recreational crabbing period, because the crabs tend to migrate into the upper estuary where food is more abundant and where recreational access is also facilitated. In both periods, large numbers of people are crabbing using traditional methods, such as trotlines and drop nets to capture this crustacean.

From those areas accessible by road, weekend crabbers often catch a bushel of crabs a day (Adkins 1972). In fact, when the conditions are right, a recreational crabber can catch twelve dozen, the daily limit, in less than an hour. Typically crabbing is a family-oriented pastime, with the recreational catch providing many families with a delightful seafood meal at nominal expense. Often the catch becomes the focus of an afternoon crab boil hosted by the crabbers, but enjoyed by family and friends.

Shrimping

Shrimp are migratory. In May, boats catch brown shrimp while white are caught in the August to December season. A special license is now required for sportsmen to harvest shrimp; a shrimping license is mandatory and the catch cannot be sold. Like their commercial counterparts, recreational shrimpers must trawl within the regulated season. Individuals can catch up to one hundred pounds a day. To improve their harvest, some build large, winged "butterfly" nets. These wharf-mounted *poupiers*, when lowered into a bayou, are an efficient way to "trap" migrating shrimp.

Frogging

Closed only during April and May, the ten-month frog season is one of the state's most popular nocturnal hunting sports. The recreational sportsman needs less than ten frogs to have enough legs for a good meal. Unfortunately, the easily accessible frog-gigging spots are often over-harvested and restaurants now import frog legs from India, Japan, and Mexico.

Crawfish

Only two Louisiana crawfish species are both available in abundance and of sufficient size to be harvested by recreationalists—the "swamp" and "river" types (*Procambarus clarkii* and *P. acutus*). These crustaceans prefer fresh to brackish water and are collected from natural water areas and cultivated ponds. But the crawfish is more than a food item in Louisiana—it is a symbol of a way of life. Found in almost every ditch, the crustacean is utilized for food, bait, income, recreation, weed control, and as a literary character. The erratic, cyclical fluctuations in supply once made consumers' satisfaction unpredictable. Now farmed in conjunction with rice production, the crustacean is readily available. Nowhere else are crawfish—often called a poor man's food—produced and consumed in such large quantities as in French Louisiana. A baited hook or a series of traps placed in nearly any waterway can yield a sack of crawfish, ideal for a backyard family crawfish boil—a South Louisiana tradition.

Principal Non-Consumptive Recreational Activities

Although the newspaper sports pages are filled with material for the recreational angler—from tide tables to tips on the best fishing spots—there are many other individuals who enjoy just being in the out-of-doors. They are not concerned with shooting or hooking a wall-mounted trophy. As a result, a large number of people use their weekends and free time for boating, canoeing/kayaking, birdwatching, camping, hiking through the state's parks or enjoying one of the coastal zone's natural and scenic rivers. Since Louisiana's estuaries sustain an abundant marine biota of fresh- and saltwater aquatic species, non-consumptive recreation activities abound.

Birdwatching

In this annual ritual, the Neotropical migration becomes the visual quarry of a large number of birders. The *chênières* and Grand Isle have developed into a mecca for birding, as more than 400 species of birds are known to occur in Louisiana, most of them in the coastal region. During the songbird migration, visitors are attracted to this "birders bonanza" looking for a rare or unusual bird (Frank 1993; Huner and Musumeche 2005).

Because of the migratory songbird population, the ground cover includes yucca, mesquite, and prickly pear cactus—plants normally associated with an arid landscape. These plants were brought in to the wetlands by the Neotropical bird migrants, who invade coastal habitats in the fall and return in the spring. In their feces are the seeds of the plants that form much of the *chênière* ground cover (Bailey 1934; Bradshaw 1997; Hanks 1988).

The *chênières* and the state's barrier islands are the last land they encounter flying south and the first land they see on their return to the North American continent. At this point in their travels, the birds are so tired that one can pick them off of the trees. Upon landfall, the birds are so exhausted that they drop from the sky in a phenomenon known as "fall out." Great numbers take refuge on the wooded *chênières* to rest and accumulate the fat reserves required to complete their journey. The *chênières* feed these birds well. Along with the vast variety of species that pass through Louisiana, the state is also the home of a number of bald eagle nesting sites, further adding to the amateur ornithologist list of birds catalogued from trips to Louisiana's swamps and marshes. (See *www.birdlouisiana.com* for more information on this annual migration.)

Swamp and marsh tours have become critical parts of the region's tourism industry, 2004. (Photo by the author.)

Eco-tourism

Since the 1970s, increasing numbers of local entrepreneurs have established local swamp tours to familiarize the traveler with Louisiana's unique swamp environments. In addition, some have established tours of the marsh.

Boating and Canoeing

Louisiana Legislative Act No. 321 makes it mandatory that all boats equipped with, or propelled by, machinery be registered, regardless of size, type, or horsepower. In Louisiana, there are hundreds of thousands of boats. About 50 percent of these are in the state's coastal parishes. Often costing more than $75,000, these outboard or inboard powered boats provide quick access to any potential hunting or fishing site from hundreds of boat launches. Further, for every registered boat there is an equal number of *bateaux*, *pirogues*, non-registered gasoline-powered boats, kayaks, and canoes. From launch sites throughout the coastal lowlands, the recreational enthusiast can travel into the marsh or swamp for a simple pleasure ride, skiing trip, or jet-ski adventure—or paddle one of the state's scenic rivers and view the landscape at water level.

CONCLUSION

For persons lacking any emotional attachment to South Louisiana's wetlands, it is easy to see how this topographical element was once labeled a "no man's land." Burdened with this moniker, the coastal lowlands became, in many ways, Louisiana's forgotten human landscape. After all, who would voluntarily live and work in—much less enjoy—a geographic province that was at times more water than land? Outside observers, overlooking the region's human occupants, described it as a virtually uninhabited expanse of unbroken vistas of near featureless grassy "wastelands" that was infested with mosquitoes, gnats, and "no-see-ums." The end result was that persons in the American mainstream believed that the coastal plain served no useful purpose. It was just a stippled pattern on a map.

It is thus hardly surprising that there was rarely any cartographic reference to the villages and small settlement enclaves that dotted the landscape. The wetlands were, according to the conventional wisdom, worthy of study only by archeologists and geologists. The area's largely European-American population was consequently ignored by researchers. They were instead consigned to rare footnotes in travel journals and even scarcer illustrations in early periodicals.

Yet, the wetlands boasted a significant human population. Marsh and swamp dwellers were a hardy, industrious group of people who thrived in their isolation thanks to their close kinship with their physical environment. Their strong work ethic and can-do attitude allowed them to prosper even in the midst of inhospitable surroundings.

Their success was the result of generations of successful environmental adaptation, an adaptive process begun millennia earlier by the region's indigenous population. Archeologists have documented this geographic province's early settlement history by systematically investigating the wide array of Indian midden sites found there and their direct connection to the area's watercourses. These studies established the intellectual framework used to establish the chronology of the Mississippi River's shifting patterns and overlapping deltas. As a result of this work, and other geologic inquiries based on radiocarbon measurements, scholars have determined that the region's alluvial wetlands are a relatively recent addition to Louisiana's coastal geography and that each deltaic lobe was outlined by prehistoric human settlement nodes.

Europeans and Asians eventually supplanted the indigenous population. These new cultural groups were physically isolated, illiterate, poor, and disconnected from the state's landed gentry. They were forgotten by the more sedentary populations on the higher natural levees, but they nevertheless transformed the wetlands into an economic province that has provided, through time, income and jobs to a sizeable population.

To put the marshland community into context, one must compare it to a more recognizable population center. The 1920 census reported 387,000 residents in New Orleans, making the Crescent City the nation's seventeenth largest municipality. In that same year, there were at least 25,000 trappers working from remote camps harvesting muskrat and alligator. Since entire families migrated into the marshes with adult male trappers, this semi-transient trapping community could easily have exceeded 100,000 persons—nearly one-third of the "Crescent City's" population. Further, there were at least fifty shrimp drying villages with an average seasonal crew of sixty support personnel and fishermen. These sites collectively housed at least 3,000 additional individuals. Oystermen operating from isolated marsh camps added to this number, as did undetermined numbers of survey crew members and roughnecks associated with the oil and gas industry. Therefore, when one begins to reflect on the eight primary categories of settlement: 1) agricultural, 2) industrial, 3) fishing,

4) trapping, 5) commercial hunting, 6) governmental service, 7) recreational, and 8) a combination of one or more of these groups, the collective number of inhabitants once occupying Louisiana's marshes was sizeable. Yet, even as late as the 1930s, the United States' Geological Survey maps labeled parts of the region as an uninhabitable "no man's land."

These marshland pioneers were easily overlooked by census-takers, because gaining entrée to their settlements was difficult, arduous, and time-consuming. Only a few journalists ventured into this flat "wilderness," and they took considerable liberty in distorting, or over-simplifying, the complexities and diversity of the area's human population. Late nineteenth-century novelists, artists, and feature writers framed the marshdwellers in the context of the area's rugged environment and physical isolation. Regardless of the problems associated with access, or the distortions of dime-novel-type pulp fiction, Louisiana's marsh and swamplands were inhabited by a highly diverse group of ethnic minorities who lived at a subsidence level, dominated by a barter economy, in which money was less important than the good of the entire community. Kinship was the key to their individual and collective happiness.

Members of the groups composing this cultural mosaic simply wanted to make a modest living from their beloved secluded homes and camps. They were not concerned about the "outside" world's misunderstanding of their values. They were not part of mainstream Louisiana. They were not involved, directly or indirectly, with the affairs of the state. They were not fascinated by the rhetoric of regional politics or interested in government subsidies. In fact, in the nineteenth century many flew the French flag with pride, and all reveled in the use of their native language. They liked the neighborly feel of their communities and worked "their" land often without clear title or any concern about ownership.

To most of the early inhabitants, the marsh was communal property to be used and enjoyed by each kinship group. Ownership was not practical, convenient, or for that matter realistic. The marsh was the marsh, not some upland parcel to be divided among migrating settlers who followed the latitude and longitudinal precepts of rectangular land ownership. Besides, surveys in the mid-nineteenth century were exhausting endeavors. They required a vast expenditure of human energy in carrying heavy equipment used to measure angles, with surveyors dragging chains, cutting trails, placing corner monuments, and blazing "witness" trees. Although practical in upland areas, the marsh was flat, wet, hot, and infested with a variety of nuisance insects and reptiles. These impediments made cadastral surveying a challenge only for the most dedicated and determined government field crews. As a result, the accuracy and precision of many if not most, of the earliest surveys are questionable.

Meticulous measurements, using more refined instruments, were not introduced to wetland surveyors until the second decade of the twentieth century. Because of problems associated with the original nineteenth century survey inaccuracies, land records were vague and hard to use to define land ownership. Yet, land records ensconced in local courthouses were of no interest to the marshdweller, as they viewed this land and the associated legal records as a community resource, held in common by everyone in the community. Private land ownership was not part of their culture. Like the Navajo and other American Indian tribes, all land was owned in common and often administered by the elder of the local kinship group.

The typical marshdweller was not a squatter, for he believed he "owned" the land upon which he worked and lived. Marshdwellers were people of the land. Until the industrialization of the wetlands, when ownership became an overriding issue, these folks occupied the largest near sea-level grassland in the coterminous United States. They tonged for oysters, caught shrimp, trapped fur-bearing animals, served as guides to wealthy industrialists, herded cattle, captained boats, helped wildcat crews find oil,

---

The Marsh is a People Place

Denise Reed, University of New Orleans, notes that: "We're managing for people here. This is a landscape of people" (Burruss 2002:10).

natural gas, and sulphur, raised vegetables, citrus, cotton, and sugarcane, engaged in market hunting, manned government outposts, and unashamedly engaged in rum-running. In short, their work schedule was dependent on the seasons and the industrial activity required to harvest the territory's renewable and non-renewable resources, but they were quite often not land owners.

The individuals that owned the marsh were entrepreneurs who purchased large tracts of land after passage of the Swamp Land Acts of 1849 and 1850, which outlined the transfer of title based on the fact that this acreage was wet and unfit for cultivation. In some cases, land conveyances were initiated by simply paying back taxes. Regardless, large marsh tracts fell under the control of a relatively small number of investors. Although, some would now label these individuals robber barons, this epithet was never applied to persons acquiring coastal property, for most buyers considered their investment unwise and irrational—pure folly. To some of these investors, the fact this real estate was wet and unfit for cultivation was not a concern, for they envisioned huge reclamation developments, reminiscent of polder-outlined fields in the Netherlands. Others were interested in hunting preserves and muskrat ranges, though a few purchased land to graze cattle. The locals thought that such schemes were crazy as the marsh was "worthless." To them—and others—this was true until oil, natural gas, and sulphur were discovered. Immediately, the coastal plain had value and ownership became an issue, and poorly or inaccurately defined boundaries became the bases for innumerable bitterly contested legal cases. The significance of these land titles was recently called into question yet again, as state and national policy planners begin to systematically define and implement a vast assortment of restoration and rehabilitation efforts.

Since Louisiana's marshlands are eroding and subsiding at a rate measured in a human time scale, not a geologic one, these efforts will require clearly defined property boundaries and ownership. The clarion call for recognition that the wetlands were eroding was initiated in early studies by the state's geological survey office. These reports were ignored and largely forgotten until the early 1970s, when a team of researchers under the direction of Dr. Sherwood Gagliano verified that the marsh was eroding coastwide (Gagliano and Van Beek 1973). To many coastal settlers, particularly persons who were fourth- or fifth-generation wetland dwellers, this was simply too hard to believe. The marsh was too large to "suddenly" begin vanishing. Other investigators became involved, new academic disciplines were created, engineers were consulted, better technology was utilized, and the analyses reached the same inescapable conclusion: the problem was real and growing ever more severe. By the early twenty-first century, marshdwellers, who were children in the late forties and fifties, began guiding reporters and academics to sites that are now underwater. The properties they surveyed with their guests were often outlined by semi-submerged fence posts—vivid reminders of the speed of this transformation.

In the first decade of the twenty-first century, the hurricanes of 2005 and 2008 heightened interest in Louisiana's sea-level citizens and the role wetlands play in protecting these inhabitants. The marsh is now viewed by many as a protective blanket that reduces the inland impact of tropical storms by diminishing the height of the storm surge and, therefore, the severity of this weather event. In the wake of this epiphany came a policy shift from benign neglect to proactive restoration, but, in many cases land ownership issues have to be clarified before this shift can be fully implemented. Given the marshes' historical experience, this is going to be a complex and time-consuming process, and, in the interim, the landscape continues to liquefy and disappear—at great human cost.

In less than five years, damage inflected by successive hurricanes has resulted in staggering personal and financial losses to the families who considered the marshlands

Engineers verses Nature

"We must remember than man's engineering skill are nothing compared with nature's. And we must also recall that today's problems were often yesterday's solutions" (Reuss 1982:148).

home. Many can trace their ancestral connection to the marsh over more than 150 years. As a result of the disasters, as well as governmental red tape making a return to the devastated settlements increasingly difficult, many marshdwellers began to consider leaving their beloved wetlands for higher ground, usually at points along the northern marsh fringe that would allow them easy access to "their" marshes.

In the long run, with sea-level rise projections increasing, coupled with natural subsidence, the coastal plain will be much different in 100 years. However, to the people of this region, radical environmental change constitutes just another complication to their lives. They love the coast and view this environment as their personal space. After all, the coast is not a place, but a process; it becomes a place only when people live there. For too long, the human population of this landscape has been deemed less important than corporate economic concerns.

In actuality, it is the people who give the marshland meaning and justify a great deal of the engineering endeavors being proposed. The fact that the coast is a "people place" gives it topographic significance; otherwise, it would not have any recognizable significance, other than esthetic. Therefore, the coastal denizens are the key factor in defining the geography of the lowlands. Yet, coastal communities are routinely overlooked in governmentally-funded research, perhaps because the human element is not easy to quantify and only after the 2005 and 2008 hurricane seasons did it become clear that socioeconomic issues associated with marshdwellers needed greater attention.

Research into the coastal communities resulting from this increased scrutiny will inevitably determine that the region's cultural landscape has many faces. Each established group has imprinted the territory with its own unique set of cultural variables. These folks—of Indian, European, and Asian ancestry—give Louisiana's near sea level marshes its "personality" while showcasing its human diversity.

Human Induced Change

There is "proof that man, by interfering with nature, has created new conditions of existence in our wet areas, and that further decline is inevitable unless some effort is made to restore the former state. . . ." (Viosca 1928:216).

BIBLIOGRAPHY

Adkins, G. (1972). *A study of the blue crab fishery in Louisiana* (Technical Bulletin No. 3). Baton Rouge, La.: Louisiana Wild Life and Fisheries Commission.

Adkins, G. (1973). Shrimp with a Chinese flavor. *Louisiana Conservationist, 25*(7-8), 20-25.

Alberstadt, M. (1975). Life on an island. *Profile, 14*(4), 19-25.

Aldrich, C. C., M. W., DeBlieux, and F. B. Kniffen. (1943). The Spanish moss industry in Louisiana. *Economic Geography, 19*(4), 347-357. Retrieved January 5, 2006, from JSTOR (http://www.jstor.org/).

Ambrose, P. M. (1965). Sulfur and pyrites. In *U. S. Bureau of Mines, minerals yearbook, 1964. vol. 1* (pp. 1019-1040). Washington, D. C.: U. S. Government Printing Office.

American Geophysical Union. (2006). *Hurricanes and the U. S. Gulf Coast: science and sustainable rebuilding.* Retrieved June 21, 2006, from http://www.agu.org/report/hurricanes/.

American Poland-China Record Association. (1914). *American Poland-China record.* Vol. 64. Retrieved August 6, 2009, from http://books.google.com/books?id=KIIIAQAAIAAJ&pg=PA794&lpg=PA794&dq=%22louisiana+delta+farms%22&source=bl&ots=AOWVjMbnwR&sig=7bMSJChWreqERJt9NwnJTJ3zy_A&hl=en&ei=8kaMSoWFBZCSMe7JxZMO&sa=X&oi=book_result&ct=result&resnum=4#v=onepage&q=%22louisiana%20delta%20farms%22&f=false

Ancelet, B. J. (1999). *From Evangeline hot sauce to Cajun ice: signs of ethnicity in south Louisiana.* Retrieved January 3, 2007, from http://www.louisianafolklife.org/LT/Articles_Essays/main _misc_hot_ sauce.html.

Ancelet, R. (1994). The present status of Louisiana's oyster fishery. *Louisiana Conservationist, 46*(1):11-14.

Anderson, B. (2008). Historic lighthouse threatened: waves lap near steps of beacon. *Baton Rouge Advocate,* (April 30):1B.

Anderson, B., and M. Dunne. (1987). Potential for storm disaster rising. *Baton Rouge Sunday Advocate,* (June 21), 1A; 14A.

Anderson, B. (1987). Future holds bigger hurricanes, longer seasons, experts say. *Baton Rouge Sunday Advocate,* (June 21), 14A.

Anderson, H. H. (1946). Recent developments in pipe-line technology. *American Petroleum Institute Proceedings, 26*(5), 20-25.

Anderson, J. M. (2006). Personal communication, September 8.

Anderson, J. M. (2006B). Personal communication, September 21.

Arpin, S., P. Arpin, and C. Alley. (1999). Reclaimer of the marsh. In E. Toups, J. B. Hebert, L. Hebert, M. H. Smith, P. Heard, and C. Rives (Eds.), *Town of Gueydan: centennial souvenir edition* (pp. 18-21).

Arthur, S. C. (1929). Report of the Division of Wildlife. In *Eighth biennial report of the Department of Conservation of the state of Louisiana, 1926-1928* (pp. 227-324). New Orleans: Department of Conservation.

Arthur, S. C. (1931). *The fur animals of Louisiana.* Baton Rouge: Ramires-Jones Printing Co.

Autin, W. J. (2002). Landscape evolution of the five islands of south Louisiana: scientific policy and salt dome utilization and management. *Geomorphology, 47*(2-4), 227-244.

Babcock, C. O. (1964). Sulfur and pyrites. In *U. S. Bureau of Mines, minerals yearbook, 1963, Vol. 1* (pp. 1075-1096). Washington, D. C.: U. S. Government Printing Office.

Babcock, C. O. and B. I. Stanley. (1963). Sulfur and pyrites. In *U. S. Bureau of Mines, minerals yearbook, 1962. Vol. 1* (pp. 1163-1187). Washington, D. C.: U. S. Government Printing Office.

Bahr, E. (2006). *Grand Isle native is determined to rebuild his home, community.* Retrieved August 30, 2006, from http://www.houmatoday.com/apps/pbcs.dll/article?AID =/20060829/NEWS/608290306.

Bahr, E. (2006B). *Island resident decides to stay.* Retrieved August 30, 2006, from an email.

Bailey, A. M. (1934). Chenier au Tigre. *Louisiana Conservation Review, 4*(2), 9-11.

Baker, M. (1946). Cheniere Caminada comes back. In *Jefferson Parish yearly review* (pp. 110-123). Jefferson, La.: Parish Publications, Inc.

Balize, the. (1992). *Down the road. Features of Plaquemines Parish and Surrounding Areas, 4*(8), 6-14.

Barataria Bay, La., and connecting waters: letter from the secretary of war. (1917). *65th Congress, 1st Session, House Document No. 200,* (House Document, vol. 33, 1917, Serial set 7298). Washington, D. C.: U. S. Government Printing Office.

Barataria La., items. (1866). *New Orleans Daily Picayune ,* (October 28).

Barataria-Terrebonne National Estuary Program. (n.d.). *Healthy estuary, healthy economy, healthy communities.* Retrieved December 6, 2006, from http://www.educators.btnep.org/client_files/video_files/2002_Indicators_Report_LowRes.pdf.

Barker, M. (1986). *A Picture history of Lockport 1835-1985.*

Barnes, K. B. and L. S. McCaslin. (1948). Kerr-McGee, Phillips and Stanolind develop spectacular Gulf of Mexico discovery. *Oil and Gas Journal, 46*(4), 96-9; 113-114.

Barras, J. A., P. E. Bourgeois, and L. R. Handley. (1994). *Land loss in coastal Louisiana 1956-90* (Open File Report 94-01). Washington, D. C.: U. S. National Biological Survey, National Wetlands Research Center.

Barras, J. A., S. Beville, D. Britsch, S. Hartley, S. Hawes, J. Johnston, et al. (2003). *Historical and projected coastal Louisiana land changes: 1978-2050* (Open File Report 03-334). Washington, D. C.: U. S. Geological Survey.

Barrett, B. B. (1970). *Water measurements of coastal Louisiana.* New Orleans: Louisiana Wild Life and Fisheries Commission.

Barrett, B. B. and M. C. Gillespie. (1973). *Primary factors which influence commercial shrimp production in coastal Louisiana* (Technical Bulletin No. 9). New Orleans, La.: Louisiana Wild Life and Fisheries Commission.

Barry, F. (1979). On the wind: island refuges. *New Orleans Times Picayune,* (March 11), (Book 71, M.J. Stevens Collection). Biloxi, Ms: Biloxi Public Library.

Barry, J. M. (1997). *Rising tide: the great Mississippi flood of 1927 and how it changed America.* New York: Simon and Schuster.

Bartlett, Z. W., C. O. Lee, and R. H. Feierabend. (1952). Development and operation of sulphur deposits in the Louisiana marshes. *Mining Engineering Transactions, 4*(August), 775-783.

Barton, D. C. (1930). Petroleum potentialities of Gulf coast petroleum province of Texas and Louisiana. *Bulletin of the American Association of Petroleum Geologists, 14*(11), 1379-1400.

Barton, D. C. and R. H. Goodrich. (1926). The Jennings oil field, Acadia Parish, Louisiana. *Bulletin of the American Association of Petroleum Geologists, 10*(1), 72-92.

Basta, D. J., M. A. Warren, T. R. Goodspeed, C. M. Blackwell, T. J. Culliton, J. J. McDonough III, et al. (1990). *A special NOAA twentieth anniversary report estuaries of the United States vital statistics of a national resource base* (U. S. Department of Commerce, National Oceanic and Atmospheric Administration National Ocean Service). Washington, D. C.: U. S. Government Printing Office.

Baumann, R. H. (1980). *Mechanisms of maintaining marsh elevation in a subsiding environment.* Unpublished Master's thesis, Louisiana State University, Baton Rouge, La.

Baumann,R. H., J. W. Day, Jr., and C. A. Miller. (1984). Mississippi deltaic wetland survival: sedimentation versus coastal submergence. *Science,* 224,1093-1095. Retrieved February 25, 2006, from JSTOR (http://www.jstor.org/).

Bay Ste. Elaine was pioneering property. (1962). *The Freeporter: 50 Years of Progress,* (July), 11.

Becnel, T. A. (1989). *The Barrow family and the Barataria and Lafourche canal: the transportation revolution in Louisiana, 1829-1925.* Baton Rouge, La.: Louisiana State University Press.

Begnaud, A. (1980). The Louisiana sugar cane industry: an overview. In *Green fields: two hundred years of Louisiana sugar* (pp. 29-50). Lafayette, La.: The Center for Louisiana Studies.

Bell, H. W. (1924). Report of Minerals Division. In *Sixth biennial report of the Department of Conservation from January 1, 1922 to December 31, 1923* (pp. 13-22). New Orleans, La.: Department of Conservation.

Bell, H. W. (1927). Report of the Division of Minerals. In *Seventh biennial report of the Department of Conservation 1924-1926* (pp. 19-44). New Orleans, La.: Department of Conservation.

Bergerie, M. (1962, reprinted 2000). *They tasted bayou water: a brief history of Iberia Parish.* Gretna, La.: A Firebird Press Book.

Bergeron, K. (1981). Bohemians link Biloxi, Baltimore as affable rivals. *Sun-Herald,* (January 25), (Book 125, M.J. Stevens Collection). Biloxi, Ms: Biloxi Public Library.

Bernard, S. K. (2001). Far from home. *Louisiana Cultural Vistas, 12*(3), 17.

Bernard, S. K. (2005). Tabasco: Edmund McIlhenny and the birth of a Louisiana pepper sauce. *Louisiana Cultural Vistas, 16*(2), 26-37.

Bertrand, A. L. and C. L. Beale. (1965). *The French and non-French in rural Louisiana: a study of the relevance of ethnic factors to rural development.* (Bulletin No. 606) Baton Rouge, La.: Louisiana State University, Agricultural Experiment Station.

Black, W. J. (1935). Beef cattle especially adapted to Gulf coast area being developed. In *U. S. Department of Agriculture, Yearbook of Agriculture* (pp. 133-136). Washington, D. C.: U. S. Government Printing Office.

Blackstone, F. B. (1949). Power plant expansion for sulphur mine. *Southern Power and Industry 67*(February), 76.

Blankenship, K. (1999). Nutria literally eating other wetland creatures out of house and home. *Chesapeake Bay Journal.* Retrieved June 21, 2006, from http://www.bayjournal.com/article.cfm?article=2118.

Block, W. T. (n.d.). *Early river boats of southwest Louisiana.* Retrieved December 11, 2006, from http://www.wtblock.com/wtblockjr/sailboats.html.

Blum, L. (n.d.). *Dried shrimp industry.* Typescript of a speech made by the author.

Blum, L. (2008). Personal communications, November 20.

Blum, L. (2009). Personal communications, May 19.

Boesch, D. F., M. N. Josselyn, A. J. Mehta, J. T. Morris, W. K. Nuttle, C. A. Simenstad, et al. (1994). Scientific assessment of coastal wetland loss, restoration and management in Louisiana. *Journal of Coastal Research,* (Special Issue No. 20.), 103.

Bolding, G. A. (1969). The New Orleans seaway movement. *Louisiana History, 10*(1), 49-60.

Bonner, J. H. (2007-2008). Louisiana: where land meets water. *Louisiana Cultural Vistas, 18*(4), 40-53.

Bonnot, P. (1932). *The California shrimp industry* (Fisheries Bulletin No. 38). Sacramento: Division of Fish and Game of California, Bureau of Commercial Fisheries.

Borne, L. A. (1945). The longest street in the world. In *Jefferson Parish yearly review* (pp. 177-208). Jefferson, La.: Parish Publications, Inc.

Boumans, R. M., J. Day, and J. W. Day. (1993). High precision measurements of sediment elevation in shallow coastal areas using a sedimentation-erosion table. *Estuaries, 15*, 375-380.

Baumans, R. M. and J. W. Day. (1994). Effects of two Louisiana marsh management plans on water and materials flux and short-term sedimentation. *Wetlands, 14*(4), 247-261.

Bourg, J. A. (1968). *A socio-economic profile of Lafourche Parish.* Unpublished Master's thesis, Louisiana State University, Baton Rouge, La.

Bourne, J. (2000). Louisiana's vanishing wetlands: going, going .... *Science, New Series, 289*(5486), 1860-1863. Retrieved February 25, 2006, from http://www.jstor.org/.

Boutwell, A. P. and G. Folse. (1997). *Terrebonne Parish: a pictorial history book then and now.* Houma, La.: The Courier.

Bowie, H. M. (1935). *Bayou Lafourche.* Unpublished Master's thesis, Louisiana State University, Baton Rouge. La.

Bowler, K. (2008). Life at the end of the road: a journey to Pilottown. *Louisiana Life, 28*(1), 42-47.

Brace, O. L. (1939). Review of developments in 1938, Gulf coast of southeast Texas and Louisiana. *Bulletin of the American Association of Petroleum Geologists, 23*(6), 871-883.

Bradley, V. (1939). The petroleum industry of the Gulf coast salt dome area. *Economic Geography, 15*(4), 395-407

Bradshaw, J. (1997). Early settlers came during days of Spanish rule. *The Daily Advertiser's History of Acadiana, 1*(June 24), 3-4.

Bradshaw, J. (1997B). Chenier au Tigre has romantic history. *The Daily Advertiser's History of Acadiana, 1*(June 24), 6.

Bradshaw, J. (1997C). Was Pecan Island the man-eaters' feasting place? *The Daily Advertiser's History of Acadiana, 1*(June 24), 7.

Bradshaw, J. (1997D). Cajun cowboys were at home on prairies. *The Daily Advertiser's History of Acadiana, 1*(June 24), 15.

Bradshaw, J. (1997E). Rice farming a key to Vermilion Parish. *The Daily Advertiser's History of Acadiana, 1*(June 24), 8.

Branan, W. (1937). Lady luck yields to science in the new bonanza land. *Louisiana Conservation Review,* (Autumn), 7-10.

Branan, W. (1938). Muskrat vs. mink. *Louisiana Conservation Review,* (Winter), 60-65.

Bryant, J. C. and R. H. Chabreck. (1998). Effects of impoundment on vertical accretion of coastal marsh. *Estuaries, 21*(3), 416-422.

Brasseaux, C. A. (1978). Acadien education: from cultural isolation to mainstream America. In G. R. Conrad (Ed.), *The Cajuns, essays on their history and culture* (pp. 212-224). Lafayette, La.: The Center for Louisiana Studies.

Brasseaux, C. A. (1985). Acadian life in the Lafourche country, 1766-1803. In P.D. Uzee (Ed.), *The Lafourche country; the people and the land* (pp. 33-42). Lafayette, La.: The Center for Louisiana Studies.

Brasseaux, C. A. (1987). *The founding of New Acadia: the beginnings of Acadian life in Louisiana, 1796-1803.* Baton Rouge, La.: Louisiana State University Press.

Brasseaux, C. A. (1991). *"Scattered to the wind": dispersal and wanderings of the Acadians, 1755-1809.* Lafayette, La.: The Center for Louisiana Studies.

Brasseaux, C. A. (2006). Personal communications, June 26.

Brassieur, C. R. (1999). *Louisiana boatbuilding: an unfathomed fortune.* Retrieved January 3, 2007, from http://www.louisianafolklife.org/LT/Articles_Essays/creole_art_boatbuild_unfat.html.

Brassieur, C. R. (2007). Personal communications, January 25.

Breaux, J. (1983). Tradition of alligator and fur trapping lives in Louisiana. *Baton Rouge Sunday Advocate,* (October 9), 26C.

Brief history of the Louisiana oyster industry, a. (n.d.). Retrieved October 24, 2006, from http://www.croatians.com/FISH-OYSTER%20HISTORY.html.

Bridaham, L.B. and G.F. Mugnier (1972). *New Orleans and bayou country.* New York, Weathervane Books.

Britsch, L. K. and E. B. Kemp, III. (1990). *Land loss rates: Mississippi River deltaic plain.* (Technical Report GL-90-2). New Orleans: U. S. U. S. Army Engineer District.

Broussard, B. (1977). *A history of St. Mary Parish.* Baton Rouge: Claitor's Publishing Division.

Broel, A. (1937). *When all else fails, it's time to try frog raising.* New Orleans: The American Frog Canning Company.

Browne, T. (1977). *Louisiana Cajuns: Cajuns de la Louisiane.* Baton Rouge, La.: Louisiana State University Press.

Bryson, M. A., Barbot, F. X., Bofinger, J. N, Howard, C. T., and J. S. Clarke. (1871). Act no. 4 incorporating the Louisiana Land Reclamation Company. In *Acts passed by the General Assembly of the state of Louisiana at the first session of the second legislature, begun and held in the city of New Orleans, January 2, 1871* (pp. 88-91). New Orleans, La.: Emile La Sere, State Printer.

BSE a vital proving ground in salt water mining of brimstone. (1959). *The Freeporter, 7*(1), 1-2.

Bultman, B. E. (2002-2003). The final hours on Isle Derniere. *Louisiana Cultural Vistas, 13*(4), 76-88; 90-91; 93.

Bultman, B. E. (2003). The saga of Louisiana rice since 1719. *Louisiana Cultural Vistas, 14*(3), 30-43.

Bultman, B. E. (2004). An ode to the pig; the transformation of a sow's ear into a rich man's feast. *Louisiana Cultural Vistas, 15*(2), 79; 83; 86-91.

Buras, J. P. (1996). *Way down yonder in Plaquemines.* Gretna, La.: Pelican Publishing Company.

Burdeau, C. (2004). Imports affect industry: locals' profits don't reflect shrimp boom. *Baton Rouge Advocate,* (March 16), 1C, 2C.

Burdeau, C. (2006). Katrina changed life on the river: navigational aids, Pilottown obliterated; Mississippi channel altered. *Baton Rouge Advocate,* (March 6), 1A, 4A.

Burdeau, C. (2009). Report: nutria efforts pays off. *Baton Rouge Advocate,* (July 17), 10B.

Burdeau, C . (2007). Study finds La. slowly sliding into Gulf. *Baton Rouge Advocate,* (January 2), 2B.

Burke, M. (2002). Louisiana's callinectes sapidus. *Louisiana Conservationist, 54*(4), 7-9.

Burke, M. (2005). A changing landscape. *Louisiana Conservationist, 58*(6), 14-21.

Burkenroad, M. D. (1931). Notes on the Louisiana conch, *Thais haemostoma Linn.,* in its relation to the oyster *Ostrea virginica. Ecology, 12*(4), 656-664. Retrieved February 25, 2006, from JSTOR (http://www.jstor.org/).

Burns, H. S. (1934). Building Grande Ecaille. *Chemical Industry, 34*(6), 503-506.

Burns, H. S. (1938). Industry on stilts; constructing an industrial city on useless tidal marsh. *Scientific American, 158*(February), 69-71.

Burst, D. (2005). Louisiana lighthouses: our forgotten treasures. part 1. *Louisiana Conservationist, 58*(3), 4-7.

Burst, D. (2005B). Louisiana lighthouses: our forgotten treasures. part 2. *Louisiana Conservationist, 58*(4), 22-25.

Burts, H. M. and Carpenter, C. W. (1975). *A guide to hunting in Louisiana: the hunter's paradise.* New Orleans: Louisiana Wild Life and Fisheries Commission.

Bush, L., and L. A. Wiltz. (1878). Act no. 52 incorporating the Louisiana Land Reclamation Company. In *Acts passed by the General Assembly of the state of Louisiana at the second session of the fifth legislature, begun and held in the City of New Orleans, January 7, 1878, and at the extra session, convened at the city of New Orleans, March 8, 1878* (pp. 88-91). New Orleans, La: Emile La Sere, State Printer.

Buskey, N. (2009). Demand for nutria pelts fades away. *The Daily Comet,* (March 22). Retrieved April 6, 2009, from http://www.dailycomet.com/article/20090322/ARTICLES/903221014/-1/OPINION?Title=Demand-for-nutria-pelts-fades-away.

Buskey, N. (2009). They're the last of the swamp-rat skinners. *The Daily Comet,* (March 22). Retrieved April 6, 2009, from http://www.dailycomet.com/article/20090322/ARTICLES/903221013.

Butler, J. T., Jr. (1985). Bayou Lafourche boats. In P. D. Uzee (Ed.), *The Lafourche country; the people and the land* (pp. 164-169). Lafayette: The Center for Louisiana Studies.

Butler, J. T., Jr. (2000). Wooden boats: refashioning history. *Louisiana Conservationist, 42*(4), 18-21.

Butler, W. E. (1980). *Down among the sugar cane: the story of Louisiana sugar plantations and their railroads.* Baton Rouge, La.: Moran Publishing Corporation.

By yellow magic of sulphur here: forty-five miles from Canal Street, industrial miracle appears. (1937). *New Orleans Times Picayune,* (January 25), 18B.

Cable, G. W. (1886). *The Creoles of Louisiana.* New York: Charles Scribner's Sons.

Cable, G. W. (1889). *Strange true stories of Louisiana.* New York: Charles Scribner's Sons..

Cagle, R. B. 1967. Formative years. In Millet, D. J. (Ed.), *The centennial history of Lake Charles, 1867-1967* (pp. 1-5). Lake Charles, La.: Lake Charles Letter Shop.

Cahoon, D. R. and R. E. Turner. (1989). Accretion and canal impacts in a rapidly subsiding wetland II, Feldspar marker horizon techniques. *Estuaries, 12*(4), 260-268.

Cahoon, D. R., P. E. Martin, B. K. Black, and J. C. Lynch. (2000). A method for measuring vertical accretion, elevation, and compaction of soft, shallow-water sediments. *Journal of sedimentary research, 70*(5), 1250-1253.

Caillou Island House. (1854). *Thibodaux Minerva*, (May 6), 1; col. 2.

Calio, A. J. (1987). Defining the estuary. *EPA Journal, 13*(6), 9-11.

Cameron Parish Development Board. (1960). *Cameron Parish resources and facilities*. Baton Rouge, La.: State of Louisiana Department of Public Works Planning Division.

Camille strikes homes, properties. (1969). *The Freeporter, 16*(71), 1, 7-10.

Camillo, C. A. and M. T. Pearcy. (2004). *Upon their shoulders: a history of the Mississippi River Commission from its inception through the advent of the modern Mississippi River and tributaries project* (Second edition, 2006). Vicksburg, Ms.: Mississippi River Commission.

Campanella, R. (2006). *Geographies of New Orleans: urban fabrics before the storm*. Lafayette, La.: The Center for Louisiana Studies.

Campanella, R.. (2007). Chinatown New Orleans. *Louisiana Cultural Vistas 18*(3), 50-57.

Campbell, M. (1999). History of the Gueydan airport. In E. Toups, J. B. Hebert, L. Hebert, M. H. Smith, P. Heard, and C. Rives (Eds.), *Town of Gueydan: centennial souvenir edition* (pp. 82-83).

Campbell, T. W. (1914). Oysters. In *Biennial report of the Department of Conservation from September 1ˢᵗ 1912 to April 1ˢᵗ 1914* (pp. 111-128). New Orleans, La.: Department of Conservation.

Capooth, W. (2006). *Tally Ho hunting and fishing club oldest in the U. S.* Retrieved March 28, 2007, from http://www.deltafarmpress.com/mag/farming_tally_ho_hunting/.

Cappiello, D. (2006). What lies beneath. *Houston Chronicle*, (November 12), A1; A8

Carleton, D. A. (1974). The minerals industry of Louisiana. In *U. S. Bureau of Mines, minerals yearbook, 1972. vol. 2.* (pp. 315-334). Washington, D. C.: U. S. Government Printing Office.

Carmen shuts down all sulphur operations. (1974). *The Freeporter, 21*(5), 1, 4-5.

Carrigan, J. A. (1963). Impacts of epidemic yellow fever on life in Louisiana. *Louisiana History, 4*(1), 5-34.

Carroll, R. (2008). Personal communications, January 30.

Carruth, T. J. (1979). *Tales of old Louisiana*. Lafayette, La.: The Center for Louisiana Studies.

Carter, H. D. (1968). Come one, come all to explore the treasures of the past and present in Chenier Perdue - Little Chenier - and Creole. Typescript.

Casada, J. (1996). The old man's boy in Louisiana. *Louisiana Conservationist, 48*(1), 16-19.

Case, G. C. (1973). *The Bayou Chene story: a history of the Atchafalaya basin and its people*. Detroit: The Harlo Press.

Casey, P. A. (1983). *Encyclopedia of forts, posts, named camps and other military installations in Louisiana, 1700-1981*. Baton Rouge, La.: Claitor's Publishing Division.

Casmier, S. (1991). Dedicated take boat to polls. *New Orleans Times-Picayune*, (November 17), B1-B2.

Castay, H. J., Jr. (2006). *The cypress industry: a tribute to what once was*. Retrieved October 11, 2006, from http://www.businessnewsonline.com/%20Web%20Site%20Files/Feature_Business/The_.

Cavendish, R. A. E. (1948). About Zebu cattle from India and the U. S. A. Gulf Coast. *Cattleman, 14*(6), 5-8.

Chabreck, R. H. (1972). *Vegetation, water and soil characteristics of the Louisiana coastal region. Agricultural Experiment Station* (Bulletin No. 664, pp. 72). Baton Rouge, La.: Louisiana State University

Chabreck, R. H. (1988). *Coastal marshes: ecology and wildlife management*. Minneapolis, Mn.: University of Minnesota Press.

Chamberlain, O. (1942). Island inventory. In *Jefferson Parish yearly review* (pp. 50-64). Jefferson, La.: Parish Publications, Inc.

Chambers, H. E. (1922). Early commercial prestige of New Orleans. *Louisiana Historical Quarterly, V* (October), 456-457.

Chandeleur Island completely torn up, lighthouse toppling over and abandoned. (1893). *New Orleans Daily Picayune*, (October 7), 1; col. 2. (Book 71, M.J. Stevens Collection). Biloxi, Ms.: Biloxi Public Library.

Chapelle, H. I. (1951). *American small sailing craft: their design, development, and construction*. New York: W.W. Norton & Company.

Chapman, C. R. (1959). Oyster drill (*Thais haemastoma*) predation in Mississippi Sound, 1958. *Proceedings of the National Shellfish Association, 49,* 87-97.

Chatry. M. and D. Chew. (1985). Freshwater diversion in coastal Louisiana: recommendations for development of management criteria. In C. F. Bryan, P. J. Zwank, and R. H. Chabreck (Eds.), *Proceedings of the fourth coastal marsh and estuary management symposium* (pp. 71-84).

Chatterton, H. J. (1944). The muskrat fur industry of Louisiana. *The Journal of Geography, 43*(2), 185-195.

Chenier Hurricane Centennial. (1994). *Réfléchir: les images des prairies tremblantes: 1840-1940.* Cut Off, La.: Chenier Hurricane Centennial.

Chenier Hurricane Centennial. (1995). *Réfléchir II: les décades: 1860-1960.* Cut Off, La.: Chenier Hurricane Centennial.

Chenier Hurricane Centennial. (1997). *Réfléchir III: épervier du memoire du bayou: a castnet of bayou memories.* Cut Off, La.: Chenier Hurricane Centennial.

Cheniere's priest tells sad story. (1893). *The Weekly Thibodaux Sentinel,* (October 14). Thibodaux, La.: Nicholls State University Archives.

Cheramie, B. (1997). *Louisiana lures and legends.* Golden Meadow, La.: REM Corporation.

Child labor and the work of mothers in oyster and shrimp canning communities on the Gulf coast. (1922). (Bureau Publication, No. 98. Washington, D. C.). In Stein, L. (Advisory ed.), *Suffer the little children: two children's bureau bulletins.* (1977). New York: Arno Press.

Chisholm W. F. (1929). Report of the division of minerals. In *Eighth biennial report of the Department of Conservation of the state of Louisiana, 1926-1928* (pp. 107-181). New Orleans, La.: Department of Conservation.

Christ, C. J. (2001). War in the Gulf: "swamp angels" conducted rescues in south Louisiana. *The Courier, Houma* (April 1). Retrieved June 23, 2005, from http://www.crt.state.la.us./crt/tourism/lawwill/courier_articles/swamp_angels.html.

China camp. (2006). Retrieved November 3, 2006, from http://www.cr.nps.gov/history/online_books/5views/5views3h19.html.

Christmas, J. Y. and D. J. Etzold (Eds.). (1977). *The shrimp fishery of the Gulf of Mexico, United States: a regional management plan.* Ocean Springs, Ms: Gulf Coast Research Laboratory.

Chung Fat platform. (2006). Retrieved November 3, 2006, from. http://www.nutrias.org/photos/grandisle/8.html.

Church, J. A., J. M. Gregory , P. Huybrechts, M. Kuhn, K. Lambeck, M. T. Nhuan, D. Qin, and P. L. Woodworth (2001). Changes in sea level. In T. Houghton, Y. Ding, D. J Griggs, M. Noguer, P. J. Van der Linden, and D. Xiaou (Eds.), *Climate change 2001: The scientific basis is the most comprehensive and up-to-date scientific assessment of past, present and future climate change* (pp. 639-694). Cambridge: Cambridge University Press.

Cipra, D. L. (1976*). Lighthouses and lightships of the Northern Gulf of Mexico.* Washington, D. C.: Department of Transportation, U. S. Coast Guard.

Clark, J. G. (1967). New Orleans and the river: a study in attitudes and responses. *Louisiana History, 8*(2), 117-135.

Claudel, C. (1945). Spanish folktales from Delacroix, Louisiana. *The Journal of American Folklore, 58*(229), 208-224. Retrieved March 6, 2006, from JSTOR (http://www.jstor.org/).

Clay, C. L. (1938). The Louisiana seafood industry. *Louisiana Conservation Review* (Autumn), 45-47.

Coalition to Restore Coastal Louisiana. (1989). *Coastal Louisiana: here today gone tomorrow?* Baton Rouge, La.: Coalition to Restore Coastal Louisiana.

Coalition to Restore Coastal Louisiana. (2000). *No time to lose: facing the future of Louisiana and the crisis of coastal land loss.* Baton Rouge, La.: Coalition to Restore Coastal Louisiana.

Coastal Louisiana. (2007). Retrieved April 13, 2007, from http://www.biology.usgs.gov/s+t/SNT/noframe/gc138.html.

Coastal protection and restoration authority integrated planning team. (2006). Comprehensive coastal protection master plan for Louisiana, preliminary draft. Baton Rouge, LA.: Louisiana Department of Natural Resources.

Coastal restoration builds on coastal science. (2007). *Water Marks, 35*(August), 1-15.

Cobb, W.F. (1946). Brahman cattle in the south. *Southern Agriculture, 76*(2), 11.

Coker, R. E. (1920). The diamond-back terrapin: past, present, and future. *The Scientific Monthly, 11*(2), 171-186.

Cole, G. (1892). An island outing. *New Orleans Daily Picayune,* (September 25), 12.

Cole, G. (1892B). The Cheniere Caminada: a visit to an old pirate village. *New Orleans Daily Picayune,* (October 2), 2; col. 1-3.

Coleman, J. M. (1966). *Recent coastal sedimentation: central Louisiana coast* (Technical Report No. 17). Baton Rouge, La.: Coastal Studies Institute, Louisiana State University.

Coleman, J. M. (1988). Dynamic changes and processes in the Mississippi River delta. *Bulletin of the Geological Society of America, 100*(July), 999-101.

Collins, J. W. and H. M. Smith. (1893). A Statistical Report on the Fisheries of the Gulf States. In *Bulletin of the United States fish commission, vol. 11 for 1891* (52nd Congress, 2d Session, House Miscellaneous Document, Number 112, pp. 93-184). Washington, D. C.: U. S. Government Printing Office.

Comeaux, M. L., (1972). Atchafalaya swamp life, settlement and folk occupations. Baton Rouge, La.: School of Geosciences, Geoscience Publications.

Comeaux, M. L. (1978). Louisiana's Acadians: the environmental impact. In G. R. Conrad (Ed.), *The Cajuns: essays on their history and culture* (pp. 142-160). Lafayette, La.: The Center for Louisiana Studies.

Comeaux, M. L. (1978B). Origin and evolution of Mississippi river fishing craft. *Pioneer America, 10*, 73-92.

Comeaux, M. L. (1985). Folk boats of Louisiana. In N. R. Spitzer (Ed.), *Louisiana folklife: a guide to the state* (pp. 161-178). Baton Rouge, La.: Moran Colorgraphics, Inc.

Comeaux, M. L. (1989). The Cajun barn. *Geographical Review, 79*(1), 47-62. Retrieved February 25, 2006, from JSTOR (http://www.jstor.org/).

Comeaux, M. L. (1999). *Introduction and use of accordions in Cajun music.* Retrieved January 3, 2007, from http://www.louisianafolklife.org/LT/Articles_Essays/intro_and_use_of_accordions.html.

Commercial value of 1928-1929 fur crop greatest ever harvested. (1929). *Louisiana Conservation News, 4*(4), 19-20.

Committee on Coastal Erosion Zone Management, Water Science and Technology Board, Marine Board, Commission on Engineering and Technical Systems and National Research Council. (1990). *Managing coastal erosion.* Washington, D. C.: National Academy Press.

Conrad, G. R. (1978). The Acadians: myths and realities. In G.R. Conrad (Ed.), *The Cajuns: essays on their history and culture* (pp. 1-20). Lafayette, La.: The Center for Louisiana Studies.

Conrad, G. R. and C. A. Brasseaux. (1994). *Crevasse! The 1927 flood in Acadiana.* Lafayette, La.: The Center for Louisiana Studies.

Conrad, G. R. and R. F. Lucas. (1995). *White gold: a brief history of the Louisiana sugar industry, 1795-1995.* Lafayette, La.: The Center for Louisiana Studies.

Conservation of Wild Life. (1914). In *Report of the conservation commission of Louisiana from April 1ˢᵗ 1912 to April 1ˢᵗ 1914* (pp. 47-62). New Orleans, La.: Palfrey-Rodd-Pursell Co., Ltd.

Constanza, R., R. d'Arge, R. de Groot, S. Farber, M. Grasso, B. Hannon, et al. (1998). The value of the world's ecosystem services and natural capital. *Ecological Economics, 25*, 3-15.

Constanza, R., W. J. Mitsch, and J. W. Day, Jr. (2006). A new vision for New Orleans and the Mississippi delta: applying ecological economics and ecological engineering. *Ecological Environment, 4*(9), 465-472.

Conte, R.L. (1967). The Germans in Louisiana in the eighteenth century (translated and edited by G. R. Conrad). *Louisiana History, 8*(1), 67-84.

Conner, W. H. and J. W. Day, Jr. (1976). Productivity and composition of a bald cypress-water tupelo site and a bottomland hardwood site in a Louisiana swamp. *American Journal of Botany, 63*(10), 1354-1364. Retrieved October 11, 2006, from JSTOR (http://www.jstor.org/).

Conner, W. H. and K Flynn. (1989). Growth and survival of baldcypress (*Taxodium distichum* (L.) Rich.) planted across a flooding gradient in a Louisiana bottomland forest. *Wetlands, 9*(2), 207-217.

Coreil, P. (2007). Personal communications, July 6.

Cortez, M. L. and L. R. Rybiski. (1980). *Memories: a story of Raceland & Bowie.* Olathe, Ks: Cookbook Publishers and the Raceland Jaycees.

Cost of doing nothing, the. (1999). *Watermarks*, (Summer), 3-11.

Cottman, E. V. (1939). Louisiana furs to the fore. *Louisiana Conservation Review, 8*(Autumn), 35-38.

Cowan, J. H., Jr., R. E. Turner, and D. R. Cahoon. (1988). Marsh management plans in practice: do they work in coastal Louisiana, USA? *Environmental Management, 12*(1), 37-53.

Cowdrey, A. E. (1977). *Land's end a history of the New Orleans district, U. S. Army Corps of Engineers, and its lifelong battle with the lower Mississippi and other rivers wending their way to the sea.* New Orleans, La.: U. S. Army Corps of Engineers, New Orleans District.

Craig, N. J., R. E. Turner, and J. W. Day, Jr. (1979). Land loss in coastal Louisiana (USA). *Environmental Management, 3*(2), 133-144.

Cramer, D. (2006). *Baymen, the point, the bay, the people.* Retrieved November 15, 2006, from http://www. baymen.org/.

Crandall, M. E. and J. L. Lindsey. (1981). Establishment of controlled freshwater diversion of the Mississippi river into Louisiana coastal zone. In R. D. Cross and D. L. Williams (Eds.), *Proceedings of the national symposium on freshwater inflow of estuaries* (pp. 138-146). Washington, D. C.: Fish and Wildlife Service.

Crété, L. (1981). *Daily life in Louisiana 1815-1830* (translated and edited by P. Gregory from the original *La Vie quotidienne en Louisiane, 1815-1830*, published in 1978 by Hachette). Baton Rouge, La.: Louisiana State University Press.

Crossett, K. M., T. J. Culliton, P. C. Wiley, and T. R. Goodspeed. (2004). *Population trends along the coastal United States: 1980-2008*. U. S. Department of Commerce, National Oceanic and Atmospheric Administration National Ocean Service. Washington, D. C.: U. S. Government Printing Office.

Culliton, T. J., M. A. Warren, T. R. Goodspeed, D. G. Remer, C. M. Blackwell, and J. J. McDonough, III. (1990). *50 years of population change along the nation's coasts 1960-2010*. Rockville, Md: Strategic Assessment Branch, Ocean Assessments Division, Office of Oceanography and Marine Assessment, National Ocean Service, National Oceanic and Atmospheric Administration.

Cunningham, W. A. (1935). Sulphur. *Journal of Chemical Education, 12*(1), 17-23.

Curry, J. Jr. (2003). 100 years later—still flying high. *Louisiana Conservationist, 55*(2), 4-7.

Curry, M.G. and J.E. Leemann. (1978). *Coastal parish management program second year planning study Terrebonne Parish, Louisiana*. Prepared for the Terrebonne Parish Coastal Advisory Committee Metairie, Louisiana: VTN Louisiana, Inc.

Cypress, wood eternal lumber industry was once king here. (1991). *Daily Review,* (March 5).

Dabney, T. E. (1944). Taming the Mississippi. In *Jefferson Parish yearly review* (pp. 44-52). Jefferson, La.: Parish Publications, Inc.

Dahl, T. E. (1990). *Wetlands losses in the United States 1780s to 1980s*. Washington, D. C.: U. S. Department of the Interior, Fish and Wildlife Service.

Daspit, A. P. (1930). Report of the fur and wild life division. In *State of Louisiana Department of Conservation sixteenth biennial report, 1942-1943* (pp. 89-111). New Orleans, La.: Department of Conservation.

Daspit, A. P. (1944). Report of the fur and wild life division. In *State of Louisiana Department of Conservation ninth biennial report, 1928-1929* (pp. 91-131). New Orleans, La.: Department of Conservation.

Daspit, A. P. (1946). Fur and refuge division. In *Department of Wild Life and Fisheries first biennial report, 1944-1945* (pp. 165-182). New Orleans, La.: Department of Wild Life and Fisheries.

Daspit, A. P. (1948). Fur and refuge division. In *Department of Wild Life and Fisheries second biennial report, 1946-1947* (pp. 267-289). New Orleans, La.: Department of Wild Life and Fisheries.

Daspit, A. P. (1948B). Louisiana's fur industry. *Louisiana Conservationist, 1*(2), 17-19.

Daspit, A. P. (1949). Fur harvest begins. *Louisiana Conservationist, 2*(3), 17-19.

Daspit, A. P. (1950.) "Migrating" nutria. *Louisiana Conservationist, 2*(5), 7-8.

Dauenhauer, J. B. Jr. (1934). Report of the Division of Fisheries. In *Eleventh biennial report of the Department of Conservation state of Louisiana, 1932-1933* (pp.161-217). New Orleans, La.: Department of Conservation.

Dauenhauer, J. B. Jr. (1938). Shrimp: an important industry of Jefferson Parish. In *Jefferson Parish yearly review* (pp. 109-131). Jefferson, La.: Parish Publications, Inc.

Davis, D. W. (1973). Louisiana canals and their influence on wetland development. Unpublished doctoral dissertation. Louisiana State University, Baton Rouge, La.

Davis, D. W. (1975). Logging canals: a distinct pattern of the swamp landscape in south Louisiana. *Forest and People, 25*(1), 14-17; 33-35.

Davis, D. W. (1976). Trainasse. Association of American Geographers, *Annals, 66*(3), 349-359.

Davis, D.W. (1977). Land-use research, one approach to coastal settlement. In H. J. Walker (Ed.), *Research techniques in coastal environments* (pp. 311-320). Baton Rouge, La.: School of Geoscience, Geoscience Publications.

Davis, D. W. (1978). Wetlands trapping in Louisiana. In S. B. Hilliard (Ed.), *Man and environment in the lower Mississippi Valley* (pp. 81-92). Baton Rouge, La.: School of Geoscience, Geoscience Publications.

Davis, D.W. (1980). New Orleans drainage and reclamation a 200 year problem. *Zeitschrift fur Geomorphology, Suppl.-Bd, 34*, 87-96.

Davis, D. W. (1981). Cattle grazing in Louisiana's coastal zone. In *Proceedings of the specialty group on marine geography, 1979-1980* (pp. 42-50). Thibodaux, La.: Nicholls State University.

Davis, D. W. (1985). Canals of the Lafourche Country. In P.D. Uzee (Ed.), *The Lafourche Country; the people and the land* (pp. 150-164). Lafayette, La.: The Center for Louisiana Studies.

Davis, D. W. (1986). Venice and New Orleans: two sinking cities. *Thalassas, 4*(1), 49-56.

Davis, D. W. (1990). Socioeconomic impacts associated with mineral exploration: Louisiana versus other mineral-producing states. *The International Journal of Social Education, 5*(2), 63-76.

Davis, D. W. (1991). Oil in the northern Gulf of Mexico. In H. D. Smith and A. Vallega (Eds.), *The development of integrated sea-use management* (pp. 139-152). New York: Routledge.

Davis, D. W. (1992). Canals and the southern Louisiana landscape. In D. G. Janelle, (Ed.), *Geographical snapshots of North American* (pp. 375-379).

New York: The Guilford Press.

Davis, D. W. (1992B). A pictorial and historical review of Louisiana's barrier islands. In J. Williams, S. Penland and A. Sallenger (Eds.), *Louisiana Barrier Island erosion study: atlas of shoreline changes in Louisiana from 1853 to 1989 U. S. Geological Survey miscellaneous investigation series 1-2150-A.* (pp. 8-23).

Davis, D. W. (2000). Historical perspective on crevasses, levees, and the Mississippi river. In C. E. Colton (Ed.), *Transforming New Orleans and its environs* (pp. 84-106). Pittsburgh, Pa.: University of Pittsburgh Press.

Davis, D. W. and J. L. Place. (1983). *The oil and gas industry of coastal Louisiana and its effect on land use and socioeconomic patterns* (Open File Report 83-118). Reston, Va.: U. S. Department of the Interior, U. S. Geological Survey.

Davis, D. W. and R. A. Detro. (1975). *Presence growth trends and environmental effects of Louisiana's wetland settlements.* Unpublished manuscript.

Davis, D. W. and R. A. Detro. (1992). *Fire and brimstone: the history of melting Louisiana's sulphur.* (Resource Information Series No. 8). Baton Rouge, La.: Louisiana Geological Survey.

Davis, E. A. (1959). *Louisiana the pelican state.* Baton Rouge, La.: Louisiana State University Press..

Davis, F. (1973). The outlaw is back in style. *Louisiana Conservationist, 25*(1,2), 26-30.

Davis, R. (1981). National strategic petroleum reserve. *Science, 213*(4508), 618-622.

Davis, J.H. (1971). Influences of man upon the coastline. In T.R. Detwyler (Ed.), *Man's Impact on Environment* (pp. 332-347). New York: McGraw Hill.

Davis, J. and L. Posey, Jr. (n.d.). *Relative selectivity of freshwater commercial fishing devices used in Louisiana.* Baton Rouge, La.: Louisiana Wild Life and Fisheries Commission.

Davis, M. (2006). Personal communications, February 4.

Davis, M. (2006B). *Planning for the future of South Louisiana, its coast and its communities: a position paper of the Coalition to Restore Coastal Louisiana, July 20..*

Day, J. W. and P. H. Template. (1989). Consequences of sea level rise: implication from the Mississippi delta. *Coastal Management, 17*(3), 241-257.

Dean, C. (2007). Will warming lead to a rise in hurricanes. *The New York Times,* (May 29), F1, F4.

Deegan, L. A., H. M. Kennedy, and C. Neill. (1984). Natural factors and human modifications contributing to marsh loss in Louisiana Mississippi river deltaic plain. *Environmental Management, 8*(6), 519-528.

Degraff, J. and T. Gresham. (2002). A hard shell to crack: the problems facing the Louisiana shrimping industry. *Louisiana Conservationist, 54*(4), 4-6.

DeGrummond, J. L. (1961). *The Baratarians and the battle of New Orleans.* Baton Rouge, La.: Legacy Publishing Company.

DeLaune, R. D., A. Jugsujinda, G. W. Peterson, and W. H. Patrick. (2003). Impact of Mississippi river freshwater reintroduction on enhancing marsh accretionary processes in a Louisiana estuary. *Estuarine, Coastal and Shelf Science, 58*(3), 653-662.

DeLaune, R. D., R. H. Baumann, and J. G. Gosselink. (1983). Relationships among vertical accretion, coastal submergence, and erosion in a Louisiana Gulf coast marsh. *Journal of Sedimentary Petrology, 53*(1), 147-157.

Dennett, D. (1876). *Louisiana as it is.* New Orleans, La.: Eureka Press.

Description of Louisiana. (1803). In *7ᵗʰ Congress, 1st Session, American State Papers, No. 164* (Miscellaneous, vol. 1, pp. 344-356). Washington, D. C.: U. S. Government Printing Office.

Detro, R. A. (1970). *Generic terms in the place names of Louisiana: an index to the cultural landscape.* Unpublished Ph.D. Dissertation, Louisiana State University, Baton Rouge, La.

Detro, R. A. and D. W. Davis. (1974). *Louisiana marsh settlement succession: a preliminary report. Paper read before Association of American Geographers.* Unpublished manuscript.

Deussen, A. (1923). Development of Gulf coast field. *Oil and Gas Journal, 22*(12), 100-102; 112.

Deutschman, P. (1949). They danced till they died. *Coronet, 25*(January):143-145.

Diamond, A.W. (1973). *Cameron's gold: gas, oil and wildlife.* Unpublished term paper. Lake Charles, La.: McNeese State University.

Diamond, J. (2005). *Collapse: how societies choose to fail or succeed.* New York: Penguin Books.

Did you know. (1917). *Abbeville Meridional,* (September 22).

Dillard, J. L. (1985). Languages and linguistic research in Louisiana. In N. R. Spitzer (Ed.), *Louisiana folklife: a guide to the state* (pp. 35-47). Baton Rouge, La.: Moran Colorgraphics, Inc.

Din, G. C. (1980). *Cimarrones* and the San Malo Band in Spanish Louisiana. *Louisiana History, 21*(3), 237-262.

Din, G. C. (1986). The Canary Islander settlements of Spanish Louisiana: an overview. *Louisiana History, 27*(4), 353-373.

Din, G. C. (1988). *The Canary islanders of Louisiana.* Baton Rouge, La.: Louisiana State University Press.

Ditto, T. B. (1980). *The longest street: a story of Lafourche Parish and Grand Isle.* Baton Rouge, La.: Moran Publishing Corporation.

Ditton, R. B. and J. Auyong. (1984). *Fishing offshore platforms, central Gulf of Mexico: An analysis of recreational and commercial fishing use at 164 major offshore petroleum structures* (OCS Monograph MMS 84−0006). Washington, D. C.: Minerals Management Service, Gulf of Mexico Regional Office.

Doak, J. (1963). Here's how one company handles liquid-sulfur distribution. *Oil and Gas Journal, 61*(25), 101-102.

Dolan, R. and H. G. Goodell. (1986). Sinking cities. *American Scientist, 74*(1), 38-47.

Dormon, J. H. (1983). *The people called Cajuns: an introduction to an ethnohistory.* Lafayette, La.: The Center for Louisiana Studies.

Doughty, R. W. (1975). *Feather fashions and bird preservation: a study in nature protection.* Berkeley, Ca.: University of California Press.

Dozier, H. L. and F. G. Ashbrook. (1950). A practical drying frame for nutria pelts. *Louisiana Conservationist, 3*(2), 16-18.

Dr. Douglas Duperier. (1915). *Abbeville Meridional,* (June 19).

Dranguet, C. A. Jr. and R. J. Heleniak. (1985). Back door to the Gulf: the Pass Manchac region, 1699-1863. *Regional Dimensions, 3,* 1-25.

Drilling on land contrasted with barge drilling in semimarsh field. (1942). *Oil and Gas Journal, 41*(December 3), 59.

Duffy, M. and Hoffpauer, C. (1966). History of waterfowl management. *Louisiana Conservationist, 18*(7,8), 6-11.

Dugan, P. (Ed.). (1993). *Wetlands in danger: a world conservation atlas.* New York: Oxford University Press.

Dugas, R. J. (1977). *Oyster distribution and density on the productive portion of state seed grounds in southeastern Louisiana.* New Orleans, La.: Louisiana Wild Life and Fisheries.

Dunbar, G. S. (1974). Geographical personality. In H.J. Walker (Ed.), *Man and cultural heritage* (pp. 25-33). Baton Rouge, La.: School of Geoscience, Geoscience Publications.

Dunbar, J. B., L. D. Britsch, and E. B. Kemp, III. (1992). *Land loss rates: report 3, Louisiana coastal plain* (Technical Report GL-90-2). New Orleans, La.: U. S. Army Corps of Engineers, New Orleans District.

Dunne, M. (1987). Louisiana evacuation plans untested. *Baton Rouge Sunday Advocate,* (June 21), 14A.

Dunne, M. (2006). La hurricanes—storms link past, present future—past: some towns disappeared after being pummeled by natural disasters. *Baton Rouge Advocate,* (February 26), 1A; 12A.

Dunne, M.. (2006B). Studies point to rising oceans: Raton Rouge could be coast by year 250". *Baton Rouge Advocate,* (March 27), 1B-2B.

Dunne, M. (2006C). Rita yields valuable data: USGS sensors track storm surge. *Baton Rouge Advocate,* (October 30), 1B-2B.

Eads: the men and the community. (1992). *Down the Road: Features of Plaquemines Parish and Surrounding Areas, 4*(8), 33-39.

Earth Search. (1995). *Cultural resources investigations on Grand Terre island, Jefferson Parish, Louisiana. Cultural Resources Series* (Report Number: COELMN/PD-95/05). New Orleans, La.: U. S. Army Corps of Engineers, New Orleans District.

Echeverria, D. (1991). *A history of Billingsgate.* Wellfleet, Ma.: The Wellfleet Historical Society.

Edred, J. S. and M. R. Johnson. (1965). Developments in Louisiana Gulf coast in 1964. *Bulletin of the American Association of Petroleum Geologists, 49*(6), 771-782.

Edwards, J. D. (1988). *Louisiana's remarkable French vernacular architecture 1700-1900.* Baton Rouge, La.: Department of Geography and Anthropology, Louisiana State University.

Eilertsen, D. E., (1969). Sulfur and pyrites. In *U. S. Bureau of Mines, minerals yearbook, 1968. vol. 1-2* (pp. 1049-1060). Washington, D. C.: U. S. Government Printing Office.

Ellet, C. Jr. (1852). Report on the overflows of the delta of the Mississippi, Senate Executive Document No. 26. In *22nd Congress, 1st session* (pp. 1-106). Washington, D. C.: U. S. Government Printing Office.

Elliott, D. O. (1932). In *The improvement of the lower Mississippi River for flood control and navigation. vol. 1* (pp. 1-158). Vicksburg, Ms.: U. S. Army Corps of Engineers, Waterways Experiment Station.

Elliott, D. O. (1932B). In *The improvement of the Lower Mississippi River for flood control and navigation. vol. 2* (pp. 159-331). Vicksburg, Ms: U. S. Army Corps of Engineers, Waterways Experiment Station.

Ellis, T. H. (n.d.). *Account of the storm on Last Island.* (Typed copy, Butler (Louise) writings, box 5, folder 2, no. 1069, S-19-21). Baton Rouge, La.: Hill Memorial Library, South Reading Room, Louisiana State University.

Ellzey, B. (2006). Terrebonne trappers were tops in the nation in 1925. *The Courier.*

Elsey, R. (2005). Managing the 'gator. *Louisiana Conservationist, 58*(5), 8-12.

Emmer, R. E. (1971). *Dutch polders and Louisiana reclamation.* Unpublished manuscript.

Engle, J. B. (1948). *Investigations of the oyster reefs of Mississippi, Louisiana, and Alabama following the hurricane of September 19, 1947* (Special Science Report 59). U. S. Department of the Interior, Fish and Wildlife Service.

Ensminger, A. (1967). They ply the marsh. *Louisiana Conservationists, 19*(9-10), 8-9.

Espina, M. E. (1988). *Filipinos in Louisiana.* New Orleans, La.: A.F. LaBorde and Sons.

Estaville, L. E., Jr. (1987). Changeless Cajuns: nineteenth-century reality or myth?. *Louisiana History, 28*(2), 117-140.

Evans, J. (1970). *About nutria and their control* (Resource Publication No. 86. U. S. Department of the Interior, Bureau of Sport Fisheries and Wildlife). Washington, D. C.: U. S. Government Printing Office.

Evans, O. (1963). Melting pot in the bayous. *American Heritage, 15*(1), 30-51.

Ewens, J. (1885). Yazoo, Tensas, and Atchafalaya basins, flood of 1884. In Q. A. Gillmore, C. B. Comstock, C. R. Suter, H. Mitchell, B. M. Harrod, S. W. Ferguson, and R. S. Taylor (Eds.), *Annual Report of the Mississippi River Commission for 1884* (pp. 102-109). Washington, D. C.: U. S. Government Printing Office.

Expedition to Barataria, La. (1814). *The Louisiana Gazette, New Orleans,* (October 11), 2.

Fahrenthold, D.A. (2008). The muskrat fur really flies at Maryland beauty pageant. *The Baton Rouge Advocate,* (March 9), 1D-2D.

Falgoux, W. (2007). *Rise of the Cajun mariners: the race for big oil.* Ann Arbor, Mi.: Edward Brothers.

Fall, R. (1893). *Cheniere Caminada, or, The wind of death: the story of the storm in Louisiana.* New Orleans, La.: Hopkins' Printing Office.

Farber. S. (1996). Economic welfare loss of projected Louisiana wetlands disintegration. *Contemporary Economic Policy, 14*(1), 92-106.

Farren, R. (2003). Let's take out the traps: "ghost" crab traps are haunting the dwindling blue crab fishery. *Shallow water angler.* Retrieved September 20, 2007, from http://www.shallowwaterangler.com/conservation/ 0307-ghost/.html.

Felsher, J. (1997). Mixing it up in coastal marshes. *Louisiana Conservationist, 49*(3), 17-19.

Ferguson, S. A. (1931). *The history of Lake Charles, Louisiana.* Unpublished Master's thesis, Louisiana State University, Baton Rouge, La.

Ferleger, L. (1982). Farm mechanization in the southern sugar section after the Civil War. *Louisiana History, 23*(1), 21-34.

Fiedler, R. H. (1932). Fisheries of Louisiana. *Louisiana Conservation Review, 2*(4), 3-8:26.

Field operations in Louisiana's marshes. (1955). *Oil and Gas Journal, 54*(10), 122-123.

Field 'sinking' a problem at Freeport properties. (1960). *The Freeporter, 7*(9), 5.

Fifth mine taking shape. (1957). *The Freeporter, 5*(2), 4.

First nutria fur coat. (1948). *Louisiana Conservationist, 1*(4), 14-15; 26.

Fisher, A. (1965). History and current status of the Houma Indians. *Midcontinent America Studies Journal, 6*(2), 149-163.

Fisher, J. L. (1931). Crabs solve Morgan City's unemployment. *Louisiana Conservation Review, 2*(2), 18-19.

Fisk, W. L. (1891). Report of Captain W.L. Fish, Corps of Engineers. In *52nd Congress, 1st session, house executive document no. 1, part 2* (Report of the Secretary of War; Being Part of the Message and Documents Communicated to the Two Houses of Congress at the Beginning of the First Session of the Fifty-Second Congress in Five Volumes, pp. 1841-1852). Washington, D. C.: U. S. Government Printing Office.

Fisk, H. N. (1944). *Geological investigation of the Alluvial Valley of the lower Mississippi River.* Vicksburg, Ms.: U. S. Army Corps of Engineers, Mississippi River Commission.

Fisk, H. N. (1952). *Geological investigations of the Atchafalaya Basin and the problem of Mississippi River diversions.* Vicksburg, Ms.: U. S. Army Corps of Engineers, Mississippi River Commission.

Follett, R. (2007). The sugar masters. *Louisiana Cultural Vistas, 18*(2), 44-55.

Fontova, H. (1997). Freestyle frogging. *Louisiana Conservationist, 49*(3), 14-16.

Fontova, H. (1997B). Ducking the delta. *Louisiana Conservationist, 49*(6), 12-14.

Ford, J. A. (1951). Greenhouse: a Troyville-Coles Creek period site in Avoyelles Parish, Louisiana. *Anthropological papers of the American Museum of Natural History, 44* (pt. 1).

Forrest, M. (n.d.). *Wasted by wind and water: a historical and pictorial sketch of the Gulf disaster.* Milwaukee, Wi.: Art Gravure and Etching Co.

Forshey, C. G. (1873). Mississippi levees. In *House miscellaneous document no. 41, 42nd Congress, 3rd session* (pp. 1-25). Washington, D. C.: U. S. Government Printing Office.

Fortier, A. (1909). *Louisiana: comprising sketches of counties, towns, events, institutions, and persons, arranged in encyclopedic form, 3 vols.* Atlanta, Ga.: Southern Historical Association.

Fortier, A. (1914). *Louisiana: comprising sketches of parishes, towns, events, institutions, and persons, arranged in cyclopedic form, 3 vols.* Madison, Wi.: Century Historical Association.

Foscue, E. J. and E. Troth. (1936). Sugar plantations of the Irish Bend district, Louisiana. *Economic Geography, 12*(4), 373-380.

Fountain, W. (1966). History of the seafood industry. *Down South,* (November-December), (Book125, M.J. Stevens Collection). Biloxi, Ms: Biloxi Public Library.

Fountain, W. (1985). Mississippi oyster pirates. *Biloxi Press* (October 9), (Book 126, M.J. Stevens Collection). Biloxi, Ms: Biloxi Public Library.

FPC high on gas. (1972). *Chemical Week, 110*(14), 15.

Frank, A. D. (1930). *The development of the federal program of flood control on the Mississippi River.* Columbia University Studies in the Social Sciences, No. 323. New York: Ams Press.

Frank, C. (1993). Fallout on southern coastal beaches. *Louisiana Conservationist, 45*(5), 4-7.

Frank, C. W., Jr. (1991). Sirens of the bayous: Louisiana decoys lure more than ducks. *Louisiana Conservationist, 43*(6), 12-15.

Frank, C. W., Jr. (1985). *Wetland heritage: the Louisiana duck decoy.* Gretna, La.: Pelican Publishing Company.

Franz, H. W. (1937). Manila Village is subject of official survey. *New Orleans Item-Tribune* (March 14), 3.

Frasch plant goes amphibious. (1952). *Chemical Engineering, 59*(May), 274-277.

Frazier, D. E. (1967). Recent deltaic deposits of the Mississippi river: their development and chronology. *Transactions Gulf Coast Association of Geological Societies, 27,* 287-315.

Freebootin porter, A. (1891). *The New Orleans Times—Democrat,* (August 23), 3.

Freeport breaks news of big sulfur find in a marshland. (1951). *Business Week, 1148*(September 1), 76-78.

Freeport commences production at Caillou Island sulfur mine. (1980). *Skillings Mining Review, 69*(November 19), 4.

Freeport opens Caillou sulphur mine. (1980). *Industrial Minerals, 159*(November), 14.

Freeport Sulphur plans to develop new mine. (1979). *Journal of Commerce* (September 27), 5.

Freeport to open sulphur mine. (1979). *Industrial Minerals, 146*(November), 18.

Freeport's find. (1951). *Time, 58*(September 3), 95-96.

Freeport Sulphur Company. (1978). *Sulphur, ally of agriculture and industry.* New Orleans, La.: Freeport Sulphur Company.

Friedrichs, A. V., Jr. (1962). Oysters through the ages. *Louisiana Conservationist, 10*(11&12), 21-23.

Fritchey, R. (2001). The Gulf coast menhaden fishery. *CoastWise, 10*(4), 6-8.

Frost, M. O. (1939). Tropical trappers' fur frontier. In *Jefferson Parish Yearly Review* (pp. 59-91; 104). Jefferson, La.: Parish Publications, Inc.

Frost, M. O. (1939B). Jefferson Parish: always original revolutionizes United States seafood industry when two women dip "seria" bush in bayou. In *Jefferson Parish yearly review* (pp. 52-73). Jefferson, La.: Parish Publications, Inc.

Frye, J. (1978). *The men all singing: the story of menhaden fishing.* Norfolk, Va.: The Donning Company.

Full story of Cheniere Isle. (1893). *New Orleans Daily Picayune* (October 6), 1; col. 1.

Fuller, R. R. (2002/2003). Pecking order. *Louisiana Life, 22*(4), 42-48.

Furlow, W. (1997). US Gulf boom leaves fabrication yards scrambling to meet rig demand. *Offshore, 57*(5), 154-155.

Gagliano, S. M. (1963). A survey of preceramic occupations in portions of south Louisiana and south Mississippi. *Florida Anthropologist, 16*(4), 105-132.

Gagliano, S. M. (1973). *Canals, dredging, and land reclamation in the Louisiana coastal zone.* Baton Rouge, La.: Center for Wetland Resources.

Gagliano, S. M. and J. L. Van Beek. (1970). *Geologic and geomorphic aspects of deltaic processes, Mississippi delta system.* Baton Rouge, La.: Coastal Studies Institute.

Gagliano, S. M. and J. L. Van Beek. (1970B). *Hydrological and geological studies of coastal Louisiana, Part 1. Vol. 1, geologic and geomorphic aspects of deltaic processes, Mississippi delta system.* Coastal Studies Institute, Department of marine Sciences, Louisiana State University, Baton Rouge.

Gagliano, S. M. and J. L. Van Beek. (1993). *A long-term plan for Louisiana's coastal wetlands*. Baton Rouge, La.: Louisiana Department of Natural Resources, Office of Coastal Restoration.

Gagliano, S. M., H. J. Kwon and J. L. Van Beek. (1973). *Hydroglogic and geologic studies of coastal Louisiana*. Report No. 2, Salinity regimes in Louisiana Estuaries (Prepared for the Department of the Army, New Orleans District, Corps of Engineers, Contract No. DACW 29-69-C-0092). Baton Rouge: Louisiana State University, Center for Wetland Resources.

Gagliano, S. M., K. J. Meyer-Arendt, and K. M. Wicker. (1981). Land loss in the Mississippi river deltaic plain. *Transactions of the Gulf Coast Association of Geological Society, 17*, 295-306.

Gagliano, S. M, L. D. Kemp, E. B. Wicker, K. Wiltenmuth, K. S. Sabatem. (2003). Neo-tectonic framework of southeast Louisiana and applications to coastal restoration. *Transactions of the Gulf Association of Geological Societies and the Gulf Coast Section, 53*, 262-272.

Gallaway, A. (2004). *Saltgrass cattlemen: they came to the Texas coast country and tamed the wild longhorn*. Draft manuscript submitted to Agricultural History.

Galtsoff, P. S. (1964). The American oyster *Crassostrea virginica* (Gmelin). *Fisheries Bulletin 64*. U. S. Department of the Interior, Fish and Wildlife Service..

Gary, D. L. and D. W. Davis. (1978). Mansions on the marsh. *Louisiana Conservationist, 30*(3), 10-13.

Gary, D. L. and D. W. Davis. (1979). *Recreation dwellings in the Louisiana marsh*. Baton Rouge, La.: Louisiana State University, Center for Wetland Resources.

Gas lack at Texas Gulf Frasch mine causes 70% layoff. (1973). *Oil and Gas Journal, 71*(9), 28.

Gates, P. W. (1956). Private land claims in the South. *The Journal of Southern History, 22*(2), 183-204.

Gates, W. G. (1910). *A few notes on oyster culture in Louisiana* (Bulletin No. 15, pp.1-32). Cameron, La.: Gulf Biologic Station.

Gautreaux, T. (2003/2004). *The clearing, 12*(4 Winter), 80-91.

Gayden, H. P. (1952). The Louisiana Brahman industry. *Gulf Coast Cattleman, 17*(12), 26-32.

GE—'the mine that couldn't be built'. (1962). *The Freeporter: 50 Years of Progress*, (July), 8-10.

Gerstner Field. (2007). Retrieved December 21, 2006, from http://www.cityoflakecharles.com/about/gerstner.asp.

Gibson, J. L., R. B. Gramling, S. T. Brazda, S. Traux, M. R. Nault, and K. M. Byrd. (1978). *Archaeological survey of the lower Atchafalaya region, south central Louisiana* (University of Southwestern Louisiana, Center for Archaeological Studies Report No. 5). Lafayette, La.: University of Southwestern Louisiana.

Gifford, J. (1892). Attakapas country. *Science, 20*(517), 372..

Gilbert, W. (1814). *Letter describing Jean Lafitte's base at Cat Island* (Gilbert [Walker] Letter). Baton Rouge, La.: Hill Memorial Library, South Reading Room, Louisiana State University.

Gillespie, G. L., A. Stickney, T. H. Handbury, H. L. Marindin, B. M. Harrod, R. S. Taylor, et al. (1897). Appendix VV, Annual Report of the Mississippi River Commission for the fiscal year ending June 30, 1897. In *Annual report of the War Department for the fiscal year ending June 30, 1897. report of the Chief of Engineers, pt. 5.* (House Document No. 2, 55th Congress, 2nd Session, pp. 3505-3835). Washington, D. C.: U. S. Government Printing Office.

Gish, E. N. (n.d.). *History of the Texas company and Port Arthur works refinery*. Retrieved Feburary 3, 2010, from http://www.texacohistory.com/History/index.htm.

Glassie, H. (1994). The practice and purpose of history. *The Journal of American History, 81*(3), 961-968. Retrieved February 25, 2006, from JSTOR (http://www.jstor.org/).

Glenk, R. (1934). Crop plants of Louisiana; how, when and where they originated. *Louisiana Conservation Review, 4*(1), 2337; 55.

Glenk, R. (1934B). Milestones of progress in the realm of sugar. *Louisiana Conservation Review, 4*(2), 23-29.

Global Warming: Early Warning Signs. (2006). Retrieved December 11, 2006, from http://www.climatehotmap.org/index.html.

Gomez, G. M. (1998). *A wetland biography: seasons on Louisiana's Chênière Plain*. Austin, Tx.: University of Texas Press.

Goodwill, D. (1938-1939). Oil development in Louisiana during 1938. *Louisiana Conservation Review, 8*(Winter), 7-8; 54-57.

Gosselink, J. G. (1980). *Tidal marshes, the boundary between land and ocean*. Washington, D. C.: Biological Services Program, U. S. Fish and Wildlife Service.

Gosselink, J. G., C. L. Cordes, and J. W. Parsons. (1979). *An ecological characterization study of the chenier plain coastal ecosystem of Louisiana and Texas. vol. 1* (Narrative report. FWS/OBS-78/9). Washington, D. C.: Office of Biological Services U. S. Fish and Wildlife Service.

Gosselink, J. G. and R. H. Baumann. (1980). Wetland inventories: wetland loss along the United States coast. *Zeitschrift for Geomorphologie, 34*, 173-187.

Gowanloch, J. N. (1952). The Louisiana crab fishery. *Louisiana Conservationists, 4*(9-10), 6-9.

Gowland, B. M. (2003). The Delacroix Isleños and the trappers' war in St. Bernard Parish. *Louisiana History, 44*(4), 411-441.

Gramling, R. (1996). *Oil on the edge: offshore development, conflict, gridlock.* Albany, NY.: State University of New York Press.

Grande Ecaille: Louisiana again bids for sulfur supremacy. (1933). *Chemical Markets, 33*(July), 19-23.

Grande Ecaille's success followed struggle with adversity. (1958). *The Freeporter, 6*(2), 1.

Grand Isle: an excursion party inspects the Ocean Club Hotel. (1891). *New Orleans Times-Democrat* (June 9), 3.

Grand Isle excursion. (1866). *New Orleans Times,* (October 5), 11.

Grand Terre island. (1893). Grand Terre island. *New Orleans Times-Democrat,* (June 17), 9; col. 5.

Grandone, P. and L. W. Hough. (1962). The mineral industry of Louisiana. In *U. S. Bureau of Mines, minerals yearbook, 1962. vol. 3* (pp. 461-492). Washington, D. C.: U. S. Government Printing Office.

Grandone, P., O. W. Jones, and L. W. Hough. (1964). The mineral industry of Louisiana. In *U. S. Bureau of Mines, minerals yearbook, 1963. vol. 3* (pp. 485-517). Washington, D. C.: U. S. Government Printing Office.

Grandone, P. (1965). The mineral industry of Louisiana. In *U.S. Bureau of Mines, minerals yearbook, 1964. vol. 3* (pp. 455-482). Washington, D. C.: U. S. Government Printing Office.

Graphic picture of poor Cheniere Caminada, a. (1893). *The Weekly Thibodaux Sentinel* (October 10). (Typed copy). Thibodaux, La.: Nicholls State University Archives.

Graves, R. A. (1930). Louisiana, land of perpetual romance. *The National Geographic Magazine, 57*(4), 393-482.

Gray, L. (1985). A town made of cypress and sweat. *River Parishes Guide,* (July 7), 3.

Gregory, H. F. (1999). *España y La Louisiana.* Retrieved January 3, 2007, from http://www.louisianafolklife.org/LT/Articles_Essays/espana_la.html.

Green fields: two hundred years of Louisiana sugar. (1980). Lafayette, La.: The Center for Louisiana Studies.

Gresham, T. (2005). Disappearing cheniers. *Louisiana Conservationist, 58*(6), 23-25.

Groat, C. (2005). Hurricane Katrina and New Orleans: "I told you so" is not enough. *Eos, 86*(38), 341.

Guidroz, W. (2008). Personal communications, August 25.

Guidry, R. (2006). Personal communications, August 3.

Guidry, R. (2007). Personal communications, April 12.

Guidry, S. (1970). *Le Terrebonne: a history of Montegut.* (n.p.).

Guilot, J. P., J.N. Nelson Gowanlocj, and E. Couloheras. (1936). Statistical summary of natural resources of Louisiana. *Louisiana Conservation Review, 5*(3), 3-8.

Guillot, J. (1977). Beefmaster - making its mark on the Gulf Coast. *Gulf Coast Cattleman, 43*(7), 8-9.

Guillory, V. (1993). Ghost fishing in blue crab traps. *North American Journal of Fisheries Management, 13*(3), 459-466.

Guillory, V. (2005). Louisiana's derelict crab trap removal program. Retrieved October 20, 2006, from http://www. derelictcrabtrap. net/.html.

Guillory, V., A. McMillen-Jackson, L. Hartman, H. Perry, T. Floyd, T. Wagner, and G. Graham. (2001). *Blue crab derelict traps and trap removal programs.* Retrieved October 20, 2006, from http://www.gsmfc.org/pubs /IJF/derelicttraps.pdf.

The Gulf House. (1855). *Thibodaux Minerva* (July 14), 2; col. 2.

Gulf Coast Wetlands Handbook. (n.d.). *Gulf coast wetlands handbook.* Alexandria, La.: U. S. Department of Agriculture, Soil Conservation Service.

Gunter, G. E. (1955). Mortality of oysters and abundance of certain associates as related to salinity. *Ecology, 36*(4), 601-605.

Gustafson, A. A. (1950). Thirteen ways a sulphur producer cut costs and improved handling. *Engineering and Mining Journal, 151*(1), 68-70.

Gutierrez, C. P. (1988). *The cultural legacy of Biloxi's seafood industry.* Biloxi, Ms.: The City of Biloxi.

H. John Heinz Center for Science, Economics and the Environment, The. (2000). *The hidden costs of coastal hazards: implications for risk assessment and mitigation.* Washington, D. C.: Island Press.

Haedrich, R. L. (1983). Estuarine fishes. In B.H. Detchum (Ed.), *Estuaries and enclosed seas* (pp. 183-207). Amsterdam: Elsevier Scientific Publishing Company.

Hahn, T. III and C. E. Pearson. (1988). *A cultural resources survey of the St. Charles Parish hurricane protection levee, St. Charles Parish, Louisiana* (Cultural Resource Series, Report Number: COELMN/PD 88/10). New Orleans, La.: U. S. Army Corps of Engineer, New Orleans District.

Hall, T. F. and W. T. Penfound. (1939). A phytosociological study of a cypress-gum swamp in southeastern Louisiana. *American Midland Naturalist, 21*(2), 378-395. Retrieved February 24, 2006, from JSTOR (http://www.jstor.org/).

Hallowell, C. (1979). *People of the bayou: Cajun life in lost America.* New York: E. P. Dutton.

Hallowell, C. (2001). *Holding back the sea: the struggle for America's natural legacy on the gulf coast.* New York: HarperCollins Publishers.

Hanks, A. S. (1988). *Louisiana paradise: the chênières and wetlands of southwest Louisiana.* Lafayette, La.: The Center for Louisiana Studies.

Hansen, E., (Ed.). (1971). *Louisiana, a guide to the state, new revised edition.* New York: Hastings House.

Harris, G. D., G. F. Atkinson, C. A. Hollick, H. Ries, and A. C. Veatch. (1899). *A preliminary report on the geology of Louisiana* (Geology and Agriculture, pt. 5). Baton Rouge, La., Louisiana Geological Survey.

Harris, W. H. (1881). *Louisiana products, resources and attractions, with a sketch of the parishes. A hand book of reliable information concerning the state.* New Orleans, La.: New Orleans Democrat Print..

Harrison, D. K. and P. McGrain. (1981). The mineral industry in Louisiana. In *U. S. Bureau of Mines, minerals yearbook, 1978-79. vol. 2.* (pp. 224-241). Washington, D. C.: U. S. Government Printing Office.

Harrison, R. W. (1951). *Swamp land reclamation in Louisiana 1849-1879: a study of flood control and land drainage in Louisiana under the swamp land grant of 1849.* Baton Rouge, La.: U. S. Bureau of Agricultural Economics.

Harrison, R. W. (1961). *Alluvial empire. vol. 1. A study of state and local efforts toward land development in the alluvial valley of the lower Mississippi River.* Washington, D. C.: U. S. Department of Agriculture, Economic Research Service.

Harrison, R. W. and S. R. Pottinger. (1931). Commercial production of menhaden fish oil for animal feeding. *Louisiana Conservation Review, 1*(12), 17-19; 37; 39.

Harrison, R. W. and W. M. Kollmorgen. (1947). Drainage reclamation in the coastal marshlands of the Mississippi River delta. *Louisiana Historical Quarterly, 30*(2), 654-709.

Hart, J. F. 1974. The spread of the frontier and the growth of population. In H. J. Walker (Ed.), *Man and cultural heritage* (pp. 73-81). Baton Rouge, La.: School of Geoscience, Geoscience Publications.

Hart, W. O. (1913). The oyster and fish industry of Louisiana. *Transactions of the American Fisheries Society, 42*, 151-156.

Harvey terminal, the. (1947). *The Freeporter,* (March), 6-7.

Hastings, D. (2007). Special delivers: Sears catalog houses, history turns to obsession. *Baton Rouge Advocate,* (April 15), 1F; 4F.

Hatton, R. S., R. D. Delaune, and J. W. H. Patrick. (1983). Sedimentation, accretion, and subsidence in marshes of Barataria Basin, Louisiana. *Limnology and Oceanography, 28*(3), 494-502.

Haynes, W. (1934). Sulfur and salt on the Gulf coast. *Chemical Industry, 34*(June), 494-502.

Hays, L. (1980). Port Eads: Plaquemines taxpayers get little from marina. *The States-Item,* (February 1), (Book 77, M.J. Stevens Collection). Biloxi, Ms: Biloxi Public Library.

Haywood, E. L. and W. M. Boshart. (1998). *West Pointe a la Hache freshwater diversion: three-year comprehensive report* (Monitoring Series No. BA-04-MSTY-0498-1). Baton Rouge, La.: Louisiana Department of Natural Resources/Coastal Restoration Division.

Hazleton, J. E. (1970). *The economics of the sulphur industry.* Washington, D.C.: Resources for the Future..

Hearn, L. (1883). Saint Malo: a lacustrine village in Louisiana. *Harper's Weekly, 27*(1371), 196-198.

Heck, R. W. (1978). Building traditions in the Acadian parishes. In G.R. Conrad (Ed.), *The Cajuns: essays on their history and culture* (pp. 167-172). Lafayette, La.: The Center for Louisiana Studies.

Hein, S. (2006). *Skimmers: their development and use in coastal Louisiana - equipment for catching shrimp - includes bibliography.* Retrieved November 3, 2006, from http://www.findarticles.com/p/articles/mi_m3089/is_n1_v57/ai_18433753/pg_1.

Heller, N. (2003). Fortifications of old New Orleans. *Louisiana Cultural Vistas, 14*(2), 8-10; 71.

Helm, R. (2000). Migratory waterfowl: how do they fly so far? *Louisiana Conservationist, 53*(6), 12-15.

Henderson. (1868). Aids for construction and repair of levees of the Mississippi River. In *Senate report no. 2, 40th Congress, 1st session* (pp. 1-8). Washington, D. C.: U. S. Government Printing Office.

Herbert, W. R. and H. E. Anderson. (1936). Proper design of drilling foundation offers problems to coast operators. *Oil and Gas Journal, 34*(March 12), 28-44.

Herbivory damage and harvest maps. (2007). Retrieved December 7, 2007, from http://www.nutria.com/site24.php.

Herring, J. L. (1976). Sound reasons for hunting seasons. *Louisiana Conservationist, 26*(11, 12), 4-8.

Hess, T. J. (1975). *An evaluation of methods of managing stands of* Scirpus olnei. Unpublished Master's thesis, Louisiana State University, Baton Rouge, La.

Hester, M. W. and I. A. Mendelssohn. (1993). Restoration of an oil access canal on Timbalier Island, Louisiana, in a dune/swale plant community. In M. C. Landin (Ed.), *Wetlands: proceedings of the 13th annual conference, Society of Wetland Scientists, New Orleans, Louisiana, June 1992* (pp. 108-111). Utica, Ms: SWS South Central Chapter.

Heuer, W. H. (1887). Improvement of various water-courses in the state of Louisiana-improvement of Sabine Pass and of Sabine and Neches Rivers, Texas. In *The executive documents of the House of Representatives for the second session of the 49th Congress in 28 vol., appendix R* (pp. 1239-1290). Washington, D. C.: U. S. Government Printing Office.

Higgins, E. (1934). The story of the shrimp industry. *The Scientific Monthly, 38*(5), 429-443. Retrieved February 25, 2006, from JSTOR (http://www.jstor.org/).

History of Bayou Boeuf Elementary. (2006). Retrieved September 11, 2006, from http://www.bbes.lafourche.k12.la.us/History%20of%2 0BBES.html.

Hollister, A. S. and B. H. S. Denny. (1989). *Where the wild goose goes, Cameron Parish, Louisiana.* Lake Charles, La.: Marshlands Publishing Co.

Holm, G. Jr. (1999). The mystical coast. *Louisiana Conservationist, 51*(3), 9-11.

Holm, G. Jr. (2003). Ted's land: the trembling prairies. *Louisiana Conservationist, 55*(2), 27-29.

Holmes, J. D. L. (1967). Indigo in colonial Louisiana and the Floridas. *Louisiana History, 8*(4), 329-349.

Hopkins, H. (1809). Henry Hopkins to Governor W.C.C. Claiborne. In Clarence E. Carter (Ed.), *Territorial papers of the United States, Vol. 9, The Territory of Orleans* (1940). Washington, D.C., U.S. Department of State.

Horn, S. F. (1943). *This fascinating lumber business.* New York: Bobbs-Merrill Company.

Horst, J. (1997). Bad press prompts search for "safe" oyster. *Louisiana Conservationist, 49*(3), 11-13.

Horst, J. M. Schexnayder, and J. Bell. (2003). Oyster fact sheet. Retrieved February 14, 2007, from http://www.seagrantfish.lsu.edu/resources/factsheets/oyster.html.

Houck, O. A. (1983). Land loss in coastal Louisiana: causes, consequences, and remedies. *Tulane Law Review, 58*(1), 3-168.

Housing at Port Sulphur. (1946). *The Freeporter* (May), 1.

Housley, G. (1913). Louisiana's terrapin: the whole world eats them. *New Orleans Daily Picayune,* (August 3), 1; col. 1-7.

Howe, H. V. and C. K. Moresi. (1932). *Geology of Iberia Parish* (Geological Bulletin No. 1). Baton Rouge, La.: Louisiana Department of Conservation, Bureau of Scientific Research of the Minerals Division.

Howe, H. V., R. J. Russell, J. H. McGuirt, B. C. Craft and M. B. Stephenson. (1935). Physiography of costal southwest Louisiana in *Reports on the Geology of Cameron and Vermilion Parishes* (Geological Bulletin 6, pp. 1-72). Baton Rouge, La: Geological Survey, Lousiana Department of Conservaion.

Howe. H. V., R. J. Russell, J. H. McGuirt, B. C. Craft and M. B. Stephenson. (1935). Submergence of Indian mounds. In *Reports on the geology of Cameron and Vermilion Parishes* (Geological Bulletin 6, pp. 64-68). Baton Rouge, La.: Geological Survey, Louisiana Department of Conservation.

How sulfur flows upriver. (1967). *The Workboat, 24*(9), 15-20.

Hubbard, H. (1990). *Shantyboat on the bayous.* Lexington: University of Kentucky Press.

Humphreys, A. A. and H. L. Abbot. (1861). Report on the physics and hydraulics of the Mississippi River; upon the protection of the alluvial region against overflow; and upon the deepening of the mouths: based upon surveys and investigations. *Professional Papers of the Corps of Topographical Engineers* (no. 4). Philadelphia, J.B. Lippincott.

Huner, J. V. and M. J. Musumeche. (2005). Coastal birding in Cameron Parish: Louisiana's premier birding destination. *Louisiana Conservationist, 58*(2), 4-7.

Hunting in Louisiana. (1931). *Louisiana Conservation Review, 1*(4), 14-15; 2626; 28.

Hurley, P. U., T. E. Jacques, and N. E. Swiek. (1973). Developments in Louisiana Gulf coast in 1972. *Bulletin of the American Association of Petroleum Geologists, 57*(8), 1532-1541.

Hurricane Laurie causes evacuation. (1969). *The Freeporter, 16*(9), 1-2.

Hurricanes in Louisiana, 1723-1860. (1865). *New Orleans Daily Picayune,* (July 15), 1; col. 1.

Hurricane study: history of hurricane occurrences along coastal Louisiana. (1972). New Orleans, La.: U. S. Army Engineer District, New Orleans Corps of Engineers.

Illinois-Indiana Land Company, the. (1917). *Abbeville Meridional*, (May 6).

Interstate compact for stabilizing industry proposed by Mr. Lamont. (1932). *Louisiana Conservation Review, 2*(6), 20-23, 40.

Irvin, D. (2007). One room. many stories. *Country Roads*, (November), 106.

Jackson, J. J. (1993). *Where the river runs deep: the story of a Mississippi River pilot*. Baton Rouge, La.: Louisiana State University Press.

Jackson and New Orleans, Number two, Lafitte, "The Pirate." (1854). *New Orleans Daily Delta*, (December 24), 1; col. 4.

Jacobi, H. J. (1937). *The Catholic family in rural Louisiana. School of Social Work, No. 8*. Washington, D. C.: Catholic University Press.

Jaworski, E. (1972). *The blue crab fishery*, Barataria estuary, *Louisiana*. Baton Rouge, La.: Louisiana State University, Center for Wetland Resources.

Jeansonne, G. (1994). Huey P. Long, Gerald L.K. Smith and Leander H. Perez as charismatic leaders. *Louisiana History, 22*(1), 5-21.

Jeansonne, G. (1995). *Leander Perez: boss of the delta* (2nd edition). Lafayette, La.: The Center for Louisiana Studies.

Job, H. K. (1910). Adrift in the Louisiana marsh. *The Outing Magazine, 56*, 450-460.

Job started to raise GIB pipelines, relay. (1965). *The Freeporter, 12*(8), 1.

Johnson, F. F. and M. M. Lindner. (1934). *Shrimp industry of the south Atlantic and Gulf States*. U. S. Department of Commerce, Bureau of Fisheries Investigational Report 21.

Johnson, L. N. (1969). Alligator, distinction or extinction. *Louisiana Conservationist, 21*(7,8), 16-18; 23.

Jones, B. (2003). Cattle ranching on the Cajun Prairie. *Louisiana Cultural Vistas, 14*(2), 58-64; 66; 68.

Jones, B. (2007). *Louisiana cowboys*. Gretna, La.: Pelican Publishing Company.

Jones, O. W. and L. W. Hough. (1967). The mineral industry of Louisiana. In *U. S. Bureau of Mines, minerals yearbook, 1966. vol. 3* (pp. 355-376). Washington, D. C.: U. S. Government Printing Office.

Jordan, D. S. (1887). The fisheries of the Pacific coast: the fisheries of San Francisco county. In *Fisheries and fishery industries of the United States* (pp. 612-618). Washington, D. C.: U. S. Government Printing Office.

Jordan, G. E. (2004). Artist of the hunt. *Louisiana Cultural Vistas, 15*(2), 52-61.

Jordan, R. A. (1985). Folklore and ethnicity: some theoretical considerations. In N.R. Spitzer (Ed.), *Louisiana Folklife: A Guide to the State* (pp. 49-54). Baton Rouge, La.: Moran Colorgraphics, Inc.

Jordan, T. G. (1969). The origin of Anglo-American cattle ranching in Texas: a documentation of diffusion from the lower south. *Economic Geography, 45*(1), 63-87. .

Jordon, T. G. (1974). Antecedents of the long-lot in Texas. *Annuals of the Association of American Geographers, 64*(1), 70-86.

Judice, M. and T. Jackson. (1997). Workers, where are you? *New Orleans Times-Picayune*, March 16, F-1. F-4.

Kammer, E. J. (1941). A socio-economic survey of the marshdwellers of four southeastern Louisiana parishes. *The Catholic University of American Studies in Sociology, Vol. III*. Washington, D. C.: The Catholic University of American Press.

Kane, H. T. (1944). *Deep delta country*. New York: Duell, Sloan and Pearce.

Keithly, W. R., Jr. (1991). *Louisiana seafood industry study: a summary*. New Orleans, La.: Louisiana Seafood Promotion and Marketing Board.

Keithly, W. R., Jr. and R. Kazmierczak, (2006). *Economic analysis of oyster lease dynamics in Louisiana*. Unpublished manuscript. Baton Rouge, La.: Louisiana Department of Natural Resources.

Keithly, W. R., Jr., K.J. Roberts, and D. Brannan. (1992). Oyster lease transfers and lending; roles in rehabilitation of Louisiana's oyster industry. *Journal of Shellfish Research, 11*(1), 125-131.

Kelly, D. B. (1988). *Archeological and historical research on Avoca Plantation: testing of site 16 SMY 130 and survey of proposed borrow areas for EABPL item E-96, St. Mary Parish, Louisiana* (Cultural Resource Series, Report Number: COELMN/PD 88/01). New Orleans, La.: U. S. Army Corps of Engineer, New Orleans District.

Kelly, R. and B. Kelly. (1993). *The Carolina watermen; bug hunters and boatbuilder*. Winston-Salem, North Carolina: John F. Blair, Publisher.

Kemp, G. P. and H. S. Mashriqui. (1996). *Forced drainage in the Mississippi River delta plain compared to the Sacramento-San Joaquin delta and Everglades*. (U. S. Geological Survey Contract No. 14-08-0001-23411). Baton Rouge, La.: Louisiana State University, Center for Coastal, Energy, and Environmental Resources.

Kemp, J. R. (1997). Manchac Swamp: Louisiana's Undiscovered Wilderness. *Louisiana Cultural Vistas, 8*(1), 8-19.

Kemp, J. R. and J. Sims. (2004). *Vanishing paradise: duck hunting in the Louisiana marsh*. Gretna, La.: Pelican Publishing Company.

Kennedy, J. G. (1981). *The astonished traveler: William Darby, frontier geographer and man of letters*. Baton Rouge, La.: Louisiana State University Press.

Kerr, E. (1953). Long live king cypress. *Forests and People, 3*(1), 10-15; 46; 48-49.

Kesel, R. H. (1988). The decline in the suspended load of the lower Mississippi River and its influence on adjacent wetlands. *Environmental Geology, 11*(3), 271-281.

Kessel, R.H. (1989). The role of the Mississippi River in wetland loss in southeastern Louisiana, U. S.A. *Environmental Geology, 13*(3), 183-193.

Kimball, D. and J. Kimball. (1969). *The market hunter*. Minneapolis, Minnesota: Dillon Press, Inc.

King, P. A. (1977). *The effects of displacement on levee dwellers, Atchafalaya Basin, Louisiana*. Unpublished Master's thesis, Louisiana State University, Baton Rouge, La.

Knapp, B. and M. Dunne. (2005). *American's wetland: Louisiana's vanishing coast*. Baton Rouge: Louisiana State University.

Knapp, F. A., Jr. (1991). *A history of the Vermilion Corporation and its predecessors (1923-1989)*. Abbeville, La: The Vermilion Corporation.

Kniffen, F. B. (1935). Historic Indian tribes of Louisiana. *Louisiana Conservation Review, 4*(July), 5-12.

Kniffen, F. B. (1936). Louisiana house types. *Association of American Geographers Annals, 26*, 179-193.

Kniffen, F. B. (1936B). Preliminary report on the Indian mounds and middens of Plaquemines and St. Bernard parishes. In R. J. Russell, H. V. Howe, J. H. McGuirt, C. R. Dohm, W. Hadley, Jr., F. B. Kniffen, and C. A. Brown (Eds.), *Lower Mississippi River delta: report on the geology of Plaquemines and St. Bernard parishes* (Geological Bulletin No. 8, pp. 407-422). Baton Rouge, La.: Geological Survey, Louisiana Department of Conservation.

Kniffen, F. B. (1945). *The Indians of Louisiana*. Baton Rouge, La.: Bureau of Educational Materials, Statistics and Research, College of Education, Louisiana State University.

Kniffen, F. B. (1951). Geography and the past. *Journal of Geography, 50*(3), 126-129.

Kniffen, F. B. (1954). Whiter cultural geography. *Annals of the Association of American Geographers Abstract, 44*, 222-223.

Kniffen, F. B. (1960). To know the land and its people. *Landscape, 9*(3), 20-23.

Kniffen, F. B. (1960B). The outdoor oven in Louisiana. *Louisiana History, 1*(1), 25-35.

Kniffen, F. B. (1965). Folk housing: key to diffusion. *Annals of the Association of American Geographers, 55*(4), 549-577.

Kniffen, F. B. (1968). *Louisiana: its land and people*. Baton Rouge, La.: Louisiana State University Press.

Kniffen, F. B. (1978). The physiognomy of rural Louisiana. In H. J. Walker and M. B. Newton, Jr. (Eds.), *Environment and culture* (pp. 199-204). Baton Rouge, La.: Department of Geography and Anthropology, Louisiana State University.

Kniffen, F. B. (1978B). To know the land and its people. In H. J. Walker and M. B. Newton, Jr. (Eds.), *Environment and culture* (pp. 163-166). Baton Rouge, La.: Department of Geography and Anthropology, Louisiana State University.

Kniffen, F. B. (1990). The Lower Mississippi Valley: European settlement, utilization and modification.. In H. J. Walker and R. A. Detro (Eds.), *Cultural diffusion and landscapes: selections by Fred B. Kniffen* (pp. 3-34). Baton Rouge, La.: School of Geoscience, Geoscience Publications.

Kniffen, F. B. and R. J. Russell. (1951). *Culture worlds*. New York: The Macmillan Company.

Kniffen, F. B. and M. Wright. (1963). Disaster and reconstruction in Cameron Parish. *Louisiana Studies, 2*(2), 74-83.

Kniffen, F. B. H. F. Gregory, and G. A. Stokes. (1987). *The historic Indian tribes of Louisiana: from 1542 to the present*. Baton Rouge, La.: Louisiana State University Press.

Knight, E. F. (n.d). Sailing. In *Chapter 5, the rigs of small boats*. Retrieved February 19, 2006, from http://www.arthur-ransome.org/ar/literary/knight5.html.

Knipmeyer, W. B. (1956). *Settlement succession in eastern French Louisiana*. Unpublished Ph.D. Dissertation, Louisiana State University, Baton Rouge, La.

Knopp, K. R. (2001). *The Confederate Spanish moss saddle blanket*. Retrieved January 5, 2006, from http://www.confederatesaddles.com/spanish_moss.htmlhttp://cond.

Ko, J. Y and J. W. Day. (2004). Wetlands: impacts of energy development in the Mississippi delta. In *Encyclopedia of energy, vol. 6* (pp. 397-408). New York: Elsevier Inc.

Koehler, G. (2005). *Duck towns. Ducks Unlimited*. Retrieved February 20, 2007, from http://www.ducks.org/media/Magazine stories/duck_towns_march_april_2002.asp.

Kolb, C. R. and J. R. Van Lopik. (1958). *Geology of the Mississippi River deltaic plain, southeast Louisiana*. (Technical Report 3-483, 2 volumes). Vicksburg, Ms.: U. S. Army Corps of Engineers Waterways Experiment Station.

Kolb, C. (2004). Voltz to Folse, Huber to Oubre, German Louisiana: a Creole history. *Louisiana Life, 24*(3), 44-49.

Kollmorgen, W. M. and R. W. Harrison. (1946). French-speaking farmers of southern Louisiana. *Economic Geography, 22*(3), 153-160. Retrieved February 24, 2006, from JSTOR (http://www.jstor.org/).

Kondert, R. (1988). *A history of the Germans of Robert Cove, 1880-1987.* Lafayette, La.: The Center for Louisiana Studies.

Kramer, T. F. (1974). *Fifty years of duck hunting.* Franklin, La: St. Mary Printers.

Kupfer, D. H. (1962). Structure of Morton Salt Company mine, Weeks Island salt dome, Louisiana. *Bulletin of the American Association of Petroleum Geologists, 46*(8), 1460-1467.

Kupfer, D. H. (1990). Anomalous features in the five islands salt stocks. *Transactions of the Gulf Coast Association Geological Societies, 40,* 425-437.

Kuratorium fuer Forschung in Kuesteningenieurwesen. (1978.) *Die Kueste, 32.*

Kuriloff, A. (2006). *Justice on the half shell.* Retrieved October 30, 2006, from http://www.legalaffairs.org/issues?May-June-2005/feature_kuriloff_mayjune05.msp.

Kutkuhn, J. H. (1966). The role of estuaries in the development and preparation of commercial shrimp resources. In *American Fisheries Society* (Special Publication Number 3, pp. 1-36).

de La Harpe, J. B. B. (1971). *The historical journal of the establishment of the French in Louisiana.* (translated and edited by J. Cain and V. Koening, edited and annotated by G. R. Conrad). Lafayette, La.: The Center for Louisiana Studies.

Labor pains. (1997). *New Orleans Times-Picayune* (April 13), A-1.

Labouisse, F. M., Jr. (1985). The Lafourche Country's plantation "big house." In P. D. Uzee (Ed.), *The Lafourche Country; the people and the land* (pp. 188-206). Lafayette, La.: The Center for Louisiana Studies.

Lacaze, M. K. (2002). The Dudley Camp story: a history of market hunting in south Louisiana. *Louisiana Conservationist, 54*(6), 15-17.

Lacaze, M. K. (2003). The Dudley Camp story: a history of market hunting in south Louisiana. *Louisiana Conservationist, 55*(1), 13-15.

Lake Pelto development moves ahead. (1960). *The Freeporter, 7*(8), 1, 5.

Lake Pelto gears for early start. (1960). *The Freeporter, 8*(1), 1.

Lake Pelto 3rd mine to use seawater process. (1961). *The Freeporter, 50 years of progress,* (July), 29.

Land claims, S.E. Land District. (1832). *22nd Congress, 1st Session, House Document N. 73* (vol.2, 1833-34, Serial Set No. 255). Washington, D. C.: U. S. Government Printing Office. 9

Landreth, J. (1819). *The journal of John Landreth surveyor* (M.B. Newton, Jr., Ed.). Baton Rouge, La.: Department of Geography and Anthropology, Louisiana State University.

Landry, L. (1999). *Shrimping in Louisiana: overview of a tradition.* Retrieved November 3, 2006, from http://www.louisianafolklife.org/LT/Articles_Essays/creole_art_shrimping_overv.html.

Landry, L. F. (2006). Personal communications, March 24.

Landry, S. P., Jr. (1996). *Frenier beach hurricane storm surge revisited.* Retrieved October 11, 2006, from http://www.tulane.edu/~biochem/biophys00/sam2.html.

Lane, R. R., J. W. Day, Jr., and J. N. Day. (2006). Wetland surface elevation, vertical accretion, and subsidence at three Louisiana estuaries receiving diverted Mississippi River water. *Wetlands, 26*(4), 1130-1142. Retrieved December 6, 2007, from http://www.bioone.org/archive/0277-5212/26/4/pdf/i0277-5212-26-4-1130.pdf.

Larson, E. (1999). *Isaac's storm.* New York: Crown Publishers.

Larson, L. P. and A. L. Marks. (1958). Sulfur and pyrites. In *U. S. Bureau of Mines, minerals yearbook, 1954, vol. 1* (pp. 1119-1143). Washington, D. C.: U. S. Government Printing Office.

Larson, L. P. and J. M. Foley. (1960). Sulfur and pyrites. In *U. S. Bureau of Mines, minerals yearbook, 1959, vol. 1.* (pp. 1035-1058). Washington, D. C.: U. S. Government Printing Office.

Last Island calamity. (1856). *New Orleans Daily Picayune,* (August 19), 1; col. 6.

Last Island inundated: shocking loss of life. (1856). *New Orleans Daily Picayune* (August 14), 2; col. 2.

Le Baron, J. F. (1905). The reclamation of river deltas and salt marshes. *Transactions of the American Society of Civil Engineers, 54*(June), 51-103.

LeBlanc, L. A. (1982). Cerveza platforms offer economic options. *Offshore, 42*(9), 49-51.

Leeper, C. D. (1976). *Louisiana places: a collection of the columns from the Baton Rouge Sunday Advocate 1960-1974.* Baton Rouge, La.: Legacy Publishing Company.

Leesburg - 1870 to Cameron - 1970. (n.d.). Cameron, La.: Cameron Home Demonstration Council.

Leighninger, R. D., Jr. (2000). What the New Deal's Public Works Administration built in Louisiana: FDR's PWA in La. *Louisiana Cultural Vistas, 11*(3), 42- 46; 48-51.

Lenski, J. (1943). Changing times along the bayou. In *Jefferson Parish Yearly Review* (pp. 94-104). Jefferson, La.: Parish Publications, Inc.

Leovy, R. S. (1930). Report of the Division of Fisheries. In *State of Louisiana Department of Conservation ninth biennial report, 1928-1929* (pp-41-69). New Orleans, La.: Department of Conservation.

Le Page du Pratz. (1774). *History of Louisiana.* London, T. Becket and P. A. De Hond.

Leslie, J. P. (1985). Laurel Valley plantation. In P.D. Uzee (Ed.), *The Lafourche Country; the people and the land* (pp. 206-224). Lafayette, La.: The Center for Louisiana Studies.

Letter from Last Island. (1852). *New Orleans The Daily Picayune* (July 28), 1; col. 7.

Lewis, P. F. (1976). *New Orleans: the making of an urban landscape.* Cambridge, Ma: Ballinger Publishing Co.

Lewis, R. W. (1968). Sulfur and pyrites. In *U. S. Bureau of Mines, minerals yearbook, 1967, vol. 1-2* (pp. 1087-1103). Washington, D. C.: U. S. Government Printing Office.

Liddell, M. (1849). *Letter describing Last Island as a popular resort.* (Liddell [Moses, St. John R. and family] papers, No. 531, U-200-209, G-21-98i). Baton Rouge, La.: Hill Memorial Library, South Reading Room, Louisiana State University.

Lighthouses: beacons of the delta. (1992). *Down the road: features of Plaquemines Parish and surrounding areas, 4*(8), 24-31.

Lindner, M. J. (1936). A discussion of the shrimp trawl; fish problem. *Louisiana Conservation Review, 5*(4), 12-17; 51.

Lindstedt, D. M., L. L. Nunn, J. C. Holmes, and E. E. Willis. (1991). *History of oil and gas development in coastal Louisiana* (Resource Information Series No. 7). Baton Rouge, La.: Louisiana Geological Survey.

Lipari, L. A. (1963). Engineering challenge: development of south Louisiana's giant Timbalier Bay field. *Journal of Petroleum Engineering, 15*(February), 127-132.

Lippincott, I. (1914). A history of river improvement. *The Journal of Political Economy, 22*(7), 630-660. Retrieved February 3, 2006, from JSTOR (http://www.jstor.org/).

List of light-houses in state of Louisiana. (1866). *New Orleans Times,* (October 12), 13; col. 2.

Little church on the move. (1979). *The Freeporter, 26*(1), 4-5.

Londenberg, R. (1972). Man, oil and the sea. *Offshore, 32*(11), 54-79.

Long Lots: How they came to be. (2006). Retrieved December 9, 2006, from http://www.geo.msu.edu/geo333/long_lots.html.

Long trail to Grande Ecaille: from beachhead to brimstone. (1947). *The Freeporter,* (June), 1-2.

Looney, B. E. (1974). *Cajun country.* Lafayette, La.: The Center for Louisiana Studies.

Louisiana blue crab, the. (n.d.). Retrieved January 12, 2006, from http://www.blue-crab.net/status.html.

Louisiana Coastal Wetlands Conservation and Restoration Task Force and the Wetlands Conservation and Restoration Authority. (1998). *Coast 2050: toward a sustainable coastal Louisiana.* Baton Rouge, La.: Louisiana Department of Natural Resources.

Louisiana Coastwide Nutria Control Program. (2006). Retrieved February 22, 2006, from http://www.nutria.com/site10.php.

Louisiana cotton and sugar plantations tokens. (2007). Retrieved January 27, 2007, from http://www.louisiana-trade-tokens.com/plantations. html.

Louisiana Department of Wildlife and Fisheries. (2004). *Comparative take of fur animals in Louisiana.* Unpublished Report. Baton Rouge, La.: Louisiana Department of Wildlife and Fisheries.

Louisiana Department of Wildlife and Fisheries. (2006). *2004-2005 Annual Report.* Retrieved May 21, 2006, from http://www.wlf.louisiana. gov/pdfs/about/LDWFAnnualReport0405r.pdf.

Louisiana Department of Wildlife and Fisheries. (2006B). *Oyster lease acreage (active/paid) leased water bottom acreage.* Retrieved May 21, 2006, from http://www.oysterweb.dnr.state.la.us/oyster/oystertable.html.

Louisiana Fur and Alligator Advisory Council. (2004). *2003-2004 Annual Report.* Retrieved February 8, 2006, from http://www. alligatorfur. com/annual.html.

Louisiana fur industry. (2003). *Nutria fur industry info.* Retrieved February 22, 2006, from http://www.nutria.com/stie4.php.

Louisiana Gulf coast swept by tidal wave. (1919). *New Orleans Daily Picayune - New Orleans,* (September 20), 1; col. 1.

Louisiana has greatest bird hatcheries in the world. (1905*). New Orleans Daily Picayune,* (December 31), 15, sec. 3; col. 1.

Louisiana lumber mill and sawmill tokens. (2007). Retrieved January 27, 2007, from http://www.louisiana-trade-tokens.com/lumber.html.

Louisiana number of trappers licensed by year. (2005). New Iberia, La.: Louisiana Department of Wildlife and Fisheries.

Louisiana oil well hits sulphur deposit. (1929). *Engineering and Mining Journal, 128*(11), 445.

Louisiana oyster industry. (2005). Retrieved October 12, 2006, from http://www.wlf.louisiana.gov/fishing/programs/research/oyster.cfm.

Louisiana seafood industry tokens. (2007). Retrieved January 27, 2007, from http://www.louisiana-trade-tokens.com/seafood.html.

Louisiana State Board of Agriculture and Immigration. (1907). *A preliminary study of the conditions for oyster culture in the waters of Terrebonne Parish, Louisiana* (Bulletin No. 9). Cameron, La.: Gulf Biologic Station.

Louisiana trade tokens. (2007). Retrieved January 27, 2007, from http://www.louisiana-trade-tokens.com/.

Louisiana's bull-frog goes to town. (1940). *Louisiana Conservation Review, 9*(Spring), 24-26; 31.

Love, T. D. (1967). Survey of the sun-dried shrimp industry of the north central Gulf of Mexico. *Commercial Fisheries Review, 29*(4), 58-61.

Lovrich, F. M. (1967). The Dalmatian Yugoslavs in Louisiana. *Louisiana History, 8*(2), 149-164.

Lowrey, W. M. (1964). The engineers and the Mississippi. *Louisiana History, 5*(3), 233-255.

Lozano, J. A. (2009). "Ike Dike" considered for storm flooding. *Baton Rouge Advocate*, (July 15), 4B.

Lucas, G. C. (1957). Flotation logging. *Southern Lumberman, 144*(2421), 53-54.

Ludlum, D. M. (1963). *Early American hurricanes, 1492-1870*. Boston, Ma.: American Meteorological Society.

Lynch, J. L. (1941). The place of burning in management of the Gulf coast wildlife refuges. *Journal of Wildlife Management, 5*(4), 454-457.

Lundy, W. T. (1934). Grande Ecaille sulphur development overcomes marsh conditions. *Chemical and Metallurgical Engineering, 41*(3), 116-120.

Lundy, W. T. (1934B). Development of the Grande Ecaille sulphur deposit. In *Transactions of the American Institute of Mining and Metallurgical Engineers, metals mining and nonmetallic minerals subsection, vol. 109* (pp. 354-369).

Lytle, S. A., C. W. McMichael, T. W. Green, and E. L. Francis. (1960). *Soil survey, Terrebonne Parish, Louisiana. Louisiana Agricultural Experiment Station*. Washington, D. C.: U. S. Soil Conservation Service.

Lytle, S. A., C.W. McMichael, T. W. Green and E. L. Francis. (1960). *Soil survey of Terrebonne Parish, Louisiana*. United States Department of Agriculture, Soil Conservation Service, Washington, D.C.

Macaluso, J. (2008). Winter affects storm's blows. *Baton Rouge Advocate*, (October 19), 18C.

Mager, A., Jr. and L. H. Hardy. (1986). *National Marine Fisheries Service habitat conservation efforts in the southeastern region of the United States for 1985*. St. Petersburg, Fl.: National Marine Fisheries Service, Habitat Conservation Division.

Magill, J. (2000). Mid-nineteenth century New Orleans by the numbers. *Louisiana Cultural Vistas, 11*(3), 38-41.

Magnaghi, R. M. (1986). Louisiana's Italian immigrants prior to 1870. *Louisiana History, 27*(1), 43-68.

Maier, E. A. (1952). *Story of sugarcane machinery*. New Orleans, La.: Sugar Journal.

Maiolo, J. R. (2004). *Hard times and a nickel a bucket*. Chapel Hill, N. C.: Chapel Hill Press, Inc..

Managing the mysterious Louisiana marshland. (1956). *Louisiana Conservationist, 8*(1), 8-11.

Mancil, E. (1960). Pullboatin' on the Blind. *Forests and People, 10*(4), 12-16.

Mancil, E. (1972). *An historical geography of industrial cypress lumbering in Louisiana*. Unpublished Ph.D. Dissertation, Louisiana State University, Baton Rouge, La.

Markland, L. K. (1945). Utopia Louisiana. *New Orleans Port Record, 3*(April), 11-14.

Martin, F. X. (1827). *The history of Louisiana from the earliest period* (reprinted in 1975). New Orleans, La.: J.A. Gresham.

Martinez, R. J. (1959). *The story of Spanish moss and its relatives; what it is and how it grows*. New Orleans, La.: Home Publications.

Massey, B. (1969). What the Brahman can contribute. *Cattlemen, 55*(9), 42-43.

Mathews, D. (2003). The birds of Chandeleur Islands. *Louisiana Conservationist, 55*(6), 22-24.

Mathews, P. F. (1977). Morgan City contributes greatly to development of oil industry technology. *Acadiana Profile, 6*(1), 76-82.

May, J.R. and L.D. Bitsch. (1987). *Geological investigation of the Mississippi River Deltaic Plain land loss and land accretion* (Techincal Report GL-87-13, Prepared for U.S. Amry Engineer District, New Orleans). Vicksburg, MS. Department of the Army, Waterways Experiment Station, Corps of Engineers.

Maygarden, B. D and J. K. Yakubik. (1999). *Bayou Chene: the life story of an Atchafalaya Basin community: preserving Louisiana heritage*. New Orleans, La.: U. S. Army Corps of Engineers, New Orleans District.

Maygarden, B. D., L. G. Santeford, J. K. Yakubik, and A. Saltus. (1995). *Cultural resources investigation on Grand Terre Island, Jefferson Parish, Louisiana* (Cultural Resource Series, Report Number: COELMN/PD 95/05). New Orleans, La.: U. S. Army Corps of Engineers, New Orleans District.

McBride, M. G. and N. M. McLaurin. (1995). The origin of the Mississippi River Commission. *Louisiana History, 36*(4), 389-411.

McBride, R. A., M. W. Hiland, S. Penland, S. J. Williams, M. R. Byrnes, K. A. Westphal, et al. (1991). In *Mapping barrier island changes in Louisiana: techniques, accuracy, and results* (pp. 1011-1026). Coastal Sediments' 91 Proceedings of the Specialty Conference WR Div./ASCE, Seattle, Washington.

McConnell, J. N. (1930). Report of the Division of Oysters. In *State of Louisiana Department of Conservation ninth biennial report, 1928-1929* (pp. 71-88). New Orleans, La.: Department of Conservation.

McConnell, J. N. (1932). Report of Division of Oysters and Water Bottoms. In *State of Louisiana Department of Conservation tenth biennial report, 1930-1931* (pp. 218-251). New Orleans, La.: Department of Conservation.

McConnell, J. N. (1934). The Louisiana oyster, its habits and value. *Louisiana Conservation Review, 4*(3), 33-37.

McConnell, J. N. (1936). Report of Division of Oysters and Water Bottoms. In *State of Louisiana Department of Conservation twelfth biennial report, 1934-1935* (pp. 230-257). New Orleans, La.: Department of Conservation.

McConnell, J. N. (1946). Division of Oysters and Water Bottoms. In *Department of Wild Life and Fisheries first biennial report, 1944-1945* (pp. 1183-212). New Orleans, La.: Department of Wild Life and Fisheries.

McConnell, J. N. (1950). Nature is greatest oyster culturist. *Louisiana Conservationist, 2*(July-August), 4-5; 23.

McConnell, J. N. (1952). Louisiana oysters' future. *Louisiana Conservationist, 4*(5), 5-9; 26.

McConnell, J. N. and L. D. Kavanagh. (1941). *The Louisiana oyster* (Bulletin No. 1 – Revised). Baton Rouge, La.: Ramires-Jones Printing Co.

McCrory, S. H. (1919). The drainage movement in the United States. In *Yearbook of the U. S. Department of Agriculture, 1918* (pp. 137-144). Washington, D. C.: U. S. Government Printing Office.

McCrory, S. H. and C. E. Soo. (1927). Historical notes on land drainage in the United States. *Proceedings of the American Society of Civil Engineers, 53*, 1629.

McCulloh, R. P., P. V. Heinrich, and B. Good. (2006). *Geology and hurricane-protection strategies in the greater New Orleans area* (Public Information Series No. 11). Baton Rouge, La.: Louisiana Geological Survey.

McDaniel, A. B. (1930). Flood waters of the Mississippi River. In *Senate document no. 127, 71st Congress, 2nd session* (pp. 1-84). Washington, D.C.: U. S. Government Printing Office.

McGhee, E. and C. Hoot. (1963). Mighty dredges little-known work horses of coastal drilling, producing, pipelining, now 25 years old. *Oil and Gas Journal, 61*(9), 150-155.

McKnight, L. (2005). Island residents stay put despite Gulf of Mexico's persistent threat. *Houma Courier*. Retrieved August 29, 2006, from http://www.houmatoday.com/apps/pbcs.dll/article?AID=/20050123/NEWS/501230316.

McIlhenny, E. A. (1918). Report of the Game Division. In *Third biennial report of the Department of Conservation, from April 1st, 1916 to April 1st, 1918* (pp. 65-80). New Orleans, La.: Palfrey-Rodd-Pursell Co, Ltd.

McIlhenny, E. A. (1930). The creating of the wild life refuges in Louisiana. *Louisiana Conservation Review, 4*(4), 23-24.

McIlhenny Company delays opening of New Orleans museum. (2006). Retrieved October 8, 2006, from http://www.tabasco.com/info_booth/news/museum.cfm.

McIntire, W. G. (1958). *Prehistoric Indian settlements of the changing Mississippi River delta* (Coastal Studies Series No. 1). Baton Rouge, La.: Louisiana State University Press.

McIntire, W. G. (1978). Methods of correlating cultural remains with stages of coastal development. In H. J. Walker and M. B. Newton, Jr. (Eds.), *Environment and Culture* (pp. 115-130). Baton Rouge, La.: Department of Geography and Anthropology, Louisiana State University.

McLaughlin, O. B. (1938). Welded highways for steam, water, sulphur; Grande Ecaille plant of Freeport Sulphur Company. *Power, 82*(February), 86-87.

McNamara, D. (2004/2005). Building barriers. *Louisiana Life, 24*(4), 48-53.

McPhee, J. (1989). *The control of nature*. New York: Farrar Straus Giroux.

McPherson, D. L. (1951). An oldtimer remembers. *Louisiana Conservationist, 3*(7), 16.

McSherry, J. M. (1980). Farmers of the sea. *Louisiana Conservationist, 32*(3), 8-13.

Means, N. (2003). Forging identity: Africa American, Cajun, and Anglo American folkways in WPA guides to the deep south. *Louisiana History, 59*(2), 211-223.

Means, T. H. (1901). Reclamation of salt marsh land. In *U.S. soils bureau* (Circular No. 8, pp. 1-10). Washington, D.C.: U.S. Government Printing Office.

Medford, C. (1999). *Crafts from the "back days."* Retrieved January 3, 2007, from http://www.louisianafolklife.org/lt/Virtual_Books/Splittin/splittin_on_the_grain.html#craftsbackdays.

Menard, D. (1997). *Hurricanes of the past: the untold story of Hurricane Audrey.* Rayne, La: Acadian Publishers and Paper Company.

Mengis, P. (1950). Port Sulphur description and history. *New Orleans Times Picayune*, (October15), mag. sec.

Meniji Japan, a sailor's visit: With a history of case-oil trade. (1996). Bath: Maine Maritime Museum.

Merrill, E. C. (1990). *The German Coast during the colonial era, 1722-1903: the evolution of a distinct cultural landscape in the lower Mississippi delta during the colonial era, with special reference to the development of Louisiana's German Coast.* Destrehan, La: The German-Acadian Coast Historical and Genealogical Society.

Merrill, E. C. (2003). The Germans of New Orleans. *Louisiana Cultural Vistas, 14*(2), 46-57; 93.

Merry, J. F. (1909). *Louisiana reclaimed lands make fertile farms: a pamphlet full of information concerning the prairie marshes and cypress swamp lands of Louisiana and how they are being reclaimed.* Chicago, Il.: Poole Brothers.

Metzler, J. A. (1978). World's largest platform set in record depths. *Ocean Industry, 13*(9), 173-180.

Meyer, J. B. (1981). *Plaquemines, the empire parish.* New Orleans, La.: Laborde Printing Company.

Meyer-Arendt, K. J. (n.d.). *The Grand Isle, Louisiana resort cycle: a case study in settlement evolution and coastal erosion.* Unpublished manuscript. Baton Rouge, La.: Louisiana State University.

Meyer-Arendt, K. J. (1981). *Recreation along the southwest Louisiana coast: cultural and physical parameters.* Unpublished manuscript. Baton Rouge, La.: Louisiana State University.

Meyer-Arendt, K. J. (1982). *Holly Beach, Louisiana - geographic perspectives on the "Cajun Riviera."* Paper presented, 78th Annual Meeting, Association of American Geographers April 25-28, 1982. San Antonio, Texas.

Meyer-Arendt, K. J. (1985). The Grand Isle, Louisiana resort cycle. *Annals of Tourism Research, 12,* 449-465.

Migchelsen, B. (n.d.). *Chaloupe verchères l' authentique.* Retrieved December 7, 2007, from http://www.duckworksmagazine.com/01/articles/chaloupe/index.htm.

Miller, G. B. (1997). Louisiana's tidelands controversy: the United States of America v. State of Louisiana maritime boundary cases. *Louisiana History, 38*(2), 203-221.

Miller, J. W. (1914). Cape Cod canal. *The National Geographic Magazine, 26*(2), 185-190.

Miller, S. (1956). Ranching in the Louisiana marshes. *Journal of Range Management, 21*(1), 284-285.

Millet, D. J. (1971*). The economic development of southwest Louisiana, 1865-1900.* Unpublished Ph.D. Dissertation, Louisiana State University, Baton Rouge, La.

Millet, D. J. (1974). The saga of water transportation into southwest Louisiana to 1900. *Louisiana History, 15*(4), 339-355.

Millet, D. J. (1983). Southwest Louisiana enters the railroad age: 1880-1900. *Louisiana History, 24*(2), 165-183.

Millet, D. J. (1987). Cattle and cattlemen of southwest Louisiana, 1860-1900. *Louisiana History, 28*(3), 311-330.

Millis, J. (1894). Report of Captain John Millis on surveys in vicinity of crevasses. In C. B., C. R. Suter, A. Stickney, H. L. Whiting, B. M. Garrod, R. S. Taylor, and H. F. Comstock (Eds.), *Annual report of the Mississippi River Commission for 1894, appendix XX* (pp. 3064-3074). Washington, D. C.: U. S. Government Printing Office.

Mine at river's mouth produced at critical time. (1962). *The Freeporter: 50 years of progress*, (July), 12.

Mizell-Nelson, M. (2009). Our daily bread. *Louisiana Cultural Vistas, 20*(2), 54-65.

Model community at Port Sulphur. (1939). *Chemical and Metallurgical Engineering, 46*(12), 762-763.

Moore, H. F. (1899). Report on the oyster-beds of Louisiana. In *United States Commission of Fish and Fisheries, part 24* (Report of the Commission for the year ending June 20, 1898, pp. 29-100). Washington, D. C.: U. S. Government Printing Office.

Moore, J. H. (1967). *Andrew Brown and cypress lumbering in the old southwest.* Baton Rouge, La.: Louisiana State University Press.

Moore, J. H. (1983). The cypress lumber industry of the old southwest and public land law, 1803-1850. *Journal of Southern History, 49*(2), 203-222. Retrieved February 25, 2006, from JSTOR (http://www.jstor.org/).

Moore, J. H. (1983B). The cypress lumber industry of the Lower Mississippi Valley during the Colonial Period. *Louisiana History, 24*(1), 25-47.

Retrieved October 11, 2006, from JSTOR (http://www.jstor.org/).

Moore, J. T. (1996). The fish factory: work and meaning for black and white fishermen of the American menhaden industry. *Journal of Southern History, 62*(2), 401-402. Retrieved February 25, 2006, from JSTOR (http://www.jstor.org/).

Morehouse, A. D. (1910). Reclamation of the southern Louisiana wet prairie lands. In *Annual report of the Office of Experiment Stations* (pp. 415-439). Washington, D. C.: U. S. Government Printing Office.

Moresi, C. K. (1934). Louisiana's sulphur mines. *Louisiana Conservation Review, 4*(1), 44-48.

Moresi, C. K. (1934B). Conservation of Louisiana's mineral resources, 1906-1935: part III—1918-1928. *Louisiana Conservation Review, 4*(4), 3-20; 41.

Moresi, C. K. (1935). Conservation of Louisiana's mineral resources, 1906-1935. Part IV—1929-1935. *Louisiana Conservation Review, 4*(5), 14-34; 45.

Moresi, C. K. (1939). A model industrial community. *Louisiana Conservation Review, 8*(Summer), 21-25.

Morey, F. (1874). Levees of the Mississippi River. In *House report no. 44, 42nd Congress, 2nd Session* (pp. 1-16). Washington, D. C.: U. S. Government Printing Office.

Morey, F. (1875). Mississippi levees. In *House report no. 418, 43rd Congress, 1st session* (pp. 1-22). Washington, D. C.: U. S. Government Printing Office.

Morgan, A. E. (1909). The alluvial lands of the lower Mississippi valley and their drainage. In *U. S. Department of Agriculture, annual report of the Office of Experiment Stations for the year ended June 30, 1908* (pp. 407-417). Washington, D. C.: U. S. Government Printing Office.

Morgan, H. W. (1902). Gulf biologic station. In *First report of the Director of the Gulf Biologic Station* (Bulletin No. 1, pp. 1-10). Baton Rouge, La.: Truth Book and Job Office.

Morgan, J. P. (1972). Impact of subsidence and erosion on Louisiana coastal marshes and estuaries. In R. H. Chabreck (Ed.), *Proceedings of the Marsh and Estuary Management Symposium* (pp. 217-233). Baton Rouge, La.: Louisiana State University Division of Continuing Education.

Morgan, J. P. and P. B. Larimore. (1957). Changes in the Louisiana Shoreline. *Transactions of the Gulf Coast Association of Geological Societies, 7,* 303-310.

Morgan, T. D. and T. O'Neil. (1976). Stalking the wild fur. *Louisiana Conservationist, 28*(9, 10), 22-27.

Morse, G. W. (1854). Report on Bayou Lafourche. *Thibodaux Minerva,* (March 11), 1; col. 3.

Morse, W. D. (n.d.). *The birth of Jennings.* Jennings, La: Jennings Chamber of Commerce.

Morton, R. A., N. A. Buster, and M. D. Kron. (2002). Subsurface controls on historical subsidence rates and associated wetland loss in southcentral *Louisiana. Transactions of the Gulf Coast Association of Geological Societies, 52,* 767-778

Mossa, J. (1996). Sediment dynamics in the lowermost Mississippi River. *Engineering geology, 45*(1-4), 457-479.

Muir, J. C. (2001). All in a day's work: San Francisco's Chinese shrimp junks. *Sea Letter, 60*(Summer), 4-9.

Murchison, J. (1978). Bio-scope fur. *Louisiana Conservationist, 30*(1), 4-7.

Murchison, S. A. and J. L. Patton. (1951). Developments in Louisiana Gulf coast. *Bulletin of the American Association of Petroleum Geologists, 35*(6), 1338-1344.

Murray, G. E. (1960). Geologic framework of the Gulf coastal province of the United States. In F. P. Shephard, F. B. Phleger, and T. H. van Andel (Eds.), *Recent sediments, northwest Gulf of Mexico* (pp. 5-33). Tulsa, Ok.: American Association of Petroleum Geologists.

Myers, R. S., G. P. Shaffer, and D. W. Llewellyn. (1995). Baldcypress (*Taxodium distichum* (L.) Rich.) restoration in southeast Louisiana: the relative effects of herbivory, flooding, competition, and macronutrients. *Wetlands, 15*(2), 141-148.

Mysterious but productive shrimp, the. (1937). *Louisiana Conservation Review,* (Autumn), 11-17.

Nardini, L.R. (1961). *No man's land: a history of El Camino Real.* New Orleans, La.: Pelican Publishing Company.

National Academy of Sciences. (1990). *Managing coastal erosion.* Washington, D. C.: National Academy Press.

National Oceanographic and Atmospheric Administration Satellite Information Service. (2006). Retrieved November 17, 2006, from http://www.ncdc.noaa.gov/oa/climate/globalwarming.html.

National Research Council, (2006). *Drawing Louisiana's new map: addressing land loss in coastal Louisiana.* Washington, D.C..: National Academies Press.

Nau, J. F. (1958). *The German people of New Orleans, 1850-1900.* Leiden: E.J. Brill.

Neal, J. T. and T. R. Magorian. (1997). Geologic site characterization (GSC) principles derived from storage and mining projects in salt, with application to environmental surety. *Environmental Geology, 29*(3/4), 165-175.

Neill, C. and L. A. Deegan. (1986). The effect of Mississippi River delta lobe development on the habitat composition and diversify of Louisiana coastal wetlands. *American Midland Naturalist, 116*(2), 296-303. Retrieved February 25, 2006, from JSTOR (http://www.jstor.org/).

Nesbit, D. M. (1885*). Tide marshes of the United States.* (U. S. Department of Agriculture, Miscellaneous Special Report No. 7). Washington, D. C.: U. S. Government Printing Office.

Netzeband, F. F., R. Early, J. P. Ryan, and W. C. Miller, (1964). *Sulfur resources and production in Texas, Louisiana, Missouri, Oklahoma, Arkansas, Kansas, and Mississippi, and markets for the sulfur* (U. S. Bureau of Mines Information Circular 8222). Washington, D. C.: U. S. Government Printing Office.

Neuman, R. W. (1970). An archaeological assessment of coastal Louisiana. *Mélanges ,11.* Baton Rouge, La.: Museum of Geoscience, Louisiana State University.

Neuman, R. W. and L. A. Simmons. (1969). *A bibliography relative to Indians of the state of Louisiana* (Anthropological Study 4). Baton Rouge, La.: Geological Survey, Louisiana Department of Conservation.

Neuman, R. W. and K. Byrd. (1977). *An archaeological survey of sections of the southern Porter Creek unit, Homochitto National Forest, Mississippi.* Washington, D. C.: U. S. Forest Service, U. S. Department of Agriculture.

Neuman, R. W. and N. W. Hawkins. (1993). *Louisiana Prehistory* (2nd edition, Anthropological Study Series No. 6). Baton Rouge, La.: Department of Culture, Recreation and Tourism..

New lands to conquer. (1944). *The Freeporter,* (April), 1.

New Orleans Daily Delta. (1850). Country correspondence of the delta. *New Orleans Daily Delta,* (February 11), 1; col. 4.

New Orleans firm sets pace for inshore drilling-barge construction. (1960). *Oil and Gas Journal, 58*(September 12), 156.

Newton, M. B., Jr. (1971*).* Louisiana house types: a field guide. *Mélanges, 2* (September 27). Baton Rouge, La.: Museum of Geoscience, Louisiana State University.

Newton, M. B., Jr. (1972.) *Atlas of Louisiana; a guide for students* (Miscellaneous Publication 72-1). Baton Rouge, La.: School of Geoscience, Geoscience Publications.

Newton, M. B., Jr. (1985). Louisiana folk houses. In N. R. Spitzer (Ed.), *Louisiana folklife: a guide to the state* (pp. 179-190). Baton Rouge, La.: Moran Colorgraphics, Inc.

Nichols, J. D., L. Vieham, R. H. Chabreck, and B. Fenderson. (1976). *Simulation of a commercially harvested alligator population in Louisiana.* (Agricultural Experiment Station, Bulletin No. 691). Baton Rouge, La.: Louisiana State University.

Ninth Biennial Report of the Department of Conservation State of Louisiana, General Conservation Bulletin, 1928-1929. (1930). New Orleans, La.: Department of Conservation.

NMFS Landings Query Results. (2006). *National Marine Fisheries Service, crab, menhaden, oyster, shrimp.* Retrieved February 8, 2006, from http://www.st.nmfs.gov/pls/webpls/MF_ANNUAL_LANDINGS.RESULTS.

NMFS Landings Query Results. (2006B) *Louisiana crabs.* Retrieved February 14, 2006, from http://www.st.nmfs.gov/pls/MS_ ANNUAL_ LANDINGS. RESULTS.

NMFS Landings Query Results. (2006C). *Louisiana oysters.* Retrieved February 14, 2006, from http://www.st.nmfs.gov/pls/MS_ ANNUAL_ LANDINGS. RESULTS.

NMFS Landings Query Results. (2006D). *Louisiana shrimp.* Retrieved February 14, 2006, from http://www.st.nmfs.gov/pls/MS_ ANNUAL_ LANDINGS. RESULTS.

Noland, L. D. (2001). From oysters to game birds: a history of the Louisiana Department of Wildlife and Fisheries. *Louisiana Conservationist, 53*(3), 16-19.

Norgress, R. E. (1935). *The history of the cypress industry in Louisiana.* Unpublished Master's thesis, Louisiana State University, Baton Rouge, La.

Nunez, A. (1979). The Isleños of St. Bernard: they arrived 200 years ago from the Canary Islands. *New Orleans Magazine, 13*(12), 50-55.

Nutria Fur Industry Info. (2003). *Nutria population dynamics: a timeline.* Retrieved February 8, 2006, from http://www.nutria.com.

Nyman, J. A. and R. H. Chabreck. (1995). Fire in coastal marshes: history and recent concerns. In S. I. Cerulean and R. T. Engstrom (Eds.), *Proceedings of the nineteenth tall timbers fire ecology conference. fire in wetlands: a management perspective* (pp. 135-141). Tallahassee, Fl.: Tall Timbers Research Station.

Occidental Petroleum plans sulphur facility in Plaquemines Parish. (1966). *Wall Street Journal,* (October 10), 13; col. 2.

Ockerson, J. A. (1901). The improvement of the lower Mississippi River. In *International Engineering Congress, Glasgow, Scotland: section II waterways and maritime works, September 4th* (pp. 3-9).

O'Donnell, L. (1933). Mining sulphur under water in Louisiana. *Chemical and Metallurgical Engineering, 40*(9), 454-458.

O'Donnell, L. and J. M. Todd. (1932). Modern steam plant furnishes hot water for sulphur mining. *Southern Power Journal, 50*(December), 10-13.

Oil and Gas in Louisiana. (1910). *U.S. Bulletin 429*, 58-89; 170; 174; 178.

Oil, salt and geology. (1968*). Science News, 94*(October), 361-362.

Okey, C. W. (1914). *The wetlands of southern Louisiana and their drainage* (Bulletin No. 71, pp. 1-82). Washington, D. C.: U. S. Department of Agriculture.

Okey, C. W. (1918). *Wetlands of southern Louisiana and their drainage* (Bulletin No. 652). Washington, D. C.: U. S. Department of Agriculture.

Okey, C. W. (1918B). The subsidence of muck and peat soils in Louisiana and Florida. *Transactions of the American Society of Civil Engineers, 82*, 396-432.

'Old Faithful' has a birthday. (1946). *The Freeporter*, (October), 18.

On a claim to land in Louisiana. (1836). In *24th Congress, 1st session, American states papers* (No. 1378; Public lands, vol. 8; pp. 341-381). Washington, D. C.: U. S. Government Printing Office.

O'Neil, T. (1949). *The muskrat in the Louisiana coastal marshes*. New Orleans, La.: Louisiana Wild Life and Fisheries Commission.

O'Neil, T. (1965). Fur future. *Louisiana Conservationist, 17*(3-4), 14-17.

O'Neil, T. (1968). From eight million muskrats: the fur industry in retrospect. *Louisiana Conservationist, 20*(9-10), 9-14.

O'Neil, T. (1969). He must walk the marshes. *Louisiana Conservationist, 21*(11-12), 8-11.

O'Neil, T. and G. Linscombe. (1975*). The fur animals, the alligator, and the fur industry in Louisiana* (Wildlife Education Bulletin, No. 109). New Orleans, La.: Louisiana Wild Life and Fisheries Commission.

Osborne, T. (2006). Personal communications. August 29.

Owens, J. A. (1999). *Holding back the waters: land development and the origins of levees on the Mississippi, 1720-1845*. Unpublished Ph.D. Dissertation, Louisiana State University, Baton Rouge, La.

Owens, M. (1999). *Louisiana's traditional cultures: an overview*. Retrieved January 3, 2007, from http://www.louisianafolklife.org/LT/Maidas_Essay/main_introduction_onepage.html.

Oysters. (1915). *Report of Conservation Commission of Louisiana September 1ˢᵗ, 1912 to April 1ˢᵗ, 1914*. New Orleans, La.: Department of Conservation.

Padgett, H. R. (1960). *The marine shell fisheries of Louisiana*. Unpublished Ph.D. Dissertation, Louisiana State University, Baton Rouge, La.

Padgett, H. R. (1963). The sea fisheries of the southern United States: retrospect and prospect. *Geographical Review, 53*(1), 22-39.

Padgett, H. R. (1966). Some physical and biological relationships to the fisheries of the Louisiana coast. *Annals of the Association of American Geographers, 56*(3), 423-439.

Padgett, H. R. (1969). Physical and cultural associations of the Louisiana coast. *Annals of the Association of American Geographers, 59*(3), 481-493. Retrieved February 25, 2006, from JSTOR (http://www.jstor.org/).

Palmisano, A. W. (1972). The alligator, a wildlife resource in Louisiana. *Louisiana Conservationist, 24*(7 and 8), 5-11.

Paradise, V. ME. (1922). Child Labor and the work of mothers in oyster and shrimp canning communities on the Gulf Coast (Bureau Publication, No. 98. Washington, D. C., 1922). In L. Stein (Advisory Ed.), *Suffer the Little Children: Two Children's Bureau Bulletins* (1977). New York: Arno Press.

Parenton, V. J. (1938). Notes on the social organization of a French village in south Louisiana. *Social Forces, 17*(1), 73-82. .

Parkerson, C. (1990). *New Orleans: America's most fortified city*. New Orleans, La.: The Quest and Rose Printing Company.

Parr, V. V. (1923). *Brahman (Zebu) cattle* (Farmers' Bulletin No. 1361). Washington, D. C.: U. S. Department of Agriculture.

Parsons, J. L. (1985). The Canary Islands and America: studies of a unique relationship. *Latin American Research Review, 20*(2), 189-199. Retrieved March 6, 2006, from JSTOR (http://www.jstor.org/).

Payne, F. T. (1914). Oysters. In *Report of the Conservation Commission of Louisiana from April 1ˢᵗ 1912 to April 1ˢᵗ 1914* (pp. 111-126). New Orleans, La.: Palfrey-Rodd-Pursell Co., Ltd.

Payne, F. T. (1916). Report of the oyster division. In *Report of the Conservation Commission of Louisiana from April 1ˢᵗ 1914 to April 1ˢᵗ 1916* (pp. 79-84). New Orleans, La.: Conservation Commission of Louisiana.

Payne, F. T. (1918). Report of the oyster division. In *Third biennial report of the Department of Conservation from April 1ˢᵗ· 1916 to April 1ˢᵗ· 1918* (pp. 163-169). New Orleans, La.: Department of Conservation.

Payne, F. T. (1920). Division of oysters and water bottoms. In *Fourth biennial report of the Department of Conservation from April 1, 1918 to April*

1, 1920 (pp. 131-153). New Orleans, La.: Department of Conservation.

Pearson, C. E., B. L. Guevin, and S. K. Reeves. (1989). *A tongue of land near La Fourche: the archaeology and history of Golden Ranch plantation, Lafourche Parish, Louisiana.* Baton Rouge, La.: Coastal Environments, Inc.

Pearson, C. E. and D. W. Davis. (1995). Cultural adaptation to landforms in the Mississippi River deltaic plain. In C. J. John and W. J. Autin (Eds.), *Geological Society of America annual meeting, guidebook of geological excursions #10* (pp. 239-267).

Pearson, C. E., G. J. Castille, D. W. Davis, T. E. Redard, and A. R. Saltus. (1989). *A history of waterborne commerce and transportation within the U. S. Army Corps of Engineers New Orleans District and an inventory of known underwater cultural resources* (Cultural Resource Series, Report Number: COELMN/PD 88/11). New Orleans, La.: U. S. Army Corps of Engineer, New Orleans District.

Pellegrin, M. (2006). Personal communications, August 8.

Pelletier, G. J. (1972). *Ile de Jean Charles.* New Orleans, La.: Pelletier.

Penfound, W. and E. S. Hathaway. (1958). Plant communities in the marshlands of southeastern Louisiana. *Ecological monographs, 8*(1), 1-56.

Penland, S., J. R. Suter, and L. Nakashima. (1986). Protecting our barrier island. *Louisiana Conservationist, 38*(1), 22-25.

Penland, S., R. Boyd, and J. R. Suter. (1988). Transgressive depositional systems of the Mississippi Delta Plain; a model for barrier shoreline and shelf sand development. *Journal of Sedimentary Petrology, 58*(6), 932-949.

Penland, S., K. E. Ramsey, R. A. McBridea, J. T. Mestayer, and K. A. Westphal. (1988). *Relative sea level rise and delta-plain development in the Terrebonne Parish Region* (Coastal Geology Technical Report No. 4). Baton Rouge: Louisiana Geological Survey.

Penland, S., K. E. Ramsey, R. A. McBride, T. F. Moslow, and K. A. Westphal. (1989). *Relative sea level rise and subsidence in Louisiana and the Gulf of Mexico* (Coastal Geology Technical Report No. 3). Baton Rouge, La.: Louisiana Geological Survey.

Penland, S. and K. E. Ramsey. (1990). Relative sea-level rise in the Louisiana and the Gulf of Mexico: 1908-1988. *Journal of Coastal Research, 6*(2), 323-342.

Penland, S., H. F. Roberts, S. J. Williams, A. H. Sallenger, Jr., D. R. Cahoon, D. W. Davis, and C. G. Groat. (1990). Coastal land loss in Louisiana. *Transactions of the Gulf Coast Association of Geological Societies, 40*, 685-700.

People long ago. (2007). Retrieved November 3, 2006, from http://www.geocities.com/tokyo/flats/4396/pla.html.

Perrault S. L. and C. E. Pearson. (1994). *Cultural resources survey and testing, Bayou L'Ours shoreline protection and marsh restoration project, Lafourche Parish, Louisiana* (Cultural Resource Series, Report Number: COELMN/PD 94/06). New Orleans, La.: U. S. Army Corps of Engineer, New Orleans District.

Perret, W. S. (1968). Menhaden or pogies, Louisiana's most valuable commercial fish. *Louisiana Conservationist, 20*(1-2), 14-15.

Perrin, P. (1985). Folklore in the Lafourche country. In P. D. Uzee (Ed.), *The Lafourche Country; the people and the land* (pp. 76-87). Lafayette, La.: The Center for Louisiana Studies.

Perrin, W.H. (1891). *Southwest Louisiana, biographical and historical.* New Orleans, La.: The Gulf Publishing Company.

Phelps, A.S. (1854). Report of the State Engineer on the Bayou Lafourche. 1854. In *Documents of the first session of the second legislature of the state of Louisiana, 1853* (pp. 8). New Orleans, La.: Emile La Sere.

Phillips, P. (1970). Archaeological survey in the Lower Yazoo Basin, Mississippi, 1949-1955. *Papers of the Peabody Museum of Archaeology and Ethnology, Harvard University, vol. 60, pt. 1.* Cambridge, Ma.: Peabody Museum.

Phillips, P., J. A. Ford, and J. B. Griffin. (1951). Archaeological survey in the Lower Mississippi alluvial valley, 1940-1947. *Papers of the Peabody Museum of Archaeology and Ethnology, Harvard University, vol. 25.* Cambridge, Ma.: Peabody Museum.

Pillsbury, R. (1964). The production of sun-dried shrimp in Louisiana. *Journal of Geography, 63*(September), 254-258.

Pipe lines supplant waterways in coastal Louisiana district. (1937). *Oil and Gas Journal, 36*(October 7), 180; 183-184.

Pitre, V. (1993). *Corn shucks, Spanish moss, and feathers: more tales of the Cajun wetlands.* Thibodaux, La.: Blue Heron Press.

Piazza, T. (2005). *Why New Orleans matters.* New York: Harper Collins Publishers Inc.

Place names of Jefferson Parish. (1971). Metairie, La.: Jefferson Parish Library.

Plaisance, E.C. (1973). Chênière: the destruction of a community. *Louisiana History, 14*(2), 179-193.

Plot line: land converts to water: mapping out the story. (2004). *Watermarks, 24*(January), 5.

Port Sulphur: a midwestern town in the marshes of Louisiana. (1950). *New Orleans Times Picayune,* (October. 15), Dixie Roto magazine sec.

Port Sulphur "navy," the. (1943). *The Freeporter,* (May), 1-5.

Post, L. C. (1962). *Cajun sketches from the prairies of southwest Louisiana.* Baton Rouge, La.: Louisiana State University Press.

Postgate, J. C. (1949). History and development of swamp and marsh drilling operations. *Oil and Gas Journal, 47*(48), 87.

Price, K. T. (1952). Freeport mines sulphur by boat and barge at Bay Ste. Elaine. *Engineering and Mining Journal, 153*(12), 98-102.

Priest, T. (2003). The history of U. S. oil and gas leasing on the outer continental shelf. Draft copy of a paper used with author's permission.

Prindiville, A.B. (1955). The dim, cool world that is your oyster. *Down South* (March/April), (Book 126, M.J. Stevens Collection). Biloxi, Ms: Biloxi Public Library.

Pritchard, E.S. (Ed.). (2005). Fisheries of the United States, 2004. *National Marine Fisheries Service, Office of Science and Technology, Fisheries Statistics Division* (Current Fishery Statistics No. 2004). Silver Spring, Md,: National Ocean and Atmospheric Administration. Retrieved November 17, 2007, from http://www.st.nmfs.gov/st1/fus/fus04/fus_2004.pdf..

Problem: build this sulfur plant in swamp. (1952). *Business Week*, (November 22), 48-50.

Production of sulfur has begun at the Caillou Island mine of Freeport Sulphur. (1981). *Mining Congress Journal, 67*(1), 6.

Prophit, W. (1982). The swamp's silent sentinel: a history of La. cypress logging. *Forests and People, 22*(2), 6-8; 32; 35.

Psuty, N. P. (1992). Estuaries: challenges for coastal management. In P. Fabbri (Ed.), *Ocean management in global change* (pp. 502-520). New York: Elsevier Applied Science.

Pulliam, L. and M. B. Newton, Jr. (1973). Country and small-town stores of Louisiana: legacy of the Greek revival and the frontier. *Mélanges, 7*(April 23). Baton Rouge, La: Museum of Geoscience.

Pumped land drainage in Jefferson Parish, Louisiana: a utility system always in the emergency response mode. (1995.). Typescript provided by the Jefferson Parish Department of Public works.

Quong Son platform. (2006). Retrieved November 3, 2006, from http://www.nutrias.org/photos/grandisle/9.html.

Rabalais, R. D. (1985). Early medical history of the Lafourche country. In P. D. Uzee (Ed.), *The Lafourche Country; the people and the land* (pp. 58-75). Lafayette, La.: The Center for Louisiana Studies.

Races attract great crowd despite stormy weather. (1915). *Houma Courier*, (July 4).

Ramsey, C. (1957). *Cajuns on the bayous*. New York: Hastings House Publishers.

Ramsey, K. E. and T. F. Moslow. (1987). A numerical analysis of subsidence and sea level rise in Louisiana. In N. C. Kraus (Ed.), *Coastal sediments '87: proceedings of a specialty conference on advances in understanding of coastal sediment processes, New Orleans, La., May 12-14, 1987* (pp. 1673-1688). New York: American Society of Civil Engineers.

Ramsey, K. E. and S. Penland. (1989). Sea-level rise and subsidence in Louisiana and the Gulf of Mexico. *Transactions of the Gulf Coast Association of Geological Societies, 39*, 491-500.

Randall, D. A., T. Landry, and I. Johnson. (1846). *Survey of Bayou Lafourche and Bayou Blue* (House Report No. 837, 29th Congress, 1st Session). Washington, D. C.: U. S. Government Printing Office.

Rangnow, D. G. and P. A. Fasullo. (1981). Rapid growth is outlook for recovered sulfur. *Oil and Gas Journal, 79*(September 28), 242-246.

Rankin, W. G. (1938). Will colonization follow our oil development? *Louisiana Conservation Review*, (Summer), 5-7.

Ransom, R. L. (1964). Canals and development: a discussion of the issues. *American Economic Review, 54*(3), 365-389.

Read, W. (1927). Louisiana place-names of Indian origin. *University Bulletin, 19*(2). Baton Rouge, La.: Louisiana State University and Agricultural and Mechanical College.

Read, W. (1931). Louisiana French. *University Studies, 5*. Baton Rouge, La.: Louisiana State University Press.

Reed, D. J. and L. Wilson. (2004). Coast 2050: a new approach to restoration of Louisiana coastal wetlands. *Physical Geography, 25*(1), 4-21.

Reeves, S.K. (1985). The settlement and cultural growth of Grand Isle Louisiana. In P. D. Uzee (Ed.), *The Lafourche Country; the people and the land* (pp. 108-120). Lafayette, La.: The Center for Louisiana Studies.

Reeves, S.K. (2007). Making groceries: a history of New Orleans markets. *Louisiana Cultural Vistas, 18*(3), 24-35.

Reeves, W. D. and D. Alario. (1996). Westwego: from cheniere to canal. *Jefferson Parish Historical Series, Monograph XIV*. Harahan, La.: Jefferson Parish Historical Commission and Mr. and Mrs. Danial Alario, Sr.

Reggio, V. C., Jr. (1987). *Rigs-to-reefs: The use of obsolete petroleum structures as artificial reefs* (OCS Report MMS 87-0015, 17 leaves). Washington, D. C.: Minerals Management Service, Gulf of Mexico Regional Office.

Rehder, J. B. (1971). *Sugar plantation settlements of southern Louisiana: a cultural geography*. Unpublished Ph.D. Dissertation, Louisiana State University, Baton Rouge, La.

Rehder, J. B. (1973). Sugar plantations in Louisiana: origin, dispersal, and responsible location factors. In J. C. Upchurch and D. C. Weaver (Eds.), *West Georgia college studies in the social sciences, vol. 12* (pp. 78-93).

Rehder, J. B. (1999). *Delta sugar: Louisiana's vanishing plantation landscape.* Baltimore: Johns Hopkins University Press.

Reilly, J. (1956). Big Bayou Pigeon makes it pay. *Oil and Gas Journal, 54*(July 23), 138-139.

Reimold, R. J., R. A. Linthurst, and P. L. Wolf. (1975). Effects of grazing on a salt marsh. *Biological Conservation, 8,* 102-125.

Reinecke, G. F. (1985). The national and cultural groups of New Orleans. In N. R. Spitzer (Ed.), *Louisiana folklife: a guide to the state* (pp. 55-64). Baton Rouge, La.: Moran Colorgraphics, Inc.

Reisner, M. (1991). *Game wars: the undercover pursuit of wildlife poachers.* New York: Viking.

Remembering Audrey's horrors. (2002/2003). *Louisiana Life, 22*(4), 72.

Report of the Conservation Commission of Louisiana from April 1st 1914 to April 1st 1916. (1916). New Orleans, La.: Department of Conservation.

Report on fur-bearing animals. (1918). In *Third biennial report of the Department of Conservation, from April 1st, 1916 to April 1st,1918* (pp. 81-98). New Orleans, La.: Palfrey-Rodd-Pursell Co, Ltd.

Residents say wastewater policy slows Holly Beach. (2006). *Baton Rouge Advocate,* (March 27), 2B.

Reuss, M. (1982). The Army Corps of Engineers and flood-control politics on the Lower Mississippi. *Louisiana History, 23*(2), 131-148.

Rhoad, A. O. and W. H. Black. (1943). *Hybrid beef cattle for sub-tropical climates* (Circular 673). Washington, D. C.: U. S. Department of Agriculture.

Richard, C. E. (2003). *Louisiana: an illustrated history.* Baton Rouge, La.: The Foundation for Excellence in Louisiana Public Broadcasting.

Richard, C. J. (1995). *The Louisiana Purchase* (Louisiana Life Series, No. 7). Lafayette, La.: The Center for Louisiana Studies.

Richardson, G. E., L. S. French, R. D. Baud, R. H. Peterson, C. D. Roark, T. M. Montgomery, et al. (2004). *Deepwater Gulf of Mexico 2004: America's expanding frontier* (OCS Report MMS 2004-021). New Orleans, La.: Minerals Management Service, Gulf of Mexico Regional Office.

Richardson, H. B. (1901). Louisiana levees. In F. H. Tompkins (Ed.), *Riparian lands of the Mississippi River past, present, prospective* (pp. 333-344). New Orleans, La.: Frank M. Tompkins.

Rickels, P. K. (1978). The folklore of the Acadians. In G. R. Conrad (Ed.), *The Cajuns: essays on their history and culture* (pp. 240-254). Lafayette, La.: The Center for Louisiana Studies.

Rita's wrath strikes wildlife, land & facilities. (2005). *Louisiana Conservationist, 58*(6), 30-31.

Roach, J. (2005). Katrina weakened, but didn't wipe out, invasive rodents. *National Geographic News.* Retrieved June 21, 2006, from http://www.news.nationalgeographic.com/news/2005/09/0909_050909_nutria.html.

Roberts, H. H. (1997). Dynamic changes of the Holocene Mississippi River delta plain: the delta cycle. *Journal of Coastal Research, 13,* 605-627.

Robinson, W. B. (1977). Maritime frontier engineering: the defense of New Orleans. *Louisiana History, 18*(1), 5-62.

Robson, J. B. (1956). *Louisiana's natural resources.* Morristown, N. J.: Silver Burdett Company.

Rochester, J. (1994). *Little St. Simons Island off the coast of Georgia.* Little St. Simons, Ga.: Little St. Simons Press.

Rogers, D. P. (1985). Retreat from the Gulf: reminiscences of early settlers of lower Lafourche. In P. D. Uzee (Ed.), *The Lafourche Country; the people and the land* (pp. 97-107). Lafayette, La.: The Center for Louisiana Studies.

Roland, D. (1984). *Mississippi provincial archives: French dominion, Vol. 4, 1729-1740.* Baton Rouge, La.: Louisiana State University Press.

Rollman, H. E. and L. W. Hough. (1957). The mineral industry of Louisiana. In *US Bureau of Mines, minerals yearbook 1954, vol. 3* (pp. 483-508). Washington, D. C.: U. S. Government Printing Office.

Rose, W. (1952). Drilling and producing report: Venice field, Plaquemines Parish, Louisiana. *Oil and Gas Journal, 51*(July 21), 62-64; 90.

Ross, J. W. (1889). Grand Isle glories. *New Orleans Daily States,* (August 7), 5; col. 1.

Ross, J. W. (1889B). Life on the Gulf. *New Orleans Daily States,* (August 7), 5; col. 1.

Roth, D. (2003). *Louisiana hurricane history: late twentieth century.* Retrieved January 27, 2006, from http://www.srh.noaa.gov/lch/ research/lalate20hur.php.

Roy, E. P. and D. Leary. (1977). Socioeconomic survey of American Indians in Louisiana. *Louisiana Agriculture, 21*(1), 14-15.

Rushton, W. F. (1979). *The Cajuns: from Acadia to Louisiana.* New York: Farrar Straus Giroux.

Russell, R. J. (1936). Physiography of the lower Mississippi River. In R. J. Russell, H. V. Howe, J. H. McGuirt, C. R. Dohm, W. Hadley, Jr., F. B. Kniffen, and C. A. Brown (Eds.), *Lower Mississippi River delta: report on the geology of Plaquemines and St. Bernard parishes* (Geological Bulletin No. 8, pp. 3-199). Baton Rouge, La.: Geological Survey, Louisiana Department of Conservation.

Russell, R. J. (1942). Flotant. *Geographical Review, 32*(1), 74-98.

Russell, R. J. and H. V. Howe. (1935). Cheniers of Southwestern Louisiana. *Geographical Review, 25*(3), 449-461.

Russell, R. J., H. V. Howe, J. H. McGuirt, C. F. Hohm, W. Hadley, Jr., F. B. Kniffen, and C. A. Brown. (1936). *Lower Mississippi River delta: reports on the geology of Plaquemines and St. Bernard parishes.* (Geological Bulletin No. 8). New Orleans, La.: Louisiana Geological Survey.

St. Amant, L. S. (1959). *Louisiana wildlife inventory and management plan.* New Orleans, La.: Pittman-Robertson Section, Fish and Game Division, Louisiana Wild Life and Fisheries Commission.

Sale of fur buyers and fur dealer's licenses. (1950). New Orleans, La.: Louisiana Department of Wildlife and Fisheries.

Salinas, L. M, R. D. DeLaune, and W. H. Patrick. (1986). Changes occurring along a rapidly submerging coastal area: Louisiana. *Journal of Coastal Research, 2*(3), 269-284.

Salute the 'Navy.' (1943). *The Freeporter*, (May), 2-5.

Sampsell, L. D. (1893). The recent storm on the Gulf coast. *Frank Leslie's Weekly Newspaper*, (October 26), 269-270.

Sand, N. H. and P. Koch. (1975). Creole carpentry in 1800: building practices and carpenters' tools that created Alexandria's Kent plantation house. *Forest and People, 25*(1), 16-19.

Sandmel, B. (1999). *Oilfield lore.* Retrieved January 3, 2007, from http://www.louisianafolklife.org/LT/Articles_Essays/creole_art_oilfield_lore.html.

Sanson, J. (2001). The Louisiana homefront during World War II. *Louisiana Cultural Vistas, 12*(3), 12-16; 18-23.

Sasser, C. E. (1994). *Vegetation dynamics in relation to nutrients in floating marshes in Louisiana, USA.* Baton Rouge, La.: Center for Coastal, Energy, and Environmental Resources.

Saucier, R. T. (1963). *Recent geomorphic history of the Pontchartrain basin* (Coastal Studies Series No. 9). Baton Rouge, La.: Louisiana State University.

Saucier, R. T. (1974). *Quaternary geology of the Lower Mississippi Valley* (Research Series No. 6). Fayetteville, Ar.: Arkansas Archeological Survey Publications.

Saucier, R. T. (1981). Current thinking on riverine processes and geologic history as related to human settlement in the southeast. In F. H. West and R. W. Neuman (Eds.), *Traces of prehistory: papers in honor of William G. Haag* (pp. 7-18). Baton Rouge, La.: School of Geoscience, Geoscience Publications.

Saving our good earth: a call to action. (1995). *Barataria-Terrebonne Estuarine System Characterization Report.* Thibodaux, La.: Barataria-Terrebonne, National Estuary Program.

Savoy, A. (1999). *Cajun music: alive and well in Louisiana.* Retrieved January 3, 2007, from http://www.louisianafolklife.org/LT/Articles_Essays/creole_art_Cajunmusic_aliv.html.

Sayre, A. (2007). Village getting LNG facility. *Baton Rouge Advocate,* (May 9), 1D; 2D.

Saxon, L. (1942). The Spaniard's beard. In *Jefferson Parish yearly review* (pp. 34-48). Jefferson, La.: Parish Publications, Inc.

Schlatre, M. (1937). The Last Island disaster of August 10, 1856 a personal narrative of one of the survivors. *Louisiana Historical Quarterly, 20*(3), 1-50.

Schlesselman, G. W. (1955). The Gulf coast oyster industry of the United States. *Geographical Review, 45*(4), 531-541. Retrieved February 25, 2006, from JSTOR (http://www.jstor.org/).

Schmalzer, P. A., C. R. Hinkle, and J.L. Mailander. (1991). Changes in community composition and biomass in *Juncus roemerianus Scheele* and *Spartina bakeri Merr.* marshes one year after a fire. *Wetlands, 11*, 67-86.

Schneider, G. R. (1952). *The history and future of flood control.* Chicago, Il.: American Society of Civil Engineers, Waterways Division.

Schneider, S. J., (1959). Bay Sainte Elaine oil field, southern Louisiana. *Bulletin of the American Association of Petroleum Geologists, 43*(10), 2470-2480.

Schoonover, F. E. (1911). In the haunts of Jean Lafitte. *Harpers Magazine, 124*(739), 80-91.

Schou, A. (1967). Pecan Island: a chenier ridge in the Mississippi marginal delta plain. *Geografiska Annaler. Series A, Physical Geography, 49*(4-2), 321-326.

Schultz. B. (1997). Trapping incentive. B*aton Rouge Sunday Advocate,* (April 6), 1A, 6A.

Schwartz, J. (2007). Can science outwit storms like Katrina? *New York Times,* (May 29), F1; F4

Schwartz, M. W. (2005). Along the present-day border between Texas and Louisiana, there once existed a No Man's Land, a lawless territory between competing colonial empires and the United States. *Louisiana Cultural Vistas, 16*(3), 56-65.

Scofield, N. B. (1919). Shrimp fisheries of California. *California Fish and Game, 5*(1), 1-2.

Scott, H. L. (1952). Production problems in water areas in south Louisiana. *Oil and Gas Journal, 51* (June 16), 222-228, 364-367.

Seaborne plant drops anchor. (1952). *Chemical Week, 71* (October. 18), 68-69.

Seaside sans souci: a visit of inspection to the new Ocean Club Hotel on Grand Isle, a. (1891). *New Orleans Daily Picayune,* (June 9).

Sea Grant Program, lagniappe. (2000). *LSU Ag Center, 24*(4).

Sea levels online. (2006). *National Oceanographic and Administration.* Retrieved October 3, 2006, from http://www.co-ops.nos.noaa.gov/sltrends/sltrends.shtml.

Segura, C. (1973). Cheniere au Tigre; journey into the past. *New Orleans Times-Picayune*, (June 24), Section 3; 6; 8.

Seglund, J. A. (1956). Geologically speaking, here's the picture in south Louisiana. *Oil and Gas Journal, 54*(June 18), 217-222.

Semple, E. C. (1904). The influence of geographic environment on the Lower St. Lawrence. *Bulletin of the American Geographic Society, 36*(8), 449-466.

Sewerage and water board of New Orleans. (1925). *Fifty-second Semi-Annual Report of the Sewerage and Water Board of New Orleans, Louisiana.* New Orleans: Sewage and Water board of New Orleans.

Shaler, N. S. (1886). The swamps of the United States. *Science, 7*(162), 232-233.

Shanabruch, C. (1977). The Louisiana immigration movement, 1891-1907: an analysis of efforts, attitudes, and opportunities. *Louisiana History, 18*(2), 203-226.

Shanklin, J. and T. T. Kozlowski. (1985). Effect of flooding of soil on growth and subsequent responses of taxodium distichum Seedlings to SO2. *Environmental Pollution (Series A), 38*(2). 199-212, 1985.

Shaw, A. M. (1917). Louisiana reclamation project grows to seven thousand acres. *Engineering News-Record, 79*(September 27), 603-605.

Shaw, J. A. (1930). Report of the Division of Minerals. In *Ninth biennial report of the Department of Conservation state of Louisiana, general conservation bulletin, 1928-1929* (pp. 140-184). New Orleans, La.: Department of Conservation.

Shaw, J. A. (1933). Annual report minerals division of the State Conservation Department, year 1932. *Louisiana Conservation Review, 3*(2), 5-12; 22.

Shaw, J. A. (1938). Report of the Division of Minerals. In *Thirteenth biennial report of the Department of Conservation state of Louisiana, 1936-1937* (pp. 175-351). New Orleans, La.: Department of Conservation.

Shaw, J. A. (1938B). Louisiana leads world in deep drilling. *Louisiana Conservation Review,* (Winter), 8-13; 66.

Sheets, K. (2009). Personal communications, May 5.

Sheffield, D. A. and D. L. Nicovich. (1979). *When Biloxi was the seafood capital of the world.* Biloxi, Ms: The City of Biloxi.

Shelton, M. (1987). Tradition endures, low prices, foreign control limiting La. fur industry. *Baton Rouge Sunday Advocate,* (February 8), 1A; 12A.

Shelton, M. (1987B). Cameron residents remember horror of Hurricane Audrey. *Baton Rouge Sunday Advocate*, (June 21), 1A; 14A.

Shields, G. (2009). State set to get millions for coastal restoration. *Baton Rouge Advocate,* (April 24), 1A; 7A.

Shiflet, T. N. (1960). Cattle walkways reclaim vital grazing areas from Louisiana marshes. *Gulf Coast Cattleman, 26*(9), 16-17.

Shiflet, T. N. (1966). Louisiana cattle drive enables rancher to use forage in season. *Soil Conservation, 32,* 15-17.

Shoemaker, J. (1957). *Spanish moss in Florida* (Bulletin No. 85). State of Florida, Department of Agriculture.

Short, E. H., Jr. (1945). Fully equipped floating tank batteries used in coastal Louisiana operations. *Oil and Gas Journal, 22* (May 26), 120-122.

Silas, U. (1890). Last Island. *Weekly Thibodaux Sentinel* (August 9): Typed copy. Thibodaux, La.: Nicholls State University Archives.

Simmons, F. E. (1940). Production and marketing of Southern (Spanish) moss in the United States.. Reprinted in N. Mayo (Ed), *Spanish moss in Florida* (Bulletin No. 85, pp. 23-26). State of Florida, Department of Agriculture.

Simpich, F. (1927). The great Mississippi flood of 1927. *National Geographic Magazine, 52*(3), 243-289.

Siry, J. V. (1984). *Marshes on the ocean shore: development of an ecological ethic.* College Station, Tx.: Texas A&M University Press.

Sketch of the Louisiana inter-coastal canal route from Morgan City to New Orleans via Houma and Lockport, a. (1910). *New Orleans: The Southern Manufacturer, 71.*

Sloane, E. (1956). *Eric Sloane's America.* New York: Promontory Press, with Harper & Row.

Sloane, E. (1965). *Eric Sloane's Sketches of America Past.* New York: Promontory Press, with Dodd, Mead & Co.

Smith, J. R. (1957). My battle with Audry. *Personnel Panorama, 6*(7), 3, 6. Retrieved September 20, 2007, from http://www.history. noaa.gov/

stories_tales/hurricaneaudrey.html.

Smith, T. L. and V. J. Parenton. (1938). Acculturation among the Louisiana French. *The American Journal of Sociology, 44*(3), 355-364. Retrieved February 25, 2006, from JSTOR (http://www.jstor.org/).

Snowden, J. O., W. B. Simmons, E. B. Traughber, and R. W. Stephens. (1977). Differential subsidence of marshland peat as a geologic hazard in the greater New Orleans area, Louisiana. *Transactions of the Gulf Coast Association of Geological Societies, 27*, 169-179.

Snowden, J. O., W. B. Simmons, and E. B. Traughber. (1979). Subsidence of marshland peat in the greater New Orleans area, Louisiana. In J. W. Day, Jr., D. O. Culley, Jr., R. E. Turner, and A. J. Mumphery, Jr., (Eds.), *Proceedings of the third coastal and estuary management symposium* (pp. 273-292). Baton Rouge, La.: Louisiana State University, Division of Continuing Education.

Snowden, J. O., W. C. Ward, and J. R. J. Studlick. (1980). *Geology of greater New Orleans: its relationship to land subsidence and flooding.* New Orleans, La.: The New Orleans Geological Society.

Soileau, C. (1977). Frog legs forever? or bye-bye bullfrog. *Louisiana Conservationist, 29*, (5-6), 4-7.

Sonderegger, V. H. (1930). Spanish moss a forest product. Reprinted In N. Mayo (Ed.), *Spanish moss in Florida* (Bulletin No. 85. , 1940, pp. 3-17) State of Florida, Department of Agriculture.

Southern, J. M. (1990). *Last Island.* Houma, La.: Cheri Publications.

South Louisiana oil; 62% in salt domes. (1965). *Oil and Gas Journal, 63*(May 3), 70-71.

Spitzer, N. R. (1985). South Louisiana: unity and diversity in a folk region. In N. R. Spitzer (Ed.), *Louisiana folklife: a guide to the state* (pp. 75-86). Baton Rouge, La.: Moran Colorgraphics, Inc.

Spitzer, N. R. (1999). *The Creole state: an introduction to Louisiana traditional culture.* Retrieved January 3, 2007, from http://www.louisianafolklife. org/LT/Articles_Essays/creole_art_creole_state.html.

Stahls, P. F., Jr. (1976). *Plantation homes of the Lafourche country.* Gretna, La.: Pelican Publishing Company.

Stahls, P. F., Jr. (2003). Evergreen blooms again. *Louisiana Life, 23*(3), 24-29.

Stanley, W. (n.d.). *The history of Johnson Bayou.* Typed manuscript.

Stanton, M. E. (1971). *The Indians in the Grand Caillou-Dulac community.* Unpublished Master's thesis, Louisiana State University, Baton Rouge, La.

Starr, S. F. (2001). The man who invented New Orleans. *Louisiana Cultural Vistas, 12*(2), 62-66.

Stein, J. K. (1986). Coring archaeological sites. *American Antiquity*, (51), 505-527.

Stephens, J. C. and E. H. Stewart. (1976). Effect of climate on organic soil subsidence. In *Proceedings of the second international symposium on land subsidence, held at Anaheim, California, 13-17 December 1976* (pp. 647-655). Ann Arbor, Mi.: International Association of Hydrological Sciences.

Sterns, S. (1887). Fisheries of the Gulf of Mexico: the fishery interests of Louisiana. In *Fisheries and Fishery Industries of the United States* (pp. 575-582). Washington, D. C.: U. S. Government Printing Office.

Steinmayer, R. A. (1932). Salt domes of Louisiana and Texas. *Chemical & Metallurgical Engineering, 39*(7), 388-389.

Stevens, E. M. and R. L. Callahan. (1974). Developments in Louisiana Gulf coast in 1973. *Bulletin of the American Association of Petroleum Geologists, 53*(8), 1621-1629.

Stielow, F. J. (1977). *Isolation and development on a Louisiana Gulf coast Island, 1781-1962.* Unpublished Ph.D. Dissertation, Indiana University, Bloomington, In.

Stielow, F. J. (1977B). The Bell Crevasse at Mavis Grove. *Louisiana History, 18*(4), 474-478.

Stielow, F. J. (1982). Grand Isle, Louisiana, and the "new" leisure, 1866-1893. *Louisiana History, 23*, 239-257.

Stielow, F. J. (1986). Francophones and Americanization on a Gulf coast island. *Louisiana History, 27*(2), 183-194.

Stokes, G. A. (1957). Lumbering and western Louisiana cultural landscape. *Annals of the Association of American Geographers, 47*(3), 250-266. Retrieved February 27, 2006, from JSTOR (http://www.jstor.org/).

Streever, B. (2001). Saving Louisiana? *The battle for coastal wetlands.* Jackson, Ms.: University Press of Mississippi.

Submerged regions of the coast explored by special methods. (1935). *Oil and Gas Journal, 33*(46), 69-71.

Subsidence and sea-level rise in southeastern Louisiana: implications for coastal management and restoration. (2007). Retrieved December 13, 2007, from http://coastal.er.usgs.gov/LA-subsidence /bibliography.html.

Sulfur mine opens. (1980). *Chemical Market Report*, Nov. 24, 7.

Sulfur mine shutdown set by Texasgulf. (1978). *Journal of Commerce*, (10), 8.

Sulphur mine to close. (1978). *Mining Magazine, 139*(3), 304.

Sulphur on the delta. (1951). *Newsweek, 38*(10), 57.

Sulphur plant makes voyage; amphibious mining plant positioned over Louisiana marshland sulphur deposit. (1952). *Engineering News Record, 149*(October 9), 25.

Sulphur plant started in Louisiana. (1931). *Chemical and Metallurgical Engineering, 38*(November), 677.

Sulfur sources shift. (1978). *Chemical Week, 123*(August 2), 19-20.

Sulfur sparks new bulk loading ideas. (1957). *Chemical Engineering, 64*(June), 164.

Surrey, N. M. M. (1916). *The commerce of Louisiana during the French regime, 1699-1763.* New York: Columbia University Press.

Surrey, N. M. M. (1922). The development of industries in Louisiana during the French regime 1673-1763. *The Mississippi Valley Historical Review, 9*(3), 227-235.

Sutherland, D. E. (1980). Looking for a home: Louisiana emigrants during the Civil War and Reconstruction. *Louisiana History, 21*(4), 341-359.

Swamp buggy helps GIB surveyors get to "inaccessible" locations. (1957). *The Freeporter, 4*(3), 7.

Swanson, B. (1975). *Historic Jefferson Parish: from shore to shore.* Greta, La.: Pelican Publishing Company.

Swanton, J. R. (1911). Indian tribes of the lower Mississippi valley and adjacent coast of the Gulf of Mexico. In *Bureau of American Ethnology, Smithsonian Institution, bulletin no. 43* (pp. 337-358). Washington, D. C.: Smithsonian Institution Press (distributed by Random House).

Swanton, J. R. (1952). The Indian tribes of North America. In *Bureau of American Ethnology, Smithsonian Institution, bulletin no. 145.* Washington, D. C.: Smithsonian Institution Press (distributed by Random House).

Swenson, E. M. (1994). *Hurricane Andrew: the inundation of the Louisiana coastal marshes* (DNR Contract No. 256081-95). Baton Rouge, La.: Louisiana Department of Natural Resources.

Swenson, E. M. and R. E. Turner. (1987). Spoil banks: effects on a coastal marsh water-level regime. *Coastal and Shelf Science, 24*(5), 599-609.

T. Baker Smith & Son, Inc. (1979). *Terrebonne's major navigable waterways delineation of function, uses, and needs.* Houma: T. Bakert Smith & Sons, Inc.

Tabberer, D. K., W. Hagg, and M. Coquat. (1985). *Pipeline impacts on wetlands* (Final environmental assessment, CS EIS/EA MMS 85-0092). New Orleans, La.: Minerals Management Service, Gulf of Mexico Regional Office.

Talfor, R. B. (1874). Survey of Bayou Lafourche, Louisiana from Lafourche Crossing to the mouth. In *House executive document no. 1, part 2, 43rd Congress, 2nd Session* (pp. 765-771). Washington, D. C.: U. S. Government Printing Office.

Tannehill, I. R. (1943). *Hurricanes: their nature and history, particularly those of the West Indies and the Southern coasts of the United States.* Princeton N. J.: Princeton University Press.

Territory submerged by the Davis crevasse. (1884). *Daily States,* (May 22), 4.

Terrebonne Parish Development Board. (1953). *Terrebonne Parish resources and facilities.* Baton Rouge, La.: State of Louisiana Department of Public Works.

Texaco built first submersible barge. (1949). *Oil and Gas Journal, 48*(December 15), 70.

Texasgulf closing Bully Camp mine. (1978). *Chemical Week, 123*(July 19), 39.

Third Biennial Report of the Department of Conservation from April 1, 1916 to April 1, 1918. (1918) Report of the Mineral Division, New Orleans, La.: Department of Conservation..

Thirty-two years of American independence in sulphur; Frasch process. (1935). *Chemical Industry, 36*(May), supp:85-87.

Thompson, J. (1982). The people of the Sacramento delta 1860 to 1880. *Sacramento County Historical Society, Golden notes, 28*(3 & 4), 1-41.

Thompson, S. (1944). Three wise men.. In *Jefferson Parish Yearly Review* (pp. 56-64; 148-152). Jefferson, La.: Parish Publications, Inc.

Thorpe, T. B. (1853). Sugar and the sugar region of Louisiana. *Harper's New Monthly Magazine,* (7), 746-767.

Those Grande Ecaille drillers. (1943). *The Freeporter,* (December), 10-13.

Tidwell, M. (2003). *Bayou farewell: the rich life and tragic death of Louisiana's Cajun coast.* New York: Pantheon Books.

Tinajero, P. T. (1980). Canarian immigration to America: the civil-military expedition to Louisiana of 1777-1779 (Translated and Edited by P. E. Hoffman). *Louisiana History, 21*(4), 377-386.

Titus, T. G., D. J. Kuo, M. J. Gibbs, T. B. LaRoche, M. K. Webb, and J. O. Waddell. (1987). Greenhouse effect, sea level rise and coastal drainage systems. *Journal of Water Resources Planning and Management, 113*(2), 216-227.

Tombs only testify to glory of Balize. (1921). *New Orleans Times-Picayune*, (October 9), 12; sec. 6, col. 2-3.

Tomlinson, F. (1926). The reclamation and settlement of land in the United States. In *International review of agricultural economics, vol. 4* (pp. 225-272). Rome, It.: The Institute.

Tompkins, S. (2006). Wimpy vegetarian nutria is one pesky rodent. *Houston Chronicle*. Retrieved June 21, 2006, from http://www.chron.com/ disp/story.mpl/outdoors/tompkins/3877375.html.

Townsite hurdled housing problem. (1962). *The Freeporter: 50 Years of Progress*, (July), 23.

Treadaway, L. W. (1971). The Louisiana oyster. *Louisiana Conservationists, 23*(5&6), 4-9.

Trow, R. B. (1952). The wettest inch. *World Oil, 135*(August), 249-252.

Transportation gets a life. (1947). *The Freeporter*, (February), 1.

Trapping ends in the parish. (1977). *Cameron Pilot* (March 3), 5; sec. B.

Trend to molten sulfur grows fast: producers build new terminal facilities and marine equipment. (1961). *Chemical and Engineering News, 39*(April 10), 23-24.

Treadway, J. (1975). Disappearing Louisiana moss may force last operating gin to close down. *New Orleans, Times-Picayune*, (June 22), (Book 153, M. J. Stevens Collection). Biloxi, Ms: Biloxi Public Library.

True, F. W. (1884). The useful aquatic reptiles and batrachians: the alligator and crocodile. In *The fisheries and fishery industries of the United States, section 1* (pp. 141-146). Washington, D. C.: U. S. Government Printing Office.

Tulian, E. A. (1916). Conservation of fisheries. In *Report of the conservation commission of Louisiana from April 1st 1914 to April 1st 1916* (pp. 84-128). New Orleans, La.: Conservation Commission of Louisiana.

Tulian, E. A. (1918). Report of the fisheries division. In *Third biennial report of the Department of Conservation, From April 1st 1916 to April 1st 1918* (pp. 135-160). New Orleans, La.: Palfrey-Rodd-Pursell Co, Ltd.

Turner, R. E. (1987). Relationship between canal and levee density and coastal land loss in Louisiana. *Biological Report, 85*(14). Washington, D. C.: U. S. Department of Interior, Fish and Wildlife Service, Research and Development, National Wetlands Research Center.

Turner, R. E. (1997). Wetland loss in the northern Gulf of Mexico: multiple working hypotheses. *Estuaries*, 20(1), 1-13.

Turner, R. E. and D. R. Cahoon. (1987). *Causes of wetland loss in the coastal central Gulf of Mexico. Vol. II: Technical Narrative* (OCS Study/MMS 87-0120). New Orleans, La.: Minerals Management Service, Gulf of Mexico Regional Office.

Turner, R. E, K. L. McKee, W. B. Sikora, J. P. Sikora, I. A. Mendelssohn, E. Swenson, et al. (1983). The impact and mitigation of man-made canals in coastal Louisiana. *Water Science and Technology, 16*(3-4), 497-504.

Turner, R. E, R. M. Lee, and C. Neill. (1994). *Backfilling canals as a wetland restoration technique in coastal Louisiana* (OCS Study/MMS 94-0026). New Orleans, La.: Minerals Management Service, Gulf of Mexico Regional Office..

Turner, R. E., R.E. and Streever. (2002). *Approaches to coastal wetland restoration: northern Gulf of Mexico*. The Hague, Netherlands: SPB Academic Publishing.

Twain, M. (1901). *Life on the Mississippi*. (Original copyright, 1874). New York: Harper and Brothers.

Tyler, M. C. (1932). Letter from the Secretary of War, transmitting a letter from the chief of engineers, United States army, dated December 8, 1932, submitting a report, together with accompanying papers and an illustration, on preliminary examination and survey of Bayou Lafourche, La., authorized by the rivers and harbor act approved July 3, 1930. In *House of representative document no. 45, 73rd Congress, 1st session* (pp. 1-35). Washington, D. C.: U. S. Government Printing Office.

Ulmer, G. (1935). *Economic and social developments of Calcasieu Parish, Louisiana, 1840-1912*. Unpublished Master's thesis, Louisiana State University, Baton Rouge, La.

Union of Concerned Scientists. (2006). Retrieved September 20, 2006, from http://www.ucsusa.org/.

Usual canal system facilitates field operations in Louisiana's marshes. (1955). *Oil and Gas Journal 54*, (July 11), 122-123.

Updated elevations for coastal Louisiana. (2006). *National Oceanographic and Administration*. Retrieved September 20, 2006, from http://www. ngs.noaa.gov/heightmod/LouisianaControl.shtml.

U. S. Army Corps of Engineers. (1957). *Water resources development of the U. S. Army Engineers in Louisiana*. Vicksburg, Ms.: U. S. Army Engineer Division, Lower Mississippi Valley.

U. S. Army Corps of Engineers. (1982). *Draft environmental impact statement: Terrebonne Parish-wide forced drainage system, Terrebonne Parish, Louisiana, 1 vol*. New Orleans, La.: U. S. Army Corps of Engineers, New Orleans District.

U. S. Army Corps of Engineers. (1983). *Final environmental impact statement: Terrebonne Parish-wide forced drainage system, Terrebonne Parish, Louisiana, 1 vol*. Louisiana. New Orleans, La.: U. S. Army Corps of Engineers, New Orleans District.

U. S. Department of Agriculture. (1986). *Lafourche-Terrebonne cooperative river basin study report.* Alexandria, La.: U. S. Department of Agriculture, Soil Conservation Service.

U. S. Environmental Protection Agency's Global Warming site. (2006). Retrieved December 11, 2006, from http://www.yosemite.epa.gov/oar/. globalwarming. nsf/content/index.html.

U.S. Geological Survey. (2003). *100+ years of land change for costal Lousiana* (U.S. Geological Survey, USGS-NWRC 2003-03-85, approximate scale 1:445,000). Lafayette, LA: National Wetlands Research Center,

Van Pelt, A. W. (1943). The Caminada storm: a night of tragedy. *New Orleans Times-Picayune, New Orleans States* (September 26), 8, mag. sec.

Van Sickle, V. R., B. B. Barrett, L.J . Gulick, and T. B. Ford. (1976). *Barataria basin: salinity changes and oyster distribution.* Baton Rouge, La.: Center for Wetland Resources, Louisiana State University.

Van Zante, G. (2006). New Orleans 1867: how an early photographer portrayed a shaken city. *Preservation, 58*(6), 32-37.

Vaughan, D. W., J. W. Smith, and M. H. Prager. (2000). *Population characteristics of Gulf menhaden,* brevoortia patronus (NOAA Technical Report NMFS 149). Seattle, Wa.: U. S. Department of Commerce.

Vermilion Historical Society. (1983). *History of Vermilion Parish, Louisiana.* Dallas, Tx.: Taylor Publishing Company.

Vileisis, A. (1997). *Discovering the unknown landscape: a history of American wetlands.* Washington, D. C.: Island Press.

Viosca, P. (1918). A survey of the Louisiana frog. In *Third biennial report of the Department of Conservation, From Aril 1st 1916 to April 1st 1918* (pp. 160-162). New Orleans, La.: Palfrey-Rodd-Pursell Co, Ltd.

Viosca, P. (1920). Division of Fisheries. In *Fourth biennial report of the Department of Conservation from April 1, 1918 to April 1, 1920* (pp. 77-130). New Orleans, La.: Department of Conservation.

Viosca, P. (1925). *A bionomical study of the mosquitoes of New Orleans and southeastern Louisiana.* (Proceedings of the New Jersey Mosquito Extermination Association 12:34-49, Discussion 49-50). New Brunswick, N.J.: Rutgers The State University of New Jersey.

Viosca, P. (1933). *Louisiana out-of-doors: a handbook and guide.* New Orleans: Published by the author.

Viosca, P. (1962). *The Louisiana shrimp story* (Wildlife Education Bulletin, No. 40). New Orleans, La.: Louisiana Wild Life and Fisheries Commission.

Viosca, P. and C. Gresham. (1953). About crabs and crabbing. *Louisiana Conservationist, 6*(1), 14-18.

Vogel, H. D. (1931). Annex no. 5, Basic data Mississippi River. In *Control of floods in the alluvial valley of the lower Mississippi River, vol. 1* (House Document 798, 71st Congress, 3rd Session, pp. 61-137). Washington, D. C.: U. S. Government Printing Office.

Voorhies, J. K. (1978). The Acadians: the search for the promised land. In G.R. Conrad (Ed.), *The Cajuns: essays on their history and culture* (pp. 97-114). Lafayette, La.: The Center for Louisiana Studies.

Vujnovich, M. M. (1974). *Yugoslavs in Louisiana.* Gretna, La.: Pelican Publishing Company.

Waddill, R. D. (1945). History of the Mississippi River levees, 1717 to 1944. In *Memorandum* (pp. 1-10): Vicksburg, Ms.: War Department Corps of Engineers, Mississippi River Commission.

Wagner, F.W. and E.J. Durabb. (1976). The sinking city. *Environment, 18*(4), 32-39.

Wailes, G. (1854). *Letter describing Last Island* (Liddell [Moses, St. John R. and family] papers, Box 10, folder 66, U-200-209,G-21-98i). Baton Rouge, La.: Hill Memorial Library, South Reading Room, Louisiana State University.

Wakefield, A. (1977). Cameron Parish. *Acadiana Profile, 6*(1), 12-21.

Waldo, E. (1957). The Louisiana oyster story. *Wild Life Education* (Bulletin No. 32). New Orleans, La.: Louisiana Wild Life and Fisheries Commission.

Waldo, E. (1958). The nutria in Louisiana. *Louisiana Conservationist, 10*(3), 45-50.

Waldo, E. (1962). The cheniers. *Louisiana Conservationist, 14*(2), 5-7; 24.

Waldo, E. (1965). Louisiana pioneer: the pirogue. *Louisiana Conservationist, 17*(1-2), 6-9.

Waldo, E. 1965B. From cattle to shrimp boats. *Louisiana Conservationist, 17*(7-8), 18-21.

Walker, H. J. and D. B. Prior. (1986). Estuarine environments. In P. G. Fookes and P. R. Vaughan (Eds.*), A handbook of engineering geomorphology* (pp. 180-192). New York: Chapman and Hall in association with Methuen, Inc.

Walker, H. J. and D. W. Davis. (2002). The Mississippi River: engineered routes to the sea. In J. Chen, D. Eisma, K. Hotta and H. J. Walker (Eds.), *Engineered coast* (pp. 61-83). Dordrecht: Kluwer Academic Publishers.

Walker, H. J., J. M. Coleman, H. H. Roberts, and R. S. Tye. (1987). Wetland loss in Louisiana. *Geografiska Annler, Series A, Physical Geography, 69A*(1), 189-200. Retrieved February 25, 2006, from JSTOR (http://www.jstor.org/).

Wallace, W. E. (1957). Fault map of south Louisiana. *Transactions of the Gulf Coast Association of Geological Societies, 7,* 240.

Walsh, H. M. (1971). *The outlaw gunner.* Centreville, Md.: Tidewater Publishers.

War Garden Victorious, The. (2007). Retrieved September 20, 2007, from http//www.earthlypursuits.com/WarGarV/WarGard6.html.2.

Ward, S. (2008). Mississippi projects shield human lives: levees just part of flood control. *Baton Rouge Advocate,* (April 28), 1A; 4A-5A.

Ward, S. (2009). Economy bites gator farmers. *The Advocate,* (Julu 4), 1A; 4A.

Ward, W. F. (1914). *Breeds of beef cattle* (Farmers' Bulletin No. 612). Washington, D. C.: U. S. Department of Agriculture.

Ware, C. (1999). *Croatians in southeastern Louisiana: overview.* Retrieved January 3, 2007, from http://www.louisianafolklife.org/LT/Articles_Essays/main_misc_croatians_s_la.html.

Warfield, A. G. (1876). Mississippi River levees. In *House report no. 494, 44th Congress, 1st session* (pp. 1-26). Washington, D. C.: U. S. Government Printing Office.

Warner, W. W. (1988). *Beautiful swimmers: watermen, crabs, and the Chesapeake Bay.* New York: Penguin Books.

Warren, G. (1973). Man and the marsh. *The Times-Picayune,* (November 25), Dixie Roto Magazine section, 16-19.

Washburn, M. (1951). Evolution of the trapping industry. *Louisiana Conservationist, 3*(1, 2), 8-9; 24.

Washburn, M. (1956). Last Island. *Louisiana Conservationist, 8*(7), 10-11; 20-22.

Watson, G. E. (1906). Cypress. *Southern Lumberman,* (December 25), 44-46.

Welder F. A. (1959). *Processes of deltaic sedimentation in the lower Mississippi River* (Technical Report No. 12). Baton Rouge, La.: Coastal Studies Institute..

Weinstein, R. A. and D. B. Kelley. (1992). *Cultural resources investigations in the Terrebonne marsh, south-central Louisiana* (Cultural Resource Series, Report Number: COELMN/PD 89/06). New Orleans: U. S. Army Corps of Engineers, New Orleans District.

Weinstein, R. A. and S. M. Gagliano (1985). The shifting deltaic coast of the Lafourche country and its prehistoric settlement. In P. D. Uzee (Ed.), *The Lafourche Country; the people and the land* (pp. 122-148). Lafayette, La.: The Center for Louisiana Studies.

Wells, J. T. and G. P. Kemp. (1982). Mudflat and marsh progradation along Louisiana's Chenier Plain: a natural reversal in coastal erosion. In D. F. Boesch (Ed.) *Proceedings of the conference on coastal erosion and wetland modification in Louisiana: causes, consequences and options: Baton Rouge, Louisiana, October 5-7* (pp. 39-51). Washington, D. C.: National Coastal Ecosystems Team, Office of Biological Services, Fish and Wildlife Service.

Wennersten, J. R. (1981). *The oyster wars of Chesapeake Bay.* Centreville, Md.: Tidewater Publishers.

Werlla, W. S. (1950). Fresh and salt water fisheries. In *Department of Wild Life and Fisheries third biennial report, 1948-1949* (pp. 83-76). New Orleans, La.: Department of Wild Life and Fisheries.

Westphal, J. A., D. B. Oster, and H. L. Deckerd. (1980). *The Mississippi and Atchafalaya rivers below Old River in relation to human settlement: 1718-present* (USACOE Contract No. DACW 29-78-C-0062). Rolla, Mo.: Institute of River Studies, University of Missouri-Rolla.

Wetland damage. (2009). Retrieved January 30, 2009, from http://www.nutria.com/site5.php.

Wetlands: Their use and regulation (OTA-0-206). (1984). Washington, D. C.: Congress of the U. S., Office of Technology Assessment.

White, C. J. (1975). *Effects of 1973 flood waters on brown shrimp in Louisiana estuaries* (Technical Bulletin No. 16). New Orleans, La.: Louisiana Wild Life and Fisheries Commission.

White Lake crops. (1915). *Abbeville Meridional,* (April 3).

Whitehead, J. H. III. (1979). *The watermen of the Chesapeake Bay.* Richmond, Va.: John Hurt Whitehead III.

White Lake Wetlands Conservation Area: an asset for Louisiana. (2006). Retrieved October 25, 2006, from http://www.lsuagcenter.com/en/our_offices/research_stations/Rice/Features/Publications/White+Lake+Wetlands+Conservation+Area+An+Asset+for+Louisiana.html.

Wicker, K. M. (1979). *The development of the Louisiana oyster industry in the nineteenth century.* Unpublished Ph.D. Dissertation, Louisiana State University, Baton Rouge, La.

Wicker, K., M. DeRouen, D. O'Connor, E. Roberts and J. Watson. (1980). *Environmental characterization of Terrebonne Parish: 1955-1978* (Final Report for the Terrebonne Parish Police Jury). Baton Rouge: Coastal Environments, Inc.

Wicker, K. M., R. E. Emmer, D. Roberts, and J. van Beek. (1989). *Pipelines, navigation channels, and facilities in sensitive coastal habitats, an analysis of outer continental shelf impacts, coastal Gulf of Mexico, Vol. 1: Technical narrative* (OCS Report/MMS 89-0051, 470). New Orleans, La: Minerals Management Service, Gulf of Mexico Regional Office.

Wicker, K. M, R. E. Emmer, D. Roberts, and J. van Beek. (1989B). *Pipelines, navigation channels, and facilities in sensitive coastal habitats, an analysis of outer continental shelf impacts, coastal Gulf of Mexico. Vol. 2: Atlas of physical, cultural, and biological parameters* (OCS Report MMS 89-0052). New Orleans, La.: Minerals Management Service, Gulf of Mexico Regional Office.

Wilby, R. T. (1991). *Clearing Bayou Teche after the Civil War, the Kingsbury Project, 1870-1871*. Lafayette, La.: The Center for Louisiana Studies.

Wilder, T. (1954). Its brimstone stake is bolstered by oil and nickel. *Barron's, 34*(April19), 17.

Wilen, J. (2008). Fuel costs rising; barrel of sweet crude in triple digits for 1st time. *Baton Rouge Advocate*, (January 3), 1A; 4A.

Wildlife Carving. (1998). *Handmade by Louisiana craftsmen*. Retrieved March 4, 2006, from http://www.crt.state.la.us/crafts/carving.html.

Wilen, J. (2007). Oil futures rise to record. *Baton Rouge Advocate*, (November 7), 1D.

Wilkinson, A. (1892). The alligator hunters of Louisiana: in the lagoons of the tidewater wilderness. *Century Magazine, 43*(3), 399-407. Retrieved January 5, 2006, from http://www.cdl.library.cornell.edu/gifcache/moa/cent/cent0043/00409.TIFG6.gif.

Williams, E. R., Jr. (1974). Louisiana public and private immigration endeavors: 1866-1893. *Louisiana History, 15*(2), 153-173.

Williams, N. (1929). Drilling for oil in the out of the way marshlands of Terrebonne Parish, Louisiana. *Oil and Gas Journal, 28*(December 19), 40-41.

Williams, N. (1933). Many hazards and uncertainties in Gulf coast operations but rewards especially good. *Oil and Gas Journal, 31*(January 19), 6; 36.

Williams, N. (1934). Practicability of drilling unit on barges definitely established in Lake Barre, Louisiana, tests. *Oil and Gas Journal, 33*(52), 14-18.

Williams, N. (1936). Laying oil line from Lafitte field is more than ordinary undertaking. *Oil and Gas Journal, 34*(January 20), 39.

Williams, N. (1936B). Lafitte, coastal Louisiana, regarded as world's deepest commercial field. *Oil and Gas Journal, 35*(July 2), 71-72.

Williams, N. (1939). Drilling in coastal Louisiana is reaching record levels. *Oil and Gas Journal, 38*(June 1), 15-16.

Williams, N. (1944). Dredging canals for servicing fields in marsh and swamp districts of Louisiana. *Oil and Gas Journal, 43*(October 2), 95-96.

Williams, N. (1957). Offshore boom: 100 fields found, 58 producing oil: Louisiana's continental shelf. *Oil and Gas Journal, 55*(April 1), 142-143.

Williams, R. E. (1955). Development and improvement of coastal marsh ranges. In *Water—Yearbook of Agriculture* (pp. 444-450). Washington, D. C.: U. S. Department of Agriculture.

Williams, R. L., P. T. Comiskey, and D. A. Lipps. (1965). Brimstone transportation. *Chemical Engineering Progress, 61*(2), 72-76.

Williams S. J. and H. A. Cichon. (1994). *Processes of coastal wetlands loss in Louisiana* (Results from a multi-year collaborative study by the U. S. Geological Survey, National Biological Survey, and Louisiana State University, as presented at Coastal Zone '93, New Orleans, Louisiana. Open-File Report 94-275). Reston, Va.: U. S. Geological Survey.

Williams, S. J., S. Penland, and A. H. Sallenger (Eds.). (1992). Louisiana barrier island erosion study: atlas of barrier shoreline changes in Louisiana from 1853 to 1989. M*iscellaneous Investigations Series I-2150-A*. Washington, D. C.: U. S. Geological Survey.

Wilson, C. A., V. Van Sickle, and D. Pope. (n.d.). *The Louisiana artificial reef plan: executive summary*. Draft report. Baton Rouge, La.: Louisiana Geological Survey.

Wilson, H. (1965). Red snapper—new frontier offshore. *Oil and Gas Journal, 64*(4), 58-60.

Wilson, J. N. O. (1850). Report of the acting secretary of the interior, relative to the swamp and overflowed lands in Louisiana. In *Senate Executive Document No. 68, 31st Congress, 1st Session* (pp. 1-8). Washington, D. C.: U. S. Government Printing Office.

Wilt, J. (2005). Logging in: is there a future for cypress?. *Louisiana Life, 24*(4), 38-43.

Wirth, F. F. (2004). *A review of the market structure of the Louisiana oyster industry; a microcosm of the United States oyster industry*. Retrieved October 13, 2006, from http://www.findarticles.com/p/articles/mi_m0QPU/is_3_23/ai_n13499597/print.

Wold, A. (2008). Panel will evaluate hurricane project. *Baton Rouge Advocate*, (May 12), 1B-2B.

Wold, A. (2009). Second surge hidden hazard of hurricanes. *Baton Rouge Advocate*, (June 15), 1A; 4A.

Wold, A. (2009B). Official: coastal talks incomplete. *Baton Rouge Advocate*, (July 17), 11A.

Wolfert, I. (1961). Thousand-mile miracle. *A Reader's Digest* Reprint (Condensed from *Shreveport Magazine*), 1-6.

Wooten, H. H. and L. A. Jones. (1955). The history of our drainage enterprises. In *Water—the yearbook of agriculture, 1955* (pp. 478-490). U. S. Department of Agriculture. Washington, D. C.: U. S. Government Printing Office.

World's largest shrimp cannery. (1938). *Louisiana Conservation Review*, (Spring), 21-24.

Working group for post-hurricane planning for the Louisiana coast, A. (2006). *A new framework for planning the future of coastal Louisiana after the hurricanes of 2005*. Cambridge, Md: University of Maryland Center for Environmental Science.

Worthy, R. (2009). Battle of the dredge: residents fight to cease operations at Lake Peigneur. *Abbeville Meridional*, (May 10), 1A; 5A.

Wright, E. (1997). Hurricane Audrey 40 years haven't dimmed pain and bitterness of some survivors. *Baton Rouge Advocate*, (June 22), 1A; 6A.

Wright, J. O. (1907). Reclamation of tide lands. In *U. S. Department of Agriculture, annual report of the Office of Experiment Stations for the year ended June 30, 1906* (pp. 373-396). Washington, D. C.: U. S. Government Printing Office.

Wright, R. L., J. J. Sperry, and D. L. Huss. (1960). *Vegetation type mapping studies of the marshes of southeastern Louisiana* (Project Number 191). College Station, Tx.: Texas A&M University Foundation.

Wurzlow, H. E. (1976). Cypress trees once abounded: forest decline was predicted. *Houma Daily Courier*, (November 2), 1A.

Wurzlow, H. E. (1976B). Spiderweb trails still visible: pullboats left their scars. *Houma Daily Courier*, (December 26), 10-F.

Yancey, R. K. (1962). Marsh Island Wildlife Refuge. *Louisiana Conservationist, 14*(3), 14-16.

Yates, D. V. (1967). *Prehistoric Indians in Louisiana: an annotated bibliography.* Unpublished Master's thesis, Louisiana State University, Baton Rouge, La.

Yearly planting of oyster shells may place Louisiana first in the rank of oyster producing states. (1929). *Louisiana Conservation News, 4*(3), 1; 14.

Zacharie, F. C. (1898). The Louisiana oyster industry. In *Bulletin of the United States Fish Commission, 17 (1897)* (pp. 297-304). Washington, D. C.: U. S. Government Printing Office.

Index

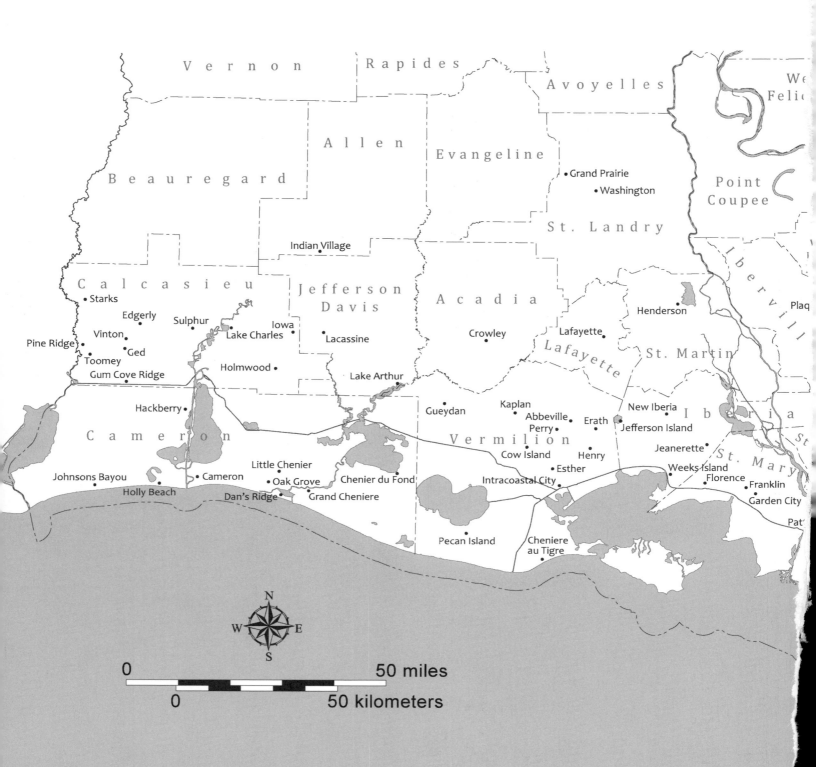